REGULATION OF CRYPTOTRANSACTIONS

■ ■ ■

Carol Goforth

University Professor and the Clayton N. Little Professor of Law
University of Arkansas School of Law

AMERICAN CASEBOOK SERIES®

American Casebook Series is a trademark registered in the U.S. Patent and Trademark Office.

© 2020 LEG, Inc. d/b/a West Academic
    444 Cedar Street, Suite 700
    St. Paul, MN 55101
    1-877-888-1330

West, West Academic Publishing, and West Academic are trademarks of West Publishing Corporation, used under license.

Printed in the United States of America

ISBN: 978-1-68467-725-2

DEDICATION AND ACKNOWLEDGMENTS

I would like to dedicate this book to members of my family, who have suffered through long conversations about all things crypto, usually (although not always) with polite expressions of almost-interest on their faces.

And, of course, I owe thanks to many people. Thank you to the University of Arkansas School of Law, for supporting me in branching out into a new area of the law. Thank you to Deans Stacy Leeds and Margaret Sova McCabe for encouraging me in this endeavor, to Associate Dean Laurent Sacharoff for his counsel throughout this process, and Associate Dean Brian Gallini for his advice. Thank you to my colleagues at the Sam M. Walton College of Business and particularly its Blockchain Center of Excellence, for your collective insights and wisdom. Thank you to Alexandra Goforth for copy editing the entire book despite an already packed schedule. Thank you to my research assistant, Courtney Baltz, for all your hard work on this project. Thanks to Professors Carl Circo, Sharon Foster, Andrew Lawson, Mary Beth Matthews, Uche Ewelukwa Ofodile, and Danielle Weatherby, and Associate Dean Will Foster, for reading and providing comments on various sections of this book. Thank you to my contact at West, Jon Harkness, for asking me on the very day I finished my manuscript, if I would submit a draft to West. Finally, thanks to all the students who sat through one of my crypto classes; every one of you helped me understand how better to teach this amazing subject. To all of you, I could not have finished this without your help. Errors that remain, of course, are all mine.

AUTHOR'S NOTE

Excerpts from administrative orders, cases, briefs, and articles have been edited. There may be formatting changes in the excerpts that appear in this book. In most instances, deletions are noted with ellipses, and additions are noted with brackets. However, footnotes, parallel citations, and string cites are often omitted without further notice. In addition, in court materials (including pleadings, briefs, and opinions), references to filed materials such as depositions, attachments, appendices, the indictment, etc. have also been omitted. Footnotes in the text of each chapter are consecutive, although footnotes from cited material generally retain the numbering from the original sources. Note that footnotes in each chapter refer back only to other footnotes in that chapter.

SUMMARY OF CONTENTS

TABLE OF CONTENTS

TABLE OF CASES

The principal cases are in bold type.

REGULATION OF CRYPTOTRANSACTIONS

CHAPTER 1

INTRODUCTION TO CRYPTOASSETS, THE BLOCKCHAIN REVOLUTION, AND REGULATORY RESPONSE

■ ■ ■

Bitcoin is not just a cryptocurrency, but also a new financial system comprised of many components. It was invented in 2008 by the mysterious Satoshi Nakamoto and released shortly after to the public. Most importantly, Bitcoin is not controlled or owned by any individual, corporation, or government. It extensively uses cryptography and relies on a peer-to-peer network. The Bitcoin protocol lays out the rules of this financial system. . . .

Nick Farrel, Jonas DeMuro, *What is Bitcoin? Understanding BTC and other crypto-currencies,* Techradar.pro (Apr. 26, 2018), available online at https://www.techradar.com/news/what-is-bitcoin

---

That "simple" explanation of Bitcoin[1] is likely to raise more questions than it answers for readers who are just entering the brave new world of blockchain, cryptocurrencies, and other cryptoassets.[2] Nonetheless, there are a number of reasons why it is critically important for lawyers to understand the crypto ecosystem. First, a tremendous amount of value has been invested in cryptoassets such as Bitcoin. As of the middle of 2019, the

---

[1] Capitalization of the word "Bitcoin" is subject to varying conventions. Some sources capitalize the word when the reference is to the system or network, but not when it refers to specific coins. Because it is akin to a proper name, this book will simply capitalize "Bitcoin" throughout, as it will the name of other cryptocoins and tokens or networks.

[2] As a famous pundit once declared: "Cryptocurrencies: Everything you don't understand about money combined with everything you don't understand about computers." John Oliver. *See* Romain Dillet, *John Oliver Helps you Explain Cryptocurrencies to your Neighbor,* TECHCRUNCH (May 2018) (available online at https://techcrunch.com/2018/03/12/john-oliver-helps-you-explain-cryptocurrencies-to-your-neighbor/).

This book focuses on cryptotransactions because it is transactions that are generally regulated, rather than the digital assets themselves. In the U.S. one of the most common labels for these assets (at least as of the time these materials were written) is "cryptocurrency," but that is a somewhat misleading term since not all kinds of cryptoassets are designed to function as currencies. These materials therefore tend to speak in terms of crypto or cryptoassets rather than cryptocurrencies, as chapter 2 explains in more detail.

total market capitalization of these "new" interests exceeded $300 billion.[3] While that may be a drop in the bucket relative to the value of the world's fiat or government-backed currencies, crypto draws the interest of developers, speculators, long-term investors, governments, regulators, and thieves alike.

The materials in this book are designed to look at cryptoassets and the expanding world of cryptotransactions to examine how the regulatory regime surrounding these interests is developing. (While federal law in the United States is the primary focus of this book, there is a chapter on state law issues and another on international aspects of crypto regulation.) This introductory chapter begins with a brief historical overview of cryptoassets and the initial regulatory issues presented by the development of these new assets. Chapter two is dedicated to the definition of terms, because this is a new and developing space and much of the jargon will be unfamiliar to many. Both of these chapters are properly regarded as an introduction to the topic of crypto in a general sense.

Chapter three focuses on FinCEN (the Financial Crimes Enforcement Network, a bureau of the Department of Treasury), one of the most important federal agencies with a role to play in overseeing how cryptoassets are regulated in the U.S. These materials provide background information about the creation and role of FinCEN in the modern financial world, including an overview of the group's authorizing legislation, its regulatory approach, and the focus of its enforcement efforts prior to the advent of cryptotransactions. Chapters four and five provide details about some of the most important situations that illustrate how cryptoassets and transactions have been used in ways that are relevant to FinCEN and its mission. Chapter six then considers the reaction of FinCEN, explaining both how the agency has reacted as well as how the real world examples discussed in chapters four and five have impacted that response. Because it is absolutely clear that FinCEN's response is still developing, potential future actions by the agency are also considered here.

Chapter seven moves from FinCEN to a different regulatory actor in the crypto space. It provides background and general information about the U.S. SEC (the Securities and Exchange Commission), and its role in modern financial markets. It focuses particularly on how the SEC and courts determine what interests are classified as securities, although other facets of the federal securities laws are also included. Chapter eight provides insight into some of the most important instances in which companies either sold cryptoassets or facilitated such transactions without registering with the SEC or complying with any exemption from the usual

---

[3]   You can check the daily market capitalization of existing cryptocurrencies by going online to sources such as CoinMarketCap.com (available at https://CoinMarketCap.com) and looking at the totals for all tracked assets. As of July 1, 2019 the total market capitalization for the 2,253 listed cryptocoins and tokens on that site was $301,803,902,489.

registration requirement imposed on the sale of securities. Chapter nine considers illustrative examples of individuals and companies engaged in fraudulent activities involving the sale of cryptoassets. Chapter ten examines the SEC's current and ongoing response to these kinds of developments, including efforts to require issuers of cryptoassets to register their coins or tokens as well as actions to curtail fraudulent businesses. Because the SEC's response to the cryptoworld continues to evolve, potential future developments are also considered here.

Chapter eleven provides an overview of the CFTC (Commodities Futures Trading Commission) and its structure, looking at both the background of this agency, its authorizing legislation, and its mission. Chapter twelve provides real world instances involving the kinds of interests and transactions in which the CFTC has expressed an interest. It also considers the evolving CFTC role in regulating crypto as well as potential directions for future responses.

Chapter thirteen presents some of the recent and current innovations and developments in the crypto space. It also discusses developing and potential reactions by regulatory authorities to these new kinds of transactions and assets.

Chapter fourteen examines state regulatory activity involving crypto, particularly focusing on money transmitter and related regulations, which have traditionally been handled at the state level. The chapter also looks at state securities laws insofar as they relate to transactions involving crypto.

Chapter fifteen offers an introduction to the international regulation of crypto. It includes information about some of the widely divergent regulatory approaches to crypto that have been taken by different countries. It also introduces some of the international organizations working towards greater uniformity with regard to some of the regulations applicable to these interests, particularly with regard to money laundering and the international funding of criminal activities such as terrorism.

The final chapter contains a relatively abbreviated discussion of issues surrounding the taxation of crypto. There are a number of reasons for the more general approach taken in this chapter. First, tax issues affect different persons than the regulations covered in the rest of the book. For the most part, the regulatory regimes discussed in this book govern the businesses that create or facilitate the distribution and use of crypto. Tax issues affect the owners and users of crypto. More importantly, it is extremely difficult to discuss the tax issues surrounding cryptocurrency in any meaningful way when a reader may have little to no background in basic tax. The issues are incredibly complicated, evolving, and require more background than is suitable for a course centered on the regulation of cryptoassets themselves. Finally, taxation of cryptotransactions is a subject the genuinely deserves its own course. It is a topic that should be dealt with by tax experts, not business or fintech lawyers who have branched out to deal with regulatory issues affecting businesses operating in the crypto sphere. Nonetheless, the issues are at least framed in chapter sixteen in a basic and relatively cursory fashion.

Because the regulatory reaction to crypto is still in the early stages, it is not really possible to create a traditional casebook that focuses only on settled judicial opinions to illustrate relevant legal issues and rules. These materials therefore look at various statutes, rules, and regulatory structures that predate the advent of crypto along with mission and informational statements promulgated by the agencies most closely involved with regulation of cryptotransactions. Press releases, complaints, and briefs on various issues are also considered. Documents such as whitepapers and other public information from lawyers and entrepreneurs is also included where relevant. Materials from administrative proceedings, and judicial opinions are also incorporated where appropriate and available.

Finally, there are a great many more footnotes and detailed citations in these materials than in many more conventional case or textbooks. The reality is that the regulatory paradigm in which crypto operates is evolving quite rapidly. It therefore seemed necessary and useful to provide sources so that an attorney or other user will be able to utilize these materials more easily as a starting point when conducting future research.

Before delving too deeply into these materials, however, it is important to understand how we got to where we are today.

1. THE MYSTERIOUS SATOSHI NAKAMOTO AND THE BYZANTINE GENERALS PROBLEM

In the early 1990s, the internet was still relatively new, and most people were struggling to understand how it worked and how they could use it efficiently. There were, however, some technological pioneers who had already discovered that the internet could be an extremely powerful tool. Some of those people believed that governmental agencies and large corporations possessed too much power. Many of them feared the burgeoning power of the internet would be used by those in position of authority for self-serving purposes, jeopardizing individual freedoms and further weakening the individual's rights of privacy and self-determination.

Fueled by a profound distrust of such centralized authority, these individuals wanted to use the internet to combat the concentration of wealth and power among governments and corporations by protecting individual liberties. They were particularly interested in giving individuals greater control over their money and their personal information. One of their highest priorities was the development of a system of digital cash independent of any government or centralized bank and over which neither governments nor banks would have control. They viewed this as an important step in guaranteeing that individuals would not see their hard-earned money wasted by government policy that could trigger inflation or by excessive transaction costs imposed by third party intermediaries like banks. They also wanted to avoid the risk that personal financial data could be traced in ways that they viewed as unwarranted invasions of personal privacy. Unfortunately for the individuals with this mindset, the first two attempts at a digital cash system, DigiCash and Cybercash, failed by the end of the nineties.

One of the principal problems in creating a true digital currency revolves around the issue of trust, or more accurately the lack of trust. When a government issues a currency (often referred to as fiat currency or sometimes simply as fiat), transactions are either handled in person or via electronic transfers. Electronic transfers are conducted with the assistance of large banks, which act as trusted third-party intermediaries. In essence, financial transaction participants are trusting that the bank will have accurate records of whether a payor has sufficient funds to pay the debt being incurred. A bank does this by keeping an accurate record, or ledger, of credits when a bank customer makes a deposit and debits when the customer make payments or withdrawals.

How do transaction participants navigate the issue of trust with a digital currency that does not rely on a trusted third party, such as a bank, to verify the legitimacy of transactions? Obviously, it is impractical to expect participants to a transaction to trust everyone on the internet. This creates a huge practical problem for potential buyers and sellers. If there is no third party verifying that a purchaser actually possesses sufficient funds, and is actually sending them to a seller, how does the seller know that it is actually receiving a valid payment? How does a buyer convince the seller to sell the goods based on nothing more than an electronic transmission when there is no third party to verify that sufficient funds are in the buyer's account? This conundrum over the lack of trust came to be known as the Byzantine Generals Problem.

The problem has been described like this: suppose that in a world before mobile communications, seven army groups surround a castle they hope to conquer. Only a simultaneous attack by at least four of the groups (i.e., a majority) will succeed. Suppose further that the groups are dispersed, meaning that the general for each group must send messages between the various groups to relay the time to attack. Complicating matters, some generals may not obey instructions, and some might actually seek to sabotage the attack, conveying incorrect timing information to others. How can the participants be assured of a coordinated attack by at least a majority of the generals?

In the context of the impersonal internet, without a solution to this problem, there is no way to proceed safely because you cannot tell if a majority of the participants have agreed on essential things such as whether they are all going to attack at a certain time. (In the context of a digital currency, the members of the group would want to agree on things such as whether they will all recognize a transaction as valid). Certainly in a decentralized, massive network, trust would not work. A middleman would require some payment for performing the tasks necessary to coordinate a transaction[4] and, in addition, the presence of a centralized authority introduces the risk that the middleman could be compromised by an outside source or hack.

The solution to this problem and the technological foundation for cryptocurrencies was first publicized in 2008, in the form of a paper entitled "Bitcoin—A Peer to Peer Electronic Cash System," which originally appeared in an online discussion of cryptography.[5] It was posted by a person or persons using the pseudonym Satoshi Nakamoto, whose real identity remains a mystery. As a result of Satoshi Nakamoto's innovations, Bitcoin was able to solve the conundrum known as the Byzantine Generals Problem by utilizing something now known as the Proof-of-Work protocol (sometimes called PoW). In this way, Bitcoin became the world's first successful digital currency system or cryptocurrency.

The PoW protocol works as follows. A transaction is reported to the network. At that point every network node (i.e., every computer with access to the network) examines the ledger (the digital record of prior transactions) to ensure the transaction is legitimate. In other words, the computers each must agree that the ledger shows that the transferor has the Bitcoins that are proposed to be transferred. Once the transaction is accepted as legitimate (i.e., the nodes verify that according to the prior records on the blockchain the transferee owns sufficient cryptoassets to complete the transfer), it becomes part of the aggregated transactions that form a potential block in the chain. However, in order to actually be added to the chain, the nodes must solve the mathematical puzzle or problem known as the "Proof-of-Work." Nodes that attempt to solve the puzzle are said to be miners, and a miner that successfully solves the puzzle sends the solution to the network for verification.

Because of the cryptographic processes used, it is difficult to solve the mathematical problem, but the solution is easy to verify once it is produced. Upon verification, that block becomes part of the chain, and the miner is rewarded for the "work" in solving the puzzle. This innovation successfully ushered in what some have started calling the blockchain era.

---

[4]   In the conventional banking world, these are generally known as clearinghouse activities.

[5]   Satoshi Kamamoto, *Bitcoin: A Peer-to-Peer Electronic Cash System*, available online at https://bitcoin.org/bitcoin.pdf.

2. BITCOIN TAKES OFF

As will be described in greater detail in chapter two, Bitcoin is a digital or virtual currency that was originally launched on January 3, 2009. In contrast to traditional fiat currencies, Bitcoin has no centralized bank, nation state, or regulatory authority backing it. "Bitcoins" have no tangible existence and instead are probably best thought of as a record of balances in the digital blockchain ledger.

The first real world Bitcoin transaction reportedly occurred when 10,000 Bitcoins were used to buy two pizzas in Florida in 2010. That would have made the then-current "value" of each Bitcoin less than $.01. Three years later, in February of 2013, Bitcoin had gone from a value of less than a penny to a price of $22 per coin.[6] That alone would seem remarkable, but the trading value of a single Bitcoin peaked at $20,000 in December of 2017, with volatile swings that sometime exceed $1000 per coin in a single day. In early May of 2018, Bitcoin was trading at less than half of that, at just slightly over $8,500 per coin. On January 2, 2019 a single Bitcoin was valued at about $3,700, and in June of 2019 it peaked again at $13,796.49 before falling back to near $10,000 on July 1, 2019. On July 1, the total market capitalization of Bitcoin was slightly under $183 billion.

This volatility in pricing is one of the characteristics that has lead so many to be skeptical of the value of crypto. In the latter half of 2018, Bitcoin was faced with widespread allegations of market manipulation that had artificially inflated the price of Bitcoin in 2017. At that time, it was reported that "at least half of the 2017 rise in bitcoin prices was due to coordinated price manipulation using another cryptocurrency called tether."[7] By the end of 2018, the price of Bitcoin was hovering around $3,400 and its total market cap was down to $59.35 billion. As noted above, however, the market bounced back significantly by mid-2019.

It is certainly fair to say that Bitcoin is not universally appreciated. The vice-chairmen of Warren Buffett's investment firm Berkshire Hathaway, Charles T. Munger, once called it "totally asinine" and a "noxious poison."[8] However, given the amount of money involved, it is not

---

[6]   Throughout this chapter, and in other places throughout the book, references may be made as to the value of individual cryptoassets, or as to the total market capitalizations (number of outstanding coins or tokens multiplied by the current trading value of a single asset). This information is all taken from CoinMarketCap.com, available online at https://coinmarketcap.com/. To obtain information about a particular coin or token, click on the name of the asset and specific data about that coin or token will appear, including a historical value and market cap chart.

[7]   Kate Rooney, *Much of Bitcoin's 2017 Boom Was Market Manipulation, Research Says*, CNBC (June 13, 2018) (available online at https://www.cnbc.com/2018/06/13/much-of-bitcoins-2017-boom-was-market-manipulation-researcher-says.html).

[8]   Julia Kollewe, *Bitcoin is 'noxious poison'*, says Warren Buffett's investment chief, THE GUARDIAN (Feb. 15, 2018) (available online at https://www.theguardian.com/technology/2018/feb/15/bitcoin-is-noxious-poison-says-warren-buffett-investment-chief).

at all surprising that a number of alternatives to Bitcoin, and a range of assets that offer opportunities not associated with the initial cryptocurrencies, have all been developed or are being developed. In fact, the underlying technology pioneered by Satoshi Yakamoto has uses far beyond cryptocurrencies, as described in more detail in the following materials.

3. WHAT IS THIS BLOCKCHAIN OF WHICH YOU SPEAK?

First utilized in 2008 in connection with the development of Bitcoin, blockchain is a technological and cryptographic process involving a digital decentralized ledger in which transactions are added in chronological order, creating a "chain" of blocks. Let's consider each of those elements separately, starting with "ledger." A "ledger" in this context is probably exactly what you would expect. It is like a stock ledger, or a record of transactions such as would be kept with a recorder of deeds. The ledger is "digital" when it is stored online rather than one paper. It is decentralized when the information contained in the ledger is shared and reconciled by a network of computers.

The information held on that distributed chain is continually being updated and reconciled. Because the information is shared in its entirety among so many computers (i.e., it is wholly distributed), it cannot be controlled by any single entity, and the system therefore has no single point of access where a hacker or other outside force can interrupt or corrupt the information on the chain. It is protected from being corrupted because altering any unit of information on the blockchain would require a huge amount of computing power to override the entire network. Blockchain technology therefore allows digital information to be distributed but not altered unilaterally.

The name "blockchain" comes from the way in which data is collected and stored. Rather than having to go through the verification process for every single transaction, the network collects a series of transactions that occur at about the same time (in much the same way as a series of transactions would fill the page of a stock ledger or real estate transactions ledger). Those transactions are aggregated into a block where the first item is a reference to the immediately preceding block (so that the system knows where it is to be placed in the chain) and the last segment includes a difficult mathematical puzzle or problem. The problem must be solved before the next block can be added to the chain. This is necessary so that the blocks are added to the chain (hence the label "blockchain") in the same sequence by everyone in the network. The first transaction in each new block is called the genesis transaction, and it will contain the record of which addresses or scripts are entitled to receive the reward for solving the mathematical problem (the final item in the preceding block). A block is thus a permanently recorded, time-stamped transaction aggregated with other transactions that occurred at about the same time, kept in a distributed, digital ledger in a virtual "chain."

As one might expect with new technology, there have been a wide variety of developments relative to the use and utility of blockchain technology. Originally conceived as a vehicle with the potential to act as a medium of exchange, blockchain has evolved into a platform for other innovations. The expanded functionality has sometimes been called "Blockchain 2.0."

In essence, while blockchain was originally designed to support applications involving cryptocurrencies like Bitcoin, Blockchain 2.0 allows for programmable transactions, which are transactions dependent on a condition or a set of conditions. Blockchain 2.0 therefore creates a range of new economic opportunities previously unavailable on the web, including such things as microtransactions, decentralized exchange, and smart contracts.

Although the first cryptoasset (Bitcoin) and most of its early progeny (all of which were so-called altcoins) were designed as virtual currencies, blockchain has numerous uses that have nothing to do with replacing fiat currencies. Potential uses for blockchain that do not depend upon the cryptoasset acting like money include (among others):

1. Facilitating payment processing

2. Monitoring supply chains

3. Data sharing

4. Equity trading

5. Digital voting

6. Recording real estate, land, and auto title transfers

7. Improving food safety and responsibility

8. Providing immutable data backup

9. Medical recordkeeping

10. Weapons tracking

11. Tracking prescription drugs

Blockchain has a particularly important role in supply chains and logistics, with retail giants like Walmart and international conglomerates like IBM being at the forefront of such applications. On the other hand, the bulk of regulatory attention has clearly been on developers and issuers who have sought to raise funds through the issuance or resale of cryptoassets. However, for the purposes of companies wishing to raise operating funds, the most important of these alternative functions may be equity trading or investing. A company can sell tokens to raise money for its operations, usually in a widespread sale that has come to be known as an "Initial Coin Offering" or ICO.

This is not surprising, given the huge sums of money involved. The first ICO involved the issuance of "Mastercoin," and raised $500,000 in 2013.[9] In 2014, Ethereum made its appearance, raising approximately $18.4 million in its September 2014 ICO.[10] This investment allowed for the expansion of the Ethereum blockchain, on which most new tokens are hosted.[11] In 2018, there were more than twice as many ICOs as in 2017; more than $11 billion was raised in more than 2,000 offerings.[12]

Most ICOs have been conducted in the U.S., Singapore, and the U.K. since 2015,[13] despite the fact that in the United States at least, the country has moved from a situation where the issuance and trading of cryptoassets was essentially unregulated, to an era of increasing scrutiny from a number of different regulatory agencies.

4. WHY TECHNOLOGY ALWAYS OUTPACES REGULATORY RESPONSE

Naturally, there are a number of reasons why regulators are reactive rather than proactive. No agency or administrator is provided a crystal ball, and therefore the regulators must wait for the natural progression of technological developments. For the most part, a "wait and see" regulatory response is inevitable, except to the extent that certain things (such as the inevitable involvement of the criminal element when large sums of money are involved) become foreseeable along the way. Had the success of Bitcoin been foreseen by regulators, they would have invested in it, become rich, and probably retired before their agencies turned their attention to how such interests should be regulated.

The problem is that not only are agencies forced to be reactive, they are also slow to react. Congress faces well known and documented political problems in trying to enact new legislation, requiring administrative

---

[9]   For more details about the initial ICO, see Chris Abraham, *The Origin Story of the Initial Coin Offering (ICO) Token Sale History*, NEWCONOMY (Oct. 13, 2018) (available online at https://newconomy.media/news/the-origin-story-of-the-initial-coin-offering-ico-token-sale-history).

[10]   For a description of the history of the Ethereum 2014 ICO, see *15 insights on how Ethereum conducted its ICO in 2014*, COINNOUNCE (June 17, 2018) (available online at https://coinnounce.com/ethereum-ico-2014/).

[11]   From a technical or programming perspective, a cryptocoin uses its own blockchain and therefore requires more in the way of programming time and expertise to set. A token is a cryptoasset that is built on top of an existing blockchain, such as the Ethereum platform.

[12]   For detailed statistics comparing the ICOs in 2017 and 2018 see Daniele Pozzi, *ICO Market 2018 vs 2017: Trends, Capitalization, Localization, Industries, Success Rate*, COINTELEGRAPH (Jan. 5, 2019) [archived at https://perma.cc/G3DZ-AKAZ].

[13]   *Id.*

agencies to engage in on rulemaking to fill in gaps in the law. While Congress occasionally mandates formal rulemaking, with substantial attendant procedures, most rulemaking in the modern era is informal.

In general terms, the procedures for rulemaking by administrative agencies at the federal level is governed by the Administrative Procedures Act (APA), codified at 5 U.S. Code §§ 551 et seq. Informal rulemaking (also referred to as notice and comment rulemaking) is governed by § 553, and that is by far the most commonly required process by which rules are adopted. Agencies may, however, choose other options, including formal, hybrid, direct final, or negotiated rulemaking. Because the burdens imposed by these procedures are more extensive, agencies naturally gravitate towards the informal process in most cases.

The ability of administrative agencies to fill in legislative gaps through the process of informal rulemaking has been heralded as one of the great innovations in modern law. In fact, administrative rules are far more prevalent and detailed than the statutory mandates which they are designed to implement. There are estimates that more than ninety percent of modern American laws are rules adopted by agencies rather than statutes imposed by legislators.[14] This makes delays in agency response of critical importance when a new paradigm is needed to respond to technological innovation, such as cryptoassets and transactions.

Greatly influenced by Thomas O. McGarity's seminal article, *Some Thoughts on "Deossifying" the Rulemaking Process,*[15] legal commentators have vigorously complained about the "ossification" of federal regulation, arguing that the administrative process is overburdened by inefficiencies and external constraints that effectively limit the ability of administrative agencies to respond to technological change. (Westlaw's online research service indicates that as of January 2019, Professor McGarity's article had been cited more than 600 time by other legal authorities.) Professor McGarity pointed to the inefficiencies caused by additional procedures, analytical requirements, and external review mechanisms that have been

---

[14] While there are many ways to look at it, no one seriously disputes that persons in the U.S. have considerably more rules than legislated statutes to contend with. As one commentator bluntly noted, "[t]he bottom line is that in today's America, most binding rules comes from agencies (unelected) rather than elected lawmakers." Clyde Wayne Crews Jr., *How Many Rules And Regulations Do Federal Agencies Issue?* FORBES (Aug. 15, 2017) (available online at https://www.forbes.com/sites/waynecrews/2017/08/15/how-many-rules-and-regulations-do-federal-agencies-issue/#51f0c7581e64), reporting that in 2016 there were 3,853 new rules as compared to only 214 bills. Nor is this a new phenomenon. A 2004 publication noted that "scholars estimate that well over 90% of the laws that regulate our lives, whether at work or at play, are now made by our public administrators, not by our legislators or traditional lawmakers." KENNETH F. WARREN, ADMINISTRATIVE LAW IN THE POLITICAL SYSTEM 260 (4th ed. 2004).

[15] Thomas O. McGarity, *Some Thoughts on "Deossifying" the Rulemaking Process,* 41 DUKE L.J. 1385 (1992).

built into the informal rulemaking process,[16] but those claims need more background in order to be understood.

As mentioned above, informal rulemaking by federal agencies is governed by section 553 of the Administrative Procedure Act (APA).[17] The text of that rule is as follows:

5 U.S. Code § 553—Rule making

(a) This section applies, according to the provisions thereof, except to the extent that there is involved—

>   (1) a military or foreign affairs function of the United States; or

>   (2) a matter relating to agency management or personnel or to public property, loans, grants, benefits, or contracts.

(b) General notice of proposed rule making shall be published in the Federal Register, unless persons subject thereto are named and either personally served or otherwise have actual notice thereof in accordance with law. The notice shall include—

>   (1) a statement of the time, place, and nature of public rule making proceedings;

>   (2) reference to the legal authority under which the rule is proposed; and

>   (3) either the terms or substance of the proposed rule or a description of the subjects and issues involved.

Except when notice or hearing is required by statute, this subsection does not apply—

>   (A) to interpretative rules, general statements of policy, or rules of agency organization, procedure, or practice; or

>   (B) when the agency for good cause finds (and incorporates the finding and a brief statement of reasons therefor in the rules issued) that notice and public procedure thereon are impracticable, unnecessary, or contrary to the public interest.

(c) After notice required by this section, the agency shall give interested persons an opportunity to participate in the rule making through submission of written data, views, or arguments with or without opportunity for oral presentation. After consideration of the relevant matter presented, the agency shall incorporate in the rules adopted a concise general statement of their basis and purpose. When

---

[16]   It was always understood that formal rulemaking would require more in the way of procedural safeguards, but this process is used far less often. In a formal rulemaking process, the agency must conduct a full hearing on the record at which evidence is presented.

[17]   For a very detailed consideration of the history of the APA, see Kathryn E. Kovacs, *Rules About Rulemaking and the Rise of the Unitary Executive*, 70 ADMIN. L. REV. 515, 528 (2018).

rules are required by statute to be made on the record after opportunity for an agency hearing, sections 556 and 557[18] of this title apply instead of this subsection.

(d) The required publication or service of a substantive rule shall be made not less than 30 days before its effective date, except—

> (1) a substantive rule which grants or recognizes an exemption or relieves a restriction;
>
> (2) interpretative rules and statements of policy; or
>
> (3) as otherwise provided by the agency for good cause found and published with the rule.

(e) Each agency shall give an interested person the right to petition for the issuance, amendment, or repeal of a rule.

* * *

This process is not particularly detailed, calling in general terms for public notice of proposed rules and an opportunity for the public to comment. To give substance to these general requirements, courts have stepped in to explain more expansively what is entailed. In some instances, the clarification offered by the courts has turned out to be quite onerous on the affected agencies.[19]

In *Vermont Yankee Nuclear Power Corp. v. NRDC*, 435 U.S. 519 (1978), the Supreme Court explicitly acknowledged that the APA left rulemaking procedure "basically . . . within the discretion of the agencies." Despite this recognition, over the past thirty years, courts have issued interpretations that obscure this original objective, with a pair of commentators recently observing that "the marvelously simple and speedy rule making procedures of 1946 . . . bear about as much resemblance to the rule making procedures of 2016 as an acorn does to a mighty seventy-year-old oak."[20]

There are a number of requirements associated with the APA that have blossomed since the statute's original enactment as a result of judicial interpretation. In this light, consider the requirement of advance notice. Section 553 requires only that notice of proposed rulemaking include "either the terms or substance of the proposed rule or a description of the

---

[18]   Author's note: These sections contain the requirements for formal rulemaking, which is more of an adjudicatory process requiring detail fact gathering, as well as detailed explanations for the rationale of any rule.

[19]   For one outline of the various steps required by the APA for informal rulemaking. *See* the Reg. Map, which can be downloaded without cost at ICF, THE REG. MAP, https://www.icf.com/resources/reports-and-research/2018/reg-map. The map of nine steps to be followed provides a glimpse into the complexities of federal rulemaking. Other commentators present the process as being even more complicated. *See, i.e.*, Mark Seidenfeld, *A Table of Requirements for Federal Administrative Rulemaking*, 27 FLA. ST. U. L. REV. 533 (2000), with 25 distinct steps.

[20]   Sidney A. Shapiro & Richard W. Murphy, *Arbitrariness Review Made Reasonable: Structural and Conceptual Reform of the Hard Look*, 92 NOTRE DAME L. REV. 331, 332–33 (2016).

subjects or issues involved." It has been held that this requires the agency to give enough notice so that interested parties are provided with "a reasonable and meaningful opportunity to participate in the rulemaking process." *Forester v. CPSC*, 559 F.2d 774, 787 (D.C. Cir. 1977).

The practice that has grown out of this requirement often involves a number of preliminary steps even before the official rulemaking process begins.[21] This includes gathering preliminary information, typically through unstructured and informal conversations with potentially interested parties. It may also publish an Advance Notice of Proposed Rulemaking in the Federal Register to gather information in a more systematic manner. This allows interested persons to help frame any eventual proposal by responding to the advance notice.

When an agency is ready to issue a proposed rule, it does so via a Notice of Proposed Rulemaking, which is the official document that announces to the public its plans. This notice is published in the Federal Register and must give the public adequate opportunity to respond. The notice will have a summary that explains the issues and proposed action along with instructions on how to submit comments on the proposal. Various supplemental information (including not only the merits of the proposal as well as information used to develop the proposal, but also the agency's legal authority to promulgate the proposed rule) must be included. It will also include either the text of the proposal or a narrative explanation of the proposed action.

The APA itself does not include extensive details about how much information the agency must include in these notices. Consider the requirement (included in 5 U.S. Code § 553(c)) that final rules have a concise general statement of the general basis and purpose. This might seem like a minimal burden, but the way in which the courts have reacted to the requirement of the "concise general statement" means that this can be a significant burden for agencies. In essence, it has resulted in substantially longer and far more detailed preambles and general statements, which in turn seems to have invited a wider range of criticisms and attacks on proposed rules.

Although there is considerable variation between the courts as to what the requirement of a "concise general statement" means, and even the consequence of failing to properly provide such a statement, federal courts are in general agreement that the statement must include significant information. In 1947, the Supreme Court noted that it is a simple but fundamental rule of administrative law that an agency must set forth clearly the grounds on which it acted. *Securities & Exchange Com. v.*

---

[21] For a more complete description of the administrative rulemaking process see Office of the Federal Register, *A Guide to the Rulemaking Process* [archived at https://perma.cc/2PLN-H2U3].

Chenery Corp., 332 U.S. 194 (1947). Without such a statement, the Court concluded, a reviewing body would be unable to determine if the decision to adopt to rule was right or wrong.

Other courts have specifically cautioned agencies against reading the requirement of a "concise" and "general" statement too literally. In *Automotive Parts & Accessories Asso. v. Boyd*, 407 F.2d 330 (DC App. 1968), the court noted that the statement must accommodate judicial requirements, reminding the agency of the "ever-present possibility of judicial review." The court specifically warned regulators that courts cannot be required to review the entire record to determine agency rationales. Instead, an agency engaged in informal rulemaking must provide an explanation of the major policy issues that were considered along with the reasons for the agency response.

The notion that the "general statement" needs to be sufficient to facilitate meaningful judicial review has been confirmed in a wide range of cases.[22] There is an impressive list of string cites in the footnote that you probably just skipped over. They are included there not because you are likely to go read the opinions, but to provide a basis for understanding how often rules are challenged, how often opponents are willing to fund their legal opposition through the federal appellate process, and how concerned the federal courts are that the "concise, general statement" be far more detailed than the language in the APA might suggest.

The reason that opponents are so persistent in opposing rules that they do not want to have adopted is clear: courts are willing to listen to complaints. Failure of an administrative agency to include sufficient and complete grounds upon which the agency relied in the "concise general statement" can render the rulemaking invalid. There is a long line of cases involving this requirement, demonstrating its impact on a wide range of rules adopted by a number of different federal agencies.[23]

---

[22]   *See St. James Hosp. v. Heckler,* 579 F. Supp. 757 (N.D. Ill. 1984), *decision aff'd,* 760 F.2d 1460 (7th Cir. 1985); *Global Van Lines, Inc. v. Interstate Commerce Com.* (1983, CA5) 714 F.2d 1290 (5th Cir. 1983); *Baltimore & O. C. T. R. Co. v. United States,* 583 F.2d 678 (3rd Cir. 1978), *cert. den.* 440 U.S. 968 (1979); *Home Box Office, Inc. v. Federal Communications Com.,* 567 F.2d 9 (DC App. 1977), *cert. den.* 434 US 829, *reh'ing den.* 434 U.S. 988 (1977); *National Welfare Rights Organization v. Mathews,* 533 F2d 637 (DC App. 1976); *National Asso. of Food Chains, Inc. v. Interstate Commerce Com.,* 535 F.2d 1308 (DC App. 1976); *Rodway v. United States Dept. of Agriculture,* 514 F.2d 809 (DC App. 1975).

[23]   The following cases illustrate the range of agencies affected by the requirement of a concise general statement:

1. *Crowley's Yacht Yard v. Pena,* 863 F. Supp. 18 (DDC 1994).
2. *Independent U.S. Tanker Owners Committee v. Dole,* 809 F.2d 847 (D.C. Cir. 1987).
3. *Lloyd Noland Hospital & Clinic v. Heckler,* 762 F.2d 1561 (11th Cir. 1985).
4. *St. James Hospital v. Heckler,* 760 F.2d 1460 (7th Cir. 1985), cert. den., 474 U.S. 902 (1985).
5. *National Asso. of Pharmaceutical Mfrs. v. Department of Health & Human Services,* 586 F. Supp. 740 (SDNY 1984).

Federal courts have also required agencies to disclose the significant, material information considered in drafting the proposed rule. In *Portland Cement Ass'n v. Ruckelshaus*, 486 F.2d 375, 393 (D.C. Cir. 1973),[24] the D.C. Circuit explained that "information should generally be disclosed as to the basis of a proposed rule at the time of issuance." In a later decision, that same court clarified that "[a]n agency commits serious procedural error when it fails to reveal portions of the technical basis for a proposed rule in time to allow for meaningful commentary." *Conn. Light & Power Co. v. NRC*, 673 F.2d 525, 530–31 (D.C. Cir. 1982) ("it is especially important for the agency to identify and make available technical studies and data that it has employed in reaching the decisions to propose particular rules"). In *United States v. Nova Scotia Food Prods. Corp.*, 568 F.2d 240, 251 (2d Cir. 1977), the Second Circuit reached a similar conclusion.

After the agency receives and considers the public comments, it must publish the final rule in the Federal Register. The final rule must also include a preamble with a summary, effective date, and supplemental information. The supplementary information must include the basis and purpose of the rule, the goals of the rule, the facts and other information relied upon in formulating the rule, responses to criticisms, and an explanation of why the rule was chosen over other alternatives.

When its work in finalizing the text of the rule is complete, the Agency must also be prepared to produce a complete record of the rulemaking process, including disclosure of the material information considered by the agency during the process. Although not directly involving informal rulemaking, the U.S. Supreme Court found in *Citizens to Preserve Overton Park, Inc. v. Volpe*, 401 U.S. 402, 415–16 (1971),[25] that the Secretary of Transportation's decision to spend federal funds on building a highway through a park in Memphis was subject to "substantial," "thorough, probing, in-depth," "searching and careful" inquiry under the APA. By 1977, the need for a complete rulemaking record in the informal rulemaking context was well established. The D.C. Circuit explained in *Home Box Office, Inc. v. FCC*, 567 F.2d 9, 36 (D.C. Cir. 1977), that the rulemaking record must be sufficient for a reviewing court "to see what

---

6. *Alexandria Hospital v. Heckler* 586 F. Supp. 581 (ED Va. 1984), *aff'd, remanded*, 769 F.2d 1017 (4th Cir. 1985).

7. *Global Van Lines, Inc. v. Interstate Commerce Com.*, 714 F.2d 1290 (5th Cir. 1983).

8. *Tabor v. Joint Board for Enrollment of Actuaries*, 566 F.2d 705 (DC App. 1977).

9. *Office of Communications of United Church of Christ v. Federal Communications Com.*, 560 F.2d 529 (2nd Cir. 1977).

10. *Rodway v. United States Dept. of Agriculture*, 514 F2d 809 (DC App. 1975).

11. *Associated Industries of New York State, Inc. v. United States Dept. of Labor*, 487 F2d 342 (2d Cir. 1973).

[24] As to the specific issue being litigated, this case was superseded by statute as stated in *American Trucking Associations, Inc. v. U.S. E.P.A.*, 175 F.3d 1027 (D.C.Cir., 1999).

[25] As to the ability of claimants to bring a direct claim, this case was abrogated by *Califano v. Sanders*, 430 U.S. 99 (1977).

major issues of policy were ventilated by the informal proceedings and why the agency reacted to them as it did."

In addition, for rules that are deemed to be significant in terms of economic impact, regulatory agencies may also be required to engage in (and document) an extensive cost-benefit analysis.[26] Failure to include sufficient consideration of the economic costs and benefits can lead to judicial invalidation of announced "final" rules, as the SEC was reminded in *Business Roundtable v. SEC,* 647 F.3d 1144 (D.C. Cir. 2011).[27]

The cumulative consequence of requirements such as these has clearly been that informal rulemaking has become a much more cumbersome process than the APA alone might suggest. Thomas McGarity, in the article referenced above, said that the "modest obligation" to provide a "concise general statement" "has blossomed" and invited abuse by regulated entities "who hire consultants and lawyers to pick apart the agencies' preambles and background documents and launch blunderbuss attacks on every detail of the legal and technical bases for the agencies' rules."[28]

There are, of course, legitimate reasons for courts to be concerned about informal rulemaking. Due process does require meaningful oversight, and courts are certainly less suited to ascertaining motives from lengthy records on an ad hoc, after-the-fact, basis. Fairness can also require a meaningful opportunity for public comment, especially since regulators (unlike legislators) are not directly selected by members of the public. These concerns do, however, place the need for efficiency and the need for due process and fairness in conflict.

Given that this is not a course in administrative procedures or federal rulemaking, what does this discussion have to do with the regulatory response to crypto? A lot.

Administrative agencies are well aware that any rules are subject to attack for failure to comply with the dictates of the APA and judicially imposed procedural requirements. Consider the SEC, one of the federal

---

[26]   For a more detailed explanation of these considerations as applicable in the context of financial regulators, see David W, Perkins & Maeve P. Carey, *Cost-Benefit Analysis and Financial Regulator Rulemaking,* CONG. RES. SERV. (Ap. 12, 2017) (available online at https://fas.org/sgp/crs/misc/R44813.pdf).

[27]   The APA requires that administrative agencies refrain from acting in an "arbitrary and capricious manner." 5 U.S.C. § 706(2)(A). On its own, this does not appear to be a particularly burdensome obligation. However, when agencies are required to take additional steps (such as engaging in a cost-benefit analysis), failure to do so can result in a finding that this standard has been violated.

With regard to the SEC, the Investment Company Act of 1940 requires that the SEC consider a rule's effect on the promotion of efficiency, competition, and capital formation. Investment Company Act of 1940, 15 U.S.C. § 80a–2(c). The Business Roundtable opinion concluded that the SEC's failure to consider the potential costs of a rule that would have changed shareholders' right to access the proxies of publicly traded corporations meant that the agency had been arbitrary and capricious. *Bus. Roundtable v. SEC,* 647 F.3d 1144, 1156 (D.C. Cir. 2011).

[28]   McGarity, *supra* note 15 at 1400.

agencies most intimately involved in the oversight of cryptotransactions. Not only does the SEC need to expend considerable resources if it wishes to promulgate new rules, but it must be prepared to defend its decisions in court if it comes to that.

As an example of what this entails, one of the issues that has long troubled the SEC is the extent to which shareholders in a publicly owned corporation ought to be allowed to use the corporation's proxy materials to nominate directors.

Although proxy regulation is mostly outside the scope of these materials, shareholders in publicly traded corporations usually do not go to vote in person. Instead, they send in "proxies," which enable a representative to "appear" at the meeting and vote in their stead. To ensure compliance with federal securities laws as well as to make sure that enough shareholders vote, public corporations expend substantial sums of money preparing and disseminating proxy solicitations materials to existing shareholders. Included in those annual proxy solicitations from the company are nominations for director. Usually the company only nominates enough individuals to fill the vacant spots, so in essence shareholders have little say in who they are voting for unless they want to expend equal amounts of money soliciting opposing proxies.

In June of 2009, concerned about the extent to which director-nominated boards were truly accountable to shareholders, the SEC proposed Exchange Act Rule 14a–11 (Rule 14a–11), which would have required publicly owned companies to include qualifying shareholder nominees on proxy ballots solicited by the company. The SEC received approximately 600 responses regarding the proposed rule over the next 15 months. Congress interceded by enacting section 971 of Dodd-Frank, specifically authorizing the SEC to expand proxy access by rule, "under such terms and conditions as the Commission determines are in the interests of shareholders and for the protection of investors." Two months after that provision became law, the SEC adopted Rule 14a–11.

The enacting release was extensive, including 19 pages in the Federal Register devoted to the SEC's cost-benefit analysis and an additional 6 pages discussing potential burdens on efficiency, competition, and capital formation. The SEC's conclusion was that Rule 14a–11 would increase corporate performance, and that any costs of the rule were a necessary consequence of enforcing traditional state law rights.

The Business Roundtable, which according to its official website is composed of the Chief Executive Officers (CEOs) of leading U.S. companies, challenged Rule 14a–11 in the Court of Appeals for the D.C. Circuit. The Roundtable argued that the SEC's decision in enacting Rule 14a–11 had been based "on a fundamentally flawed assessment of the rules' costs, benefits, and effects on efficiency, competition, and capital formation."[29] The SEC stayed enforcement of the new rule pending the outcome of the case, and in 2011, the District Court for the District of Columbia concluded that the SEC had acted "arbitrarily and capriciously" in enacting the rule.[30] The SEC elected not to appeal.

That opinion, and others like it, reflects the reality faced by federal administrative agencies, and it helps explain why regulatory reaction seems so slow. Nonetheless, regulators are not free to ignore technological innovations that directly impact their mission and their responsibilities. This is certainly the case with crypto.

This, not surprisingly, causes a number of problems. In the absence of specific regulations, innovators may abuse the situation. Alternatively, persons desiring to implement legally compliant protocols and policies may be uncertain of how they should act. In addition, regulators themselves may be forced to attempt to fit square pegs into round holes as they attempt to shoehorn new innovations into an existing regulatory scheme. Again, this appears to be the case in the new and evolving world of crypto-based enterprises.

Before delving much further into the realm of cryptoassets and cryptotransactions, however, it is probably important to make sure that the relevant terminology associated with crypto is understood. The next chapter therefore focuses on important terms and concepts, providing definitions for a wide range of terms that are important in this space.

---

[29]   Opening Brief of Petitioners, *Business Roundtable v. SEC*, 647 F.3d 1144 (Nov. 31, 2010, No. 10–1305), 2010 WL 5116461, at *31.

[30]   The rule in question was subject to a specific requirement not generally applicable to rules under the APA requiring the SEC to consider economic costs and efficiency considerations when adopting such rules. The plaintiffs and court objected to a perceived failure to follow this cost-benefit analysis during the rulemaking process.

CHAPTER 2

CRYPTO-SPEAK: UNDERSTANDING THE LANGUAGE OF CRYPTOASSETS

■ ■ ■

Bitcoin is not just a cryptocurrency, but also a new financial system comprised of many components. It was invented in 2008 by the mysterious Satoshi Nakamoto and released shortly after to the public. Most importantly, Bitcoin is not controlled or owned by any individual, corporation, or government. It extensively uses cryptography and relies on a peer-to-peer network. The Bitcoin protocol lays out the rules of this financial system. . . .

Nick Farrel, Jonas DeMuro, *What is Bitcoin? Understanding BTC and other crypto-currencies,* Techradar.pro (Apr. 26, 2018), available online at https://www.techradar.com/news/what-is-bitcoin

---

Chapter one of this book started with precisely this quote, along with a notation that this "simple" explanation of Bitcoin is likely to raise more questions than it answers for readers who are just learning about Cryptoassets. What does it mean when the first sentence says Bitcoin is not just a "cryptocurrency?" What is a Cryptocurrency? What is the difference between a "Cryptocurrency" and a "Cryptoasset"?[1] How was Bitcoin "invented," and who is Satoshi Nakamoto? How can it not be controlled by any person or government? What does it mean to say Bitcoin "uses cryptography," and what is a Peer-to-Peer network"? What is a "Protocol" in this context? While some of these questions were introduced in the first chapter, the following materials are designed to provide a more complete explanation of these concepts as well as definitions for other terms that are important in understanding how Cryptoassets and Cryptotransactions are being regulated today.

---

[1] While commentators in the U.S. often continue to use "Cryptocurrency" when speaking of Cryptocoins and tokens, this terminology is problematic. Most importantly, it implies that all Cryptoassets share the purpose and function of being a currency (further implying that all Crypto should all be regulated as such). Given that this is clearly no longer an accurate reflection even though the initial Cryptoassets were in fact all designed as virtual currencies, this book generally utilizes "Cryptoasset" rather than "Cryptocurrency."

Suffice it to say that understanding Cryptoassets is not easy, which makes it even more challenging to understand how they are regulated. This chapter therefore considers a wide range of specialized terms and concepts that are important in understanding the legal environment applicable to Cryptoassets. Rather than trying to fit these terms into a logical framework that would explain all of the relevant jargon and terminology, this chapter is organized along the lines of a traditional dictionary. Terms are listed and defined alphabetically.[2] For those of you who prefer to be very precise and consistent in your grammar (and I applaud you for that), in order to make it clearer as to when there is a definition available, defined terms are capitalized throughout this chapter, even if the words would normally be written in lower case. This convention applies only in the words contained in this introduction and Part 1 of this chapter.

Because these materials focus on legal regulation of Cryptoassets, various legal terms, abbreviations, and acronyms are also introduced here. (A more complete list of acronyms used in the book may be found in the Appendix.) Note that this is far from a comprehensive list of every term that might be important in understanding Cryptotransactions,[3] but the goal is to provide a starting point for communicating about Crypto and how it is regulated. All of the terms and definitions related to regulation of Crypto contained in this chapter refer to U.S. laws and authorities. Different rules and agencies are obviously in place in other jurisdictions.

The materials in this section are organized as follows. Part I of this chapter contains is a list of numbered definitions and explanations. Part II provides readings and questions designed to enable you to check to make sure that you have a basic understanding of the most important concepts.

1. DEFINITIONS

Defined terms in this section are arranged in alphabetical order, along with an explanation of each such term or phrase. Some of the terms appear throughout the book and are central to an understanding of the nature of

---

[2]   Many of these terms are also defined in Carol Goforth, *The Lawyer's Cryptionary: A Resource for Talking to Clients about Crypto-transactions*, 41 CAMPBELL L. REV. 47 (2019).

[3]   There are a growing number of unusual terms and slang associated with Crypto, including made-up words such as "hodl," which apparently originated when "hold" was mistyped. It has come to mean holding a Cryptoasset rather than selling it. Sometimes, acronyms are used in place of complete phrases, such as "FUD," which means "fear, uncertainty, and doubt." Abbreviations may also be used. A "sat," for example is short for a Satoshi, the smallest increment of a Bitcoin that may be transferred. Other words have been created through the combination of two other words, such as "cryptojacking," derived from both cryptocurrency and hijacking and referring to a relatively new form of malware that inserts itself on devices to steals computing resources in order to Mine Cryptocurrencies such as Bitcoin. Finally, there are some words that have simply been coopted and given a new meaning in the Crypto ecosystem, such as "whale," which generally refers to a very large Crypto investor. No attempt is made in this book to include all of such terms, given the continually evolving language being used in the Crypto community. This chapter does, however, offer a starting point that should be helpful in communicating about how the law is reacting to this new technology.

Cryptoassets. For example, a student reading about these concepts for the first time would be well advised to make sure to understand the meanings of and distinctions between Coins, Cryptocurrency, Digital Currency, Tokens, and Virtual Currency. In addition, it will probably be helpful to keep in mind some of the history and attributes that make Bitcoin, Ether, and Ripple (or its XRP token) so distinctive.

On the other hand, some of the terms are included here as technical background appropriate for a general understanding of how Crypto works. This includes words and phrases such as Cryptographic Hash, ERC-20 Token Standard, Masternodes, PoS and PoW, and Signature, each of which appears only a few places throughout the book. Students should not expect to spend a lot of time on the details of these definitions, and instead should seek to understand these concepts in general terms.

The definitions also include information about a few of the more commonly encountered Cryptoassets, including Dash, Ether, Litecoin, Ripple's XRP Token, and Zcash as well as Bitcoin. Given that there are thousands of Coins and Tokens, it is not realistic to expect anyone to be familiar with the attributes of every Cryptoasset. The included examples deal with some of the most popular Cryptoassets, and some of those involved in the few recorded cases and administrative actions that have been brought in the context of Crypto. The definitions or explanations in this chapter are included to provide basic insights into how Crypto can be structured. If the details are important, they will generally be highlighted in later materials when the Coin or Token is encountered again.

Some of the following terms do not directly deal with Cryptoassets. For example, these definitions include introductory references to regulatory authority (such as the Bank Secrecy Act or Securities Acts or the *Howey* test) and agencies (such as FinCEN or the SEC) that will be important in later chapters. The descriptions included here are designed to prepare students for the more detailed information about these agencies and rules that will appear later in the book.

Keep in mind that it is always possible to refer back to these definitions if needed when terms are used in context later. In addition, remember that if a word is capitalized in these definitions, it is likely to have its own definition here to which you may refer as needed. Finally, for all the acronyms scattered throughout these pages and the rest of the book, remember there is an appendix following the last chapter which contains a list of acronyms for easier reference.

1) *Address (Cryptocurrency Address)*

In the context of Cryptoassets, an Address (or technically speaking a Cryptocurrency Address) is typically a string of alphanumeric characters used to send or receive information about transactions on a network in the same way that an internet protocol (IP) address allows for the routing of communications on the internet. In fact, when Bitcoin was first presented to potential users, it was possible to send Bitcoin to IP addresses, but developers realized that this could compromise the security of transactions because IP addresses often are relatively insecure. As a result, changes were made so that Cryptocurrency Addresses are now based on a series of cryptographic algorithms. The technical details of Addresses and the algorithmic processes used to keep them secure are far beyond the scope of these materials, but it is important to know that current configuration of Addresses generally ensures that they are relatively easy to use and cannot be disrupted by outside parties.

2) Airdrop

An Airdrop (which may sometimes be called a Crypto Airdrop, a Coin Airdrop, or a Cryptocurrency Airdrop) occurs when a Coin or Token project wants to promote their Cryptoasset by distributing it to an active community without the expectation of immediate payment in any form of currency. Instead of seeking payment, for a limited period of time, the project will distribute its Coins or Tokens for free, without requiring an investment of money or other property. While a free Coin Airdrop can be done on any Blockchain, Ethereum has been the dominant Blockchain for these kinds of distributions.

The project uses this distribution as a way to create a community around their Coin or Token, while creating a potential customer database at the same time. It is both an advertising ploy and a way to generate interest and value in a Cryptoasset, since holders of any specific kind of Crypto are more inclined to give it value than are persons who have not heard of the asset in question.

Different Airdrops may have different requirements, such as an obligation to provide certain personal information (for example to enable the Project to comply with its Know-Your-Customer obligations), an obligation to follow the project on Twitter or to join its Telegram account, or the need to be demonstrably active in the Crypto community.

3) Altcoin

"Altcoin" is the general term for Cryptocurrencies that are specifically designed as alternatives to Bitcoin. Most of these promote themselves as better than Bitcoin in one or more ways and were launched after the initial successes of Bitcoin. Altcoins include a wide variety of Cryptocurrencies that have special attributes in addition to being a potential medium of exchange, unit of account, or store of value (the typical characteristics of conventional currency). Altcoins may possess a range of specialized attributes, such as offering increased privacy or security. They may utilize Consensus Protocols that are more egalitarian or less potentially harmful to the environment. Alternatively, it is also possible for an Altcoin to offer specialized applications for particular platforms such as serving as a developer tool or providing a means or mechanism for sharing data.

4) Anti-Money Laundering (AML) Requirements

Under the Bank Secrecy Act (BSA), as amended by the U.S.A. PATRIOT Act, "financial institutions" are required to develop a risk assessment policy that insures compliance with federal AML requirements.[4] "Financial Institutions" are broken into a number of different subcategories, with category-specific rules.

While many of the BSA requirements apply only to institutions that work with "real" (Fiat) currency, such as national banks or savings and loans, exchangers and administrators of Virtual Currencies that are convertible into such currency are subject to certain requirements as Money Transmitters. In very general terms, the BSA imposes on Money Transmitter businesses three kinds of requirements: (1) the business must register with FinCEN; (2) it must possess risk-based know-your-customer (KYC) and anti-money-laundering (AML) programs; and (3) it must maintain records and file various reports such as suspicious activity reports (SARs) with FinCEN. Mere "users" of Cryptocurrencies are not subject to these requirements, but the definition of user is restricted to persons who obtain a Cryptocurrency solely for the purpose of purchasing goods or services, and not for investment, charitable contribution, gift, or non-exchange reason.

5) Bank Secrecy Act (BSA)

Congress passed the BSA in 1970 in order to fight money laundering in the U.S. The purpose of the BSA, aside from making money laundering more difficult to perpetrate, is to prevent banks from becoming unknowing intermediaries in illicit activity. The BSA has been amended several times, including by the USA PATRIOT Act of 2001, which included provisions specifically designed to strengthen U.S. measures to prevent, detect and prosecute international money laundering and the financing of terrorism. The BSA, as amended, is enforced by the Financial Crimes Enforcement Network (FinCEN), to which required reports must be made.

The BSA requires U.S. financial institutions to work with and report suspected money laundering and fraud. Covered financial institutions not only include banks, but also broker dealers, casinos and dealers in gemstones and precious metals, and businesses that issue and redeem money orders. Cryptocurrencies do not currently fall within these general categories, but do fit within the broader categories of "Money Service

---

[4] The general parameters of the Bank Secrecy Act are discussed in significantly more detail in chapter 3. Those materials also contain a more thorough explanation of AML and other requirements.

Business" and potentially "Money Transmitters," which are also subject to the BSA AML (Anti-Money Laundering) and KYC (Know-Your-Customer) requirements.

6) Bitcoin

Although there are more than 2000 distinct Cryptoassets, a particularized examination of "Bitcoin" is important because of the dominating space Bitcoin occupies in the Crypto and financial worlds. Bitcoin is a Cryptocurrency launched in 2009 when the Bitcoin network went public, making Bitcoin available to anyone who successfully "Mined" it. In contrast to traditional government-backed currencies ("Fiat"), Bitcoin has no centralized bank, nation state, or regulatory authority backing it. "Bitcoins" have no tangible existence and instead are balances on the Blockchain ledger, controlled by digital keys[5] stored in a digital wallet[6] that can exist online or on an investors' own hardware. Despite significant volatility, the total capitalization of Bitcoin has not been below $100 Billion since the end of October 2017. Despite wide fluctuation in the value of individual Bitcoins, as of the start of July 1, 2019, the total market capitalization of Bitcoin exceeded $200 billion. This is not to say that Bitcoin is universally applauded, with some financial experts characterizing it as not being suitable for investment because it lacks any intrinsic value. Nonetheless, as the first successfully established Cryptocurrency, Bitcoin has been the "de facto standard" for all Cryptocurrencies.

The technological foundation for Bitcoin was first publicized in 2008 in a paper entitled *Bitcoin—A Peer to Peer Electronic Cash System* that originally appeared in an online discussion of cryptography. It was posted under the pseudonym Satoshi Nakamoto, whose real identity still remains a mystery. The paper presented the innovative idea of Consensus Protocols in the form of Proof-of-Work, which provides a solution to the issue of how consensus can be reached as to the validity of transactions on a decentralized network absent the ability to trust the other parties who are involved.

---

[5]   Keys are basically very long numbers that work with a cryptographic algorithm to protect electronically transmitted data from being intercepted and translated. The details of public key cryptography are far beyond the scope of these materials, and it is not really necessary to understand the intricacies of the process. In general terms, a public key is made available to everyone, while a private key remains confidential with its owner. Whatever is encrypted with a public key may only be decrypted with the corresponding private key. This means that if a wallet owner loses his or her private key, he or she will also lose access to any Crypto associated with that wallet.

[6]   A digital wallet does not act like a conventional storage device. It does not, for example, actually "hold" any Crypto. Instead, it stores the private key needed to decrypt messages and to generate the digital Signature needed to verify ownership of assets held on a Blockchain associated with the wallet.

Given both the speed with which Bitcoin has risen to prominence (far outpacing effective regulation and oversight) and the sheer amount of money involved, it is not surprising that there have been bumps along the way. For example, in 2011, MyBitcoins, a wallet service, suddenly disappeared from the web, reportedly because the site was hacked. In 2012, Bitcoinica, an early Bitcoin Exchange, was hacked multiple times before being closed, and several other Exchanges were also shutdown. In January 2014, the world's largest Bitcoin Exchange at the time, Mt. Gox, suddenly declared bankruptcy, and 850,000 Bitcoins (then valued at approximately $460 million) were apparently lost to hackers. Hackers have continued to exploit weaknesses in various Bitcoin Exchanges and wallet services, while regulators attempt to insure that there are protocols in place to protect customers.

On the other hand, these insecurities all relate to sites that trade in or host ownership of Bitcoin, with the Decentralized Blockchain Ledger technology underlying the success of Bitcoin proving to be remarkably secure and successful. The economic success and longevity of Bitcoin has at least proven that its underlying technology is workable and can be reliable. Its history also proves that service providers who offer platforms on which such assets can be stored or traded may not be as secure, and that there are a variety of potential risks with investment in or utilization of Cryptoassets.

7) *Block*

In the context of Blockchains, a "Block" is a permanently recorded, time-stamped transaction aggregated with other transactions that occurred at about the same time. One of the simplest ways to think about this is as if a "Block" is the equivalent of a page in a ledger or record book. Each Block includes a reference to the immediately preceding Block (so that the system knows where it is to be placed in the chain) and ends with a difficult mathematical puzzle or problem. The problem must be solved before the Block can be verified and added to the chain. Blocks are then added to the chain (the "Blockchain") in the same sequence by everyone in the network. The first transaction in each new Block is called the genesis transaction, and for Crypto that is issued to Miners, it will contain the record of which addresses or scripts are entitled to receive the reward for solving the mathematical problem.

It is possible for the chain to have temporary splits or Forks, which would happen, for example, if two computers performing Mining operations coincidentally arrive at two different valid solutions for the problem in the most recent Block at the same time. The Peer-to-Peer Network is designed to resolve these splits within a short period of time, so that only one branch of the chain survives. The surviving chain is the one with the most combined difficulty.

8) Blockchain

First utilized in 2008 in connection with the development of Bitcoin, Blockchain is a technological and cryptographic process involving a digital decentralized Distributed Ledger in which transactions are added in chronological order, creating a "chain" of Blocks. The information held on that distributed chain is continually being updated and reconciled. Because the information is shared in its entirety among so many computers (i.e., it is wholly distributed), it cannot be controlled by any single entity, and the system therefore has no single point of access where a hacker or other outside force can interrupt or corrupt the information on the chain. It is protected from being corrupted because altering any unit of information on the Blockchain would mean using a huge amount of computing power to override the entire network. Blockchain technology therefore allows digital information to be distributed but not altered unilaterally.

9) Blockchain 2.0

As one might expect with new technology, there have been a number of developments relative to the use and utility of Blockchain technology since its introduction. Originally conceived as a vehicle with the potential to act as a medium of exchange, Blockchain has evolved into a platform for other innovations. The expanded functionality is sometimes called "Blockchain 2.0."

In essence, while Blockchain was originally designed to support applications involving Cryptocurrencies, Blockchain 2.0 allows for programmable transactions, which are transactions dependent on a condition or a set of conditions. Blockchain 2.0 therefore creates a range of new economic opportunities previously unavailable on the web, including such things as microtransactions, decentralized exchange, and Smart Contracts.

10) Blockchain Consensus Protocol (Consensus Protocol)

As a caveat, these materials are not designed to provide technical operational information. With that understanding, Consensus Protocols are Crypto's solution to the problems created by the fact that disperse participants in a network cannot reasonably trust everyone else in the network. In other words, Consensus Protocols allow for the establishment of peer-to-peer decentralized ledgers such as currency systems even absent trust or the involvement of an independent intermediary.

The original Consensus Protocol, utilized by Bitcoin following Satoshi Nakamoto's innovative solution as published in a 2009 whitepaper, can be described in simplified terms as follows. A proposed transaction is reported to the network. At that point every network Node (i.e., every computer with access to the network) examines the ledger to ensure the transaction is legitimate (i.e., verifies that the previously approved ledger shows that the transferor has the Bitcoins that are proposed to be transferred). Once the transaction is accepted as legitimate, it becomes part of the aggregated transactions that form a potential Block in the chain. However, in order to actually be added to the chain, the Nodes must solve a mathematical puzzle or problem, known as the "Proof-of-Work." Nodes that attempt to solve the puzzle are said to be Miners, and a Miner that successfully solves the puzzle sends the solution to the network for verification. Upon verification, that Block becomes part of the Chain, the pending transactions that are part of the Block are added to the ledger, and the Miner is rewarded for the "work" in solving the puzzle (in Bitcoin's case, the reward takes the form of a number of Bitcoins).

The Proof-of-Work (PoW) mechanism successfully solved the trust problem, but there are some issues with it as a consensus protocol. First and foremost, PoW is an inefficient process because of the sheer amount of power and energy that it consumes. Moreover, given that Cryptocurrencies were often lauded for their democratic character, the fact that wealthier people and organizations who can afford faster and more powerful application-specific integrated circuit (ASIC) devices have a better chance of Mining than others has been viewed as incompatible with the egalitarian goals behind the technology. (This was certainly true for Bitcoin, although subsequent Altcoins have relied on different algorithms to help ameliorate this problem.)

In response to these concerns, several Cryptoasset projects have been working on alternatives to the Proof-of-Work Consensus Protocol. The first of the alternatives involves Proof-of-Stake (PoS) Protocols. The idea behind this approach is simple: the more you invest in the Coin or Token, the more you gain by Mining it with this protocol. Proof-of-Stake requires a functional consensus distribution algorithm that rewards earnings based on the number of Coins or Tokens a Node owns or holds (or other attributes such as age or duration). The environmental reason for this shift is readily apparent; instead of thousands of computers Mining simultaneously, all a user needs is a single computer with all of the user's holdings on it. Reportedly, the first Cryptoasset to adopt the Proof-of-Stake method was Peercoin.

Cardano, a fully open-source, decentralized public Blockchain project, has developed a Smart Contract Proof-of-Stake platform based on its Ouroboros algorithm. Because of its innovative work in this area, it has been described as a leader in this space. The Cardano project explains its commitment to the Ouroboros algorithm as being based on concern for the extreme environmental impact of Proof-of-Work Protocols.

Ethereum is also planning to move from Proof-of-Work to Proof-of-Stake, under a process that is somewhat different from that proposed by

Cardano. The Ethereum project is working on a network upgrade known as Casper, which will allow users to "stake" their Ether Tokens. Validators, who must own enough Ether to be eligible to participate, will lock up some of their Ether in order to support bets. If they act maliciously, they lose their stake; those who act honestly will be rewarded with an interest proportional to the amount of Ether that they chose to stake. This project has taken longer than originally projected, although there are reports that, as of mid-2019, Ethereum plans on moving to PoS in one way or another in the next twelve months.

Other Blockchain Consensus Protocols have also been considered, including Proof-of-Activity, Proof-of-Burn, Proof-of-Capacity, and Proof-of-Elapsed-Time. Currently, none of these seem to have gained widespread acceptance.

11) Byzantine Generals Problem

This is the label that was applied to the problem that stood in the way of successful decentralized, Peer-to-Peer networks before the innovations announced by Satoshi Nakamoto in 2009.

The Byzantine Generals Problem is framed in a world before mobile communications. In that fictitious environment, several army groups surround a castle they hope to conquer. Only a simultaneous attack by at least a majority of the group will succeed. Suppose further that the groups are dispersed, meaning that the general for each group must send messages between the various groups to relay the time to attack. Complicating matters, some generals may not obey instructions, and some might actually seek to sabotage the attack, conveying incorrect information about when the attack is to occur to others. How can the participants be assured of a coordinated attack by at least a majority of the generals?

In the context of modern Blockchains, absent a solution to that problem, there is no way to proceed safely because other participants cannot be trusted. There must be a way to ensure that a sufficient number of participants in the network agree on things (such as whether they are all going to recognize a transaction as valid). Certainly in a decentralized, massive network, trust does not work. The conventional solution of a trusted intermediary would require some payment for coordinating a transaction and, in addition, a single middleman could be compromised by internal malfeasance, an outside source, or a hack.

Satoshi Nakamoto solved the Byzantine Generals Problem by inventing something now known as the Proof-of-Work Protocol (sometimes called PoW). As described earlier in this chapter, PoW works as follows: A transaction is reported to the network. At that point every network Node (i.e., every computer with access to the network) examines the ledger to ensure the transaction is legitimate. Once the transaction is accepted as legitimate, it becomes part of the aggregated transactions that form a potential Block in the chain. In order to be added to the chain, the Nodes must solve a mathematical puzzle or problem which is known as the "Proof-of-Work." Nodes that attempt to solve the puzzle are said to be Miners, and a Miner that successfully solves the puzzle sends the solution to the network for verification. Upon verification, that Block becomes part of the Chain, and the Miner is rewarded for the "work" in solving the puzzle. This protocol enables the network to function without the need to trust any individual participant or third party.

12) Coinbase

Coinbase is a digital trading platform founded in June of 2012, with headquarters in San Francisco, California. It claims 10 million or more users with more than $50 billion in Cryptoassets traded. Coinbase has often been listed as one of the "most popular" and "well-known" brokers and trading platforms for Crypto.[7] The goal of the platform is to make it easy to buy, store and trade Digital Currency securely. The company allows purchases of certain Cryptocurrencies (which vary depending on the country in which the trader is located) through a digital wallet or through trading on the company's Coinbase Pro subsidiary, which was formerly called Global Digital Asset Exchange (GDAX).

Coinbase Pro operates in a number of countries, including the U.S., and has been praised as having a "[g]ood reputation, security, reasonable fees, [being] beginner friendly, [and having] stored currency [that] is covered by Coinbase insurance." On the other hand, it has also been described as lacking adequate customer support, and having "limited payment methods, limited countries supported, [and] non-uniform rollout of services worldwide," with the conclusion by some that it is "suitable for technical traders only." In mid-2019, according to the Coinbase Pro website (https://pro.coinbase.com/fees), the base cost for this platform was a 4% fee on U.S. based transactions, although the exact amount charged varied depending on size of the transaction and a variety of other factors.

13) Coincheck

Coincheck is a Tokyo-based Cryptocurrency Exchange (or trading platform) that promoted itself as having the number one Bitcoin trading volume in Japan. In early 2018, it was hacked, infamously losing $530 million in NEM Tokens. Coincheck froze transactions on its platform following the hack. For more than a year, the official Coincheck webpage stated that "[c]urrently, we have suspended various features on our platform including new registrations."

---

[7] *See, i.e.,* Shanthi Rexaline, *Best Cryptocurrency Trading Platform*, BENZINGA (Aug. 13, 2019) (available online at https://www.benzinga.com/money/best-brokers-cryptocurrencies/).

Coincheck is only one of a number of digital currency trading platforms, but this experience should serve as a cautionary warning about some of the risks associated with trading on platforms based outside of the U.S. Of course, regulation in the U.S. is also lagging behind technological developments, and there are no widely accepted standards by which such trading platforms are evaluated or rated.

14) CoinDesk and CoinTelegraph

CoinDesk is a news site focusing on Blockchain technology and digital currencies. It describes itself on its webpage as "the leading digital media, events and information services company for the crypto asset and Blockchain technology community. Its mandate is to inform, educate and connect the global community as the authoritative daily news provider dedicated to chronicling the space."[8]

CoinTelegraph describes itself in very similar terms. On its webpage, CoinTelegraph claims that it "is the leading independent digital media resource covering a wide range of news on blockchain technology, crypto assets, and emerging fintech trends. Each day our team delivers the most accurate and up-to-date news from both the decentralized and centralized worlds."[9]

Both of these services provide an incredible range of current sources about what is going on in the crypto ecosystem. Reports cover events on a state, national, and global scale.

15) CoinMarketCap

CoinMarketCap.com is a website that lists all Coins and Tokens (either separately, or combined into what it calls "All Cryptocurrencies"), along with each asset's Market Capitalization, price, volume, circulating supply, and percent change in price over the preceding 24 hours. Valuation can be in US Dollars, Bitcoin, Ether, or based on the trading price of a few other Cryptoassets. CoinMarketCap describes itself as the "world's cryptocurrency data authority,"[10] and its pricing charts are accessible online without charge.

16) Coins (Cryptocoins)

From a technical or programming standpoint a "Cryptocoin" is a form of Cryptoasset that operates independently of other platforms. Bitcoins and early Altcoins (alternatives to Bitcoins) are examples of this kind of

---

[8]   *About CoinDesk, Inc.*, COINDESK (available online at https://www.coindesk.com/about).

[9]   *About CoinTelegraph*, COINTELEGRAPH [archived at https://perma.cc/X794-LCSF].

[10]   COINMARKETCAP.COM (slogan appearing at https://coinmarketcap.com/api/ with page archived at https://perma.cc/Z9LJ-Q7DM). The homepage, with lists of cryptoassets and market capitalization appears at https://coinmarketcap.com/. [A sample CoinMarketCap page from Oct. 17, 2018 is archived at https://perma.cc/9CAH-KALJ.]

Cryptoasset. Aside from this programming aspect, some commentators prefer to use "Coin" when referring to a form of Crypto specifically designed to act as an alternative to Fiat Currency. This would have applied to Bitcoin and all the early Altcoins. On the other hand, some Cryptoassets that are hosted on their own Blockchain, independent of any other platform, may have functionality beyond merely serving as a medium of exchange, store of value, or unit of account (the traditional hallmarks of currency). As a result, sometimes "Cryptocoin" means any Crypto that operates on its own Blockchain regardless of its intended function, and sometimes it means any Crypto that serves solely as a currency regardless of whether it is hosted on a third-party Blockchain. The actual meaning of "Coin" or "Cryptocoin" may therefore have to be determined by context, with the understanding that not all users agree when the label should be applied.

17) Commodities Futures Trading Commission (CFTC)

Futures trading occurs where two parties enter into a contract purporting to call for the delivery of something at a future date when no bona fide delivery is actually contemplated.[11] As early as 1921, Congress recognized that futures trading (while it might look like gambling) could also protect farmers in particular from the uncertainties of the market. To balance the legitimate need for a ready market for agricultural commodities, in 1921 Congress tried to require that all grain futures contracts occur on an exchange approved by the Secretary of Agriculture. When that legislation was struck down, Congress reacted with the Grain Futures Act, which became the Commodities Exchange Act (CEA) a few years later.[12] In 1974 the CEA was amended to authorize the Commodities Futures Trading Commission (CFTC), and its reach has expanded far beyond agricultural products.

Under the current version of the CEA, the term "commodity" includes all agricultural products except onions, "and all services, rights, and interests (except motion picture box office receipts. . .) in which contracts for future delivery are presently or in the future dealt in."[13] As noted in 2014 by the then-Chairman Timothy Massad, in testimony before a U.S. Senate Committee, "[t]he CEA defines the term commodity very broadly so that in addition to traditional agricultural commodities, metals, and energy, the CFTC has oversight of derivatives contracts related to

---

[11] This kind of transaction was originally regarded as being akin to gambling, and in *Justh v. Holliday*, 2 Mackey 346 (D.C. Sup. 1883), the U.S. Supreme Court struck down a contract between a young General Custer as a gaming contract that was void for being "contrary to public policy." *Id.* at 348. On the other hand, the liquidity provided by the presence of speculators was a great boon to farmers in particular, who were able to utilize the futures markets to guarantee a return on their operations notwithstanding price instability and uncertainties for the agricultural produce itself.

[12] The Commodities Exchange Act (CEA) is codified at 7 U.S. CODE §§ 1 et seq.

[13] 7 U.S. CODE § 1a(9).

Treasury securities, interest rate indices, stock market indices, [and] currencies . . . to name just a few underlying products."[14]

This definition is important because every futures and derivative contract has an underlying commodity, and commodities as well as a variety of derivatives based on those commodities can be traded. The way in which different kinds of transactions are regulated by the CFTC varies. Transactions in the actual commodity involving immediate delivery of the item are said to occur in the "spot," or "physical," or "actual" market, and are not subject to CFTC regulation except to the extent necessary to prevent fraud or manipulation. Even forward contracts, derivative arrangements which involve contracts calling for deferred delivery (where delivery is in fact contemplated), are subject to regulation by the CFTC only to the extent that fraud or price manipulation is involved. If, however, the transaction involves a futures contract, or in other words a contract that does not genuinely contemplate the actual delivery of the underlying commodity, the CFTC has exclusive jurisdiction over the transaction and can impose requirements in order for the transaction to be legally compliant. Under current rules, a futures contract must be conducted through an exchange that is a "designated contract market" regulated by the CFTC. Each regulated exchange imposes standardized terms on all transactions that take place on that exchange, with the only non-standard term being price of the commodity (which is negotiated).

This is relevant to a discussion of Cryptoassets because the CFTC treats Virtual Currencies as commodities, and at least one court has agreed with this approach.[15] The CFTC's approach to Crypto is discussed more fully in chapters eleven and twelve.

18) Cryptoasset (Crypto)

Cryptoasset or Crypto is a word that has been developed to more clearly convey that the reference is intended to include all Cryptocoins and Tokens, regardless of how they are classified or regulated. The word "Cryptocurrency" is sometimes intended to exclude those assets that are not intended to serve as a replacement for conventional of Fiat currency. The word "Tokens" sometimes excludes "Coins," and vice versa, although this is not universally accurate. To minimize potential confusion or ambiguity, some sources (including this book) generally use "Cryptoasset" or "Crypto" as the broader term, encompassing all of the potential categories of Cryptocoins and Tokens.

---

[14]   U.S. CFTC *Testimony of Chairman Timothy Massad before the U.S. Senate Committee on Agriculture, Nutrition & Forestry* (Dec. 10, 2014), https://www.cftc.gov/PressRoom/Speeches Testimony/opamassad-6.

[15]   *CFTC v. McDonnell*, 287 F. Supp.3d 213 (E.D.N.Y. Mar. 6, 2018).

19) *Cryptocurrency*

"Cryptocurrency" is a term that is very widely used, but unfortunately it does not always mean precisely the same thing. That is the primary reason why this book will rely on other words, such as Cryptoasset or simply Crypto when there is no specific type of Cryptoasset in mind or when the comment applies to all kinds of Crypto. Similarly, these materials will generally use "Coin" or "Token" or "Virtual Currency" if a specific kind of interest or function is important to the discussion. Readers should be aware that other sources, including some materials excerpted in this book, may use the word "Cryptocurrency" differently, and the meaning of that word will then depend on context.

Often, "Cryptocurrency" is used to describe both Coins and Tokens, regardless of how they are intended to function. One source, for example, says that Cryptocurrency is generally understood as covering the realm of exchangeable value Coins and Tokens.[16] CoinMarketCap.com, a website that tracks what it calls Cryptocurrency capitalization, divides Cryptocurrencies into Coins and Tokens, with the platforms utilized by each listed Token also being specified.

Some sources disagree with this taxonomy and instead would limit Cryptocurrency to digital assets that meet certain characteristics. These may include possessing attributes such as being public, open-source, and decentralized. For example, some commentators have objected to classifying the JPMorgan JPM Coin as a Cryptocurrency because it does not share these characteristics.[17]

In other contexts, the word Cryptocurrency is meant to describe only Cryptoassets that are designed and intended to function as replacements for traditional, Fiat currency.[18] In this case, the designation refers to the

---

[16] "It is important to note that all coins or tokens are regarded as cryptocurrencies, even if most of the coins do not function as a currency or medium of exchange." Aziz, *Coins, Tokens & Altcoins: What's the Difference?*, MASTERTHECRYPTO (available online at https://masterthecrypto. com/differences-between-cryptocurrency-coins-and-tokens/).

[17] Madhvi Mavadiya, *Stop Calling JPMorgan's JPM Coin A Cryptocurrency, Because It's Not*, Forbes (Feb.17, 2019) (available online at https://www.forbes.com/sites/madhvimavadiya/ 2019/02/17/jp-morgans-cryptocurrency-jpm-coin-is-not-a-cryptocurrency/#4cb3795d21d1). Even more established assets such as Ripple have been criticized as not being true cryptocurrencies. *See* Joe Liebkind, *Why Some Claim Ripple Isn't a 'Real' Cryptocurrency*, INVESTOPEDIA (updated Dec. 14, 2017) (available online at https://www.investopedia.com/news/why-some-claim-ripple-isnt-real-cryptocurrency-0/).

[18] For example, one online dictionary simply defines "cryptocurrency" as "a digital currency in which encryption techniques are used to regulate the generation of units of currency and verify the transfer of funds, operating independently of a central bank." *Cryptocurrency*, GOOGLE ONLINE DICTIONARY (available online at https://www.google.com/search?rlz=1C5CHFA_enUS784US784 &q=Dictionary#dobs=cryptocurrency). On the other hand, dictionary.com would be more expansive, defining the term as "a digital currency *or decentralized system of exchange* that uses advanced cryptography for security." *See Cryptocurrency*, DICTIONARY.COM (available online at https://www.dictionary.com/browse/cryptocurrency) (definition as of August 15, 2019; emphasis added).

currency function of the Cryptoasset, rather than describing a presumed technical difference between Coins and Tokens.

There is no consensus on whether any particular usage is more correct. Instead, it is important to realize that "Cryptocurrency" may be used to mean Coins alone; both Coins and Tokens; only those Coins or Tokens that are designed to function as currencies; or to either kind of Cryptoasset, regardless of whether its function is to serve as a currency replacement. In fact, this lack of precision in terminology is one of the many factors that makes basic research into this emerging field so difficult. Since various sources discussing concepts relevant to Cryptoassets are inconsistent in their use of the technical terms, care must be taken in trying to understand the context in which particular comments are made.

20) *Cryptocurrency Exchange (Exchange; Crypto Exchange)*

Cryptocurrency Exchanges are websites where Cryptoassets may be bought, sold, or exchanged for other forms of Crypto or Fiat currencies such as U.S. dollars or Euro. Not all Exchanges will support all Cryptoassets. Professional traders may seek out an Exchange such as Kraken or Bittrex. Those kinds of Exchanges require participants to register, verify their identification, and have an account. Occasional traders may rely on trading platforms that do not require an account, although this is increasingly unusual. Such platforms are websites that connect buyers and sellers and typically take a fee from each transaction. They may involve direct trading, where sellers set their own exchange rates, or may involve a broker who sets the exchange rate on the broker's website. Exchanges are increasingly subject to regulatory requirements, and violation of applicable rules can result in substantial penalties being imposed although there are still many unregulated exchanges in operation in various countries.

21) *Cryptographic Hash*

The fixed and unchanging nature of a Blockchain ledger stems from the aggregation of time-stamped transactions into linear-sequenced Blocks. It is the aggregation into Blocks that permits the creation of links between transactions—the proverbial "chain" in the Blockchain. Each Block contains a unique Cryptographic Hash derived from the Block before it. The function of the Cryptographic Hash is to authenticate the data in the Block. The resulting relationship between all the Blocks makes it virtually impossible to alter a prior entry in the digital ledger. This security feature is often regarded as one of the most attractive attributes of Blockchain technology, rendering it impervious to after-the-fact alteration or tampering.

22) Dash

Dash is an Altcoin that has been described as "a more secretive version of Bitcoin." The Dash website promotes the Coin as "Digital Cash You Can Spend Anywhere," and suggests that users can "make instant, private payments online or in-store using our secure open-source platform hosted by thousands of users around the world."[19] This product was originally launched in January of 2014 as "Darkcoin," but was rebranded in March of 2015 to become Dash (which stands for digital cash). Dash is self-funded, meaning that when new Dash are minted, 10% are set aside to improve the functionality of the Cryptocurrency. Another difference between Dash and Bitcoin is that Dash has a two-tiered structure involving "Masternodes" that perform essential functions such as determining which projects are funded and which private transactions are enabled.

23) Decentralized Applications (DApps)

Decentralized Applications (DApps) are a new sort of software, intended to be more flexible, transparent, distributed, and resilient than traditional software models. There is general agreement about what kinds of applications qualify as DApps. For example, most commentators agree that a DApp should be fully open-source, with consensus of participants being required before the DApps' protocols can be modified. A DApp's data and operating reports must be encrypted and stored on a decentralized Blockchain. A DApp must require a cryptographic Coin or Token (such as Bitcoin or an original application Token) in order to access the application. Validation input contributed by Miners or others must be rewarded in the DApp's Tokens. In more technical words, a DApp is an application that is open source, operates autonomously, has its data stored on a Blockchain, is incentivized in the form of cryptographic Tokens, and operates on a protocol that shows Proof-of-Value.

24) Decentralized Autonomous Organization (DAO)

Not to be confused with "The DAO," which was a specific Decentralized Autonomous Organization,[20] in the more general sense a Decentralized

---

[19] *Dash website* (available online at https://www.dash.org/). (This language was current as of mid-summer 2019, but had changed by September. As of September 2019 the website stated: "Real world vendors accept Dash currency. Dash is accepted globally by businesses of all shapes and sizes. Our low fees and instant transaction time make Dash the preferred method of payment around the world." This language is likely to change again, as Dash continues to promote characteristics that are likely to be seen by users and regulators as positive or at least neutral.

[20] The DAO was supposed to be a decentralized organization that would fund other blockchain projects, based on investment decisions voted on by the token holders themselves." David Siegal, *Understanding The DAO Attack*, COINDESK (June 25, 2016, 4:00 PM), https://perma. cc/U7HL-4UUF. The DAO attracted approximately $150 million worth of Ether in exchange for DAO tokens, which was remarkably successful for a coin offering. Unfortunately, hackers exploited a technical vulnerability in the programming that resulted in millions of dollars being in value being drained from the project before a "fix" could be implemented. See Emma Avon, *The DAO Hack—What Happened and What Followed?*, COINCODEX (2017) (available online at https://coin

Autonomous Organization is a group that has done away with hierarchical management. Instead, it relies on Smart Contracts, or pre-programmed rules that describe how the system is to operate. The primary problem with this characteristic, and one which caused The DAO to fail after some months, is that it is very difficult to change a DAO, or the Smart Contracts underpinning it, once the system is in operation. This can be a positive attribute, because no one person can unilaterally change the rules under which the system operates, but it is also a potentially huge disadvantage. If there is a problem, such as a bug or exploitable weakness in the underlying code, developers cannot necessarily remedy the problem efficiently. Even if participants in the community agree that there is a problem, they may not agree on how to address it. A change imposed on participants who disagree with a particular course of action may cause divisions in the community that impair its viability or potential for long-term success.

25) Digital Currency

Digital Currency is a term that traditionally referred to a non-physical (i.e., electronic or digital) representation of traditional money or Fiat currency. When used in this way, "Digital Currency" can be distinguished from "Virtual Currency," which has no corresponding external value or existence. Unfortunately, while many sources use Digital Currency in this more limited sense, that is not always the case. Coinbase, for example, used to promote itself as "the easiest and most trusted place to buy, sell, and manage your digital currency." Obviously, this was intended to convey the fact that it could be used with Cryptoassets such as Bitcoin, Bitcoin Cash, Ethereum, and various other interests. Under the more limited definition of the phrase, these assets would not be considered "Digital Currency," which may explain why Coinbase changed to talking about Cryptocurrency in mid-2019. Nonetheless, because the term can have different meanings, it is very important to carefully consider the context in which the words are used.

26) Distributed Ledger

In the context of Blockchains, a ledger is simply a digital version of a database or spreadsheet that can store all sorts of information, which everyone can trust to be accurate. An online ledger maintained by Distributed Ledger technology is "distributed" because transactions are stored on up to several thousand computers connected to a common network via the internet. Changes and updates to the ledger may only be made if the network of computers, relying on common software, reaches a

---

codex.com/article/50/the-dao-hack-what-happened-and-what-followed/) and Antonio Madeira, *The DAO, The Hack, The Soft Fork and The Hard Fork*, CRYPTOCOMPARE (Jan 12, 2018) [archived at https://perma.cc/6R49-Q42N], for additional information about the DAO.

consensus that the change or update is valid. This means that the ledger must incorporate a system-wide consensus protocol to maintain its integrity.

A Blockchain is therefore one type of Distributed Ledger; it is a decentralized, Peer-to-Peer network of independent computers recording, sharing, and synchronizing data according to preset protocols. The Blocks of data stored on the Blockchain are in essence a ledger of accepted transactions.

27) Equity Token

It is very difficult to come up with a meaningful way to distinguish between Tokens that is useful to lawyers and regulators while still being comprehensible to those in the Crypto community. Some of the suggestions made by members of the Crypto community have been quite complex, with one suggestion attempting to evaluate tokens by classifying them according to their technical layer, their intended purpose, the utility provided by the token, their legal status, and their underlying value.[21] This "multi-dimensional" approach resulted in 15 distinct categories that have not gained much traction as a way to categorize Cryptoassets. Other sources offer their own taxonomies, but from a legal perspective, the underlying technical layer does not appear to be a particularly useful way of thinking about or describing Cryptoassets.

The presence or absence of a function or utility, while important to many developers, users, and commentators, has generally been less than persuasive in shaping how regulators view Cryptoassets. Certainly, the law does not care how the developer labels a particular Coin or Token. The actual function of an asset (regardless of its potential usefulness) and how it is marketed or promoted and to whom are more likely to be important to regulators.

Given that regulators appear to have their own approaches for evaluating Cryptoassets, it is not surprising that some Tokens have been developed and described as having the specific objective of mimicking traditional ownership rights. Thus, an "Equity Token" is generally a subcategory of Tokens (or potentially Coins if the asset is located on its own Blockchain and one is using those words in a technical programming sense), that represents certain ownership rights in the underlying developer group. In this way, the Token would be like an equity interest, and hence the label "Equity Token."

---

[21] *See* Thomas Euler, *The Token Classification Framework: A multi-dimensional tool for understanding and classifying crypto tokens*, UNTITLED, INC. (Jan. 18, 2018)(available online at http://www.untitled-inc.com/the-token-classification-framework-a-multi-dimensional-tool-for-understanding-and-classifying-crypto-tokens/).

Perhaps the most famous Equity Token to date has been offered by tZero, the Blockchain-focused subsidiary of Overstock, a well-established e-commerce company. tZero filed documents with the SEC explicitly acknowledging that it was raising money through the sale of "tZero Preferred Equity Tokens."[22] In August of 2018, the company announced that it had raised $134 million through the offering.[23]

28) ERC-20 Token Standard

ERC-20 is the name given to the particular technical standards for Smart Contracts hosted on the Ethereum Blockchain. "ERC" stands for "Ethereum Request for Comment," and "20" refers to the number assigned to this particular project. As described in the Abstract for ERC-20, the standard "allows for the implementation of a standard API for tokens within smart contracts. . . . [It] provides basic functionality to transfer tokens, as well as allow[ing] tokens to be approved so they can be spent by another on-chain third party."[24] Although the standard has since been updated, many Tokens continue to operate by ERC-20 guidelines. By mid-October, 2018, there were nearly 500 ERC-20 compliant Tokens with associated Smart Contracts, and the number has continued to increase, involving more than 1100 Tokens by mid-2019.[25]

29) Ether (ETH) and Ethereum Classic (ETC)

Ether (ETH) is a digital Token offered on the Ethereum network. The terms Ether and Ethereum have come to be used interchangeably, although speaking technically Ethereum is the Blockchain network or platform on which Ether operates. Ether facilitates the development and functioning of applications on the Ethereum Blockchain, and may be used to create a wide range of DApps, including things such as online voting protocols, financial products, and games, among others.[26]

Note that the original Ethereum Token was split via a Hard Fork into Ether (ETH) and Ethereum Classic (ETC) following the infamous 2016

---

[22]   tZero, *Confidential Private Placement Offering Memorandum* (as of March 1, 2018) (available online at https://www.sec.gov/Archives/edgar/data/1130713/000110465918013731/a18-7242_1ex99d1.htm).

[23]   Stan Higgins & Nikhilesh De, *Overstock Blockchain Spin-Off Raises $134 Million—With Millions More Committed*, COINDESK (Aug. 9, 2018) (available online at https://www.coindesk.com/overstock-blockchain-subsidiary-raises-134-million-in-token-sale).

[24]   Fabian Vogelsteller & Vitalin Buterin, *ERC-20 Token Standard* (available online at https://github.com/ethereum/EIPs/blob/master/EIPS/eip-20.md).

[25]   *ERC20 Tokens list*, EIDOO (available online at https://eidoo.io/erc20-tokens-list/) [archived at https://perma.cc/6HMA-PSWX as of October 17, 2018, and archived at https://perma.cc/U9M7-29G2 on July 5, 2019]. Eidoo conveniently reports this data in a single place, but it takes its information from CoinMarketCap, and cannot guarantee that this is a complete list. Thus, the number of ERC-20 Tokens may actually be greater than reported.

[26]   Ethereum website (online at https://www.ethereum.org/).

hack of The DAO.[27] Ether is the Token that has achieved considerable economic success, and it is one of two widely-traded Tokens that the head of the Division of Corporation Finance at the SEC has to date declared not to be a security.[28]

30) *Ethereum (the Platform)*

Ethereum is a "a decentralized software platform that enables Smart Contracts and Distributed Applications to be built and run without any downtime, fraud, control or interference from a third party."[29] No one owns it, and there are no investors backing it, because there is no "Ethereum, Inc." Although there is no conventional business organization behind Ethereum, the team backing the project and encouraging innovation has been recognized for possessing an exceptional level of talent. As a result, it is not surprising that Ethereum's primary Token, ETH (which is confusingly sometimes also called simply Ethereum), has had a market capitalization second only to Bitcoin. Ether reached a peak market capitalization of more than $122 billion in January 2017 but has declined substantially in value since that time. Its value generally tracks that of Bitcoin, with substantial volatility in pricing. By the mid-2019, its total market capitalization was around $30 billion. (All of this pricing information can be confirmed by looking at the historical data on CoinMarketCap.com.)

31) *Exchange Traded Fund (ETF)*

An Exchange Traded Fund (or ETF) is essentially an investment vehicle that allows investors to buy and sell a "basket of securities" through a brokerage firm on a stock exchange. This is an innovative investment product that allows purchasers to enjoy the benefits of diversification usually associated with mutual funds, alongside the ease of trading typically associated with investment in stocks. The ETF provider owns the underlying assets, tracks their performance, and sells shares in the fund to investors. Purchasers do not own the underlying assets, and instead own a portion of the fund. ETFs are particularly popular with institutional investors, which helps explain why multiple observers have concluded that a Crypto ETF is crucial to bringing legitimacy to Crypto trading.[30]

---

[27] For more about The DAO and the resulting Hard Fork, see David Siegal, *Understanding The DAO Attack,* COINDESK (June 25, 2016, 4:00 PM) (available online at https://www.coindesk.com/understanding-dao-hack-journalists), and Emma Avon, *The DAO Hack—What Happened and What Followed?*, COINCODEX (available online at https://coincodex.com/article/50/the-dao-hack-what-happened-and-what-followed/).

[28] SEC Speech, William Hinman, *Digital Asset Transactions: When Howey Met Gary (Plastic)* (June 14, 2018) [archived at https://perma.cc/SES3-DVFF].

[29] Ethereum, *supra* note 26.

[30] The consensus in the investment community appears to be that a Bitcoin ETF would give much needed legitimacy to the Crypto market. For an explanation of this, see Bob Pisani, *The*

ETFs for securities have had to obtain exemptive relief in order to comply with Investment Company Act of 1940, a time-consuming and uncertain process. In 2018, the SEC proposed rule 6c–11 to exempt certain "vanilla" ETFs from various statutory provisions in order to streamline the approval process, but the SEC continues to hold off on approving Bitcoin ETFs. Its stated rationale has been that the proposals created too much of a risk of market manipulation and fraud.

On August 12, 2019, the SEC yet again postponed its decision on three pending Bitcoin ETF proposals (by asset managers VanEck SolidX, Bitwise Asset Management and Wilshire Phoenix), signaling that it was not yet ready to move forward with these projects.

32) *Fiat (Fiat Currency)*

"Fiat Currency" originally referred to something that had value as a medium of exchange, not because of any intrinsic or underlying value, but because people were willing to accept that it had value. For the most part, in common usage, "Fiat" or "Fiat Currency" refers to currency that is issued or backed by a governmental authority without being tied to any tangible asset (such as gold). For example, American dollars have value as a medium of exchange because the U.S. government has declared that the dollar will be legal tender and because the public generally accepts that this is true.

One of the driving theoretical underpinnings of Cryptocurrencies such as Bitcoin was that they offer comparative advantages over Fiat currencies, particularly in developing economies. Cryptocurrencies are not, for example, subject to hyperinflation because the supply of particular coins can be set as finite, preventing the problems that can occur when a government begins to print more and more cash. It can also avoid the problems of counterfeit currency because a widely distributed Blockchain ledger is not susceptible to forgery or alteration. Concerns over Fiat currency being rigged (by either governments or larger institutions), coercive, favoring the wealthy, and leading to an increasingly unhealthy concentration of wealth have also been raised as reasons to prefer Cryptocurrencies. Finally, ownership can be kept confidential since governments and large financial institutions do not oversee the creation or transfer of Cryptocurrencies.

33) *Financial Crimes Enforcement Network (FinCEN)*

Established in 1990 by order of the Secretary of the Treasury (Treasury Order Number 105–08), FinCEN merged with the Treasury Department's Office of Financial Enforcement in 1994. Following the

---

Next Step for Bitcoin is ETFs, CNBC (updated Nov. 29, 2017) (available online at https://www.cnbc.com/2017/11/29/the-next-step-for-bitcoin-is-etfs.html).

enactment of the USA PATRIOT Act in 2002, FinCEN became an official bureau in the Department of the Treasury. Its primary mission is "to safeguard the financial system from illicit use, combat money laundering and promote national security through the collection, analysis, and dissemination of financial intelligence and strategic use of financial authorities."[31] FinCEN therefore has responsibility to "implement, administer, and enforce compliance with the authorities contained in what is commonly known as the 'Bank Secrecy Act.' "[32]

On March 18, 2013, FinCEN released official guidance on how FinCEN's Regulations should be applied to "Persons Administering, Exchanging, or Using Virtual Currencies."[33] Under this guidance, mere users of Virtual Currencies are not money transmitters, but administrators and exchanges are treated as Money Transmitters, making them subject to ongoing reporting obligations and subjecting them to FinCEN jurisdiction under the terms of the Bank Secrecy Act (BSA).

In very general terms, FinCEN is focused on regulating the flow of money so that it is not used to fund illegal operations such as terrorism and cannot be funneled out of illegal operations through laundering schemes. It does this in part by subjecting persons under its jurisdiction to a wide range of monitoring, record-keeping, and reporting obligations. Persons that might facilitate illegal activities through transactions involving Cryptoassets must therefore comply with the BSA's Anti-Money Laundering (AML) and Know-Your-Customer (KYC) requirements, as overseen by FinCEN.

34) Fintech

Distributed Ledger Technology has particular significance in the financial sector, with the potential to make financial technology ("Fintech") more efficient, resilient, and reliable. Fintech generally refers to companies and projects that are designed to use technology in innovative ways to improve financial services. Experts predict particularly rapid changes in this sector of the world economy as a result of ongoing developments relating to Blockchain. There are specific resources devoted to an analysis

---

[31] FinCEN, *Mission*, https://www.fincen.gov/about/mission, archived at https://perma.cc/BYJ9-6HW7.

[32] FinCEN, *FinCEN's Mandate from Congress*, available online at https://www.fincen.gov/resources/fincens-mandate-congress.

[33] FinCEN, *Application of FinCEN's Regulations to Persons Administering, Exchanging, or Using Virtual Currencies*, FIN–2013–G001 (Mar. 18, 2013), available online at https://www.fincen.gov/resources/statutes-regulations/guidance/application-fincens-regulations-persons-administering.

of various Blockchain and Cryptoasset innovations and developments as they relate specifically to Fintech.[34]

35) *Fork*

Normally, a Blockchain consists of a series of transactions accumulated into "blocks" that are added to the chain in the same order by every computer or Node in the network. It is, however, possible for the chain to have temporary splits or Forks, which would happen, for example, if two computers performing Mining operations coincidentally arrive at two different valid solutions for the same Block at the same time. The Peer-to-Peer network is designed to resolve these splits within a short period of time, so that only one branch of the chain survives. The surviving chain is the one with the most combined difficulty.[35]

Forks therefore create an alternate version of the Blockchain, leaving two Blockchains to run simultaneously on different parts of the network until the discrepancy is resolved. A hard Fork renders some previously invalid transactions valid, and vice versa. This type of Fork requires all Nodes and users to upgrade to a new version of the protocol software. A soft Fork differs from a hard Fork in that previously valid transactions are still valid, but the updated Nodes will no longer accept new transactions like the old ones. Since old Nodes recognize the new Blocks as valid, a soft Fork is essentially backward-compatible.[36]

Hard forks generally occur when there is a seemingly unreconcilable difference of opinion among the Nodes. For example, while the Ethereum platform has never been compromised, there was an attack on The DAO[37] in 2016, pursuant to which 3.6 million Ether was hacked.[38] The community could not agree on an appropriate response. As a consequence, Ethereum was split via a hard Fork into Ethereum (ETH) and Ethereum Classic (ETC).[39]

---

[34]   *See, e.g.,* FINTECH CRYPTO NEWS (available online at https://www.fintechcryptonews. com/), and *Cryptocurrencies,* FINTECH RANKING (available online at http://fintechranking.com/ category/crypto/).

[35]   This is to prevent someone from creating a split or Fork in the chain and rapidly creating a large number of low-difficulty Blocks that it is programmed to solve, thereby having it accepted by the network as "longest."

[36]   For a description of the soft Fork considered by and the hard Fork taken by Ethereum Foundation in response to the hacking of The DAO, see *infra* note 20.

[37]   "DAO" generally refers to Decentralized Autonomous Organization as described *supra* at notes 20–23 and accompanying text. However, "The DAO" was a specific DAO programmed and launched on April 30, 2016. Siegal, *supra* note 20. The DAO attracted approximately $150 million worth of Ether in exchange for DAO tokens, which it was then going to use as a kind of venture capital fund for decentralized cryptocurrency projects. Avon, *supra* note 20.

[38]   The drained Ether has not been accessed, but its sudden removal from the system triggered a rapid drop in the value of Ether from over $20 to under $13. Siegal, *supra* note 20.

[39]   Prableen Bajpai, *The 6 Most Important Cryptocurrencies Other Than Bitcoin,* INVESTOPEDIA (Dec. 7, 2017) available online at https://www.investopedia.com/tech/most-important-cryptocurrencies-other-than-bitcoin/.

36) Howey *(or the* Howey *Test or the* Howey *Investment Contract Test)*

Both the Securities Act of 1933 and the Securities Exchange Act of 1934 contain lengthy definitions of what constitutes a security,[40] and in both instances the definition includes "investment contracts." The *Howey* test is named for a 1946 Supreme Court opinion that set out the test for what constitutes an investment contract subject to regulation under the Securities Act of 1933. *SEC v. W.J. Howey Co.*, 328 U.S. 293, 298–99 (1946). Speaking generally, this test looks at these factors to determine if a particular transaction involves a security: (i) whether there exists an investment of money (or something else of value); (ii) whether there exists a common enterprise; (iii) whether there exists an expectation of profits; and (iv) whether the expectation of profits is from the essential entrepreneurial efforts of others. All of these elements must be present in order for a particular interest to be an investment contract under *Howey*.

37) *Initial Coin Offering (ICO)*

An ICO is a way in which Blockchain-based projects raise funds by selling their underlying Cryptocoins or Tokens for other Cryptoassets or occasionally for Fiat currencies. Most ICOs have been conducted by having investors send funds (usually Bitcoin or Ether) to a Smart Contract. Those assets are stored until closing, at which time the investors are automatically provided with an equivalent value in the new Token pursuant to the programming in the Smart Contract.

The first year in which ICOs appeared to take off in a major way was 2013. At that time, Ripple had pre-mined 1 billion XRP Tokens, and it conducted an ICO in which it sold those Tokens to investors in exchange for Fiat Currencies or Bitcoin. ICOs quickly became very popular. In early 2014, in what was then the largest ICO that had ever been conducted, Ethereum raised a little over $18 million selling its Tokens to investors. It is now not uncommon to hear of ICOs raising tens or even hundreds of millions of dollars. There have even been ICO "unicorns," (another word popular in the Crypto community), meaning that the value of the sale exceeded a billion dollars.[41]

Originally there was significant doubt as to how such Token sales would be seen by regulators with eager entrepreneurs expecting that these

---

[40] The Securities Act of 1933 is codified at 15 U.S. CODE § 77 (with the definition of security appearing in section 2(a)(1) of the '33 Act, codified at 15 U.S. CODE § 77b(a)(1)), and the Securities Exchange Act of 1934 is codified at 15 U.S. CODE § 78 (with the definition of security appearing at section 3(a)(10) of the '34 Act, codified at 15 U.S. CODE § 78c(a)(10)).

[41] Jon Russell, *The first ICO Unicorns are Here,* TechCrunch (Aug. 31, 2017) (available online at https://techcrunch.com/2017/08/31/the-first-ico-unicorns-are-here/?guccounter=1&guce_referrer_us=aHR0cHM6Ly93d3cuZ29vZ2xlLmNvbS8&guce_referrer_cs=JRrDZX359XbLPP4cv_1r3w) ("It was always likely to happen, but the speed in which the first ICOs worth more than $1 billion have arrived is surprising.")

sales would often be outside the purview of existing regulations. By early 2018, however, the Chairman of the SEC was being widely quoted as saying that he had never seen an ICO that does not have the hallmarks of a securities offering.[42] Under the *Howey* test, this conclusion makes some sense because while some individuals doubtless purchase Tokens to access an underlying product or service at some future point in time, it does appear that most Token purchases are fueled by speculation.

More recently, the term "ICO" has come into some disfavor because of its obvious resemblance to "IPO," which stands for "Initial Public Offering." An initial public offering of a conventional security implies that there is a full-scale registration with the SEC, while most compliant tokenized offerings actually rely on one or more exemptions from registration even if the issuers call the distribution an "ICO."

38) *Know Your Customer (KYC)*

As applied to Money Transmitter Businesses, which under the Bank Secrecy Act would include both administrators and exchangers of Cryptoassets, KYC requirements obligate such businesses to adopt and follow a risk-based Know-Your-Customer policy. Combined with the requirement to report to FinCEN suspicious activities (including those that might involve money laundering or the funding of illegal activities), the KYC rules are designed to minimize the risk that such businesses will be facilitating the transfer of currencies (whether Fiat or Crypto based) into or out of illegal activities.

39) *Libra*

On June 18, 2019, Facebook announced that it was planning to launch a Cryptocurrency in 2020, to be called Libra.[43] Facebook does not intend to fully control Libra, but will have a vote along with other founding members of the Libra Association, a non-profit group based in Switzerland. The Libra Association was originally planned to include Facebook along with parties like Mastercard, Visa, PayPal, eBay, Kiva, and Uber, each of which is expected or has paid $10 million to join the exclusive group. That group will then oversee Libra's development, the real-world reserves that are designed to provide a stable value for Libra, and the Libra Blockchain's governance rules. (Visa, Mastercard, PayPal and eBay have since backed

---

[42] In fact, in early 2018 the Commissioner of the SEC asserted, without equivocation, that "ICOs are securities offerings that must either be registered with the SEC or qualify for a private placement exemption." Michael H. Krimminger, et. al., *SEC and CFTC Testimony on Virtual Currencies: Is More Regulation on the Horizon?*, CLEARY FINTECH UPDATE (Feb. 14, 2018) (available online at https://www.clearyfintechupdate.com/2018/02/sec-cftc-testimony-virtual-currencies-regulation-horizon/).

[43] *See generally* Nick Statt, *Facebook Confirms it will Launch a Cryptocurrency Called Libra in 2020*, THE VERGE (June 18, 2019) (available online at https://www.theverge.com/2019/6/18/18682290/facebook-libra-cryptocurrency-visa-mastercard-digital-currency-calibra-wallet-announce).

out.) Members will have the right to become a validator Node, be given a vote on the Association council, and be entitled to a share of dividends from interest earned on the Libra reserves, in an amount that is proportionate to their investment.

Libra itself will be designed as a "stablecoin," with value pegged to a basket of bank deposits and short-term government securities for a group of historically-stable Fiat currencies, including the dollar, pound, euro, Swiss franc, and yen. The precise mix of currencies has not been released, and the Association can change its composition if deemed necessary to offset price fluctuations in any particular Fiat. The plan is to start the value somewhere close to the dollar, euro, or pound to make it easier to adopt the new Cryptoasset.

Facebook intends to use a subsidiary, Calibra, to handle its dealings with Libra apart from its Facebook operations. This is intended to help preserve the privacy of Libra users. Calibra will serve as an initial wallet for the virtual currency and is anticipated to be built into Facebook Messenger and WhatsApp, as well as being a standalone product.

This development is discussed in chapter thirteen, in large part because of the immediate levels of doubt expressed by legislators and others about the proposal. Officials in numerous nations have expressed a wide range of concerns about the proposal. Some have questioned whether Facebook will really protect the privacy of users. Others have worried that Libra could threaten the stability of the existing international monetary system. There is also the fear that Libra might become "too big to fail" (potentially requiring governments to back up a private enterprise in order to protect the global economy). Others have expressed concern that Libra could be used for money laundering or funding of criminal enterprises.

40) Litecoin (LTC)

Litecoin is an Altcoin introduced in 2011, with the stated objective of becoming the "silver" to Bitcoin's "gold." As of mid-October 2018, Litecoin market capitalization was just over $3 billion, and by mid-2019 it was over $7.4 billion.[44] While it falls considerably below Bitcoin's and Ether's capitalization, this is certainly not an insignificant amount.

There are certain attributes that distinguish Litecoin from Bitcoin. One difference, which may be more apparent than real, is that Bitcoin is limited to 21 million Coins, while Litecoin can issue up to 84 million Coins. This is not likely to have any practical significance because both Coins can be divided into extremely small fractional amounts.

---

[44] COINMARKETCAP.COM (Oct. 17, 2018), archived at https://perma.cc/VA37-UD6Q as of October 17, 2018 and archived at https://perma.cc/99DY-HXYR on July 5, 2019.

A potentially more significant difference is the speed with which transactions are confirmed. While transactions themselves occur instantaneously, it takes an average of 10 minutes for the Bitcoin network to confirm transactions, while the equivalent figure for Litecoin is approximately 2 ½ minutes. Litecoin also offers lower transaction fees than Bitcoin.

Perhaps the most significant difference between the two Coins involves the cryptographic algorithms which they each employ. Bitcoin utilizes the SHA-256 algorithm, while Litecoin makes use of a newer algorithm known as Scrypt, which affects how the Coins are Mined. The SHA-256 algorithm employed by Bitcoin has allowed specialized hardware systems to become quite successful and overwhelmingly prevalent as Bitcoin Mining operations, while Scrypt was intentionally designed to be less susceptible to ASIC-based mining, which allows Nodes that can afford expensive, custom hardware an advantage in the mining process.[45]

41) Masternodes

A Node is a computer that participates in the Peer-to-Peer network that hosts a Blockchain. In some cases, not all computers are "equal," meaning that the system is not truly Peer-to-Peer, because not all Nodes in the system have equal power or authority.

A Masternode keeps a complete copy of the blockchain in real-time, but it is more than that. It also has unique functions not accessible to ordinary Nodes. For example, it might have the power to conduct private transactions, or might be the only way in which other transactions can be validated.

Because of their increased capabilities, Masternodes typically require a sizable investment. This barrier to entry, or stake in the game, is necessary to prevent Masternodes from acting in a malicious manner. Normally, this means that in order to be a Masternode, the owner must hold a minimum number of Coins of that particular Crypto. For example, for DASH MN a Masternode requires 1000 DASH units; for PIVX MN 10,000 PIVX units are required.[46] The minimum stake varies from one Cryptoasset to another.

The Masternode must also have a server and dedicated IP address on which the wallet can be hosted continuously, and the system must have storage space sufficient to save the entire Blockchain.

---

[45] Steven Buchko, *How Long do Bitcoin Transactions Take?*, COINCENTRAL (Dec. 12, 2017) (available online at https://coincentral.com/how-long-do-bitcoin-transfers-take/).

[46] Cryptoslate maintains a list of Cryptoassets utilizing Masternodes. The list can be found online at https://cryptoslate.com/cryptos/masternode/.

42) *Mining (Miners)*

Mining is the process by which transactions are verified and added to the public ledger in a Blockchain. In the case of Bitcoin and several other Cryptocurrencies, it is also the means through which new Coins are released. Anyone with access to the internet and suitable hardware can participate in Mining, although not all participating computers will be equally able to solve the problems. (In some cases, a Cryptoasset will be released to the public only after it has been pre-mined by the developers.)

The Mining process involves compiling recent transactions into Blocks and trying to solve a computationally difficult puzzle that appears at the end of each Block when it is added to the "chain." The participant ("Miner") who first solves the puzzle automatically places the next Block on the Blockchain and claims the rewards. The rewards, which may take the form of Coins or other agreed payment, incentivize Mining and act as the transaction fees associated with the transactions compiled in the Block.

"Bitcoin Mining" is the process by which transactions in Bitcoin are verified and added to the Bitcoin ledger or chain. As of mid-2019, the process results in the issuance of 12.5 new Bitcoins to the successful Miner for each Block verified.[47] Bitcoin mining, in particular, has been criticized because those who can afford faster and more powerful application-specific integrated circuit (ASIC) devices have a better chance of Mining than others, and this has been viewed as incompatible with the egalitarian and democratic goals behind Blockchain technology. It has also been criticized for significant environmental costs, since there are large scale mining operations or farms with specially designated computers using vast amounts of energy, almost equal to the entire energy consumption of Ireland, for example.[48]

43) *Money Transmitter*

Under the Bank Secrecy Act, "money transmission services" include "the acceptance of currency, funds, or other value that substitutes for currency from one person and the transmission of currency, funds, or other value that substitutes for currency to another location or person by any means."[49] Any administrator or exchanger that (1) accepts and transmits a Cryptocurrency or (2) buys or sells Cryptocurrency is a Money Transmitter under FinCEN's regulations, unless a limitation to or exemption applies. A

---

[47]　Originally, the reward was 50 Bitcoins per Block mined, but the reward has been halved every 210,000 Blocks. As of the end of 2018, there had been two such halving events. The mining reward will halve again sometime around April 30, 2020. For the time until the next halving event, see https://www.bitcoinclock.com/.

[48]　Timothy Lee, *New study quantifies bitcoin's ludicrous energy consumption*, ARS TECHNICA (May 17, 2018) (available online at https://arstechnica.com/tech-policy/2018/05/new-study-quantifies-bitcoins-ludicrous-energy-consumption/).

[49]　31 C.F.R. § 1010.100(ff)(5)(i)(A).

user who obtains Cryptocurrency solely for the purpose of buying real or virtual goods or services is not engaged in "money transmission services" and therefore is not subject to FinCEN's registration, reporting, and recordkeeping regulations.

Under these definitions, a legal person who creates a Cryptoasset and uses it to purchase real or virtual goods and services is a user (as opposed to an administrator or exchanger) and is therefore not subject to regulation as a Money Transmitter. Anyone who creates a Cryptoasset and sells it for Fiat currency or other Crypto that is convertible into Fiat currency is engaged in transmission to another location and is a Money Transmitter, as is anyone who accepts Crypto and transmits it to another person as part of the acceptance and transfer of Fiat or Crypto.

44) Nodes

A Node is a computer connected to the Blockchain network that performs the task of validating and relaying transactions. While every computer that downloads the Blockchain and has a record of ownership is a member of the network, it takes a certain amount of dedicated computing resources in order to be a Node (and on some Blockchains other requirements are imposed, as well). The computer serving as a Node obtains a copy of the Blockchain, which is downloaded automatically when the computer joins the network. In a fully decentralized network, every Node acts as an "administrator" of the Blockchain upon joining. In other words, the fact that every Node can access the entire ledger or history of the Blockchain makes the network decentralized. Nodes may be full or lightweight, with a full Node having a copy of the entire Blockchain and therefore having the power to validate Blocks and transactions from other Nodes, while a lightweight Node essentially operates by trusting the full Nodes to perform the validation functions.

45) Peer-to-Peer (P2P)

Peer-to-Peer computing is a distributed application organizational structure in which the peer computers are equally empowered participants. The peers form a network of Nodes, in which each computer that is connected to the network via the internet functions both as a client and server to other Nodes. Files are therefore shared directly without the need of a central server or host.

In the context of Cryptoassets, Peer-to-Peer generally refers to the exchange or sharing of Cryptoassets without the involvement of a central banking or governmental authority. In some cases, where only some Nodes have full functionality and other Masternodes are relied upon to perform some of the essential functions of the Blockchain, the network may not be truly Peer-to-Peer.

46) Pre-Functional Token

In the recent past, many developers and Token projects attempted to sell interests in Tokens that were not yet fully functional. Either the network or the application was not developed at the time that funding was sought, and in this sense if the issuer was selling interests in the "Tokens," they were really pre-functional Tokens, at best. This was part of the impetus for the SAFT project, which attempted to create a contract (the "Simple Agreement") which would give a purchaser of the SAFT the right to acquire the "Future Token" when it is finally completed and available. The SAFT was designed to be a security (presumably under the *Howey* test), while the resulting Token (assuming it was a fully functional Utility Token) would have fallen outside the scope of the securities laws.[50]

47) Privacy Coin

Some Altcoins have been designed to further obscure the identities of owners of a particular Cryptoasset and to hide the amounts involved in any transaction in that asset. Privacy Coins will be examined in greater detail in chapter thirteen, but in very general terms, these Coins are all designed to enhance anonymity of and privacy for owners of the asset, beyond what is available with Bitcoin. There are a number of different ways in which such privacy can be enhanced, and these are also explained later. Because distrust of governmental and other authorities was a driving factor in the creation of Bitcoin, these features continue to be of significant interest to a number of individuals within the Crypto community. Unfortunately, this privacy comes with a cost, as Privacy Coins can also be used by criminals to facilitate money laundering or to support illegal activities, including terrorism.

48) Profits Token

"Profits Token" is a label that some commentators have attached to Tokens that are specifically designed to function as a replacement for traditional investments that entitle a purchaser to a share of the issuer's profits. A Profits Token is thus specifically designed as a substitute for a traditional investment vehicle and is essentially a digital security set up to utilize a Blockchain infrastructure. Ownership of a Profits Token would entitle the owner to a share of the issuer's profits.

There are a number of possible benefits of having such a Token instead of a conventional equity interest like a share of stock or a debt interest that

---

[50]   For one explanation of this history and process, see Lukas Schor, *Explaining The "Simple Agreement For Future* Tokens" *Framework*, MEDIUM (Nov. 29, 2017) (available online at https://medium.com/@schor/explaining-the-simple-agreement-for-future-tokens-framework-15d5e 7543323). Another good source of information is the SAFT whitepaper. Juan Batiz-Benet, Jesse Clayburgh, & Marco Santori, *The SAFT Project: Toward a Compliant Token Sale Framework*, PROTOCOL LABS (Oct. 2, 2017), https://saftproject.com/static/SAFT-Project-Whitepaper.pdf archived at https://perma.cc/EQ8N-E3TJ (hereinafter called the SAFT White paper).

carries a right to profits rather than interest. Tokens are digital, making them trackable and impossible to counterfeit; they do not incur significant transaction costs; and they may appeal to a larger or different pool of investors. Depending on future regulatory developments, Profits Tokens may provide greater liquidity, may entail fewer mandatory disclosures which impose significant expenses on the issuer, and may allow for greater flexibility.

49) Proof-of-Stake (PoS) and Proof-of-Work (PoW)

Proof-of-Stake (PoS) and Proof-of-Work (PoW) are two different options for how consensus can be achieved in a decentralized, Peer-to-Peer network, and both are described in more detail in the definition of Blockchain Consensus Protocol. PoW was the original protocol, utilized by Bitcoin and most of the initial Altcoins that followed, while PoS is a more recent option designed to solve some of the problems that have arisen with PoW protocols.

50) Ripple (and Ripple's XRP Token)

Founded in 2012 under the name "OpenCoin," Ripple was designed to facilitate fast, low-cost transactions between financial institutions. As has been true for the Ethereum platform and Ether, there is often confusion about the naming of the project, the platform, and the relevant Token. One source simply asserts that "Ripple is the name for both a digital currency (XRP) and an open payment network within which that currency is transferred."[51] A simple google search on whether investment in Ripple is a good idea pulls up a plethora of articles, reinforcing the notion that many people simply say Ripple when they really mean the XRP Token.

In essence, Ripple (the Token) is intended to eliminate the limitations of conventional financial transactions caused when intermediaries are involved, particularly between unaffiliated banks. Ripple is based on conventional SWIFT banking principles and currently works with more than 100 banks. Ripple's market capitalization peaked at over $119 billion in January of 2018, but its value has declined precipitously, to approximately $18.5 billion in October of 2018 and $16 billion by mid-2019.[52]

Ripple has been criticized for lacking many of the fundamental characteristics that are the traditional hallmarks of Blockchain-based Cryptoassets. The XRP Token was not designed to function as a currency, and Ripple has generally chosen to focus on strengthening the underlying Blockchain rather than giving any priority to supporting the value of the

---

[51] Ariella Brown, *10 things you need to know about Ripple,* COINDESK (May 17, 2013) (available online at https://www.coindesk.com/10-things-you-need-to-know-about-ripple/).

[52] *Ripple, Historical Charts,* COINMARKETCAP.COM, archived at https://perma.cc/BK3Y-SSUT on July 5, 2019.

XRP Token. There are other characteristics that distinguish Ripple's XRP from conventional Cryptocurrencies. For one, XRP has no Miners and relies on a "centralized" Blockchain for speed and security. Its Blockchain is not open, and although information is safely stored and protected through cryptography, only trusted operators in the network are allowed access. Even the founders of Ripple recommend against using XRP as currency or an investment, but given the surge in trading value during 2017, clearly not everyone agrees.

Despite concerns by some that XRP should not be regarded as a "true" Cryptocurrency, it has serious financial weight behind it, and it is at least now listed as a trading option on a number of Exchanges. From a legal perspective, Ripple's XRP is most likely to be important to Banking clients because of its functionality for inter-bank and transnational banking services.

51) SAFT ("Simple Agreement for Future Tokens")

SAFT stands for "Simple Agreement for Future Tokens," a nod to the successful SAFE startup documentation project pioneered several years ago by Y Combinator.[53] In essence, a SAFT is a contract in which an investor makes a payment in exchange for a contractual right to receive Tokens when certain conditions (often including development of the Token itself) are met.

Although it was not the first project to propose a contract calling for the delivery of tokens in the future, Cooley LLP, working in conjunction with Protocol Labs, various Token creators, legal experts, and investors, produced its SAFT project in late 2017.[54] The whitepaper on this project explained that its goal was to provide framework that would operate in compliance with existing federal regulations pursuant to which investors would fund development of a network that would generate "genuinely functional utility tokens" that would then be delivered to the investors.[55] The paper readily conceded that the SAFT transaction itself would involve the sale of interests that would be investment contracts under the U.S. securities laws, but the plan was that the resulting Utility Tokens would not be securities under the *Howey*[56] investment contract test.

While this may be relatively easy to state, it would be a profound mistake to believe that the scope and details of the SAFT project are easy to understand. At least one commentator apparently took the idea that

---

[53]   To review the SAFE Financing documents developed by Y Combinator, see Carolyn Levy, *SAFE Financing Documents*, Y COMBINATOR (Sept. 3, 2018) (available online at https://www.ycombinator.com/documents/).

[54]   *Announcing The SAFT Project*, PROTOCOL LABS BLOG (Oct. 2, 2017) (available online at https://protocol.ai/blog/announcing-saft-project/ and archived at https://perma.cc/DUP2-JJ4K).

[55]   SAFT White paper, *supra* note 50.

[56]   *SEC v. W.J. Howey, Co.*, 328 U.S. 293, 298–99 (1946).

prefunded Utility Tokens should escape regulation as securities upon issuance as evidence that any company with a functional Utility Token probably would not need to worry about the project being a security. This is certainly inconsistent with the position announced by the SEC, which has generally treated virtually all ICOs as involving the sale of securities regardless of whether the Token in question has a functional utility. Uncertainty about market regulation has led most Token sales, even those in reliance on presale agreements, to be limited to investors from outside the United States.

Additional information about the SAFT is provided in chapters eight and thirteen.

52) Satoshi

"Satoshi" is the pseudonymous first name of the initial developer of Blockchain technology that allowed for the creation of Bitcoin and succeeding Blockchain-based endeavors. In honor of this name, "the minimum quantity of transferable bitcoin is one hundred millionth of a bitcoin (0.00000001 bitcoins) known colloquially as one 'satoshi.' "[57]

53) Securities Act of 1933 (the '33 Act) and Securities Exchange Act of 1934 (the '34 Act)

The Securities Act of 1933[58] and the Securities Exchange Act of 1934[59] are two of the primary pieces of legislation establishing the regime under which securities are regulated by the U.S. government. While these are not the only federal securities laws, they are among the most important to Crypto developers and entrepreneurs. Both of these statutes were enacted in response to the stock market crash of 1929.

There are a number of things that are counted as securities under these two acts, including: stock; certain kinds of debt instruments; various derivatives like options, warrants, puts, calls, and straddles; and interests that are categorized as "investment contracts." The *Howey* Investment Contract Test (described above and in greater detail in chapter seven), explains what that phrase means.

The primary focus of the '33 Act was to make information (including financial data about the issuer of securities) more available and transparent in order to allow potential purchasers of securities to make informed investment decisions. It was also designed to provide federal relief in the event of misrepresentation or fraud in connection with the

---

[57]   Jason Fernando, *Bitcoin vs. Litecoin: What's the Difference?*, INVESTOPEDIA (Feb 15, 2018, 3:38 PM) (available online at https://www.investopedia.com/articles/investing/042015/bitcoin-vs-litecoin-whats-difference.asp).

[58]   The Securities Act of 1933 is codified at 15 U.S. CODE § 77.

[59]   The Securities Exchange Act of 1934 is codified at 15 U.S. CODE § 78.

issuance and sale of securities. The '33 Act does this by imposing disclosure obligations on issuers of securities, who generally may not sell anything classified as a security unless that security is first "registered" or there is an available exemption from registration.

The '34 Act, which created the Securities and Exchange Commission (SEC), includes ongoing reporting and other informational requirements for companies that have a class of securities that is publicly held. This legislation also covers rules for securities agents, broker-dealers, and for exchanges on which publicly held securities are traded.

54) *Securities and Exchange Commission (SEC)*

The SEC was created following enactment of the Securities Exchange Act of 1934. It is the federal agency charged with enforcement of federal securities laws in the U.S. It is composed of five commissioners appointed by the President with the advice of the Senate. No more than three of the commissioners may be from the same political party. Commissioners serve for five-year terms. The SEC has the legal power to administer oaths, subpoena witnesses, take evidence and request documentation from any issuer that may have violated federal securities law. The SEC may suspend trading in any security for up to 10 days.

55) *Security Token*

The phrase "Security Token" has been used in different ways by different people. For example, some commentators use this phrase to signify only that a particular Token has been classified by the applicable regulatory authorities as a security. A more helpful definition, and one that appears to be gaining in acceptance, is that the Token in question is specifically designed and intended to serve as a substitute for conventional securities such as a debt or equity interests. For example, both Equity and Profits Tokens would be particular kinds of Securities Tokens, since both of those kinds of Cryptoasset are designed to replace conventional securities.

To minimize ambiguity, this book will typically use the label "tokenized securities" rather than the less consistently-used "Security Token." Note, however, that "Security Token" appears far more often in popular literature and commentary on Crypto.

56) *Signature*

A digital Signature is the mathematical operation used to validate the legitimacy of an electronic message or digital document. In the context of Cryptocurrencies, it is the process through which someone can prove their sole ownership over their Coin, wallet, etc. The user does this through use of an asymmetric key pair: a public and a private key. Used in tandem, the two cryptographic keys allow the message to be authenticated. To prove that a message is legitimate, the user encrypts the message or transaction data using the private key. The user's public key is accessible to everyone, so the recipient can decrypt the message. This serves as a digital Signature verification, since only the private key could have encrypted that message.

The details of how the encryption, authentication, and decryption processes work is outside the scope of these materials and not really necessary to understand how Cryptoassets and transactions are regulated.

57) Smart Contract

A "Smart Contract" is not really a "contract" at all. Instead, it is (1) pre-programmed logic written in computer code, (2) stored and replicated on a distributed platform or Blockchain, (3) that is executed or run by a network of computers (typically the same computers that host the Blockchain), (4) which results in ledger updates pursuant to the terms of the agreement as specified in the computer code. In other words, a Smart Contract is a computer program set up to enforce predetermined outcomes. A slightly more technical definition was provided by the programmer behind Ethereum, Vitalik Buterin, who explained the Smart Contract approach as starting when "an asset or currency is transferred into a program 'and the program runs this code and at some point it automatically validates a condition and it automatically determines whether the asset should go to one person or back to the other person, or whether it should be immediately refunded to the person who sent it or some combination thereof.' "[60]

The potential benefits of Smart Contracts have been widely lauded. They include increased accuracy, transparency, the potential for increased autonomy, a decreased need to "trust" the other parties to an arrangement, automatic backup for data, security for documents as a result of the cryptographic encryption of data, increased speed for transactional processes, and savings since many intermediaries (such as notaries) become unnecessary in the Smart Contract context. The clear intent is that Smart Contracts will be "smart, irrevocable, transparent, and secure." These benefits may be possible in a wide range of situations since Smart Contracts can function as "multi-signature" accounts, manage bilateral agreements, add utility to other contracts, and store records such as registration or membership information.

Bitcoin was the first Smart Contract, allowing the transfer of value from one person to another upon verification of the transaction by the network of Nodes. The Bitcoin Blockchain can process Bitcoin transactions,

---

[60]   Pukis3891, *Matrix Fixes the Blockchain: Security Vulnerabilities*, MEDIUM (Oct. 10, 2018) (available online at https://medium.com/@pukis3891/matrix-fixes-the-blockchain-security-vulnerabilities-57730d28827e).

but was not designed to execute other kinds of Smart Contracts. Ethereum is currently "the most advanced for coding and processing smart contracts," and has the advantage of being public; on the other hand, a user must pay for computing power with Ether tokens.[61]

The fact that Ethereum is the most advanced platform does not mean that Smart Contracts executed on it are exempt from some potentially serious problems. First, there are the problems inherent in setting up an immutable transaction. Those have been explained as follows: "What happens if I send the wrong code, or . . . I send the right code, but my apartment is condemned (i.e., taken for public use without my consent) before the rental date arrives? If this were the traditional contract, I could rescind it in court, but the blockchain is a different situation. The contract performs, no matter what."[62] Second, there are the potential regulatory and legal problems. How will governments tax transactions executed via Smart Contract? How will they be regulated? Which agencies and which courts will have jurisdiction? Finally, what happens if there is an error or bug in the code used in a Smart Contract or a weakness that can be exploited by a hacker? Each of these questions raises legal issues about which clients may seek advice, making it important that lawyers understand the basics of what a Smart Contract might involve.

58) Token

Technically speaking, from a programmer's perspective the difference between a Coin and a Token is that a Coin is a Cryptoasset that operates independently of other platforms. For example, Bitcoin possesses its own Blockchain, where transactions relating to Bitcoin are recorded. Many Altcoins work the same way, with those Coins having a unique Blockchain on which they operate. Conversely, Tokens are built on top of another platform in order to function.

Although this may be important for programmers and developers, for the purposes of legal regulation this is a distinction that is likely to be more form than substance. Regulators are more concerned with various functional characteristics of the Cryptoassets, not necessarily with being able to identify how they operate from a programming standpoint.

From a regulatory perspective, any Cryptoasset (regardless of whether it is hosted on its native Blockchain or it functions on top of another Blockchain) can fulfill a number of distinct functions, and a single Coin or Token can have more than one such purpose. For example, it is possible for a Cryptoasset to serve as a medium of exchange, like a currency, in which it acts as a payment system between participants. In the same way, it can

---

[61]   Ameer Rosic, *Smart Contracts: The Blockchain Technology that will Replace Lawyers,* BLOCKGEEKS (2016) [archived at https://perma.cc/28KU-RWY2].

[62]   *Id.*

act as a store of value if the purchaser holds it for appreciation or even safe-keeping. The same Coin or Token can also act as a digital asset or in other words as a digital right; owning it can represent ownership of an interest in any kind of property. Crypto (whether or not it also acts as a medium or exchange or otherwise) can also serve as a means of access or membership to a community or group. It can function as a share of or stake in a business venture. It can be a means of rewarding those who contribute to the system. Moreover, even if a particular Cryptoasset is designed for functionality rather than as an investment, it may still be possible that it will be viewed and traded as an investment. Because there are so many options, it is often difficult to appropriately and consistently classify any particular Cryptoasset, especially because in many instances Tokens are a cross between shares, an internal currency, and accounting units.

Some "kinds" of Tokens have been talked about more than others (and are therefore defined in these materials). Those include Equity Tokens, Profit Tokens, Security Tokens, and Utility Tokens. Each of those has a separate definition in this chapter. It is worth emphasizing, however, that this is not the only way of looking at Tokens. In fact, a wide variety of classification schemes for Tokens have been suggested.[63] Because most of those do not have a direct impact on or relevance to legal regulation, and because none of them appear to be in widespread use, they will not be considered in detail here.

59) *Token Generation Event (TGE)*

While Bitcoin and many of the early Altcoins add Coins or Tokens to the community through the process of Mining, some newer Cryptoassets do not require Mining in order to add Coins or Tokens to the outstanding supply. Instead, the project will use a Token Generation Event that may take the form of a private or public distribution, perhaps involving an ICO or an Airdrop. Note that, as is true with many terms used in the Crypto space, "TGE" is not always used consistently. It appears that most people tend to speak of a Token Generation Event as any action by the developer or promoter that leads to the creation and issuance of additional Coins or Tokens. On the other hand, some sources use TGE to cover only widespread distributions designed to raise funds, and some use Token Generation (or Token Launch) as an alternative to ICO if a Token is involved instead of a Coin.[64]

---

[63]   *Compare* Thomas Euler, *supra* note 21 (offering a multi-dimensional framework for Token classification) with Alexander Lielacher, *Tokenomics: What are the Classifications of ICO Tokens?*, ICOALERT BLOG (Mar. 13, 2018) (archived at https://perma.cc/XX7Q-V5SE) (a list of five categories); or Mercury Protocol, *Crypto-Token Classifications*, MEDIUM (Jul 17, 2018) (available online at https://medium.com/mercuryprotocol/crypto-token-classifications-3c9c8b18b4f2).

[64]   For example, compare Josiah Wilmoth, *ICO 101: How to Participate in a Token Generation Event*, STRATEGIC COIN (available online at https://medium.com/@Strategic_Coin/ico-101-how-to-participate-in-a-token-generation-event-f094b2b29561) (suggesting that ICO is just another name for a Token Generation Event), with Zach LeBeau, *What's the Difference Between*

60) *Uniform Regulation of Virtual-Currency Businesses Act*

The Uniform Regulation of Virtual-Currency Businesses Act (Uniform Act) was released by the Uniform Law Commission (ULC) on October 9, 2017, after having been approved at the annual meeting in July of that year.[65] Although as of mid-2019, no state had enacted the Uniform Act, bills to consider the act were introduced in three states in 2018 and an additional five states in the first half of 2019. While past experience indicates that uniform legislation promulgated by ULC is often influential on state legislators, the slow start for this project does not suggest that it will result in substantial uniformity in state regulation of Crypto businesses.

One of the stated goals of the Uniform Act is to provide "a balanced and reasonable regulatory structure that should validate good business practice and thus enhance trust for users of virtual currency, and may lead to SEC approval of virtual-currency offerings."[66] The Uniform Act is also clearly drafted with both state money transmission laws and Financial Crimes Enforcement Network (FinCEN) money services business regulations in mind, with the express observation that the Uniform Act provides protections and obligations that are generally similar to those legal regimes.

In essence, with certain exemptions, the Uniform Act requires a license in order for a business to legally "engage in virtual-currency business activity" or to hold oneself out as doing so.

61) *Utility Token*

Few terms in the Crypto space are used as inconsistently as "Utility Token." Very generally (and unhelpfully), a Utility Token is a Token that is designed to have some function or utility beyond serving as a substitute for Fiat currency. What does that mean? The answer is that it depends on who you are listening to.

At one end of the spectrum, some people have used this term to refer to any Token that is not a Security Token, or possibly to any Token that is not intended to act as a security. This is such a broad definition that it is probably not helpful in very many contexts. Moreover, because the

---

an 'ICO' and a 'Token Launch'? MEDIUM (Dec. 29, 2017) (available online at https://medium.com/@BreakerWorldwide/whats-the-difference-between-an-ico-and-a-token-launch-d892d4d689a4) (suggesting that a Token Launch is to be distinguished from an ICO).

[65] The Uniform Act (with comments) is available for download at the ULC website, ULC, UNIFORM REGULATION OF VIRTUAL-CURRENCY BUSINESSES ACT (WITH COMMENTS), https://www.uniformlaws.org/viewdocument/final-act-with-comments-72?CommunityKey=e104aaa8-c10f-45a7-a34a-0423c2106778&tab=librarydocuments.

[66] UNIF. REG. VIRTUAL-CURRENCY BUSINESSES ACT (with comments), *Development of the Act, Balances Achieved,* Pt. B., at p. 12.

parameters of which Tokens will be securities are unclear, it is not very precise.

At the other end, the Merriam-Webster online definition of Utility Token is that it is a "digital token or cryptocurrency that is issued in order to fund development of the cryptocurrency and that can be later used to purchase a good or service offered by the issuer of the cryptocurrency."[67] This definition is probably too narrow and a little off the mark. First, not all Cryptoassets are accurately described as Cryptocurrencies, and certainly a Utility Token is generally not intended to be a currency even if it may act as such under some circumstances. Second, it is not accurate to think of a Utility Token as something that is issued only in order to fund development of the Cryptoasset. If that was the case, you could never have a functional Utility Token, and that is definitely not the intent of the Crypto community. Finally, this definition limits the functionality to purchasing goods or services. This is also too narrow, as it is entirely possible that such Tokens will have other functionality, such as providing access to a group.

Probably the most helpful definition, and the one that is increasingly used, is that a Utility Token is a digital interest that has a function (other than acting as a substitute for traditional Fiat or traditional investment), which the purchaser is interested in paying for. The functionality or utility of the Token is limited only by the imagination of designers.

62) *Virtual Currency*

From a regulatory standpoint, "Virtual Currency" probably should be understood as being more precise than "Cryptocurrency," which is a phrase of variable meanings that can be used to cover all Coins and Tokens. Many of the existing regulatory authorities, and the Uniform Act proposed by the Uniform Law Commission, use the term "Virtual Currency" to describe what is being regulated. Unfortunately, just as is the case with the word "Cryptocurrency," there is less than complete agreement among these authorities as to what "Virtual Currency" means.

Not surprisingly, the definitions vary most significantly depending on the background in which the applicable regulatory authority is used to acting. Consider the I.R.S., which is charged with helping taxpayers "understand and meet their tax responsibilities and enforce the law with integrity and fairness to all." The I.R.S. uses the following definition of Virtual Currency:

> Virtual currency is a digital representation of value that functions as a medium of exchange, a unit of account, and/or a store of value. In some environments, it operates like "real" currency—i.e., the

---

[67]   *Utility Token,* Merriam-Webster online (online at https://www.merriam-webster.com/dictionary/utility%20token?utm_campaign=sd&utm_medium=serp&utm_source=jsonld).

coin and paper money of the United States or of any other country that is designated as legal tender, circulates, and is customarily used and accepted as a medium of exchange in the country of issuance—but it does not have legal tender status in any jurisdiction.[68]

While the I.R.S. has stated that Virtual Currency does not have legal status, as of March 2018 that is no longer completely accurate, although no American state recognizes it as such. Regardless of this particular development, treating Virtual Currency as property allows the I.R.S. to maximize certain taxes, by denying taxpayers favored rates that might have been applicable if Virtual Currency was treated like a foreign currency.

On the other hand, banking authorities tend to have a significant interest in regulating Virtual Currencies as currencies. For example, the U.S. Treasury Department's Financial Crimes Enforcement Network (FinCEN) defines "Virtual Currency" to be "a medium of exchange that operates like a currency in some environments, but does not have all the attributes of real currency." FinCEN's guidance is limited to convertible Virtual Currencies, which means Virtual Currency that "either has an equivalent value in real currency, or acts as a substitute for real currency." The guidance was issued despite the fact that at that point in time, "Virtual Currency [did] . . . not have legal tender status in any jurisdiction."

State Banking authorities, again not surprisingly, take an approach similar to that used by FinCEN. For example, the Conference of State Bank Supervisors (CSBS) has determined that, for its purposes:

> Virtual Currency is a digital representation of value used as a medium of exchange, a unit of account, or a store of value, but does not have legal tender status as recognized by the United States Government. Virtual Currency does not include the software or protocols governing the transfer of the digital representation of value. Virtual Currency does not include stored value redeemable exclusively in goods or services limited to transactions involving a defined merchant, such as rewards programs.[69]

This definition builds in certain exclusions, probably in recognition of the limits of state banking authorities' power.

The New York Department of Financial Services took an extraordinarily broad approach to what is meant by Virtual Currencies, carving out limited exceptions from the scope of specialized regulations

---

[68]   I.R.S. *Virtual Currency Guidance*, I.R.S. Notice 2014–21, 2014–16 I.R.B. 938 (released March 26, 2014; published April 14, 2104) (available online at https://www.irs.gov/pub/irs-drop/n-14-21.pdf) [archived at https://perma.cc/W5DL-XBLB].

[69]   CSBS, *State Regulatory Requirements for Virtual Currency Activities—CSBS Model Regulatory Framework* (Sept. 15, 2015) [archived at https://perma.cc/NMV8-WMLT] at p. 2.

governing Virtual Currencies in that state. Under the New York regulations:

> *virtual currency* means any type of digital unit that is used as a medium of exchange or a form of digitally stored value. Virtual Currency shall be broadly construed to include digital units of exchange that have a centralized repository or administrator; are decentralized and have no centralized repository or administrator; or may be created or obtained by computing or manufacturing effort.[70]

Certain narrow exclusions are carved out from this definition, so that "Virtual Currency" as used in the New York regulations does not include digital units that are: (1) non-convertible and non-redeemable, and are designed to be used solely within online gaming platforms; (2) issued as part of loyalty or rewards program that can only be used with the issuer or designated merchants as part of that program; or (3) used as part of prepaid cards.

63) Walmart Crypto

On August 5, 2019, Walmart announced that it had applied for a Cryptocurrency patent for a new Blockchain based mobile payments. Although the patent was filed January 29, 2019, the news broke in August, alongside official comment from Walmart that it was not actively pursuing the Coin at that time.[71]

The new Crypto, which as of the writing of these materials has not been officially named, appears to be a stablecoin, to be pegged to the value of the dollar. Although some commentators have hypothesized that the Walmart Coin might have an easier time with American regulators than Facebook's Libra,[72] that observation does not mean that this particular project will come to fruition.

64) Zcash (ZEC)

Zcash is a decentralized and open-source Cryptocurrency launched in the latter part of 2016. It has described itself like this: "If Bitcoin is like http for money, Zcash is https."[73] Zcash offers selective transparency of transactions in order to offer enhanced security. Transactions are recorded

---

[70]   N.Y. COMP. CODES R. & REGS. tit. 23, § 200.2(p) (italics in original).

[71]   *Walmart's Answer To Facebook's Libra: The Walmart Coin*, PYMNTS (Aug. 5, 2019) (available online at https://www.pymnts.com/news/retail/2019/walmarts-coin-facebooks-libra/).

[72]   *See, i.e.,* Max Boddy, *Expert: Walmart Crypto Project More Agreeable to Lawmakers Than Libra*, COINTELEGRAPH (Aug. 5, 2019) [archived at https://perma.cc/UJ7N-HYBS].

[73]   ZCASH, https://z.cash/. As of August, 2018, this webpage proclaimed "[i]f Bitcoin is like http for money, Zcash is https—a secure transport layer." [Archived on August 25, 2018 at https://perma.cc/38DZ-GY2D]. By mid-October, 2018, that language had been replaced, but the site still touts the security and privacy aspects of Zcash. [Archived on Oct. 17, 2018 at https://perma.cc/SC6N-D43R].

and transmitted via the Blockchain, but details including the identity of the sender, the recipient, and the amounts involved are not published. One source suggests that "Zcash's privacy strategy is essentially to erase the 'memory'—that is, the transaction history—of coins whenever a transaction occurs. . . . [B]y obfuscating transaction history, Zcash makes it impossible to trace transactions."[74]

2. PUTTING THESE TERMS INTO CONTEXT

First, you might go back and read the quote that appears at the start of this chapter. You should now understand that Bitcoin represented a significant technological innovation by proving the viability of blockchains. Hence, it is accurate to say that Bitcoin is not just a cryptocurrency, although it certainly serves that purpose. Ideally, you also know a little bit about how Bitcoin came to be "invented," and you should know that the public does not know the true identify of Satoshi Nakamoto. You should also understand why proponents (accurately) claim that Bitcoin is not controlled by any person or government. And even if you lack any background in computer programming, you should be aware of Bitcoin's connection to cryptography. Finally, the preceding materials should at least give you a general understanding of how the Bitcoin blockchain involves a peer-to-peer network.

To further check your understanding of these definitions, consider the following short excerpt from a relatively recent post intended to help persons new to the Crypto space to navigate some of the new and confusing terminology.

PRELIMINARY NOTES AND QUESTIONS

1.   What terms are defined here in ways that are different from the definitions set out in part 1 of this chapter?

2.   Some of the differences in definitions simply reflect the fact that the author of this post chooses to use various words differently than they are used in these materials. On the other hand, some of his definitions contradict the definitions offered above (and indicate to a high degree of certainty that the author below is not a U.S.-trained attorney). Can you find at least a couple of terms that are used below in ways that are inaccurate or misleading (if you assume that the author of this book is correct about the state of American law)?

---

[74]   NASDAQ, Frank Etto, *Know Your Coins: Public vs. Private Cryptocurrencies* (Sept. 22, 2017) (available online at https://www.nasdaq.com/article/know-your-coins-public-vs-private-cryptocurrencies-cm849588). Zcash relies on an advanced cryptographic technique called zk-SNARKs to ensure privacy. *Id.*

UTILITY TOKENS VS SECURITY TOKENS: LEARN THE DIFFERENCE

Rajarshi Mitra, *Ultimate Guide*, BLOCKGEEKS (Mar. 2019)[75]

If you are new to the crypto space then you must be overwhelmed by the sheer volume of terminology. For the uninitiated, terms like "cryptocurrency", "tokens", "securities", "utility tokens" etc. must get extremely overwhelming.

In this guide, we are going to tackle all those terms and make life much simpler for you.

. . . .

It can be a little complicated to pinpoint on an exact definition of a "token". To give you a very wide, non-generalized definition, a token is a representation of something in its particular ecosystem. It could [be] value, stake, voting right, or anything. A token is not limited to one particular role; it can fulfill a lot of roles in its native ecosystem.

Before we go any further, however, we must make one more difference clear. The difference between a cryptocurrency coin and a token.

A cryptocurrency coin, like BTC, Ether etc. . . . is independent of a platform. They can be used as a form of currency outside their native environment.

. . . .

However, on the other hand, OmiseGO, Golem etc. are examples of tokens which exist on a particular platform, in this case, Ethereum.

A token represents a security or utility that a company has and they usually give it away to their investors during a public sale called ICO (Initial Coin Offering), in the case of utility tokens. . . .

ICOs or Initial Coin Offerings are basically crowd sales, the cryptocurrency version of crowdfunding.

. . . .

Because most of the ICOs are investment opportunities in the company itself, most tokens qualify as securities.

. . . .

———————

Now consider these questions, and see how you do at understanding what is being asked and in constructing at least a preliminary response

———————

[75]   The complete article is online, archived with permission from BLOCKGEEKS at https://perma.cc/TWG9-RUWR.

based on the terms and definitions in Part 1 above, adding in whatever you might know about economics, world finances, and current events.

NOTES AND QUESTIONS

1.   Why might it not matter to most U.S. regulatory authorities that there is a technical distinction between cryptocoins (which are hosted on their own blockchain) and cryptotokens (which rely on another blockchain to serve as their platform)?

2.   What is the difference, in your mind, between a cryptocoin, a cryptocurrency, a digital currency, a virtual currency, and a cryptoasset?

3.   What is the difference between a tokenized security and a security token? If you would define them to be synonymous, are there some tokens that do not act like traditional securities (like debt or equity interests—terms which you may need to look up) but which might still be an investment contract under the *Howey* Test? Are you sure the words should mean the same thing?

4.   How is it possible for a single asset to be simultaneously property for the I.R.S., currency (or funds) for FinCEN, a commodity for the CFTC, and a security for the SEC?

CHAPTER 3

CRYPTO AND THE REGULATORS—FinCEN

∎ ∎ ∎

As mentioned in the introductory chapter, this book assumes no significant prior exposure to the mission and role of the Department of Treasury's Financial Crimes Enforcement Network (FinCEN), the Securities and Exchanges Commission (SEC), the Commodities Futures Trading Commission (CFTC), the Internal Revenue Service (IRS),[1] or the statutes and regulations applicable to or promulgated by any of these agencies. Instead, there are chapters dedicated to the history and regulatory focus and mission of each of these agencies. In the case of FinCEN, this introductory chapter explains the underlying problems that led to the creation of FinCEN, as well as explaining the basics of how FinCEN operates to oversee and regulate money services businesses and money transmitters at the federal level.

These materials are not designed to fully explain the scope of the federal requirements that are overseen by FinCEN. These materials will generally introduce the Bank Secrecy Act (BSA) (as amended) and the regulations that have been promulgated under it by or on the authority of the Secretary of the Treasury. Some of the regulatory language will be discussed, but the purpose of these materials is not to fully explain the way in which the BSA operates. These materials are provided to give context to the efforts of FinCEN to impose various regulatory requirements on persons acting in the crypto space. Thus, there is a consideration of the history of the laws and regulations, as well as a brief consideration of the kinds of activities that the BSA is designed to help combat, but only to the extent necessary to shed light on how FinCEN operations impact crypto.

Following this introductory chapter, there are two chapters that describe developments in the world of crypto that have significantly influenced FinCEN in how it views cryptoassets and transactions. These materials take the form of abbreviated case studies designed to illustrate how real world events have shaped the reaction of FinCEN to crypto. Those case studies involve the Silk Road (Chapter 4) and various crypto businesses that act or acted in ways that FinCEN has chosen to see as money transmitters, including Mt. Gox and Ripple (Chapter 5). Chapter 6

---

[1]   The Appendix to this book contains a list of acronyms, although for convenience, the full name of various agencies, statutes, and various concepts are also included in this chapter the first time that an acronym is used. In later chapters, these terms may be referred to solely by their acronyms.

then specifically considers how FinCEN has reacted to these kinds of developments, given the real world context provided in the case studies.

Later chapters will introduce the other regulatory agencies active in this space and their reactions to the innovations and new issues being presented by the development and release of various cryptoassets and increasingly sophisticated and diverse cryptotransactions.

1. THE PROBLEM OF MONEY-LAUNDERING

According to the federal government (as set forth on the FinCEN website):

> Money laundering is the process of making illegally-gained proceeds (i.e. "dirty money") appear legal (i.e. "clean"). Typically, it involves three steps: placement, layering and integration. First, the illegitimate funds are furtively introduced into the legitimate financial system. Then, the money is moved around to create confusion, sometimes by wiring or transferring through numerous accounts. Finally, it is integrated into the financial system through additional transactions until the "dirty money" appears "clean." Money laundering can facilitate crimes such as drug trafficking and terrorism, and can adversely impact the global economy.[2]

Money laundering became a significant focus of law enforcement efforts during the 1970 and increased in priority throughout the 1980s. There was a widespread perception that massive amounts of money were being funneled into and out of the narcotics trade in particular. Over the past several decades, problems associated with money laundering and the financing of criminal and terrorist activities have been a topic of perennial concern for federal legislators. This has resulted in a large number of federal laws addressing these problems.[3]

The earliest legislation focused on indirect methods of attacking the problem, generally imposing reporting requirements for transactions

---

[2]   FinCEN, *History of Anti-Money Laundering Laws*, https://www.fincen.gov/history-anti-money-laundering-laws [archived at https://perma.cc/UA7Y-Y8MF].

[3]   The list of federal acts addressing such behavior includes all of the following:

1. Bank Secrecy Act (1970) (generally referred to as the BSA)
2. Money Laundering Control Act (1986)
3. Anti-Drug Abuse Act of 1988
4. Annunzio-Wylie Anti-Money Laundering Act (1992)
5. Money Laundering Suppression Act (1994)
6. Money Laundering and Financial Crimes Strategy Act (1998)
7. Uniting and Strengthening America by Providing Appropriate Tools Required to Intercept and Obstruct Terrorism Act of 2001 (known as the USA PATRIOT Act or simply the Patriot Act)
8. Intelligence Reform & Terrorism Prevention Act of 2004

involving currency. The first direct attack on money laundering came in 1986, when money laundering itself was made a federal offense. In general, those statutes prohibit participation in certain kinds of transactions involving money derived from illegal operations or funds intended to support such activity. They penalize not only the person who originally earned the illicit funds, but also others who engage in financial and other transactions knowing that the source of the funding is "dirty money."

Although there were legislative enactments throughout the 1990s, it was the USA PATRIOT Act of 2001 (the Patriot Act), enacted in the wake of the September 11, 2001, terrorist attacks in the United States that most significantly expanded the anti-money laundering (AML) legislation. The Patriot Act added new recordkeeping requirements, expanded reporting and record-keeping requirements to a variety of nonbank financial institutions such as broker-dealers and insurance companies, and broadened the reach of the already expansive money-laundering laws.

As explained by the Office of the Comptroller of the Currency, money-laundering continues to be a major threat to the American financial system:

> Criminals have long used money-laundering schemes to conceal or "clean" the source of fraudulently obtained or stolen funds. Money laundering poses significant risks to the safety and soundness of the U.S. financial industry. With the advent of terrorists who employ money-laundering techniques to fund their operations, the risk expands to encompass the safety and security of the nation.[4]

The amount of money involved is staggering. Estimates of the amount of money derived from illegal operations and criminal enterprises and then laundered globally each year suggest that $800 billion (between 2–5% of global GDP) is involved. In the U.S. alone, estimates from the U.S. Treasury place the total amount being laundered each year at approximately $300 billion in U.S. Dollars.

In order to understand the applicable regulatory landscape, a more detailed examination of some of the statutes and regulations is necessary.

2. THE BANK SECRECY ACT

The Financial Recordkeeping and Reporting of Currency and Foreign Transactions Act of 1970 is generally referred to as the Bank Secrecy Act (BSA).[5] The statute itself does not actually impose specific reporting or

---

[4]   Office of the Comptroller of the Currency, U.S. Dept. of the Treasury, *Bank Secrecy Act (BSA)* (available online at https://www.occ.treas.gov/topics/compliance-bsa/bsa/index-bsa.html).

[5]   The BSA is codified at 31 U.S. Code §§ 5311 et seq.

recording requirements, and instead enables the Secretary of the Treasury to adopt appropriate regulations to achieve the objectives of the BSA.

The BSA is divided into two titles. Title I authorizes the Secretary of the Department of the Treasury to impose record-keeping requirements. Title II authorizes the adoption of more specific record-keeping, reporting, and registration requirements, as well as setting out both civil and criminal penalties. The statutory provisions include a declaration of purpose, definitions, record keeping requirements for financial institutions,[6] registration requirements for certain businesses, and various penalties for non-compliance.

The stated purpose of the BSA was originally "to require certain reports or records where they have a high degree of usefulness in criminal, tax, or regulatory investigations or proceedings."[7] The Patriot Act added an additional purpose at the end, so that the BSA now includes a focus on protecting against international terrorism.

Section 5312 of the BSA includes a number of definitions applicable to the Act. As it currently stands for purposes of this act, "financial institution" is broadly defined to cover any:

> licensed sender of money or any other person who engages as a business in the transmission of funds, including any person who engages as a business in an informal money transfer system or any network of people who engage as a business in facilitating the transfer of money domestically or internationally outside of the conventional financial institutions system.[8]

Neither funds[9] nor currency are defined in the statute, but there is a definition of "monetary instruments," which are limited to:

---

[6]   "Financial Institution" is defined generally in title 18 as including banks, depository institutions, and similar organizations. *See* 18 U.S. Code § 20. The BSA, however, has a more specific definition that governs its provisions, as will be described in the next few paragraphs of text.

[7]   31 U.S. Code § 5311.

[8]   31 U.S. Code § 5312(a)(2)(R).

[9]   The word "funds" is used repeatedly in the BSA, but it defined neither in the statute nor its implementing regulations. The appropriate definition of the term has, however, been the subject of litigation.

("Financial transaction") . . . captures all movements of "funds" by any means, or monetary instruments. "Funds" is not defined in the statute and is therefore given its ordinary meaning. "Funds" are defined as "money, often money for a specific purpose." *See* Cambridge Dictionaries Online [archived at https://perma.cc/K3SG-LUBV]. "Money" is an object used to buy things. Put simply, "funds" can be used to pay for things in the colloquial sense.

United States v. Ulbricht, 31 F. Supp. 3d 540, 570 (S.D.N.Y. 2014) (internal citations omitted). More extensive excerpts from this case are included in chapter 4 of this book.

The word "funds" is also discussed extensively in *United States v. Murgio*, 209 F. Supp. 3d 698, 704 (S.D.N.Y. 2016), which is excerpted in chapter 6. In that case, a criminal defendant argued specifically that Bitcoin could not qualify as "funds." In rejecting that argument, the District Court

(A) United States coins and currency;

(B) as the Secretary may prescribe by regulation, coins and currency of a foreign country, travelers' checks, bearer negotiable instruments, bearer investment securities, bearer securities, stock on which title is passed on delivery, and similar material; and

(C) as the Secretary of the Treasury shall provide by regulation for purposes of sections 5316 and 5331 . . . [instruments] drawn on or by a foreign financial institution . . . not in bearer form.[10]

The heart of the record-keeping and reporting directive appears in section 5313. That section specifies that:

When a domestic financial institution is involved in a transaction for the payment, receipt, or transfer of United States coins or currency (or other monetary instruments the Secretary of the Treasury prescribes), in an amount, denomination, or amount and denomination, or under circumstances the Secretary prescribes by regulation, the institution and any other participant in the transaction the Secretary may prescribe shall file a report on the transaction at the time and in the way the Secretary prescribes. A participant acting for another person shall make the report as

---

agreed that the word should be given its "ordinary meaning." *Id.* at 707, citing *Taniguchi v. Kan Pac. Saipan, Ltd.*, 566 U.S. 560 (2012). The court in *Murgio* went on to explain:

> The ordinary meaning of "funds," according to Webster's Dictionary, is "available pecuniary resources." Webster's Third New International Dictionary 921 (2002). "Pecuniary" is defined as "taking the form of or consisting of money." *Id.* at 1663. And "money," in turn, is defined as "something generally accepted as a medium of exchange, a measure of value, or a means of payment." *Id.* at 1458. This definition of "funds," and the corresponding definition of "money," have consistently been adopted by courts in this circuit. In *United States v. Faiella*, Judge Rakoff defined "funds," in the context of interpreting § 1960, as " 'available money' or 'an amount of something that is available for use.' " 39 F.Supp.3d 544, 545 (S.D.N.Y.2014) (citation omitted). And as the Court does here, he also defined "money" as "something generally accepted as a medium of exchange, a measure of value, or a means of payment." *Id.* (citation omitted).

Id. This led the court to ultimately decide that " 'funds,' for the purposes of § 1960, means pecuniary resources, which are generally accepted as a medium of exchange or a means of payment. Applying that definition here, it is clear that bitcoins are funds within the plain meaning of that term." *Id.*

It is worth noting that there is contrary authority. Two Florida decisions have concluded that Bitcoins are not payment instruments under Florida law. *See Florida v. Espinoza*, No. F14–293 (Fla. Cir. Ct. July 22, 2016) (rev'd on appeal), and *United States v. Petix*, 2016 WL 7017919 (WDNY 2016) (not reported in F. Supp.). Excerpts from *Petix* also appear in chapter 6, including the analysis that would limit the meaning of the word "funds" to "money" capable of being deposited in typical financial institutions. These two opinions do, however, appear to represent the minority position on this issue, and *Espinoza* was subsequently reversed. *State v. Espinoza*, 264 So.3d 1055 (Fla. App. 2019).

    [10]   31 U.S. Code § 5312(a)(3). (The definitions section of the BSA contains no reference to virtual currency.)

the agent or bailee of the person and identify the person for whom the transaction is being made.[11]

With regard to substantive requirements of the statute that may have application to crypto-based businesses, section 5330 is also of particular importance. That provision requires registration of money transmitting businesses. In general, "[a]ny person who owns or controls a money transmitting business shall register the business (whether or not the business is licensed as a money transmitting business in any state) with the Secretary of the Treasury not later than the end of the 180-day period beginning on . . . the date on which the business is established."[12] "Money transmitting business" is defined in § 5330(d) as:

any business other than the United States Postal Service which—

(A) provides check cashing, currency exchange, or money transmitting or remittance services, or issues or redeems money orders, travelers' checks, and other similar instruments or any other person who engages as a business in the transmission of funds, including any person who engages as a business in an informal money transfer system or any network of people who engage as a business in facilitating the transfer of money domestically or internationally outside of the conventional financial institutions system;

(B) is required to file reports under section 5313; and

(C) is not a depository institution . . . .[13]

As a result of the BSA and regulations promulgated thereunder, financial institutions operating in the U.S. are required to take a number of concrete steps. Depending on the precise nature of the financial institution, it may be required to register with FinCEN. The business may need to establish effective BSA compliance programs and customer due diligence systems and monitoring programs. The institution may also be obligated to have an effective suspicious activity monitoring and reporting process pursuant to which cash transactions that exceed an aggregate of $10,000 during any single day are reported to FinCEN. In addition, activity that might signal criminal activity such as money laundering, tax evasion, or the like may need to be promptly reported. Proposed transactions may need to be screened against Office of Foreign Assets Control (OFAC) and other government lists.

---

[11]   31 U.S. Code § 5313(a). (While the BSA does not set dollar limits, the Treasury has established $10,000 as the applicable transaction threshold. Applicable regulations are codified at 31 C.F.R. Chapter X. This particular requirement is found in 31 C.F.R. § 1010.311 and further clarified in § 1010.330.)

[12]   31 U.S. Code § 5330(a)(1).

[13]   31 U.S. Code § 5330(d).

These record-keeping and reporting obligations, not surprisingly, were not popular with financial institutions or many customers, and an early action was brought to enjoin enforcement of these kinds of obligations on constitutional grounds.

PRELIMINARY NOTES AND QUESTIONS

1.　This case arose long before Bitcoin was foreseen as a possibility. What is the relevance of the issues discussed in this opinion to cryptoassets and transactions?

2.　As you read through the opinion, try to decide whether the particular obligations being discussed and challenged would apply in the context of crypto, and if so, to whom.

3.　Do you personally agree with the reasoning and conclusions of the Court?

CALIFORNIA BANKERS ASS'N V. SHULTZ
416 U.S. 21 (1974)

MR. JUSTICE REHNQUIST delivered the opinion of the Court.

These appeals present questions concerning the constitutionality of the so-called Bank Secrecy Act of 1970 (Act), and the implementing regulations promulgated thereunder by the Secretary of the Treasury.

The Act was enacted by Congress in 1970 following extensive hearings concerning the unavailability of foreign and domestic bank records of customers thought to be engaged in activities entailing criminal or civil liability. Under the Act, the Secretary of the Treasury is authorized to prescribe by regulation certain recordkeeping and reporting requirements for banks and other financial institutions in this country.

. . . .

The express purpose of the Act is to require the maintenance of records, and the making of certain reports, which 'have a high degree of usefulness in criminal, tax, or regulatory investigations or proceedings.' Congress was apparently concerned with two major problems in connection with the enforcement of the regulatory, tax, and criminal laws of the United States.

First, there was a need to insure that domestic banks and financial institutions continue to maintain adequate records of their financial transactions with their customers. Congress found that the recent growth of financial institutions in the United States had been paralleled by an increase in criminal activity which made use of these institutions. While many of the records which the Secretary by regulation ultimately required to be kept had been traditionally maintained by the voluntary action of many domestic financial institutions, Congress noted that in recent years some larger banks had abolished or limited the practice of photocopying checks, drafts, and similar instruments drawn on them and presented for payment. The absence of such records, whether through failure to make them in the first instance or through failure to retain them, was thought to seriously impair the ability of the Federal Government to enforce the myriad criminal, tax, and regulatory provisions of laws which Congress had enacted. At the same time, it was recognized by Congress that such required records would 'not be made automatically available for law enforcement purposes (but could) only be obtained through existing legal process.'

In addition, Congress felt that there were situations where the deposit and withdrawal of large amounts of currency or of monetary instruments which were the equivalent of currency should be actually reported to the Government. While reports of this nature had been required by previous regulations issued by the Treasury Department, it was felt that more precise and detailed reporting requirements were needed. The Secretary was therefore authorized to require the reporting of what may be described as large domestic financial transactions in currency or its equivalent.

Second, Congress was concerned about a serious and widespread use of foreign financial institutions, located in jurisdictions with strict laws of secrecy as to bank activity, for the purpose of violating or evading domestic criminal, tax, and regulatory enactments.

. . . .

While most of the recordkeeping requirements imposed by the Secretary under the Act merely require the banks to keep records which most of them had in the past voluntarily kept and retained, and while much of the required reporting of domestic transactions had been required by earlier Treasury regulations in effect for nearly 30 years, there is no denying the impressive sweep of the authority conferred upon the Secretary by the Bank Secrecy Act of 1970. While an Act conferring such broad authority over transactions such as these might well surprise or even shock those who lived in an earlier era, the latter did not live to see the time when bank accounts would join chocolate, cheese, and watches as a symbol of the Swiss economy. Nor did they live to see the heavy utilization of our domestic banking system by the minions of organized crime as well as by millions of legitimate businessmen. The challenges made here to the Bank Secrecy Act are directed not to any want of legislative authority in Congress to treat the subject, but instead to the Act's asserted violation of specific constitutional prohibitions.

I

Title I of the Act, and the implementing regulations promulgated thereunder by the Secretary of the Treasury, require financial institutions to maintain records of the identities of their customers, to make microfilm copies of certain checks drawn on them, and to keep records of certain other items. Title II of the Act and its implementing regulations require reports of certain domestic and foreign currency transactions.

A.   TITLE I—THE RECORDKEEPING REQUIREMENTS

Title I of the Act contains the general recordkeeping requirements for banks and other financial institutions, as provided by the Secretary by regulation.

. . . .

Although an initial draft of Title I would have compelled the Secretary to promulgate regulations requiring banks to maintain copies of all items received for collection or presented for payment, the Act as finally passed required the maintenance only of such records and microfilm copies as the Secretary determined to have a 'high degree of usefulness.' Upon passage of the Act, the Treasury Department established a task force which consulted with representatives from financial institutions, trade associations, and governmental agencies to determine the type of records which should be maintained. Whereas the original regulations promulgated by the Secretary had required the copying of all checks, the task force decided, and the regulations were accordingly amended, to require check copying only as to checks in excess of $100. The regulations also require the copying of only 'on us' checks: checks drawn on the bank or issued and payable by it. The regulations exempt from the copying requirements certain 'on us' checks such as dividend, payroll, and employee benefit checks, provided they are drawn on an account expected to average at least one hundred checks per month. The regulations also require banks to maintain records of the identity and taxpayer identification number of each person maintaining a financial interest in each deposit or share account opened after June 30, 1972, and to microfilm various other financial documents. In addition, the Secretary's regulations require all financial institutions to maintain a microfilm or other copy of each extension of credit in an amount exceeding $5,000 except those secured by interest in real property, and to microfilm each advice, request, or instruction given or received regarding the transfer of funds, currency, or other money or credit in amounts exceeding $10,000 to a person, account, or place outside the United States.

Reiterating the stated intent of the Congress, the regulations provide that inspection, review, or access to the records required by the Act to be maintained is governed by existing legal process.

. . . .

B.   TITLE II—FOREIGN FINANCIAL TRANSACTION REPORTING REQUIREMENTS

Chapter 3 of Title II of the Act and the regulations promulgated thereunder generally require persons to report the transportation of monetary instruments into or out of the United States, or receipts of such instruments in the United States from places outside the United States, if the transportation or receipt involves instruments of a value greater than $5,000. Chapter 4 of Title II of the Act and the implementing regulations generally require United States citizens, residents, and businessmen to file reports of their relationships with foreign financial institutions. The legislative history of the foreign-transaction reporting provisions indicates that the Congress was concerned with the circumvention of United States regulatory, tax, and criminal laws which United States citizens and residents were accomplishing through the medium of secret foreign bank transactions.

Section 231 of the Act requires anyone connected with the transaction to report, in the manner prescribed by the Secretary, the transportation into or out of the country of monetary instruments exceeding $5,000 on any one occasion. As provided by the Secretary's regulations, the report must include information as to the amount of the instrument, the date of receipt, the form of instrument, and the person from whom it was received. The regulations exempt various classes of persons from this reporting requirement, including banks, brokers or other dealers in securities, common carriers, and others engaged in the business of transporting currency for banks. Monetary instruments which are transported without the filing of a required report, or with a materially erroneous report, are subject to forfeiture . . .; a person who has failed to file the required report or who has filed a false report is subject to civil [and criminal] penalties . . . .

Section 241 of the Act authorizes the Secretary to prescribe regulations requiring residents and citizens of the United States, as well as nonresidents in the United States and doing business therein, to maintain records and file reports with respect to their transactions and relationships with foreign financial agencies. Pursuant to this authority, the regulations require each person subject to the jurisdiction of the United States to make a report on yearly tax returns of any 'financial interest in, or signature or other authority over, a bank, securities or other financial account in a foreign country.' Violations of the reporting requirement of § 241 as implemented by the regulations are also subject to civil and criminal penalties . . . .

C. TITLE II—DOMESTIC FINANCIAL TRANSACTION REPORTING REQUIREMENTS

In addition to the foreign transaction reporting requirements discussed above, Title II of the Act provides for certain reports of domestic transactions where such reports have a high degree of usefulness in criminal, tax, or regulatory investigations or proceedings. Prior to the enactment of the Act, financial institutions had been providing reports of their customers' large currency transactions pursuant to regulations promulgated by the Secretary of Treasury which had required reports of all currency transactions that, in the judgment of the institution, exceeded those 'commensurate with the customary conduct of the business, industry or profession of the person or organization concerned.' In passing the Act, Congress recognized that the use of financial institutions, both domestic and foreign, in furtherance of activities designed to evade the regulatory mechanisms of the United States, had markedly increased. Congress recognized the importance of reports of large and unusual currency transactions in ferreting out criminal activity and desired to strengthen the statutory basis for requiring such reports. In particular, Congress intended to authorize more definite standards for determining what constitutes the type of unusual transaction that should be reported.

Section 221 of the Act therefore delegates to the Secretary the authority for specifying the currency transactions which should be reported, 'if they involve the payment, receipt, or transfer of United States currency, or such other monetary instruments as the Secretary may specify.' Section 222 of the Act provides that the Secretary may require such reports from the domestic financial institution involved or the parties to the transactions or both. Section 223 of the Act authorizes the Secretary to designate financial institutions to receive such reports.

In the implementing regulations promulgated under this authority, the Secretary has required only that financial institutions file certain reports with the Commissioner of Internal Revenue. The regulations require that a report be made for each deposit, withdrawal, exchange of currency, or other payment or transfer 'which involves a transaction in currency of more than $10,000.' The regulations exempt from the reporting requirement certain intrabank transactions and 'transactions with an established customer maintaining a deposit relationship (in amounts) commensurate with the customary conduct of the business, industry, or profession of the customer concerned.' Provision is also made in the regulations whereby information obtained by the Secretary may in some instances and in confidence be available to other departments or agencies of the United States. There is also provision made in the regulations whereby the Secretary may in his sole discretion make exceptions to or grant exemptions from the requirements of the regulation. Failure to file the required report or the filing of a false report subjects the banks to criminal and civil penalties.

II

This litigation began in June 1972 in the United States District Court for the Northern District of California. Various plaintiffs applied for a temporary restraining order prohibiting the defendants, including the Secretary of the Treasury and heads of other federal agencies, from enforcing the provisions of the Bank Secrecy Act, enacted by Congress on October 26, 1970, and thereafter implemented by the Treasury regulations. The plaintiffs below included several named individual bank customers, the Security National Bank, the California Bankers Association, and the American Civil Liberties Union (ACLU), suing on behalf of itself and its various bank customer members.

The plaintiffs' principal contention in the District Court was that the Act and the regulations were violative of the Fourth Amendment's guarantee against unreasonable search and seizure. The complaints also alleged that the Act violated the First, Fifth, Ninth, Tenth, and Fourteenth Amendments. The District Court issued a temporary restraining order enjoining the enforcement of the foreign and domestic reporting provisions of Title II of the Act, and requested the convening of a three-judge court . . . to entertain the myriad of constitutional challenges to the Act.

The three-judge District Court unanimously upheld the constitutionality of the recordkeeping requirements of Title I of the Act and the accompanying regulations, and the requirements of Title II of the Act and the regulations for reports concerning the import and export of currency and monetary instruments and relationships with foreign financial institutions. The District Court concluded, however, with one judge dissenting, that the domestic reporting provisions . . . were repugnant to the Fourth Amendment of the Constitution. The court held that since the domestic reporting provisions of the Act permitted the Secretary of the Treasury to require detailed reports of virtually all domestic financial transactions, including those involving personal checks and drafts, and since the Act could conceivably be administered in such a manner as to compel disclosure of all details of a customer's financial affairs the domestic reporting provisions must fall as facially violative of the Fourth Amendment. Their enforcement was enjoined.

Both the plaintiffs and the Government defendants filed timely notices of appeal from the portions of the District Court judgment adverse to them. We noted probable jurisdiction over three separate appeals from the decision below.

. . . .

III

. . . .

We proceed then to consider the initial contention of the bank plaintiffs that the recordkeeping requirements imposed by the Secretary's regulations under the authority of Title I deprive the banks of due process by imposing unreasonable burdens upon them, and by seeking to make the banks the agents of the Government in surveillance of its citizens. Such recordkeeping requirements are scarcely a novelty. . . . [T]his Court has been faced with numerous cases involving similar recordkeeping requirements . . . [and has held that if] there was 'a sufficient relation between the activity sought to be regulated and the public concern so that the government can constitutionally regulate or forbid the basic activity concerned, . . . [it] can constitutionally require the keeping of particular records, subject to inspection. . . .'

. . . .

We see no reason to reach a different result here. The plenary authority of Congress over both interstate and foreign commerce is not open to dispute, and that body was not limited to any one particular approach to effectuate its concern that negotiable instruments moving in the channels of that commerce were significantly aiding criminal enterprise.

. . . .

The bank plaintiffs contend, however, that the Act does not have as its primary purpose regulation of the banks themselves, and therefore the requirement that the banks keep the records is an unreasonable burden on the banks. . . . But provisions requiring reporting or recordkeeping by the paying institution, rather than the individual who receives the payment, are by no means unique. The Internal Revenue Code and its regulations, for example, contain provisions which require businesses to report income payments to third, employers to keep records of certain payments made to employees, corporations to report dividend payments made to third parties, cooperatives to report patronage dividend payments, brokers to report customers' gains and losses, and banks to report payments of interest made to depositors.

. . . .

In this case . . . Congress determined that recordkeeping alone would suffice for its purposes, and that no correlative substantive legislation was required. Neither this fact, nor the fact that the principal congressional concern is with the activities of the banks' customers, rather than with the activities of the banks themselves, serves to invalidate the legislation on due process grounds.

The bank plaintiffs proceed from the premise that they are complete bystanders with respect to transactions involving drawers and drawees of their negotiable instruments. But such is hardly the case. A voluminous body of law has grown up defining the rights of the drawer, the payee, and the drawee bank with respect to various kinds of negotiable instruments. The recognition of such rights, both in the various States of this country and in other countries, is itself a part of the reason why the banking business has flourished and played so prominent a part in commercial transactions. The bank is a party to any negotiable instrument drawn upon it by a depositor, and upon acceptance or payment of an instrument incurs obligations to the payee. While it obviously is not privy to the background of a transaction in which a negotiable instrument is used, the existing wide acceptance and availability of negotiable instruments is of inestimable benefit to the banking industry as well as to commerce in general.

Banks are therefore not conscripted neutrals in transactions involving negotiable instruments, but parties to the instruments with a substantial stake in their continued availability and acceptance. Congress not illogically decided that if records of transactions of negotiable instruments were to be kept and maintained, in order to be available as evidence under customary legal process if the occasion warranted, the bank was the most easily identifiable party to the instrument and therefore should do the recordkeeping. We believe . . . there is a sufficient connection between the evil Congress sought to address and the recordkeeping procedure it required to pass muster under the Due Process Clause of the Fifth Amendment.

The bank plaintiffs somewhat halfheartedly argue, on the basis of the costs which they estimate will be incurred by the banking industry in complying with the Secretary's recordkeeping requirements, that this cost burden alone deprives them of due process of law. They cite no cases for this proposition, and it does not warrant extended treatment. . . . The cost burdens imposed on the banks by the recordkeeping requirements are far from unreasonable, and we hold that such burdens do not deny the banks due process of law.

. . . .

Plaintiffs urge that when the bank makes and keeps records under the compulsion of the Secretary's regulations it acts as an agent of the Government, and thereby engages in a 'seizure' of the records of its customers. But all of the records which the Secretary requires to be kept pertain to transactions to which the bank was itself a party. The fact that a large number of banks voluntarily kept records of this sort before they were required to do so by regulation is an indication that the records were thought useful to the bank in the conduct of its own business, as well as in reflecting transactions of its customers. We decided long ago that an

Internal Revenue summons directed to a third-party bank was not a violation of the Fourth Amendment rights of either the bank or the person under investigation by the taxing authorities.

. . . .

IV

We proceed now to address the constitutional challenges directed at the reporting requirements of the regulations authorized in Title II of the Act. Title II authorizes the Secretary to require reporting of two general categories of banking transactions: foreign and domestic.

. . . .

As noted above, the regulations issued by the Secretary under the authority of Title II contain two essential reporting requirements with respect to foreign financial transactions. Chapter 3 of Title II of the Act and the corresponding regulation require individuals to report transportation of monetary instruments into or out of the United States, or receipts of such instruments in the United States from places outside the United States, if the instrument transported or received has a value in excess of $5,000. Chapter 4 of Title II of the Act and the corresponding regulation generally require United States citizens, residents, and businessmen to file reports of their relationships with foreign financial institutions.

The domestic reporting provisions of the Act as implemented by the regulations, in contrast to the foreign reporting requirements, apply only to banks and financial institutions. In enacting the statute, Congress provided in § 221 that the Secretary might specify the types of currency transactions which should be reported:

> 'Transactions involving any domestic financial institution shall be reported to the Secretary at such time, in such manner, and in such detail as the Secretary may require if they involve the payment, receipt, or tansfer of United States currency, or such other monetary instruments as the Secretary may specify, in such amounts, denominations, or both, or under such circumstances, as the Secretary shall by regulation prescribe.'

Section 222 of the Act authorizes the Secretary to require such reports from the domestic financial institution involved, from the parties to the transactions, or from both. In exercising his authority under these sections, the Secretary has promulgated regulations which require only that the financial institutions make the report to the Internal Revenue Service; he has not required any report from the individual parties to domestic financial transactions. The applicable regulation requires the financial institution to 'file a report of each deposit, withdrawal, exchange of currency or other payment or transfer, by, through, or to such financial institution, which involves a transaction in currency of more than $10,000.'

The regulation exempts several types of currency transactions from this reporting requirement, including transactions 'with an established customer maintaining a deposit relationship with the bank, in amounts which the bank may reasonably conclude do not exceed amounts commensurate with the customary conduct of the business, industry or profession of the customer concerned.'

A. FOURTH AMENDMENT CHALLENGE TO THE FOREIGN REPORTING REQUIREMENTS

The District Court, in differentiating for constitutional purposes between the foreign reporting requirements and the domestic reporting requirements imposed by the Secretary, relied upon our opinion in *United States v. United States District Court*, 407 U.S. 297 (1972), for the proposition that Government surveillance in the area of foreign relations is in some instances subject to less constitutional restraint than would be similar activity in domestic affairs. Our analysis does not take us over this ground.

The plenary authority of Congress to regulate foreign commerce, and to delegate significant portions of this power to the Executive, is well established. Plaintiffs contend that in exercising that authority to require reporting of previously described foreign financial transactions, Congress and the Secretary have abridged their Fourth Amendment rights.

The familiar language of the Fourth Amendment protects '(t)he right of the people to be secure in their persons, houses, papers, and effects, against unreasonable searches and seizures . . . .' Since a statute requiring the filing and subsequent publication of a corporate tax return has been upheld against a Fourth Amendment challenge, reporting requirements are by no means per se violations of the Fourth Amendment. Indeed, a contrary holding might well fly in the face of the settled sixty-year history of self-assessment of individual and corporate income taxes in the United States. This Court has on numerous occasions recognized the importance of the self-regulatory aspects of that system, and interests of the Congress in enforcing it:

> 'In assessing income taxes the Government relies primarily upon the disclosure by the taxpayer of the relevant facts. This disclosure it requires him of make in his annual return. To ensure full and honest disclosure, to discourage fraudulent attempts to evade the tax, Congress imposes sanctions. Such sanctions may confessedly be either criminal or civil.' *Helvering v. Mitchell*, 303 U.S. 391, 399 (1938).

To the extent that the reporting requirements of the Act and the settled practices of the tax collection process are similar, this history must be overcome by those who argue that the reporting requirements are a violation of the Fourth Amendment.

. . . .

Of primary importance . . . is the fact that the information required by the foreign reporting requirements pertains only to commercial transactions which take place across national boundaries.

. . . .

If reporting of income may be required as an aid to enforcement of the federal revenue statutes, and if those entering and leaving the country may be examined as to their belongings and effects, all without violating the Fourth Amendment, we see no reason to invalidate the Secretary's regulations here. The statutory authorization for the regulations was based upon a conclusion by Congress that international currency transactions and foreign financial institutions were being used by residents of the United States to circumvent the enforcement of the laws of the United States. The regulations are sufficiently tailored so as to single out transactions found to have the greatest potential for such circumvention and which involve substantial amounts of money. They are therefore reasonable in the light of that statutory purpose, and consistent with the Fourth Amendment.

B. FOURTH AMENDMENT CHALLENGE TO THE DOMESTIC REPORTING REQUIREMENTS

The District Court examined the domestic reporting requirements imposed on plaintiffs by looking to the broad authorization of the Act itself, without specific reference to the regulations promulgated under its authority. The District Court observed:

> '(A)lthough to date the Secretary has required reporting only by the financial institutions and then only of currency transactions over $10,000, he is empowered by the Act, as indicated above, to require, if he so decides, reporting not only by the financial institution, but also by other parties to or participants in transactions with the institutions and, further, that the Secretary may require reports, not only of currency transactions but of any transaction involving any monetary instrument—and in any amount—large or small.'

The District Court went on to pose, as the question to be resolved, whether 'these provisions, broadly authorizing an executive agency of government to require financial institutions and parties (thereto) . . . to routinely report . . . the detail of almost every conceivable financial transaction . . . (are) such an invasion of a citizen's right of privacy as amounts to an unreasonable search within the meaning of the Fourth Amendment.'

Since, as we have observed earlier in this opinion, the statute is not self-executing, and were the Secretary to take no action whatever under his authority there would be no possibility of criminal or civil sanctions being imposed on anyone, the District Court was wrong in framing the question in this manner. The question is not what sort of reporting requirements might have been imposed by the Secretary under the broad authority given him in the Act, but rather what sort of reporting requirements he did in fact impose under that authority.

. . . .

The question for decision, therefore, is whether the regulations relating to the reporting of domestic transactions violations of which could subject those required to report to civil or criminal penalties, invade any Fourth Amendment right of those required to report. To that question we now turn.

The regulations issued by the Secretary require the reporting of domestic financial transactions only by financial institutions.

. . . .

We have no difficulty then in determining that the Secretary's requirements for the reporting of domestic financial transactions abridge no Fourth Amendment right of the banks themselves. The bank is not a mere stranger or bystander with respect to the transactions which it is required to record or report. The bank is itself a party to each of these transactions, earns portions of its income from conducting such transactions, and in the past may have kept records of similar transactions on a voluntary basis for its own purposes. The regulations presently in effect governing the reporting of domestic currency transactions require information as to the personal and business identity of the person conducting the transaction and of the person or organization for whom it was conducted, as well as a summary description of the nature of the transaction. It is conceivable, and perhaps likely, that the bank might not of its own volition compile this amount of detail for its own purposes, and therefore to that extent the regulations put the bank in the position of seeking information from the customer in order to eventually report it to the Government. But as we have noted above, 'neither incorporated nor unincorporated associations can plead an unqualified right to conduct their affairs in secret.'

The regulations do not impose unreasonable reporting requirements on the banks. The regulations require the reporting of information with respect to abnormally large transactions in currency, much of which information the bank as a party to the transaction already possesses or would acquire in its own interest. To the extent that the regulations in connection with such transactions require the bank to obtain information from a customer simply because the Government wants it, the information is sufficiently described and limited in nature, and sufficiently related to a tenable congressional determination as to improper use of transactions of that type in interstate commerce, so as to withstand the Fourth Amendment challenge made by the bank plaintiffs. "(T)he inquiry is within the authority of the agency, the demand is not too indefinite and the information sought is reasonably relevant. 'The gist of the protection is in the requirement, expressed in terms, that the disclosure sought shall not be unreasonable.' "

. . . .

V

All of the bank and depositor plaintiffs have stressed in their presentations to the District Court and to this Court that the recordkeeping and reporting requirements of the Bank Secrecy Act are focused in large part on the acquisition of information to assist in the enforcement of the criminal laws. While, as we have noted, Congress seems to have been equally concerned with civil liability which might go undetected by reason of transactions of the type required to be recorded or reported, concern for the enforcement of the criminal law was undoubtedly prominant in the minds of the legislators who considered the Act. We do not think it is strange or irrational that Congress, having its attention called to what appeared to be serious and organized efforts to avoid detection of criminal activity, should have legislated to rectify the situation. We have no doubt that Congress, in the sphere of its legislative authority, may just as properly address itself to the effective enforcement of criminal laws which it has previously enacted as to the enactment of those laws in the first instance. In so doing, it is of course subject to the strictures of the Bill of Rights, and may not transgress those strictures. But the fact that a legislative enactment manifests a concern for the enforcement of the criminal law does not cast any generalized pall of constitutional suspicion over it. Having concluded that on the record in these appeals, plaintiffs have failed to state a claim for relief under the First, Fourth, and Fifth Amendments, and having concluded that the enactment in question was within the legislative authority of Congress, our inquiry is at an end.

. . . .

[Concurrence of Justices Powell and Blackmun, as well as separate dissents by Justices Douglas, Brennan, and Marshall are omitted.]

NOTES AND QUESTIONS

1. A number of issues were left open in this case. One of those open issues was whether bank customers have a protected Fourth Amendment right in records of their transactions held by their banks. This question was specifically addressed in *United States v. Miller*, 425 U.S. 435 (1976). In that case, a bank customer had been convicted in part based on banking records that had been obtained via grand jury subpoena. The records in question had been maintained by the bank pursuant to requirements imposed by the BSA.

The customer was originally convicted, but the Fifth Circuit reversed on the grounds that the government's procurement of those records violated the customer's Fourth Amendment rights. *U.S. v. Miller,* 500 F.2d 751, 756–58 (5th Cir. 1974), *judgment rev'd,* 425 U.S. 435 (1976). The Supreme Court reinstated the conviction, finding that the customer/defendant had no legitimate expectation of privacy in business records owned by a third party (in this case, the bank).

2.   Would you agree that FinCEN needs all of the procedures and power described in the preceding opinion in order to effectively administer and enforce the mandates of the Bank Secrecy Act? In your opinion, do the provisions of that Act, as expanded by the Patriot Act, strike a fair and reasonable balance between the needs of the government and the privacy interests of individuals?

3.   Do you think the intrusions on privacy that the BSA required helped create the environment and mindset that led to the desire for and proliferation of Bitcoin and other cryptocurrencies?

3.   THE PATRIOT ACT AND EXPANSION OF AML REQUIREMENTS

In the years since the U.S. Supreme Court originally upheld the oversight, record-keeping, and reporting requirements authorized under the BSA against various constitutional challenges, the reach of its requirements has been significantly expanded. One of the most critical developments was the early establishment of the Financial Crimes Enforcement Network (FinCEN).[14]

As mentioned earlier, prior to September 11, 2001, FinCEN was primarily engaged in efforts to combat traditional money laundering (the use of increasingly sophisticated techniques to make money derived from illegal operations appear to have been legitimately earned) and to aid in the investigation of criminal activities such as tax evasion and the drug trade. Title III of the Patriot Act broadened the scope of the BSA to require financial institutions to perform "enhanced due diligence" on private accounts and further expanded the BSA to include foreign financial institutions with assets within the borders of the United States. It also extended extraterritorial jurisdiction over persons suspected of money laundering. Under provisions added to the BSA by the Patriot Act financial institutions must adopt a customer identification program and maintain adequate records of cash purchases of negotiable instruments. Section 314 of the Patriot Act also includes special information sharing procedures for

---

[14]   FinCEN was established by Treasury Order 105–08 on April 25, 1990. Its mission was expanded in May, 1994 to include certain regulatory responsibilities, and in October of that year its precursor, the Office of Financial Enforcement, merged with FinCEN.

information related to money laundering or terrorist activities, but these special procedures are limited to those two categories of illegal activity.

While traditional financial institutions such as banks and savings and loans were subject to extensive regulations prior to the Patriot Act, many non-bank businesses were not regulated closely until after September 11, 2001. As mentioned above, the Patriot Act expanded the BSA to include not only reports potentially useful in criminal, tax, or regulatory investigations but also to cover to protect against international terrorism. The Patriot Act also extended the definition of "financial institution" to include a number of non-bank entities such as credit unions, futures commission merchants, commodity trading advisers, commodity pool operators, and individuals engaging in informal money-transfer systems. In addition, it adopted a number of changes to the regulatory reporting framework, adding the requirement that financial institutions adopt and maintain AML programs.

After enactment of the Patriot Act, FinCEN became an official bureau within the Department of the Treasury.[15] FinCEN's duties and powers now include the obligation to implement, administer, and enforce compliance with the BSA.[16] In essence, FinCEN collects and analyzes information about financial transactions in order to combat domestic and international money laundering, terrorist financing, and other financial crimes. This is all done in furtherance of its official mission, which (as reflected on the FinCEN website) is "to safeguard the financial system from illicit use, combat money laundering, and promote national security through the strategic use of financial authorities and the collection, analysis, and dissemination of financial intelligence."[17]

FinCEN does not actually bring criminal actions, and instead partners with law enforcement at the appropriate level. For example, FinCEN has close relationships with the largest Federal law enforcement agencies through a number of arrangements. There are direct information sharing agreements and full-time detailed assignments at FinCEN and with the U.S. Attorneys' Offices as well as information sharing arrangements with the DoJ's National Advocacy Center. FinCEN also coordinates and shares information with all 50 states and numerous major local authorities across the nation.

---

[15]   *See* Treasury Order 180–01. This is now reflected in 31 U.S. Code § 310(a), which confirms FinCEN as "a bureau in the Department of the Treasury."

[16]   More specifically, this includes: maintaining a government-wide data access service covering a range of financial transactions information; analyzing and disseminating information in support of law enforcement investigation at the federal, state, local, and international levels; ascertaining emerging trends and developments in money laundering and other financial crimes; serving as the financial intelligence unit of the United States; and carrying out other regulatory responsibilities delegated to it.

[17]   FinCEN, *What We Do*, available online at https://www.fincen.gov/what-we-do.

Rather than citing the specific regulations here, the following materials describe how the various requirements of federal law as overseen by FinCEN apply.

4. MONEY LAUNDERING AND MONETARY TRANSACTIONS INVOLVING SPECIFIED UNLAWFUL ACTIVITY

The Money Laundering Control Act of 1986 contains two distinct provisions:[18] 18 U.S. Code § 1956 dealing with the laundering of monetary instruments, and § 1957 prohibiting monetary transactions involving property derived from a specified unlawful activity. In general terms, § 1956 applies to criminals who act either to hide the source of money derived from illegal operations or to use funds to further their criminal activities. Section 1957 is broader, and criminalizes the knowing acceptance of tainted funds by anyone interacting with criminals.

More specifically, § 1956 is divided into three parts; the first part covers financial-transaction money laundering. A § 1956(a)(1) violation occurs whenever a defendant (1) knows that the property involved in a financial transaction represents the proceeds of some form of unlawful activity, (2) conducts or attempts to conduct a financial transaction that (3) involves the proceeds of a specified unlawful activity, and (4) acts with the requisite knowledge or intent.

In comparison, § 1957 provides that an offense is committed by "[w]hoever, in any of the circumstances set forth in subsection (d), knowingly engages or attempts to engage in a monetary transaction in criminally derived property that is of a value greater than $10,000 and is derived from specified unlawful activity. . . ." Subsection (d) provides extraterritorial reach of the provision, so long as the defendant is a U.S. person.

Probably the easiest way to consider the differences between these two provisions is to look at their major components in a side-by-side comparison.

---

[18]   The two sections are codified at 18 U.S. Code §§ 1956 & 1957. Both of these provisions were enacted as part of the Anti-Drug Abuse Act of 1986. Together, they are generally known as the Money Laundering Control Act of 1986. The Senate drafted 18 U.S. Code § 1956, while the House of Representatives drafted 18 U.S. Code § 1957. Although both sections were enacted at the same time, and both have been expanded significantly since being originally enacted, the two provisions contain significant differences.

	18 U.S. CODE § 1956	18 U.S. CODE § 1957
Conduct criminalized	All commercial transactions affecting interstate commerce, including those by or through financial institutions	Limited to transactions by or through financial institutions
Transaction threshold	None	Over $10,000
Knowledge requirement	Knowledge that funds are criminally derived; includes only felony violations	Knowledge that funds are criminally derived; includes felonies and may include misdemeanors
Intent	To promote specified unlawful activity; to engage in tax-evasion conduct; to conceal or disguise proceeds; to avoid (evade) reporting requirements	No intentional activity required
Penalty	20 years/$500,000	10 Years/$250,000
Asset forfeiture	Applies to property involved and proceeds	Applies to property involved and proceeds

Section 1956 therefore applies to conventionally criminal behavior and requires proof that the defendant intended to engage in illegal activity. Section 1957 can apply even in the absence of criminal intent, so long as there is evidence that a covered financial institution knew that the funds were derived from illegal activity included within the scope of the statute.

In order to insure that they are not subject to liability under these provisions, financial institutions are required to adopt AML compliance programs that include policies and procedures designed to detect and report certain sizable transactions and certain suspicious activities. A suspicious activity includes any transaction that appears to be outside the business norm for a customer for which the bank has been unable to obtain a reasonable explanation after reasonable investigation.

The Comptroller of the Currency has suggested a list of suspicious activities that are characterized as "money laundering red flags."[19] These include "customers who provide insufficient or suspicious information"; customers who engage in "efforts to avoid reporting or record keeping requirement"; certain fund transfers such as wire transfers to or from foreign or high-risk locations without apparent business justification; "activity inconsistent with the customer's business"; frequent exchanges of smaller denominations for larger bills; a large number of large transactions under ordinary reporting thresholds; "changes in bank-to-bank transactions"; and suspicious behavior by bank employees.[20]

A financial institution participating in a transaction without reasonable investigation may run the risk of a prosecution based on willful blindness. In *United States v. Campbell*, 777 F. Supp. 1259 (WDNC), *aff'd in part, rev'd in part*, 977 F.2d 854 (4th Cir. 1992), *cert. denied*, 507 U.S. 938 (1993), a broker was charged under 18 U.S. Code § 1957 in connection with the sale of a home to a buyer who turned out to be a narcotics trafficker. The jury would have found the defendant guilty, but the trial court entered a verdict of acquittal. The Fourth Circuit reversed, finding that there was sufficient evidence that the broker could have been on notice of the illegal source of the funds based on the purchaser's extravagant lifestyle and the "under the table" payment at closing. *United States v. Campbell*, 977 F.2d 854, 856–860 (4th Cir. 1992), *cert. denied*, 507 U.S. 938 (1993) (remanded for new trial).

5.　MONEY-TRANSMITTING BUSINESSES

Under current law[21] it is a crime to engage in an illegal money-transmitting business. As amended, 18 U.S. Code § 1960 criminalizes the behavior of anyone who "knowingly conducts, controls, manages, supervises, directs, or owns all or part of an unlicensed money transmitting business."[22] The statue does not impose any requirements with regard to the source of funds used in the business, and instead only requires that the business be operated illegally.[23] Under the terms of the statute, this occurs

---

[19]　*See* Office of the Comptroller of the Currency, *Money Laundering: A Banker's Guide to Avoiding Problems* (Dec. 2002, replacing the Second Edition issued June, 1993), online at https://www.hsdl.org/?abstract&did=3617 (last accessed March 2019).

[20]　*Id.*

[21]　The relevant section of the BSA was added in 1992 by the Annunzio-Wylie Anti-Money Laundering Act, as codified at 18 U.S. Code § 1960.

[22]　In addition, "money transmitting" includes "transferring funds on behalf of the public by any and all means." *Id.* at § 1960(b)(2).

[23]　Section 1960 defines "unlicensed money transmitting business" to include any businesses (so long as interstate or foreign commerce is affected), if it:

(A)　is operated without an appropriate money transmitting license in a State where such operation is punishable as a misdemeanor or a felony under State law, whether or not the defendant knew that the operation was required to be licensed or that the operation was so punishable;

if the business is operated without being licensed as required by either federal or applicable state law. In addition, § 1960 was substantially broadened by the Patriot Act to remove any requirement that the defendant knew the operation was required to be licensed by either federal or state law. The Patriot Act also amended § 1960 so that it now covers any business that involves the movement of funds where the defendant knows the funds are being used to promote or support unlawful activity. Under this provision, there is no requirement to show that the funds come from a tainted source if the financial transaction or transmission is intended to promote or support a new offense.

6. TO WHOM DO FEDERAL AML REQUIREMENTS APPLY?

As originally enacted, the BSA imposed AML requirements on federal banks, savings and loans, and federal branches of foreign banking institutions.[24] The Patriot Act,[25] however, substantially expanded the reach of BSA requirements by adding a number of non-banks to the definition of financial institution.[26] Some of these non-bank financial institutions are obligated to comply with many of the same requirements that apply to banks, such as developing AML programs, complying with the reporting and recordkeeping requirements of the BSA, and the obligation to report suspicious activity. Other of these organizations have exemptions or threshold requirements, or other limitations applicable to their operations.

(B)   fails to comply with the money transmitting business registration requirements under [31 U.S. Code § 5330] . . .; or

(C)   otherwise involves the transportation or transmission of funds that are known to the defendant to have been derived from a criminal offense or are intended to be used to promote or support unlawful activity

18 U.S. Code § 1960(b)(1).

[24]   For a description of the evolution of the BSA and its requirements, see Eric J. Gouvin, *Bringing out the Big Guns: The USA Patriot Act, Money Laundering, and the War on Terrorism,* 55 BAYLOR L. REV. 955, 971 (2003).

[25]   The Patriot Act is more formally known as Uniting and Strengthening America by Providing Appropriate Tools Required to Intercept and Obstruct Terrorism Act of 2001, Pub. L. No. 107–56, § 301–77 115 Stat. 272, 296–342.

[26]   *See* 31 U.S. Code § 5312(a)(2. This subsection defines "financial institution" to include without limitation: insured banks; commercial banks or trust companies; private bankers; credit unions; thrifts; registered brokers and dealers; investment bankers and investment companies; currency exchanges; dealers in travelers checks; credit card system operators; insurance companies; dealers in precious metals and the like; pawnbrokers; loan and finance companies; travel agencies; persons in the business of the transmission of funds; vehicle sales; persons involved in real estate closings; and casinos. Futures commission merchants, commodity trading advisors, and commodity pool operators required to register under the Commodity Exchange Act are also added to the definition pursuant to § 5312(c)(1)(A).

Pursuant to regulations adopted by FinCEN, financial institution specifically includes money services businesses (MSBs). 31 C.F.R. § 1010.100(t).

There are therefore various problems for businesses wishing to insure that they are acting appropriately under these definitions. Obviously, a business needs to know if it is subject to the BSA's AML requirements, because the penalties for non-compliance can be significant. However, some exemptions and limitations apply to certain kinds of operations but not to others, complicating the appropriate classification of businesses.

Some covered operations are quite broad and may well come into play when a business develops a business plan that calls for it to issue, sell, convert, transmit, or exchange interests that are not properly regarded as traditional or fiat currency. Crypto can qualify as such an interest.

One such category that may apply to some crypto businesses is that of "money services business" (MSB), which encompasses a number of different business operations.[27] It is particularly critical to know if and when MSB requirements will apply because, with limited exceptions, MSBs are subject to the full range of BSA regulatory requirements, including AML compliance program requirements, suspicious activity and currency transaction reporting requirements, and various other mandates. Most MSBs are also required to register with FinCEN. In addition, many states have established supervisory requirements for MSBs, often including the requirement that an MSB be licensed with the state(s) in which it is incorporated or does business.

FinCEN defines MSB as a legal person doing business in one or more of a number of different capacities.[28] Included in the list of possibilities is acting as a "money transmitter."[29] While some of the other possibilities have monetary thresholds, any money transmission, regardless of amount, may result in a person being an MSB. In addition, under BSA regulations, persons (individuals or entities) conducting money transmission (or other listed) activities within the U.S. are considered MSBs regardless of where

---

[27]   MSBs are defined in 31 C.F.R. § 1010.100(ff).

[28]   An MSB includes any business acting as a dealer in foreign exchange; check casher; issuer or seller of traveler's checks or money orders; money transmitter; provider of prepaid access; seller of prepaid access; and the U.S. Postal Service. Some of these activities have monetary thresholds (i.e., dealers in foreign exchange, check cashers and issuers of traveler's checks are not MSBs unless their transactions exceed $1,000 for a single person on a single day).

[29]   MSBs are defined in 31 C.F.R. § 1010.100(ff)(5) to include money transmitters, which are:

(i)   In general.

(A)   A person that provides money transmission services. The term "money transmission services" means the acceptance of currency, funds, or other value that substitutes for currency from one person and the transmission of currency, funds, or other value that substitutes for currency to another location or person by any means. "Any means" includes, but is not limited to, through a financial agency or institution; a Federal Reserve Bank or other facility of one or more Federal Reserve Banks, the Board of Governors of the Federal Reserve System, or both; an electronic funds transfer network; or an informal value transfer system; or

(B)   Any other person engaged in the transfer of funds.

they are located or doing business and "whether or not on a regular basis or as an organized or licensed business concern."

Money transmitters are subject to many of the same requirements as traditional financial institutions, although they generally do not function in the same way as banks or savings and loans. This obviously raises the question of how broadly "money transmitter" Will be construed. Under current definitions, a person is a money transmitter if that person "provides money transmission services" or is engaged in the transfer of funds. In addition, FinCEN finalized a rule in 2011 that expanded "money transmission" to include "the acceptance of currency, funds, or other value that substitutes for currency from one person and the transmission of currency, funds, or other value that substitutes for currency to another location or person by any means."[30] (As will be discussed in more detail later, it was the expansion of the definition to cover "other value that substitutes for currency" that has provided the primary basis for applying AML and know-your-customer (KYC) requirements to actors in the crypto space under the rubric of regulating money transmitters.)

When it comes to applying these definitions to businesses operating in the real world, various kinds of business operations can fall within the ambit of these rules. Rulings from FinCEN emphasize that the term's application depends on the totality of facts and circumstances, including a consideration of for whose benefit the business is being operated.[31]

7. ENFORCEMENT ACTIONS

A. TRADITIONAL MONEY LAUNDERING

Traditionally, money laundering involved efforts to conceal any illegal source of funds. This could be accomplished through any of a number of techniques. For example, funds from criminal enterprises could (and still can) be laundered by introducing the funds into the financial system in carefully orchestrated placement efforts. This can include breaking large amounts into many different deposits and investments. In order to obscure sources, funds can also be "layered," which occurs when money is shuffled around between various entities to create distance between the funds and their criminal source. The goal of this process is to integrate "clean" funds back into the hands of the criminal instigators.

Regardless of how the laundering is structured, at the heart of each of these techniques is the reality that the transactions are "designed . . . to conceal . . . the nature, the location, the source, the ownership or the

---

[30]   *Bank Secrecy Act Regulations; Definitions and Other Regulations Relating to Money Services Businesses,* 76 Fed. Reg. 43585 (July 21, 2011).

[31]   *See* 31 C.F.R. § 1010.100(ff)(5)(ii), imposing a facts and circumstances approach on determining whether a person is a money transmitter.

control" of assets.[32] What does this entail? This issue is discussed in the following case, which involves traditional fiat currency rather than any kind of crypto but helps set the stage for how crypto is being regulated today by FinCEN.

UNITED STATES V. GARCIA-EMANUEL
14 F.3d 1469 (10th Cir. 1994)

[Headings have been added to this opinion.]

MCKAY, CIRCUIT JUDGE.

On April 1, 1991, a jury in the Northern District of Oklahoma convicted Mario R. Garcia-Emanuel of one count of conspiracy to possess with intent to distribute and to distribute cocaine, one count of continuing criminal enterprise (hereinafter CCE), five counts of income tax evasion, one count of conspiracy to launder money, and seventeen counts of money laundering. The district court . . . granted a judgment of acquittal pursuant to Rule 29(c) on all seventeen money laundering counts . . . . [The government appealed.]

II   [Analysis]

. . .[T]he government asserts that the trial court erred in granting a judgment of acquittal on the money laundering . . . counts. The district court found the evidence insufficient to sustain any of these counts.

The record, viewed in the light most favorable to the government as required by *Sanders [United States v. Sanders,* 928 F.2d 940, 944 (10th Cir.)], shows that Defendant and his wife engaged in a wide variety of transactions involving the proceeds of his criminal enterprise. They paid their mortgage, bought some land, invested in an insurance company, collected Paso Fino riding horses, built a riding area, bought a pickup truck and horse trailers, and wired money to someone in Colombia. They paid in either cash, personal checks, or cashier's checks. While not all transactions were conducted in Defendant's name (some were in his wife's name, others were in the name of the Guadalajara Restaurant, which he owned), Defendant or his restaurant, or both, were conspicuously involved in each transaction. All told, the government charged that seventeen of the transactions constituted money laundering under 18 U.S. Code § 1956(a)(1)(B)(i) (1988).

The district court granted a judgment of acquittal with respect to all the money laundering counts based on the discussion of money laundering in *Sanders,* which it read as requiring the government to prove that the transactions were structured to "conceal[ ] . . . the identity of the person providing the illicit proceeds." Because Defendant was so conspicuously

---

[32]   This requirement is embodied in the BSA itself. *See* 18 U.S. Code § 1956(a)(1)(B)(i).

involved in the transactions, and because it found that "[t]he Guadalajara Restaurant, for our purposes here, was Mario Garcia," the court granted the judgment of acquittal.

We agree that on twelve of the seventeen counts the government failed to prove a violation of § 1956(a)(1)(B)(i). However, because we disagree with the district court's view of *Sanders*, we reinstate five of the convictions.

A [Statutory elements]

A review of the statute reveals that in order to prevail at trial, the government was required to prove four elements beyond a reasonable doubt: (1) that Defendant engaged in a financial transaction; (2) that Defendant knew that the property involved in that transaction represented the proceeds of his unlawful activities; (3) that the property involved was in fact the proceeds of that criminal enterprise; and (4) that Defendant knew that "the transaction [was] designed in whole or in part to conceal or disguise the nature, the location, the source, the ownership or the control" of the proceeds of the specified unlawful activities. 18 U.S. Code § 1956(a)(1)(B)(i). In this appeal, the only challenge is to the fourth element, which we will refer to as the "design requirement."

This circuit first addressed the design requirement of the money laundering statute in *Sanders*, where we reversed the conviction of a man charged with using drug proceeds to purchase two automobiles. Even though one of the cars was placed in the name of the defendant's daughter, and even though the defendant's wife signed the daughter's name, we found that the purchase was so open as to negate any inference of a design to conceal. *Id.* at 946.

It is true that *Sanders* stated that "the purpose of the money laundering statute is to reach commercial transactions intended (at least in part) to disguise the relationship of the item purchased with the person providing the proceeds. . . ." *Id.* Defendant contended successfully in the trial court that this statement requires a judgment of acquittal unless there is evidence that the transactions were structured to conceal Defendant's identity. We disagree. As we explained in *United States v. Lovett*, 964 F.2d 1029 (10th Cir.), *cert. denied*, 506 U.S. 857 (1992), there is "no requirement in the statute or in *Sanders* that every money laundering conviction must be supported by evidence of intent to conceal the identity of the participants to the transaction." *Id.* at 1034. Rather, "the statute is aimed broadly at transactions designed in whole or in part to conceal or disguise in any manner the nature, location, source, ownership or control of the proceeds of unlawful activity." *Id.* at 1034 n.3.

B   [Statutory Interpretation]

Although the trial court based its judgment of acquittal on an erroneous view of *Sanders*, we nevertheless affirm on twelve of the counts.

Since 1991, challenges to the design requirement of money laundering have become a growth industry, with at least fifteen reported cases from the various courts of appeals. Given the wide range of money laundering claimed by the government in this case, and the prevalence of appeals on this point, it is useful to review both the statute and the recent case law to discern the principles that govern these appeals.

1   [What knowledge is required]

The core issue in *Sanders* was the government's contention that the money laundering statute should be interpreted broadly to include all purchases made by persons with knowledge that the money used represents the proceeds of illegal activity. We rejected that argument.

To so interpret the statute would, in the court's view, turn the money laundering statute into a "money spending statute." This interpretation would be contrary to Congress' expressly stated intent that the transactions being criminalized in the statute are those transactions "designed to conceal or disguise the nature, the location, the source, the ownership or the control of the proceeds of specified unlawful activity." *Sanders*, 928 F.2d at 946 (quoting § 1956(a)(1)(B)(i)).

Implicit in the *Sanders* formulation is the difficult task of separating money laundering, which is punishable by up to twenty years in prison, from mere money spending, which is legal. This, of course, is an issue of congressional intent.

We agree with the Executive Branch statements quoted by the prosecution as to the purposes of the money laundering statute. The President's Commission on Organized Crime described money laundering as schemes designed to assist criminals who "seek to change large amounts of cash . . . into an ostensibly legitimate form, such as business profits or loans, *before using those funds for personal benefit. . . .*" President's Commission on Organized Crime, *The Cash Connection: Organized Crime, Financial Institutions, and Money Laundering*, at 7 (Interim Report, Oct. 1984) (quoted in *United States v. Cuevas*, 847 F.2d 1417, 1424 n.19 (9th Cir.1988), *cert. denied*, 489 U.S. 1012 (1989)) [hereinafter *The Cash Connection*] (emphasis added). Similarly, the Department of the Treasury described the purpose of money laundering as "conceal[ing] the illicit sources of their monies *by creating the appearance of legitimate wealth.*" United States Department of the Treasury, *Layering*, Money Laundering Updates, Mar. 1991, at 9, 9 [hereinafter *Layering*] (emphasis added).

These statements reveal the heart of the difficulty in applying the money laundering statute. In speaking of transactions that are "designed

. . . to conceal . . . the nature, the location, the source, the ownership or the control" of assets, 18 U.S. Code § 1956(a)(1)(B)(i), the statute is aimed at transactions that are engaged in for the purpose of concealing assets. Merely engaging in a transaction with money whose nature has been concealed through other means is not in itself a crime. In other words, the government must prove that the specific transactions in question were designed, at least in part, to launder money, not that the transactions involved money that was previously laundered through other means. If transactions are engaged in for present personal benefit, and not to create the appearance of legitimate wealth, they do not violate the money laundering statute.

2   ["Designed" to conceal]

The statute speaks in terms of transactions that are "designed" to conceal the proceeds of unlawful activity. Whenever a drug dealer uses his profits to acquire any asset—whether a house, a car, a horse, or a television—a jury could reasonably suspect that on some level he is motivated by a desire to convert his cash into a more legitimate form. The requirement that the transaction be "designed" to conceal, however, requires more than a trivial motivation to conceal.

The Seventh Circuit encountered a similar problem regarding the level of proof required to show that the assets involved were the proceeds of a crime. The court stated that "[i]t will be a rare case in which [the design] requirement[ ] will be satisfied without proof that the funds used in the charged transaction were derived in substantial measure from 'specified unlawful activities' rather than from other legal or illegal conduct." *United States v. Jackson*, 935 F.2d 832, 840 (7th Cir.1991). In a like vein, were we to hold that an inference of a trivial motivation to conceal was sufficient to support a conviction, we would essentially "turn the money laundering statute into a 'money spending statute.'" *Sanders*, 928 F.2d at 946.

In reviewing the sufficiency of the evidence, the most difficult cases are those in which the defendant acquires an asset which both brings a present personal benefit and has substantial resale value, and thus is a potential tool for money laundering. On the one hand, cases involving investments made with illegal proceeds are close to the core of the statute's purpose of criminalizing changing cash into an "ostensibly legitimate form, such as business profits or loans, before using those funds for personal benefit. . . ." *The Cash Connection, supra*, at 7. On the other hand, when the defendant has merely acquired an asset that brings a significant present personal benefit to himself or his family, the inference becomes more difficult to draw.

In these cases, our requirement that the jury verdicts of guilt beyond a reasonable doubt be based on substantial evidence, and not mere suspicion, *Sanders*, 928 F.2d at 944; *United States v. Ortiz*, 445 F.2d 1100,

1103 (10th Cir.), *cert. denied,* 404 U.S. 993 (1971), becomes paramount. It is not enough for the government to show that a defendant probably is guilty; in our system, guilt must be proven beyond a reasonable doubt.

3   [Proof required]

While there are many things that criminals can do with their profits that would arouse suspicion of an intent to launder the money, actions that are merely suspicious and do not provide substantial evidence of a design to conceal will not alone support a conviction. There are many examples of suspicious behavior that we have held will not, standing alone, justify a finding of a design to conceal beyond a reasonable doubt. We held in *Sanders* that the defendant's decision to register a car in his daughter's name would not alone support his conviction. *Sanders,* 928 F.2d at 946. Likewise in *Lovett,* 964 F.2d 1029 at 1036, we reversed a conviction based on similar circumstances—the purchase of a vehicle registered in a family member's name with proceeds of an illegal transaction. We concluded in that case that even the additional evidence that the defendant "created the impression with the salesman that his siding business was a lucrative business, going so far as to offer the salesman a job" was insufficient additional evidence of intent to conceal. *Id.*

It also can fairly be discerned from our cases that the mere fact that a defendant was convicted of money laundering arising out of some transactions is not sufficient to sustain a money laundering conviction involving other transactions. In *Lovett,* the court reversed the conviction relating to an automobile purchase notwithstanding evidence of other money laundering activities which were sustained in the same case. *Id.*

A final example is our conclusion in *Sanders,* 928 F.2d at 945–46, that even the additional evidence of the use of a large amount of cash to purchase a car was not sufficient to satisfy the proof necessary to sustain a money laundering conviction.

By way of contrast, a variety of types of evidence have been cited by this and other circuits as supportive of evidence of intent to disguise or conceal. They include, among others, statements by a defendant probative of intent to conceal; unusual secrecy surrounding the transaction; structuring the transaction in a way to avoid attention; depositing illegal profits in the bank account of a legitimate business; highly irregular features of the transaction; using third parties to conceal the real owner; a series of unusual financial moves cumulating in the transaction; or expert testimony on practices of criminals.

This is not an exclusive list. It is obvious from the proliferation of details of evidence that no list of categories can govern the decision about what is sufficient evidence to sustain a conviction of money laundering beyond a reasonable doubt. However, it is clear from our decision in *Lovett* that trial courts, upon motion for directed verdict, and juries, upon proper instruction, must rigorously enforce two disciplines. The first is our decision in *Sanders*, reaffirmed in *Lovett*, that this is a concealment statute—not a spending statute. The second is the requirement that the evidence of concealment must be substantial.

An examination of *Lovett* and *Sanders* illustrates our holding. In *Lovett*, the conviction on other money laundering counts, evidence of placing the purchased vehicle in the name of a relative, and even a conversation which created the impression that the defendant's business was a lucrative one were not sufficient, alone or in combination, to support concealment beyond a reasonable doubt. Similarly, in *Sanders* we reversed a conviction supported only by the evidence that ownership of a vehicle was placed in the name of a relative and that the defendant used a large amount of cash. Taken together, these cases make clear that the mere accumulation of non-concealing behavior is not enough to sustain a conviction for money laundering. Rather, there must be evidence that the transaction was "designed in whole or in part [ ] to conceal or disguise the nature, the location, the source, the ownership, or the control of the proceeds of specified unlawful activity." 18 U.S. Code § 1956(a)(1)(B)(i).

C   [Application to this case]

With these principles in mind, we turn to the details of the individual counts against the present Defendant.

In counts 9 and 10, Defendant withdrew $9,000 from his bank account in the form of a cashier's check on which he was named as remitter and then used it to pay his residential mortgage. No other evidence was presented to establish a design to conceal. While we acknowledge that all mortgage payments increase the owner's investment in his home, the mere fact that Defendant made the payment with a cashier's check purchased with drug money is insufficient to sustain a money laundering conviction. We AFFIRM the grant of a judgment of acquittal on counts 9 and 10.

In count 11, Defendant presented a cashier's check, on which his restaurant was listed as remitter, to pay for some land. The transaction not only creates the false impression that the restaurant was his source of wealth, but it creates documentary evidence in support of that deception that could mislead an investigator. This furthers a launderer's goal of "plac[ing] illicit bulk cash in an economy, [so] it becomes increasingly difficult to uncover their money laundering operation." *Layering, supra,* at 1474. We REVERSE the district court and REMAND with instructions to reinstate the conviction on count 11.

In count 12, Defendant made a second payment on the same land, using a cashier's check on which he, not his restaurant, was named as remitter. Consistent with our holding on counts 9 and 10, we do not believe that this, alone, demonstrates a design to conceal. Moreover, the record on appeal does not indicate whether the land in question was essentially an investment or whether it was used in significant part for present personal enjoyment. Accordingly, the government has not met its burden of persuasion to overturn the judgment of acquittal below. We AFFIRM the grant of a judgment of acquittal on count 12.

In count 13, Defendant first bought a Certificate of Deposit with cash then used the CD as collateral for a loan to an insurance company he partially owned. This is classic money laundering where Defendant, through a complex series of transactions, transformed the cash he received selling drugs into a legitimate business investment that allowed him to display his wealth without arousing suspicion. We REVERSE and REMAND with instructions to reinstate the conviction on count 13.

In count 14, unlike count 13, Defendant and his wife made no effort to conceal cash, but rather, spent $15,000 in cash as partial payment for a Paso Fino horse. The evidence on appeal shows that Defendant and his wife had a hobby of raising Paso Fino horses. Therefore, while a horse in some instances could be essentially an investment, there was a significant aspect of present personal benefit in this case. The record also shows that it is not unusual for horse purchasers to use cash when making a down payment. At some point in their dealings with the seller and after agreeing to purchase the horse, Defendant and his wife misrepresented the source of the cash to the seller, indicating that the money came from the weekend profits at their restaurant. While it is true that this misrepresentation brings an element of concealment into the transaction, we do not believe that, standing alone and in the face of other circumstances present, this single misrepresentation can amount to substantial evidence that the transaction was designed to conceal illegal funds.

As we discussed *supra*, the most difficult cases are those in which the defendant acquires an asset that both brings a present personal value and has substantial investment value. It is in these borderline cases that the substantial evidence requirement becomes paramount. The only evidence of concealment in count is the oral misrepresentation which Defendant made to the seller. However, Defendant initially negotiated and signed the contract for the horse in his own name. He made the subsequent payments on the horse with a cashier's check in which he was the sole remitter. The oral misrepresentation occurred after the parties had already agreed to the transaction, and only after a paper trail had already been created that clearly connected Defendant to the cash. Unlike count 11, Defendant did not transfer money to his restaurant, use his restaurant as a remitter, involve his restaurant as a named party in any kind of transaction, or design a paper trail that would lead an investigator to believe that the money for the horse came from some source other than Defendant.

Thus, it appears from the totality of the evidence that the transaction was not designed to conceal the source of his money. Instead, the evidence only supports the conclusion that Defendant entered into the transaction for his present personal benefit, for which he paid in cash. The single false comment about the source of the cash is not substantial evidence that the transaction itself was designed, in whole or in part, to conceal money under the circumstances in which it was made. We AFFIRM the grant of a judgment of acquittal on count 14.

In count 22, Defendant made another payment on the same horse from count 14. To do so, he used a cashier's check with Defendant as remitter. Because there is no new evidence of a design to conceal, count 22 is controlled by our analysis in count 14. We AFFIRM the grant of a judgment of acquittal on count 22.

In count 15, Defendant's wife purchased another Paso Fino horse in Defendant's name with a $20,000 check drawn on their joint checking account. In the week prior to the issuance of the check, $23,000 in currency was deposited into their checking account in three units of $7,000, $8,000, and $8,000. Ordinarily, this pattern of deposits would be prosecuted under § 1956(a)(1)(B)(ii) as designed to avoid a transaction reporting requirement—in this case, the currency transaction report banks must issue when they receive deposits of over $10,000 cash. See 31 U.S. Code § 5313(a) (1988); 31 C.F.R. § 103.22 (1992). Were the case to have proceeded under this theory, the proof would have been quite straightforward.

The government, however, has chosen to prosecute not the deposits under (B)(ii), but the subsequent purchase under (B)(i) which criminalizes money laundering. The inference under this theory, that the design to conceal in the first transaction (the purchase of the cashier's check) can be imputed to the second (the purchase of the horse), is considerably weaker. Nevertheless, this is evidence of a design to conceal, and we are constrained to reverse. "If we had sat on the jury, we might not have convicted [Defendant] for money laundering. But in reviewing [his] conviction on appeal, we are unable to hold that the jury's conclusion was unreasonable." *United States v. Posters 'N' Things Ltd.*, 969 F.2d 652, 661 (8th Cir.1992), *cert. granted on other grounds,* 507 U.S. 971 (1993). We REVERSE and REMAND with instructions to reinstate the conviction on count 15.

In counts 16 and 17, Defendant bought a pickup truck and a horse trailer with cash and placed them both in his wife's name. Ordinarily, this would not be sufficient to convict of money laundering. However, the government also presented testimony from a co-conspirator that Defendant indicated that he planned to place assets in his wife's name to deceive the IRS. This testimony is probative of a design to conceal. We REVERSE and REMAND with instructions to reinstate the convictions on counts 16 and 17.

In counts 18, 19, 20, 24 and 25, Defendant purchased horses, another horse trailer, a covered riding arena, and a round pen with cash or checks. In each instance, Defendant's name appears on the contract of sale or the check. The government has not shown evidence that any of these assets were placed in his wife's name nor any other evidence of a design to conceal. Given Defendant's hobby of raising horses and the appearance of his name on documents accompanying each sale, the evidence is insufficient to support the convictions for money laundering. We AFFIRM the grant of a judgment of acquittal on counts 18, 19, 20, 22, 24, and 25.

In count 21, Defendant purchased a watch with a cashier's check on which he appears as remitter. The government's sole evidence of a design to conceal is a business card for Defendant's restaurant attached to the sales receipt. This is insufficient evidence that the purchase of the watch was designed to conceal anything. We AFFIRM the grant of a judgment of acquittal on count 21.

In count 23, Defendant wired $4,440 from his bank to the Florida bank account of a Colombian national. The government presented no evidence of an unusual structure to this transaction, of undue secrecy surrounding it, or of any attempt to avoid attention. The government has also not presented any expert testimony about the pattern of drug dealers in wiring funds. Under these circumstances, the evidence is insufficient to support the conviction. We AFFIRM the grant of a judgment of acquittal on count 23.

. . . .

NOTES AND QUESTIONS

1.   Based on your reading of the preceding case, what is meant by the phrase "traditional money laundering"?

2.   The preceding excerpt from *Garcia-Emanuel* centered around a particular kind of behavior. What was it that the defendant did with funds that was illegal (aside from the defendants' involvement in distributing cocaine and any attempted tax evasion)? What government or public interests are being protected by making these actions illegal? Most importantly (for the purposes of this book), how might crypto be used in connection with this kind of behavior?

3.   As of the date this note was written, crypto was accepted by relatively few merchants. Wouldn't that make it more difficult to use crypto for money laundering? How can you launder crypto when so few merchants accept it?

B. REVERSE MONEY LAUNDERING

As mentioned earlier, sometimes money laundering does not involve the traditional pattern of taking funds from a criminal enterprise and introducing it to the financial system in such a way as to obscure its criminal origins. Sometimes the issue is that legitimately derived funds are being diverted to support criminal activity, in what is sometimes known as reverse money laundering. This can also be a federal crime under current U.S. law.

UNITED STATES V. HAMILTON
931 F.2d 1046 (5th Cir. 1991)

THORNBERRY, CIRCUIT JUDGE:

The defendant was convicted . . . for mailing drug proceeds . . . . The defendant appeals his conviction arguing that . . . the money laundering statute under which he was convicted, 18 U.S.C. § 1956(a)(1), does not prohibit mailing drug proceeds between two points within the United States. Finding no error, we AFFIRM.

FACTS AND PROCEDURAL HISTORY

. . . .

Charlie McVey, a Mississippi Bureau of Narcotics Sergeant, spotted Hamilton driving towards Columbus, Mississippi. McVey, who had [previously] arrested Hamilton for [marijuana possession] . . . had received information that the defendant was continuing to deal in drugs. . . . McVey decided to follow Hamilton and requested assistance from other agents. The agents followed Hamilton to the Columbus post office where they later determined that Hamilton had mailed a package addressed to Sesar Lopez Perez in Chula Vista, California. Sergeant McVey contacted law enforcement officials in Chula Vista, as well as others familiar with Perez, and determined that Perez was involved in illicit drug activity. Based on this information, McVey obtained a federal warrant to seize and search the package. Inside the package, narcotics agents discovered clothing, a throw pillow, and three sections of PVC pipe with caps on each end. The agents discovered $18,100.00 in cash inside of the PVC pipes.

. . . .

After a one day non-jury trial, Hamilton was convicted of . . . attempting to conduct a financial transaction affecting interstate commerce with proceeds from unlawful activities (i.e., mailing drug money), see 18 U.S.C.A. § 1956(a)(1). . . .

DISCUSSION

Hamilton . . . claims that he was erroneously convicted under section 1956(a)(1) of title 18 for attempting to mail the proceeds of drug transactions from Mississippi to California. That statute provides, in relevant part, as follows:

(a)(1) Whoever, knowing that the property involved in a financial transaction represents the proceeds of some form of unlawful activity, conducts or attempts to conduct such a financial transaction which in fact involves the proceeds of specified unlawful activity—

(A)(i)   with the intent to promote the carrying on of a specified unlawful activity; . . .

shall be sentenced to a fine of not more than $500,000 or twice the value of the property involved in the transaction, whichever is greater, or imprisonment for not more than twenty years, or both.

18 U.S.C.A. § 1956. "[T]he term 'financial transaction' means a transaction involving the movement of funds by wire or other means or involving one or more monetary instruments, which in any way or degree affects interstate or foreign commerce." 18 U.S.C.A. § 1956(c)(4). "[T]he term 'transaction' includes a purchase, sale, loan, pledge, gift, transfer, delivery, or other disposition." 18 U.S.C.A. § 1956(c)(3). Thus, the terms of the statute prohibit mailing the proceeds of drug sales, and absent a clearly expressed legislative intent to the contrary, that language must be regarded as conclusive unless exceptional circumstances dictate otherwise. *See Burlington Northern R. Co. v. Oklahoma Tax Com'n*, 481 U.S. 454, 461 (1987).

Notwithstanding this language, Hamilton argues that the statute does not prohibit mailing drug money from one point in the United States to another point in the United States. He cites no authority for this conclusion, but he attempts to reach it through the following interpretation of the statute. Section 1956(a)(2) of title 18 specifically prohibits "transport[ing], transmit[ing] or transfer[ing] . . . a monetary instrument or funds" between the United States and a foreign country.

Hamilton argues that if section 1956(a)(1) prohibits all mailings of drug proceeds, as the government argues, then section 1956(a)(2)'s prohibition against international mailings adds nothing. Hamilton, therefore, concludes that the "mere act of mailing money is not covered by Section 1956(a)(1), but is covered only by Section 1956(a)(2)."

Hamilton's interpretation of the statute misconstrues the plain language of the two subsections of the statute. The two provisions seek to attack two different types of criminal conduct. Section 1956(a)(1) specifically refers to "transactions" involving "proceeds of some form of unlawful activity." 18 U.S.C.A. § 1956(a)(1). Section 1956(a)(2), on the other hand, prohibits the international "transport[ation], transmit[al], or transfer[al] [of] . . . a monetary instrument or funds" in cases where such funds are intended to promote unlawful activities. A person could, in effect, violate section 1956(a)(2) without actually participating in an unlawful transaction as defined by section 1956(a)(1). For example, a foreign drug cartel might transfer proceeds from a legitimate business enterprise into a bank account in the United States. Such a transfer would not violate section 1956(a)(1), because the proceeds would not represent "proceeds of unlawful activities."

Under section 1956(a)(2), however, the same transfer would be criminalized if the legitimate proceeds of that bank account were intended to provide the capital necessary for expanding a drug enterprise in the United States. Unlike section 1956(a)(1), section 1956(a)(2) reaches beyond individual drug transactions and encompasses the international transportation of "monetary instruments or funds" that would contribute to the growth and capitalization of the drug trade or other unlawful activities.

Section 1956(a)(1) clearly prohibits the mailing of drug money. Although there may be some overlap between the two subsections in that the "monetary instrument or funds" of section 1956(a)(2) might, themselves, be the "proceeds of unlawful activity," this does not change the fact that the two subsections were passed to address two completely different problems. Hamilton was correctly convicted under the statute.

. . . .

CONCLUSION

For the foregoing reasons, we AFFIRM the district court's judgment.

NOTES AND QUESTIONS

1.   This case involved traditional currency in the form of U.S. dollars, and it certainly predates the rise of cryptocurrencies such as Bitcoin. How might the rules announced and applied in this case impact the use of crypto?

2.   "Money laundering" is often thought of as taking the proceeds of a criminal enterprise and "cleaning" it in some form, so that the taint of the illegal origins is obscured. While this is certainly prohibited, and is sometimes referred to as "traditional" money laundering, it is important to remember that is not the only kind of activity that can fall within the criminal money laundering provisions. In the preceding case, the problem was not that the funds were clearly derived from illegal activities. Instead, the government based its case on the theory that the funds were being mailed in order to facilitate unlawful activities (the drug trade). This is sometimes referred to as "reverse" money laundering. Can crypto be used for reverse money laundering? How?

3.   In your opinion, given what you currently understand about crypto, is crypto likely to be a bigger problem in "reverse money laundering" as compared to "traditional money laundering"? Why or why not?

Consider the following perspective on this problem. Again, this analysis predates the advent of crypto, but think about how the issues discussed in this excerpt might apply to crypto.

'REVERSE' MONEY LAUNDERING POSES NEW DUE DILIGENCE CHALLENGES FOR BANKS

Janis M. Meyer, Esq., 18 No. 4 White-Collar Crime Rep. 5 (Jan. 2004)

A recent Internal Revenue Service announcement serves as a reminder that financing of terrorist activity does not always follow money laundering's traditional patterns. In May 2003 the IRS asked for input on guidance with respect to the international activities of not-for-profit organizations to "reduce the possibility of diversion of assets for non-charitable purposes." The IRS noted that law enforcement authorities "have identified situations in which charitable organizations have been a significant source of terrorist funding."

Also in May, the Treasury Department announced designation of the Al-Aqsa Foundation as a "specially designated global terrorist entity" on the ground that Al-Aqsa funnels money to the Hamas terrorist organization under the guise of providing humanitarian relief.

. . . .

Al-Aqsa is the 18th charity to be designated as a financier of terrorism by the Treasury Department since President Bush issued Executive Order 13224 shortly after Sept. 11, 2001. That order identified individuals and entities who support terrorism, froze their financial assets, and prohibited U.S. individuals and businesses from conducting transactions with them.

. . . .

These recent announcements underscore the recognition that terrorism is often funded by "clean" money which, in a process of "reverse" laundering, is used for "dirty" purposes. In a highly publicized case last year, the Justice Department arrested Enaam Arnaout, the head of the Benevolence International Foundation, an Islamic charity, which the government claimed was a source of terrorist funding. BIF's assets were frozen after the Sept. 11 attacks, and Arnaout was charged with perjury in denying his connections to known terrorist leaders in documents he filed in an effort to lift the freeze. Arnaout claimed that BIF was a faith-based humanitarian organization that performed charitable works, such as building wells and providing for orphans and refugees, and was not involved in funding terrorist activity. The government, however, accused BIF of using its charitable mission as a front to secretly finance terrorism around the world.

The seizure of BIF's assets and Arnaout's subsequent indictment (he pleaded guilty in February 2003 to one count of racketeering conspiracy), as well as the designation of Al-Aqsa as a "specially designated global terrorist entity," are just two examples of the larger effort to freeze assets of charities with suspected links to terrorism, a process accelerated in the wake of Sept. 11.

. . . .

U.S. law enforcement officials have become increasingly aware of the use of "clean" money to finance terrorism. In 2002 the Treasury and Justice Departments noted that investigation and analysis by the law enforcement and intelligence communities has yielded information indicating that terrorist organizations utilize charities and non-governmental organizations to facilitate funding and to funnel money. Charitable donations to NGOs are commingled and then often diverted or siphoned to groups or organizations that support terrorism.

The same report noted that many of the contributors to terrorist activity do not know the intended purpose of their contribution. This use of charities and other non-governmental organizations as well as the diversion of the proceeds of legitimate business to fund terrorist activity has posed new challenges to and placed new burdens on financial institutions.

Banks and other financial institutions have long been familiar with the procedures for detecting and reporting traditional money-laundering activities. In a traditional money-laundering scheme, proceeds obtained from illicit sources, such as drug sales, are filtered through a series of transactions so that they appear to be from legal activities. The goal of traditional money laundering, long used by drug traffickers and organized crime, has been financial gain. Combating money laundering by traditional criminal organizations requires financial institutions to look in the first instance to the source of the funds, not their ultimate destination. Therefore, to prevent conventional money laundering, financial institutions have developed procedures to know their customers, monitor account activity and make inquiries concerning the source of funds.

With the increased focus on terrorism, however, banks and other financial institutions are now charged with the task of detecting suspicious activity where the source of the funds is "clean," and the purpose of the laundering is not to amass wealth for the criminal but rather to distinguish the source of the funds from the ultimate "dirty," that is, illegal, purpose.

Although terrorist activities are funded in part by illegal activities such as kidnapping and drug trafficking, the funding of terrorist groups differs from that of traditional criminal organizations because terrorists often receive "clean" money from sources such as sympathetic individuals, legitimate businesses with ideologically radical ownership, foreign states and legitimate, or illegitimate, charities. Terrorist groups utilize these financial transactions not only to hide the source of funds, as traditional money launderers do, but also to sever any link between the original, seemingly legitimate, "clean" source and the subsequent "dirty" use of the proceeds.

Recent guidance from the Financial Action Task Force[33] provides some illustrations of this phenomenon. In one example, several wealthy individuals were suspected of using the financing of a place of worship and other activities of a nonprofit as a front for aiding a terrorist organization's activities. In another example, a nonprofit claimed it was raising money for widows and orphans when in reality it was funding a major terrorist leader. In a third, the foreign branch office of a not-for-profit organization falsified its records to obtain additional funds from the organization's main office which in turn were used to finance terrorist activities. In each of these cases, the source of the funding was "clean"—charitable donations—while the end result was illicit activity.

Further complicating the issue is the fact that a terrorist's primary goal is not monetary gain. "Terrorist groups usually have non-financial goals such as seeking publicity, political legitimacy, political influence and dissemination of an ideology. Terrorist fund-raising is a means to these ends." In addition, terrorists often finance their schemes through small transactions that are typical of normal retail activity, and not the large transactions that are ordinarily the focus of traditional anti-money-laundering programs. Thus, a financial institution may adhere to all of its procedures, know its customers and monitor accounts for suspicious activity and still unwittingly facilitate terrorist activities.

Financial institutions have an obvious incentive in ensuring that they do not become conduits for payments to terrorist groups. If they fail to adopt and follow the appropriate due diligence procedures, they run the risk of being charged that they knew or should have known that funds would be used for an illegal purpose. Nevertheless, development of these procedures is not necessarily a simple task. It is clear that using funds, clean or dirty, to finance terrorist activity violates current money-laundering laws. Money "dirtying" is prohibited by 18 U.S. Code § 1956(a)(2), which makes it a crime to transport, transmit or transfer monetary instruments or funds into or out of the United States with the intent to promote specified unlawful activity, including terrorism. The larger problem facing financial institutions as well as law enforcement is how to detect and prevent it.

. . . .

---

[33] Author's note: The Financial Action Task Force (FATF) is an international organization focused on setting standards and overseeing implementation of measures to combat money laundering and terrorist financing as well as related threats to the integrity of the international financial system. It is discussed in more detail infra, in Part 2.D. of chapter 15 of this book.

NOTES AND QUESTIONS

1.   That comment was written in 2004, more than 15 years ago. To what extent does it raise issues that continue to be relevant to fiat currencies?

2.   To what extent could crypto fit into the preceding discussion of terrorist fund-raising?

3.   How might crypto make fighting fund-raising that supports terrorism even more challenging?

C. FAILURE TO REGISTER WITH FINCEN OR COMPLY WITH OTHER BSA REQUIREMENTS

As described above, a money transmitter is a kind of MSB under BSA regulations. Remember that an MSB includes any "person that provides money transmission services" which includes "the acceptance of currency, funds, or other value that substitutes for currency from one person and the transmission of currency, funds, or other value that substitutes for currency to another location or person by any means."[34]

Money transmitter businesses must register with FinCEN; must implement an AML program based on an individualized and comprehensive risk assessment of their risk of participation in money laundering activities; and must comply with monitoring, recordkeeping, and reporting requirements established by FinCEN.[35] To illustrate the extent of these record-keeping and reporting obligations, a money transmitter must file currency transaction reports for transactions involving more than $10,000 and suspicious activity reports if there is evidence that transactions are facilitating criminal activity. If the company's activities involve the "transmittal of funds" under FinCEN's regulations, the company must also comply with requirements relating to certain transmittals in excess of $3,000.

And what happens if a business does not comply? In 1992, Congress criminalized unlicensed money transmission. Under 18 U.S. Code § 1960, it is a crime if a defendant "knowingly conducts, controls, manages, supervises, directs, or owns all or part of an unlicensed money transmitting business."

---

[34]   FinCEN, *Request for Administrative Ruling on the Application of FinCEN's Regulations to a Virtual Currency Payment System*, FIN–2014–R012 at 5 (Oct. 27, 2014).

[35]   Rather than citing again to specific BSA provisions, if you are interested in reading more about the operation of these compliance requirements, see the FinCEN website which has a range of resources geared towards MSBs. Included are documents such as FinCEN, *Fact Sheet on MSB Registration Rule* [archived at https://perma.cc/SS6K-AT58]; FinCEN, *Guidance on Existing AML Program Rule Compliance Obligations for MSB Principals with Respect to Agent Monitoring*, FIN–2016–G001 (March 11, 2016) [archived at https://perma.cc/22RK-AYP9].

UNITED STATES V. DIMITROV

546 F.3d 409 (7th Cir. 2008)

ROVNER, CIRCUIT JUDGE.

Stefan Dimitrov entered a conditional guilty plea to one count of operating an unlicensed money transmitting business in violation of 18 U.S.C. § 960(a). He was sentenced to three months' imprisonment to be followed by three years of supervised release. Dimitrov now appeals, challenging the constitutionality of § 1960 and the district court's ruling on a motion in limine decided before his guilty plea. For the reasons explained herein, we affirm.

I.   [Facts]

In 1998 Dimitrov, a Bulgarian immigrant, began operating an institution known as the Bulgarian Cultural Center on Irving Park road in Chicago. Dimitrov and his wife at the time, Tatiana Dimitrova, offered a number of services to the Bulgarian community through the Cultural Center, including document translation and assistance with everything from green card applications to locating employment. The Cultural Center also contained a library of Bulgarian books and videos, jewelry from Bulgaria for sale, and a small kitchen. According to Dimitrov, people began asking for assistance transferring money to Bulgaria. Initially he assisted others by translating the money transmitting forms into English and using his personal checking account to transfer the funds. As the number of requests for help transferring money increased, he opened a separate account at TCF Bank to transmit money to Bulgaria.

The money transmitting service supplied the bulk of any income that Stefan and Tatiana made running the Cultural Center. The Dimitrovs charged a flat $20 fee for the service in addition to a small (usually .5%) percentage of the total amount transferred. The Department of Immigration and Customs Enforcement began investigating the Dimitrovs' business after reviewing bank records from TCF Bank suggesting that the Dimitrovs may not have a required license to operate a money transmitting business. The bank records revealed deposits into an account named "B Connection," which Dimitrov used to wire money to the Bulgarian Post Bank in Sofia, Bulgaria. Investigating agents then used the bank records to identify Bulgarians who had used Dimitrov's money transmitting business. One of these individuals agreed to cooperate with the agents and explained that he had wired money to Bulgaria using B Connection on multiple occasions. He would give one of the Dimitrovs the cash for wiring, the name of the intended recipient of the money, and the Bulgarian equivalent of the Social Security number of the recipient. The cooperating individual recounted that his family members later retrieved the money from the Bulgarian Post National Bank. In later transactions, Dimitrov made the process more secure by having customers deposit their funds for transfer directly into the account at TCF Bank. Between January 2003 and April 2005 the Dimitrovs transmitted approximately $3,000,000 to Bulgaria on behalf of their customers.

Although the Dimitrovs' money transmitting business was by all accounts a legitimate one, it lacked the license required by Illinois for money transmitting. That oversight amounted to a felony by virtue of 18 U.S.C. § 1960(a), which prohibits operating . . . without an appropriate money transmitting license where the failure to have a license is punishable "as a misdemeanor or felony under State law, whether or not the defendant knew that the operation was required to be licensed or that the operation was so punishable." § 1960(b)(1)(A). . . .

Instead of the required money transmitting license, Dimitrov obtained a Limited Business License from the City of Chicago "for general sales, service and office operations/or businesses that do not fall under another license category and are not exempt from City licenses," . . . which he believed discharged his licensing obligations. That belief, if genuine, became less tenable in September 2004, when TCF Bank sent him the first of several letters requesting verification of the registration and licensing status of his money transmitting business. The letter included a form entitled "Verification of Licensing and Registration for Money Service Business" which Dimitrov was instructed to complete and sign. When it received no response from Dimitrov, TCF Bank sent him a second letter in November 2004 requesting that he verify his licensing status and warning him that failure to do so would result in closure of his account. In December, TCF Bank sent Dimitrov a third letter informing him that it had reviewed his account and determined that he was operating a business that provided money services. That letter requested a current copy of B Connection's state license and its anti-money laundering policy and procedures as well as the IRS acknowledgment that B Connection was registered with the Financial Crimes Enforcement Network. The letter warned that failure to respond with the requested verifications within 30 days would result in closure of his accounts.

Presumably prompted by the letters from TCF Bank, Dimitrov looked into obtaining a money transmitting license in late 2004 or early 2005. Dimitrov and a business associate, Hamid Rusef, traveled to Springfield and met with Phil Sanson, a senior examiner for Illinois in the Department of Financial and Professional Regulation. Sanson explained to Dimitrov and Rusef the process for obtaining a money transmitting license and also gave them the application packet, which contains a checklist of the required materials. Dimitrov, however, never completed the application materials. When Dimitrov failed to respond to its warnings, TCF Bank ultimately closed the accounts associated with his money transmitting business. He then transferred the accounts to Bank One, where he continued transmitting money through April 2005.

Dimitrov and his wife Tatiana were charged in July 2005 with one count of violating § 1960(a). Tatiana pleaded guilty pursuant to a written plea agreement, but Dimitrov initially intended to proceed to trial. On the day Dimitrov's trial was scheduled to begin, he elected to enter a conditional guilty plea . . . . Dimitrov chose to plead guilty, but reserved his right to challenge the constitutionality of § 1960(a) to the extent that it does not require the defendant to know that his conduct is illegal.

II. [Analysis]

On appeal, Dimitrov argues that § 1960(a) is unconstitutionally vague. Specifically, Dimitrov claims that the statute lacks a mens rea element and so fails to give fair notice of prohibited conduct. To understand Dimitrov's argument, a brief history of § 1960 is in order.

A. 18 U.S.C. § 1960(a)

Congress enacted § 1960(a) in 1992 in response to concerns that nonbank financial institutions (money transmitters, check cashers, and foreign exchange dealers) were increasingly being used to transfer the proceeds of illegal activity. See S.Rep. No. 101–460 (September 12, 1990); *United States v. Velastegui,* 199 F.3d 590, 593 (2d Cir.1999). The original version of § 1960 provided in pertinent part as follows:

(a) Whoever conducts, controls, manages, supervises, directs, or owns all or part of a business, *knowing the business is an illegal money transmitting business,* shall be fined in accordance with this title or imprisoned not more than 5 years, or both.

(b) As used in this section—

(1) the term "illegal money transmitting business" means a money transmitting business which affects interstate or foreign commerce in any manner or degree and—

(A) is *intentionally operated without an appropriate money transmitting license* in a State where such operation is punishable as a misdemeanor or felony under State law; or

(B) fails to comply with the money transmitting business registration requirements under [31 U.S.C. § 5330], or regulations prescribed under such section. . . .

18 U.S.C. § 1960 (1992) (emphasis supplied).

As part of the Patriot Act, Congress amended § 1960 on October 26, 2001, in an attempt to make it easier to prosecute those responsible for funneling money to terrorism. The amended version reads in pertinent part as follows:

(a) Whoever *knowingly* conducts, controls, manages, supervises, directs, or owns all or part of *an unlicensed money transmitting business*, shall be fined in accordance with this title or imprisoned not more than 5 years, or both.

(b) As used in this section—

(1) the term *"unlicensed* money transmitting business" means a money transmitting business which affects interstate or foreign commerce in any manner or degree and—

(A) is operated without an appropriate money transmitting license in a State where such operation is punishable as a misdemeanor or a felony under State law, *whether or not the defendant knew that the operation was required to be licensed or that the operation was so punishable;*

18 U.S.C. § 1960 (emphasis added).

The 2001 amendments thus removed the scienter requirement of the former version, making § 1960 a "general intent crime for which a defendant is liable if he knowingly operates a money transmitting business." Under the amended § 1960, the government no longer need prove that a defendant was aware of state licensing requirements or that he knew about the federal registration requirements found at 31 U.S.C. § 5330 (requiring owners or controllers of money transmitting businesses to register with the Secretary of the Treasury) . . . .

B. Dimitrov's Vagueness Challenge to § 1960(a)

According to Dimitrov, § 1960 "does not contain a mens rea element," and therefore fails to give fair notice of prohibited conduct. Dimitrov also maintains that because § 1960 is broader than necessary "to satisfy the legislature's intent," it invites arbitrary enforcement. A criminal statute is unconstitutionally vague if it fails to sufficiently define prohibited conduct so that ordinary individuals understand what is prohibited or fails to establish minimal guidelines to prevent arbitrary or discriminatory enforcement.

In *United States v. Talebnejad*, 460 F.3d 563, 568 (4th Cir.2006), the Fourth Circuit considered and rejected a vagueness challenge to the amended version of § 1960. In considering the defendant's contention that § 1960 was unconstitutional by virtue of its failure to recognize ignorance of state licensing requirements as a defense to liability, the Fourth Circuit noted that, "[t]here is no question that, at least under some circumstances, Congress may dispense with a mens rea element, as it has clearly done with respect to § 1960(b)(1)(A)." By failing to acknowledge this, Dimitrov conflates legal knowledge with factual knowledge. True, the statute no longer contains any requirement that a money transmitting operator know that what he is doing is prohibited by state law. But "[t]he rule that 'ignorance of the law will not excuse' is deep in our law." *Lambert v. State of California,* 355 U.S. 225, 228 (1958) (internal citation omitted); see also *Cheek v. United States,* 498 U.S. 192, 199 (1991) ("[I]gnorance of the law or a mistake of law is no defense to criminal prosecution."). *Lambert* itself is the only Supreme Court case to recognize a "mistake of law" defense. The registration statute invalidated in *Lambert* criminalized the act of being present in Los Angeles as a convicted felon without registering, regardless of one's knowledge of the registration requirement.

Unlike the statute at issue in *Lambert,* § 1960(a) requires the affirmative action of knowingly operating a money transmitting business. *See Talebnejad,* 460 F.3d at 570 (contrasting passive presence regulated in *Lambert* with the "unquestionably active conduct of operating a business"). This is in contrast to the registration statute in *Lambert,* where the Court noted that "[v]iolation of its provisions is unaccompanied by any activity whatsoever, mere presence in the city being the test." *Lambert,* 355 U.S. at 229. Moreover, the *Lambert* Court emphasized that there were no surrounding circumstances "which might move one to inquire as to the necessity of registration." *Id.* Here, however, Dimitrov operated his business in a highly regulated industry, and could reasonably have been expected to know that there may be licensing requirements. *See Papachristou v. City of Jacksonville,* 405 U.S. 156, 162 (1972) ("In the field of regulatory statutes governing business activities, where the acts limited are in a narrow category, greater leeway is allowed."). The fact that § 1960 does not include knowledge of the licensing requirement as an element of the crime does not by itself render it unconstitutionally vague. It is enough that the statute requires a defendant to know the facts that make his conduct illegal—i.e., that he is operating an unlicensed money transmitting business.

Nor are we convinced by Dimitrov's argument that ordinary individuals will not be able to differentiate between an "appropriate" money transmitting license and an inadequate one. Unlike the vagrancy ordinance invalidated in *Papachristou,* 405 U.S. at 157–171, on which Dimitrov relies, § 1960 provides objective criteria for determining what is an "appropriate" license. The reference to "State law" in § 1960(b) makes it plain that an appropriate license is whatever is required under state law. Moreover, *Papachristou* explicitly distinguished "the average householder" subject to the vagrancy ordinance at issue from an individual in "business," who would presumably be alerted to the regulatory schemes governing his conduct. *See Papachristou,* 405 U.S. at 162–63. We thus conclude that by referencing state law, the phrase "appropriate money transmitting license" provides individuals of "ordinary intelligence a reasonable opportunity to know what is prohibited." *Grayned v. City of Rockford,* 408 U.S. 104, 108

(1972). Given the language of the statute, a reasonable person would understand that a generic city business license would not pass muster as a "money transmitting license."

. . . .

For the foregoing reasons, we AFFIRM Dimitrov's conviction and sentence.

NOTES AND QUESTIONS

1.   Americans may be very familiar with the maxim that "ignorance of the law is no excuse," but consider that the defendant in the preceding case was not American, but Bulgarian. Under Bulgarian law, "(1) Crime shall be an act dangerous to society (action or inaction), which has been culpably committed and which has been declared punishable by law."[36] That Code expressly incorporates the requirement of culpability or fault involving at least negligence.[37] Moreover, it is almost certain that English was not the defendant's native language, making it more likely that Dimitrov may not have understand all that was required of him. Do you believe that Dimitrov should have been able to argue that he did not know that he was violating the law and was not negligent (given his situation) in failing to understand what was required of him? Does the fact that he voluntarily pled guilty, reserving only his constitutional claims, make you more or less sympathetic to his case?

2.   Given that the reach of the BSA includes acts not only of persons within the United States, but also foreign actors who transmit funds to or for persons in America, do you have an opinion about whether strict liability is appropriate or fair? Note that given the inherent global or extra-territorial potential of crypto, the ability of foreign actors to interact with persons in the U.S. may be particularly problematic for regulators.

---

[36]   *See* Bulgarian Criminal Code, Art. 9 (2009), archived at https://perma.cc/Y7HK-3S75 (as translated into English).

[37]   *Id.* at Article 11.

CHAPTER 4

SILK ROAD AND ITS IMPACT ON CRYPTO

■ ■ ■

For true believers in crypto, and for many others as well, one of the most problematic aspects of the new technology is how susceptible it is to abuse. The reality is that without some degree of regulation and oversight, which also happen to be two of the very things the originators of blockchain pushed against, there is the very real risk that nefarious individuals will exploit cryptoassets to further criminal agendas and activities. Cryptoassets, even those not specifically designed as currency substitutes, can be used to launder money arising out of criminal activities, finance terrorist activity, evade taxes, and purchase illegal items such as drugs, unless they are properly monitored.

Two of the attributes of blockchain and crypto that make it so attractive to the criminal element are anonymity and ease of cross-border transactions. For example, illegal drugs or weapons can be sold for fiat, which can then be converted to crypto, traded multiple times potentially across borders and in countries where there are no regulations governing crypto exchanges, and then converted back into fiat currency at a later date, either with or without the assistance of regulated exchanges. The illegal origins of the funds would be obscured through the multiple online transactions. Crypto can similarly be used to fund illegal activity from the outset, if payment is taken in something like Bitcoin. Crypto can also be channeled to terrorist organizations or states through as many steps as it takes, regardless of whether the source of the funds is from the sale of illegal goods or services. Similarly, individuals seeking to prevent the government from linking them to income (again regardless of whether derived from illegal or fraudulent activity) can turn to crypto to evade tax laws. By hiding their assets in crypto and not reporting gains or earnings, taxpayers may deprive their governments of significant amounts of tax revenue.

The anonymity of blockchain transactions is central to the very working of cryptoassets. Blockchain transactions are recorded by digital addresses that are not easily or directly tied to anyone's real identity. Instead, they are designed to be anonymous or pseudonymous. Because the payer can conduct the transaction without the assistance of a third party, such as a major bank, there is no exchange of sensitive personal information which jeopardizes privacy and security of the transactions, but this also makes it difficult for governmental authorities to trace where the funds originated. Moreover, because cryptoassets are used and exchanged through the internet, it is easy to have cross-border transactions where even the location of the parties is unknown and difficult to trace.

Obviously, internet protocol addresses may be associated with particular transactions, but there are a number of ways that parties can obscure their real identities and locations. Individuals can use pseudonyms to conduct these transactions, and it is possible to add layers of encryption and security through things such as onion routers, mixers, tumblers, and protocols designed to create fictitious identifiers.[1]

All of these characteristics make cryptoassets a development that is of profound interest to FinCEN. FinCEN's entire mission is centered on minimizing the harms of money laundering and limiting the flow of funds to criminal enterprises. With the background of FinCEN's mission and the basics of its empowering legislation in mind, consider the following early instance where Bitcoin, the first cryptocurrency, was used to facilitate a wide variety of illegal transactions.

1. THE SILK ROAD—BITCOIN AND MONEY LAUNDERING

One of the most notorious examples of how cryptocurrencies have been used in furtherance of illegal schemes was the Silk Road. The Silk Road operation illustrates how the anonymity, decentralization, and lack of regulatory oversight of cryptocurrencies made them susceptible to abuse. In this case, Bitcoin was utilized to facilitate large-scale international money laundering and funding of a wide variety of illegal activities.

Silk Road was launched early in 2011 as part of the modern "dark web." Its name was derived from historical trade routes between Europe, India, China, and certain countries in Northern Africa, dating back more than 2000 years to the Han Dynasty. The modern Silk Road was also

---

[1]   Onion routing simply refers to layers of encryption that facilitate anonymity. Tor was built on this principle, and is therefore sometimes called "the onion router." *See* Andy Greenberg, *The Grand Tor: How To Go Anonymous Online*, WIRED (Sept. 12, 2017) (available online at https:// www.wired.com/story/the-grand-tor/). More specifically, "Tor" is a software browser that "protects you by bouncing your communications around a distributed network of relays run by volunteers all around the world: it prevents somebody watching your Internet connection from learning what sites you visit, [and] it prevents the sites you visit from learning your physical location. . . ." Tor Project (available online at https://www.torproject.org/projects/torbrowser.html).

A mixer combines coins with the coins of others. Everyone using this service sends their coins to a central addresses, and the mixer sends a transaction back to each user from the key controlling the central address. By mixing stolen or tainted coins with "clean" coins, they become very difficult to trace.

Tumblers work by swapping coins between users, sending transactions in various amounts to keys under its control in order to simulate other transactions. For a description of mixing and tumbling, Best Bitcoin Mixers is a website that maintains a list of mixing and tumbling services. They also describe how these processes work. This source can be found online at https://bestbitcoin mixers.com/.

intended to facilitate trade, and was operated by the pseudonymous "Dread Pirate Roberts" (named after the fictional character from The Princess Bride). In reality, the founder of the site was Ross Ulbricht, a gifted computer programmer and charismatic resident of San Francisco who was a self-proclaimed libertarian known for his anti-regulatory sentiments.[2]

Ross Ulbricht is an interesting character. He graduated from the University of Texas with a degree in Physics and later earned a masters degree in Materials Science and Engineering from Penn State. It was apparently at Penn State where he solidified his libertarian leanings, eventually viewing taxation and government regulations as a form of coercion. His thinking was heavily influenced by Austrian economist Ludwig von Mises, who argued that economic freedom was a prerequisite to either political or moral freedom.

He tried both day trading and traditional entrepreneurship before developing the online trading site that he named Silk Road. According to statements made by him, he envisioned this as a free market experiment that would emphasize user anonymity. This accorded with his belief that people should have the right to buy and sell whatever they want as long as they do not harm others.[3]

There is certainly evidence that, early on especially, Silk Road operated differently from other dark web alternatives. It looked like a legitimate marketplace, where users could rate their satisfaction with prior transactions. When Silk Road was first launched, the terms of service agreed to by sellers prohibited the sale of anything whose purpose was to "harm or defraud." This included child pornography, stolen credit cards, assassinations, and weapons. Some of the goods sold, such as erotica and art, were not illegal.

While Ulbricht may have originally envisioned his online marketplace as a way to distance recreational drug usage and sales from the world of hardened criminals, as Silk Road grew and the amount of money exchanging hands exploded, it morphed into a site where all manner of illegal items and services were for sale. Although Silk Road is still best known for facilitating the sale of illegal drugs, it clearly brokered transactions in other illicit goods and services. Some sources suggested that from 2011 to 2013 (when the site was finally shut down) you could buy almost anything on the Silk Road, including not only drugs but also child

---

[2]   Andy Greenberg, *Collected Quotations Of The Dread Pirate Roberts, Founder Of Underground Drug Site Silk Road And Radical Libertarian*, FORBES (Ap. 29, 2013) (available online at https://www.forbes.com/sites/andygreenberg/2013/04/29/collected-quotations-of-the-dread-pirate-roberts-founder-of-the-drug-site-silk-road-and-radical-libertarian/#37b4faaf1b0c).

[3]   These claims were made by Ulbricht in a sentencing letter filed with the court after his ultimate conviction. Ross Ulbricht, *Sentencing Letter to Judge Forrestt* (May 22, 2015) [archived at https://perma.cc/PG29-WNHF].

pornography, arranged murders, and hacked credit cards.[4] "There were even discussions of selling body parts, such as livers and kidneys."[5]

Silk Road was both extensive and sophisticated, operating as a Tor[6] hidden service, offering users anonymity. It also promised no oversight or monitoring of transactions. Silk Road accepted only Bitcoins, meaning that users (both senders and receivers of the cryptocurrency) were identified only by an anonymous Bitcoin address or account.

Originally, there were a limited number of new seller accounts, each of which had to be purchased at auction. Later, this was changed to a fixed fee for each new account. This was a particularly popular development in the life of the Silk Road, because the change allowed users to utilize different addresses for each transaction in order to further hide their real identities. Finally, Silk Road used a tumbler for every transaction, sending all payments through (as the site itself explained) "a complex, semi-random series of dummy transactions."

In June 2011, Gawker published an article about the site, notifying readers that they could use Silk Road to buy illegal drugs anonymously, stating that "[i]t's Amazon—if Amazon sold mind-altering chemicals."[7] Not surprisingly, this led to a substantial increase in website traffic and visibility. Also not surprisingly, as soon as it became publicly known there were a number of calls for it to be shut down including a demand from U.S. Senator Charles Schumer that federal authorities take action.

As it turns out, it was easier to recognize the need to close the site than it was to actually identify the individuals responsible for its operation. It wasn't until October 2013 that the Federal Bureau of Investigation (FBI) was able to shut down the website and arrest Ross Ulbricht on charges of being the site's pseudonymous founder, "Dread Pirate Roberts." In February 2014, the Department of Justice (DoJ) indicted Ulbricht on charges of participating in a narcotics trafficking conspiracy, engaging in a criminal enterprise, conspiring to commit computer hacking, and conspiring to commit money laundering. For this book, the most important of those claims was conspiracy to commit money laundering.

---

[4]   Robert Anthony, *The Craziest Things You Could've Bought on Silk Road, the Black Market of the Internet*, ELITE DAILY (Oct. 9, 2013) (available online at http://elitedaily.com/envision/the-craziest-things-you-couldve-bought-on-silk-road-the-black-market-of-the-internet/).

[5]   Nick Bilton, *Silicon Valley Murder Mystery: How Drugs and Paranoia Doomed Silk Road*, VANITY FAIR (online posting April 26, 2017) (available online at https://www.vanityfair.com/news/2017/04/silk-road-ross-ulbricht-drugs-murder).

[6]   *See supra* note 1.

[7]   Adrian Chen, *The Underground Website Where You Can Buy Any Drug Imaginable*, GAWKER (June 1, 2011) (available online at https://gawker.com/the-underground-website-where-you-can-buy-any-drug-imag-30818160).

2. *U.S. V. ULBRICHT* AND ULBRICHT'S MOTION TO DISMISS

Ross Ulbricht was arrested on October 2, 2013, at a branch of the San Francisco Public Library. He was originally indicted on charges of money laundering, computer hacking, conspiracy to traffic narcotics, and attempting to have six people killed.[8]

The first line of defense was a motion to dismiss the charges in the DoJ indictment before the trial. In particular, with respect to the count regarding money laundering, Ulbricht alleged that he could not "have engaged in money laundering because all transactions occurred through the use of Bitcoin and thus there was therefore no legally cognizable 'financial transaction.' "[9] His attorney claimed that Bitcoins were not monetary instruments, and therefore that the transactions involving Bitcoin could not be the basis for a money laundering conspiracy. The following is an excerpt from the ruling on that motion to dismiss.

PRELIMINARY NOTES AND QUESTIONS

1. What was Ross Ulbricht's connection to Bitcoin and the crypto community? Did his libertarian impulses make him more likely to be involved with crypto or was it simply a desire to make money that drove him?

2. What was it about the background of this case that made it particularly likely that FinCEN would feel the need to be involved in regulating crypto?

3. Why do you suppose commentators point to the "lasting legacy of Silk Road" as a primary reason why FinCEN continues to be so active in enforcing various regulations and requirements in the context of crypto? Do you agree that the fallout from the Silk Road continues to drive regulation of crypto? Should it?

UNITED STATES V. ULBRICHT [MOTION TO DISMISS]
31 F. Supp. 3d 540 (S.D.N.Y. 2014)

KATHERINE B. FORREST, DISTRICT JUDGE:

On February 4, 2014, a Grand Jury sitting in the Southern District of New York returned [an] Indictment, charging Ross Ulbricht ("the defendant" or "Ulbricht") on four counts for participation in a narcotics

---

[8]   Prosecutors originally alleged that Ulbricht had paid $730,000 to have various individuals who Ulbricht suspected of betraying him killed, although none of the murders actually occurred (probably because Ulbricht had asked undercover officers to carry out some of those killings). Ulbricht was neither charged with nor convicted of any of the alleged murder attempts (quite probably because two of those same undercover officers themselves had been sucked into criminal activities and were eventually convicted of various crimes associated with their involvement in the Silk Road).

[9]   *United States v. Ulbricht*, 31 F. Supp. 3d at 548.

trafficking conspiracy (Count One), a continuing criminal enterprise ("CCE") (Count Two), a computer hacking conspiracy (Count Three), and a money laundering conspiracy (Count Four). Pending before the Court is the defendant's motion to dismiss all counts. For the reasons set forth below, the Court DENIES the motion in its entirety. [Author's note: the following excerpt concentrates only on Counts One and Four; the first to provide background into the extent of Silk Road's illegal operations and the last to focus on matters within the purview of FinCEN.]

The Government alleges that Ulbricht engaged in narcotics trafficking . . . and money laundering conspiracies by designing, launching, and administering a website called Silk Road ("Silk Road") as an online marketplace for illicit goods and services. These allegations raise novel issues as they relate to the Internet and the defendant's role in the purported conspiracies.

A conspiracy claim is premised on an agreement between two or more people to achieve an unlawful end. The Government alleges that by designing, launching, and administering Silk Road, Ulbricht conspired with narcotics traffickers and hackers to buy and sell illegal narcotics . . . and to launder the proceeds using Bitcoin.

. . . .

The Government alleges that Silk Road was designed to operate like eBay: a seller would electronically post a good or service for sale; a buyer would electronically purchase the item; the seller would then ship or otherwise provide to the buyer the purchased item; the buyer would provide feedback; and the site operator (i.e., Ulbricht) would receive a portion of the seller's revenue as a commission. Ulbricht, as the alleged site designer, made the site available only to those using Tor, software and a network that allows for anonymous, untraceable Internet browsing; he allowed payment only via Bitcoin, an anonymous and untraceable form of payment.

Following the launch of Silk Road, the site was available to sellers and buyers for transactions. Thousands of transactions allegedly occurred over the course of nearly three years—sellers posted goods when available; buyers purchased goods when desired. As website administrator, Ulbricht may have had some direct contact with some users of the site, and none with most. This online marketplace thus allowed the alleged designer and operator (Ulbricht) to be anywhere in the world with an Internet connection (he was apprehended in California), the sellers and buyers to be anywhere, the activities to occur independently from one another on different days and at different times, and the transactions to occur anonymously.

A number of legal questions arise from conspiracy claims premised on this framework. In sum, they address whether the conduct alleged here can serve as the basis of a criminal conspiracy—and, if so, when, how, and with whom.

. . . .

The defendant also raises the following additional arguments[:]. . . the rule of lenity, the doctrine of constitutional avoidance, the void-for-vagueness doctrine, constitutionally defective over-breadth, and a civil immunity statute for online service providers. The Court refers to these collectively as the "Kitchen Sink" arguments.

. . . Finally, with respect to Count Four, the defendant alleges that he cannot have engaged in money laundering because all transactions occurred through the use of Bitcoin.

. . . .

I. THE INDICTMENT

Rule 7(c)(1) of the Federal Rules of Criminal Procedure provides that an indictment "must be a plain, concise, and definite written statement of the essential facts constituting the offense charged." It need not contain any other matter not necessary to such statement. ("A count may allege that the means by which the defendant committed the offense are unknown or that the defendant committed it by one or more specified means.").

An indictment must inform the defendant of the crime with which he has been charged. . . . The Second Circuit has "consistently upheld indictments that do little more than track the language of the statute charged and state the time and place (in approximate terms) of the alleged crime."

Nevertheless, "[a] criminal defendant is entitled to an indictment that states the essential elements of the charge against him." "[F]or an indictment to fulfill the functions of notifying the defendant of the charges against him and of assuring that he is tried on the matters considered by the grand jury, the indictment must state some fact specific enough to describe a particular criminal act, rather than a type of crime."

. . . .

As with all motions to dismiss an indictment, the Court accepts as true the allegations set forth in the charging instrument for purposes of determining the sufficiency of the charges.

The Indictment here alleges that Ulbricht designed, created, operated, and owned Silk Road, "the most sophisticated and extensive criminal marketplace on the Internet." Silk Road operated using Tor, software and a network that enables users to access the Internet anonymously—it keeps users' unique identifying Internet Protocol ("IP") addresses obscured, preventing surveillance or tracking. All purchases occurred on Silk Road using Bitcoin, an anonymous online currency.

Silk Road allegedly functioned as designed—tens of thousands of buyers and sellers are alleged to have entered into transactions using the site, violating numerous criminal laws. Over time, thousands of kilograms of heroin and cocaine were allegedly bought and sold, as if the purchases were occurring on eBay or any other similar website.

Count One charges that, from in or about January 2011 up to and including October 2013, the defendant engaged in a narcotics trafficking conspiracy. To wit, "the defendant . . . designed [Silk Road] to enable users across the world to buy and sell illegal drugs and other illicit goods and services anonymously and outside the reach of law enforcement." The defendant allegedly "controlled all aspects of Silk Road, with the assistance of various paid employees whom he managed and supervised." "It was part and object of the conspiracy" that the defendant and others "would and did deliver, distribute, and dispense controlled substances by means of the Internet" and "did aid and abet such activity" in violation of the law. The controlled substances allegedly included heroin, cocaine, and lysergic acid diethylamide ("LSD"). The defendant allegedly "reaped commissions worth tens of millions of dollars, generated from the illicit sales conducted through the site." According to the Indictment, the defendant "pursued violent means, including soliciting the murder-for-hire of several individuals he believed posed a threat to that enterprise."

. . . .

Count Four alleges that Ulbricht "designed Silk Road to include a Bitcoin-based payment system that served to facilitate the illegal commerce conducted on the site, including by concealing the identities and locations of the users transmitting and receiving funds through the site." "[K]nowing that the property involved in certain financial transactions represented proceeds of some form of unlawful activity," Ulbricht and others would and did conduct financial transactions with the proceeds of specified unlawful activity, "knowing that the transactions were designed . . . to conceal and disguise the nature, the location, the source, the ownership and the control of the proceeds."

II. THE LAW OF CONSPIRACY

A. Elements of a Conspiracy

"The essence of the crime of conspiracy . . . is the agreement to commit one or more unlawful acts." Put differently, a conspiracy is the " 'combination of minds for an unlawful purpose.' " [Detailed consideration of the elements of criminal conspiracy are omitted. . . .]

III. DISCUSSION OF CONSPIRATORIAL AGREEMENT

The Indictment alleges that Ulbricht designed Silk Road specifically to enable users to anonymously sell and purchase narcotics and malicious software and to launder the resulting proceeds. On this motion to dismiss, the Court's task is a narrow one—it is not concerned with whether the Government will have sufficient evidence to meet its burden of proof as to each element of the charged conspiracies at trial. Instead, the Court is concerned solely with whether the nature of the alleged conduct, if proven, legally constitutes the crimes charged, and whether the defendant has had sufficient notice of the illegality of such conduct.

. . . .

According to the Indictment, Ulbricht purposefully and intentionally designed, created, and operated Silk Road to facilitate unlawful transactions. Silk Road was nothing more than code unless and until third parties agreed to use it. When third parties engaged in unlawful narcotics transactions on the site, however, Ulbricht's design and operation gave rise to potential conspiratorial conduct. The subsequent sale and purchase of unlawful narcotics and software on Silk Road may, as a matter of law, constitute circumstantial evidence of an agreement to engage in such unlawful conduct. Additionally, the Indictment charges that Ulbricht obtained significant monetary benefit in the form of commissions in exchange for the services he provided via Silk Road. He had the capacity to shut down the site at any point; he did not do so. The defendant allegedly used violence in order to protect the site and the proceeds it generated.

Ulbricht argues that his conduct was merely as a facilitator—just like eBay, Amazon, or similar websites. Even were the Court to accept this characterization of the Indictment, there is no legal prohibition against such criminal conspiracy charges provided that the defendant possesses (as the Indictment alleges here) the requisite intent to join with others in unlawful activity.

Moreover, in this case, the charges in the Indictment go further than Ulbricht acknowledges. The Indictment alleges that Ulbricht engaged in conduct that makes Silk Road different from other websites that provide a platform for individual buyers and sellers to connect and engage in transactions: Silk Road was specifically and intentionally designed for the purpose of facilitating unlawful transactions. The Indictment does not allege that Ulbricht is criminally liable simply because he is alleged to have launched a website that was—unknown to and unplanned by him—used for illicit transactions. If that were ultimately the case, he would lack the mens rea for criminal liability. Rather, Ulbricht is alleged to have knowingly and intentionally constructed and operated an expansive black market for selling and purchasing narcotics and malicious software and for laundering money. This separates Ulbricht's alleged conduct from the mass of others whose websites may—without their planning or expectation—be used for unlawful purposes.

. . . .

[Sections IV, V, and VI are omitted.]

VII. THE "KITCHEN SINK" ARGUMENTS

Ulbricht also alleges that since his alleged conduct . . . has never before been found to constitute the crimes charged, a variety of legal principles preclude criminal liability. Those principles include the rule of lenity, the doctrine of constitutional avoidance, void-for-vagueness, and overbreadth. In addition, the defendant argues that the presence of a civil immunity statute for online providers indicates congressional "support for a free-wheeling [I]nternet, including one in which providers or users of interactive computer services can operate without fear of civil liability for the content posted by others." These arguments do not preclude the criminal charges here.

As an initial matter, as set forth above, the conduct charged fits within existing law. It is certainly true that case law to date has not been applied to the type of conduct that forms the basis for the Government's charges—but that is not fatal.

. . . . The fact that a particular defendant is the first to be prosecuted for novel conduct under a pre-existing statutory scheme does not ipso facto mean that the statute is ambiguous or vague or that he has been deprived of constitutionally appropriate notice.

The defendant's Kitchen Sink arguments are also premised on a view of his alleged conduct as being sufficiently common—i.e., that he is doing nothing more than that done by other designers and operators of online marketplaces—that he could not have known or been on notice of its illegality.

The Court disagrees. Again, on a motion to dismiss an indictment, the Court accepts as true the Government's allegations; whether and how those allegations can be proven is not a question for this stage in the proceedings.

A. The Rule of Lenity and the Doctrine of Constitutional Avoidance

The defendant's arguments with respect to the rule of lenity and the doctrine of constitutional avoidance are based on the incorrect premise that the statutes under which he has been charged . . . are ambiguous when applied to his alleged conduct.

The rule of lenity provides that when a criminal statute is susceptible to two different interpretations—one more and one less favorable to the defendant—"leniency" requires that the court read it in the manner more favorable.

The rule of lenity is a principle of statutory construction: it comes into play only if and when there is ambiguity. It should not be viewed as a general principle requiring that clear statutes be applied in a lenient manner.

. . . .

Here, . . . the defendant does not allege that a word or phrase in a statute requires construction or is susceptible to more than one interpretation. Instead, he argues that even if the elements of, for instance, a narcotics conspiracy are well known, his particular conduct in designing and operating the website does not clearly fall within what the statute is intended to cover. The Court disagrees.

Sections 841 and 846 are intended to cover conduct in which two or more people conspire to distribute or possess with the intent to distribute narcotics. If the Government can prove at trial that Ulbricht has the requisite intent, then these statutory provisions clearly prohibit his conduct. These statutory provisions do not, for instance, require that only one type of communication method be used between coconspirators (for instance, cellular telephone versus the Internet); they do not prescribe what the various roles of coconspirators must be or are limited to; and they have been applied in the past to individuals alleged to be middlemen in drug transactions. Here, there is no statutory ambiguity and thus no basis for application of the rule of lenity.

The doctrine of constitutional avoidance provides that when a "statute is susceptible of two constructions, by one of which grave and doubtful constitutional questions arise and by the other of which such questions are avoided, [a court's] duty is to accept the latter."

This doctrine is inapplicable for the same reason as the rule of lenity: there is no ambiguity. . . .

B. Void-for-Vagueness and Constitutional Overbreadth

The defendant also argues that the statutes, as applied to his conduct in particular, are void on the basis that they are either unconstitutionally vague or overbroad. The Court disagrees.

The void-for-vagueness doctrine is inapplicable. It addresses concerns regarding (1) fair notice and (2) arbitrary and discriminatory prosecutions. To avoid a vagueness challenge, a statute must define a criminal offense in a manner that ordinary people must understand what conduct is prohibited and in a manner that does not encourage arbitrary and discriminatory enforcement. The question, in short, is whether an ordinary person would know that engaging in the challenged conduct could give rise to the type of criminal liability charged.

The Government argues that this prosecution is not particularly novel. "[B]oth the narcotics conspiracy statute and continuing criminal enterprise statute have specifically been applied in a previous prosecution of defendants involved in operating online marketplaces for illegal drugs." "[T]he computer hacking statute has previously been applied to persons involved in providing online services used by others to distribute malicious software." The citations by the Government in support of these assertions are, however, merely to indictments. And neither case has yet resulted in a published decision which could reasonably have provided notice to the defendant, or which demonstrates an ineffectual legal challenge.

As the Supreme Court has recognized, however, "due process requirements are not designed to convert into a constitutional dilemma the practical difficulties in drawing criminal statutes both general enough to take into account a variety of human conduct and sufficiently specific to provide fair warning that certain kinds of conduct are prohibited." Here, the charged conduct is not merely designing some benign marketplace for bath towels. The conduct is alleged to be specific and intentional conduct to join with narcotics traffickers or computer hackers to help them sell illegal drugs or hack into computers, and to be involved in enforcing rules (including using murder-for-hire) regarding such sales and taking commissions. No person of ordinary intelligence could believe that such conduct is somehow legal. Indeed, no reasonable person could assume that such conduct is in any way equivalent to designing and running eBay, for example. There is nothing vague about the application of the statute to the conduct charged.

. . . .

C. Civil Immunity for Online Service Providers

The defendant argues that the existence of a civil statute for certain types of immunity for online service providers expresses a congressional intent to immunize conduct akin to that in which Ulbricht is alleged to have engaged. This Court disagrees. Even a quick reading of the statute makes it clear that it is not intended to apply to the type of intentional and criminal acts alleged to have occurred here. *See* 47 U.S. Code § 230.

. . . .

VIII.   COUNT FOUR

Count Four charges the defendant with participation in a money laundering conspiracy in violation of 18 U.S. Code § 1956(h). The Government has alleged the requisite statutory elements. First, the Government has alleged that a conspiracy existed between the defendant and one or more others, the object of which was to engage in money laundering. . . . [T]he Indictment recites the specific elements required for money laundering:

> It was a part and an object of the conspiracy that . . . the defendant, and others known and unknown, . . . knowing that the property involved in certain financial transactions represented proceeds of some form of unlawful activity, would and did conduct and attempt to conduct such financial transactions, which in fact involved the proceeds of specified unlawful activity, to wit,

narcotics trafficking and computer hacking . . . with the intent to promote the carrying on of such unspecified unlawful activity . . . .

The defendant argues that the factual allegation that Bitcoins constituted the exclusive "payment system that served to facilitate [ ] illegal commerce" on Silk Road cannot constitute the requisite "financial transaction." The Court disagrees.

As an initial matter, an allegation that Bitcoins are used as a payment system is insufficient in and of itself to state a claim for money laundering. The fact that Bitcoins allow for anonymous transactions does not ipso facto mean that those transactions relate to unlawful activities. The anonymity by itself is not a crime. Rather, Bitcoins are alleged here to be the medium of exchange—just as dollars or Euros could be—in financial transactions relating to the unlawful activities of narcotics trafficking and computer hacking. It is the system of payment designed specifically to shield the proceeds from third party discovery of their unlawful origin that forms the unlawful basis of the money laundering charge.

The money laundering statute defines a "financial transaction" as involving, inter alia, "the movement of funds by wire or other means, or [ ] involving one or more monetary instruments, [ ] or involving the transfer of title to any real property, vehicle, vessel, or aircraft." 18 U.S.C. § 1956(c)(4). The term "monetary instrument" is defined as the coin or currency of a country, personal checks, bank checks, and money orders, or investment securities or negotiable instruments. 18 U.S.C. § 1956(c)(5).

The defendant argues that because Bitcoins are not monetary instruments, transactions involving Bitcoins cannot form the basis for a money laundering conspiracy. He notes that the IRS has announced that it treats virtual currency as property and not as currency. The defendant argues that virtual currencies have some but not all of the attributes of currencies of national governments and that virtual currencies do not have legal tender status. In fact, neither the IRS nor FinCEN purport to amend the money laundering statute (nor could they). In any event, neither the IRS nor FinCEN has addressed the question of whether a "financial transaction" can occur with Bitcoins. This Court refers back to the money laundering statute itself and case law interpreting the statute.

It is clear from a plain reading of the statute that "financial transaction" is broadly defined. *See United States v. Blackman*, 904 F.2d 1250, 1257 (8th Cir.1990) (citation omitted). It captures all movements of "funds" by any means, or monetary instruments. "Funds" is not defined in the statute and is therefore given its ordinary meaning. "Funds" are defined as "money, often money for a specific purpose." See Cambridge Dictionaries Online. "Money" is an object used to buy things.

Put simply, "funds" can be used to pay for things in the colloquial sense. Bitcoins can be either used directly to pay for certain things or can act as a medium of exchange and be converted into a currency which can pay for things. Indeed, the only value for Bitcoin lies in its ability to pay for things—it is digital and has no earthly form; it cannot be put on a shelf and looked at or collected in a nice display case. Its form is digital—bits and bytes that together constitute something of value. And they may be bought and sold using legal tender. Sellers using Silk Road are not alleged to have given their narcotics and malicious software away for free—they are alleged to have sold them.

The money laundering statute is broad enough to encompass use of Bitcoins in financial transactions. Any other reading would—in light of Bitcoins' sole raison d'etre—be nonsensical. Congress intended to prevent criminals from finding ways to wash the proceeds of criminal activity by transferring proceeds to other similar or different items that store significant value. With respect to this case, the Government has alleged that Bitcoins have a value which may be expressed in dollars. ([citation to Indictment, alleging that Ulbricht "reaped commissions worth tens of millions of dollars, generated from the illicit sales conducted through the site").

There is no doubt that if a narcotics transaction was paid for in cash, which was later exchanged for gold, and then converted back to cash, that would constitute a money laundering transaction.

One can money launder using Bitcoin. The defendant's motion as to Count Four is therefore denied.

IX. CONCLUSION

For the reasons set forth above, the defendant's motion to dismiss is DENIED in its entirety. The clerk of the Court is directed to terminate the motion. . . .

NOTES AND QUESTIONS

1. The preceding excerpt includes a consideration of various transactions that took place on the Silk Road. As Judge Forrest notes in Part III dealing with the requirements of a conspiratorial agreement, "[t]he Indictment alleges that Ulbricht designed Silk Road specifically to enable users to anonymously sell and purchase narcotics and malicious software and to launder the resulting proceeds." It is safe to say that allegations about Ulbricht's not-so-shining character were well within the contemplation of the judge in determining how broadly to construe and apply the various money laundering provisions at issue later in the opinion. If this case had involved someone who had simply assisted his friends in buying Bitcoin, do you think that could have influence the interpretation of the money laundering statute in Part VII of the opinion?

2. The judge signals a degree of distain for some of the defense's arguments by bundling them together and calling them the "kitchen sink"

arguments. Not surprisingly all of those arguments are rejected. As a matter of strategy, was it tactically wise to make all of those arguments or should the defense have focused only on the strongest points? Were any of the "kitchen sink" arguments stronger than the others (in your mind, after considering what the judge had to say about them)?

3. Consider this example of a logical fallacy. A dog is an animal with four legs. Cats have four legs. Therefore, cats are dogs. The first two of those statements are generally true. The conclusion, however, is false. What is the difference between that fallacy and the following line of reasoning: Money is used to pay for things. Bitcoin is used to pay for things. Therefore Bitcoin is money. That is essentially the analysis employed in the preceding opinion. Judge Forrest writes as if there is no real doubt as to whether Bitcoin transactions can support a charge of money laundering, because she concludes that Bitcoins are "funds." In fact, there is no definition of "funds" in the statute. The lists of things that are monetary transactions sufficient to support a charge of money laundering do not include intangible assets such as Bitcoin or other forms of crypto. Moreover, as we will see later, not all courts are in agreement with Judge Forrest on this point.

Ulbricht's actual trial did not begin until mid-January, 2015. It took place in Federal Court in Manhattan. From the outset, Ulbricht admitted to founding Silk Road, but he claimed to have transferred control of the enterprise shortly after it was up and running. His attorneys argued[10] that Mark Karpelès was the "real" Dread Pirate Roberts and that Karpelès had arranged for Ulbricht to take the fall by transferring ownership back to him when the FBI investigation got too close. The judge eventually ruled that evidence there had been substantial speculation during the investigation about whether someone else ran Silk Road was not admissible. In response to the general argument that he had transferred control over Silk Road, the prosecution presented evidence from Ulbricht's computer that purportedly indicated how he had administered Silk Road for months. Ulbricht's attorney responded with allegations that the evidence had been planted by a program, BitTorrent, which had been running on the computer at the time of Ulbricht's arrest.

Apparently, the jury believed the prosecution rather than Ulbricht. On February 4, 2015, the jury convicted Ulbricht of seven charges, including charges that he had engaged in a continuing criminal enterprise, narcotics trafficking, money laundering, and computer hacking. Following his conviction, in a pre-sentencing letter to the judge, Ulbricht stated that he had founded Silk Road out of an excess of "libertarian idealism," and that "Silk Road was supposed to be about giving people the freedom to make

---

[10] Ross Ulbricht did not testify at trial, but it would be improper to draw any conclusions from that fact.

their own choices." Instead, he acknowledged that Silk Road had been a "terrible mistake" that "ruined his life." On May 29, 2015, Ulbricht was given five sentences to be served concurrently, including two for life imprisonment without the possibility of parole. He was also ordered to forfeit $183 million. His lawyer appealed to the Second Circuit, resulting in the following opinion.

Given that Bitcoin transactions were supposed to be generally anonymous, and that the Silk Road website was further shrouded in as much secrecy and anonymity as possible, many people are curious about how Ulbricht was caught and successfully prosecuted. The answer to that is, at least in part, that the government obtained a wide range of data from Ulbricht's computer. Although not directly relevant to how crypto is regulated, understanding how the government proved its case may be useful in some contexts. It is particularly relevant in understanding why so many crypto enthusiasts continue to push the need for increased privacy protections, and why even persons with no criminal aspirations may be supporters of developments like so-called privacy coins.

Only certain issues relating to evidence allowed at trial are included in the following excerpt.

UNITED STATES V. ULBRICHT [ON APPEAL]
858 F.3d 71 (2d Cir. 2017), *cert. denied*, 138 S. Ct. 2708 (2018)

GERARD E. LYNCH, CIRCUIT JUDGE:

Defendant Ross William Ulbricht appeals from a judgment of conviction and sentence to life imprisonment entered in the United States District Court for the Southern District of New York (Katherine B. Forrest, J.). A jury convicted Ulbricht of drug trafficking and other crimes associated with his creation and operation of Silk Road, an online marketplace whose users primarily purchased and sold illegal goods and services. He challenges several aspects of his conviction and sentence. . . . Because we identify no reversible error, we AFFIRM Ulbricht's conviction and sentence in all respects.

BACKGROUND

In February 2015, a jury convicted Ross William Ulbricht on seven counts arising from his creation and operation of Silk Road under the username Dread Pirate Roberts ("DPR"). Silk Road was a massive, anonymous criminal marketplace that operated using the Tor Network, which renders Internet traffic through the Tor browser extremely difficult to trace. Silk Road users principally bought and sold drugs, false identification documents, and computer hacking software. Transactions on Silk Road exclusively used Bitcoins, an anonymous but traceable digital currency.[3] The site also contained a private message system, which allowed users to send messages to each other (similar to communicating via email), a public forum to discuss topics related to Silk Road, and a "wiki," which is like an encyclopedia that users could access to receive advice about using the site. Silk Road customers and vendors could also access a support section of the website to seek help from the marketplace's administrators when an issue arose.

According to the government, between 2011 and 2013, thousands of vendors used Silk Road to sell approximately $183 million worth of illegal drugs, as well as other goods and services. Ulbricht, acting as DPR, earned millions of dollars in profits from the commissions collected by Silk Road on purchases. In October 2013, the government arrested Ulbricht, seized the Silk Road servers, and shut down the site.

I.   Silk Road Investigation

After Ulbricht created Silk Road in 2011, the site attracted the interest of at least two separate divisions of the Department of Justice: the United States Attorney's Offices for the District of Maryland and for the Southern District of New York. Throughout the investigations, law enforcement agents knew that the person using Dread Pirate Roberts [DPR] as his or her Silk Road username had created and managed the site, but they did not know DPR's actual identity. In 2012 and 2013, agents from both offices investigated several individuals who the government suspected were operating Silk Road as DPR. Those individuals included Ulbricht, Anand Athavale, and Mark Karpelés. Ultimately, the New York office identified Ulbricht as DPR, but the Maryland office had investigated and later abandoned the theory that either Athavale or Karpelés might have been Dread Pirate Roberts.

Two aspects of the pre-arrest investigation into Ulbricht are particularly relevant to this appeal: (1) the pen/trap orders that the government obtained to monitor Internet Protocol ("IP") address traffic to and from various devices associated with Ulbricht; and (2) the corrupt behavior of two Baltimore agents who worked on the Silk Road investigation.

---

[3]   Bitcoins allow vendors and customers to maintain their anonymity in the same way that cash does, by transferring Bitcoins between anonymous Bitcoin accounts, which do not contain any identifying information about the user of each account. The currency is "traceable" in that the transaction history of each individual Bitcoin is logged in what is called the blockchain. The blockchain prevents a person from spending the same Bitcoin twice, allowing Bitcoin to operate similarly to a traditional form of currency. Bitcoin is also a completely decentralized currency, operating free of nation states or central banks; anyone who downloads the Bitcoin software becomes part of the Bitcoin network. The blockchain is stored on that network, and the blockchain automatically "self-updates" when a Bitcoin transaction takes place.

A.   The Pen/Trap Orders[11]

In September 2013, after Ulbricht became a primary suspect in the DPR investigation, the government obtained five "pen/trap" orders. *See* 18 U.S.C. §§ 3121–27 ("Pen/Trap Act"). The orders authorized law enforcement agents to collect IP address data for Internet traffic to and from Ulbricht's home wireless router and other devices that regularly connected to Ulbricht's home router. According to the government's applications for the pen register and trap and trace device, "[e]very device on the Internet is identified by a unique number" called an IP address. "This number is used to route information between devices, for example, between two computers." In other words, an "IP address is analogous to a telephone number" because "it indicates the online identity of the communicating device without revealing the communication's content." Ulbricht does not dispute that description of how IP addresses function.

The pen/trap orders thus did not permit the government to access the content of Ulbricht's communications, nor did the government "seek to obtain[ ] the contents of any communications." According to Ulbricht, the government's use of his home Internet routing data violated the Fourth Amendment because it helped the government match Ulbricht's online activity with DPR's use of Silk Road. Ulbricht argues that he has a constitutional privacy interest in IP address traffic to and from his home and that the government obtained the pen/trap orders without a warrant, which would have required probable cause.

B.   Corrupt Agents Force and Bridges

One of the many other tactics that the government used to expose DPR's identity was to find low-level Silk Road administrators who helped DPR maintain the site, obtain their cooperation, take over their Silk Road usernames, and chat with DPR under those identities. The true owners of the administrator accounts would assist in the investigation by helping the government chat with DPR and access various aspects of the site. Government agents would also create their own new usernames and pose as drug dealers or buyers to purchase or sell narcotics and occasionally contact DPR directly. One of the government's principal trial witnesses, Special Agent Jared Der-Yeghiayan, used the former technique to chat with DPR under the name Cirrus. Cirrus had been a member of the Silk Road support staff before the government took over his account, and Der-Yeghiayan frequently used Silk Road's messaging system to communicate

---

[11]   Author's note: A pen/trap order involves a pen register or a trap and trace device. A pen register traditionally shows what numbers a phone has called (i.e., outgoing calls), while a trap and trace device shares what numbers have called a specific phone (i.e., incoming calls). The modern interpretation of these terms includes electronic communications so that pen/traps orders cover IP addresses. A pen/trap order may be entered by any court of competent jurisdiction following a government's certification "that the information likely to be obtained is relevant to an ongoing criminal investigation being conducted by that agency." This information is expanded upon later in this opinion.

with DPR and other administrators as Cirrus. Cirrus also gave the government access to the staff chat, a separate program allowing DPR to communicate only with his employees.

Two undercover agents involved in the Silk Road investigation are of particular import to this appeal: Secret Service Special Agent Shaun Bridges and Drug Enforcement Administration ("DEA") Special Agent Carl Force, both of whom were assigned to the Baltimore investigation. Both Force and Bridges used their undercover access to exploit the site for their own benefit in various ways, and they eventually pleaded guilty to criminal charges in connection with their work on the Silk Road investigation.[6]

For example, Force and Bridges took over an administrator account belonging to Curtis Green, who worked for Silk Road under the name Flush. According to the criminal complaint against Force and Bridges, in January 2013, Bridges used the Flush username to change other users' passwords, empty their Bitcoin wallets, and keep $350,000 in Bitcoins in offshore bank accounts, all while attempting to hide his activity through a series of transactions. Specifically, the complaint against Force and Bridges alleges that Bridges "act[ed] as an administrator to reset pins and passwords on various Silk Road vendors' accounts," then exchanged the Bitcoins for U.S. dollars using the Mt. Gox exchanger. Shortly after he committed the January 2013 thefts, Bridges asked Force to chat with DPR as Nob, Force's authorized undercover username, to get advice about how to liquidate Bitcoins. He also sought Force's help in convincing Curtis Green (formerly Flush) to help him transfer Bitcoins to other accounts, and he ultimately tried to blame Green for the theft.

With the government's approval, Force also posed as a drug dealer and communicated with DPR as Nob. As part of his official undercover work as Nob, Force agreed to sell fraudulent identification documents to DPR for $40,000 in Bitcoins. According to the criminal complaint against the agents, Force kept the Bitcoins received by his Nob account in connection with that transaction for his personal use. On another occasion, again as part of his authorized undercover work, Force advised DPR that he had access to information about Silk Road from an invented corrupt government employee. DPR paid Force $50,000 in Bitcoins for purported inside law enforcement information; Force allegedly purloined that payment as well. Moreover, outside his authorized undercover work, Force operated another account under the name French Maid, through which he again offered to sell DPR information about the government's Silk Road investigation. Acting as French Maid, Force received about $100,000 in Bitcoins that he kept for his personal use.

---

[6] Both Force and Bridges pleaded guilty to money laundering and obstruction of justice; Force also pleaded guilty to extortion. Force was sentenced to 78 months in prison, and Bridges received a 71-month sentence.

Force created yet another unauthorized Silk Road account, under the name DeathFromAbove, which was unknown to law enforcement until the defense identified it during trial. Force used the DeathFromAbove account to try to extort money from DPR. For example, in one such chat that took place on April 16, 2013, DeathFromAbove told DPR that he knew that DPR's true identity was Anand Athavale. DeathFromAbove demanded a payment of $250,000 in exchange for which DeathFromAbove would remain silent about DPR's identity. There is no evidence that DPR made the requested payment to DeathFromAbove; indeed, DPR shrugged off the attempted blackmail as "bogus."

As will be explained in more detail below, the district court prevented Ulbricht from introducing evidence at trial related to Force's corruption because doing so would have exposed the ongoing grand jury investigation into Force's conduct. The district court also denied Ulbricht discovery related to the investigation and excluded certain hearsay statements that arguably revealed Force's corruption. Ulbricht contends on appeal that the district court's various rulings concerning evidence related to Force deprived him of a fair trial. Additionally, Ulbricht did not learn of Bridges's corrupt conduct until after trial when the criminal complaint against both agents was unsealed. Thus, in his motion for a new trial, he argued that the belated disclosure violated his due process rights under *Brady v. Maryland,* 373 U.S. 83 (1963). Ulbricht contends on appeal that the district court incorrectly denied that motion.

II. Ulbricht's Arrest

Ulbricht was arrested in a San Francisco public library on October 1, 2013, after the government had amassed significant evidence identifying him as Dread Pirate Roberts. The arrest was successfully orchestrated to catch Ulbricht in the act of administering Silk Road as DPR. Federal agents observed Ulbricht enter the public library, and a few minutes later Dread Pirate Roberts came online in the Silk Road staff chat. Der-Yeghiayan, under the undercover administrator username Cirrus, initiated a chat with DPR, asking him to go to a specific place on the Silk Road site to address some flagged messages from users. Der-Yeghiayan reasoned that this would "force [Ulbricht] to log in under . . . his Dread Pirate Roberts account" in the Silk Road marketplace, as well as in the staff chat software.

Once Der-Yeghiayan knew that DPR had logged onto the flagged message page in the marketplace, he signaled another agent to effect the arrest. Ulbricht was arrested, and incident to that arrest agents seized his laptop. The same chat that Der-Yeghiayan had initiated with Dread Pirate Roberts a few minutes earlier was open on Ulbricht's screen. Ulbricht also visited the flagged post in the marketplace that Der-Yeghiayan (as Cirrus) had asked DPR to look at during their chat. While he was chatting with

Cirrus, moreover, Ulbricht had accessed Silk Road by using the "Mastermind" page. That page was available only to Dread Pirate Roberts.

A great deal of the evidence against Ulbricht came from the government's search of his laptop and his home after the arrest. On the day of Ulbricht's arrest, the government obtained a warrant to seize Ulbricht's laptop and search it for a wide variety of information related to Silk Road and information that would identify Ulbricht as Dread Pirate Roberts. Ulbricht moved to suppress the large quantity of evidence obtained from his laptop, challenging the constitutionality of that search warrant. Ulbricht argues on appeal that the district court erred in denying his motion to suppress. More details concerning the search warrant will be described in context below.

III. The Trial

Ulbricht's trial lasted approximately three weeks, from January 13 through February 4, 2015. Judge Forrest handled the complex and contentious trial with commendable patience and skill. . . . [W]e summarize the evidence presented at trial as context for the issues raised on appeal.

A. The Government's Case

The government presented overwhelming evidence that Ulbricht created Silk Road in 2011 and continued to operate the site throughout its lifetime by maintaining its computer infrastructure, interacting with vendors, crafting policies for site users, deciding what products would be available for sale on the site, and managing a small staff of administrators and software engineers. Defense counsel conceded in his opening statement that Ulbricht did in fact create Silk Road.

According to Ulbricht's own words in a 2009 email, Ulbricht originally conceived of Silk Road as "an online storefront that couldn't be traced back to [him] . . . where [his] customers could buy [his] products" and pay for them "anonymously and securely." From 2009 through 2011, Ulbricht worked to get the site up and running, relying on computer programming assistance from others, including his friend Richard Bates. According to one of the journal entries discovered on his laptop, in 2010 Ulbricht began to grow hallucinogenic mushrooms to sell on the site "for cheap to get people interested." As the site began to garner significant interest in 2011, Ulbricht wrote in his journal that he was "creating a year of prosperity and power beyond what I have ever experienced before. Silk Road is going to become a phenomenon and at least one person will tell me about it, unknowing that I was its creator."

1. Evidence Linking Ulbricht to Dread Pirate Roberts

Around January 2012, the Silk Road user who represented himself as the lead administrator of the site adopted the username Dread Pirate

Roberts. The name alludes to the pseudonym of a pirate in the popular novel and film The Princess Bride that is periodically passed on from one individual to another. In order to assure users that posts purporting to be authored by DPR were indeed his own, DPR authenticated his posts using an electronic signature known as a PGP key. Silk Road users had access to a public PGP key, and DPR had a private PGP key that he alone could use to sign his Silk Road posts. When DPR signed a post using his private key, Silk Road users could run the code in the public key, and if the post was signed with the correct private key the user would receive a message that the authentication was successful. The government recovered DPR's private PGP key on Ulbricht's laptop. Importantly, the public PGP key did not change during the site's life span, meaning that DPR used the same private key to sign his posts throughout the time that he administered Silk Road.

Additional evidence supported the conclusion that Ulbricht was Dread Pirate Roberts. For example, the instructions that DPR provided to Cirrus (the account that Der-Yeghiayan later used for undercover work) for how to access the staff chat and contact DPR directly were found in a file on Ulbricht's laptop. The government also discovered the following evidence, covering the entire period during which DPR managed the Silk Road site, on Ulbricht's computer: thousands of pages of chat logs with Silk Road employees; detailed journal entries describing Ulbricht's ownership of the site; a list that tracked Ulbricht's tasks and ideas related to Silk Road; a copy of Silk Road's database; and spreadsheets cataloguing both the servers that hosted Silk Road and expenses and profits associated with the site. The government seized approximately $18 million worth of Bitcoins from the wallet on Ulbricht's laptop and analyzed their transaction history (through blockchain records) to determine that about 89% of the Bitcoins on Ulbricht's computer came from Silk Road servers located in Iceland.

A search of Ulbricht's home yielded additional evidence linking him with the site. That evidence included two USB hard drives with versions of documents related to Silk Road that were also stored on Ulbricht's laptop. There were also handwritten notes crumpled in Ulbricht's bedroom trash can about ideas for improving Silk Road's vendor rating system—an initiative that Dread Pirate Roberts had just revealed through a post in a discussion forum on the site.

. . . .

2.   Murders Commissioned by Dread Pirate Roberts

The government also presented evidence that DPR commissioned the murders of five people to protect Silk Road's anonymity, although there is no evidence that any of the murders actually occurred.

. . . .

B. The Defense Case

As noted above, Ulbricht conceded at trial that he had created Silk Road, and he was caught red-handed operating the site at the end of the investigation. His principal defense strategy at trial—more of an effort at mitigation than outright denial of his guilt of the conspiracy and other charges in the indictment—was to admit his role at the beginning and end of the site's operation, but to contend that he sold Silk Road to someone else in 2011 and abandoned his role as its administrator, only to be lured back by the successor DPR near the end of its operation to take the blame for operating the site. The defense attempted on several occasions to implicate as alternative suspects Karpelés and Athavale, both of whom the government had investigated for a possible connection to Silk Road but later abandoned as candidates for DPR's real-world identity. As part of his alternative-perpetrator defense, Ulbricht theorized that the person or persons who operated as the true Dread Pirate Roberts during the purported interim period planted incriminating evidence on his laptop in order to frame him. For the most part, the defense advanced this theory through cross-examination of government witnesses. Ulbricht did not testify at trial.

One point in the testimony of Richard Bates exemplifies the defense's approach and the government's response. Bates, Ulbricht's friend who assisted with computer programming issues when Ulbricht launched Silk Road, testified for the government. According to Bates, Ulbricht told him in November 2011 that he had sold Silk Road to someone else, a claim that Bates believed at the time to be true. Moreover, in a February 2013 Google chat between Bates and Ulbricht, Ulbricht wrote that he was "[g]lad" that Silk Road was "not [his] problem anymore." Bates understood that to mean that Ulbricht no longer worked on the site.

To mitigate any damage from Bates's testimony, the government introduced a December 9, 2011 Tor chat between Ulbricht and vj. In that chat, vj asked Ulbricht whether anyone else knew about his involvement in Silk Road. Ulbricht responded: "[U]nfortunately yes. There are two, but they think I sold the site and got out and they are quite convinced of it." He further wrote that those two people thought he sold the site "about a month ago," which roughly corresponds to the November 2011 conversation between Bates and Ulbricht. Significantly, it was shortly after this conversation that vj suggested that Ulbricht change his online identity to DPR. In view of the fictional character it referenced, the government contended that the online moniker DPR was deliberately adopted to support the cover story that the lead administrator of Silk Road changed over time.

Thus, although the government elicited testimony that Ulbricht told Bates that he sold the site in 2011, it also presented evidence that Ulbricht had lied to Bates about that sale and continued to operate the site in secret.

1.   Cross-Examination of Government Witnesses

Ulbricht's defense depended heavily on cross-examination of government witnesses, much of which was designed to support the argument that either Karpelés or Athavale was the real DPR, or that multiple people operated as Dread Pirate Roberts during Silk Road's life span. The district court limited his cross-examination in two ways that Ulbricht challenges on appeal. First, the district court prevented Ulbricht from exploring several specific topics with Der-Yeghiayan, the government's first witness, through whom it introduced much of its evidence. Those topics included, inter alia, Der-Yeghiayan's prior suspicions that Karpelés was DPR. Second, the district court limited Ulbricht's ability to cross examine FBI computer scientist Thomas Kiernan, who testified about evidence that he discovered on Ulbricht's laptop, concerning several specific technical issues related to software on Ulbricht's computer. More details about those attempted cross-examinations will be discussed in context below.

2.   Hearsay Statements

Ulbricht also attempted to introduce two hearsay statements in his defense, both of which the district court excluded as inadmissible. Those hearsay statements comprise: (1) chats between DPR and DeathFromAbove (Force) concerning Force's attempt to extort money from DPR in exchange for information about the government's investigation of Silk Road; and (2) the government's letter describing a statement by Andrew Jones, a site administrator, concerning one particular conversation that he had with DPR.

. . . .

C.   The Verdict and Post-Trial Motion

After deliberating for about three and a half hours, the jury returned a guilty verdict on all seven counts in the Indictment.

. . . .

IV. Sentencing

The United States Probation Office prepared the Pre-Sentence Investigation Report ("PSR") in March 2015. It described the offense conduct in detail and discussed the five murders that Ulbricht allegedly hired RedandWhite [Author's note: a Silk Road seller who allegedly agreed to act as a hitman] to commit.

. . . .

Ulbricht's sentencing hearing took place on May 29, 2015. The district court concluded that Ulbricht's offense level was 43—the highest possible offense level under the Sentencing Guidelines—and that his criminal history category was I. The high offense level largely resulted from the massive quantity of drugs trafficked using Silk Road, as well as several enhancements, including one for directing the use of violence. . . .

At the sentencing hearing, the district court resolved several disputed issues of fact. For example, because Ulbricht contested his responsibility for the five commissioned murders for hire, the district court found by a preponderance of the evidence that Ulbricht did in fact commission the murders, believing that they would be carried out. The district court characterized the evidence of the murders for hire, which included Ulbricht's journal, chats with other Silk Road users, and the evidence showing that Ulbricht actually paid a total of $650,000 in Bitcoins for the killings, as "ample and unambiguous."

. . . .

DISCUSSION

On appeal, Ulbricht raises a number of claims of error. For purposes of organizational clarity, we group them . . . and present them in the order in which the issues arose in the district court. Accordingly, we discuss first Ulbricht's claims that much of the evidence against him should have been suppressed because it was obtained in violation of his Fourth Amendment rights; second, his arguments that the district court's evidentiary errors denied him a fair trial. . . .

I. Fourth Amendment Issues

Ulbricht claims that the district court erred in denying his motion to suppress evidence obtained in violation of the Fourth Amendment. On appeal from a denial of a suppression motion, "we review a district court's findings of fact for clear error, and its resolution of questions of law and mixed questions of law and fact de novo." *United States v. Bohannon*, 824 F.3d 242, 247–48 (2d Cir. 2016). Ulbricht raises two principal arguments. First, he contends that the pen/trap orders that the government used to monitor IP address traffic to and from his home router violated the Fourth Amendment because the government obtained the orders without a warrant. Second, he claims that the warrants authorizing the government to search his laptop as well as his Google and Facebook accounts violated the Fourth Amendment's particularity requirement. We reject those contentions and affirm the denial of Ulbricht's motion to suppress.

A. Pen/Trap Orders

Pursuant to orders issued by United States magistrate judges in the Southern District of New York, the government used five pen registers and trap and trace devices to monitor IP addresses associated with Internet traffic to and from Ulbricht's wireless home router and devices that regularly connected to that router. The government obtained the orders pursuant to the Pen/Trap Act, which provides that a government attorney "may make [an] application for an order . . . authorizing or approving the installation and use of a pen register or a trap and trace device . . . to a court of competent jurisdiction." 18 U.S.C. § 3122(a)(1). A "pen register" is defined as a "device or process which records or decodes dialing, routing, addressing, or signaling information transmitted by an instrument or facility from which a wire or electronic communication is transmitted," and "shall not include the contents of any communication." *Id.* § 3127(3). A "trap and trace" device means "a device or process which captures the incoming electronic or other impulses which identify the originating number or other dialing, routing, addressing, and signaling information reasonably likely to identify the source of a wire or electronic communication." *Id.* § 3127(4). Like pen registers, trap and trace devices may not capture the "contents of any communication." *Id.* The statute does not require a search warrant for the use of a pen register or trap and trace device, nor does it demand the kind of showing required to obtain such a warrant. Rather, the statute requires only that the application contain a "certification . . . that the information likely to be obtained is relevant to an ongoing criminal investigation." *Id.* § 3122(b)(2).

The orders in this case authorized the government to "use a pen register and trap and trace device to identify the source and destination [IP] addresses, along with the dates, times, durations, ports of transmission, and any Transmission Control Protocol ('TCP') connection data, associated with any electronic communications sent to or from" various devices, including Ulbricht's home wireless router and his laptop. In each order, the government specified that it did not seek to obtain the contents of any communications. Instead, it sought authorization to collect only "dialing, routing, addressing, and signaling information" that was akin to data captured by "traditional telephonic pen registers and trap and trace devices." Ulbricht claims that the pen/trap orders violated the Fourth Amendment because he had a reasonable expectation of privacy in the IP address routing information that the orders allowed the government to collect.

The Fourth Amendment to the United States Constitution provides that: "The right of the people to be secure in their persons, houses, papers, and effects, against unreasonable searches and seizures, shall not be violated, and no Warrants shall issue, but upon probable cause, supported by Oath or affirmation, and particularly describing the place to be searched, and the persons or things to be seized." The "cornerstone of the modern law of searches is the principle that, to mount a successful Fourth Amendment challenge, a defendant must demonstrate that he personally has an expectation of privacy in the place searched." *United States v. Haqq,*

278 F.3d 44, 47 (2d Cir. 2002) (internal quotation marks omitted). Thus, a "Fourth Amendment 'search [ ]' . . . does not occur unless the search invades an object or area [in which] one has a subjective expectation of privacy that society is prepared to accept as objectively reasonable." *United States v. Hayes,* 551 F.3d 138, 143 (2d Cir. 2008).

The Supreme Court has long held that a "person has no legitimate expectation of privacy in information he voluntarily turns over to third parties," including phone numbers dialed in making a telephone call and captured by a pen register. *Smith v. Maryland,* 442 U.S. 735, 743–44 (1979). This is so because phone users "typically know that they must convey numerical information to the phone company; that the phone company has facilities for recording this information; and that the phone company does in fact record this information for a variety of legitimate business purposes." Similarly, "e-mail and Internet users . . . rely on third-party equipment in order to engage in communication." *United States v. Forrester,* 512 F.3d 500, 510 (9th Cir. 2008). Internet users thus "should know that this information is provided to and used by Internet service providers for the specific purpose of directing the routing of information." *Id.* Moreover, "IP addresses are not merely passively conveyed through third party equipment, but rather are voluntarily turned over in order to direct the third party's servers." *United States v. Christie,* 624 F.3d 558, 574 (3d Cir. 2010) (internal quotation marks omitted).

Ulbricht notes that questions have been raised about whether some aspects of modern technology, which entrust great quantities of significant personal information to third party vendors, arguably making extensive government surveillance possible, call for a re-evaluation of the third-party disclosure doctrine established by Smith. *See, e.g., United States v. Jones,* 565 U.S. 400, 417–18 (2012) (Sotomayor, J., concurring). We remain bound, however, by that rule until and unless it is overruled by the Supreme Court.

Moreover, whatever novel or more intrusive surveillance techniques might present future questions concerning the appropriate scope of the third-party disclosure doctrine, the orders in this case do not present such issues. The recording of IP address information and similar routing data, which reveal the existence of connections between communications devices without disclosing the content of the communications, are precisely analogous to the capture of telephone numbers at issue in Smith. That is why the orders here fit comfortably within the language of a statute drafted with the earlier technology in mind. The substitution of electronic methods of communication for telephone calls does not alone create a reasonable expectation of privacy in the identities of devices with whom one communicates. Nor does it raise novel issues distinct from those long since resolved in the context of telephone communication, with which society has lived for the nearly forty years since Smith was decided. Like telephone companies, Internet service providers require that identifying information be disclosed in order to make communication among electronic devices possible. In light of the Smith rule, no reasonable person could maintain a privacy interest in that sort of information.

We therefore join the other circuits that have considered this narrow question and hold that collecting IP address information devoid of content is "constitutionally indistinguishable from the use of a pen register."

. . . .

Where, as here, the government did not access the contents of any of Ulbricht's communications, it did not need to obtain a warrant to collect IP address routing information in which Ulbricht did not have a legitimate privacy interest. We therefore reject Ulbricht's contention that the issuance of such orders violated his Fourth Amendment rights.

. . . .

B.   Search Warrants

Ulbricht also contends that the warrants authorizing the search and seizure of his laptop . . . violated the Fourth Amendment's particularity requirement. The Fourth Amendment explicitly commands that warrants must be based on probable cause and must "particularly describ[e] the place to be searched, and the persons or things to be seized." U.S. Const. amend. IV. "It is familiar history that indiscriminate searches and seizures conducted under the authority of 'general warrants' were the immediate evils that motivated the framing and adoption of the Fourth Amendment." *Payton v. New York,* 445 U.S. 573, 583 (1980). Those general warrants "specified only an offense," leaving "to the discretion of the executing officials the decision as to which persons should be arrested and which places should be searched." *Steagald v. United States,* 451 U.S. 204, 220 (1981). The principal defect in such a warrant was that it permitted a "general, exploratory rummaging in a person's belongings," *Andresen v. Maryland,* 427 U.S. 463, 480 (1976) (internal quotation marks omitted), a problem that the Fourth Amendment attempted to resolve by requiring the warrant to "set out with particularity" the "scope of the authorized search," *Kentucky v. King,* 563 U.S. 452, 459 (2011).

To be sufficiently particular under the Fourth Amendment, a warrant must satisfy three requirements. First, "a warrant must identify the specific offense for which the police have established probable cause." *United States v. Galpin,* 720 F.3d 436, 445 (2d Cir. 2013). Second, "a warrant must describe the place to be searched." *Id.* at 445–46. Finally, the "warrant must specify the items to be seized by their relation to designated crimes." *Id.* at 446 (internal quotation marks omitted).

"Where, as here, the property to be searched is a computer hard drive, the particularity requirement assumes even greater importance." *Id.* A general search of electronic data is an especially potent threat to privacy because hard drives and e-mail accounts may be "akin to a residence in terms of the scope and quantity of private information [they] may contain." *Id*. The "seizure of a computer hard drive, and its subsequent retention by the government, can [therefore] give the government possession of a vast trove of personal information about the person to whom the drive belongs, much of which may be entirely irrelevant to the criminal investigation that led to the seizure." *United States v. Ganias*, 824 F.3d 199, 217 (2d Cir. 2016) (en banc). Such sensitive records might include "[t]ax records, diaries, personal photographs, electronic books, electronic media, medical data, records of internet searches, [and] banking and shopping information." *Id*. at 218. Because of the nature of digital storage, it is not always feasible to "extract and segregate responsive data from non-responsive data," *id*. at 213, creating a "serious risk that every warrant for electronic information will become, in effect, a general warrant," *Galpin*, 720 F.3d at 447 (internal quotation marks omitted). Thus, we have held that warrants that fail to "link [the evidence sought] to the criminal activity supported by probable cause" do not satisfy the particularity requirement because they "lack[ ] meaningful parameters on an otherwise limitless search" of a defendant's electronic media. *United States v. Rosa*, 626 F.3d 56, 62 (2d Cir. 2010).

The Fourth Amendment does not require a perfect description of the data to be searched and seized, however. Search warrants covering digital data may contain "some ambiguity . . . so long as law enforcement agents have done the best that could reasonably be expected under the circumstances, have acquired all the descriptive facts which a reasonable investigation could be expected to cover, and have insured that all those facts were included in the warrant." *Galpin*, 720 F.3d at 446 (internal quotation marks omitted).

Moreover, it is important to bear in mind that a search warrant does not necessarily lack particularity simply because it is broad. Since a search of a computer is "akin to [a search of] a residence," *id.*, searches of computers may sometimes need to be as broad as searches of residences pursuant to warrants. Similarly, traditional searches for paper records, like searches for electronic records, have always entailed the exposure of records that are not the objects of the search to at least superficial examination in order to identify and seize those records that are. And in many cases, the volume of records properly subject to seizure because of their evidentiary value may be vast. None of these consequences necessarily turns a search warrant into a prohibited general warrant.

1. Laptop Search Warrant

The warrant authorizing the search and seizure of Ulbricht's laptop (the "Laptop Warrant") explicitly incorporated by reference an affidavit listing the crimes charged . . . . The affidavit also described the workings of

Silk Road and the role of Dread Pirate Roberts in operating the site and included a wealth of information supporting a finding that there was probable cause to believe that Ulbricht and DPR were the same person. Based on that information, the Laptop Warrant alleged that Ulbricht "use[d] [the laptop] in connection with his operation of Silk Road," and that there was "probable cause to believe that evidence, fruits, and instrumentalities of the [charged offenses]" would be found on the laptop.

Generally speaking, the Laptop Warrant divided the information to be searched for and seized into two categories. The first covered evidence concerning Silk Road that was located on the computer, including, inter alia, "data associated with the Silk Road website, such as web content, server code, or database records"; any evidence concerning servers or computer equipment connected with Silk Road; emails, private messages, and forum postings or "other communications concerning Silk Road in any way"; evidence concerning "funds used to facilitate or proceeds derived from Silk Road," including Bitcoin wallet files and transactions with Bitcoin exchangers, or "information concerning any financial accounts . . . where Silk Road funds may be stored"; and "any evidence concerning any illegal activity associated with Silk Road."

The second category of information in the Laptop Warrant included "evidence relevant to corroborating the identification of Ulbricht as the Silk Road user 'Dread Pirate Roberts.' " In order to connect Ulbricht with DPR, the Laptop Warrant authorized agents to search for: "any communications or writings by Ulbricht, which may reflect linguistic patterns or idiosyncra[s]ies associated with 'Dread Pirate Roberts,' or political/economic views associated with [DPR] . . ."; "any evidence concerning any computer equipment, software, or usernames used by Ulbricht, to allow comparison with" computer equipment used by DPR; "any evidence concerning Ulbricht's travel or patterns of movement, to allow comparison with patterns of online activity of [DPR]"; "any evidence concerning Ulbricht's technical expertise concerning Tor, Bitcoins," and other computer programming issues; any evidence concerning Ulbricht's attempts to "obtain fake identification documents," use aliases, or otherwise evade law enforcement; and "any other evidence implicating Ulbricht in the subject offenses."

After careful consideration of the warrant, the supporting affidavit, and Ulbricht's arguments, we conclude that the Laptop Warrant did not violate the Fourth Amendment's particularity requirement. We note, at the outset of our review, that the warrant plainly satisfies the basic elements of the particularity requirement as traditionally understood. By incorporating the affidavit by reference, the Laptop Warrant lists the charged crimes, describes the place to be searched, and designates the information to be seized in connection with the specified offenses. Each category of information sought is relevant to Silk Road, DPR's operation thereof, or identifying Ulbricht as DPR. We do not understand Ulbricht's arguments to contest the Laptop Warrant's basic compliance with those requirements.

Rather, Ulbricht's arguments turn on the special problems associated with searches of computers which, as we have acknowledged in prior cases, *Galpin*, 720 F.3d at 447; *Ganias*, 824 F.3d at 217–18, can be particularly intrusive. These arguments merit careful attention. For example, Ulbricht questions the appropriateness of the protocols that the Laptop Warrant instructed officers to use in executing the search. Those procedures included opening or "cursorily reading the first few" pages of files to "determine their precise contents," searching for deliberately hidden files, using "key word searches through all electronic storage areas," and reviewing file "directories" to determine what was relevant. Ulbricht, supported by amicus the National Association of Criminal Defense Lawyers ("NACDL"), argues that the warrant was insufficiently particular because the government and the magistrate judge failed to specify the search terms and protocols ex ante in the warrant.

We cannot agree. As illustrated by the facts of this very case, it will often be impossible to identify in advance the words or phrases that will separate relevant files or documents before the search takes place, because officers cannot readily anticipate how a suspect will store information related to the charged crimes. Files and documents can easily be given misleading or coded names, and words that might be expected to occur in pertinent documents can be encrypted; even very simple codes can defeat a pre-planned word search. For example, at least one of the folders on Ulbricht's computer had a name with the misspelling "aliaces." For a more challenging example, Ulbricht also kept records of certain Tor chats in a file on his laptop that was labeled "mbsobzvkhwx4hmjt."

The agents reasonably anticipated that they would face such problems in this case. Operating Silk Road involved using sophisticated technology to mask its users' identities. Accordingly, although we acknowledge the NACDL's suggestions in its amicus submission for limiting the scope of such search terms, the absence of the proposed limitations does not violate the particularity requirement on the facts of this case. We therefore conclude that, in preparing the Laptop Warrant, "law enforcement agents [did] the best that could reasonably be expected under the circumstances, [had] acquired all the descriptive facts which a reasonable investigation could be expected to cover, and [had] insured that all those facts were included in the warrant." *Galpin*, 720 F.3d at 446 (internal quotation marks omitted).

The fundamental flaw in Ulbricht's (and the NACDL's) argument is that it confuses a warrant's breadth with a lack of particularity. As noted above, breadth and particularity are related but distinct concepts. A warrant may be broad, in that it authorizes the government to search an identified location or object for a wide range of potentially relevant material, without violating the particularity requirement. For example, a warrant may allow the government to search a suspected drug dealer's entire home where there is probable cause to believe that evidence relevant to that activity may be found anywhere in the residence. Similarly, "[w]hen the criminal activity pervades [an] entire business, seizure of all records of the business is appropriate, and broad language used in warrants will not offend the particularity requirements." *U.S. Postal Serv. v. C.E.C. Servs.*, 869 F.2d 184, 187 (2d Cir. 1989). Ulbricht used his laptop to commit the charged offenses by creating and continuing to operate Silk Road. Thus, a broad warrant allowing the government to search his laptop for potentially extensive evidence of those crimes does not offend the Fourth Amendment, as long as that warrant meets the three particularity criteria outlined above.

It is also true that allowing law enforcement to search his writings for linguistic similarities with DPR authorizes a broad search of written materials on Ulbricht's hard drive. That fact, however, does not mean that the warrants violated the Fourth Amendment. The Laptop Warrant clearly explained that the government planned to compare Ulbricht's writings to DPR's posts to confirm that they were the same person, by identifying both linguistic patterns and distinctive shared political or economic views. Ulbricht and the NACDL similarly claim that searching for all evidence of his travel patterns and movement violates the Fourth Amendment's particularity requirement. Again, the warrant explained that it sought information about Ulbricht's travel "to allow comparison with patterns of online activity of 'Dread Pirate Roberts' and any information known about his location at particular times." Thus, the Laptop Warrant connects the information sought to the crimes charged and, more specifically, its relevance to identifying Ulbricht as the perpetrator of those crimes.

We remain sensitive to the difficulties associated with preserving a criminal defendant's privacy while searching through his electronic data and computer hard drives. In the course of searching for information related to Silk Road and DPR, the government may indeed have come across personal documents that were unrelated to Ulbricht's crimes. Such an invasion of a criminal defendant's privacy is inevitable, however, in almost any warranted search because in "searches for papers, it is certain that some innocuous documents will be examined, at least cursorily, in order to determine whether they are, in fact, among those papers authorized to be seized." *Ganias,* 824 F.3d at 211, quoting *Andresen,* 427 U.S. at 482 n.11. The Fourth Amendment limits such "unwarranted intrusions upon privacy," *id.* (internal quotation marks omitted), by requiring a warrant to describe its scope with particularity. The Laptop Warrant satisfied that requirement. Ulbricht has challenged only the facial validity of the Laptop Warrant and not its execution. Because we have no reason to doubt that the officers faithfully executed the warrant, its execution did not result in an undue invasion of Ulbricht's privacy.

Finally, we note that the crimes charged in this case were somewhat unusual. This case does not involve a more typical situation in which officers searched for evidence of a physician's illegal distribution of pain medications, to use the NACDL's example, which may have electronically-stored data associated with the alleged crimes on a hard drive that largely contains non-criminal information. Here the crimes under investigation were committed largely through computers that there was probable cause to believe included the laptop at issue, and the search warrant application gave ample basis for the issuing magistrate judge to conclude that evidence related to Silk Road and Ulbricht's use of the DPR username likely permeated Ulbricht's computer. Thus, given the nature of Ulbricht's crimes and their symbiotic connection to his digital devices, we decline to rethink the well-settled Fourth Amendment principles that the Laptop Warrant may implicate. A future case may require this Court to articulate special limitations on digital searches to effectuate the Fourth Amendment's particularity or reasonableness requirements. Such a case is not before us.

. . . .

II. The District Court's Trial Rulings . . .

Ulbricht contends that he did not receive a fair trial . . . [among other things because of the district court's rulings surrounding corrupt agents Force and Bridges.]

A. Corrupt Agents Force and Bridges

Ulbricht's principal fair trial argument is that the district court erred in numerous ways by preventing him from relying on information related to the corruption of two federal agents, Force and Bridges, involved in the investigation of the Silk Road site. Before trial, the district court (1) precluded Ulbricht from referring at trial to the secret grand jury proceeding against Force; (2) denied Ulbricht discovery related to the Force investigation; and (3) denied Ulbricht an adjournment of the trial until the Force investigation was complete. During trial, the district court excluded as hearsay certain chats that related to Force's illicit use of Silk Road. Finally, Ulbricht learned after trial that the government was investigating a second corrupt agent, Bridges. Ulbricht contends that the failure to disclose Bridges's corruption until after the trial violated *Brady v. Maryland,* 373 U.S. 83 (1963), and that the district court erroneously denied his motion for a new trial on that ground.

Without question, the shocking personal corruption of these two government agents disgraced the agencies for which they worked and embarrassed the many honorable men and women working in those agencies to investigate serious criminal wrongdoing. Even more importantly, when law enforcement officers abuse their offices for personal gain, commit other criminal acts, violate the rights of citizens, or lie under oath, they undermine the public's vital trust in the integrity of law enforcement. They may also compromise the investigations and prosecutions on which they work.

At the same time, the venality of individual agents does not necessarily affect the reliability of the government's evidence in a particular case or become relevant to the adjudication of every case in which the agents participated. Courts are obligated to ensure that probative evidence is disclosed to the defense, carefully evaluated by the court for its materiality to the case, and submitted for the jury's consideration where admissible. But courts must also take care that wrongdoing by investigators that has no bearing on the matter before the court not be used as a diversion from fairly assessing the prosecution's case. Like any other potential evidence, information about police corruption must be evaluated by reference to the ordinary rules of criminal procedure and evidence, a task to which we now turn.

1. Background: Pretrial Disclosure of the Force Investigation

The government disclosed its investigation into Force's corruption to the defense about six weeks before trial. Initially, on November 21, 2014, the government wrote a sealed ex parte letter to the district court seeking permission to disclose to the defense information about the Force grand jury investigation subject to a protective order. The district court granted the application. On December 1, the government provided a copy of the November 21 letter, which otherwise remained sealed, to defense counsel. According to the letter, Force leaked information to DPR in exchange for payment and "corruptly obtain[ed] proceeds from the Silk Road website and convert[ed] them to his personal use." The government then undertook to purge its trial evidence of anything arguably traceable to Force.

Ulbricht moved to unseal the entire November 21 letter so that he could rely on the information in the letter that related to Force's corruption at trial, arguing that the letter included Brady information and that he therefore had a particularized need to disclose the information that outweighed the presumption of grand jury secrecy. He also requested discovery and subpoenas . . . to learn more about the scope of Force's corruption. In the alternative, Ulbricht sought an adjournment of the trial until the Force investigation concluded and information about his corruption might become public through the filing of charges against him. . . .[T]he district court issued a sealed and partially redacted opinion denying all of Ulbricht's requests.

. . . .

2.   Preclusion of Force Investigation Evidence: Rule 6(e)

On appeal, Ulbricht claims that the district court erred in denying his motion to unseal the November 21 letter because he demonstrated a particularized need that rebutted the presumption of secrecy that attaches to grand jury investigations. We disagree.

"[T]he proper functioning of our grand jury system depends upon the secrecy of grand jury proceedings." *Douglas Oil Co. of California v. Petrol Stops Nw.*, 441 U.S. 211, 218 (1979). We have described five rationales for such secrecy:

> (1) To prevent the escape of those whose indictment may be contemplated; (2) to insure the utmost freedom to the grand jury in its deliberations, and to prevent persons subject to indictment or their friends from importuning the grand jurors; (3) to prevent subornation of perjury or tampering with the witnesses who may testify before the grand jury and later appear at the trial of those indicted by it; (4) to encourage free and untrammeled disclosures by persons who have information with respect to the commission of crimes; (5) to protect the innocent accused who is exonerated from disclosure of the fact that he has been under investigation, and from the expense of standing trial where there was no probability of guilt.

In re Grand Jury Subpoena, 103 F.3d 234, 237 (2d Cir. 1996). Rule 6(e)(6) of the Federal Rules of Criminal Procedure implements this policy of secrecy by requiring that "all records, orders, and subpoenas relating to grand jury proceedings [must] be sealed."

Information falling within Rule 6(e)'s protections is entitled to a "presumption of secrecy and closure." *Id.* at 239. To rebut the presumption of secrecy, the party "seeking disclosure [must] show a particularized need that outweighs the need for secrecy." *Id.* (internal quotation marks omitted). To prove a particularized need, parties seeking disclosure must show that the "material they seek is needed to avoid a possible injustice in another judicial proceeding, that the need for disclosure is greater than the need for continued secrecy, and that their request is structured to cover only material so needed." *Id.* (internal quotation marks omitted). "A district court's decision as to whether the burden of showing a particularized interest has been met will be overturned only if the court has abused its discretion." *Id.*

We cannot say that the district court abused its discretion when it denied Ulbricht's request to unseal the November 21 letter discussing the Force grand jury investigation. It is undisputed that the letter contained information related to a grand jury proceeding that, if made public, would disclose matters occurring before the grand jury. Ulbricht did not demonstrate a particularized need for disclosure because he did not show that the need for disclosure was greater than the need for continued secrecy or that a possible injustice would result if the grand jury investigation was not disclosed. Specifically, the district court did not err in concluding that revealing the entire letter could have compromised the Force grand jury investigation in a number of ways. For example, potential co-conspirators might have learned of the investigation and attempted to intimidate witnesses or destroy evidence. The investigation was also likely to garner significant media attention, a fact that might influence witnesses or grand jurors. And, although Force knew of the investigation, revealing its existence to the public might have harmed him if the allegations had ultimately proved untrue. Finally, Ulbricht's request was not structured to cover only the information needed to avoid any possible injustice; instead, he sought to unseal the entire November 21 letter and did not propose a more narrowly tailored disclosure.

In redacted portions of its opinion, the district court also considered ex parte arguments concerning how the Force investigation might be relevant to Ulbricht's defense. In general terms, Ulbricht argued that the agents' corruption was critical to his defense because it would reveal the agents' ability to falsify evidence against him and demonstrate their motive to do so. According to the district court's characterization of his ex parte letters, Ulbricht speculated that Force may have used Curtis Green's (Flush) administrative capabilities to impersonate DPR; Force's corrupt conduct might have demonstrated technical vulnerabilities in the site that would render it susceptible to hacking; and learning that Force had good information about the Silk Road investigation might have caused the true DPR to recruit Ulbricht as his successor.

The district court reasoned that much of the information that might have arguably supported any of those theories was made available to the defense in discovery. The only new information in the November 21 letter concerned the investigation of Force's corruption; the fact of that investigation and its scope does not bolster any of the defense theories that Ulbricht described before the district court or on appeal. That Force was personally corrupt and used his undercover identity to steal money from Silk Road and DPR does not suggest either a motive or an ability on his part to frame Ulbricht as DPR. Absent any explanation of how Force could have orchestrated a massive plant of incriminating information on Ulbricht's personal laptop, his larcenous behavior does not advance the claim that such a frame-up was possible beyond mere speculation. Thus, Ulbricht was equally capable of presenting his various defense theories to the jury with or without the November 21 letter.

The government's commitment to eliminating all evidence that came from Force's work on the Silk Road investigation further undermines Ulbricht's claim that he needed the information to avoid a possible injustice. Had Force been called as a government witness, or had any of the government's evidence relied on his credibility, his character for truthfulness would have been at issue during the trial, and information that impeached his credibility would have become highly relevant. Ulbricht's reliance on the general fact of cooperation among different government agencies and different U.S. Attorney's Offices does not undermine the government's explicit representations that none of the evidence presented at trial derived from Force, and nothing in the record suggests that those representations were false. Ulbricht had no need to rely on the grand jury investigation of Force to attack the credibility of the actual government witnesses or the integrity of its other evidence.

In sum, Ulbricht has not shown that the district court abused its discretion in maintaining the secrecy of the Force grand jury investigation. He did not demonstrate to the district court, and has not demonstrated on appeal, that keeping the November 21 letter under seal resulted in any injustice, or that his need for disclosing the investigation was greater than the need for continued secrecy.

. . . .

CONCLUSION

For the foregoing reasons, we AFFIRM the judgment of the district court in all respects.

NOTES AND QUESTIONS

1. The preceding excerpt from the Second Circuit opinion in *Ulbricht* is not intended to serve as a substantive guide to evidentiary rules, Fourth Amendment jurisprudence, or standards on appeal. It is included here to illustrate the difficulty that the government can face when collecting information needed to obtain a conviction even in the face of overwhelming evidence of illegality. It also provides clear evidence of the fact that regulation of cryptocurrency is not a topic that fits well within a single traditional law school course. It requires some familiarity with a range of federal regulations, and also an understanding of a significant number of issues generally associated with criminal and constitutional law.

2. Are you surprised that the sentencing protocol described in the preceding opinion allowed consideration of crimes for which Ulbricht was never indicted nor convicted? Do you think that two consecutive life sentences are warranted for Ulbricht's convicted offenses?

Part of the argument on appeal that was omitted from the preceding opinion involved the decision to include evidence from some of the parents whose children had died from drug overdoses ostensibly from drugs purchased via Silk Road. At the oral argument on this appeal, the appellate judges appeared to question how fair it was to present this evidence.

. . .[T]he judges criticized a portion of the sentencing hearing in which parents of Silk Road buyers who had died of drug overdoses were called to testify. That testimony "put an extraordinary thumb on the scale that shouldn't be there," argued appellate judge Gerald Lynch. He went on to call the sentence "quite a leap."

"Does this [testimony] create an enormous emotional overload for something that's effectively present in every heroin case?" Lynch asked at one point. "Why does this guy get a life sentence?"[12]

Nonetheless, as the preceding excerpt indicates, the sentence was affirmed, sending Ross Ulbricht to jail for life, with no possibility for parole. The Supreme Court's denial of certiorari in the case was the final nail in the coffin for the once promising young entrepreneur.

3.   Consider the Fourth Amendment and privacy arguments raised by Ulbricht in light of the breadth of the pen/trap warrants order and eventual search warrants. A significant proportion of the information used to link Ulbricht to the criminal enterprise was obtained without a warrant under the pen/trap orders described in the case. The only showing to a judge to obtain those orders was a certification that the information was "relevant" to a pending criminal investigation. In addition, the vagueness of the search warrant's terms allowed essentially unfettered access to the browser history and contents (including deleted files) of Ulbricht's computer. Consider the range of information that could include. Obviously, Ulbricht is far from sympathetic as a defendant. The privacy concerns that he raised, however, deserve reflection. What would the government learn if it could simply access all of your online communications and browsing history? Do you agree that you have no expectation of privacy in regard to which websites you might choose to access in the privacy of your own home?

3.   FURTHER FALLOUT FROM SILK ROAD

As described in the Second Circuit opinion in *Ulbricht,* "Dread Pirate Roberts" was not the only person involved in significant criminal behavior in connection with the operation of the Silk Road. Obviously, everyone who bought or sold illegal items or services was also engaged in criminal behavior. However, there were also significant additional activities that ran afoul of the money laundering laws overseen by FinCEN.

In late March 2015, a criminal complaint issued by the United States District Court for the Northern District of California led to the arrest of two former federal agents who had worked undercover in the Baltimore Silk Road investigation of Ulbricht, former Drug Enforcement Administration agent Carl Mark Force IV and Secret Service agent Shaun Bridges. The agents were alleged to have kept funds that Ulbricht transferred to them in exchange for purported information about the investigation. The agents were charged with wire fraud and money

---

[12]   Andy Greenberg, *Judges Question Ross Ulbricht's Life Sentence in Silk Road Appeal,* WIRED (Oct. 6, 2016) (available online at https://www.wired.com/2016/10/judges-question-ulbrichts-life-sentence-silk-road-appeal/).

laundering. They both pled guilty, and Force was sentenced to 78 months (6 ½ years) with three years of probation while Bridges was sentenced to 71 months.[13]

The Silk Road scandal also resulted in the indictment of Charles Shrem, former vice chairman of the Bitcoin Foundation and chief executive officer of a Bitcoin exchange company, and Robert Faiella, an underground Bitcoin exchanger who went by the moniker "BTCKing," on grounds of operating an unlicensed money transmitting business in violation of 18 U.S. Code § 1960 and conspiracy to commit money laundering in violation of 18 U.S. Code § 1956(h).

Their companies engaged in Bitcoin exchange for the Silk Road website, which essentially means that they facilitated the conversion of fiat currency into Bitcoin, or Bitcoins into fiat currencies. As in *U.S. v. Ulbricht*, 31 F. Supp. 3d 540, 546 (S.D.N.Y. 2014), the defendants in these cases also argued that Bitcoin was not "money" and that therefore operating a Bitcoin exchange could not constitute money transmitting under federal law.

The judge's response to this in the context of the prosecution of Robert Faiella was relatively short and to the point.

UNITED STATES V. FAIELLA
39 F. Supp. 3d 544 (S.D.N.Y. 2014)

Memorandum Order

JED S. RAKOFF, DISTRICT JUDGE.

Defendants in this case are charged in connection with their operation of an underground market in the virtual currency "Bitcoin" via the website "Silk Road." Defendant Faiella is charged with one count of operating an unlicensed money transmitting business in violation of 18 U.S.C. § 1960, and one count of conspiracy to commit money laundering in violation of 18 U.S.C. § 1956(h). Following indictment, Faiella moved to dismiss Count One of the Indictment on three grounds: first, that Bitcoin does not qualify as "money" under Section 1960; second, that operating a Bitcoin exchange does not constitute "transmitting" money under Section 1960; and third that Faiella is not a "money transmitter" under Section 1960. Following full briefing, the Court heard oral argument on August 7, 2014. Upon consideration, the Court now denies defendant Faiella's motion, for the following reasons:

First, "money" in ordinary parlance means "something generally accepted as a medium of exchange, a measure of value, or a means of

---

[13]   For a detailed description of the cases against Force and Bridges, see Cyrus Farivar & Joe Mullin, *Stealing Bitcoins With Badges: How Silk Road's Dirty Cops Got Caught*, ARS TECHNICA (Aug. 17, 2016) (available online at https://arstechnica.com/tech-policy/2016/08/stealing-bitcoins-with-badges-how-silk-roads-dirty-cops-got-caught/).

payment." Merriam-Webster Online, http://www.merriam-webster.com/ dictionary/money (last visited Aug. 18, 2014). As examples of this, Merriam-Webster Online includes "officially coined or stamped metal currency," "paper money," and "money of account"—the latter defined as "a denominator of value or basis of exchange which is used in keeping accounts and for which there may or may not be an equivalent coin or denomination of paper money" Further, the text of Section 1960 refers not simply to "money," but to "funds." In particular, Section 1960 defines "money transmitting" as "transferring *funds* on behalf of the public by any and all means." 18 U.S.C. § 1960(b)(2) (emphasis added). Merriam-Webster Online defines "funds" as "available money" or "an amount of something that is available for use: a supply of something."

Bitcoin clearly qualifies as "money" or "funds" under these plain meaning definitions. Bitcoin can be easily purchased in exchange for ordinary currency, acts as a denominator of value, and is used to conduct financial transactions.

If there were any ambiguity in this regard—and the Court finds none—the legislative history supports application of Section 1960 in this instance. Section 1960 was passed as an anti-money laundering statute, designed "to prevent the movement of funds in connection with drug dealing." Congress was concerned that drug dealers would turn increasingly to "nonbank financial institutions" to "convert street currency into monetary instruments" in order to transmit the proceeds of their drug sales. Section 1960 was drafted to address this "gaping hole in the money laundering deterrence effort." Indeed, it is likely that Congress designed the statute to keep pace with such evolving threats, which is precisely why it drafted the statute to apply to any business involved in transferring "funds . . . by any and all means." 18 U.S.C. § 1960(b)(2).

Second, Faiella's activities on Silk Road constitute "transmitting" money under Section 1960. Defendant argues that while Section 1960 requires that the defendant sell money transmitting services to others for a profit, see 31 C.F.R. § 1010.100(ff)(5)(1)(2013) (defining "money transmission services" to require transmission of funds to "another location or person"), Faiella merely sold Bitcoin as a product in and of itself. But, as set forth in the Criminal Complaint that initiated this case, the Government alleges that Faiella received cash deposits from his customers and then, after exchanging them for Bitcoins, transferred those funds to the customers' accounts on Silk Road. These were, in essence, transfers to a third-party agent, Silk Road, for Silk Road users did not have full control over the Bitcoins transferred into their accounts. Rather, Silk Road administrators could block or seize user funds. Thus, the Court finds that in sending his customers' funds to Silk Road, Faiella "transferred" them to others for a profit.

Third, Faiella clearly qualifies as a "money transmitter" for purposes of Section 1960. The Financial Crimes Enforcement Network ("FinCEN") has issued guidance specifically clarifying that virtual currency exchangers constitute "money transmitters" under its regulations. See FinCEN Guidance at 1 ("[A]n administrator or exchanger [of virtual currency] is an MSB [money services business] under FinCEN's regulations, specifically, a money transmitter, unless a limitation to or exemption from the definition applies to the person." (emphasis in original)). FinCEN has further clarified that the exception on which defendant relies for its argument that Faiella is not a "money transmitter," 31 C.F.R. § 1010.100(ff)(5)(ii)(F), is inapplicable. See FinCEN Guidance at 4 ("It might be argued that the exchanger is entitled to the exemption from the definition of 'money transmitter' for persons involved in the sale of goods or the provision of services. . . . However, this exemption does not apply when the only services being provided are money transmission services.").

Finally, defendant claims that applying Section 1960 to a Bitcoin exchange business would run afoul of the rule of lenity, constituting such a novel and unanticipated construction of the statute as to operate like an ex post facto law in violation of the Due Process Clause. The Supreme Court has repeatedly stated that the rule of lenity is "reserved . . . for those situations in which a reasonable doubt persists about a statute's intended scope even after resort to 'the language and structure, legislative history, and motivating policies' of the statute'" Moskal v. United States, 498 U.S. 103, 108 (1990). Here, as noted, there is no such irreconcilable ambiguity requiring resort to the rule of lenity. Further, defendant's argument that this case constitutes ex post facto judicial lawmaking that violates the Due Process Clause is undermined by Faiella's own statements to the operator of Silk Road that Bitcoin exchanges have "to be licensed," and that law enforcement agencies might "seize [his] funds."

For the reasons above, defendant's motion to dismiss is denied.

Some observations about how this all played out are important. Note that these cases involved criminal enforcement actions brought by the Department of Justice on behalf of the United States. Nonetheless, at the heart of each prosecution was the allegation that the actions of the defendants violated federal money transmitter that are regulated under the auspices of FinCEN. FinCEN partners with federal law enforcement in these matters, and while the details of the investigation of any criminal action are confidential, it is clear that FinCEN's expertise and assistance in these prosecutions is an important part of successful prosecutions.

For those who wonder what happened to all the Bitcoins that were in transit, or that were held by Ulbricht, on June 23, 2013, it was first reported that the DEA had seized 11.02 Bitcoins, then worth a total of

$814, which the media suspected was a result of a Silk Road honeypot sting.[14] At the time of Ulbricht's arrest, the FBI seized 26,000 Bitcoins from accounts on Silk Road, worth approximately $3.6 million at the time. The FBI announced that it would hold those coins until the conclusion of Ulbricht's trial. In October of that year, the FBI reported that it had seized an additional 144,000 Bitcoins, then worth approximately $28.5 million, and that those Bitcoins had belonged to Ulbricht. The seized Bitcoins were eventually sold at auction in lots during 2014 and 2015 for just over $48 million (an average of $334 per coin). Ironically, if the federal government had waited until late 2017 to sell the assets, it might have netted hundreds of millions of dollars more, as the average trading price of Bitcoin between October and December of 2017 never dropped below $4,000 per coin and went as high as $20,000 per Bitcoin.

4. SILK ROAD'S SUCCESSORS

Closing down Silk Road and incarcerating "Dread Pirate Roberts" for life were significant milestones for federal law enforcement, but they are far from the end of the story or the problems that crypto has posed for FinCEN. In May of 2015, THE ECONOMIST reported that "closing down the web's biggest drug shop has simply cleared the way for competitors."[15] In 2017, the government shutdown dark web marketplaces AlphaBay and Hansa. AlphaBay had been described as the largest online marketplace for illegal goods prior to its closure on July 4, 2017, while Hansa was reportedly the third largest then in operation. Both of those sites had grown to prominence following the closure of Silk Road, with AlphaBay in particular growing tremendously large. When Silk Road went dark, it had approximately 14,000 online sales offers; by comparison AlphaBay had more than 100,000 listings when it was shuttered.

Acting FBI Director Andrew McCabe compared shutting these websites to playing whack-a-mole, but also cautioned that this is simply the name of the game. As reported by many sources, McCabe acknowledged the difficulty of law enforcement's task. "Our critics will say as we shutter one site, another will emerge . . . But that is the nature of criminal work. It never goes away, you have to constantly keep at it, and you have to use every tool in your toolbox."[16]

---

[14]   A honeypot sting involves a fake site set up to gather intelligence, and in this instance apparently involved FBI representatives who purported to be interested in selling drugs on the site.

[15]   *Silk Road successors*, THE ECONOMIST (May 29, 2015) (available online at https://www.economist.com/graphic-detail/2015/05/29/silk-road-successors), listing sources such as Agora, Pandora and Evolution as illicit websites that each provide thousands of listings of illegal drugs.

[16]   Tom Winder, *AlphaBay, Hansa Shut, but Drug Dealers Flock to Dark Web DreamMarket*, NBC NEWS (July 20, 2017) (available online at https://www.nbcnews.com/news/us-news/alphabay-hansa-shut-drug-dealers-flock-dark-web-dreammarket-n785001).

CHAPTER 5

ILLEGAL MONEY TRANSMITTERS

■ ■ ■

1. BACKGROUND REGULATION

As the preceding chapter should illustrate, FinCEN has significant motivation to be active in the crypto space. In the case of Silk Road (and many other dark web marketplaces), transactions are often structured in Bitcoin or other cryptocurrencies in an effort to avoid detection and identification. This can facilitate both money laundering in a traditional sense and also reverse money laundering, where legitimately derived funds are funneled into criminal enterprises. This is, however, not the only kind of activity that has sparked FinCEN's interest.

Remember that FinCEN not only helps investigate money launderers, but also oversees the regulation of money transmitters who are in a position to provide information about money laundering activities. FinCEN has consistently taken the position that any person assisting others in the transfer of funds requires a money transmitter license. FinCEN treats cryptoassets that are convertible into real world currency at any point as "funds," and therefore companies that facilitate the transfer of convertible cryptoassets from one person to another are "money services businesses" (MSBs) which are required to possess a money transmitter license. According to FinCEN, exchangers and administrators of cryptocurrencies are expected to register with FinCEN as an MSB, and any such firm working with cryptocurrencies is expected to comply with anti-money laundering (AML) and Know-Your-Customer (KYC) regulations.

This means that cryptoasset platforms designed to facilitate the exchange of cryptoassets, such as Binance, CoinEgg, BitForex, BitMart, or Coinbase Pro to name a few,[1] are expected to register with FinCEN if they do business with U.S. customers. In addition, they must make regular reports, including Suspicious Activity Reports (SARs) on customer transactions that exceed specified thresholds. This kind of cryptocurrency exchange must also allow the federal government to access its records, and

---

[1]   CoinMarketCap, referenced in many places in this book, contains a list of coins and tokens and their market capitalizations. It also maintains a list of crypto exchanges, arranged by trading volume. The list can be found at COINMARKETCAP.COM (available online at https://coinmarketcap.com/rankings/exchanges/) [image archived at https://perma.cc/ABW4-NP7J on July 8, 2019]. As of that date, this particular list was still in its beta version. CoinMarketCap.com has announced updates to its services, so live images of the site after 2019 may look different.

FinCEN must be able to perform random audits to ensure that the company is complying with regulatory requirements.

As was the case for money launderers, the regulators became most interested in crypto exchanges when problems arose. One of the earliest incidents involving a virtual currency exchange involved Mt. Gox, a Bitcoin exchange based in Japan.

2. MT. GOX

Mt. Gox was created in 2010 by a talented U.S. programmer, Jed McCaleb (who will be mentioned again in the next section of this chapter for his role in founding Ripple). The name "Mt. Gox" somewhat oddly stands for "Magic: The Gathering Online eXchange" in an apparent reference to the popular trading card game created by Richard Garfield. Mt. Gox was purchased by Mark Karpelés (a French developer and Bitcoin enthusiast)[2] in March 2011.

Shortly after being sold to Karpelés, the first sign of trouble occurred for Mt. Gox. The exchange was hacked in June 2011, with evidence pointing to a computer belonging to a company auditor being compromised. This incident involved an artificial alteration in the nominal value of Bitcoin down to one cent, followed by the transfer of an estimated 2,000 Bitcoins from customer accounts at that price. Those coins were then sold at the actual market price.[3] In addition, approximately 650 Bitcoins were purchased by Mt. Gox customers at the deflated price, and none of those were ever recovered. In response, Mt. Gox adopted new security measures, including placing a substantial amount of its Bitcoin holdings in "cold storage," meaning that the records associated with ownership of those coins were not connected to the internet and thus not subject to theft in this way.

Despite this setback, by 2013 Mt. Gox had become the largest Bitcoin exchange in the world. This happened just as the public interest in the coin was growing, and the price was increasing rapidly (growing from approximately $13 per coin in January of 2013 to a peak of $1,200 by June of that year).

The outward success of the exchange masked some serious internal issues. Apparently, or at least according to varied reports from former employees following the organization's eventual collapse, the business was disorganized and poorly run, with a number of serious issues relating to security, website source codes, and business operations. At about this same

---

[2]   Karpelés is also the individual that Ross Ulbricht claimed was the "real" Dread Pirate Roberts in the Silk Road enterprise. For a discussion of these claims, see chapter 4 and the discussion of *United States v. Ulbricht,* 858 F.3d 71 (2d Cir. 2017).

[3]   Reports from that time suggest that the market price of the coins would have been around $10 per BTC. BitcoinWiki, *Bitcoin History* (available online at https://en.bitcoinwiki.org/wiki/Bitcoin_history#Bitcoin_in_2011).

time, and also pointing to problems with the way in which Mt. Gox conducted business, the exchange was sued by CoinLab, Inc. for $75 million arising out of an alleged breach of contract.

A. THE COINLAB LAWSUIT

The complaint in *CoinLab, Inc. v. Mt. Gox* was filed in the U.S. District Court for the Western District of Washington on May 2, 2013 by Breskin, Johnson & Townsend, PLLC. The allegations of the complaint establish the legal theories on which CoinLab intended to proceed against Mt. Gox. (Note that the complaint was subsequently amended as discovery filled in additional details, but the initial complaint is indicative of the claims that might have been pursued had Mt. Gox not chosen to declare bankruptcy.)

The contents of the complaint (minus certain formatting as well as the signature blocks, headings, and footers) are reprinted below with permission from Roger M. Townsend, who signed the complaint on behalf of his firm and his client, CoinLab:

COINLAB, INC. V. MT. GOX KK
No. 2:13-cv-00777 (W.D. Wash. 2013)

COMPLAINT JURY TRIAL DEMANDED

COMES NOW, Plaintiff CoinLab, Inc. ("CoinLab"), by and through their undersigned attorneys, brings this action against the Defendants, Mt. Gox KK, a Japanese corporation ("Mt. Gox"), and Tibanne KK, a Japanese corporation ("Tibanne"). Plaintiff states and alleges as follows:

I. INTRODUCTION

1. CoinLab brings this suit against Mt. Gox to remedy breach of the parties' exclusive license agreement for the United States and Canada. Both parties are among the world's largest providers of technology and services for the digital currency Bitcoin. In November 2012, the parties entered into a contract under which Mt. Gox granted CoinLab access to Mt. Gox computer servers and the exclusive right to certain intellectual property necessary for CoinLab to provide digital currency exchange services to North American customers. CoinLab offered its credibility, market insights, relationships with established banks and investors, and intellectual property and agreed to manage and market the exchange services in North America.

2. Mt. Gox has willfully failed to perform its obligations under this contract. Mt. Gox has continued to market to customers in North America and has accepted business from customers there. Mt. Gox has also failed to provide CoinLab with account reconciliation data, server access, and other information promised in the agreement that is essential for CoinLab to market exchange services and service its customers as contemplated in the

agreement. These breaches have caused CoinLab to lose customers and threaten to cause substantial damage to CoinLab's business. As a result, CoinLab brings this action for breach of contract and related claims.

II. JURISDICTION AND VENUE

3. Jurisdiction is proper in this Court under 28 U.S.C. § 1332. Plaintiff CoinLab is a resident of Delaware and Washington State. Defendants Mt. Gox and Tibanne are residents of Japan. This is an action for damages in excess of $75,000,000.00 . . . .

4. CoinLab is a Delaware corporation with its principal place of business in King County Washington.

5. . . . Mt. Gox and Tibanne (collectively "Defendants") are corporations organized under the laws of Japan with their principal places of business in Tokyo, Japan.

6. On or about November 22, 2012, Defendants and CoinLab entered into a fully integrated "Exclusive License Agreement for the USA & Canada agreement" (the "Agreement"). A true and accurate copy of the Agreement is attached hereto as Exhibit A.

7. The Agreement provides that the Defendants "irrevocably consent to the personal jurisdiction of and venue in the state and federal courts located in King County, Washington with respect to any action, claim or proceeding arising out of or relating to this Agreement."

8. The Agreement provides that it shall be governed, construed and interpreted in accordance with the laws of the State of Washington.

III. FACTS

A. The Bitcoin Market

9. Bitcoin is the most successful digital currency in the world. Bitcoins were first described in a paper published on the Internet in 2008 and were introduced to the market in early 2009. Bitcoins are a currency that is not issued or directly overseen by any government, but that is instead managed through a peer-to-peer network operating over the Internet. Bitcoins use complex cryptography to protect the security of the Bitcoin system and prevent counterfeiting.

10. When first introduced, a single Bitcoin was valued at less than one penny. The value of a Bitcoin has increased substantially since introduction. At times a single Bitcoin has been valued as high as $266. Bitcoins may be used to purchase goods and services through a number of websites or from any merchant that accepts Bitcoins.

11. A company offering Bitcoin exchange services will trade "fiat" or "sovereign" based currency such as U.S. dollars for Bitcoins and also trade Bitcoins for U.S. dollars or other currencies. The annualized exchange

volume for Bitcoin exchanges has grown to over $12 billion/year as of April 2013.

12. While Bitcoins are not a traditional fiat based currency, they are subject to regulation by United States Financial Crimes Enforcement Network ("FinCEN").

13. In March 2013, FinCEN issued regulatory guidance for exchanges dealing in digital currency such as Bitcoins.

B. CoinLab and Mt. Gox Provide Bitcoin Services.

14. The Defendants provide Bitcoin exchange services via the Internet. They operate an interactive website available at <https://mtgox. com/> (the "the Mt. Gox website") which accepts orders for Bitcoin exchanges. Through the Mt. Gox website, users can exchange currency for Bitcoins. Mt. Gox has been widely reported to be the largest operating Bitcoin exchange in the world.

15. CoinLab is engaged in the operation and development of Bitcoin software and technology products, services and platforms. CoinLab is prepared to provide Bitcoin exchange services directly to customers in the United States and Canada. CoinLab has established relationships with banks in the United States that will allow CoinLab to operate an exchange in North America. Because of its relationships with these financial institutions and respected venture capitalists and because of its adherence to applicable regulatory frameworks, CoinLab has established a very positive reputation in the Bitcoin business community.

16. CoinLab is registered with FinCEN to provide Bitcoin exchange services in the United States and has fully complied with FinCEN's March 2013 guidance for digital currency exchanges.

C. The Agreement Provides CoinLab With Exclusive Rights.

17. On November 22, 2012 Mt. Gox and CoinLab entered into the Agreement to service the Bitcoin exchange market in a mutually beneficial manner that provided for stability and liquidity in that market.

18. Mt. Gox has no established banking relationships in North America and is unable to process transactions through banks in the United States or Canada. Through the Agreement, Mt. Gox greatly increased its ability to service the North American market.

19. Through the Agreement, Mt. Gox was enriched through its relationship with CoinLab and CoinLab's intellectual property, expertise, standing in the Bitcoin ecosystem, and relationships.

20. Pursuant to the Agreement, Defendants granted CoinLab an exclusive license in the North American market to use the Defendants' software and other intellectual property in providing digital currency exchange services (the "Licensed Materials").

21. The Agreement further provides that Defendants shall not grant anyone else the right to use the Licensed Materials to provide Bitcoin exchange services anywhere in the United States or Canada.

22. In consideration for this exclusive license and promise of cooperation, CoinLab promised, among other things, to assume responsibility for managing and marketing the exchange services in the United States and Canada. CoinLab also offered Mt. Gox the ability to service North American customers in a manner that it could not otherwise achieve.

23. Failure to comply with the exclusivity provisions of the Agreement is expressly specified to be a material breach of the Agreement.

D. The Defendants Have Breached The Exclusivity Provisions.

24. Defendants have breached the exclusivity provisions of the Agreement by directly servicing customers in the United States and Canada since the Agreement took effect.

25. The Agreement provides that beach of the exclusivity provisions of the Agreement alone provides for liquidated damages in the amount of $50,000,000.00 as a nonexclusive remedy. The liquidated damages clause was defined at the time of the Agreement because of the uncertain nature of the Bitcoin exchange market and likely underestimates the actual damages incurred by Bitcoin as a result of Mt. Gox's breach of the exclusivity provisions of the Agreement.

26. Defendants have, in email and other written exchanges, and in public statements to the press acknowledged that they have directly serviced customers in the United States and Canada since entering the Agreement. This conduct constitutes a breach of the Agreement, including the exclusivity provisions in the Agreement.

E. The Defendants Have Breached Other Provisions Of The Agreement.

27. The Agreement further provides for a transition period whereby United States and Canadian customers are transitioned from Mt. Gox to CoinLab by March 22, 2013. Mt. Gox is required to cooperate with CoinLab to transfer North American customers, defined as "CoinLab Customers" in the Agreement, from Mt. Gox to CoinLab.

28. Mt. Gox has failed to cooperate in facilitating the timely and seamless transfer of CoinLab Customers to Coinlab since the Agreement took effect.

29. Among other things, Defendants agreed to provide necessary technology, software, and know-how to CoinLab during the transition period and to establish promised connections from CoinLab's computer network to Mt. Gox's computer network.

30. Defendants have breached their promises to provide necessary technology, software, and know-how to CoinLab and have refused or failed to establish promised connections from CoinLab's computer network to Mt. Gox's computer network.

31. In the Agreement, Mt. Gox promised to deliver all passwords, Yubikeys, administrative logins and any other security information required for CoinLab to assume operation of the Bitcoin exchange services for customers in the United States and Canada if Mt. Gox has a service interruption or is otherwise unable to maintain its exchange.

32. Despite repeated requests to do so, Mt. Gox has failed to deliver all passwords, Yubikeys, administrative logins and any other security information required so that CoinLab may assume operation of the Bitcoin exchange services for customers in the United States and Canada in case of a service interruption.

33. The Agreement requires that Mt. Gox shall make available to CoinLab on-demand and read-only access to Mt. Gox's databases and other related records and data pertaining to any and all accounts for customers in the United States and Canada.

34. Despite repeated requests to do so, Mt. Gox has failed to make available to CoinLab on-demand and read-only access to Mt. Gox's databases and other related records and data pertaining to any and all accounts for customers in the United States and Canada.

35. The Agreement provides for a revenue share for customers in the United States and Canada (defined as "CoinLab Customers") at different levels, depending upon the date that the customer began using Defendants' services to exchange Bitcoins.

36. Defendants have failed to comply with the revenue share requirements set forth in the Agreement and timely remit funds due to Coinlab.

37. Pursuant to the Agreement, Mt. Gox agreed to deposit Bitcoin and other funds (however denominated) of CoinLab Customers in an account or accounts controlled by CoinLab (the "Liquidity Funds") in accordance with CoinLab's instructions on transaction types, timing of transactions and wire transfer or other deposit instructions.

38. Mt. Gox has failed to timely deposit Liquidity Funds in the manner instructed by CoinLab.

39. Pursuant to the Agreement, the Parties were required to reconcile revenue and customer trade imbalances on a weekly or more frequent basis.

40. Defendants have failed to timely reconcile revenue and customer trade imbalances.

41. The Agreement provides that CoinLab shall, for a period of five (5) years following termination, receive trailing revenues for users in the United States or Canada that use the Mt. Gox website or otherwise are serviced by Defendants for purposes of operating a Bitcoin exchanges or other purposes.

42. CoinLab stood ready to perform its obligations under the Agreement at all times and informed the Defendants of this fact.

43. At all times during the Agreement, CoinLab has complied with its representations and warranties under the Agreement.

44. CoinLab has, at all times during the term of the Agreement, operated in compliance with all applicable laws.

45. CoinLab has provided assurances of compliance with its representations and warranties and reasonable course of action for compliance with potential future changes in regulatory requirements applicable to operation of a Bitcoin exchange.

[Allegations relating to specific causes of action for Breach of Contract, Breach of the Implied Duty of Good Faith and Fair Dealing, and claims seeking an Accounting are omitted.]

NOTES AND QUESTIONS

1.   In most law student texts, the emphasis is on reported decisions. This is an excerpt not from a judicial opinion, but a complaint drafted by attorneys seeking redress for a client. What was the basis of CoinLab's complaint? Which of the facts included in the complaint are background information to help frame the issues, and which are the essential facts that support the legal theories upon which the case was brought? Why were so many background facts deemed necessary?

2.   The complaint illustrates one possible source of redress for problems such as those created when a crypto-based business fails to live up to its contractual obligations. In cases where private causes of action exist, there may be little reason for heavy-handed regulatory oversight. On the other hand, there are limits on private claims. After reading through the complaint, can you think of reasons why a regulatory response might still be required? Are there potential advantages to regulatory oversight that private litigation cannot provide? At this point, what sort of regulatory oversight would you think could be important?

B. INVESTIGATION BY THE U.S. DEPARTMENT OF HOMELAND SECURITY

Although it was not yet public information, by mid-2013 the U.S. Department of Homeland Security was also actively investigating a Mt. Gox subsidiary operating an unregistered money transmitter business in the U.S. In June 2013, the government obtained a warrant to seize money from the Mt. Gox U.S. subsidiary as well as Karpelés' personal accounts. The basis for the warrant was that the U.S. company had violated the BSA by failing to register as a money transmitter business as required by federal law.

The contents of the warrant, which led to the seizure of $5,000,000 by the U.S. investigators, are reprinted on the following page.

PRELIMINARY NOTES AND QUESTIONS

1. Civil forfeitures have recently been in the news. In February 2019, the U.S. Supreme Court ruled that the Constitution limits the ability of states to seize cash and other property used to commit crimes. *Timbs v. Indiana,* 586 U.S. ___, 139 S. Ct. 682 (2019). In that case, the state of Indiana had attempted to seize a $42,000 Land Rover from Tyson Timbs, a small-time drug offender, after a guilty plea in connection with the sale of $225 of heroin. The trial court and court of appeals in Indiana both held that the civil forfeiture would be disproportionate to the offense, but the Indiana Supreme Court reversed, on the grounds that the Excessive Fines Clause did not apply to the states. On certiorari to the U.S. Supreme Court, the Court reversed, holding that the Eighth Amendment's Excessive Fines Clause was incorporated and applicable to the states under the Fourteenth Amendment's Due Process Clause. The case was therefore remanded back to the Indiana Supreme court.

While it is true that individual clients of Mt. Gox may have lost millions of dollars, and it is true that the money seized by the U.S. investigators pursuant to the following warrant may have been used to commit a crime (operating an unregistered money transmitter business), would the seizure of this amount of money be disproportionate to the "crime"? If so, what remedy might Mt. Gox or Karpelés have?

2. Note how general the warrant is. What showing was made in order to seize the bank accounts? How would Mt. Gox's or Karpelés' attorneys formulate a response to a warrant like this?

3. Note the name of the special agent to whom the warrant is issued. Where have you seen that name before (in this course)?

JUN 1 9 2013

AT BALTIMORE

UNITED STATES DISTRICT COURT
DISTRICT OF MARYLAND

In the Matter of the Seizure of
(Address or brief description of property to be seized)

The contents of one
Wells Fargo Bank account, and
up to $50,000 in another Wells
Fargo Bank account.

SEIZURE WARRANT
CASE NUMBER:

13-1085SAG

TO: Shaun Bridges, Special Agent, United States Secret Service, and any Authorized Officer of the United States:

An Affidavit having been made before me by Shaun Bridges, Special Agent, United States Secret Service, who has reason to believe that in Maryland, and elsewhere there is now certain property which is subject to forfeiture to the United States, namely (describe the property to be seized)

the contents of Wells Fargo Bank account 7657841313 in the name of
Mutum Sigillum LLC and up to $50,000 contained in
Wells Fargo Bank account 6836757515 in the name of Mark Karpeles.

I am satisfied that the affidavit establishes probable cause to believe that the property so described is subject to seizure and forfeiture and that grounds exist for the issuance of this seizure warrant.

YOU ARE HEREBY AUTHORIZED to seize within fourteen (14) days, the property specified, serving this warrant and making the seizure in the daytime - 6:00 AM to 10:00 PM - leaving a copy of this warrant and receipt for the property seized, and prepare a written inventory of the property seized and promptly return this warrant to any U.S. Magistrate Judge, as required by law. Service of this seizure warrant may be made by facsimile, provided that a hard copy is thereafter served by regular mail, overnight mail, or personal delivery.

Issued May 9, 2013, at Baltimore, Maryland, by
       Date Issued

Honorable Stephanie A. Gallagher
United States Magistrate Judge

C. "TEMPORARY" SHUTDOWN OF MT. GOX LEADING TO BANKRUPTCY

As a result of the federal investigation into its business, Mt. Gox announced a "temporary," one-month suspension of withdrawals from the exchange in U.S. dollars. Although the suspension was supposed to last for a single month, customers at this time were reporting delays of up to 3 months in withdrawing cash from their accounts. Few withdrawals in U.S.

dollars were successfully completed. These problems resulted in Mt. Gox losing its place as the largest Bitcoin exchange. This was a serious setback to a company that at one time had reported owning 100,000 Bitcoins, worth approximately $50 million at the time.[4] By the end of 2013 there were two other exchanges reporting larger trading volumes.

The long-term fallout from the U.S. government investigation of Mt. Gox and the seizure of its assets in this country was profound. On February 7, 2014, Mt. Gox halted all Bitcoin withdrawals. Initially, the company claimed that this was to be a brief hiatus in operations needed "to obtain a clear technical view of the currency process."[5] The remainder of the month resulted in total uncertainty and confusion, until the exchange abruptly suspended all trading and went offline on February 24. An internal corporate document, leaked that same week, reported a theft of almost 750,000 Bitcoins belonging to customers as well as the loss of an additional 100,000 coins that belonged to Mt. Gox itself. This theft left the exchange insolvent, and the next day, on February 28, 2013, Mt. Gox filed for bankruptcy in Japan. Two weeks later, a U.S. bankruptcy filing followed.

The precise details about what happened and when those events took place may never be unraveled,[6] but subsequent investigations have suggested that hackers actually started the massive theft as early as September of 2011. Some evidence suggests that as many as 80,000 Bitcoins had been stolen even before Mark Karpelés bought the company from Jed McCaleb in 2011. As a result of the extended period in which these thefts took place, it appears that Mt. Gox had been insolvent for almost two years before it actually declared bankruptcy. In fact, it had lost most of its Bitcoins by mid-2013.

Although somewhat technical, because it is relevant to how regulators perceive and react to crypto operations, it is worth looking a little more closely at the mechanics of how Mt. Gox went so quickly from being the largest Bitcoin exchange to filing for bankruptcy protection. It appears that at some point prior to September, 2011, the Mt. Gox private key was in an unencrypted file. Someone (either a hacker or insider) obtained a copy of that unencrypted key presumably by copying a wallet.dat file. At that

---

[4]   For more details about the Mt. Gox exchange and its fall from grace, see Robert McMillan & Cade Metz, *The Rise and Fall of the World's Largest Bitcoin Exchange*, WIRED (Nov. 6, 2013, 6:30 AM) (available online at https://www.wired.com/2013/11/mtgox/), & Robert McMillan, *The Inside Story of Mt. Gox, Bitcoin's $460 Million Disaster*, WIRED (Mar. 3, 2014, 6:30 AM) (available online at https://www.wired.com/2014/03/Bitcoin-exchange/).

[5]   Andrew Norry, *The History of the Mt Gox Hack: Bitcoin's Biggest Heist*, BLOCKONOMI (Nov. 19, 2018) (available online at https://blockonomi.com/mt-gox-hack/).

[6]   For a fascinating look at attempts to revive Mt. Gox, and claims that the CoinLab lawsuit referenced earlier in this chapter is meritless and actively interfering with the possibility of justice for original clients of the exchange, see Josh Constine, *The Plot to Revive Mt. Gox and Repay Victims' Bitcoin*, TECHCRUNCH (Feb. 2019) (available online at https://techcrunch.com/2019/02/06/the-plot-to-revive-mt-gox-and-repay-victims-bitcoin/).

point, someone or perhaps multiple individuals, had unauthorized access to Mt. Gox's private key.

To understand what that means, remember that cryptoassets such as Bitcoins have no tangible existence and instead are records maintained in digital form on the Blockchain. "Ownership" is based on records that are stored electronically in a web-based wallet, confirmable by participants in the blockchain network through use of cryptographic keys. The wallet stores secure digital codes, known as private keys, which are used to show ownership of a public digital code (the public key). The public key is shown to the network in order to verify transactions involving that wallet. Because possession of the private key allows access to currency addresses needed to effectuate transactions in the recorded cryptoasset, anyone with the private key can cause the accessed wallets to transfer cryptoassets that it holds.

In this case, once the file containing the private key was accessed, whether by a hacker(s) or insider(s), the private key gave access to Bitcoins held by Mt. Gox. Once the wallets "holding" Bitcoins were accessed, the hacker or insider could simply cipher Bitcoins gradually from the wallets associated with those private keys. Mt. Gox appeared to be oblivious to the thefts for some time, apparently interpreting transfers as the shifting of deposits to more secure systems.

In March 2014, Mt. Gox reported to the bankruptcy court that it had found 200,000 Bitcoins. They had apparently been stored in older digital wallets that had been in use prior to June 2011. The newly discovered Bitcoins were placed in trust for the benefit of creditors during the bankruptcy.

The Japanese court appointed a trustee to track down assets and investigate claims. On May 25, 2016, the trustee announced that 24,750 claims, primarily from former Mt. Gox customers, had been approved. The trustee froze the value of the Bitcoins that had been hacked at $483 (the market value at the time of the bankruptcy), thus setting total claims at approximately $432 million.[7] This has created a highly unusual situation because of the drastically higher trading price of Bitcoin in today's markets. The bankruptcy estate holds nearly 170,000 each of Bitcoins and Bitcoin Cash. As of January 1, 2019, the market value of Bitcoin was just over $3741 and Bitcoin Cash was trading at about $162. Thus, even though the value of these assets is down considerably from the billions that those cryptoassets would have worth at the height of the Bitcoin "craze," the

---

[7]   For more information about the bankruptcy, and the assets subsequently determined to be held by the estate, see Adrianne Jeffries, *Inside the Bizarre Upside-Down Bankruptcy of Mt. Gox,* THE VERGE (Mar. 22, 2018) (available online at https://www.theverge.com/2018/3/22/171514 30/bankruptcy-mt-gox-liabilities-Bitcoin).

estate is still worth $663.5 million, more than the total of outstanding claims.

As a result of the fact that Mt. Gox is no longer technically insolvent, the Tokyo District Court halted the bankruptcy proceedings in June of 2018, beginning a process known in Japan as civil rehabilitation.[8] At that time, the Bitcoins held in trust were worth about $1.2 billion. The civil rehabilitation process was still continuing as of the end of 2018, with claimants being given to December 26, 2018 to file rehabilitation claims.[9]

D. *GREENE V. MT. GOX*

The failure of Mt. Gox to return investments to its clients led to private litigation in the U.S. On February 27, 2014, an individual Bitcoin owner, Gregory Greene, brought a class action against Mt. Gox, Inc. (a Delaware subsidiary of the exchange); Mt. Gox KK (the Japanese corporation operating the exchange), and Mark Karpelés, in the U.S. District Court for the Northern District of Illinois.

The complaint itself recognized the need to educate the judge about the unusual nature of the case, and the first several paragraphs therefore focused on describing Bitcoin, in the context of Mt. Gox's alleged fraud. After explaining the history of Bitcoin, the complaint introduced how "Bitcoin exchanges" (including Mt. Gox) generally function. It then concluded that "while it was relatively easy to join the Mt. Gox exchange and deposit cash and Bitcoins, withdrawing one's money or Bitcoins" became impossible because of the way in which Mt. Gox operated. (Complaint ¶ 4.) The initial explanation was that withdrawals were halted in February 2014 because of a "computer bug." This burgeoned into reports of a multi-year security breach at the exchange.

The essence of Greene's complaint, brought on his own behalf and on behalf of similarly situated persons, was that the exchange "intentionally and knowingly failed to provide its users with the level of security protection for which they paid." (Complaint ¶ 5.) Various details about the

---

[8] Civil rehabilitation became appropriate when the massive increase in Bitcoin value left Mt. Gox with enough value to repay all creditors, whose claims had been frozen at much lower rates. For more information about these valuations, see Jen Wieczner, *$1 Billion Bitcoins Lost in Mt. Gox Hack to Be Returned to Victims*, FORTUNE (June 22, 2018) (available online at http://fortune.com/2018/06/22/Bitcoin-price-mt-gox-trustee/).

[9] In early 2019, the prospect for payouts looked good, although no payments had been made as of January, 2019. Calogero Boccadutri, *Italy: A Treasure For Former Mt. Gox Clients*, MONDAQ (Jan. 22, 2019) (available online at http://www.mondaq.com/italy/x/773564/fin+tech/A+Treasure+for+Former+Mt+Gox+Clients). Despite optimistic estimates that payments were inching forward, in April 2019, the head of the largest organized creditor group resigned, claiming that the payouts could take up to two more years. Nikhilesh De, *Advocate for Mt Gox Creditors Quits, Saying Bitcoin Payouts Could Take Years*, COINDESK (Ap. 9, 2019) (available online at https://www.coindesk.com/coinlabs-mt-gox-claim-may-hold-up-payouts-for-another-2-years). *Accord* Alex Cohen, *'CoinLab is a Big Stopping Block': Mark Karpeles Talks Mt. Gox Creditor Claims and Life after Trial*, COINTELEPGRAPH (Jun. 16, 2019) [archived at https://perma.cc/S8EW-SKUR].

Mt. Gox operation were included as the backbone of the complaint, including its claim that it was the "world's most established Bitcoin exchange," handling "over 80% of all Bitcoin trade" worldwide. (Complaint ¶ 18.) The Complaint also referenced Mt. Gox's claim that it was the leader in Bitcoin exchanges because it allowed consumers to "quickly and securely trade Bitcoins with other people around the world." (*Id.*)

The details of the Mt. Gox trading rules were included in the complaint, along with the events leading up to the February 2014 freeze of user accounts, and the February 23, 2014 removal of the Mt. Gox media webpage. This led to a reported "loss of hundreds of millions of dollars worth of its users' Bitcoins (approximately 744,000 of them)." (Complaint ¶ 27.)

In addition to naming Mt. Gox, the complaint in this action also named Mark Karpelés, the sole shareholder and CEO of the exchange.

> On information and belief, Mr. Karpelés, as the sole shareholder of Mt. Gox, personally profited by shutting down Mt. Gox and obtaining users' Fiat Currency and Bitcoins worth millions of dollars. Mr. Karpelés was and is aware of the conduct and security problems underlying the widespread loss of Bitcoins, and was and is aware that he and his co-defendants were wrongfully obtaining Bitcoins and Fiat Currency by shutting down the Mt. Gox exchange and capturing its users' property. Mr. Karpelés personally participated in, and had direct control over, Mt. Gox's public statements, the design and development of its website, the maintenance of its hardware and software, its customer service, banking regulatory affairs, interactions with government entities, and events leading to the loss of its users' Bitcoins and Fiat Currency and the closing of the Mt. Gox exchange. On information and belief, Mr. Karpelés was personally responsible for making the decision to shut down Mt. Gox without releasing any of Plaintiff's or the putative Classes' Bitcoins or Fiat Currency.

(Complaint ¶ 28.)

The action has been incredibly complicated, with more than 300 distinct pleadings and orders being filed by the end of 2018. Obviously, the bankruptcy filings for Mt. Gox in both Japan and the U.S. stayed the proceeding against the companies, and the action against the companies was settled in May, 2014. The claims against Mt. Gox CEO Mark Karpelés, however, have continued.[10] In addition, as discovery progressed, the complaint has been amended various times to add defendants and

---

[10] In March 2019, the Tokyo district court found Karpelés guilty of tampering with Mt. Gox's financial records, and he received a suspended jail sentence as a result. Marie Huillet, *Japanese Court find Ex-Mt. Gox CEO Guilty of Record Tampering*, COINTELEGRAPH (Mar. 15, 20190 [archived at https://perma.cc/6ZYZ-ZDZ5].

additional allegations, but the claims against other defendants have been dismissed on various procedural grounds.

In August of 2018, Karpelés filed a motion to dismiss for lack of personal jurisdiction. Karpelés' attorneys argued that the plaintiffs had abandoned any claim that Karpelés had conducted businesses in the United States by failing to allege that any wrongful conduct occurred outside Japan. The motion also argued that Karpelés never "purposefully availed" himself of the privilege of doing business in Illinois. The motion also relies on various difficulties that the action presents, given that Japan has precluded Karpelés from leaving that country. Finally, his attorneys argued that the fiduciary shield doctrine, which applies when an individual's acts were done on behalf of a principal, should prevent the court from exercising personal jurisdiction over Karpelés. However, in a brief notice filed by the court on January 11, 2019, the parties were directed to "proceed on the assumption that Defendant Karpelés's motion to dismiss will be denied."

As a result, *Greene v. Mt. Gox et al.* continued under the name *Greene v. Karpelés*, and on March 12, 2019, Karpelés' motion to dismiss was denied. Greene v. Karpelés, No. 14 C 1437, 2019 WL 1125796, at *11 (N.D. Ill. Mar. 12, 2019). The dispute over what really happened with the Mt. Gox exchange continues. In addition to the allegations against Karpelés and the question of how to distribute the proceeds that are in the company's bankruptcy estate, approximately 650,000 Bitcoins remain unaccounted for as a result of the Mt. Gox hack.

In addition, in July 2017, Alexander Vinnick, a Russian national, was arrested by U.S. authorities in Greece. He was charged with having a major role in the laundering of Bitcoin stolen from Mt. Gox. Vinnick is reported to be associated with BTC-e, another Bitcoin exchange, which the FBI raided as part of the investigation. Also as part of the investigation, the BTC-e exchange was shut down and the domain seized by the FBI.

Note that the cases referenced against Mt. Gox are private actions rather than administrative enforcement proceedings or criminal actions. The Mt. Gox fiasco occurred very early on, before regulators had fully decided how to respond to crypto, even initially. Moreover, by the time FinCEN may have been ready to intervene, the business was bankrupt and no longer operating. Given that private claims were relatively prompt, it is worth asking what regulators might have done that private citizens could not do? What kinds of regulation might have been helpful? Would regulating Mt. Gox as a money transmitter have protected its clients?

3. RIPPLE

One of the most significant early interactions directly between FinCEN and the crypto world involved a company known as Ripple and its XRP token.

PRELIMINARY NOTES AND QUESTIONS

As you read through the following materials, consider the following questions about Ripple, its XRP token, and its interactions with FinCEN.

1.   Did FinCEN get involved with Ripple because of concern that Ripple was knowingly participating in money laundering (or reverse money laundering) activities?

2.   Were any of Ripple's activities criminal in the sense of supporting illegal activities of others? If Ripple did not knowingly aid criminal enterprises, why did the U.S. Attorney for the Northern District of California get involved?

3.   How does forcing Ripple into compliance with the BSA AML requirements further the goals of FinCEN?

4.   If you assume that Ripple was not intentionally engaged in criminal or illegal activities, why would it knowingly (or at least recklessly) fail to register as a money transmitter until forced to do so by these proceedings?

A. THE EARLY HISTORY OF RIPPLE AND XRP

While Bitcoin is generally regarded as the first successful cryptocurrency, having been initially introduced to the public in 2009, the history of Ripple begins before that date. In 2004, Ryan Fugger (a web and decentralized systems developer from Vancouver, Canada) founded a company he called RipplePay. Fugger's idea was that instead of running financial transactions through traditional banks, a peer-to-peer network of customers could be established that would avoid the costs of dealing with multiple banks as well as the delays that often accompanied financial transactions. In this network, which was to be based on trust, customers could simply deal with each other directly without the need for a bank to serve as an intermediary.

The basic theory behind RipplePay was fairly simple. In essence, banks exist to make and receive loans. A bank deposit is, in reality, a loan from the customer to the bank. The bank maintains a record of that "loan" on its ledgers, and the customer trusts that the bank's records are accurate. A payment from that customer to another customer causes the bank to update its loan balances on its records (its ledgers), with the first customer's loan balance decreasing by the amount of the payment made, and the second customer's bank balance increasing by the amount "received." Banks coordinate with one another in the case of a payment from one bank's customer to the customer of another bank. Each bank trusts that the other bank has an accurate record of how much has been lent from each customer, or in more ordinary terms, how much is in each customer's account.

RipplePay wanted to establish a peer-to-peer trust network where customers could "lend" to each other directly (without the assistance of banks as middlemen). Payments would result in alterations to the "balances" of payers and recipients without the expense or delay associated with bank mediated transactions.

For a large number of reasons, this framework never took off. The ability to "trust" one another even in a limited peer-to-peer network is simply lacking, and any resulting system would likely be unstable or limited to a few large banks similar to the existing system. The growth of Bitcoin, however, led to substantial revisions to the original model for Ripple, making the system that now exists as Ripple very different from the original idea behind RipplePay.

As mentioned in the preceding section of this chapter, Jed McCaleb, an early Bitcoin participant, founded the Mt. Gox Bitcoin exchange in 2010 and sold it in March of 2011. In May of that year, he was hired by Ryan Fugger and given responsibility for the Ripple project. At this time, McCaleb apparently brought Arthur Britto and David Schwartz on board. Britto and Schwartz were both programmers with significant software development experience. Some sources credit Britto with helping design XRP's technical structure and even being the "real guy behind Ripple." Schwartz, who continues to work at Ripple, is now the company's Chief Technology Officer, and the Ripple website describes him as "one of the original architects of the Ripple consensus network."

In 2012, McCaleb hired Chris Larsen, a Stanford M.B.A. and the co-founder and former chairman and CEO of E-Loan, a company Larsen helped take public in 1999 at the peak of the tech bubble. In 2005, Larsen oversaw the sale of E-Loan to Banco Popular for $300 million. He then went on to found Prosper Marketplace, the first peer-to-peer, on-line lending platform that was at one time valued at more than $1 billion. Larsen left Prosper to join Ripple. Larsen continues (as of November 2019) to serve as Executive Chairman on Ripple's board, and is listed on Ripple's website as co-founder. As will be described later, McCaleb is no longer associated with Ripple.

When Ripple hired Larsen, RipplePay changed its name to OpenCoin, which became the first of three name changes for the company between 2012 and 2015. (In September of 2013, OpenCoin became Ripple Labs, and in October, 2015, the company shortened its name to Ripple, the name it continues to use today.)

More than the name of the company changed. With the increasing successes of Bitcoin, Ripple (then OpenCoin) initiated plans to allow

Bitcoin payments on its network. Realizing that the peer-to-peer trust structure originally contemplated would not work, the company decided to form gateways to maintain network integrity. These designated gateways would be independent participants that other users in the network would be able to trust. These validating users would use a consensus process to maintain integrity of the shared public database that contains transaction information stored through cryptographic processes in order to maintain privacy of users. This is a hybrid approach to the problem of trust, somewhere between a fully decentralized, peer-to-peer system, and a system relying totally on centralized authorities to monitor and oversee transactions. This choice was seen as a compromise necessary in order to induce ordinary users of the Ripple platform to trust the legitimacy of transactions. (This lack of a truly peer-to-peer system is also one reason why some crypto enthusiasts have complained that Ripple's XRP is not a "true" cryptocurrency.)

In late 2012, OpenCoin received seed round investments of approximately $200,000 from Jesse Powell, the founder and CEO of the Kraken exchange (launched in 2011) and close friend of McCaleb. Roger Ver, a Bitcoin enthusiast, libertarian, and self-proclaimed anarcho-capitalist with a felony record for selling explosives on eBay, is also reported to have been an early investor in Ripple.

OpenCoin used these early funds to finance the launch of the XRP token in January of 2013. As with Bitcoin, XRP is based on a public chain of cryptographic signatures. XRP can be sent directly between users, just as is the case with Bitcoin. The company set the total supply of XRP at 100 billion tokens.

In April 2013, the company (still operating as OpenCoin) received $1.5 million in funding from some of the most respected venture-capital companies in existence, including Google Ventures, Andreessen Horowitz, IDG Capital Partners, FF Angel, Lightspeed Venture Partners, the Bitcoin Opportunity Fund, and Vast Ventures. This was the first in many rounds of venture funding for the company.

Sometime between June 2013 and May 2014, McCaleb left the project. He has claimed that his departure occurred in June 2013, at the same time as Stefan Thomas took over as Chief Technology Officer of the company (a position Thomas held until May 2018). Prior to joining Ripple, Thomas founded WeUseCoins.com, a website for novice Bitcoin users, and was the creator of BitcoinJS, a software package used by a range of Bitcoin-based businesses.

Reports suggest that the cause of McCaleb's departure was not the promotion of Thomas, but rather disagreements with Larsen about corporate strategy and priorities. Although McCaleb continues to be active and successful in the crypto world, founding Stellar in 2014,[11] it appears that his departure from Ripple was neither completely voluntary nor on the friendliest of terms.

In May 2014, Jesse Powell (an early investor in Ripple) described the situation in the following terms. In his opinion, the management of the company had departed from the original vision, and he denounced the decision of the founders to allocate 20% of XRP to themselves. He also alleged that McCaleb had wanted to return the XRP that he held to the company while Larsen had been hostile to that idea.

This public pronouncement prompted a reply from Ripple to the effect that Powell was spreading defamatory and inaccurate information in violation of his duties as a member of the Ripple board of directors. Powell persisted in his allegations that McCaleb and Larsen had in effect stolen large amounts of XRP (20 billion tokens, or 20% of the total available supply) from the company as a result of the allocation of tokens to themselves. Many of Powell's complaints were made online in Ripple forums and were particularly directed at Larsen. In response, the company eventually announced the creation of a foundation, "Ripple Works," to distribute 7 billion of Larsen's XRP to "the underbanked and financially underserved." This action apparently addressed a growing level of discontent in the Ripple community, although there continues to be some issue with the extent to which Larsen has actually made all of the donations that he initially announced.[12]

Following McCaleb's departure, OpenCoin changed its name to Ripple Labs. In February 2014 it implemented a new "balance freeze" feature. This modification to the original protocols went active in August 2014, and set a new default protocol allowing Ripple gateways[13] to freeze or confiscate coins from any user of its gateway. The stated purpose of the modification was to facilitate compliance with regulatory requirements and court orders. Although the decision to disable the freeze option was given to

---

[11] Stellar is an open-source, decentralized protocol for digital currency to fiat currency transfers, designed to function by "making money more fluid, markets more open, and people more empowered." *See* Stellar, https://www.stellar.org/. The description of how Steller functions changes over time as the company decides which attributes to emphasize and how best to communicate their objectives. This was the description on their webpage as of September 10, 2019.

[12] Obviously, this degree of detail may not seem important to understanding at a general level why and how U.S. regulators got involved with Ripple. It is, however, relevant to understanding how opaque the internal operations of crypto-based enterprises can be. Ordinary purchasers of Ripple's tokens, for example, were very unlikely to know much about the background and internal disagreements that plagued the company. Remember that at this time it was not clear that there were any mandatory disclosures for crypto-business such as Ripple. On the other hand, investors probably would have wanted to know about the internal disagreements, missing data, and unclear operating history with regard to who had been issued tokens at what time and for what consideration. It is this disconnect between the information that was voluntarily disclosed and what investors would reasonably have wanted to know that helps explain some of the SEC's involvement with crypto.

[13] A Ripple gateway is a business that serves as a point of entry onto the XRP Ledger network, allowing transfer of fiat and crypto in and out of the network.

individual gateways, the largest gateway at the time, Bitstamp, did not choose to opt out.

B. FINCEN, RIPPLE LABS, AND THE BANK SECRECY ACT

At about this time Ripple Labs, and its subsidiary, XRP II, LLC, came under investigation by FinCEN, acting pursuant to its mandates in the Bank Secrecy Act (BSA). Acting in conjunction with the U.S. Attorney's Office for the Northern District of California, the two companies were charged with failing to comply with various BSA requirements, including failure to register with FinCEN, and failure to implement and maintain proper anti-money laundering (AML) and know-your-customer (KYC) protocols. According to FinCEN, Ripple's failure to comply with these FinCEN requirements was facilitating the use of cryptocurrencies by money launderers and terrorists.

This action did not proceed to trial, with Ripple Labs settling the charges by agreeing to pay a $700,000 fine and further agreeing to take immediate remedial steps to bring the companies into compliance with BSA requirements. The settlement was announced by FinCEN on May 5, 2017, with the following press release.

FinCEN Fines Ripple Labs Inc. in First Civil Enforcement Action Against a Virtual Currency Exchanger

FinCEN Press Release (May 5, 2015)
https://www.fincen.gov/sites/default/files/shared/20150505.pdf

Company Agrees to $700,000 Penalty and Remedial Actions

Washington, DC—The Financial Crimes Enforcement Network (FinCEN), working in coordination with the U.S. Attorney's Office for the Northern District of California (USAONDCA), assessed a $700,000 civil money penalty today against Ripple Labs Inc. and its wholly owned subsidiary, XRP II, LLC (formerly known as XRP Fund II, LLC). Ripple Labs willfully violated several requirements of the Bank Secrecy Act (BSA) by acting as a money services business (MSB) and selling its virtual currency, known as XRP, without registering with FinCEN, and by failing to implement and maintain an adequate anti-money laundering (AML) program designed to protect its products from use by money launderers or terrorist financiers. XRP II later assumed Ripple Labs' functions of selling virtual currency and acting as an MSB; however, like its parent company, XRP II willfully violated the BSA by failing to implement an effective AML program, and by failing to report suspicious activity related to several financial transactions.

"Virtual currency exchangers must bring products to market that comply with our anti-money laundering laws," said FinCEN Director Jennifer Shasky Calvery. "Innovation is laudable but only as long as it does not unreasonably expose our financial system to tech-smart criminals eager to abuse the latest and most complex products."

FinCEN's assessment is concurrent with the USAO-NDCA's announcement of a settlement agreement with Ripple Labs and XRP II. In that settlement, the companies resolved possible criminal charges and forfeited $450,000. The $450,000 forfeiture in that action will be credited to partially satisfy FinCEN's $700,000 civil money penalty. A Statement of Facts and Violations, describing the underlying activity and details of the BSA violations, is incorporated into FinCEN's assessment as well as the USAO-NDCA's settlement.

Both actions were accompanied by an agreement by Ripple and XRP II to engage in remedial steps to ensure future compliance with AML/CFT obligations, as well as enhanced remedial measures. Among these steps are agreements to only transact XRP and "Ripple Trade" activity through a registered MSB; to implement and maintain an effective AML program; to comply with the Funds Transfer and Funds Travel Rules; to conduct a three-year "look-back" to require suspicious activity reporting for prior suspicious transactions; and a requirement for the companies to retain external independent auditors to review their compliance with the BSA every two years up to and including 2020. Pursuant to the agreement, Ripple Labs will also undertake certain enhancements to the Ripple Protocol to appropriately monitor all future transactions.

"By these agreements, we demonstrate again that we will remain vigilant to ensure the security of, and prevent the misuse of, the financial markets," said U.S. Attorney Melinda Haag. "Ripple Labs Inc. and its wholly-owned subsidiary both have acknowledged that digital currency providers have an obligation not only to refrain from illegal activity, but also to ensure they are not profiting by creating products that allow would-be criminals to avoid detection. We hope that this sets an industry standard in the important new space of digital currency."

"Federal laws that regulate the reporting of financial transactions are in place to detect and stop illegal activities, including those in the virtual currency arena," said Richard Weber, Chief, IRS Criminal Investigation. "Unregulated, virtual currency opens the door for criminals to anonymously conduct illegal activities online, eroding our financial systems and creating a Wild West environment where following the law is a choice rather than a requirement."

Ripple Labs Inc., headquartered in San Francisco, CA, facilitated transfers of virtual currency and provided virtual currency exchange transaction services. XRP II, LLC is a wholly-owned subsidiary of Ripple

Labs that was incorporated as XRP Fund II, LLC in South Carolina on July 1, 2013; the company changed its name to XRP II in July 2014. As of 2015, Ripple is the second-largest cryptocurrency by market capitalization, after Bitcoin. On March 18, 2013, FinCEN released guidance clarifying the applicability of regulations implementing the BSA, and the requirement for certain participants in the virtual currency arena—namely, virtual currency exchangers and administrators—to register as MSBs with FinCEN pursuant to federal law.

Director Shasky Calvery expressed her appreciation to the U.S. Attorney's Office for the Northern District of California and to the Internal Revenue Service-Criminal Investigation Division for their contributions to the investigation and strong partnership with FinCEN.

FinCEN seeks to protect the U.S. financial system from being exploited by illicit activity. Its efforts are focused on compromised financial institutions and their employees; significant fraud; third-party money launderers; transnational organized crime and security threats; and cyber threats. FinCEN has a broad array of enforcement authorities to target both domestic and foreign actions affecting the U.S. financial system.

The charges against Ripple were based at least in part on conduct that predated any currency guidance from FinCEN, and it might therefore be argued that this action was unfair to Ripple Labs because the company might not have known it was subject to the BSA AML and KYC requirements. On the other hand, and possibly in order to address this concern, FinCEN was careful to point out Ripple Labs' prior history of describing itself as "a currency exchange service providing on-line, real-time currency trading and cash management."[14] FinCEN also emphasized that there was no need under the statute or regulations for the government to prove that the defendant had knowledge that it violated the BSA with its conduct.[15] In addition, FinCEN carefully alleged that both Ripple Pay and XRP II continued their illegal conduct after the release of official guidance establishing FinCEN's position that virtual currency businesses could be regulated as money transmitters and therefore subject to AML and KYC requirements.

---

[14]   *See* FinCEN, *Assessment of Civil Money Penalty*, p. 4, ¶ 16 [archived at https://perma.cc/ 2FMW-57WR].

[15]   *Id.* at p. 2, n.3.

C. RIPPLE'S ACTIONS FOLLOWING FINCEN INTERVENTION

In addition to agreeing to a $700,000 fine, Ripple Labs also agreed to a variety of remedial measures to be put into place. These measures included all of the following:

1. Ripple Labs agreed to register with FinCEN.

2. It agreed that if Ripple (the company) gave away any more XRP, recipients would be required to register their account information and provide identification details to Ripple.

3. It agreed to comply with AML regulations and appoint a compliance officer.

4. It agreed that it would be subject to external audits.

5. It agreed to provide data or tools to the regulators in order to allow the regulators to analyze Ripple transactions and potentially trace the flow of funds.

The company's final name change occurred in October 2015, when Ripple Labs was shortened to Ripple, the name under which the company continues to operate. Ripple has had both remarkable success as well as some significant setbacks since settling with FinCEN in 2015.

In September 2016, Ripple successfully raised $55 million in a financing round lead by SBI Holdings, Japan's leading online retail stock-brokerage company. SBI acquired a 10.5% ownership interest in Ripple as part of this funding round. In addition, SBI has now partnered with Ripple to create SBI Ripple Asia, a joint venture that is 60% owned by SBI and 40% by Ripple. In November of that year, the project announced the final launch of a new network based on Ripple's blockchain by a consortium of 42 Japanese banks. In March 2017, the joint venture and this consortium of banks "successfully" implemented RC Cloud on a pilot basis, Ripple's unified platform for both domestic and cross-border payments. In September 2018, Japanese regulators granted SBI Ripple Asia a license to operate as an electronic payment service in that country. In October 2018, a Ripple-power payments app offering real-time settlement of transactions was launched in Japan. Over time, the consortium expanded to include more than 60 Japanese banks.

On the other hand, not all news has been positive for Ripple. In September 2017, another blockchain-based company, R3, sued Ripple in both Delaware and New York for alleged breach of contract. R3 alleged that Ripple had agreed in a September 2016 partnership agreement between the two companies to give R3 an option to buy 5 billion XRP at $0.0085 per token, exercisable at any time prior to September 2019. (At the time of the lawsuit's filing, the value of the XRP at issue under the option would have been about $1 million, but at the peak of XRP pricing, in January of 2018, the value of the call option would have been worth approximately $19 billion.) R3 further alleged that in June 2017, Ripple terminated the contract in violation of its terms. According to Ripple, R3 had failed to comply with the terms of the original 2016 agreement by failing to introduce Ripple to a sufficient number of banking clients or to promote XRP for usage in those banking systems. Ripple also alleged that R3 had concealed material evidence that some of its members, including Goldman Sachs and Banco Santander, intended to leave the group rather than following through on promises to promote the use of XRP. Following the dismissal of both the California and Delaware actions, leaving only the New York action intact, the case was settled in September 2018 on undisclosed terms.

Ripple's XRP token is also subject to the same volatility that plagues the entire crypto market. According to CoinMarketCap, the pricing of XRP, as well as the total market capitalization based on the number of XRP in circulation, in roughly 6 months intervals from August 2013 to July 2019 is shown in the following table:

The Rise of Ripple's XRP (2013–2019)

Date	XRP Price (USD)	Total Market Cap (USD, in millions)
Aug. 6, 2013	.005847	45.9
Jan. 1, 2014	.026443	211.4
July 2, 2014	.003537	27.6
Jan. 1, 2015	.024272	751.9
July 1, 2015	.011211	357.7
Dec. 31, 2015	.006071	203.6
July 1, 2016	.006787	239.9
Jan. 2, 2017	.006319	229.6
July 1, 2017	.253714	9,715.1
Dec. 31, 2017	2.32	89,951.1
July 2, 2018	.487171	19,127.4
Jan. 2, 2019	.370664	15,120.9
July 1, 2019	.406862	17,318.7

D. WHO OWNS THE 100 BILLION XRP?

Unlike Bitcoin, when XRP was released, all 100 billion tokens were completely pre-issued (so there are no tokens to be earned by mining). Of those, 80 billion XRP was allocated to the company and 20 billion was given to the three founders: McCaleb, Larsen, and Britto.

The original, approximate breakdown of that allocation is as follows:

Ripple   80 billion XRP
Larson   9.5 billion XRP[16]
McCaleb   9.5 billion XRP
Britto   1 billion XRP

At some point, Schwartz was also allegedly given 1 billion XRP, but that could have come from the company's original share of 80 billion.

Plans called for the company to sell or give away the 80 billion of XRP that it had retained over time, and to use the funds for company operations, and to seed global money-transfer gateways. The exact way in which the company has released its tokens (including timing of allocations and information relating to how many tokens were sold as opposed to being given away) is obscured by the fact that more than 30,000 blocks of data are missing from the start of the ledger, so that the transactions recorded in those blocks can no longer be accessed or reconstructed. According to Schwartz, now CTO of Ripple, the lost blocks don't "mean anything for the average Ripple user. In January of 2013, a bug in the Ripple server caused ledger headers to be lost. All data from all running Ripple servers was collected, but it was insufficient to construct the ledgers."[17]

When McCaleb left Ripple, he or his relatives retained 7.5 billion XRP. The other 1.5 billion of his original 9.5 billion XRP were given to charity and other relatives. Because of concerns that McCaleb might "dump" his XRP and crash its market price, he agreed with the Company and other participants that his tokens would be subject to a lock-up agreement, restricting the timing of sales. It is not clear whether some of the XRP had been given to relatives prior to this agreement. (Britto's XRP is also apparently subject to restrictions on resale.) McCaleb's lock-up was revised in 2016 after Ripple asserted that he was not complying with the terms of the original arrangement.

According to Ripple, as of June 30, 2015, the company held slightly more than 65.7 billion XRP, having issued, sold, or given away the remaining tokens. Thereafter the company placed 55 billion of its XRP into escrow, according to Ripple specifically to "alleviate concerns surrounding

---

[16]   Seven billion of Larsen's XRP are supposedly committed to the Ripple Works charitable foundation, although it is not at all clear how much of that amount has been contributed at this time.

[17]   *See, Why is Ripple's effective genesis ledger at 32570?* (Answer by David Schwartz) BITCOIN STACKEXCHANGE (Oct. 2, 2013) (available online at https://bitcoin.stackexchange.com/ questions/13558/why-is-ripples-effective-genesis-ledger-at-32570).

XRP supply."[18] As of early January, 2019,[19] Ripple reported the following information relating to the outstanding supply XRP:

Total XRP Held By Ripple 6,451,319,755

Total XRP Distributed 41,040,405,095*

Total XRP Placed In Escrow 52,500,000,013

In addition, the escrow arrangements, which are also detailed on the Ripple website, are cryptographically-secured. Pursuant to the escrow terms, Ripple is limited in how many additional XRP tokens may be issued each month, in order to assure supply predictability and limit concerns about market manipulation.[20]

E. THE BITSTAMP RIPPLE FREEZE INCIDENT

As mentioned earlier, one of the changes that took place very shortly after McCaleb's departure in 2013 was the adoption of the freeze feature designed to allow gateways to comply with law enforcement requirements. Somewhat ironically, the first use of the feature came when Ripple itself sent Bitstamp, then the largest Ripple gateway, a freeze order that affected funds allegedly belonging to one of McCaleb's relatives.

It appears that one of McCaleb's relatives (later identified as Jacob Stephenson, a cousin of McCaleb) sold 96 million XRP back to Ripple for approximately $1 million. It is not clear whether those tokens had been transferred prior to the lock-up agreement or whether the tokens were in fact subject to the limitation on how quickly McCaleb's XRP could be sold. Regardless, Ripple asked Bitstamp to use its freeze option to confiscate the $1 million payment. Bitstamp reacted by taking both Ripple and McCaleb to court in the Northern District of California in order to determine how to proceed.

Among the allegations that were made in the complaint were questions about how Ripple had "agreed" to structure the repurchase. Certainly, the repurchase from Stephenson involved a complicated transaction, and there was at least the possibility that part of the intent was to manipulate the market to "improperly inflate the price per XRP of

---

[18]　Ripple, *Market Performance* [archived on Mar. 11, 2019 at https://perma.cc/W52W-AEBR]. The live page is available online at https://www.ripple.com/xrp/market-performance/, but the current numbers are considerably different that those reported in the text. In summer 2019, Ripple released a considerable amount of the XRP that it had been holding, leading some holders of XRP tokens to threaten to fork the Ripple blockchain to limit such distributions. *See, i.e.,* George Gerogiev, *Ripple Releases $130M Worth of XRP Despite Recent Fork Threats,* CRYPTOPOTATO (Sept. 4, 2019) [archived at https://perma.cc/3H2S-UAEE].

[19]　This data comes from Ripple's website, Ripple, *XRP Market Performance,* on January 10, 2019 [archived at https://perma.cc/8D7Y-NNVT]. The amount distributed figure (with the asterisk) was accurate as of December 31, 2018.

[20]　Ripple, *Insights: Ripple Escrows 55 Billion XRP for Supply Predictability* [archived at https://perma.cc/FWX7-DSKD].

the transaction and mislead other purchasers."[21] As part of the deal, Ripple paid more than the cost and then asked Stephenson to return $75,000. Thereafter, Ripple asked Bitstamp to confiscate the entire $1 million.

Bitstamp's complaint[22] asserted that it was a "disinterested stakeholder," and that it needed the court to determine which side should prevail. The dispute continued until settlement was reached in 2016.

The dispute between McCaleb and Ripple continued until a final resolution in February 2016, when the company, implying that McCaleb had violated the 2014 XRP lock-up agreement, stated that a final settlement had been reached. As part of the settlement, the $1 million payment was unfrozen, Ripple paid all legal fees, and 2 billion XRP were freed for donation to charity. The lock-up terms were renegotiated, with a new schedule of permissible sales being adopted.

4.　OBSERVATIONS

Much of the information in this chapter focuses on disputes involving two distinct companies. Mt. Gox was a Bitcoin exchange plagued by thefts, mismanagement, and potential misconduct by its executives throughout its life. Ripple was and is a very different company, designed to operate its own platform with a new token that it created. It has created a very successful platform and token, and over the years has produced substantial evidence of willingness to work with regulators. Nonetheless, it also appears to have been subject to a wide variety of disputes, both internal and external. The primary external dispute described above, instigated by FinCEN, relates to the regulatory paradigm that is developing in the context of cryptoassets. However, the internal disputes, primarily relating to control over XRP and its supply, including accusations of theft and market manipulation, are likely to have a profound role in how crypto is perceived by regulators.

Similarly, the involvement of the same players in many of these ventures is also likely to be relevant to how crypto-focused businesses are perceived. For example, Jed McCaleb founded both Mt. Gox and Ripple, although he was no longer involved with either at the time when most of the external disputes occurred. Prior to his involvement with Mt. Gox, however, McCaleb had founded another company, MetaMachine, Inc., and had released an eDonkey2000 application,[23] which lead to copyright infringement claims. In 2006, McCaleb's company and its top executives

---

[21]　*The Ripple Story*, BITMEX BLOG (Feb. 6, 2018) (available online at https://blog.bitmex.com/the-ripple-story/).

[22]　*Bitstamp Ltd, v. Ripple Labs Inc. et al.*, U.S. D.C. N.D. Cal., Case No. 3:15–cv–1503, Complaint for Interpleader Under FRCP 22 (filed April 1, 2015).

[23]　The eDonkey application was a decentralized, P2P file-sharing network primarily geared at sharing large files. For a more detailed explanation, see *eDonkey Network (eD2k)*, TECHOPEDIA (available online at https://www.techopedia.com/definition/25241/edonkey-network-ed2k).

agreed to "immediately cease distributing eDonkey, eDonkey2000, Overnet and other software" and to pay $30 million to avoid copyright infringement lawsuits. With regard to Mt. Gox, there have been allegations that systematic thefts of Bitcoin had begun prior to McCaleb's departure, although none of those have been proven. In the case of Ripple, McCaleb's honesty was called into questions by a variety of persons, although those may have been based in part on his reputation having been tainted by association with Mt. Gox.

Mark Karpelès is also a name that shows up repeatedly in crypto ventures, and his involvement with criminal enforcement agencies is more direct. Complaints against him were filed in 2005 alleging that he had transferred "a large quantity of stored date" from his employer's services, and in 2010, Karpelès was convicted in absentia of fraud after he had left France for Japan.[24] He was sentenced to a suspended year in jail. (This predates his involvement with Mt. Gox.) In 2012, after he was associated with Mt. Gox, he was sued in Japan by a customer who claimed he had paid Karpelès more than $20,000 for a website that he had never developed. The Tokyo District court made Karpelès refund the payment. In connection with his involvement with Mt. Gox, he was subpoenaed by FinCEN to provide testimony on April 18, 2014 in Washington, D.C. He declined to appear after claiming he did not have an attorney for the matter. He was also involved to some extent in the Silk Road market place, with lawyers for Ross William Ulbricth claiming at one point that Karpelès was the mastermind behind "Dread Pirate Roberts." Karpelès publicly denied the claim, and Ulbricht was eventually found guilty. Karpelès is still a defendant in the on-going Mt. Gox class action suit alleging fraud in connection with the hacking of Bitcoins from the exchange.[25]

Individuals like Roger Ver have a smaller role, but the fact that Ver is a convicted felon and self-described anarchist makes his role in the funding and direction of crypto-based businesses a matter of concern to regulators.

This is not to suggest that everyone, or even a majority, of those involved in crypto-based businesses operate with improper or illegal motives. However, the fact that there are repeated allegations of fraud and mismanagement, combined with the amounts of money involved and the speed with which virtual fortunes can be made and lost, has regulators concerned and vigilant.

---

[24]   Cyrus Farivar, *Why the Head of Mt. Gox Bitcoin Exchange Should be in Jail*, ARS TECHNICA (Aug. 1, 2014) (available online at https://arstechnica.com/tech-policy/2014/08/why-the-head-of-mt-gox-Bitcoin-exchange-should-be-in-jail/), citing Pierre Alonso, "*En France, le passé trouble de l'ancien "baron du Bitcoin"* " [Old Bitcoin baron's old trouble in France], LE MONDE (in French) (Aug. 1, 2014).

[25]   *See Pearce v. Karpelés*, 2019 WL 3409495 (E.D. Pa, July 26, 2019) (denying Karpelés' motion to dismiss).

CHAPTER 6

HOW CRYPTO HAS SHAPED FinCEN'S RESPONSE

■ ■ ■

1. REVIEW OF THE SCOPE OF FINCEN'S MANDATE PRIOR TO CRYPTO

As described in Chapter three, FinCEN is primarily concerned with the twin problems of traditional money-laundering and the related issue of how to combat the funding of criminal activities, with a particular focus (since September 11, 2001) on terrorism. As a Bureau of the Treasury Department, FinCEN's official mission, as reflected on the FinCEN website, is "to safeguard the financial system from illicit use, combat money laundering, and promote national security through the strategic use of financial authorities and the collection, analysis, and dissemination of financial intelligence."[1]

In connection with this mandate, FinCEN relies on a number of federal provisions that form the underpinnings of the agency's current approach to cryptoassets, which it generally calls "virtual currencies." It is worth emphasizing that Congress has not amended the statutes pursuant to which FinCEN operates in order to make the legislative mandates apply to cryptocurrencies or other cryptoassets. Similarly, FinCEN has proposed no new rules to accomplish this task. Instead, it has sought to bring cryptoassets within the scope of pre-existing regulations. Thus, there is a focus on the direct and indirect prohibitions and requirements that have applied to other kinds of financial operations. For example, FinCEN investigates persons who use cryptoassets to engage in money laundering (both traditional, where the illegal source of funds is obscured, and reverse, where funds are channeled into illegal operations, both as described in chapter three). FinCEN also investigates crypto-based businesses to insure compliance with money transmitter requirements (which are generally focused on registration, AML, and KYC requirements).

Within this context, remember that federal law contains a number of provisions that criminalize money laundering activities. For example, 18 U.S. Code § 1956 (enacted as part of the Money Laundering Control Act of 1986) makes it a crime to knowingly or intentionally hide the source of

---

[1]   The mission statement can be found at FinCEN, *Mission*, https://www.fincen.gov/about/mission.

money derived from illegal operations or to use funds to further criminal activities. In addition, 18 U.S. Code § 1957 (enacted as part of the same legislation) is broader, criminalizing the knowing acceptance of tainted funds by anyone interacting with criminals. Furthermore, 18 U.S. Code § 1960 (as amended by the USA PATRIOT Act) makes it a crime to engage in an illegal money-transmitting business without any requirement of knowledge or intent. An illegal money-transmitting business is one that fails to comply with federal or state requirements, and the obligation to register is applied broadly. In general, "[a]ny person who owns or controls a money transmitting business shall register the business (whether or not the business is licensed as a money transmitting business in any State) with the Secretary of the Treasury not later than the end of the 180-day period beginning on . . . the date on which the business is established."[2]

"Money transmitting business" is further defined in § 5330(d)[3] as:

any business other than the United States Postal Service which—

> (A) provides check cashing, currency exchange, or money transmitting or remittance services, or issues or redeems money orders, travelers' checks, and other similar instruments or any other person who engages as a business in the transmission of funds, including any person who engages as a business in an informal money transfer system or any network of people who engage as a business in facilitating the transfer of money domestically or internationally outside of the conventional financial institutions system;
>
> (B) is required to file reports under section 5313; and
>
> (C) is not a depository institution.

. . . .

2. JUSTIFICATION FOR OVERSIGHT OF "VIRTUAL CURRENCY"

Nowhere in these statutes or implementing regulations is there a definition of "virtual currency," or "cryptocurrency." One might therefore wonder why FinCEN is so active in the space given that there is no specific legislative direction.

In answering this question, it is hard to overestimate the legacy of the Silk Road, described in some detail in chapter four. Recall that the Silk Road was essentially a "dark web" equivalent of Amazon. It operated as an online marketplace for illegal goods and services, where Bitcoin was the

---

[2]   31 U.S. Code § 5330(a)(1).

[3]   31 U.S. Code § 5330(d).

only form of payment allowed, and it was used to buy and sell cocaine, weapons, fake IDs, and even contracts for illegal services. The role of Bitcoin, the world's first successful cryptocurrency, in funding these illegal transactions has had a profound and on-going impact on how crypto-currencies are regulated. Marco Santori, a leading fintech lawyer who was then associated with the Cooley LLP law firm, has publicly commented about having attended a meeting with representatives from a wide array of regulatory agencies, including "FinCEN, IRS, FBI, DEA, SEC, CFPB, CFTC ... just about any agency with a potential interest" in cryptocurrencies.[4] Santori's impression was that every regulator came to that meeting predisposed to believe that "[B]itcoin is for criminals." As he explained, the government's interest in regulation peaked along with recognition that cryptocurrencies could be used for illicit activity. In fact, government interest in regulating cryptocurrencies paralleled increasing realization about how easily cryptocurrencies could be used to fund criminal enterprises. "As Silk Road gained global notoriety, cryptocurrencies became synonymous with illegal activity—and not just drugs. Reports began circulating that Bitcoin was being used to fund terrorism, and commentators estimated that the majority of transactions were illegal."[5]

The groundwork for FinCEN's current conclusions about cryptoassets was laid in 2011, when FinCEN finalized a rule that expanded the meaning of the phrase "money transmission services" to include "the acceptance of currency, funds, or other value that substitutes for currency from one person and the transmission of currency, funds, or other value that substitutes for currency to another location or person by any means."[6] While not explicitly mentioning crypto or "virtual currency," this expansion of money transmission to cover "other value that substitutes for currency" provided the primary basis for applying AML and KYC requirements to actors in the crypto space.

3. THE 2013 OFFICIAL GUIDANCE

FinCEN's first major guidance that specifically addressed the applicability of BSA requirements to crypto-based businesses came in 2013, making it one of the earliest regulators in the world to address the regulation of cryptoassets. While FinCEN has expanded on this Guidance,

---

[4]   Marco Santori, *Silk Road Goes Dark: Bitcoin Survives Its Biggest Market's Demise*, COINDESK (May 5, 2017, 11:30 AM) (available online at https://www.coindesk.com/bitcoin-milestones-silk-road-goes-dark-bitcoin-survives-its-biggest-markets-demise).

[5]   *The Silk Road to Bitcoin: Has the Crypto Escaped Its Dark Past?*, IG ANALYST (Feb. 5, 2018, 8:58 AM) (available online at https://www.ig.com/au/trading-opportunities/the-silk-road-to-bitcoin--has-the-crypto-escaped-its-dark-past--41990-180205).

[6]   *Bank Secrecy Act Regulations; Definitions and Other Regulations Relating to Money Services Businesses*, 76 FED. REG. 43585 (July 21, 2011).

for the most part, the rules announced in 2013 continue to frame the way in which crypto is treated by FinCEN.

DEPT. OF THE TREASURY, FINCEN GUIDANCE, *APPLICATION OF FINCEN'S REGULATIONS TO PERSONS ADMINISTERING, EXCHANGING, OR USING VIRTUAL CURRENCIES*
FIN–2013–G001 (Mar. 18, 2013)

The Financial Crimes Enforcement Network ("FinCEN") is issuing this interpretive guidance to clarify the applicability of the regulations implementing the Bank Secrecy Act ("BSA") to persons creating, obtaining, distributing, exchanging, accepting, or transmitting virtual currencies.[1] Such persons are referred to in this guidance as "users," "administrators," and "exchangers," all as defined below. A user of virtual currency is not an MSB [Ed.—"Money Services Business"] under FinCEN's regulations and therefore is not subject to MSB registration, reporting, and recordkeeping regulations. However, an administrator or exchanger is an MSB under FinCEN's regulations, specifically, a money transmitter, unless a limitation to or exemption from the definition applies to the person. An administrator or exchanger is not a provider or seller of prepaid access, or a dealer in foreign exchange, under FinCEN's regulations.

Currency vs. Virtual Currency

FinCEN's regulations define currency (also referred to as "real" currency) as "the coin and paper money of the United States or of any other country that [i] is designated as legal tender and that [ii] circulates and [iii] is customarily used and accepted as a medium of exchange in the country of issuance." In contrast to real currency, "virtual" currency is a medium of exchange that operates like a currency in some environments, but does not have all the attributes of real currency. In particular, virtual currency does not have legal tender status in any jurisdiction. This guidance addresses "convertible" virtual currency. This type of virtual currency either has an equivalent value in real currency, or acts as a substitute for real currency.

Background

On July 21, 2011, FinCEN published a Final Rule amending definitions and other regulations relating to money services businesses ("MSBs").[4] Among other things, the MSB Rule amends the definitions of

---

[1]   FinCEN is issuing this guidance under its authority to administer the Bank Secrecy Act. *See* Treasury Order 180–01 (March 24, 2003). This guidance explains only how FinCEN characterizes certain activities involving virtual currencies under the Bank Secrecy Act and FinCEN regulations. It should not be interpreted as a statement by FinCEN about the extent to which those activities comport with other federal or state statutes, rules, regulations, or orders.

[4]   *Bank Secrecy Act Regulations—Definitions and Other Regulations Relating to Money Services Businesses*, 76 FR 43585 (July 21, 2011) (the "MSB Rule"). This defines an MSB as "a person wherever located doing business, whether or not on a regular basis or as an organized or

dealers in foreign exchange (formerly referred to as "currency dealers and exchangers") and money transmitters. On July 29, 2011, FinCEN published a Final Rule on Definitions and Other Regulations Relating to Prepaid Access (the "Prepaid Access Rule"). This guidance explains the regulatory treatment under these definitions of persons engaged in virtual currency transactions.

Definitions of User, Exchanger, and Administrator

This guidance refers to the participants in generic virtual currency arrangements, using the terms "user," "exchanger," and "administrator."[6] A user is a person that obtains virtual currency to purchase goods or services. An exchanger is a person engaged as a business in the exchange of virtual currency for real currency, funds, or other virtual currency. An administrator is a person engaged as a business in issuing (putting into circulation) a virtual currency, and who has the authority to redeem (to withdraw from circulation) such virtual currency.

Users of Virtual Currency

A user who obtains convertible virtual currency and uses it to purchase real or virtual goods or services is not an MSB under FinCEN's regulations. Such activity, in and of itself, does not fit within the definition of "money transmission services" and therefore is not subject to FinCEN's registration, reporting, and recordkeeping regulations for MSBs.[9]

Administrators and Exchangers of Virtual Currency

An administrator or exchanger that (1) accepts and transmits a convertible virtual currency or (2) buys or sells convertible virtual currency for any reason is a money transmitter under FinCEN's regulations, unless a limitation to or exemption from the definition applies to the person.[10] FinCEN's regulations define the term "money transmitter" as a person that provides money transmission services, or any other person engaged in the transfer of funds. The term "money transmission services" means "the acceptance of currency, funds, or other value that substitutes for currency

---

licensed business concern, wholly or in substantial part within the United States, in one or more of the capacities listed in paragraphs (ff)(1) through (ff)(7) of this section. This includes but is not limited to maintenance of any agent, agency, branch, or office within the United States." 31 CFR § 1010.100(ff).

6   These terms are used for the exclusive purpose of this regulatory guidance. Depending on the type and combination of a person's activities, one person may be acting in more than one of these capacities.

9   31 CFR § 1010.100(ff)(1–7).

10   FinCEN's regulations provide that whether a person is a money transmitter is a matter of facts and circumstances. The regulations identify six circumstances under which a person is not a money transmitter, despite accepting and transmitting currency, funds, or value that substitutes for currency. 31 CFR § 1010.100(ff)(5)(ii)(A)–(F).

from one person and the transmission of currency, funds, or other value that substitutes for currency to another location or person by any means."[11]

The definition of a money transmitter does not differentiate between real currencies and convertible virtual currencies. Accepting and transmitting anything of value that substitutes for currency makes a person a money transmitter under the regulations implementing the BSA. FinCEN has reviewed different activities involving virtual currency and has made determinations regarding the appropriate regulatory treatment of administrators and exchangers under three scenarios: brokers and dealers of e-currencies and e-precious metals; centralized convertible virtual currencies; and de-centralized convertible virtual currencies.

a.   E-Currencies and E-Precious Metals

The first type of activity involves electronic trading in e-currencies or e-precious metals.[13] In 2008, FinCEN issued guidance stating that as long as a broker or dealer in real currency or other commodities accepts and transmits funds solely for the purpose of effecting a bona fide purchase or sale of the real currency or other commodities for or with a customer, such person is not acting as a money transmitter under the regulations.[14]

However, if the broker or dealer transfers funds between a customer and a third party that is not part of the currency or commodity transaction, such transmission of funds is no longer a fundamental element of the actual transaction necessary to execute the contract for the purchase or sale of the currency or the other commodity. This scenario is, therefore, money transmission. Examples include, in part, (1) the transfer of funds between a customer and a third party by permitting a third party to fund a customer's account; (2) the transfer of value from a customer's currency or commodity position to the account of another customer; or (3) the closing out of a customer's currency or commodity position, with a transfer of proceeds to a third party. Since the definition of a money transmitter does not differentiate between real currencies and convertible virtual currencies, the same rules apply to brokers and dealers of e-currency and e-precious metals.

---

[11]   31 CFR § 1010.100(ff)(5)(i)(A).

[13]   Typically, this involves the broker or dealer electronically distributing digital certificates of ownership of real currencies or precious metals, with the digital certificate being the virtual currency. However, the same conclusions would apply in the case of the broker or dealer issuing paper ownership certificates or manifesting customer ownership or control of real currencies or commodities in an account statement or any other form. These conclusions would also apply in the case of a broker or dealer in commodities other than real currencies or precious metals. A broker or dealer of e-currencies or e-precious metals that engages in money transmission could be either an administrator or exchanger depending on its business model.

[14]   Application of the Definition of Money Transmitter to Brokers and Dealers in Currency and other Commodities, FIN–2008–G008, Sept. 10, 2008. The guidance also notes that the definition of money transmitter excludes any person, such as a futures commission merchant, that is "registered with, and regulated or examined by. . .the Commodity Futures Trading Commission."

b. *Centralized Virtual Currencies*

The second type of activity involves a convertible virtual currency that has a centralized repository. The administrator of that repository will be a money transmitter to the extent that it allows transfers of value between persons or from one location to another. This conclusion applies, whether the value is denominated in a real currency or a convertible virtual currency. In addition, any exchanger that uses its access to the convertible virtual currency services provided by the administrator to accept and transmit the convertible virtual currency on behalf of others, including transfers intended to pay a third party for virtual goods and services, is also a money transmitter.

FinCEN understands that the exchanger's activities may take one of two forms. The first form involves an exchanger (acting as a "seller" of the convertible virtual currency) that accepts real currency or its equivalent from a user (the "purchaser") and transmits the value of that real currency to fund the user's convertible virtual currency account with the administrator. Under FinCEN's regulations, sending "value that substitutes for currency" to another person or to another location constitutes money transmission, unless a limitation to or exemption from the definition applies. This circumstance constitutes transmission to another location, namely from the user's account at one location (e.g., a user's real currency account at a bank) to the user's convertible virtual currency account with the administrator. It might be argued that the exchanger is entitled to the exemption from the definition of "money transmitter" for persons involved in the sale of goods or the provision of services. Under such an argument, one might assert that the exchanger is merely providing the service of connecting the user to the administrator and that the transmission of value is integral to this service. However, this exemption does not apply when the only services being provided are money transmission services.

The second form involves a de facto sale of convertible virtual currency that is not completely transparent. The exchanger accepts currency or its equivalent from a user and privately credits the user with an appropriate portion of the exchanger's own convertible virtual currency held with the administrator of the repository. The exchanger then transmits that internally credited value to third parties at the user's direction. This constitutes transmission to another person, namely each third party to which transmissions are made at the user's direction. To the extent that the convertible virtual currency is generally understood as a substitute for real currencies, transmitting the convertible virtual currency at the direction and for the benefit of the user constitutes money transmission on the part of the exchanger.

c. De-Centralized Virtual Currencies

A final type of convertible virtual currency activity involves a de-centralized convertible virtual currency (1) that has no central repository and no single administrator, and (2) that persons may obtain by their own computing or manufacturing effort. A person that creates units of this convertible virtual currency and uses it to purchase real or virtual goods and services is a user of the convertible virtual currency and not subject to regulation as a money transmitter. By contrast, a person that creates units of convertible virtual currency and sells those units to another person for real currency or its equivalent is engaged in transmission to another location and is a money transmitter. In addition, a person is an exchanger and a money transmitter if the person accepts such de-centralized convertible virtual currency from one person and transmits it to another person as part of the acceptance and transfer of currency, funds, or other value that substitutes for currency.

Providers and Sellers of Prepaid Access

A person's acceptance and/or transmission of convertible virtual currency cannot be characterized as providing or selling prepaid access because prepaid access is limited to real currencies.[18]

Dealers in Foreign Exchange

A person must exchange the currency of two or more countries to be considered a dealer in foreign exchange.[19] Virtual currency does not meet the criteria to be considered "currency" under the BSA, because it is not legal tender. Therefore, a person who accepts real currency in exchange for virtual currency, or vice versa, is not a dealer in foreign exchange under FinCEN's regulations.

---

[18]   This is true even if the person holds the value accepted for a period of time before transmitting some or all of that value at the direction of the person from whom the value was originally accepted. FinCEN's regulations define "prepaid access" as "access to funds or the value of funds that have been paid in advance and can be retrieved or transferred at some point in the future through an electronic device or vehicle, such as a card, code, electronic serial number, mobile identification number, or personal identification number." 31 CFR § 1010.100(ww). Thus, "prepaid access" under FinCEN's regulations is limited to "access to funds or the value of funds." If FinCEN had intended prepaid access to cover funds denominated in a virtual currency or something else that substitutes for real currency, it would have used language in the definition of prepaid access like that in the definition of money transmission, which expressly includes the acceptance and transmission of "other value that substitutes for currency." 31 CFR § 1010.100(ff)(5)(i).

[19]   FinCEN defines a "dealer in foreign exchange" as a "person that accepts the currency, or other monetary instruments, funds, or other instruments denominated in the currency, of one or more countries in exchange for the currency, or other monetary instruments, funds, or other instruments denominated in the currency, of one or more other countries in an amount greater than $1,000 for any other person on any day in one or more transactions, whether or not for same-day delivery." 31 CFR § 1010.100(ff)(1).

The foregoing publication (which will be referred to in this text as the 2013 Guidance) defines virtual currency quite broadly, as "a medium of exchange that operates like a currency in some environments, but does not have all the attributes of real currency" (notably the lack of legal tender status). However, in order to be subject to BSA requirements, the crypto in question must also be convertible into real currency. (The BSA Regulations define real currency as coin and paper money of any country that is also designated as legal tender, circulates and is customarily used and accepted as a medium of exchange in the country of issuance.) Note that because convertible virtual currency is not "real" currency, FinCEN's Prepaid Access regulations do not apply. Similarly, FinCEN's regulations regarding dealers in foreign exchange do not apply to transactions involving crypto, because crypto is not a "real" currency.

Actually, and to be technical about it, when the 2013 Guidance was issued there were no government-issued cryptocurrencies, but this is no longer universally true. The Marshall Islands, countries associated with the Eastern Caribbean Central Bank, Senegal, Tunisia, and Venezuela have all acted to create government-back cryptoassets.[7] There are also other nations that are considering the issuance of their own cryptocurrencies, although the eventual fate of these projects remains uncertain as of mid-2019.[8]

Despite the technical possibility that a few cryptocurrencies might be legal tender in some places, most cryptoassets continue to be something other than legal tender, and U.S. regulators continue to treat crypto in that way. FinCEN has therefore categorized persons who act in the crypto space in one of three ways: (1) users of the cryptoasset, (2) crypto administrators, and (3) exchangers of the crypto. Because FinCEN takes a different regulatory approach to these different categories, it is important to determine what causes a person to fit within one group and not another.

4. APPLICATION OF REQUIREMENTS TO VARIOUS PERSONS

A. USERS

According to FinCEN's 2013 Guidance (excerpted earlier in this chapter), a user is "a person that obtains virtual currency to purchase goods or services on the user's own behalf." FinCEN has specifically determined that this kind of activity (in and of itself) is insufficient to cause a person to become an MSB. In fact, FinCEN's 2013 Guidance, concludes that "[a] user of virtual currency is not [a money service business] under FinCEN's

---

7   *See infra* chapter 15, part 4.G.

8   This includes nations such as China, Iran, and potentially Russia. For a discussion of these nations, *see infra* chapter 15, part 4.G.

regulations and therefore is not subject to MSB registration, reporting, and recordkeeping regulations."

Subsequent determinations from FinCEN further support the notion that classification of the person as a user or otherwise is based on "how that person uses the convertible virtual currency, and for whose benefit."[9] Thus, "investors" in virtual currencies who buy for their own account, and not to benefit or at the request of any other person, are to be considered "users" and therefore are not money transmitters.[10]

FinCEN also considered in its 2013 Guidance how this analysis would apply to miners of cryptoassets (i.e., persons who obtain a reward for transaction verification services in the form of a cryptoasset that would be characterized by FinCEN as a virtual currency). FinCEN originally concluded (in the 2013 Guidance) that a miner who uses the mined crypto to purchase goods or services would be a user, and not a money transmitter, while a miner who "sells those units to another person for real currency or its equivalent is engaged in transmission to another location and is a money transmitter." FinCEN relatively quickly reconsidered its approach to mining, and in January 2014 issued a revised view of this kind of operation. Under its revised approach, the determination of whether a miner is engaged in money transmission depends on what the miner "uses the convertible virtual currency for, and for whose benefit."[11] In the context of a specific request for a ruling from a Bitcoin mining company, FinCEN concluded in its 2014 response that:

> To the extent that a user mines Bitcoin and uses the Bitcoin solely for the user's own purposes and not for the benefit of another, the user is **not** an MSB under FinCEN's regulations, because these activities involve neither "acceptance" nor "transmission" of the convertible virtual currency and are not the transmission of funds within the meaning of the Rule.

In the ruling, neither the fact that the company might (for its own purposes) convert Bitcoin into another currency or might distribute it to its own shareholders, is enough to make the company "in and of itself" a money transmitter. FinCEN did note that "transfers to third parties at the behest of sellers, creditors, owners, or counterparties involved in these transactions should be closely scrutinized, as they may constitute money transmission."

---

[9]   FinCEN, *Request for Administrative Ruling on the Application of FinCEN's Regulations to a Virtual Currency Trading Platform*, FIN–2014–R011 at 6 (Oct. 27, 2014).

[10]   FinCEN, *Application of FinCEN's Regulations to Virtual Currency Software Development and Certain Investment Activity*, FIN–2014–R002 (Jan. 30, 2014).

[11]   FinCEN, *Application of FinCEN's Regulations to Virtual Currency Mining Operations*, FIN–2014–R001 (Jan. 30, 2014).

B. ADMINISTRATORS

Also as articulated in the original 2013 Guidance, FinCEN defines an administrator as "a person engaged as a business in issuing (putting into circulation) a virtual currency, and who has the authority to redeem (to withdraw from circulation) such virtual currency." It is the authority to redeem the asset that is likely to be most significant in this approach. Unless the issuer of a cryptoasset also has the right to redeem it (i.e., repurchase, reacquire, or cancel it on terms that the issuer decides), under FinCEN's 2013 Guidance, a person who creates and issuers units of convertible virtual currency is not a money transmitter.

However, an issuer may well desire such a redemption feature. For example, it may be an important part of the issuer's planned security measures that it can undo certain transactions (for example those that manipulate flaws in the underlying smart contracts). If the smart contracts give a cryptoasset's issuer not only the power to issue but also the authority to redeem the asset, then it may well be that the issuer will be an administrator under FinCEN's guidance, thereby triggering money transmitter requirements.

In addition, when a person acts as an intermediary for two other parties or acts on behalf of another or at the direction of that other to consummate a transaction with a third person, such activity may also count as money transmission. According to FinCEN's 2013 Guidance, the administrator of a centralized virtual currency repository will, for example, "be a money transmitter to the extent that it allows transfers of value between persons or from one location to another." The 2013 Guidance makes it clear that accepting real (or fiat currency) from a user to create a cryptoasset account with the centralized administrator is classified as money transmission.

C. EXCHANGERS

FinCEN defines an exchanger as "a person engaged as a business in the exchange of virtual currency for real currency, funds, or other virtual currency." This means that a person is an exchanger if it is in the business of accepting and converting a real currency into virtual currency, or vice versa, or converting one form of crypto into another, on behalf of third parties. In an October 27, 2014 ruling,[12] the bureau explained:

> An exchanger will be subject to the same obligations under FinCEN regulations regardless of whether the exchanger acts as a broker (attempting to match two (mostly) simultaneous and offsetting transactions involving the acceptance of one type of currency and the transmission of another) or as a dealer

---

[12] FinCEN, *Request for Administrative Ruling on the Application of FinCEN's Regulations to a Virtual Currency Payment System*, FIN–2014–R012 (Oct. 27, 2014).

(transacting from its own reserve in either convertible virtual currency or real currency).

This particular ruling came in response to a request from a company proposing to establish a system to "provide virtual currency-based payments to merchants in the United States and (mostly) Latin America, who wish to receive payment for goods or services sold in a currency other than that of the legal tender in their respective jurisdictions." The company intended to maintain its own supply of Bitcoin and use those reserves to facilitate payments to merchants who wanted to avoid foreign exchange risk when dealing with international customers. The company intended to deal only with the merchants, and not the merchants' customers.

FinCEN concluded that the company would be an exchanger under the proposed system notwithstanding the fact that payments would come from the company's own reserves of Bitcoin. It would not qualify as a payment processor (which would make it exempt from the exchanger requirements) because it did not plan to operate through BSA-regulated financial institutions.

In a separate ruling issued the same day,[13] FinCEN also considered the request of a company that proposed operating a "convertible virtual currency trading and booking platform." The company wanted to avoid being a money transmitter and argued that it should be a "user" rather than an "exchanger." As explained to FinCEN, the company planned to establish "a trading system . . . to match offers to buy and sell convertible virtual currency for currency of legal tender . . . and a set of book accounts in which prospective buyers or sellers of one type of currency or the other [customers] can deposit funds to cover their exchanges." Transactions were conditioned upon the company finding a match. FinCEN disagreed with the customer's analysis, determining that the proposed platform would be a money transmitter and an exchanger.

Relying on its 2013 Guidance, FinCEN explained that "a person is an exchanger and a money transmitter if the person accepts convertible virtual currency from one person and transmits it to another person as part of the acceptance and transfer of currency, funds, or other value that substitutes for currency." The method of funding for the transactions (i.e., considering the source of any virtual currency being exchanged) is not relevant to the determination of whether the company is a money transmitter or exchanger. Similarly, the fact that any particular transaction would be subject to conditions (such as the ability to find a match for the proposed trade) would not be enough to prevent the proposed business from being a money transmitter and exchanger.

---

[13]   FinCEN, *Request for Administrative Ruling on the Application of FinCEN's Regulations to a Virtual Currency Trading Platform*, FIN–2014–R011 (Oct. 27, 2014).

5. RULES APPLICABLE TO ADMINISTRATORS AND EXCHANGERS

As described above, simple "users" of a virtual currency are not subject to regulation under the BSA. However, both administrators and exchangers are, and the rules applicable to these two categories of persons are extensive.

Businesses that fall within the definition of administrator or exchanger are categorized as money services businesses (MSBs) which must register with FinCEN. They must also comply with various requirements of the BSA and implementing regulations unless there is an available limitation or exemption from the regulatory requirements. This means they must design, implement, and maintain an effective, risk-based AML program.[14] The program must be designed to prevent funds from being used to launder income from illegal sources (traditional money laundering) or to finance terrorist or other illegal activities (reverse money laundering). The AML program must be based on an individualized and "comprehensive risk assessment," and it must include all of the following elements:

- It must include policies, procedures and internal controls to verify customer identification, file reports, create and retain records, and respond appropriately and efficiently to law enforcement requests;

- To the extent applicable, it must integrate AML compliance procedures with automated data processing systems;

- It must include the designation of an AML program compliance officer;

- It must include the provision of appropriate AML education and training for relevant personnel; and

- It must provide for independent periodic review and monitoring to ensure continuing adequacy of the program.

MSBs are also subject to a range of monitoring, recordkeeping and reporting requirements. This includes the obligation to report currency transactions that exceed $10,000, suspicious activities reports if there are transactions or patterns that should create a suspicion of illegal activity, record-keeping if negotiable instruments are conveyed, and compliance

---

[14] For an explanation of current AML requirements, see the FinCEN website which has a range of resources geared towards MSBs. Included are documents such as FinCEN, *Fact Sheet on MSB Registration Rule* [archived at https://perma.cc/SS6K-AT58]; FinCEN, *Guidance on Existing AML Program Rule Compliance Obligations for MSB Principals with Respect to Agent Monitoring*, FIN–2016–G001 (March 11, 2016) [archived at https://perma.cc/22RK-AYP9].

with funds transfer and travel rules that require identifying information for certain transactions in excess of $3,000.

The most powerful enforcement tools for federal authorities are the statutes that criminalize money laundering. These include the Money Laundering Control Act of 1986, which is codified at 18 U.S. Code §§ 1956 & 1957, and 18 U.S. Code § 1960. As mentioned earlier, these provisions make it illegal to intentionally seek to hide the illegal origin of funds, to knowingly use funds to further criminal activity, to knowingly accept tainted funds, or to operate an illegal money transmission business. The last of these prohibitions does not have a scienter requirement, so that failure to appropriately register a money transmission business is a crime regardless of whether there is any intent to disregard the law or knowledge of the requirement.

6. USE OF CRYPTOASSETS TO ENGAGE IN MONEY LAUNDERING ACTIVITIES

The criminalization of money laundering, as described briefly above and in more detail in chapter three, occurred prior to the advent of Bitcoin and other cryptoassets. The application of these rules to crypto may not have been immediately obvious to crypto businesses since neither the statutes themselves nor any legislative history mentions cryptocurrency or other such assets as the subject of the laws.

A. ARE "VIRTUAL" ASSETS CURRENCY?

In a wide variety of contexts, criminal defendants engaged in virtual currency businesses have sought to have criminal indictments against them dismissed on the grounds that they were not dealing in "money" and therefore could not have been engaged in "money laundering" under the federal statutes. In an early case that predates the rise of modern cryptocurrencies, the defendants, who owned and operated an internet-based "digital currency" payment system known as E-Gold, were indicted for conspiring to engage in money laundering and to operate an unlicensed money transmitting business.[15]

E-Gold, Ltd. had designed e-Gold as an alternative payment system that operated over the internet. A person desiring to utilize e-Gold was first required to open an account and then to convert "national currency" into e-Gold. The account holder could then utilize the e-Gold to buy goods, services, or to pay a third party, or could convert the e-Gold back into national currency. E-Gold Ltd. charged a transaction fee for each transfer, as well as a monthly storage fee for the gold bullion that was supposedly stored in Europe in order to back up the virtual e-Gold. In addition to E-

---

[15]   *United States v. E-Gold, Ltd.*, 550 F. Supp. 2d 83 (DDC 2008).

Gold Ltd., a digital exchange service known as OmniPay operated to exchange national currency into e-Gold and vice versa. OmniPay was operated by Gold & Silver Reserve, Inc., which was also a named defendant, along with three individuals heavily involved in the E-Gold operations.

Defendants in *E-Gold* filed a motion to dismiss charges filed against them of operating an illegal money transmission business under 18 U.S. Code § 1960 on the grounds that they did not deal in cash or "currency" and therefore did not come within the ambit of the statute. The court rejected the defendants' arguments and instead determined that the prohibition on illegal money transmission businesses included businesses engaged in the transmission of the value of currency through some medium of exchange.[16] This opinion helped form the backdrop for cryptocurrency cases such *U.S. v. Murgio*, 209 F. Supp. 3d 698 (S.D.N.Y. 2016), excerpted here.

PRELIMINARY NOTES AND QUESTIONS

1.   What was the business that Murgio was alleged to have operated as an unregistered money transmission business? How did it function?

2.   Why would FinCEN care if the business was allowed to operate? What part of FinCEN's mission was implicated by the Coin.mix operation?

UNITED STATES V. MURGIO
209 F. Supp. 3d 698 (S.D.N.Y. 2016)

ALISON J. NATHAN, DISTRICT JUDGE:

. . . . The allegations in the Indictment stem from Murgio's alleged operation . . . of Coin.mx, a website that the Government characterizes as an unlawful Bitcoin exchange. . .

I.   BACKGROUND

. . . . Murgio is charged . . . with operating, and conspiring to operate, Coin.mx as an unlicensed money transmitting business. The Government alleges that Murgio and his co-conspirators attempted to shield the true nature of his Bitcoin exchange business by operating through several front companies, including one known as "Collectables Club," to convince financial institutions that Coin.mx was just a members-only association of individuals interested in collectable items, like stamps and sports memorabilia. Counts Six and Seven of the Indictment charge Murgio with committing, and conspiring to commit, wire fraud by virtue of making material misrepresentations to the financial institutions he was allegedly attempting to deceive. In Counts Eight and Nine, he is charged with engaging in, and conspiring to engage in, money laundering. . . .

---

[16]   *Id.* at 88–97.

... Murgio filed a motion to dismiss Counts One and Two of the Indictment, as well as a series of omnibus pre-trial motions. . . .

II. MURGIO'S MOTION TO DISMISS COUNTS ONE AND TWO

Murgio moves to dismiss Counts One and Two of the Indictment, pursuant to Federal Rule of Criminal Procedure 12(b)(3)(B), on the grounds that those counts fail to state an offense. Because "federal crimes are solely creatures of statute, a federal indictment can be challenged on the ground that it fails to allege a crime within the terms of the applicable statute."
. . . .

Count One of the Indictment charges Murgio with conspiring to commit an offense against the United States, in violation of 18 U.S.C. § 371. The object of that alleged conspiracy is the operation of an unlicensed money transmitting business, in violation of 18 U.S.C. § 1960. This underlying substantive offense . . . is the focus of Murgio's motion to dismiss.

Section 1960 makes it a crime to "knowingly conduct[ ], control[ ], manage[ ], supervise[ ], direct[ ], or own[ ] all or part of an unlicensed money transmitting business." 18 U.S.C. § 1960(a). The key phrase in § 1960, for purposes of this motion, is "unlicensed money transmitting business." Breaking that phrase down into its component parts, first, the statute defines "money transmitting" to include "transferring funds on behalf of the public by any and all means including but not limited to transfers . . . by wire, check, draft, facsimile, or courier." Id. § 1960(b)(2). Whether Coin.mx handled "funds," and if so, whether it "transferr[ed]" them on behalf of the public, are key questions here.

Next, the statute does not provide a particularized definition of "business," other than to specify that a "money transmitting business" must "affect[ ] interstate or foreign commerce" in order to fall within § 1960. Id. § 1960(b)(1).

Finally, the statute lists three ways in which a "money transmitting business" can be deemed "unlicensed." First, a money transmitting business is unlicensed if it "is operated without an appropriate money transmitting license in a State where such operation is punishable as a misdemeanor or a felony." Id. § 1960(b)(1)(A). Second, such a business is unlicensed if it fails to comply with federal "money transmitting business registration requirements." Id. § 1960(b)(1)(B). And third, a money transmitting business is unlicensed if it "involves the transportation or transmission of funds that are known to the defendant to have been derived from a criminal offense or are intended to be used to promote or support unlawful activity." Id. § 1960(b)(1)(C).

In sum, to qualify as an "unlicensed money transmitting business" under § 1960, a business must a) transfer, on behalf of the public, b) funds, and c) do so in violation of state or federal licensing and registration requirements, or with knowledge that the funds were derived from a criminal offense.

Murgio raises three principal arguments in support of dismissing Counts One and Two of the Indictment. First, he argues that bitcoins do not qualify as "funds" under § 1960. Second, he claims that the Indictment fails to allege that Coin.mx transferred funds so as to be a "money transmitting business" under § 1960. And third, he contends that the Indictment inadequately alleges that Coin.mx failed to comply with state and federal licensing and registration requirements. For the reasons that follow, the Court rejects each of these arguments.

A.   Bitcoins Are "Funds" Under § 1960

Section 1960 does not specify what counts as "money" that is "transmitted," other than to note that it "includes . . . funds." 18 U.S.C. § 1960(b)(2). This raises the question of whether bitcoins are "funds" under the statute. The Court concludes that they are.

"When a term goes undefined in a statute," courts give the term "its ordinary meaning." *Taniguchi v. Kan Pac. Saipan, Ltd.*, 566 U.S. 560 (2012). The ordinary meaning of "funds," according to Webster's Dictionary, is "available pecuniary resources." Webster's Third New International Dictionary 921 (2002). "Pecuniary" is defined as "taking the form of or consisting of money." *Id.* at 1663. And "money," in turn, is defined as "something generally accepted as a medium of exchange, a measure of value, or a means of payment." *Id.* at 1458. This definition of "funds," and the corresponding definition of "money," have consistently been adopted by courts in this circuit. In *United States v. Faiella*, Judge Rakoff defined "funds," in the context of interpreting § 1960, as " 'available money' or 'an amount of something that is available for use.' " 39 F.Supp.3d 544, 545 (S.D.N.Y.2014) (citation omitted). And as the Court does here, he also defined "money" as "something generally accepted as a medium of exchange, a measure of value, or a means of payment." *Id.* (citation omitted). Similarly, Judge Forrest has explained that " '[f]unds' are defined as 'money, often money for a specific purpose,' " and that " '[m]oney' is an object used to buy things." *United States v. Ulbricht*, 31 F.Supp.3d 540, 570 (S.D.N.Y.2014) (citation omitted). Although Judge Forrest reached that conclusion in a case involving a different statute—18 U.S.C. § 1956, which prohibits money laundering—she did so by engaging in the same analysis the Court must perform here. *See id.* (noting that " '[f]unds' is not defined in the statute and is therefore given its ordinary meaning"). In light of this consensus as to the term's ordinary meaning, the Court concludes that "funds," for the purposes of § 1960, means pecuniary resources, which are generally accepted as a medium of exchange or a means of payment.

Applying that definition here, it is clear that bitcoins are funds within the plain meaning of that term. Bitcoins can be accepted "as a payment for goods and services" or bought "directly from an exchange with [a] bank account." They therefore function as "pecuniary resources" and are "used as a medium of exchange" and "a means of payment." As Judge Rakoff explained, bitcoins "clearly qualif[y] as 'money' or 'funds'" under § 1960 because they "can be easily purchased in exchange for ordinary currency, act[ ] as a denominator of value, and [are] used to conduct financial transactions." 39 F.Supp.3d at 545; *see also Ulbricht*, 31 F.Supp.3d at 570 (holding that bitcoins are "funds" because they "can be either used directly to pay for certain things or can act as a medium of exchange and be converted into a currency which can pay for things"). Courts considering other virtual currencies have reached the same conclusion—those currencies also count as "funds" under § 1960. *See Budovsky*, 2015 WL 5602853, at *14 (relying on *Faiella* for the proposition that "LR," another virtual currency, "qualifies as 'funds' for purposes of § 1960"); *see also United States v. E-Gold, Ltd.*, 550 F.Supp.2d 82, 88 (D.D.C.2008) (noting that "[s]ection 1960 defines 'money transmitting' broadly to include transferring 'funds,' not just currency, by 'any and all means'").

The legislative history of § 1960 supports the conclusion that bitcoins fall within the statute's purview. Section 1960 was enacted to address the fact that "money launderers with illicit profits ha[d] found new avenues of entry into the financial system." S. Rep. No. 101–460 (1990). From its inception then, § 1960 sought to prevent innovative ways of transmitting money illicitly. It appears that Congress "designed the statute to keep pace with . . . evolving threats," and this Court must accordingly give effect to the broad language Congress employed—namely, that § 1960 "appl[ies] to any business involved in transferring 'funds . . . by any and all means.'" *Faiella*, 39 F.Supp.3d at 546 (emphases added) (quoting 18 U.S.C. § 1960(b)(2)). Dictionaries, courts, and the statute's legislative history all point to the same conclusion: bitcoins are funds.

Murgio, however, urges the Court to reject this straightforward conclusion. He asks the Court to adopt a more narrow definition of "funds," contending that the term should mean only "currency." The path that leads him to that conclusion is as follows: First, he claims that Black's Law Dictionary defines "funds" as "[a] sum of money or other liquid assets established for a specific purpose." *Id.* (alteration in original) (quoting Black's Law Dictionary 788 (10th ed. 2014)). Second, he cites Black's definition of "money." *Id.* Black's defines "money" as "[a]ssets that can be easily converted to cash," and, more narrowly, as "the medium of exchange authorized or adopted by a government as part of its currency." Black's Law Dictionary, *supra,* at 1158. As Murgio notes, the narrower of the two definitions of "money" is taken from the Uniform Commercial Code ("UCC"). Third, and finally, Murgio argues that "funds" must mean only "currency" because the other definition of "money" from Black's—i.e., assets easily converted to cash—would render § 1960 "meaningless and overly broad." Each step in this chain of reasoning is flawed.

First, Murgio's resort to Black's—a legal dictionary—as the starting point for defining "funds" ignores the rule that an undefined term in a statute is given its "ordinary meaning." The definitions of "money" and "funds" from Black's "would only be relevant if Congress intended that these terms be given special meaning as legal 'terms of art.'" There is no evidence that Congress intended such a specialized meaning here.

Second, even if Black's were the right dictionary to consult, Murgio errs in three respects in consulting it. First, the definition of "funds" that he cites is actually the definition of "fund," singular. *See* Black's Law Dictionary, *supra,* at 788 ("A *sum* of money or other liquid assets established for a specific purpose." (emphasis added)). That definition is inapplicable here because "funds," as used in § 1960, clearly refers to the money or liquid assets themselves, rather than the kind of "fund" that is comprised of a sum of assets. *Compare* Black's Law Dictionary, *supra,* at 788 (providing example of "a fund reserved for unanticipated expenses"). And in fact, Black's provides a definition of the plural of "fund," defining "funds" as "[m]oney or other assets, such as stocks, bonds, or working capital, available to pay debts, expenses, and the like." *Id*. Murgio's second error is ignoring the second half of this definition—i.e., that "funds" includes "other assets." The examples of "other assets" that Black's provides—stocks, bonds, or working capital—are clearly broader than just "currency." Finally, even if the Court were to ignore half of the definition of "funds" and rely only on Black's definition of "money," it would reject the narrower of the two definitions of money that Black's provides. The narrower definition relies expressly on the UCC, which is evidence that "money" only has a restricted meaning in specialized contexts, like commercial law. *See* U.C.C. § 1–103 (Unif. Law Comm'n) (explaining that the UCC's purpose is to "modernize the law governing commercial transactions").

Third, Murgio's concern about overbreadth—i.e., that interpreting "funds" to mean more than just "currency" would render § 1960 overly broad—is meritless. Murgio argues that using the ordinary meaning of "funds," as outlined above, would require treating commodities like copper, hogs, or coffee as "funds," thereby bringing those commodities within the purview of the money transmitter statute. But no one would consider coffee or hogs "pecuniary resources," and although such commodities are traded on exchanges, they do not themselves function as a "medium of exchange." Murgio's concerns about absurd results are therefore unfounded.

Murgio attempts to buttress his argument in favor of a narrower definition of funds by relying on various government documents that discuss virtual currencies. None of those documents, however, address the meaning of "funds" in the context of § 1960. For instance Murgio cites the Department of Treasury's Financial Crimes Enforcement Network's ("FinCEN") guidance on virtual currencies. *See* Application of FinCEN'S Regulations to Persons Administering, Exchanging, or Using Virtual Currencies, FIN–2013–G001 (Mar. 18, 2013) ("FinCEN Guidance") That document defines "funds" for the limited purpose of explaining when a person has provided or sold "prepaid access," and concludes that prepaid access to "funds or the value of funds" is limited to "real currencies." *Id.* at 3 & n.18. But the FinCEN Guidance does not even mention § 1960, much less purport to interpret the statute's use of the word "funds." Similarly, the fact that the IRS treats virtual currency as "property," rather than "currency," for tax purposes is irrelevant to the inquiry here. *See* I.R.S. Notice 2014–21, available at http://www.irs.gov/pub/irs-drop/n-14-21.pdf. In fact, the IRS Notice that Murgio cites makes clear that it "addresses *only the U.S. federal tax consequences* of transactions in, or transactions that use, convertible virtual currency." *Id.* at 1 (emphasis added). The document does not speak to the definition of "funds" or have anything to do with § 1960. *See Budovsky*, 2015 WL 5602853, at *14 (rejecting both the FinCEN Guidance and the IRS Notice as "inapposite" because the documents "do not suggest that the term 'funds' should not be read to encompass virtual currencies"). Finally, Murgio's invocation of the fact that the Commodity Futures Trading Commission ("CFTC") has classified Bitcoin as a commodity is similarly unmoored from § 1960 and from the Court's responsibility to determine the plain meaning of "funds." *See . . . In re Coinflip, Inc.,* CFTC No. 15–29, 2015 WL 5535736 (Sept. 17, 2015). To the extent the CFTC's decision in *Coinflip* is relevant, it actually defines Bitcoin as "a digital representative of value that functions as a medium of exchange, a unit of account, and/or a store of value, but not does not have legal tender status." *Coinflip*, 2015 WL 5535736 at *1 n.2. That definition places bitcoins squarely within the plain meaning of § 1960's term "funds."

Finally, Murgio invokes the rule of lenity and the doctrine of constitutional avoidance. Like the other federal courts to have considered the issue, this Court rejects the claim that applying the plain meaning of "funds" to encompass bitcoins runs afoul of the rule of lenity or the Constitution. First, the rule of lenity is reserved "for those situations in which a reasonable doubt persists about a statute's intended scope even after resort to the language and structure, legislative history, and motivating policies of the statute." *Moskal v. United States*, 498 U.S. 103, 108 (1990) (emphasis in original) (internal quotation marks and citation omitted). Here, "[h]aving considered the text, purpose, and legislative history of § 1960, there is no ambiguity that would require resort to the rule of lenity." *Budovsky,* 2015 WL 5602853, at *14; *see also Faiella,* 39 F.Supp.3d at 547 (finding no "irreconcilable ambiguity" in § 1960 that would require "resort to the rule of lenity"). Second, Murgio's invocation of the doctrine of constitutional avoidance presumably relies on the risk that interpreting "funds" in § 1960 to encompass bitcoins would constitute "an unforeseeable and retroactive judicial expansion of narrow and precise statutory language." *Bouie v. City of Columbia*, 378 U.S. 347, 352 (1964). But Murgio "does not point to any prior law that failed to apply § 1960 to virtual currencies," nor does he explain how its application here would constitute an unforeseeable statutory enlargement. *Budovsky*, 2015 WL 5602853, at *15. To the contrary, the analysis above reinforces that applying § 1960 to Bitcoin is consistent with the statute's plain meaning. Bitcoins are "funds," and treating them as such is constitutional.

1. The Indictment Sufficiently Alleges that Coin.mx Failed to Comply with Florida Licensing Requirements

A money transmitting business that operates "without an appropriate money transmitting license in a State where such operation is punishable as a misdemeanor or a felony" is "unlicensed." 18 U.S.C. § 1960(b)(1)(A). The state at issue here is Florida, and Florida law provides that "[a] person may not engage in the business of a money services business . . . in this state unless the person is licensed or exempted from licensure under this chapter." Fla. Stat. § 560.125(1). Chapter 560 defines a "money services business" as "any person" who "acts as a . . . money transmitter." *Id.* § 560.103(22). And the statute further defines "money transmitter" as an entity that "receives currency, monetary value, or payment instruments for the purpose of transmitting the same by any means, including transmission by wire, facsimile, electronic transfer, courier, the Internet, or through bill payment services." *Id.* § 560.103(23).

Murgio's arguments as to why these Florida provisions do not apply to the charged conduct principally mirror his claims about § 1960 more broadly. First, he contends that bitcoins are not covered by Florida's definition of "money transmitter" because, just as he argues that bitcoins are not "funds" under federal law, he contends that they are not "currency, monetary value, or payment instruments" under Florida law. The Court disagrees. Florida defines "monetary value" as "a medium of exchange, whether or not redeemable in currency." Fla. Stat. § 560.103(21). Bitcoins, as explained previously, function as a "medium of exchange." They therefore fall within Chapter 560's express definition of "monetary value." Bitcoins also fall within the statute's express definition of "payment instruments." Chapter 560 defines "payment instrument" as "a check, draft, warrant, money order, travelers check, electronic instrument, or other instrument, payment of money, or monetary value whether or not negotiable." *Id.* § 560.103(29) (emphases added). Because bitcoins are "monetary value," they are also "payment instruments."

Murgio also invokes the rule of lenity to argue that the Court should not apply Chapter 560's definition of "monetary value" or "payment instrument" to bitcoins. But there is no "statutory ambiguity" here. *See Moskal,* 498 U.S. at 107. Again, bitcoins function as a medium of exchange, and they are therefore both monetary value and payment instruments, as Florida defines those terms. Moreover, the rule of lenity is particularly inapt in the context of Chapter 560, given that Bitcoin's raison d'être is to serve as a form of payment. It does not raise the specter of unconstitutionality to apply a law that specifically mentions "payment instruments" to a virtual currency designed to serve as a form of payment.

Murgio's second challenge to applying Florida's Chapter 560 here is that, for the "same reasons" that Coin.mx is not a "money transmitting business" under § 1960, it is not a "money transmitter" under Chapter 560. Murgio points to no reason that a "money transmitting business" under federal law is not a "money transmitter" under Florida law. . . .

The one distinct argument that Murgio raises with respect to Florida law relates to a recently decided Florida case. While the pending pre-trial motions in this case were being briefed, a Florida trial court issued an opinion addressing the applicability of Chapter 560 to Bitcoin. *See Florida v. Espinoza,* No. F14–293 (Fla. Cir. Ct. July 22, 2016). The court in *Espinoza* dismissed the information, which charged the defendant with operating an unlicensed money services business because he sold bitcoins to an undercover officer. *Id.* at 2–3. Relying on many of the arguments that Murgio raises here, the Florida court held that bitcoins are not "payment instruments" under Florida law. *Id.* at 5. It also held that the defendant did not "transmit" bitcoins because he was only a seller of bitcoins, rather than a middleman, and therefore did not transmit bitcoins "from one person or place to another." *Id.* at 4 (internal quotation marks and citation omitted). The court explained that although "[t]he Florida Legislature may choose to adopt statutes regulating virtual currency in the future," applying existing law regulating money services business to Bitcoin would be "like fitting a square peg in a round hole." *Id.* at 6. This Court respectfully disagrees.

To the Court's knowledge, the *Espinoza* court is the first Florida court to have considered the reach of Chapter 560 in the context of Bitcoin, and neither the state's Supreme Court nor the District Courts of Appeal have weighed in. This Court is therefore not bound by the decision in *Espinoza,* though it owes the decision "proper regard." *Tyler v. Bethlehem Steel Corp.,* 958 F.2d 1176, 1190 (2d Cir.1992) (quoting *C.I.R. v. Bosch's Estate,* 387 U.S. 456, 465 (1967)). After carefully considering the analysis in *Espinoza,* the Court determines that the Florida Supreme Court, if faced with the question, would hold that Murgio is properly charged with violating Chapter 560. As an initial matter, the Court finds that there is no plausible interpretation of "monetary value" or "payment instruments," as the terms are used in Chapter 560, that would place bitcoins outside the statute's ambit. With respect to "monetary value," the Court has already explained that Bitcoin plainly is "a medium of exchange, whether or not redeemable in currency" (though Bitcoin is in fact redeemable in currency). Fla. Stat. § 560.103(21). The *Espinoza* court did not contemplate the possibility that bitcoins qualify as "monetary value"—the court limited its discussion to "currency" and "payment instruments." *See Espinoza*, slip op. at 4–5. *Espinoza* therefore does not squarely address this Court's reasoning for holding that Chapter 560's definition of "money transmitter" applies to businesses that transmit bitcoins. Moreover, with respect to the meaning of "payment instrument," the only reason the *Espinoza* court cites for concluding that bitcoins are not "payment instruments" is that the IRS "has decided to treat virtual currency as property for federal tax purposes." *Id.* at 5. As an initial matter, this argument ignores the fact that Chapter 560 defines "payment instrument" as including "monetary value." Fla. Stat. § 560.103(29). But more to the point, the *Espinoza* court offers no explanation as to why a decision by the IRS is relevant to the question of whether bitcoins, which are used as (and designed to be) an instrument of payment, qualify as "payment instruments" under Florida law. The IRS's classification is divorced from the basic statutory interpretation question at issue here. Accordingly, the Court remains persuaded that Chapter 560 regulates businesses that transmit bitcoins.

Additionally, the *Espinoza* court's holding that the defendant in that case did not "transmit" bitcoins because he was only a seller of bitcoins, rather than a middleman, does not alter this Court's conclusion that the Indictment sufficiently alleges a failure to comply with Chapter 560. *See Espinoza,* slip op. at 4. As explained above, the fact that the Indictment alleges that Coin.mx was a "money transmitting business" is sufficient to survive a motion to dismiss, and the Court therefore does not need to reach the question of whether the *Espinoza* court's "middleman" requirement is correct. Moreover, the evidence at trial may in fact show that Coin.mx "operate[d] much like a middleman in . . . financial transaction[s]," which would satisfy the standard set forth by *Espinoza* and advocated by Murgio. *Id.* Finally, there are key factual differences between this case and Murgio's that cast doubt on the applicability of the *Espinoza* court's holding. The defendant in *Espinoza* was an individual who did nothing more than sell bitcoins to one undercover officer on several occasions. *Id.* at 2–3. There were no allegations in that case about running a website, transfers between Bitcoin wallets, or processing credit card payments. In other words, it appears that the conduct charged in *Espinoza* is meaningfully different from the allegations against Murgio. In light of those considerations, the Court holds that the Indictment properly charges Murgio with failing to comply with Florida's licensing requirements for money transmitters.

. . . .

[These motions are Denied.]

_____

At the time that *Murgio* was decided, the only reported decision holding that Bitcoin and other cryptocurrencies did not constitute "funds" within the meaning of a money transmitter statute was the Florida trial court opinion in *Espinoza*, referenced in *Murgio*. *See State v. Espinoza*, No. 14–cr–2923 (Fla. Cir. Ct. July 22, 2016) (granting a motion to dismiss on the grounds that Bitcoins were not payment instruments under Florida law). On January 30, 2019, the intermediate Florida appellate court reversed the trial court determination, in *Florida v. Espinoza*, 264 So.3d 1055 (Fla. App. 2019). The appellate court flatly concluded that it agreed "with the district court's conclusion in *Murgio* that 'there is no plausible interpretation of 'monetary value' or 'payment instruments,' as those terms are used in Chapter 560 that would place bitcoins outside of the statute's ambit.'" 264 So.3d at 1066, citing *Murgio*, 209 F. Supp.3d at 713.

On the other hand, a few months later a federal magistrate in the Western District of New York reached a conclusion similar to the one reached by the district court in *Espinoza*. The case is an unusual one in that it arose out of a supervised release violation where the defendant had lied to his probation officer about using Bitcoins.

UNITED STATES V. PETIX
2016 WL 7017919 (W.D.N.Y. 2016) (not reported in F. Supp.)

HONORABLE HUGH B. SCOTT, UNITED STATES MAGISTRATE JUDGE.

I. INTRODUCTION

In Count Two of the superseding indictment that it has filed, the Government accuses defendant Richard Petix ("Petix") of running an unlicensed money transmitting business in violation of 18 U.S.C. § 1960. The financial instrument at the heart of the alleged unlawful business, however, is not cash, checks, notes, or other aspects of the United States monetary system. The financial instrument in question is the digital virtual currency known as Bitcoin. Does the transmission of Bitcoin come within the reach of Section 1960?

Petix says no and has filed a motion to dismiss Count Two accordingly. Petix argues that Bitcoin is private property like precious metals and that he did not operate any business connected to Bitcoin that would fall under Section 1960. The Government counters that Bitcoin is just the latest example of a medium of exchange that Section 1960 was written to regulate.

. . . .

II. BACKGROUND

This case concerns allegations that Petix lied to his probation officers about using computers, in particular using them in connection with the decentralized virtual currency known as Bitcoin. Petix's relationship with the USPO stemmed from a criminal conviction in this District for knowingly transporting child pornography in interstate commerce, in violation of 18 U.S.C. § 2252A(a)(1). On January 16, 2009, District Judge Charles J. Siragusa sentenced Petix to a term of imprisonment of 60 months and a term of supervised release of 30 years. As a special condition of supervision, Judge Siragusa required Petix to give the USPO advance notice of any computer usage and gave the USPO broad authority to manage that usage. In October 2015, after his release, Petix filled out paperwork for the USPO pertaining to the special condition about computer usage. Among other information that Petix gave in that paperwork, he explicitly denied being a computer user. The paperwork contained a notice that false statements could lead to prosecution under 18 U.S.C. § 1001.

As alleged by the Government, Petix's compliance with the special condition of release did not last long. Between August 2014 and December 2015, Petix engaged in numerous transactions involving the buying and selling of bitcoins. Given the nature of Bitcoin, Petix's transactions necessarily would have required the use of a computer. . . . On December 3, 2015, agents and probation officers observed Petix at a local coffee shop using a computer and other electronic devices. When the agents and probation officers confronted Petix, he denied ownership of the devices, even when his girlfriend, sitting in a car outside the coffee shop, confirmed his ownership. The open screen of the computer displayed information indicating that Petix had just completed a transaction involving 37 bitcoins with a value, at the time, of approximately $13,000. The agents and probation officers took Petix into custody that evening.

. . . .

. . .[T]he Government accuses Petix of running an unlicensed money transmitting business in violation of 18 U.S.C. § 1960. The superseding indictment also contains a notice of forfeiture for electronic devices seized on December 3, 2015 and a notice of intent to seek a money judgment. [Petix has moved to dismiss this charge.]

. . . .

Petix argues that what he allegedly did . . . "was the functional equivalent of selling any other chattel—e.g. a silver dollar, collectable currency, a diamond, gold jewelry, etc." By proposing that the Court treat Bitcoin as chattel, Petix effectively is arguing that Bitcoin is not "money" or "funds" as Section 1960 uses those terms. Additionally, Petix argues that what he allegedly did ... does not constitute "transmitting" or "transferring" the proceeds from sales of bitcoins as understood in Section 1960. In supplemental briefing, Petix develops this argument further by arguing that his alleged conduct does not constitute a "business" that he was "operating" for purposes of Section 1960. The Government counters that Bitcoin qualifies as "funds" under Section 1960 because "virtual currencies such as Bitcoin have no intrinsic value or purpose beyond serving as a means of transferring wealth." The Government argues further that what Petix allegedly did counts as a business that he operated because "[a]ny transfer or non-transfer of the defendant's fees, proceeds, or profits from selling bitcoins is irrelevant. . . . The transfer of the bitcoins is the service that the defendant performed on behalf of any paying member of the public, wherever situated. . . .

III. DISCUSSION

A. Motions to Dismiss Indictments Generally

Petix is arguing that the Government's allegations . . . taken at face value, do not amount to a criminal offense. The Court accordingly will review Petix's motion under Rule 12(b)(3)(B)(v), which allows for pretrial motions to dismiss indictments for "failure to state an offense."

. . . .

B. Bitcoin and Section 1960

. . . .

Section 1960 has two subsections, an operational subsection and a definitional subsection. The operational subsection appears simple enough: It runs one sentence long. "Whoever knowingly conducts, controls, manages, supervises, directs, or owns all or part of an unlicensed money transmitting business, shall be fined in accordance with this title or imprisoned not more than 5 years, or both." 18 U.S.C. § 1960(a). Analysis of the statute quickly becomes complicated, though; of all the terms and phrases used in the operational subsection, the definitional subsection partially defines only two of them. For purposes of Section 1960, and ignoring language not relevant to this case, "the term 'unlicensed money transmitting business' means a money transmitting business which affects interstate or foreign commerce in any manner or degree and . . . fails to comply with the money transmitting business registration requirements under section 5330 of title 31, United States Code, or regulations prescribed under such section." *Id.* § 1960(b)(1)(B). The definitional subsection also addresses the term "money transmitting," but it does not truly define the term. Whatever "money transmitting" is, the definitional subsection states only that it "*includes* transferring funds on behalf of the public by any and all means including but not limited to transfers within this country or to locations abroad by wire, check, draft, facsimile, or courier." *Id.* § 1960(b)(2) (emphasis added). At its irreducible core, then, Section 1960 declares that, under the right conditions including deficiencies in licensing and registration, certain conduct involving "money" or "funds" is unlawful. Section 1960 does not define "money"; the Government has acknowledged that "Section 1960 also does not define 'transferring' or 'funds.'" Getting a better handle on the terms "money" and "funds" is a good next step in the Court's analysis; as noted above, the Government has argued explicitly that Petix's bitcoins themselves, and not any "fees, proceeds, or profits from selling bitcoins," lie at the heart of [the charge]. . . .

C. Are Bitcoins "Money" or "Funds" Under Section 1960?

Defining the terms "money" and "funds" requires using a few principles of statutory interpretation. "Our first step in interpreting a statute is to determine whether the language at issue has a plain and unambiguous meaning with regard to the particular dispute in the case. Our inquiry must cease if the statutory language is unambiguous and the statutory scheme is coherent and consistent. The plainness or ambiguity of statutory language is determined by reference to the language itself, the specific context in which that language is used, and the broader context of the statute as a whole." *Robinson v. Shell Oil Co.,* 519 U.S. 337, 340–41 (1997) (internal quotation marks and citations omitted). When courts have to examine specific terms in statutes, and the statutes do not provide definitions for those terms, judges will assign an ordinary, common-sense meaning consistent with the broader context of the statute. *EMI Christian Music Grp., Inc. v. MP3tunes, LLC,* 840 F.3d 69 (2d Cir. 2016) (citations omitted). "A 'common and ordinary' meaning may include another statutory definition from a similar context, a dictionary definition, or a common-law definition." 2A Norman Singer and Shambie Singer, Sutherland Statutory Construction § 47:7 (7th ed. and 2016 Supp.) (citations omitted); *see also, e.g., Boumediene v. Bush,* 553 U.S. 723, 776 (2008) ("When interpreting a statute, we examine related provisions in other parts of the U.S. Code.") (citations omitted); *Walters v. Metro. Educ. Enterprises, Inc.,* 519 U.S. 202, 207 (1997) ("In the absence of an indication to the contrary, words in a statute are assumed to bear their ordinary, contemporary, common meaning.") (internal quotation marks and citation omitted). Courts have to use caution when relying solely on dictionary definitions of terms that ordinary people in everyday life would understand in a different way. "Whether a statutory term is unambiguous, however, does not turn solely on dictionary definitions of its component words. . . . Ordinarily, a word's usage accords with its dictionary definition. In law as in life, however, the same words, placed in different contexts, sometimes mean different things." *Yates v. United States,* 135 S. Ct. 1074, 1081–82 (2015) (citations omitted).

Taking the two undefined terms in Section 1960 in reverse order, the Supreme Court already has applied the above principles of interpretation to the term "funds." "The ordinary meaning of 'fund[s]' is 'sum[s] of money . . . set aside for a specific purpose.'" *Clark v. Rameker*, ___ U.S. ___, 134 S. Ct. 2242, 2246 (2014) (ellipsis and brackets in original) (citation omitted). The Supreme Court happened to look at a dictionary to define "funds" in *Clark*, but consistent with the principle expressed in *Yates*, that definition aligns with how ordinary people would understand that term. The Supreme Court's understanding of "funds" also is consistent with legislative materials that use the term in similar or analogous contexts. For example, when the House of Representatives prepared a report for the proposed Financial Anti-Terrorism Act of 2001, it discussed "funds" that supported terrorism using examples such as cash, checks, credit cards, and "seed money." H.R. Rep. 107–250(I), 2001 WL 1249988, at *34 (2001). The civil forfeiture statute, 18 U.S.C. § 981, treats the term "funds" as something that, inter alia, can be deposited in established and regulated financial institutions. Some of the banking statutes use the term "funds" to describe something that can be deposited into and withdrawn from the United States Treasury. *See generally, e.g.,* 12 U.S.C. § 1735. From one source to another, the exact meaning of "funds" might change a little, but the uses of the term in the United States Code and in everyday life have in common the description that the Supreme Court used: designated or allocated sums of money.

The ordinary understanding of "funds," with its reference to "money," necessarily brings the Court to an assessment of that other term. Legal authorities abound with uses of the term "money." The Constitution gave Congress the enumerated power "[t]o coin Money, [and to] regulate the Value thereof." U.S. Const. art. I, § 8, cl. 5. The United States Code, under a subchapter titled "Monetary System," has a definition of legal tender that covers coins, currency, and notes. 31 U.S.C. § 5103. Another provision of Title 31 refers to "money" and "public money" as something that can be deposited in the United States Treasury. 31 U.S.C. § 3302. A portion of the tax code refers to estate transfers that occur "for a consideration in money or money's worth." 26 U.S.C. § 2043. Portions of the judicial code refer to "receiving and paying over money" compared to "disposing of such property," 28 U.S.C. § 1921(c)(1); and to plural "moneys paid into any court of the United States," 28 U.S.C. § 2041. Countless other examples exist, written before and after Section 1960, and of course the exact use of the term "money" will vary somewhat across very different statutes and cases.

What all of the above examples have in common, though, is the involvement of a sovereign. Across all of the legal authorities that make some reference to money, and despite new technologies that have emerged over the years within the United States monetary system, there has been a consistent understanding that money is not just any financial instrument or medium of exchange that people can devise on their own. "Money," in its common use, is some kind of financial instrument or medium of exchange that is assessed value, made uniform, regulated, and protected by sovereign power. *See, e.g.,* David G. Oedel, *Why Regulate Cybermoney?*, 46 Am. U. L. Rev. 1075, 1077 (1997) ("[I]n the background of most functional definitions are suggestions that money serves as a tool for governments to exercise macroeconomic control and to channel financial commerce along preferred routes.") (citations omitted). Ordinary people in everyday life know this intuitively; the average person who hears the term "money" will think of government-issued "dollars" or instruments, like checks, money orders, credit cards, or notes, directly connected to dollars. *Cf. Nix v. Hedden,* 149 U.S. 304, 307 (1893) (giving "the common language of the people" priority over scientific definitions, for purposes of statutory construction). The Supreme Court years ago expressed the ordinary understanding of money as a regulated instrument when, quoting Blackstone, it wrote that "[t]he coining of money is the act of the sovereign power, that its value may be known on inspection." *Legal Tender Cases,* 79 U.S. 457, 491 (1870) (emphasis in original), abrogated in part on other grounds by *Tahoe-Sierra Pres. Council, Inc. v. Tahoe Reg'l Planning Agency,* 535 U.S. 302, 326 n.21 (2002). The Ninth Circuit once wrote a succinct yet fairly comprehensive description of how money draws its usefulness from governmental authority:

> The broad and comprehensive national authority over the subjects of revenue, finance and currency is derived from the aggregate of the powers granted to the Congress, embracing the powers to lay and collect taxes, to borrow money, to regulate commerce with foreign nations and among the several states, to coin money, regulate the value thereof, and of foreign coin, and fix the standards of weights and measures, and the added express power to make all laws which shall be necessary and proper for carrying into execution the other enumerated powers. The constitution was designed to provide the same currency, having a uniform legal value in all the States. It was for that reason that the power to regulate the value of money was conferred upon the federal government, while the same power, as well as the power to emit bills of credit, was withdrawn from the states. The states cannot declare what shall be money, or regulate its value. Whatever power there is over the currency is vested in the Congress. The power includes [t]he authority to impose requirements of uniformity and parity (which) is an essential feature of this control of the currency. The Congress is authorized to provide a sound and uniform currency for the country, and to secure the benefit of it to the people by appropriate legislation.

Laycock v. Kenney, 270 F.2d 580, 590 (9th Cir. 1959) (internal quotation marks and citations omitted). Criminal monetary statutes exist in part to protect a uniform, regulated monetary system; that is, they aim to prevent any implicit lending of sovereign power or legitimacy to criminal enterprises. *Cf., e.g., United States v. Fernando,* 745 F.2d 1328, 1330 (10th Cir. 1984) ("Thus, it may be fair to assume that Congress, perceiving the possibility that misuse of currency could occur more easily, intended the scope of § 649 to be restricted to currency only and not to include negotiable documents. Finally, the existence of other criminal statutes, such as 18 U.S.C. § 641, which has a scope clearly broad enough to make criminal any conversion to personal use of checks as well as money, persuades us that a broad reading of the term 'money' is not imperative."); Lawrence Trautman, *Virtual Currencies; Bitcoin & What Now After Liberty Reserve, Silk Road, and Mt. Gox?,* 20 Rich. J.L. & Tech. 13 (2014) (noting that part of the mission of the Department of the Treasury's Financial Crimes Enforcement Network ("FinCEN") "is to safeguard the financial system from illicit use"); Oedel, 46 Am. U. L. Rev. at 1084 ("In its traditional forms, money gives to its users the chance to buy or sell valuables more quickly and more anonymously than in a barter economy. This feature may be useful not only to legitimate businesspersons seeking to streamline commerce, but also to parties hoping to hide illegal transactions, illicit sources of funding, and taxable income from public scrutiny. To prevent the use of money for such fraudulent purposes, governments sometimes oblige financial institutions to report unusual cash transactions and to disclose monetary flows that appear to be linked to fraudulent activities.") (citations omitted).

The above context demonstrates that Bitcoin is not "money" as people ordinarily understand that term. Bitcoin operates as a medium of exchange like cash but does not issue from or enjoy the protection of any sovereign; in fact, the whole point of Bitcoin is to escape any entanglement with sovereign governments. Bitcoins themselves are simply computer files generated through a ledger system that operates on block chain technology. *See, e.g.,* Shahla Hazratjee, *Bitcoin: The Trade of Digital Signatures,* 41 T. Marshall L. Rev. 55, 59 (2015) ("The Bitcoin system operates as a self-regulated online ledger of transactions. These transactions are currently denoted by the change of ownership in Coins. This ledger, also referred to as the 'block chain,' has certain built-in mechanisms that eradicate the risk of double spending or tampering with the master record of all transactions."). Like marbles, Beanie Babies™, or Pokémon™ trading cards, bitcoins have value exclusively to the extent that people at any given time choose privately to assign them value. No governmental mechanisms assist with valuation or price stabilization, which likely explains why Bitcoin value fluctuates much more than that of the typical government-backed fiat currency. *See, e.g.,* Jennifer R. Bagosy, *Controversial Currency: Accepting Bitcoin As Payment for Legal Fees,* Orange County Lawyer, June

2014, at 42 ("Bitcoin has other key features that make it very different from other methods of payment. First, the value of Bitcoin is highly volatile. In January 2013, one Bitcoin was worth about $13. By December 4, 2013, the price had skyrocketed to $1,061 per Bitcoin. By April 15, 2014, the value had dropped to $500 per Bitcoin.") (citation omitted). As for experiences in daily life, ordinary people do not receive salaries in bitcoins, cannot deposit them at their local banks, and cannot use them to pay bills. The Court cannot rule out the possibility that widespread, ordinary use of bitcoins as money could occur someday, but that simply is not the case now:

> Bitcoin may have some attributes in common with what we commonly refer to as money, but differ in many important aspects. While Bitcoin can be exchanged for items of value, they are not a commonly used means of exchange. They are accepted by some but not by all merchants or service providers. The value of Bitcoin fluctuates wildly and has been estimated to be eighteen times greater than the U.S. dollar. Their high volatility is explained by scholars as due to their insufficient liquidity, the uncertainty of future value, and the lack of a stabilization mechanism. With such volatility they have a limited ability to act as a store of value, another important attribute of money.

State v. Espinoza, No. F14–2923, slip op. at 5–6 (Fla. 11th Judicial Cir. Ct. July 22, 2016) (unpublished decision) . . . (last visited Dec. 1, 2016).

The ordinary understanding of money, and Bitcoin's status outside of that understanding, bring the Court back to the case at hand. The Government's aphorisms aside, there might be ways to prosecute Petix if he had conspired with others to engage in activity that violated other criminal statutes. Here, though, and as noted above, the Government has chosen to focus on the transfer of bitcoins in itself. The Government's theory of prosecution requires treating Bitcoin as money in the ordinary understanding of that term. Because Bitcoin does not fit an ordinary understanding of the term "money," Petix cannot have violated Section 1960 in its current form. As a matter of law, then, [the charge] . . . fails no matter what amount of factual evidence the Government might have at its disposal.

The principal authorities that the Government has cited do not change the above analysis. *United States v. E-Gold, Ltd.,* 550 F. Supp. 2d 82 (D.D.C. 2008), did not attempt to define the terms "money" or "funds," and neither did the FinCEN regulations cited in the Government's papers. In *United States v. Faiella,* 39 F. Supp. 3d 544 (S.D.N.Y. 2014)—a.k.a. the "Silk Road case"—the court turned directly to a dictionary to define both "money" and "funds" and then equated an ordinary understanding of those terms with the dictionary definitions. *Accord United States v. Budovsky,* 2015 WL 5602853 (S.D.N.Y. Sept. 23, 2015); *United States v. Murgio,* 2016

WL 5107128 (S.D.N.Y. Sept. 19, 2016). Perhaps there were circumstances in that line of Southern District cases that justified a first and exclusive resort to a dictionary. "Dictionary definitions of 'money,' however, are not helpful in determining congressional intent in employing that term in [a criminal statute]." *United States v. Jackson*, 759 F.2d 342, 344 (4th Cir. 1985). As the Court noted above, there are several problems with a straight dictionary approach. First, a dictionary approach overlooks the numerous times in the United States Constitution and Code when the term "money" consistently has referred to some kind of instrument issued and regulated by a sovereign. Second, the approach does not address the Supreme Court's determination of the ordinary meaning of the term "funds." Third, as the Supreme Court noted in *Yates,* terms in ordinary life do not always line up with dictionary definitions, and ordinary people simply would not think of any private medium of exchange as money. Finally, resorting exclusively to a dictionary does not address the desire, implicit in Section 1960, to keep the United States monetary system away from criminal activity and transactions that support it. The weight of those authorities, experiences, and statutory objectives must be allowed to control here over broad technical definitions that lack context.

To be clear, the Court reminds the parties that it is only interpreting the language of Section 1960 in its current form. The Court takes no position on whether and how Congress should amend Section 1960 to define "money" and "funds" for purposes of that section. The Court also takes no position on the deeper issue of whether block chain technology and virtual currencies should be fit into existing regulatory schemes, as opposed to devising new schemes to address a completely new technology. Given the options available for future regulation, any discussion about regulating virtual currencies is best left to the political process.

. . . .

IV. CONCLUSION

For all of the foregoing reasons, the Court respectfully recommends granting Petix's motion to dismiss . . . .

NOTES AND QUESTIONS

1.   Note that the preceding excerpt from *Petix* was the opinion of a magistrate judge, and therefore comes in the form of a recommendation to the trial court. The defendant accepted a plea deal before this recommendation was accepted or rejected by the district court. What is the legal impact of a magistrate's recommendation that is neither adopted nor rejected by a court?

2.   Do you find the reasoning of *Murgio* or *Petix* more convincing? Why?

3.   Were the facts of one case more compelling than those in the other, or are there other reasons why the *Murgio* court would conclude that Bitcoin

can constitute "money" or "funds," while the *Petix* magistrate reached a contrary result?

B. EXTRATERRITORIAL APPLICATION OF THE BSA REQUIREMENTS

One issue of critical importance to federal enforcement efforts is the extent to which BSA requirements may apply to businesses that are located or at least headquartered or founded in another country. This is important because of the reality that virtual businesses may be headquartered outside of the territorial confines of the U.S. but nonetheless have a huge impact here. In *U.S. v. Budovsky*, 2015 WL 5602853 (S.D.N.Y. Sept. 23, 2015), an opinion cited in both of the preceding decisions, this issue was discussed extensively.

PRELIMINARY NOTES AND QUESTIONS

1.   Are there any legitimate reasons why a bank would be so interested in secrecy for its customers? Consider in this regard the Swiss banking system, which operated for decades under the Banking Act of 1934, which (among other things) made it a crime to disclose client information to third parties without their consent. The era of absolute secrecy has ended, with Swiss banks now being required to cooperate with various taxing authorities, albeit in strictly constrained ways.[17] Swiss banks still protect privacy to a considerable extent, for example restricting when Swiss authorities can see what citizens have in their bank accounts.

2.   Since most of the questionable activity discussed in the following case took place in other countries, why is it not sufficient to allow the other countries to regulate the behavior? Certainly Costa Rico had rules in place as evidenced by the requirement that the business register with appropriate officials in that country.

UNITED STATES V. BUDOVSKY

No. 2015 WL 5602853 (S.D.N.Y. Sept. 23, 2015) (not reported in F. Supp.3d)

DENISE COTE, DISTRICT JUDGE.

Defendant Arthur Budovsky ("Budovsky") has moved to dismiss the three-count Indictment filed against him, his company Liberty Reserve S.A. ("Liberty Reserve"), and other codefendants on May 28, 2013.

---

[17]   Michael Shields, *Era of Bank Secrecy Ends as Swiss start Sharing Account Data*, Reuters (Oct. 5, 2018) (available online at https://www.reuters.com/article/us-swiss-secrecy/era-of-bank-secrecy-ends-as-swiss-start-sharing-account-data-idUSKCN1MF13O). Initially, Swiss banks were to share data with taxing authorities from other countries in the European Union as well as Australia, Canada, Guernsey, Iceland, Isle of Man, Japan, Jersey, Norway and South Korea. Some disclosures were delayed for technical reasons or because the countries in question failed to adopt sufficient cyber security and confidentiality protocols.

. . . .

Budovsky, the principal founder of Liberty Reserve, is charged under several statutes with creating and operating an unlicensed money transmitting business designed to facilitate illegal financial transactions and launder criminal proceeds. For the following reasons, Budovsky's motion is denied.

BACKGROUND

The following allegations are taken from the Indictment. Liberty Reserve, a company incorporated in Costa Rica in 2006, operated one of the world's most widely used digital currencies. Through its website, Liberty Reserve provided access to "instant, real-time currency for international commerce," which could be used to "send and receive payments from anyone, anywhere on the globe." With its virtual currency, known commonly as "LR," Liberty Reserve touted itself as the Internet's "largest payment processor and money transfer system," serving "millions" of people around the world, including those in the United States. An established Liberty Reserve user could receive and transfer LR with any other user, with Liberty Reserve collecting a one-percent fee per transaction.

Budovsky and his co-defendants are alleged to have intentionally created, structured, and operated Liberty Reserve as a business venture designed to help criminals conduct illegal transactions and launder the proceeds of their crimes. According to the Indictment, Liberty Reserve emerged as the "financial hub of the cyber-crime world, facilitating a broad range of online criminal activity, including credit card fraud, identity theft, investment fraud, computer hacking, child pornography, and narcotics trafficking." Liberty Reserve's user base was global, with more than one million users worldwide, including more than 200,000 users in the United States. The Indictment further alleges that from 2006 to 2013, Liberty Reserve processed an estimated 55 million separate financial transactions and laundered more than $6 billion in criminal proceeds. At no point did Liberty Reserve register with the United States Department of the Treasury as a money transmitting business.

The Indictment describes how Liberty Reserve took steps to allow its users to hide their identities. Unlike traditional banks or legitimate online payment processors, Liberty Reserve did not require users to validate their identity information. For an additional privacy fee of 75 cents per transaction, users could hide their account numbers when transferring funds, effectively making the transfer untraceable. To add additional layers of anonymity, Liberty Reserve prohibited users from depositing or withdrawing funds directly. Rather, users were required to exchange real currency for LR and vice-versa through third-party exchangers, a number of whom were pre-approved on the Liberty Reserve website. These recommended exchangers were often foreign unregulated and unlicensed money transmitting businesses that charged high transaction fees for their services.

The Indictment alleges that through these layers of anonymity, Liberty Reserve became the "bank of choice for the criminal underworld." Liberty Reserve users routinely established accounts under false names, including blatant criminal aliases such as "Russian Hackers" and "Hacker Account." Criminal users, including computer hackers for hire, drug-dealing websites, and traffickers of stolen credit card and personal identity information used Liberty Reserve to process payments for illegal goods and services. Other cyber-criminals used Liberty Reserve to launder criminal proceeds and transfer funds among criminal associates. Users of Liberty Reserve included credit-card theft and computer hacking rings operating in countries around the world, including China, Nigeria, and the United States. The Indictment also alleges that Budovsky and his associates were well aware of Liberty Reserve's function as an unlawful money laundering enterprise and deliberately attracted a criminal customer base by making financial activity anonymous and untraceable.

The Indictment further describes the circumstances surrounding Budovsky's founding of Liberty Reserve. In or about 2006, Budovsky, along with co-defendant Vladimir Kats, operated a company called Gold Age, Inc., which functioned as an exchanger for e-gold, a popular digital currency of that time. In December 2006, Budovsky and Kats were convicted in New York State of operating Gold Age, Inc. as an unlicensed money transmitting business. At or about the same time, "E-Gold and several of its principals" were charged with various offenses, including money laundering. In the wake of his conviction, Budovsky emigrated to Costa Rica where, in 2006, he and codefendant Ahmed Yassine Abdelghani incorporated Liberty Reserve in an effort to evade U.S. law enforcement. In or about 2011, Budovsky renounced his United States citizenship and became a Costa Rican citizen.

The Indictment also contains allegations concerning Budovsky's efforts to conceal Liberty Reserve's operations and assets. For example, in or around 2009, the Costa Rican agency Superintendencia General de Entidades Financieras ("SUGEF") notified Liberty Reserve that it needed to apply for a license to operate as a money transmitting business in Costa Rica. Upon reviewing Liberty Reserve's application, SUGEF refused to grant a license due to concerns that Liberty Reserve did not have basic anti-money laundering controls. In response, Budovsky and co-defendants Allan Esteban Hidalgo Jimenez, Mark Marmilev, and Maxim Chukharev created a computer portal for Costa Rican regulators to access and monitor transactional information for suspicious activity. According to internal communications among the defendants, however, this data was mostly fake and could be manipulated to hide incriminating information from regulators.

Moreover, on November 18, 2011, the U.S. Department of the Treasury's Financial Crimes Enforcement Network ("FinCEN") issued a notice to financial institutions about the risks associated with providing financial services to Liberty Reserve. In response, Liberty Reserve falsely informed Costa Rican officials that its business had been sold and that it would no longer be operating in Costa Rica. Instead, Liberty Reserve continued to operate in Costa Rica with a reduced staff out of office space held in the name of a shell company controlled by Budovsky. At the same time, Budovsky and co-defendants Jimenez and Azzeddine El Amine began transferring millions of dollars from Liberty Reserve's Costa Rican accounts to a bank account in Cyprus held by a shell company controlled by Budovsky and El Amine. This money was then transferred to a bank account in Russia held by yet another shell company. Shortly afterward, the Costa Rican government seized pursuant to a request by United States law enforcement approximately $19.5 million in Costa Rican bank accounts held by Liberty Reserve. After this seizure, Budovsky, Jimenez, and El Amine moved Liberty Reserve funds into more than two dozen shell-company accounts around the world to evade further seizures.

The Indictment charges Budovsky in three counts with (1) conspiracy to commit money laundering in violation of 18 U.S.C § 1956(h); (2) conspiracy to operate an unlicensed money transmission business in violation of 18 U.S.C. § 371; and (3) operation of an unlicensed money transmission business in violation of 18 U.S.C. § 1960. On June 23, 2015, Budovsky moved to dismiss each of these counts. . . .

I.   Motion to Dismiss the Indictment

Budovsky moves to dismiss all counts of the Indictment.

. . . .

Budovsky seeks an Order: (i) dismissing the Indictment as a whole due to a lack of nexus between Budovsky's alleged conduct and the United States. . . . [Other grounds to dismiss are not excerpted here.]

A.   Nexus Between the Alleged Conduct and the United States

Budovsky first seeks dismissal of the Indictment in its entirety on the ground that the alleged conduct has no nexus with the United States and therefore violates the Due Process Clause of the Constitution. "[A]s a general proposition, 'Congress has the authority to enforce its laws beyond the territorial boundaries of the United States.'" *United States v. Yousef*, 327 F.3d 56, 86 (2d Cir.2003) (quoting *EEOC v. Arabian Am. Oil Co.*, 499 U.S. 244, 248 (1991)). "When the text of a criminal statute is silent" regarding extraterritorial effect, the Congressional intent to apply the statute extraterritorially is "inferred from the nature of the offense."

United States v. Al Kassar, 660 F.3d 108, 118 (2d Cir. 2011) (citation omitted).

While the Supreme Court has not yet applied the Due Process Clause to limit Congress's authority to apply criminal statutes to extraterritorial conduct, the Second Circuit has held that in order to extraterritorially apply a federal criminal statute to a defendant in accordance with due process, "there must be a sufficient nexus between the defendant and the United States, so that such application would not be arbitrary or fundamentally unfair." *Id.* (citation omitted). A jurisdictional nexus exists "when the aim of that activity is to cause harm inside the United States or to U.S. citizens or interests." *Id.* Given this formulation, it should come as no surprise that cases in which extraterritorial application of a federal criminal statute is deemed a due process violation are rare.

Budovsky's nexus argument is meritless. Assuming that the Government is required to state the nexus of the alleged crimes to the United States in an indictment, the Indictment includes several allegations that establish a sufficient nexus with the United States. The Indictment alleges, among other things, that Liberty Reserve had over 200,000 users in the United States; the site's users included criminal rings operating in the United States; Budovsky moved $13.5 million from a Costa Rican bank account held by Liberty Reserve through a correspondent bank account in the Southern District of New York; and Budovsky engaged in money laundering with the object of transferring funds in and out of the United States.

Budovsky argues that his conduct and Liberty Reserve's operations occurred wholly outside the United States, that Liberty Reserve targeted a global market rather than the United States, and that the Indictment's claim that Liberty Reserve had 200,000 users in the United States could "only be supposition." Since in a motion to dismiss an indictment the facts alleged by the Government are taken as true, Budovsky's evidentiary arguments do not require dismissal.

Budovsky further argues that even if the existence of a large user base in the United States constitutes a sufficient nexus, "any operator of any web business-located anywhere in the world-could be hauled into United States courts." While the advent of the web may create a theoretical concern about the extraterritorial reach of U.S. criminal laws, in this case the Indictment has sufficiently alleged the conduct of a criminal business with the aim of causing harm to U.S. citizens and U.S. interests. *See Al Kasser,* 660 F.3d at 118; *see also United States v. Rowe,* 414 F.3d 271, 279 (2d Cir.2005) (upholding venue in a child pornography case based on viewing of defendant's Internet advertisement in the forum state).

. . .

[Motion is denied.]

NOTES

1.   Budovsky also alleged that the Indictment failed to disclose precisely how Liberty Reserve, which had been operating out of Costa Rico, had violated 18 U.S. Code § 1960. In addressing this particular allegation, the court specifically noted the convoluted nature of the statutes at issue.

Section 1960 makes it a crime to knowingly conduct, control, manage, supervise, direct, or own an "unlicensed money transmitting business." An unlicensed money transmitting business is one that affects interstate or foreign commerce in any manner or degree and which fulfills at least one of the three other listed requirements. One of those three requirements is that the business fails to comply with the registration requirements under 31 U.S. Code § 5330. Section 5330's registration requirement hinges in part on the duty to file reports pursuant to § 5313. Section 5313 provides that:

> When a domestic financial institution is involved in a transaction for the payment, receipt, or transfer of United States coins or currency (or other monetary instruments the Secretary of the Treasury prescribes), in an amount . . . or under circumstances the Secretary prescribes by regulation, the institution and any other participant in the transaction the Secretary may prescribe shall file a report on the transaction at the time and in the way the Secretary prescribes.

31 U.S. Code § 5313.

"Domestic financial institution" applies not merely to financial institutions located in the United States, but to any financial institution, wherever located, that acts in the United States. *United States v. Mazza-Alaluf*, 621 F.3d 205, 210–11 (2d Cir.2010) (finding foreign-located money transmitting business qualified as a "domestic financial institution" based on the maintenance of bank accounts in the United States). Additional provisions in the BSA make it clear that the Secretary of the Treasury is authorized to determine that financial services include "any activity . . . similar to, related to, or a substitute for any activity in which any business described in this paragraph is authorized to engage; or any other business designated by the Secretary whose cash transactions have a high degree of usefulness in criminal . . . matters." 31 U.S. Code §§ 5312(a)(2)(Y)–(Z).

Under these authorities, the court found that Budovsky had sufficient notice under the indictment that Liberty Reserve was being charged with failure to register a covered business activity. The court also specifically noted that the registration requirements in 18 U.S. Code § 1960 can apply to foreign-located businesses. It is enough if the pertinent business activities occur wholly or in material part within the United States, and allegations that 200,000 "customers" were U.S. residents met this requirement.

2.   Budovsky also alleged that the indictment failed to explain how Liberty Reserve's operations affected interstate or foreign commerce. The court noted that the requirements for an indictment do not require it to specify how such commerce is affected but also found that allegations of 200,000 issuers

residing in the U.S. and use by the site by many U.S.-based criminal rings, if proven, could meet the requirements for conviction.

3.   In addition, Budovsky argued that the complaint should be dismissed because "virtual currency does not constitute "funds," as required for charges brought under §§ 1956 and 1960." 2015 WL 5602853 at *13. For the reasons relied upon in cases such as *United States v. Ulbricht*, 31 F.Supp.3d 540, 568–70 (S.D.N.Y.2014) and the other opinions that are excerpted in these materials, the court concluded that "funds" includes substitutes for traditional "money" and is not limited to fiat currency.

U.S. v. Budovsky is not an isolated example of FinCEN enforcing U.S. laws by applying them to businesses "located" outside of the country. In 2017, FinCEN announced that it was imposing a $110 million fine on BTC-e for facilitating Ransomware and illegal drug transactions. The text of the official announcement from FinCEN follows:

FinCEN Press Release, *FinCEN Fines BTC-e Virtual Currency Exchange $110 Million for Facilitating Ransomware*
Dark Net Drug Sales (July 27, 2017)
https://www.fincen.gov/news/news-releases/fincen-fines-btc-e-virtual-currency-exchange-110-million-facilitating-ransomware

Treasury's First Action Against a Foreign-Located Money Services Business

WASHINGTON—The Financial Crimes Enforcement Network (FinCEN), working in coordination with the U.S. Attorney's Office for the Northern District of California, assessed a $110,003,314 civil money penalty today against BTC-e a/k/a Canton Business Corporation (BTC-e) for willfully violating U.S. anti-money laundering (AML) laws. Russian national Alexander Vinnik, one of the operators of BTC-e, was arrested in Greece this week, and FinCEN assessed a $12 million penalty against him for his role in the violations.

BTC-e is an internet-based, foreign-located money transmitter that exchanges fiat currency as well as the convertible virtual currencies Bitcoin, Litecoin, Namecoin, Novacoin, Peercoin, Ethereum, and Dash. It is one of the largest virtual currency exchanges by volume in the world. BTC-e facilitated transactions involving ransomware, computer hacking, identity theft, tax refund fraud schemes, public corruption, and drug trafficking.

"We will hold accountable foreign-located money transmitters, including virtual currency exchangers, that do business in the United States when they willfully violate U.S. anti-money laundering laws," said

Jamal El-Hindi, Acting Director for FinCEN. "This action should be a strong deterrent to anyone who thinks that they can facilitate ransomware, dark net drug sales, or conduct other illicit activity using encrypted virtual currency. Treasury's FinCEN team and our law enforcement partners will work with foreign counterparts across the globe to appropriately oversee virtual currency exchangers and administrators who attempt to subvert U.S. law and avoid complying with U.S. AML safeguards."

FinCEN acted in coordination with law enforcement's seizure of BTC-e and Vinnik's arrest. The Internal Revenue Service-Criminal Investigation Division, Federal Bureau of Investigation, United States Secret Service, and Homeland Security Investigations conducted the criminal investigation.

Among other violations, BTC-e failed to obtain required information from customers beyond a username, a password, and an e-mail address. Instead of acting to prevent money laundering, BTC-e and its operators embraced the pervasive criminal activity conducted at the exchange. Users openly and explicitly discussed criminal activity on BTC-e's user chat. BTC-e's customer service representatives offered advice on how to process and access money obtained from illegal drug sales on dark net markets like Silk Road, Hansa Market, and AlphaBay.

BTC-e also processed transactions involving funds stolen between 2011 and 2014 from one of the world's largest bitcoin exchanges, Mt. Gox. BTC-e processed over 300,000 bitcoin in transactions traceable to the theft. FinCEN has also identified at least $3 million of facilitated transactions tied to ransomware attacks such as "Cryptolocker" and "Locky." Further, BTC-e shared customers and conducted transactions with the now-defunct money laundering website Liberty Reserve. FinCEN previously issued a finding under Section 311 of the USA PATRIOT Act that identified Liberty Reserve as a financial institution of primary money laundering concern.

BTC-e has conducted over $296 million in transactions of bitcoin alone and tens of thousands of transactions in other convertible virtual currencies. The transactions included funds sent from customers located within the United States to recipients who were also located within the United States. BTC-e also concealed its geographic location and its ownership. Regardless of its ownership or location, the company was required to comply with U.S. AML laws and regulations as a foreign-located MSB including AML program, MSB registration, suspicious activity reporting, and recordkeeping requirements. This is the second supervisory enforcement action FinCEN has taken against a business that operates as an exchanger of virtual currency, and the first it has taken against a foreign-located MSB doing business in the United States.

In addition to direct enforcement actions against international businesses, FinCEN has the power to issue advisories against regimes that are seen as likely to promote illegal activities, particularly terrorism. Obviously, FinCEN cannot initiate criminal enforcement activities against a foreign government. However, by releasing information about illicit activities conducted by these nation states, FinCEN can put any business that it does regulate on notice that their AML programs must include safeguards against doing business with or on behalf of such countries. Such an advisory release was issued in late 2018 with respect to Iran.

FinCEN, *ADVISORY ON THE IRANIAN REGIME'S ILLICIT AND MALIGN ACTIVITIES AND ATTEMPTS TO EXPLOIT THE FINANCIAL SYSTEM*
FIN–2018–A006 at 9–10 (Oct. 11, 2018)[18]

Virtual Currency

Since 2013, Iran's use of virtual currency includes at least $3.8 million worth of bitcoin-denominated transactions per year. While the use of virtual currency in Iran is comparatively small, virtual currency is an emerging payment system that may provide potential avenues for individuals and entities to evade sanctions. Despite public reports that the CBI has banned domestic financial institutions from handling decentralized virtual currencies, individuals and businesses in Iran can still access virtual currency platforms through the Internet. For example, virtual currency can be accessed through: (1) Iran-located, Internet-based virtual currency exchanges; (2) U.S.- or other third country-based virtual currency exchanges; and (3) peer-to-peer (P2P) exchangers.

Institutions should consider reviewing blockchain ledgers for activity that may originate or terminate in Iran. Institutions should also be aware that the international virtual currency industry is highly dynamic; new virtual currency businesses may incorporate or operate in Iran with little notice or footprint. Further, P2P exchangers—natural or legal persons who offer to buy, sell, or exchange virtual currency through online sites and in-person meetups—may offer services in Iran.

These P2P exchangers may operate as unregistered foreign MSBs in jurisdictions that prohibit such businesses; where virtual currency is hard to access, such as Iran; or for the purpose of evading the prohibitions or restrictions in place against such businesses or virtual currency exchanges and other similar business in some jurisdictions. Institutions can utilize technology created to monitor open blockchains and investigate transactions to or from P2P exchange platforms.

---

[18]   This advisory is archived at https://perma.cc/6QSA-HBMT.

Activity of these exchangers may involve wire transactions from many disparate accounts or locations combined with transfers to or from virtual currency exchanges. These transactions may occur when account holders fund an account or withdraw value from an account, especially if the foreign exchanger operates in multiple currencies. Financial institutions and virtual currency providers that have BSA and U.S. sanctions obligations should be aware of and have the appropriate systems to comply with all relevant sanctions requirements and AML/CFT obligations. Sanctions requirements may include not only screening against the SDN List but also appropriate steps to comply with other OFAC-administered sanctions programs, including those that impose import and/or export restrictions with respect to particular jurisdictions. Further, a non-U.S.-based exchanger or virtual currency provider doing substantial business in the United States is subject to AML/CFT obligations and OFAC jurisdiction.

U.S. individuals and institutions involved in virtual currency should be aware of OFAC's March 2018 Frequently Asked Questions (FAQs) on sanctions issues associated with virtual currencies. The FAQs remind U.S. persons that their compliance obligations with respect to transactions are the same, regardless of whether a transaction is denominated in virtual currency or not. OFAC also states as a general matter that U.S. persons and persons otherwise subject to OFAC jurisdiction, including firms subject to OFAC jurisdiction that facilitate or engage in online commerce or process transactions using "digital currency," are responsible for ensuring that they do not engage in unauthorized transactions prohibited by OFAC sanctions, such as dealings with blocked persons or property, or engaging in prohibited trade or investment-related transactions. Prohibited transactions include transactions that evade or avoid, have the purpose of evading or avoiding, cause a violation of, or attempt to violate prohibitions imposed by OFAC under various sanctions authorities. Additionally, persons that provide financial, material, or technological support for or to a designated person may be designated by OFAC under the relevant sanctions authority.

C. WHAT MAKES A MONEY TRANSMITTER BUSINESS "ILLEGAL"?

As the preceding cases make clear, the mere fact that a business utilizes cryptoassets rather than fiat currencies, or is headquartered outside the United States, will not prevent it from being subject to potential liability under U.S. federal financial laws. All of the cases discussed so far involve defendants who appear to have been acting to further criminal behavior, and it certainly seems appropriate to treat their activities as criminal. The federal money-laundering rules, however, do not require participation in criminal enterprises such as terrorism or the drug trade in order to find criminal behavior.

One of the broadest federal anti-money laundering provisions is 18 U.S.C. § 1960, which criminalizes the operation of an unlicensed money transmitter business. The statute makes it a crime if a defendant "knowingly conducts, controls, manages, supervises, directs, or owns all or part of an unlicensed money transmitting business." In addition, 18 U.S.C. § 1960(b)(1) defines "unlicensed money transmitting business" to include any of the following (so long as interstate or foreign commerce is affected, as noted in *Budovsky*):

1. Operating a business without a license in a state where such operation is a crime under state law, regardless of whether the defendant knew that a state license was required;

2. Operating a business without complying with the federal money transmitting business registration requirements; or

3. Conducting a business that involves the transmission of funds known to the defendant to have been derived from a criminal offense, or intended to promote unlawful behavior.

Under these provisions, a defendant engaged in money transmitting (including transmission of virtual currencies), could be committing a federal crime if he or she fails to comply with either federal or state registration requirements.

Most criminal prosecutions result in plea bargains where the defendant(s) plead guilty to lesser charges or agree to cooperate in exchange for reduced sentences. This pattern is as true in criminal prosecutions involving crypto as in any other kind of matter. The following opinion is a result of two defendants' request to withdraw a guilty plea based upon a determination that they might have an argument invalidating the legal claims against them. The issue discussed is one that helps explain the parameters of criminal liability for operating an illegal money transmission business.

UNITED STATES V. LORD

2017 WL 1424806 (W.D. La. Apr. 20, 2017) (not reported in F. Supp.)

MEMORANDUM RULING

S. MAURICE HICKS, JR., UNITED STATES DISTRICT JUDGE.

Before the Court is Defendants Michael A. Lord ("Michael Lord") and Randall B. Lord's ("Randall Lord") (collectively "Defendants") Motion to Withdraw their guilty pleas. The Government opposes Defendants' Motion. For the reasons contained in the instant Memorandum Ruling, Defendants' Motion is DENIED.

FACTUAL AND PROCEDURAL BACKGROUND

Randall Lord is a former chiropractor and resident of Shreveport, Louisiana. Michael Lord is Randall Lord's son, and he lives with his father in Shreveport. Beginning in 2013, Defendants began operating a business in which they exchanged cash, credit card payments, and other forms of payment for bitcoins. The bitcoin is a decentralized form of online currency that is maintained in an online "wallet." Bitcoins can be purchased from online exchangers or brokers, who often charge a fee for making such an exchange. Bitcoins can then be exchanged for other goods or services online and transferred to another person's wallet. That person can then either use such bitcoins to purchase other goods and services or convert them back to U.S. dollars or some other traditional form of currency.

Defendants operated their bitcoin business through a website called localbitcoins.com, on which they posted advertisements for bitcoin exchange services. Persons who engaged Defendants' services would transfer money to Defendants by some traditional means, such as cash or wire transfer. Then, Defendants would purchase bitcoins from Coinbase, another online bitcoin broker, and transfer the bitcoins back to the buyer after subtracting their commission. Though Defendants initially used personal bank accounts for these transactions, they eventually used accounts associated with the following: (1) Randall Lord's former chiropractic clinic, Jewella Chiropractic Clinic; (2) two "doing business as" designations, Crypto Processing Solutions and Quantum Health; and (3) two newly-formed Nevada limited liability companies, Data Security LLC and Pelican Mining LLC.

At some point in the spring of 2014, Coinbase contacted Defendants regarding the volume of activity that had been occurring in their account and its consequences. Coinbase informed Defendants that because they were acting as bitcoin exchangers they were required to register with the Federal Crimes Enforcement Network ("FinCEN"), a division of the Department of the Treasury, under March 2013 guidance from FinCEN that clarified that bitcoin exchangers were subject to registration requirements. In July 2014, Defendants represented to Coinbase that they were registered with FinCEN, though they were not registered with FinCEN at that time. Defendants did not register with FinCEN until November 2014. By that time, Defendants' bitcoin business had exchanged more than $2.5 million for bitcoins for customers all around the United States. Defendants continued operating the bitcoin exchange business through 2015.

. . . .

On November 18, 2015, a federal grand jury for the Western District of Louisiana issued a 15-count indictment against Defendants. Count 1 of the indictment charged Defendants with conspiracy to operate an unlicensed money service business in violation of 18 U.S.C. § 371 (conspiracy) and 18 U.S.C. § 1960 (unlicensed money transmitting businesses). Counts 2–14 charged Defendants with various other crimes associated with operating their bitcoin exchange business. [Material related to Count 15, a drug charge against Michael Lord, is omitted.] On April 19, 2016, Defendants appeared before this Court and pleaded guilty to Count 1 of the indictment . . . . Defendants filed the instant Motion to Withdraw their guilty pleas on February 21, 2017. The Government opposes the Motion, and the Motion is fully briefed.

LAW AND ANALYSIS

I. Legal Standards

Federal Rule of Criminal Procedure 11 (d)(2)(B) states that a criminal defendant may withdraw a plea of guilty after the court accepts the plea but before the imposition of a sentence when "the defendant can show a fair and just reason for requesting the withdrawal." Thus, a defendant "does not have an absolute right to withdraw a plea," and a defendant bears the burden of persuading the Court that the reason advanced for withdrawal is "fair and just." *United States v. Conroy*, 567 F.3d 174, 177 (5th Cir. 2009); Fed. R. Crim. P. 11(d)(2)(B). A district court has discretion to grant or deny such a motion, and a district court's decision on such a motion is reviewed for an abuse of discretion.

In deciding a motion to withdraw a guilty plea, the Court must consider the following factors: (1) whether or not the defendant has asserted his innocence . . . . [Discussion of other factors omitted.]

II. Analysis

The parties' arguments center on the first factor that must be considered in deciding a motion to withdraw a guilty plea, whether Defendants have asserted their innocence. Defendants argue that they "have always believed that their buying and selling of bitcoins did not make them a money services business ("MSB") and therefore, they were not required to obtain a license to operate their business." Defendants also argue that they have now confirmed with the State of Louisiana's Office of Financial Institutions ("OFS") that the State of Louisiana does not require a license for persons to engage in exchanging or brokering bitcoins.

The Government concedes that Defendants were not required to obtain an MSB license from the State of Louisiana to operate such a business. However, the Government argues that this concession is not fatal to the charges against Defendants in Count 1 of the indictment because the failure to obtain a state license was but one theory upon which Count 1 is based. The Government also argues that most of the other factors that must be considered weigh in favor of denying the Motion.

. . . .

The Government's argument on the first factor, whether Defendants have asserted their innocence, is correct. Defendants correctly argue, and the Government has conceded, that the fact that the State of Louisiana does not require a license to operate an MSB precludes one theory upon which Count 1 of the indictment is based.

However, Count 1 of the indictment charged Defendants with conspiracy to operate an unlicensed MSB under 18 U.S.C. § 371 (conspiracy) and 18 U.S.C. § 1960 (unlicensed money transmitting businesses). Under 18 U.S.C. § 1960, a person commits an offense when he "knowingly conducts, controls, manages, supervises, directs, or owns all or part of an unlicensed money transmitting business." The statute defines the term "unlicensed money transmitting business" as "a money transmitting business which affects interstate or foreign commerce in any manner or degree" and either (A) is operated without an appropriate money transmitting license in a State; or (B) fails to comply with the money transmitting business registration requirements under 31 U.S.C. § 5330 or regulations thereunder. 18 U.S.C. § 1960(b)(1)(A) and (B). Thus, the statute sets forth two separate methods by which the Government may prove that a defendant is an "unlicensed money transmitting business": failure to obtain a state license where such a license is necessary, or failure to comply with separate federal registration requirements.

Though the Government now concedes that it cannot prove the first method, the evidence the Government presented at the guilty plea hearing is nonetheless sufficient to prove the second method. Regulations promulgated under 31 U.S.C. § 5330 and other statutes define a "money service business" as a business engaging in at least one of several different varieties of financial business. 31 C.F.R. § 1010.100(ff). One such variety is a "money transmitter," a person that engages in "the acceptance of currency, funds, or other value that substituted for currency from one person and the transmission of currency, funds, or other value that substituted for currency to another location or person by any means." 31 C.F.R. § 1010.100(ff)(5)(A). All businesses that meet the definition of "money services businesses" must register with FinCEN through the registration procedures set forth in 31 C.F.R. § 1022.380. One such requirement is that an MSB must submit its registration form to FinCEN within 180 days of the date the business is established.

As stated in the Factual and Procedural Background, *supra*, FinCEN released interpretive guidance in March 2013 clarifying the application of these regulations to businesses like that of Defendants. This guidance clarified that though a user of a virtual currency like bitcoin is not an MSB, "an administrator or exchanger is an MSB under FinCEN's regulations, specifically, a money transmitter, unless a limitation to or exemption from the definition applies to the person." It is undisputed that Defendants failed to register with FinCEN until November 2014, well past the 180-day deadline for such registration, which commenced sometime in 2013 when Defendants first began their bitcoin exchange business. Thus, because "it is unlawful to do business [as an MSB] without complying with 31 U.S.C. § 5330 and [31 C.F.R. § 1022.380]" regardless of compliance with any state licensing requirements, the Court finds that Defendants have not asserted their actual innocence of the crime to which they pleaded guilty in Count 1 of the indictment.

. . . .

Therefore, Defendants' Motion to Withdraw their guilty pleas is DENIED.

NOTES AND QUESTIONS

1.   As the preceding excerpt makes clear, criminal defendants are not completely free to withdraw guilty pleas once they are made in open court. Federal rules of criminal procedure require the defendant to show "a fair and just reason for requesting the withdrawal," with the trial court having a significant measure of discretion to grant or deny the request. Do you agree that the trial court did not abuse its discretion in refusing to allow the Lords to revoke their guilty plea to the first count of the indictment against them?

2.   The Lords represented to Coinbase that they were registered with FinCEN in July of 2014, and in fact they were registered within 180 days of that representation. It is not clear whether that registration occurred within 180 days of being notified by Coinbase that they needed to be registered. Assuming that they were registered within 180 days after they first discovered that they needed to register their business, would that have made a difference to their potential liability as illegal money transmitters? Should it matter?

7.   ON-GOING CONFUSION ABOUT FINCEN'S ROLE AND ACTIVITIES

The preceding materials may make it appear that FinCEN's position is consistent and clear, and that there is no reason for anyone failing to understand the position taken by this agency with regard to virtual currencies. This is not an accurate reflection of reality.

First, there are a number of different levels of authority within FinCEN. The Director of FinCEN is appointed by the Secretary of the Treasury, and when official reports or testimony is required, it is most often the Director (or acting Director) who will respond. On occasion, however, Deputy Directors and Associate Directors have spoken to Congress to provide testimony about the Bureau. FinCEN employs hundreds of individuals, including persons working intelligence, enforcement, policy, liaison, technology, and management divisions. A variety of anonymous sources from within the Bureau have been quoted in the press over the years about different aspects of FinCEN policy and operations. It is not surprising that their testimony or reported opinions do not always align precisely.[19] In addition, FinCEN is a Bureau within the Department of the Treasury, and while the Secretary of the Treasury appoints the FinCEN Director, he or she actually reports to the Under Secretary for Terrorism and Financial Intelligence. Thus, persons at Treasury may also weigh in on FinCEN issues.

One of the most recent and significant issues about the future direction of FinCEN involved widely distributed reports about a "FinCEN letter" that ostensibly announced a decision to apply federal banking regulations to anyone conducting an ICO (initial coin offering). The reports all contained essentially this information:

> The Financial Crimes Enforcement Network (FinCEN) published a letter Tuesday that indicates the U.S. agency will apply its regulations to those who conduct initial coin offerings (ICOs). . . . [U]nder this interpretation of the law, a group that conducts an ICO that involves U.S. residents but hadn't registered with FinCEN as a money transmitter and adhere to KYC regulations may be charged with a felony under federal law.[20]

This would, if true, be a huge deal for crypto-entrepreneurs. The reports, despite being widely circulated, appear to have significantly misconstrued the letter. In fact, it was not issued by FinCEN, and was not intended to announce any change in FinCEN policy. One source explained the truth as follows:

> The March 6 publication of a letter describing the ability of the Financial Crimes Enforcement Network (FinCEN) to regulate and monitor the use of virtual currencies has prompted a wave of coverage focusing on its apparent implications for Initial Coin Offerings (ICOs). . . . Coverage of this development has neglected to notice that this "FinCEN Letter" was not actually from FinCEN, was not mainly about ICOs, and states policies that should be unsurprising to anyone familiar with U.S. laws and regulations on AML/CFT.[21]

---

[19]   In 2013, the FinCEN Director, while speaking about the "potential, perplexities, and promise" of the virtual economy, specifically noted that different individuals will have different perspectives, while quoting a number of headlines that illustrate this reality. *See* FinCEN, *Remarks of Jennifer Shasky Calvery, Director, Financial Crimes Enforcement Network* (June 13, 2013) [archived at https://perma.cc/67XR-XKB6].

[20]   Nikhilesh De, *FinCEN: Money Transmitter Rules Apply to ICOs*, COINDESK (Mar. 6, 2018) (available online at https://www.coindesk.com/fincen-money-transmitter-rules-apply-ico-developers-exchanges).

[21]   Robert Kim, *FinCEN's ICO Letter: Not FinCEN's, Not ICO Focused, and Not Surprising*, BLOOMBERG NEWS (Ap. 6, 2018) [archived at https://perma.cc/KAT8-GDVV]. Reproduced with permission. Published April 6, 2018. Copyright 2018 by The Bureau of National Affairs, Inc. (800-372-1033) http://www.bna.com.

In fact, the letter was actually prepared and signed by the Assistant Secretary for Legislative Affairs at the Department of the Treasury. His purpose was to explain FinCEN's activities, and to address how various regulatory requirements were being applied to virtual currency exchangers and administrators. Only a few paragraphs in the letter are devoted to ICOs, and those appear at the end of the letter. While it might be appropriate for businesses contemplating an ICO to consider the potential impact of BSA requirements, the letter does not suggest that FinCEN intends to apply BSA requirements to everyone who participates in such transactions.

To allow you to assess the truth of the situation, the letter[22] is reprinted on the following pages.

PRELIMINARY NOTES AND QUESTIONS

1. Who was the author of the letter, and what authority did they have to speak for or to bind FinCEN?

2. What did the letter actually say about the responsibilities of issuers conducting ICOs?

3. Based on what you know about FinCEN and the rules and regulations under which it operates, when should issuers conducting an ICO be worried about needing to comply with BSA requirements such as registering with FinCEN, adopting risk-based AML plans, record-keeping, and reporting requirements?

4. What are some potential consequences of the widespread reports that the letter meant FinCEN would thereafter be requiring issuers of all ICOs to be done in compliance with BSA requirements?

---

[22]   For readers desiring an electronic version, the letter is archived at https://perma.cc/ 4QJB-CSSL and may be accessed there.

DEPARTMENT OF THE TREASURY
WASHINGTON, D.C. 20220

February 13, 2018

The Honorable Ron Wyden
Ranking Member
Committee on Finance
United States Senate
Washington, DC 20510

Dear Senator Wyden:

Thank you for your December 14, 2017 letter requesting information on the oversight and enforcement capabilities of the Financial Crime Enforcement Network (FinCEN) over virtual currency financial activities. I am pleased to have the opportunity to highlight some of the work FinCEN has done in this space to advance its crucial mission of administering the Bank Secrecy Act (BSA) and protecting the U.S. financial system from the potential illicit financing risks you highlight in your letter.

FinCEN shares your desire to promote the positive financial innovations associated with this technology, while protecting our financial system from criminals, hackers, sanctions-evaders, and hostile foreign actors. Together with other components of the Office of Terrorism and Financial Intelligence (TFI), FinCEN has worked diligently to ensure that anti-money laundering/combating the financing of terrorism (AML/CFT) rules apply to virtual currency exchangers and administrators that are in the United States or do business in whole or in substantial part within the United States, but do not have a physical presence in this country.

Combating the abuse of existing and emerging payment systems by illicit financiers is a priority issue for FinCEN. We establish our regulatory, examination, and enforcement priorities based on numerous factors that help us assess potential harm, including, e.g., the nature and impact of the underlying crime; the size of the illicit financing flows; the scale of the financial product or service; and its vulnerability to abuse. To identify risks and illicit use of virtual currency and other emerging payments systems, including the abuse of virtual currency to facilitate cybercrime, black market sales of illicit products and services, and other high-tech crimes, FinCEN maintains a team of analysts to examine BSA filings from virtual currency money services businesses (MSB) and other emerging payments providers, including filings pertaining to digital coins, tokens, and Initial Coin Offerings (ICOs), to proactively identify trends and risks for money laundering, terrorist financing, and other financial crimes, and provide this information to U.S. law enforcement and other government agencies.

Virtual currency exchangers and administrators have been subject to the BSA's money transmitter requirements since 2011.[1] In 2013, FinCEN clarified this by issuing guidance that

---

[1] Amendments to Bank Secrecy Act Regulations; Definitions and Other Regulations Relating to Money Services Businesses, 76 FR No. 140, (Jul. 21, 2011), https://www.gpo.gov/fdsys/pkg/FR-2011-07-21/pdf/2011-18309.pdf.

explicitly stated that virtual currency exchangers and administrators are money transmitters and must comply with the BSA and its implementing regulations.[2] These requirements include: registering with FinCEN as a MSB; preparing a written AML compliance program that is designed to mitigate risks (including money laundering risks) associated with the entity's specific business and customer mix, and to ensure compliance with other BSA requirements; filing BSA reports, including suspicious activity and currency transaction reports; keeping records for certain types of transactions at specific thresholds; and obtaining customer identification information sufficient to comply with the AML Program and recordkeeping requirements. In addition, a virtual currency money transmitter that is a U.S. person must, like all U.S. persons, comply with all Office of Foreign Assets Control financial sanctions obligations.

Regulated virtual currency businesses provide FinCEN with Suspicious Activity Reports that may include the identity of the account owner in their records. In cases where a bitcoin address is identified in the course of an investigation, blockchain analysis can often enable investigators to tie it to a virtual currency exchanger, hosted wallet, or other virtual currency money transmitter that may have the identity of the account owner. Blockchain network analytic tools can also tie a targeted bitcoin address to other potentially identifiable persons that have transacted with the particular bitcoin address and may have information that could potentially help identify beneficial owners. Like other investigative techniques, this process requires expenditure of investigative resources to try to follow bitcoin transactions through addresses to a real world identity, and can involve subpoenas for records at virtual currency businesses. FinCEN supports law enforcement and regulators' efforts to identify and trace bitcoin by providing information and analysis used to investigate criminal use of virtual currency.

In 2014, FinCEN, working with its delegated examiner, the Internal Revenue Service Small Business/Self-Employed Division, began to implement comprehensive, periodic examinations of exchangers and administrators. To date, these efforts have included the examination of about one-third of the approximately 100 virtual currency exchangers and administrators registered with FinCEN. In addition, FinCEN has also initiated investigations into the activities of some exchangers and administrators. As your letter notes, this has included enforcement actions against exchangers like Ripple Labs (2015) and BTC-e (2017), and against individuals that operate exchangers, such as Alexander Vinnik (2017). It has also included action under Section 311 of the USA PATRIOT Act against Liberty Reserve (2013), the administrator of a centralized virtual currency. FinCEN will continue its efforts to ensure that MSBs, including virtual currency exchangers and administrators, meet their AML/CFT obligations, and will continue to take appropriate action when they fail to do so.

There are significant challenges to investigating foreign virtual currency businesses, because most jurisdictions do not regulate and supervise virtual currency businesses, and therefore do not require them to maintain customer records. FinCEN works to identify foreign-located money transmitters that may be enabling financial crime, and evaluates them for potential enforcement actions when they violate U.S. law, as in the BTC-e matter. FinCEN and other Treasury components actively encourage other countries to regulate virtual currency activities, consistent

---

[2] The BSA is codified at 12 U.S.C. §§ 1829b, 1951–1959 and 31 U.S.C. §§ 5311–5314, 5316–5332. Regulations implementing the Bank Secrecy Act currently appear at 31 C.F.R. Chapter X.

with the international AML/CFT standards, and to cooperate in investigations of the criminal exploitation of virtual currencies. We deliver this message bilaterally and through multilateral fora such as the Financial Action Task Force and the Egmont Group of Financial Intelligence Units.

FinCEN is working closely with the Securities Exchange Commission (SEC) and the Commodities Futures Trading Commission (CFTC) to clarify and enforce the AML/CFT obligations of businesses engaged in Initial Coin Offering (ICO) activities that implicate the regulatory authorities of these agencies. The application of AML/CFT obligations to participants in ICOs will depend on the nature of the financial activity involved in any particular ICO. This is a matter of the facts and circumstances of each case.

Generally, under existing regulations and interpretations, a developer that sells convertible virtual currency, including in the form of ICO coins or tokens, in exchange for another type of value that substitutes for currency is a money transmitter and must comply with AML/CFT requirements that apply to this type of MSB.[3] An exchange that sells ICO coins or tokens, or exchanges them for other virtual currency, fiat currency, or other value that substitutes for currency, would typically also be a money transmitter.

However, ICO arrangements vary. To the extent that an ICO is structured in a way that it involves an offering or sale of securities or derivatives, certain participants in the ICO could fall under the authority of the SEC, which regulates brokers and dealers in securities, or under the authority of the CFTC, which regulates merchants and brokers in commodities. In such a case, the AML/CFT requirements imposed by SEC or CFTC regulations would apply to such ICO participants. Treasury expects businesses involved in ICOs to meet the BSA obligations that apply to them.

Thank you again for contacting FinCEN on this important matter. If you have any further questions or concerns, please feel free to contact me or Mrs. Kelly Whitney, FinCEN's Congressional Advisor, at (703) 839-4131 or kelly.whitney@fincen.gov.

Sincerely,

Drew Maloney
Assistant Secretary for Legislative Affairs

---

[3] *See*, FIN-2013-G001 (explaining that convertible virtual currency administrators and exchangers are money transmitters under the BSA), and FIN-2014-R001, Application of FinCEN's Regulations to Virtual Currency Mining Operations, January 30, 2014 (explaining that persons that create units of virtual currency, such as miners, and use them in the business of accepting and transmitting value are also money transmitters).

- 3 -

FinCEN continues to take steps to make its position clear to affected persons. In May of 2019 it issued a 30 page guidance again explaining how

FinCEN's regulations apply to certain virtual currency businesses.[23] FinCEN explicitly noted that it was not establishing new regulations or requirements with the 2019 Guidance, and instead was acting to "consolidate[ ] current FinCEN regulations, and related administrative rulings and guidance issued since 2011, and then appl[y] these rules and interpretations to other common business models . . . ."[24]

The 2019 Guidance continues FinCEN's focus on crypto as a currency substitute, which is not surprising given the bureau's overall mission. The label applied in the document is "convertible virtual currency" or CVC, which FinCEN says can include any "digital currency," "cryptocurrency," "cryptoasset," "digital asset," etc., that lacks some of the attributes of "real" currency (such as legal status), but which "either has an equivalent value as currency, or acts as a substitute for currency."[25] As explained in the Guidance, FinCEN treats crypto as a "value that substitutes for currency" either when it is created "(a) specifically for the purpose of being used as a currency substitute or (b) originally for another purpose but then repurposed to be used as a currency substitute by an administrator (in centralized payment systems) or an unincorporated organization, such as a software agency (in decentralized payment systems)."[26] This is not necessarily a change in the FinCEN approach, but certainly clarifies that actions of parties other than the issuer or development team can result in crypto being treated as a currency substitute for purposes of the BSA.

The new guidance does remind businesses that if they are registered with and regulated by the SEC or CFTC, they will not be "money services businesses," although they may be required to register with FinCEN and comply with requirements by another authority.[27] Natural persons who occasionally provide what would otherwise be considered money transmission services without seeking gain or profit are not regulated as MSBs by FinCEN.[28] Natural persons engaged in peer-to-peer (P2P) exchange services as a business as subject to regulation as an MSB,[29] even if they perform such services informally or irregularly.

The new guidance does address some business models that have become popular that were not fully explored in the 2013 Guidance. Rather than an editorialized explanation of those expanded explanations, here is

---

[23]   FinCEN Guidance, *Application of FinCEN's Regulations to Certain Business Models Involving Convertible Virtual Currencies*, FIN–2019–G001 (May 9, 2019) [archived at https://perma.cc/K5JT-ZSBJ] (referred to in these materials as the 2019 Guidance).

[24]   *Id.* at 1.

[25]   *Id.* at 7.

[26]   *Id.* at 4.

[27]   *Id.*

[28]   *Id.* at 4–5.

[29]   *Id.* at 14.

an excerpt from the 2019 Guidance, covering various business operations that were not specifically identified or examined in 2013.

Preliminary Notes and Questions

1.   If the 2019 Guidance really is not intended to change existing rules and regulations, what is its purpose?

2.   Note the extensive attention paid to anonymizing services. Why is this topic deserving of so much specificity and detail?

Dept. of the Treasury, FinCEN Guidance, Application of FinCEN's Regulations to Certain Business Models Involving Convertible Virtual Currencies
FIN–2019–G001 (May 9, 2019)[30]

. . . .

4.   Guidance on Application of BSA Regulations to Common Business Models Involving the Transmission of CVC

This guidance sets forth examples of how FinCEN's money transmission regulations apply to several common business models involving transactions in CVC. The description of each business model does not intend to reflect an industry standard or cover all varieties of products or services generally referred by the same label, but only highlight the key facts and circumstances of a specific product or service on which FinCEN based its regulatory interpretation.

4.1. Natural Persons Providing CVC Money Transmission (P2P Exchangers)

FinCEN's definition of an MSB includes both natural and legal persons engaged as a business in covered activities, "whether or not on a regular basis or as an organized business concern." Peer-to-Peer (P2P) exchangers are (typically) natural persons engaged in the business of buying and selling CVCs. P2P exchangers generally advertise and market their services through classified advertisements, specifically designed platform websites, online forums, other social media, and word of mouth. P2P exchangers facilitate transfers from one type of CVC to a different type of CVC, as well as exchanges between CVC and other types of value (such as monetary instruments or payment products denominated in real currency). P2P exchangers may provide their services online or may arrange to meet prospective customers in person to purchase or sell CVC. Generally, once there is confirmation that the buyer has delivered or

---

[30]   The guidance is archived at https://perma.cc/D6MA-LLWM.

deposited the requested currency or CVC, the P2P exchanger will electronically provide the buyer with the requested CVC or other value.

A natural person operating as a P2P exchanger that engages in money transmission services involving real currency or CVCs must comply with BSA regulations as a money transmitter acting as principal. This is so regardless of the regularity or formality of such transactions or the location from which the person is operating. However, a natural person engaging in such activity on an infrequent basis and not for profit or gain would be exempt from the scope of money transmission.

As a money transmitter, P2P exchangers are required to comply with the BSA obligations that apply to money transmitters, including registering with FinCEN as an MSB and complying with AML program, recordkeeping, and reporting requirements (including filing SARs . . . .).

4.2. CVC Wallets

CVC wallets are interfaces for storing and transferring CVCs. There are different wallet types that vary according to the technology employed, where and how the value is stored, and who controls access to the value. Current examples of different types of CVC wallets that vary by technology employed are mobile wallets, software wallets, and hardware wallets. Wallets may store value locally, or store a private key that will control access to value stored on an external server. Wallets may also use multiple private keys stored in multiple locations. Wallets where user funds are controlled by third parties are called "hosted wallets" whereas wallets where users control the funds are called "unhosted wallets."

The regulatory interpretation of the BSA obligations of persons that act as intermediaries between the owner of the value and the value itself is not technology dependent. The regulatory treatment of such intermediaries depends on four criteria: (a) who owns the value; (b) where the value is stored; (c) whether the owner interacts directly with the payment system where the CVC runs; and, (d) whether the person acting as intermediary has total independent control over the value. The regulatory treatment of each type of CVC wallet based on these factors is described in the next subsection.

4.2.1.   Hosted and Unhosted Wallet Providers

Hosted wallet providers are account-based money transmitters that receive, store, and transmit CVCs on behalf of their accountholders, generally interacting with them through websites or mobile applications. In this business model, the money transmitter is the host, the account is the wallet, and the accountholder is the wallet owner. In addition, (a) the value belongs to the owner; (b) the value may be stored in a wallet or represented as an entry in the accounts of the host; (c) the owner interacts directly with the host, and not with the payment system; and (d) the host has total independent control over the value (although it is contractually obligated to access the value only on instructions from the owner).

The regulatory framework applicable to the host, including the due diligence or enhanced due diligence procedures the host must follow regarding the wallet owner, varies depending on: (a) whether the wallet owner is a non-financial institution (in this context, a user, according to the 2013 VC Guidance), agent, or foreign or domestic counterparty; and (b) the type of transactions channeled through the hosted wallet, and their U.S. dollar equivalent.

When the wallet owner is a user, the host must follow the procedures for identifying, verifying and monitoring both the user's identity and profile, consistent with the host's AML program. When the wallet owner is an agent of the host, the host must comply with regulations and internal policies, procedures and controls governing a principal MSB's obligation to monitor the activities of its agent. When the wallet owner is a financial institution other than an agent, the host must comply with the regulatory requirements applicable to correspondent accounts (or their MSB equivalents).

Similarly, the regulatory requirements that apply to the transactions that host channels from or for the wallet owner will depend on the nature of the transaction. For example, where the transactions fall under the definition of "transmittal of funds," the host must comply with the Funds Travel Rule based on the host's position in the transmission chain (either as a transmittor's, intermediary, or recipient's financial institution), regardless of whether the regulatory information may be included in the transmittal order itself or must be transmitted separately.

Unhosted wallets are software hosted on a person's computer, phone, or other device that allow the person to store and conduct transactions in CVC. Unhosted wallets do not require an additional third party to conduct transactions. In the case of unhosted, single-signature wallets, (a) the value (by definition) is the property of the owner and is stored in a wallet, while (b) the owner interacts with the payment system directly and has total independent control over the value. In so far as the person conducting a transaction through the unhosted wallet is doing so to purchase goods or services on the user's own behalf, they are not a money transmitter.

4.2.2.   Multiple-signature wallet providers

Multiple-signature wallet providers are entities that facilitate the creation of wallets specifically for CVC that, for enhanced security, require more than one private key for the wallet owner(s) to effect transactions. Typically, multiple-signature wallet providers maintain in their possession one key for additional validation, while the wallet owner maintains the other private key locally. When a wallet owner wishes to effect a transaction from the owner's multiple-signature wallet, the wallet owner will generally submit to the provider a request signed with the wallet owner's private key, and once the provider verifies this request, the provider validates and executes the transaction using the second key it houses. With respect to an un-hosted multiple-signature wallet, (a) the value belongs to the owner and is stored in the wallet; (b) the owner interacts with the wallet software and/or payment system to initiate a transaction, supplying part of the credentials required to access the value; and (c) the person participating in the transaction to provide additional validation at the request of the owner does not have total independent control over the value.

If the multiple-signature wallet provider restricts its role to creating un-hosted wallets that require adding a second authorization key to the wallet owner's private key in order to validate and complete transactions, the provider is not a money transmitter because it does not accept and transmit value. On the other hand, if the person combines the services of a multiple-signature wallet provider and a hosted wallet provider, that person will then qualify as a money transmitter. Likewise, if the value is represented as an entry in the accounts of the provider, the owner does not interact with the payment system directly, or the provider maintains total independent control of the value, the provider will also qualify as a money transmitter, regardless of the label the person applies to itself or its activities.

4.3. CVC Money Transmission Services Provided Through Electronic Terminals (CVC Kiosks)

CVC kiosks (commonly called "CVC automated teller machines (ATMs)" or "CVC vending machines") are electronic terminals that act as mechanical agencies of the owner-operator, to enable the owner-operator to facilitate the exchange of CVC for currency or other CVC. These kiosks may connect directly to a separate CVC exchanger, which performs the actual CVC transmission, or they may draw upon the CVC in the possession of the owner-operator of the electronic terminal.

An owner-operator of a CVC kiosk who uses an electronic terminal to accept currency from a customer and transmit the equivalent value in CVC (or vice versa) qualifies as a money transmitter both for transactions receiving and dispensing real currency or CVC. FinCEN issued guidance clarifying that owners/operators of ATMs that link an accountholder with his or her account at a regulated depository institution solely to verify balances and dispense currency do not meet the definition of a money transmitter. The guidance addressing BSA coverage of private ATMs does not apply to the owner-operator of a CVC kiosk because CVC kiosks do not link accountholders to their respective accounts at a regulated depository institution. Accordingly, owners-operators of CVC kiosks that accept and transmit value must comply with FinCEN regulations governing money transmitters.

4.4. CVC Money Transmission Services Provided Through Decentralized Applications (DApps)

[Discussion of why DApps are treated like kiosks omitted.]

4.5. Anonymity-Enhanced CVC Transactions

Anonymity-enhanced CVC transactions are transactions either (a) denominated in regular types of CVC, but structured to conceal information otherwise generally available through the CVC's native distributed public ledger; or (b) denominated in types of CVC specifically engineered to prevent their tracing through distributed public ledgers (also called privacy coins).

A money transmitter that operates in anonymity-enhanced CVCs for its own account or for the accounts of others (regardless of the frequency) is subject to the same regulatory obligations as when operating in currency, funds, or nonanonymized CVCs. In other words, a money transmitter cannot avoid its regulatory obligations because it chooses to provide money transmission services using anonymity-enhanced CVC. The regulatory framework that applies to a person participating in anonymity-enhanced CVC transactions depends on the specific role performed by the person, as set forth below in Section 4.5.1.

4.5.1. Providers of anonymizing services for CVCs

Providers of anonymizing services, commonly referred to as "mixers" or "tumblers," are either persons that accept CVCs and retransmit them in a manner designed to prevent others from tracing the transmission back to its source (anonymizing services provider), or suppliers of software a transmittor would use for the same purpose (anonymizing software provider).

4.5.1(a) Anonymizing services provider

An anonymizing services provider is a money transmitter under FinCEN regulations. The added feature of concealing the source of the transaction does not change that person's status under the BSA. FinCEN previously issued a regulatory interpretation that concluded that persons who accept and transmit value in a way ostensibly designed to protect the privacy of the transmittor are providers of secure money transmission services and are not eligible for the integral exemption. In order to be exempt from status as a money transmitter under the integral exemption, the person's business must be different from money transmission itself, and the money transmission activity must be necessary for the business to operate. The subject of this previous regulatory interpretation accepted and transmitted funds in a way designed to protect a consumer's personal and financial information from a merchant, when the consumer purchased goods or services through the Internet. FinCEN determined that the added feature of protecting consumers' information did not constitute an activity separate from the funds transmission itself, because the need to protect the consumers' personal and financial information only arose in connection with the transmission of funds. FinCEN concluded that the company was engaged in the business of offering secure money transmission, rather than security for which money transmission is integrally required. Accordingly, the company qualified as a money transmitter subject to BSA obligations.

The same analysis applies to anonymizing services providers: their business consists exclusively of providing secured money transmission. Therefore, a person (acting by itself, through employees or agents, or by using mechanical or software agencies) who provides anonymizing services by accepting value from a customer and transmitting the same or another type of value to the recipient, in a way designed to mask the identity of the transmittor, is a money transmitter under FinCEN regulations.

4.5.1(b) Anonymizing software provider

An anonymizing software provider is not a money transmitter. FinCEN regulations exempt from the definition of money transmitter those persons providing "the delivery, communication, or network access services used by a money transmitter to support money transmission services." This is because suppliers of tools (communications, hardware, or software) that may be utilized in money transmission, like anonymizing software, are engaged in trade and not money transmission.

By contrast, a person that utilizes the software to anonymize the person's own transactions will be either a user or a money transmitter, depending on the purpose of each transaction. For example, a user would employ the software when paying for goods or services on its own behalf, while a money transmitter would use it to engage as a business in the acceptance and transmission of value as a transmittor's or intermediary's financial institution.

Lastly, FinCEN issued guidance stating that originating or intermediary financial institutions that replace the proper identity of a transmittor or recipient in the transmittal order with a pseudonym or reference that may not be decoded by the receiving financial institution (i.e., substituting the full name of the transmittor with a numeric code) are not complying with their obligations under the Funds Travel Rule.

4.5.2. Providers of anonymity-enhanced CVCs

A person that creates or sells anonymity-enhanced CVCs designed to prevent their tracing through publicly visible ledgers would be a money transmitter under FinCEN regulations depending on the type of payment system and the person's activity. For example:

(a)   a person operating as the administrator of a centralized CVC payment system will become a money transmitter the moment that person issues anonymity enhanced CVC against the receipt of another type of value.

(b)   a person that uses anonymity-enhanced CVCs to pay for goods or services on his or her own behalf would not be a money transmitter under the BSA. However, if the person uses the CVC to accept and transmit value from one person to another person or location, the person will fall under the definition of money transmitter, if not otherwise exempted.

(c)   a person that develops a decentralized CVC payment system will become a money transmitter if that person also engages as a business in the acceptance and transmission of value denominated in the CVC it developed (even if the CVC value was mined at an earlier date). The person would not be a money transmitter if that person uses the CVC it mined to pay for goods and services on his or her own behalf.

4.5.3.   Money Transmitters that accept or transmit anonymity-enhanced CVCs

Many money transmitters involved in CVC transactions comply with their BSA obligations, in part, by incorporating procedures into their AML Programs that allow them to track and monitor the transaction history of a CVC through publicly visible ledgers.

As mentioned above, FinCEN has issued guidance stating that transmittor's or intermediary's financial institutions that replace the proper identity of a transmitter or recipient in the transmittal order with a pseudonym or reference that may not be decoded by the receiving financial institution (i.e., substituting the full name of the transmittor with a numeric code) are not complying with their obligations under the Funds Travel Rule. A money transmitter must follow its AML risk assessment policies and procedures to determine under which circumstances the money transmitter will accept or transmit value already denominated in anonymity-enhanced CVCs. When knowingly accepting anonymity-enhanced CVCs (or regular CVC that has been anonymized), money transmitters engaged in CVC transactions subject to the Funds Travel Rule must not only track a CVC through the different transactions, but must also implement procedures to obtain the identity of the transmittor or recipient of the value.

4.6. Payment   Processing   Services   Involving   CVC   Money Transmission

CVC payment processors are financial intermediaries that enable traditional merchants to accept CVC from customers in exchange for goods and services sold. CVC payment processors sometimes integrate with a merchant's point of sale or online shopping cart solution so that the value of goods being purchased is quoted in CVC. The CVC payment processor may collect the CVC from the customer and then transmit currency or funds to the merchant, or vice versa.

CVC payment processors fall within the definition of a money transmitter and are not eligible for the payment processor exemption because they do not satisfy all the required conditions for the exemption. Under the payment processor exemption, a person is exempt from the definition of "money transmitter" when that person only "[a]cts as a payment processor to facilitate the purchase of, or payment of a bill for, a good or service through a clearance and settlement system by agreement with the creditor or seller." To be eligible for the payment processor exemption, a person must:

(a) facilitate the purchase of goods or services, or the payment of bills for goods or services (not just the money transmission itself);

(b) operate through clearance and settlement systems that admit only BSA regulated financial institutions;

(c) provide its service pursuant to a formal agreement; and

(d) enter a formal agreement with, at a minimum, the seller or creditor that provided the goods or services and also receives the funds.

A person providing payment processing services through CVC money transmission generally is unable to satisfy the second condition because such money transmitters do not operate, either in whole or in part, through clearing and settlement systems that only admit BSA-regulated financial institutions as members. This condition is critical, because BSA-regulated financial institutions have greater visibility into the complete pattern of activities of the buyer or debtor, on the one hand, and the seller or creditor, on the other hand. Having BSA-regulated financial institutions at either end of the clearance and settlement of transactions reduces the need to impose additional obligations on the payment processor. The CVC payment processor in that ruling received real currency payments from the buyer through a clearing and settlement system that only admits BSA-regulated financial institutions as members (specifically, a credit card network), but made payment of the Bitcoin equivalent to the merchant, to a merchant-owned virtual currency wallet or to a larger virtual currency exchange that admits both financial institution and non-financial institution members, for the account of the merchant. This same visibility simply does not exist when a CVC payment processor operates through a clearance and settlement system involving non-BSA regulated entities unless the CVC payment processor complies with the reporting obligations of a money transmitter.

Accordingly, in general, persons providing payment processing services in CVC will be money transmitters under the BSA, regardless of whether they accept and transmit the same type of CVC, or they accept one type of value (such as currency or funds) and transmit another (such as CVC).

. . . .

NOTES AND QUESTIONS

1.   If you buy Bitcoin for a couple of friends to show them how it is done, are you operating a money transmission business? If you accept a "gift" in return for the service, does that make you subject to BSA requirements? What if it is more like a dozen friends and acquaintances, and you charge a small fee for your time? Does the answer to this question depend on whether you know about the BSA requirements?

2.   What is the difference between a hosted and unhosted wallet service and why does it matter to FinCEN for purposes of this guidance?

3.   FinCEN has previously acknowledged that ATMs which link customers with fiat accounts in conventional banks or financial institutions are not acting as money transmitters. Why are CVC kiosks generally required to comply with FinCEN regulations applicable to money transmitters? How can a kiosk be expected to satisfy AML and KYC requirements?

4.   As mentioned in the notes preceding this excerpt, several sections of the 2019 Guidance relate to anonymizing services. Under what circumstances can a legal person employing anonymizing procedures be in compliance with FinCEN requirements?

5.   Does it seem that the 2019 Guidance sufficiently clarifies and simplifies application of BSA requirements to CVC businesses so that future businesses will clearly understand the rules applicable to their operation? Will these rules result in greater compliance?

8. THE POTENTIAL FOR LEGISLATIVE INTERVENTION

The general direction likely to be taken by FinCEN appears to be set, but this assumes that there is no legislative intervention. Representative Tom Emmer introduced a house bill, the Blockchain Regulatory Certainty Act, on January 14, 2019.[31] If enacted, this act would exempt blockchain developers and providers of blockchain services that do not take control of consumer funds from certain financial reporting and licensing requirements. In essence, the bill would prevent blockchain developers and providers from being money transmitters or money services businesses unless they have "in the regular course of business, control over digital

---

[31]   H.R. 528, 116th Cong. (2019–2020).

currency to which a user is entitled under the blockchain service or the software created, maintained, or disseminated by the blockchain developer." It also preempts state law money transmitter requirements. The act defines "digital currency" as "a medium of exchange, a unit of account, or a store of value that is represented by entries in a distributed ledger generated by a blockchain network." "Regular course of business" is not defined.

While it does not appear that this particular act is designed to prevent application of the BSA requirements to most of the businesses in which FinCEN would have a current interest, it does add some uncertainty by adding the requirement that the developer or provider be involved with digital currency in "the regular course of business."

As of the date these materials were written, there was no indication that this particular bill will be adopted. However, if federal legislation is enacted it could significantly impact the direction taken by FinCEN in its future actions involving cryptoassets and businesses.

CHAPTER 7

CRYPTO AND THE REGULATORS—
THE SEC

■ ■ ■

This chapter is designed to provide a high-level overview of the mission, role, and regulatory reach of the Securities and Exchange Commission (SEC), including the history and framework of the agency's authorizing legislation, the basic structure and mission of the agency, and the scope of its activities (in a general sense) in the modern financial world. Chapters eight and nine will introduce developments in the world of crypto that have shaped and are continuing to shape the reaction of the SEC to this new technology. Chapter ten will focus a little more clearly on the current state of the SEC's enforcement initiatives in the crypto space, along with an abbreviated consideration of where future changes in approach might occur, and what those changes might involve.

1. AN OVERVIEW OF THE FEDERAL REGULATORY SCHEME

The Securities Act of 1933 (codified at 15 U.S. Code § 77, and often referred to as the Securities Act or the '33 Act) and the Securities Exchange Act of 1934 (codified at 15 U.S. Code § 78, and often referred to as the Exchange Act or the '34 Act) helped establish the regime under which securities are regulated by the U.S. government. Both pieces of legislation were enacted in response to the stock market crash of 1929. Those two statutes form the basis for federal regulation of securities, although other statutes are also involved in specific situations.[1]

The SEC was created following enactment of the Securities Exchange Act of 1934 as the federal agency charged with enforcement of federal securities laws in the U.S. It is composed of five commissioners appointed by the President with the advice of the Senate. No more than three of the commissioners may be from the same political party. Commissioners serve for five-year terms. The SEC has a wide range of powers, including the legal power to administer oaths, subpoena witnesses, take evidence, and request documentation from any issuer that may have violated federal

---

[1]   Included in the more specific statutes is the Investment Company Act of 1940 (codified at 15 U.S. Code §§ 80a–1 to 80a–64, and often referred to as the Investment Company Act or 1940 Act). The 1940 Act will be mentioned briefly later in this chapter, particularly in connection with the regulation of ETFs.

securities law. The SEC may suspend trading in any security for up to 10 days, and may initiate administrative enforcement proceedings. It may also pursue criminal sanctions with the assistance of the federal Department of Justice. Except as otherwise provided, the federal legislation does not preempt state regulation of securities transactions,[2] so the federal regime generally acts alongside state securities laws (which are often referred to as Blue Sky laws).

Under the '33 Act, all offers and sales of interests that fit within the applicable definition of security must be registered, or the sales must comply with available exemptions from registration. Registration requires filing of extensive (and very expensive) disclosure documents in a form acceptable to the SEC. It is a painstaking and time-consuming process that most issuers prefer to avoid by finding an available exemption from registration as long as reasonably possible. However, regardless of whether an exemption from registration can be found, the sale of securities subjects the issuer to potential liability for fraud in connection with the transaction. Thus, an issuer who conducts a sale of securities may be liable under both federal and state law for securities fraud regardless of whether the sale was registered or an exemption was relied upon. (Fraud may include not only false and misleading statements, but conduct such as market manipulation that would amount to a fraud or deceit upon investors.)

An unregistered sale of securities that is not exempt gives the SEC a range of enforcement options. A violation of the securities laws may result in cease and desist orders, injunctions against further sales, the imposition of civil penalties, and/or criminal penalties in the event of willful or intentional violations. The issuer might also find itself ineligible to use certain exemptions for future deals. In addition to these administrative and criminal penalties, the improper sale of a security may also result in the seller incurring liability to the buyer for damages even in the absence of any fraud or other wrongdoing. Alternatively, a buyer might have an automatic right to rescind the deal, which would require the seller to buy back the security for the price paid plus interest.

The following material provides a little more detail, still in overview format, as to how the U.S. securities laws work.

---

[2]   Preemption of inconsistent state securities regulation dates back to 1996, when Congress enacted the National Securities and Markets Improvement Act of 1996 (NSMIA). Among other things, NSMIA preempted state regulations of "covered securities," which was defined so as to include securities traded on national exchanges and securities sold in reliance on the then-current version of Rule 506 of Reg. D. To give an idea of how important issuers and their counsel viewed the ability to avoid application of state securities laws, in short order "some 99% of the amounts of securities sold, approaching $1 trillion annually," relied on that single exemption. The JOBS Act of 2012, however, amended the definition of "covered" security to specifically apply to shares issued in compliance with certain other regulations. As a result, offerings conducted in accordance with Reg. A (tier 2), Reg. D (Rule 506), and Reg. CF need not be conducted in accordance with state law requirements that might otherwise apply.

2. APPLICATION OF THE SECURITIES LAWS— WHEN IS AN INTEREST A "SECURITY"?

A. IN GENERAL

When a company decides to raise funds by selling something that the purchaser is not buying for consumption or use (such as a car that will be driven, food that will be eaten, or computers that will be used), one of the first inquiries should be whether the company plans on selling a security. If the answer is yes, in securities parlance, the company in this scenario will be acting as the issuer. This matters because when an issuer offers or sells a security, a whole panoply of laws and regulations are triggered, at both the federal and state levels.

The '33 Act was obviously enacted long before anything like crypto existed (and similarly before business enterprises like limited liability companies or limited liability partnerships existed). The likelihood of future developments was foreseen, even if particular changes were not predictable. Given the virtual certainty of continuing innovation, it was important for the securities statutes to include definitions that explained as clearly as possible what kinds of interests would be regulated as securities, while being flexible enough to apply to new interests, such as cryptoassets.

Section 2 of the Securities Act of 1933 Act contains the following definition of "security," which includes terms with specific, well-understood meanings as well as words that are more elastic and possess less defined parameters. The definition follows the phrase, "unless the context otherwise requires" so keep in mind that some of the named interests may not always be securities:

The term "security" means any note, stock, treasury stock, bond, debenture, evidence of indebtedness, certificate of interest or participation in any profit-sharing agreement, collateral-trust certificate, preorganization certificate or subscription, transferable share, investment contract, voting-trust certificate, certificate of deposit for a security, fractional undivided interest in oil, gas or other mineral rights, any put, call, straddle, option, or privilege on any security, certificate of deposit, or group or index of securities (including any interest therein or based on the value thereof), or any put, call, straddle, option, or privilege entered into on a national securities exchange relating to foreign currency, or, in general, any interest or instrument commonly known as a 'security' or any certificate of interest or participation in, temporary or interim certificate for, receipt for, guarantee participation in, temporary or interim certificate for, receipt for, guarantee of, or warrant or right to subscribe to or purchase, any of the foregoing.[3]

This statutory definition of security is the obvious starting point for any analysis of whether particular interests sold by a business to raise funds will be classified as securities. The statute contains lists of specific interests that are "securities," but does not purport to include a substantive definition applicable to all such interests. If the issuer is not selling an interest that fits within these categories, the securities laws (including antifraud provisions) will not apply. If the interest is a security, the issuer will have to comply with the securities laws.

B. INVESTMENT CONTRACTS

Some of the categories of interests in the statutory definition of security have a relatively well-understood meaning. This is true for interests such as stock, notes, bonds, etc. When it comes to "investment contract," however, there is no generally accepted meaning of the phrase outside the securities laws context. This makes "investment contract" a very important concept, because it is broad and general enough to cover potential investment vehicles that did not exist at the time the '33 Act and '34 Act were being promulgated. As the material later in this chapter will make clear, that includes cryptoassets.

For purposes of the federal securities laws, the term "investment contract" is analyzed under the general framework announced by the U.S. Supreme Court in *SEC v. W.J. Howey Co.*, 328 U.S. 293 (1946):

SECURITIES AND EXCHANGE COMMISSION
V. W. J. HOWEY CO. ET AL.
328 U.S. 293 (1946)

MURPHY, J.

This case involves the application of § 2(1) of the Securities Act of 1933 to an offering of units of a citrus grove development coupled with a contract for cultivating, marketing and remitting the net proceeds to the investor.

The Securities and Exchange Commission instituted this action to restrain the respondents from using the mails and instrumentalities of interstate commerce in the offer and sale of unregistered and nonexempt securities in violation of § 5(a) of the Act, 15 U.S. Code § 77e(a). The District Court denied the injunction, and the Fifth Circuit Court of Appeals affirmed the judgment. We granted certiorari on a petition alleging that the ruling of the Circuit Court of Appeals conflicted with other federal and state decisions and that it introduced a novel and unwarranted test under

---

[3]   15 U.S. Code § 77b(1).

the statute which the Commission regarded as administratively impractical.

Most of the facts are stipulated. The respondents, W. J. Howey Company and Howey-in-the-Hills Service Inc., are Florida corporations under direct common control and management. The Howey Company owns large tracts of citrus acreage in Lake County, Florida. During the past several years it has planted about 500 acres annually, keeping half of the groves itself and offering the other half to the public 'to help us finance additional development.' Howey-in-the-Hills Service, Inc., is a service company engaged in cultivating and developing many of these groves, including the harvesting and marketing of the crops.

Each prospective customer is offered both a land sales contract and a service contract, after having been told that it is not feasible to invest in a grove unless service arrangements are made. While the purchaser is free to make arrangements with other service companies, the superiority of Howey-in-the-Hills Service, Inc., is stressed. Indeed, 85% of the acreage sold during the 3-year period ending May 31, 1943, was covered by service contracts with Howey-in-the-Hills Service, Inc.

The land sales contract with the Howey Company provides for a uniform purchase price per acre or fraction thereof, varying in amount only in accordance with the number of years the particular plot has been planted with citrus trees. Upon full payment of the purchase price the land is conveyed to the purchaser by warranty deed. Purchases are usually made in narrow strips of land arranged so that an acre consists of a row of 48 trees. During the period between February 1, 1941, and May 31, 1943, 31 of the 42 persons making purchases bought less than 5 acres each. The average holding of these 31 persons was 1.33 acres and sales of as little as 0.65, 0.7 and 0.73 of an acre were made. These tracts are not separately fenced and the sole indication of several ownership is found in small land marks intelligible only through a plat book record.

The service contract, generally of a 10-year duration without option of cancellation, gives Howey-in-the-Hills Service, Inc., a leasehold interest and 'full and complete' possession of the acreage. For a specified fee plus the cost of labor and materials, the company is given full discretion and authority over the cultivation of the groves and the harvest and marketing of the crops. The company is well established in the citrus business and maintains a large force of skilled personnel and a great deal of equipment, including 75 tractors, sprayer wagons, fertilizer trucks and the like. Without the consent of the company, the land owner or purchaser has no right of entry to market the crop; thus there is ordinarily no right to specific fruit. The company is accountable only for an allocation of the net profits based upon a check made at the time of picking. All the produce is pooled by the respondent companies, which do business under their own names.

The purchasers for the most part are non-residents of Florida. They are predominantly business and professional people who lack the knowledge, skill and equipment necessary for the care and cultivation of citrus trees. They are attracted by the expectation of substantial profits. It was represented, for example, that profits during the 1943–1944 season amounted to 20% and that even greater profits might be expected during the 1944–1945 season, although only a 10% annual return was to be expected over a 10-year period. Many of these purchasers are patrons of a resort hotel owned and operated by the Howey Company in a scenic section adjacent to the groves. The hotel's advertising mentions the fine groves in the vicinity and the attention of the patrons is drawn to the groves as they are being escorted about the surrounding countryside. They are told that the groves are for sale; if they indicate an interest in the matter they are then given a sales talk.

It is admitted that the mails and instrumentalities of interstate commerce are used in the sale of the land and service contracts and that no registration statement or letter of notification has ever been filed with the Commission in accordance with the Securities Act of 1933 and the rules and regulations thereunder.

Section 2(1) of the Act defines the term 'security' to include the commonly known documents traded for speculation or investment. This definition also includes 'securities' of a more variable character. . . . The legal issue in this case turns upon a determination of whether, under the circumstances, the land sales contract, the warranty deed and the service contract together constitute an 'investment contract' within the meaning of § 2(1). An affirmative answer brings into operation the registration requirements of § 5(a), unless the security is granted an exemption under § 3(b). The lower courts, in reaching a negative answer to this problem, treated the contracts and deeds as separate transactions involving no more than an ordinary real estate sale and an agreement by the seller to manage the property for the buyer.

The term 'investment contract' is undefined by the Securities Act or by relevant legislative reports. But the term was common in many state 'blue sky' laws in existence prior to the adoption of the federal statute and, although the term was also undefined by the state laws, it had been broadly construed by state courts so as to afford the investing public a full measure of protection. Form was disregarded for substance and emphasis was placed upon economic reality. An investment contract thus came to mean a contract or scheme for 'the placing of capital or laying out of money in a way intended to secure income or profit from its employment.' This definition was uniformly applied by state courts to a variety of situations where individuals were led to invest money in a common enterprise with the expectation that they would earn a profit solely through the efforts of the promoter or of some one other than themselves.

By including an investment contract within the scope of § 2(1) of the Securities Act, Congress was using a term the meaning of which had been crystallized by this prior judicial interpretation. It is therefore reasonable to attach that meaning to the term as used by Congress, especially since such a definition is consistent with the statutory aims. In other words, an investment contract for purposes of the Securities Act means a contract, transaction or scheme whereby a person invests his money in a common enterprise and is led to expect profits solely from the efforts of the promoter or a third party, it being immaterial whether the shares in the enterprise are evidenced by formal certificates or by nominal interests in the physical assets employed in the enterprise. Such a definition .... embodies a flexible rather than a static principle, one that is capable of adaptation to meet the countless and variable schemes devised by those who seek the use of the money of others on the promise of profits.

The transactions in this case clearly involve investment contracts as so defined. The respondent companies are offering something more than fee simple interests in land, something different from a farm or orchard coupled with management services. They are offering an opportunity to contribute money and to share in the profits of a large citrus fruit enterprise managed and partly owned by respondents. They are offering this opportunity to persons who reside in distant localities and who lack the equipment and experience requisite to the cultivation, harvesting and marketing of the citrus products. Such persons have no desire to occupy the land or to develop it themselves; they are attracted solely by the prospects of a return on their investment. Indeed, individual development of the plots of land that are offered and sold would seldom be economically feasible due to their small size. Such tracts gain utility as citrus groves only when cultivated and developed as component parts of a larger area. A common enterprise managed by respondents or third parties with adequate personnel and equipment is therefore essential if the investors are to achieve their paramount aim of a return on their investments. Their respective shares in this enterprise are evidenced by land sales contracts and warranty deeds, which serve as a convenient method of determining the investors' allocable shares of the profits. The resulting transfer of rights in land is purely incidental.

Thus all the elements of a profit-seeking business venture are present here. The investors provide the capital and share in the earnings and profits; the promoters manage, control and operate the enterprise. It follows that the arrangements whereby the investors' interests are made manifest involve investment contracts, regardless of the legal terminology in which such contracts are clothed. The investment contracts in this instance take the form of land sales contracts, warranty deeds and service contracts which respondents offer to prospective investors. And respondents' failure to abide by the statutory and administrative rules in making such offerings, even though the failure result from a bona fide mistake as to the law, cannot be sanctioned under the Act.

This conclusion is unaffected by the fact that some purchasers choose not to accept the full offer of an investment contract by declining to enter into a service contract with the respondents. The Securities Act prohibits the offer as well as the sale of unregistered, non-exempt securities. Hence it is enough that the respondents merely offer the essential ingredients of an investment contract.

We reject the suggestion of the Circuit Court of Appeals that an investment contract is necessarily missing where the enterprise is not speculative or promotional in character and where the tangible interest which is sold has intrinsic value independent of the success of the enterprise as a whole. The test is whether the scheme involves an investment of money in a common enterprise with profits to come solely from the efforts of others. If that test be satisfied, it is immaterial whether the enterprise is speculative or non-speculative or whether there is a sale of property with or without intrinsic value. The statutory policy of affording broad protection to investors is not to be thwarted by unrealistic and irrelevant formulae.

Reversed.

———————

As explained in *Howey*, an investment contract is a contract, transaction, or scheme where purchasers are "led to invest money in a common enterprise with the expectation that they would earn a profit solely through the efforts of the promoter or of someone other than themselves." This test, now widely referred to simply as the "*Howey* test," has been substantially expanded and clarified over the past decades, but it continues to provide the basis for determining whether a number of interests that are not specifically enumerated in the '33 Act are securities.

Speaking very broadly, an interest will be classified as an investment contract under *Howey* if it satisfies all of the following elements:

(i)   there is an investment of money (or something else of value);

(ii)   in a common enterprise;[4]

(iii) where the purchaser expects to receive profits; and

———————

[4]   While cases and academic commentators alike have relied on these elements for decades, officials at the SEC have taken issue with the "common enterprise" requirement, suggesting in recent documents that the SEC "does not . . . view a 'common enterprise' as a distinct element of the term 'investment contract.'" SEC FinHub, *Framework for 'Investment Contract' Analysis of Digital Assets* (Ap. 3, 2019) at n.10 [available online at https://www.sec.gov/files/dlt-framework. pdf]. Ironically, the text to which the note is appended (and the note itself) specifically recognize that courts do treat the *Howey* test as requiring a common enterprise as a distinct element.

(iv) the expectation of profits is from the essential entrepreneurial efforts of others.

The SEC has specifically noted that "[t]his definition . . . embodies a flexible rather than a static principle, one that is capable of adaptation to meet the countless and variable schemes devised by those who seek the use of the money of others on the promise of profits." *Howey,* 328 U.S. at 299. It is also consistent with the U.S. Supreme Court's admonition that in the context of applying the securities laws, "form should be disregarded for substance," and the focus should be on the economic reality underlying transactions rather on the name they are given. *See Tcherepnin v. Knight,* 389 U.S. 332, 336 (1967).

Note that there continues to be a great deal of discussion about what is meant by some of these elements. Having at least a general understanding of the requirements for there to be an investment contract is important because this is likely to be the focus of future disputes about whether particular cryptoassets or transactions involve the sale of securities.

Some of the elements seem deceptively simple. How hard, for example, is it to determine if there is an investment of money (or something else of value)? In actuality, even this element can be tricky. What if the question is whether the contribution is partially for investment and partially for the potential or actual usefulness of the crypto being acquired? Is speculation ever different from investment? What if there is no money (fiat or crypto) involved, but the transaction involves contribution of some minimal service, such as joining a Telegram account? Is that an investment of something of value? Do you consider value from the perspective of the person acquiring the interest or the person with whom the interest originates? Answers to these questions may actually be dispositive in certain cases.

There is no doubt about the complexity of the second element. The requirement that there be a "common enterprise" has probably spawned the widest disagreement, with a considerable split among the federal circuits as to what this requires.[5] And again, the requirements of commonality may be important in determining whether securities laws apply to specific interests and transactions.

Horizontal commonality exists when investors' funds are pooled and investors share in the profits and losses of the venture. On the other hand, some courts look at whether there is a common interest in a vertical sense, between the investor and promoter(s). Strict vertical commonality exists if investor fortunes are directly tied with those of the promoters. Broad vertical commonality is satisfied if investors' profits (or losses) correlate

---

[5]   This disagreement carries over to the SEC, as noted above.

with the efforts and expertise of the promoters. Further complicating matters, some courts apply a mix of these tests, or have offered inconsistent approaches to the question of what is meant by commonality.[6]

The third element of *Howey*, the expectation of profits, may also help some crypto escape regulation as securities. If a particular token has a function (or in other words it is a functioning utility token), and purchasers are acquiring the token in order to take advantage of that function, there is a strong argument that the securities laws should not be involved. Keep in mind, however, that the mere existence of a function is not enough; it is the motive of the purchasers that matters. This, of course, is complicated

---

[6]   Although not necessary to place the SEC's approach to crypto in context, it may be helpful to understand just how much disagreement there is among the federal circuits with regard to what is required to prove that there is a common enterprise.

Horizontal commonality appears to be the preferred test in the Second Circuit, although strict vertical commonality may also suffice. In *Revak v. SEC Realty Corp.*, 18 F.3d 81, 88 (2d Cir. 1994), the Second Circuit explained that "[i]f a common enterprise can be established by the mere showing that the fortunes of investors are tied to the efforts of the promoter, two separate questions posed by *Howey* . . . are effectively merged into a single inquiry." *Accord Copeland v. Hill*, 680 F. Supp. 466, 468 (D. Mass. 1988).

Courts in the Fourth Circuit also accept horizontal commonality, with the status of the vertical commonality approach being unclear. In *Teague v. Bakker*, 35 F.3d 978, 986 n.8 (4th Cir. 1994), the Fourth Circuit found that horizontal commonality existed, and noted that the district court was therefore not required to have determined whether vertical commonality was present. In *SEC v. Pinckney*, 923 F. Supp. 76, 81–82 (E.D.N.C. 1996), a district court surveyed Fourth circuit cases on commonality and concluded that vertical commonality would be sufficient.

The Fifth Circuit appears to accept a showing of broad vertical commonality. *See, i.e., SEC v. Koscot Interplanetary, Inc.*, 497 F.2d 473, 478 (5th Cir. 1974) (holding that "the critical factor is not the similitude or coincidence of investor input, but rather the uniformity of impact of the promoter's efforts"); *SEC v. Cont'l Commodities Corp.*, 497 F.2d 516, 522 (5th Cir. 1974) (holding pooling of investors' funds is not necessary to establish a common enterprise). On the other hand, a more recent decision casts some doubt on how broadly the Fifth Circuit will be willing to define the requirement of commonality. In *Long v. Shultz Cattle Co.*, 896 F.2d 85, 86, 88 (5th Cir. 1990), the Fifth Circuit declined to reconsider its standard under the facts of that case, but also recognized that its approach was "at odds with the stricter approaches taken in other circuits."

Courts in the Eighth Circuit have not been entirely consistent in the approaches that have been taken. For example, in *Sias v. Herzog*, Civil No. 04–3832, 2006 WL 2418950, at *8 (D. Minn. Aug. 21, 2006), one district the court acknowledged the split among the courts and analyzed the schemes in question for horizontal commonality and strict vertical commonality, but not broad vertical commonality. *Id.* at *13 n.8. On the other hand, in *Top of Iowa Coop. v. Schewe*, 6 F. Supp. 2d 843, 852–53 (N.D. Iowa 1998), a different district court looked at horizontal commonality and both of the vertical commonality approaches.

The Ninth Circuit permits the "common enterprise" element to be shown either by strict vertical commonality or horizontal commonality. *See, e.g., SEC v. R.G. Reynolds Enters., Inc.*, 952 F.2d 1125, 1130–31 (9th Cir. 1991) (requiring proof of either strict vertical commonality or horizontal commonality).

While the Tenth Circuit will accept horizontal commonality, it has also indicated that this is not a rigid requirement. *McGill v. Am. Land & Exploration Co.*, 776 F.2d 923, 925 (10th Cir. 1985) (rejecting notion that horizontal commonality is required by *Howey*). Narrow vertical commonality was relied upon in *Walsh v. Int'l Precious Metals Corp.*, 510 F. Supp. 867, 871 (D. Utah 1981), although the Tenth Circuit does not appear to have formally accepted this approach.

The Eleventh Circuit has adopted the broad vertical approach. *See SEC v. ETS Payphones, Inc.*, 300 F.3d 1281, 1284 (11th Cir. 2002) (affirming the circuit's adoption of the "broad vertical commonality" approach, which "only requires a movant to show that the investors are dependent upon the expertise or efforts of the investment promoter for their returns"), *rev'd on other grounds*, 540 U.S. 389 (2004), *remanded* 408 F.3d 727 (11th Cir. 2005).

by the reality that motives of different purchasers may not be the same, and even a single purchaser may have mixed motives.

Finally, the expectation of profits must be based on the efforts of others. This element may also be missing in the case of crypto, especially where a particular coin or token is so widely held that it is decentralized market forces rather than any identifiable person or group of others who will presumably affect the asset's value.

Before moving on, it is also worth noting that this discussion has focused on the federal definition of "investment contract." Many state securities laws are also triggered if a particular transaction involves the offer or sale of an investment contract, but while many states have adopted the federal investment contract analysis, not all states have done so. A minority of states rely on what is generally known as the "risk capital" test to determine when an issuer is selling an investment contract under state law, meaning that additional research may be required in order to figure out if a particular state's securities laws will be implicated in any given transaction.[7]

3. SECURITIES MUST BE REGISTERED OR EXEMPT IN ORDER TO BE SOLD

Once a determination is made that a particular interest is a security under federal law, the '33 Act comes into play. This Act governs offers and sales of securities and, in general, requires the registration of offers and sales unless an exemption from registration is available. The focus of the '33 Act is on making sure that offers and sales of securities are free from fraud, and that investors are provided with enough information in order to evaluate the merits of a proposed investment.

A primary means of accomplishing these goals is the disclosure of important financial information through the registration process. As part

---

[7] For a more detailed consideration of what the risk capital test requires, the following law review articles provide a good amount of information and detail:

- Miriam R. Albert, *The Howey Test Turns 64: Are the Courts Grading this Test on a Curve?*, 2 WM. & MARY BUS. L. REV. 1, 32–35 (2011) (discussing the application of the *Howey* test under blue-sky laws and its codification in the Uniform Securities Act).

- Elaine A. Welle, *Limited Liability Company Interests as Securities: An Analysis of Federal and State Actions Against Limited Liability Companies Under the Securities Laws*, 73 DENV. U.L. REV. 425, 465 (1996), noting that there are actually several versions of the risk capital test, but all are considered to be broader than the *Howey* test. *Id.* at 465–470.

- Mark A. Sargent, *Are Limited Liability Company Interests Securities?*, 19 PEPP. L. REV. 1069, 1092–93 (1992).

- Gregory J. Pease, Note, *Bluer Skies in Tennessee—The Recent Broadening of the Definition of Investment Contract as a Security and an Argument for a Unified Federal-State Definition of Investment Contract*, 35 U. MEM. L. REV. 109, 114 (2004) (noting that the majority of states follow the *Howey* test while a minority follow the broader "risk capital" approach, most commonly associated with *State v. Hawaii Market Center, Inc.*, 485 P.2d 105 (Haw. 1971)).

of that process, an issuer must file a detailed registration statement with the SEC. The filing must include a prospectus containing a variety of mandatory disclosures to be provided to all purchasers. The information in those documents enables investors, not the government, to make informed judgments about whether to purchase a company's securities. While the SEC requires that the information provided be accurate, it is not a guarantor of the document's veracity. Investors who purchase securities and suffer losses have important legal rights if they can prove that there was incomplete or inaccurate disclosure of material information.

The required disclosures include a description of the company's properties and business; a description of the security to be offered for sale; information about the management of the company; and financial statements certified by independent accountants. The documents become public shortly after filing with the SEC. If filed by U.S. domestic companies, the statements are available on the EDGAR database accessible at www.sec.gov, a searchable database maintained by the SEC. There is no charge to view these documents.

A. REGISTRATION PROCESS

Although registration is required every time an issuer wants to conduct a public sale of its securities, the first time a company makes a public distribution of its shares (or sometimes debt securities), it is said to be conducting an initial public offering (IPO). The required disclosures make registration a relatively cumbersome and costly process, especially for an IPO. One survey found that 83% of CFOs estimated spending more than $1 million on one-time costs associated with the IPO, not including underwriters' fees.[8] This source put the average total cost of an IPO (with underwriting, legal, and accounting fees included) at a minimum of $3 million for offerings of less than $100 million, scaling up from there.[9] In addition to the expense, the time required is also significant. Various sources say that an IPO takes between 90 days to 6 months or between 6 and 9 months to complete (from the company's decision to go public up through the SEC's declaration that the registration is "effective"), depending on the complexity of the underlying transactions necessary to get the company in shape for the sale.

If that expense alone is not enough to prevent a company from wanting to register a sale of shares or other securities, there are additional follow-up costs of being public. Publicly held companies (i.e., companies with any class of publicly registered securities) must file specific and detailed annual, quarterly, and special reports. They become subject to federal

---

[8]   *Considering an IPO to fuel your company's future? Insight into the costs of going public and being public*, PWC (Nov, 2017) (available online at https://www.pwc.com/hu/hu/szolgaltatasok/konyvvizsgalat/szamviteli-tanacsadas/kiadvanyok/cost_of_an_ipo_2017.pdf), at p. 5.

[9]   *Id.* at 7.

regulation of their proxies, and rules regarding how they must handle shareholder proposals. They become subject to insider trading rules, and various accounting and board standards. The survey referenced earlier found that that 2/3 of CFOs estimate the annual cost of being public is between $1 million and $1.9 million.[10]

This is an extremely simplistic overview of the registration process and the contents of the registration statement. Entire law school classes are taught around the kinds of information required from someone seeking to register securities for sale, as well as the kinds of communications that are permitted during each stage of the registration process. This material should, however, provide important background into why crypto entrepreneurs would rather not have their cryptoassets classified as securities, and why the availability of exemptions and the requirements of such exemptions are important.

B. IMPORTANT EXEMPTIONS

Absent an exemption from registration, every securities transaction that uses the U.S. mails or other means of interstate commerce must be registered with the SEC. In general, § 3 of the '33 Act lists certain types of securities that need not be registered. These securities may be sold and resold without registration, but are not necessarily exempt from the antifraud provisions of the federal securities laws. (In general terms, those exemptions apply to narrow classes of securities, such as those issued by state or local governments, by charitable organizations, by regulated banks, or by insurance companies in the form of insurance contracts and annuities.) Section 4 of the '33 Act lists certain transactions that are exempt from the registration requirements of § 5 of the Act. Securities sold pursuant to one of these exemptions cannot be resold without registration or availability of a new exemption (although sales by anyone other than an "issuer, underwriter, or dealer" are exempt under § 4(a)(1)).[11] Sales in accordance with § 4 exemptions are also subject to the antifraud requirements of federal law. The SEC has promulgated various regulations either to explain or effectuate many of these authorized exemptions.

Some of the most important issuer exemptions under the Securities Act include:

Section 3(a)(11) and Rules 147 and 147A;

Section 4(a)(2)[before the JOBS Act, this was Section 4(2)];

---

[10]   *Id.* at 14.

[11]   As a warning, this exemption is not as broad as it may first appear, because of the extremely broad definition given to "underwriter" in the securities laws. A discussion of who counts as an underwriter is far outside the scope of this book, but for those who are interested, a general discussion of the term can be found in ELGA A. GOODMAN, ET AL, BUSINESS LAW DESKBOOK, NEW JERSEY PRACTICE SERIES (Nov. 2018 update) at § 30:3, *The Underwriter Concept.*

Section 4(a)(5);

Regulation A (Reg. A)

Regulation D (Reg. D), including Rules 504, 506(b) and 506(c);

Regulation S (Reg. S); and

Regulation CF (Reg. CF).

The following materials contain a general overview of and introduction to each of these exemptions. More detailed footnotes are primarily to serve as a research resource. Remember that this is not an exclusive listing of potential exemptions, but merely some of the more commonly used ones, which also happen to be ones that may be relevant when it comes to understanding how the securities laws apply to cryptotransactions in the U.S.

Despite the lack of detail and specificity, this material is important for a variety of reasons. First, it gives a glimpse into the complexity of these regulations. It also provides a basis for understanding why it is difficult for issuers to comply with the available exemptions. Second, it explains why issuers of cryptoassets really want their cryptocoins and tokens to be excluded from the definition of security. Third, it sets the stage for considering what the issuer of a cryptoasset might be able to do in order to conduct a compliant offering if they are selling a security. Finally, it illustrates why being a securities attorney is not something that should generally be done on a part-time basis, as well as why securities lawyers often charge fairly high rates for their services. The expense of retaining experience securities counsel also explains why businesses that have operated on the cheap are likely to have proceeded without appropriate legal advice, and are therefore more likely to run into problems under the federal securities laws.

With that in mind, here is the general explanation of the most commonly used exemptions from registration.

1)   § 3(a)(11)—Intrastate Offerings

The intrastate offering exemption is found in § 3(a)(11) of the '33 Act. This provision exempts "[a]ny security which is part of an issue offered and sold only to persons within a single State . . . where the issuer of such security is a person resident and doing business, or, if a corporation, incorporated by and doing business within, such State. . . ."[12]

The primary argument made in favor of this exemption is that state regulation should be sufficient to protect investors in any offering that

---

[12]   This language appears in the "Exempted Securities" provisions of § 3 rather than the "Exempt Transactions" of § 4, but this placement is viewed as a legislative accident rather than being intentional. In Exchange Act Release No. 5450, the SEC made it clear that § 3(a)(11) covers the transaction, not the security.

occurs completely within a single state. On the other hand, there is considerable evidence that state securities laws vary considerably, with some requiring not only disclosure but imposing requirements based on the presumed merit of offerings.[13] In addition, although most intrastate offerings are small, and all must be "local in character," some are quite large, involving millions of dollars and hundreds of investors.[14]

The problem with the statutory exemption is that it contains very little in the way of certainty. What does it mean when the provision says that the offering may be sold only to persons "within" the state? What does it mean for an issuer to be "doing business" in a state? Case law tended to interpret the exemption very strictly, leading to considerable uncertainty as to the scope of the exemption. Because of the need for more certainty, the SEC adopted regulatory safe harbors to give issuers a degree of predictability. In essence, these safe harbors provide that the exemption is available if 80% of an issuer's assets are located in the state, or 80% of their gross receipts come from in-state operations, most employees are based in the state, and/or at least 80% of the proceeds are to be used in the state.[15]

---

[13]   Merit requirements vary by state and may include things such as prohibiting multiple classes of shares, a requirement for voting rights, escrow requirements, etc. For a list of various merit review standards, see Nancy Fallon-Houle, *Blue Sky Merit Review States*, VELOCITY LAW (available by searching "Blue Sky Merit Review" at https://www.velocitylaw.com/).

[14]   SEC Release No. 33–4434 explained that the intrastate exemption was originally designed to apply only to issues offered and sold exclusively to residents of one state; a single offer to a non-resident destroyed exemption.

[15]   The original safe harbor was Rule 147, and if an issuer complied with the articulated standards of that rule, it was automatically deemed to have complied with the statutory exemption.

Rule 147, as originally implemented, had many stringent requirements. Among the limitations on the exemption were requirements that (1) the issuer be organized in-state and (2) all offers had to be directed to in-state residents. Moreover, the issuer was not entitled to rely on simple representations of residency, instead bearing the burden of establishing actual residency of all purchasers and offerees.

On October 26, 2016, the Commission modernized some of the Rule 147 requirements, adopting final rules that amended Rule 147 and implementing a new intrastate exemption in the form of Rule 147A. Securities Act Rule 147A allows offers (although not sales) to be accessible to out-of-state residents and makes the exemption available to issuers that are incorporated or organized out-of-state.

Under both Rule 147 as it currently exists and 147A, those in control of the issuer must primarily direct, control, and coordinate the issuer's activities within the applicable state. This is the "principal place of business" requirement. The issuer must also be doing business in the state, which requires at least one of the following: the issuer derives at least 80% of its consolidated gross revenues from the operation of a business or of real property located in-state or from the rendering of services in-state; the issuer has at least 80% of its consolidated assets located in-state; the issuer intends to use and does use at least 80% of the net proceeds from the offering towards the operation of a business or of real property in-state, the purchase of real property located in-state, or the rendering of services in-state; or a majority of the issuer's employees are based in-state. Sales are limited to in-state residents, or to those whom the issuer reasonably believes to be in-state residents. The issuer must obtain a written representation from each purchaser as to residency. Finally, for six months from the sale, resales may be made only to persons residing in-state. Issuers must disclose the limitation on resale on the certificate or other document evidencing the security.

Compliance with this exemption does not affect any applicable state laws. It also does not remove the requirement that the offering comply with the antifraud provisions of the federal securities laws.

2) § 4(a)(2)—Private Offering Exemption

Section 4(a)(2) of the '33 Act[16] exempts any "transaction by an issuer not involving any public offering." Unfortunately, there is no statutory definition of what constitutes a "public offering."[17] In general terms, to conduct a compliant § 4(a)(2) offering (generally referred to as a "private placement"), the issuer must make sure that the offering does not involve any general solicitation or advertising. All offerees should be appropriately qualified,[18] meaning that the issuer must have a basis for believing that they are capable of understanding the risk of investment. This obligation can be satisfied if the issuer has a prior relationship with the potential investors or conducts reasonable inquiry to make sure that investors are sufficiently sophisticated. The investors must also have meaningful access to material information relevant to the investment decision. The total number of investors does not have to be extremely small, but does need to be reasonably limited. Finally, the issuer needs to take reasonable care to make sure that an investor is not buying the security with the intent of turning around and reselling to someone else. In securities jargon, this means the shares must "come to rest" before they can be resold.[19]

---

[16]   This provision was found at § 4(2) prior to the 2012 JOBS Act.

[17]   A 1935 Securities Act release from General Counsel's office said that under ordinary circumstances, if offering was to fewer than 25 persons, it was not public (Release No. 285) and that certain other facts also had to be examined:

  1.   the number of offerees and their relationship to each other and the issuer;

  2.   the number of units offered;

  3.   the size of the offering; and

  4.   the manner of the offering.

The leading early case looking at the meaning of "public offering" was *SEC v. Sunbeam Gold Mines*, 95 F.2d 699 (9th Cir. 1938), which held that loans from 530 individuals involved a public offering, even though the sale was limited to company's shareholders.

[18]   The critical inquiry was whether all offerees (not just purchasers) needed the protection of the securities laws.

It was traditionally good advice to require sellers to prequalify offerees by using information sheets to obtain background (suitability standards); by keeping records of the number of offers; and by numbering any offering documents distributed to offerees. Courts are split as to whether an issuer can make a private placement to a small number of unsophisticated investors. The Tenth Circuit has both suggested that sophistication is a necessary condition and that it is only one of four factors. The Fifth Circuit emphasizes whether offerees are actually entitled to and do receive appropriate disclosures. The use of offeree representatives to help the offeree understand the disclosures is sometimes expressly permitted (as in the Reg. 506(b) safe harbor in Reg. D) and sometimes allowed by implication. (No court has said an issuer cannot consider the aid of an offeree representative in determining sophistication.) Outside of certain safe harbors, the ability of the offeree to withstand the risk of the investment has not emerged as a major factor, although some commentators have suggested that it should be considered.

[19]   If a resale occurs before a security has come to rest, it is treated as part of the original transaction. A resale to an impermissible purchaser may result in the entire deal being treated as a public offering. To avoid this, issuers often place legends on securities, issue stop orders, require

For purposes of this exemption, an issuer can be almost any judicial "person," including an individual, corporation, partnership, unincorporated association, government, etc. The word "issuer" includes persons who propose to issue securities as well as those who follow through and actually complete the transaction(s); a promotor who takes pre-incorporation subscriptions is also an issuer.

The most common type of private placement involves offers and sales to institutions that are accredited investors, defined in Reg. D[20] and further described in this next section of this chapter. If offerees are all accredited institutional investors, they cannot claim to be unsophisticated, and cases hold that they can fend for themselves; in their case, sophistication is a substitute for actual disclosure.

Because the boundaries of this exemption are so unclear, few issuers rely on this exemption unless they inadvertently violate the terms of the various exemptions that are spelled out in the SEC's regulations, such as Reg. D. Instead, they will seek to comply with one of the exemptions set out in the regulations adopted by the SEC pursuant to '33 Act authorizations.

3)   § 4(a)(5)—Offers and Sales Solely to Accredited Investors

Section 4(a)(5) of the '33 Act exempts transactions solely to one or more accredited investors so long as there is no public advertising or general solicitation, and so long as the amount raised does not exceed a specified maximum, which as of 2019 is set at $5,000,000.[21] The term "accredited investor" is actually defined as part of Reg. D. Although the rest of Reg. D is described in a later section of this chapter, the meaning of "accredited investor" will be considered here. In general, in order to be accredited, an

---

consent of the issuer for resales within a defined period of time, or use other techniques to limit resales. In general, if the securities are acquired for investment purposes, and come to rest, they can be resold without affecting the exemption, but even then the securities must be registered or the resale must be conducted in compliance with an available exemption.

[20]   Reg. D is discussed *infra*, in section 3.B.5 of this chapter.

[21]   15 U.S. Code § 77(d) exempts from registration:

transactions involving offers or sales by an issuer solely to one or more accredited investors, if the aggregate offering price of an issue of securities offered in reliance on this paragraph does not exceed the amount allowed under section 77c(b)(1) of this title, if there is no advertising or public solicitation in connection with the transaction by the issuer or anyone acting on the issuer's behalf, and if the issuer files such notice with the Commission as the Commission shall prescribe.

As of 2019, the cap on the amounts that can be raised pursuant to § 77c(b)(1) governing "small issues" is $5,000,000, although the SEC does have general exemptive authority under § 77z–3 to exempt any "class of classes of persons, securities or transactions . . . to the extent that such exemption is necessary or appropriate in the public interest, and is consistent with the protection of investors." 15 U.S. Code § 77z–3.

investor has to be an institutional investor, a wealthy individual, or someone relatively high-up in the issuer's management.[22]

---

[22]   To give some idea of the complexity of who qualifies as an "accredited investor," the entire definition (which appears in Rule 501(a) as codified at 17 C.F.R. § 501(a)) is excerpted here, with internal cross references to other sections of the '33 Act being omitted:

17 C.F.R. § 230.501 **Definitions and terms used in Regulation D**.

As used in Regulation D (§ 230.500 et seq. of this chapter), the following terms shall have the meaning indicated:

(a)   **Accredited investor.** Accredited investor shall mean any person who comes within any of the following categories, or who the issuer reasonably believes comes within any of the following categories, at the time of the sale of the securities to that person:

(1)   Any bank, or any savings and loan association or other whether acting in its individual or fiduciary capacity; any broker or dealer registered pursuant to section 15 of the Securities Exchange Act of 1934; any insurance company; any investment company registered under the Investment Company Act of 1940 or a business development company as defined in section 2(a)(48) of that Act; any Small Business Investment Company licensed by the U.S. Small Business Administration under section 301(c) or (d) of the Small Business Investment Act of 1958; any plan established and maintained by a state, its political subdivisions, or any agency or instrumentality of a state or its political subdivisions, for the benefit of its employees, if such plan has total assets in excess of $5,000,000; any employee benefit plan within the meaning of the Employee Retirement Income Security Act of 1974 if the investment decision is made by a plan fiduciary, as defined in section 3(21) of such act, which is either a bank, savings and loan association, insurance company, or registered investment adviser, or if the employee benefit plan has total assets in excess of $5,000,000 or, if a self-directed plan, with investment decisions made solely by persons that are accredited investors;

(2)   Any private business development company as defined in section 202(a)(22) of the Investment Advisers Act of 1940;

(3)   Any organization described in section 501(c)(3) of the Internal Revenue Code, corporation, Massachusetts or similar business trust, or partnership, not formed for the specific purpose of acquiring the securities offered, with total assets in excess of $5,000,000;

(4)   Any director, executive officer, or general partner of the issuer of the securities being offered or sold, or any director, executive officer, or general partner of a general partner of that issuer;

(5)   Any natural person whose individual net worth, or joint net worth with that person's spouse, exceeds $1,000,000.

(i)   Except as provided in paragraph (a)(5)(ii) of this section, for purposes of calculating net worth under this paragraph (a)(5):

(A)   The person's primary residence shall not be included as an asset;

(B)   Indebtedness that is secured by the person's primary residence, up to the estimated fair market value of the primary residence at the time of the sale of securities, shall not be included as a liability (except that if the amount of such indebtedness outstanding at the time of sale of securities exceeds the amount outstanding 60 days before such time, other than as a result of the acquisition of the primary residence, the amount of such excess shall be included as a liability); and

(C)   Indebtedness that is secured by the person's primary residence in excess of the estimated fair market value of the primary residence at the time of the sale of securities shall be included as a liability;

(ii)   [Transition rules applicable to rights as of July 20, 2010.] . . .

(6)   Any natural person who had an individual income in excess of $200,000 in each of the two most recent years or joint income with that person's spouse in excess of $300,000 in each of those years and has a reasonable expectation of reaching the same income level in the current year;

Over time, there have been attempts to both restrict and expand the definition of accredited investor. Arguments for restricting the definition include the reality that the $1,000,000 asset cap (which was in place when the definition was first adopted in 1982) is not worth nearly as much today, and the amount involved is not enough to assure sophistication or access to reliable financial advice. (The most recent change along these lines was the removal of primary residence from the assets that can be counted in reaching the $1,000,000 threshold to qualify as an accredited investor. Other efforts to adjust asset and income requirements upward have so far failed, although the SEC is required to assess whether to raise the threshold amounts on a regular basis in the future, not less frequently than every four years.) Arguments for relaxing the requirement include the reality that these thresholds exclude poorer individuals from many of the most lucrative investments available, which are often snapped up by well-financed accredited investors without ever being offered to the public. In addition, certain persons may be sufficiently sophisticated by reason of education or experience without meeting income and asset thresholds. When the SEC considered increasing the threshold amounts in 2014, comments from a number of sources made suggestions along these lines, but as of mid-2019 none have been implemented, although the SEC is again considering the issue.

4) Reg. A—Conditional Small Issues

For many years, Reg. A fell out of favor as unduly limited and overly expensive. However, recent amendments to the securities laws[23] have

---

(7) Any trust, with total assets in excess of $5,000,000, not formed for the specific purpose of acquiring the securities offered, whose purchase is directed by a sophisticated person as described in § 230.506(b)(2)(ii); and

(8) Any entity in which all of the equity owners are accredited investors.

As of mid-2019, the SEC is actively considering whether and how to update these definitions. *See* SEC Press Release, *SEC Seeks Public Comment on Ways to Harmonize Private Securities Offering Exemptions*, 2019–97 (Jun. 18, 2019) [archived at https://perma.cc/Y389-ASZ2] (seeking comment on a number of issues, including who can invest in certain exempt offerings).

[23]   Prior to 2012, § 3(b) of the '33 Act gave the SEC authority to exempt offerings up to $5,000,000. Following the JOBS Act of 2012, this authority was moved to § 3(b)(1), and a new subsection was added requiring the SEC to add a class of exempted securities where sales are up to $50,000,000 and various requirements are imposed. The terms of the provision authorizing Reg. A (and Reg. CF as well, which will be discussed later) are as follows:

15 U.S. CODE § 77c **Exempted Securities** . . .

(b)   **Additional exemptions**

(1) **Small issues exemptive authority**

The Commission may from time to time by its rules and regulations, and subject to such terms and conditions as may be prescribed therein, add any class of securities to the securities exempted as provided in this section, if it finds that the enforcement of this subchapter with respect to such securities is not necessary in the public interest and for the protection of investors by reason of the small amount involved or the limited character of the public offering; but no issue of securities shall be exempted under this subsection where the aggregate amount at which such issue is offered to the public exceeds $5,000,000.

made this an important potential exemption for a variety of securities offerings. Reg. A[24] now actually consists of two distinct potential offerings.

(2) Additional issues

The Commission shall by rule or regulation add a class of securities to the securities exempted pursuant to this section in accordance with the following terms and conditions:

(A) The aggregate offering amount of all securities offered and sold within the prior 12-month period in reliance on the exemption added in accordance with this paragraph shall not exceed $50,000,000.

(B) The securities may be offered and sold publicly.

(C) The securities shall not be restricted securities within the meaning of the Federal securities laws and the regulations promulgated thereunder.

(D) The civil liability provision in section 77l(a)(2) of this title shall apply to any person offering or selling such securities.

(E) The issuer may solicit interest in the offering prior to filing any offering statement, on such terms and conditions as the Commission may prescribe in the public interest or for the protection of investors.

(F) The Commission shall require the issuer to file audited financial statements with the Commission annually.

(G) Such other terms, conditions, or requirements as the Commission may determine necessary in the public interest and for the protection of investors, which may include—

    (i) a requirement that the issuer prepare and electronically file with the Commission and distribute to prospective investors an offering statement, and any related documents, in such form and with such content as prescribed by the Commission, including audited financial statements, a description of the issuer's business operations, its financial condition, its corporate governance principles, its use of investor funds, and other appropriate matters; and

    (ii) disqualification provisions under which the exemption shall not be available to the issuer or its predecessors, affiliates, officers, directors, underwriters, or other related persons. . . .

(3) Limitation

Only the following types of securities may be exempted under a rule or regulation adopted pursuant to paragraph (2): equity securities, debt securities, and debt securities convertible or exchangeable to equity interests, including any guarantees of such securities.

(4) Periodic disclosures

Upon such terms and conditions as the Commission determines necessary in the public interest and for the protection of investors, the Commission by rule or regulation may require an issuer of a class of securities exempted under paragraph (2) to make available to investors and file with the Commission periodic disclosures regarding the issuer, its business operations, its financial condition, its corporate governance principles, its use of investor funds, and other appropriate matters, and also may provide for the suspension and termination of such a requirement with respect to that issuer.

(5) Adjustment

Not later than 2 years after April 5, 2012, and every 2 years thereafter, the Commission shall review the offering amount limitation described in paragraph (2)(A) and shall increase such amount as the Commission determines appropriate. If the Commission determines not to increase such amount, it shall report to the Committee on Financial Services of the House of Representatives and the Committee on Banking, Housing, and Urban Affairs of the Senate on its reasons for not increasing the amount.

[24] Reg. A, entitled a "Conditional Small Issues Exemption," is codified at 17 C.F.R. §§ 230.251–.263.

Tier 1 exempts certain offerings raising up to $20 million,[25] and Tier 2 exempts offerings up to $50 million in any 12-month period.[26]

A Tier 1 offering requires the issuer to prepare and file a disclosure document (generally called an offering circular), which must include a wide range of information, with the SEC before sales can commence. The SEC will review that document and must qualify the offering. Investors must be given a copy of or access to the offering circular. Members of the general public may invest regardless of whether they are accredited, and the issuer may raise up to $20 million. One major drawback of this process is that state law is not preempted, meaning that the issuer must also comply with the state securities laws of every state in which any offeree or purchaser resides.

A Tier 2 offering allows the issuer to raise up to $50 million, but has a number of additional requirements beyond the preparation, filing, and distribution of the offering circular. There are specific limits on the amount of money that non-accredited investors may invest; the required financial statements must be audited; and the issuer becomes subject to substantial ongoing reporting obligations. However, state law is preempted so the required documents need not be reviewed by state securities administrators.[27]

While these requirements look at first glance to be reasonably simple, there are additional considerations. On the downside, the first major obstacle to this exemption is the expense. One source estimates that "[f]rom start to finish a Regulation A+ offering will cost between $250,000 and $500,000 mostly depending on how big the marketing budget is."[28] Another concern is the lack of institutional investor acceptance for this kind of deal, but this could easily change over time.

Perhaps the biggest obstacle to the widespread use of Reg. A is the SEC itself. In a Reg. A offering, the issuer must have their offering documents "qualified" by the SEC.[29] Rules suggest that the required offering circular may receive the same level of scrutiny as the registration statement associated with public offerings. This has meant substantial delays and is a significant potential drawback of Reg. A. Moreover, when the SEC is dealing with new technologies and unfamiliar issues, as is often

---

[25] 17 C.F.R. § 230.251(a)(1).

[26] 17 C.F.R. § 230.251(a)(2).

[27] For a more detailed explanation of the requirements of Reg. A, see SEC, *Amendments to Regulation A: A Small Entity Compliance Guide** (June 18, 2015 (revised February 4, 2019)) [archived at https://perma.cc/7BTY-7L58].

[28] Louis A. Bevilacqua, *MicroCap Review: So What's Wrong with Reg A+?* STOCK NEWS NOW (Sept. 23, 2016) (reprinted from MicroCap Review Fall 2016 print issue) (available online at https://stocknewsnow.com/showcommentary.php?newsartid=ANEWSID23092016100001&title= MicroCap-Review-So-What%27s-Wrong-with-Reg-A-).

[29] 17 C.F.R. § 230.251(d)(1)(iii).

then case in the crypto world, any approval may be particularly slow to come.[30]

5)   Reg. D—Limited Offering Exemptions

One of the most popular exemptions from the federal registration requirement is Reg. D. This regulation consists of Rules 500 to 508[31] and actually contains three distinct exemptions: Rules 504, 506(b), and 506(c).

As currently written, Rule 504 exempts sales up to $5,000,000 by non-reporting issuers only (i.e., only companies that are not publicly held are eligible to use this option). The total amount sold by the issuer in any other Rule 504 offering held within 12 months will reduce the $5,000,000 cap on proceeds. There is no requirement that sales be directed only to accredited investors or a limited number of un-accredited persons. No general

---

[30]   The first crypto offering to receive SEC approval under Regulation A came on July 10, 2019 when the SEC qualified an offering of Blockstack tokens. *Blockstack PBV Preliminary Offering Circular* (July 10, 2019) (available online at https://www.sec.gov/Archives/edgar/data/ 1693656/000110465919039757/a18-15736_1partiiandiii.htm). *See* Max Boddy, *US SEC Approves Blockstack Token Offering Under Regulation A+*, COINTELEGRAPH (Jul 11, 2019) [archived at https://perma.cc/AV8U-AP8W].

[31]   Reg. D is codified at 17 CFR §§ 230.500–.508.

Rule 500 sets out how Reg. D is to be used. Subsection (a) states that the exemption only applies to the registration requirement (not the antifraud provisions). Subsection (b) reminds issuers they still need to comply with state law (although there is a second provision that preempts inconsistent state law in the case of offerings under 506(b) or (c)). Subsection (c) says an attempt to use any part of Reg. D is not exclusive, so even if the offering fails one part, another exemption (i.e., under § 4(a)(2)) might still be available. Subsection (d) limits Reg. D to issuers; (e) says it cannot be used for business combinations, and (f) says it cannot be used as part of a scheme to evade the requirements of law.

Rule 501 contains definitions, the most important of which is probably the definition of "accredited investor," which is described in section 3.B.3) of this chapter. In essence, high level insiders of the issuer are accredited, as are a number of institutional investors (either those that are very regulated such as banks, S&Ls, investment advisors, business development companies, etc., or those with more than $5,000,000 in assets such as retirement plans). In addition to that, certain wealthy individuals are accredited. The rules accredit any natural person whose net worth alone or with a spouse exceeds $1,000,000 excluding their primary residence, or a natural person who earned at least $200,000 in each of the last two years (or $300,000 with their spouse) and reasonably expects the same in the current year. Trusts with assets over $5,000,000 are accredited only so long as they were not formed for the purpose of acquiring the securities and so long as they are directed by someone sophisticated enough to evaluate the merits of the investment. Finally, any entity where all of the equity owners are accredited is also accredited.

Rule 502 imposes certain general requirements, including the condition that so long as the issuer does not make any sales within the period that starts six months before an offering and lasts to six months after the offering, sales outside that period will not be "integrated" with the Reg. D offering (i.e., treated as part of the same offering). It also lists the kinds of information that must be available to investors to the extent material, including specific financial data. It prohibits general solicitation or advertising in the case of Rule 506(b) deals, and it limits the ability of purchasers to resell their securities for a year (and potentially even longer for affiliates).

Rule 503 requires form D to be filed with the SEC at the start and end of the offering. Form D notifies the SEC of basic information about the offering.

As for the actual exemptions, as mentioned above there are three of them. Prior to amendments that were adopted in order to comply with the JOBS Act, Reg. D was broken into three distinct exemptions (Rules 504, 505, and 506), and only Rule 506 was available if an issuer wanted to raise more than $5 million. As amended, Rule 505 has disappeared, and Rule 506 has been expanded to include two distinct exemptions: Rule 506(b) and 506(c).

solicitation or public advertising is permitted unless the issuer registers its offering under the laws of every state where the offering is conducted.[32] Material information must be provided, and it must be free of fraudulent misrepresentations. In most cases securities purchased in a 504 offering may only be resold after a holding period of six months or a year. Compliance with this exemption does not preempt state law, so the issuer will also have to comply with state securities requirements in every state where the securities are to be sold.

Rule 506(b) allows an issuer to raise an unlimited amount from sales to accredited investors and a limited number of others (a maximum number of 35 non-accredited investors) who meet sophistication requirements, but this alternative does not allow general solicitation or public advertising. If there are any unaccredited investors, certain specified information must be provided (not just be made available) a "reasonable time prior to sale." Inconsistent state regulation is prohibited, although a state can require a notice filing and may collect a fee. One advantage to this offering is that the issuer can legally sell to up to 35 unaccredited investors. There are, however, more detailed information requirements than those associated with Rule 504. The biggest drawback is that no general solicitation or advertising is permitted.

Rule 506(c) also allows an issuer to raise unlimited amounts so long as all investors are accredited. The biggest advantage of a 506(c) offering is that it permits the issuer to conduct public advertising and a general solicitation of offers. Rule 506(c) does have a potentially significant drawback in that it restricts sales to carefully "verified" accredited investors, which requires considerably more detailed recordkeeping than was customary prior to the JOBS Act (or than is required for Rule 506(b) sales). While the rules do not purport to set out the only ways in which an investor's status may be verified, all of the examples suggest that the issuer (or a registered attorney, broker-dealer, or CPA providing a verification document to the issuer) will have to carefully review current documentation in order to assure the accuracy of the investor's claim to being accredited. As is the case with 506(b), inconsistent state regulation is preempted.

---

[32]   The actual requirement is slightly more complicated. *See* 17 C.F.R. § 230.504(b)(1). In essence, general solicitation and advertising is allowed for offers that take place exclusively:

1. under one or more state laws that require registration, public filing and delivery to investors of a substantive disclosure document before sale;

2. in one or more states that do not require registration so long as such registration has occurred in at least one such state and all purchasers receive the filed disclosure document, regardless of where they reside; or

3. to accredited investors who reside in a state that permits general solicitation and advertising.

6) Reg. S—Offshore Offers and Sales

Reg. S, "Rules Governing Offers and Sales Made Outside the United States Without Registration Under the Securities Act of 1933," is known as the exemption for Offshore Offers and Sales.[33] Reg. S exempts offerings of debt and equity securities from the registration requirements of the '33 Act, for offerings made outside the U.S. It applies to sales by both U.S. and foreign issuers. The safe harbor is non-exclusive, meaning that other exemptions may also apply if the issuer fails to satisfy all Reg. S requirements. However, it is far more difficult to comply with this exemption than one might suspect.

Reg. S is quite complex, involving three distinct categories of transactions,[34] based on the kind of securities being sold, whether the issuer is U.S. or foreign, whether the issuer is a reporting company (i.e., has a class of securities that are publicly traded in the U.S.), and whether there is a "substantial U.S. market interest" in the securities being offered. The first category is the least likely to come back to the U.S., and consequently the only requirements for this kind of offering are that the transaction must be offshore and no directed selling efforts may be made in the U.S. The other two categories are subject to additional number of restrictions and requirements for the duration of the "distribution compliance period," which ranges from 40 days to six months for reporting companies and one year for non-reporting issuers selling equity securities.

---

[33] This exemption is codified at 17 C.F.R. §§ 230.901–905.

[34] Category 1 includes the following offerings:

1. securities by foreign issuers who reasonably believe at the commencement of the offering that there is no substantial U.S. market interest in the offered certain securities;

2. securities by either a "foreign issuer" or, in the case of non-convertible debt securities, a U.S. issuer, in an "overseas directed offering";

3. securities backed by the full faith and credit of a foreign government or sovereign, including; and

4. securities from foreign issuers pursuant to an employee benefit plan established under foreign law.

Category 2 transactions involve the following:

1. equity securities of a reporting foreign issuer;

2. debt securities of a reporting U.S. or foreign issuer; and

3. debt securities of a non-reporting foreign issuer.

Note that the presence of a substantial U.S. market interest in these securities does not make this option unavailable. However, persons relying on this exemption must ensure that any person to whom they sell securities is a non-U.S. person, and is not buying for the account of a U.S. person.

Category 3 transactions apply to all transactions not eligible for either of the first two options. This therefore includes:

1. debt or equity offerings by non-reporting U.S. issuers;

2. equity offerings by U.S. reporting issuers; and

3. equity offerings by non-reporting foreign issuers for which there is a substantial U.S. market interest.

In general terms, in order to satisfy Reg. S, the offer or sale must be made in an "offshore transaction," and the issuer and those acting for it may not make any "directed selling efforts" in the U.S. A transaction will be considered to be an "offshore transaction" only if the following requirements are met: (1) no offer is made to a person in the U.S.; and (2) the seller reasonably believes the buyer is physically outside the U.S., or the transaction takes place on an established foreign securities exchange and the seller is unaware of any pre-arranged resale to a U.S. purchaser.

"Directed selling efforts" include "any activity undertaken for the purpose of, or that could reasonably be expected to have the effect of, conditioning the market in the United States for any of the securities being offered. . . . Such activity includes placing an advertisement in a publication 'with a general circulation in the United States' that refers to the offering of securities being made in reliance upon this Regulation S."[35]

One of the most important aspects of a Reg. S offering is that sales in compliance with this exemption will not be integrated with private placements in the U.S. Thus, an issuer may simultaneously conduct a Reg. D offering in the U.S., and the two offerings will not be treated as part of the same transaction so as to disrupt either exemption.[36]

7) Reg. CF—Crowdfunding

The JOBS Act of 2012 authorized the SEC to adopt regulations to facilitate crowdfunding initiatives, and Reg. CF was the result.[37]

Pursuant to the terms of Reg. CF, eligible companies[38] may raise up to a specified amount ($1,070,000 as of the start of 2019) through an offering

---

[35]   17 C.F.R. § 230.902(c). Legally required notices that specify only that the securities are not registered and may not be sold in the U.S., and other limited notices and specified actions are excluded from the definition of "directed selling efforts" under 17 C.F.R. § 230.902(c)(3).

[36]   For the official explanation of the Reg. S, see SEC, *Final Rule: Offshore Offers and Sales (Regulation S)* (Release No. 33–7505, 34–39668) (available online at https://www.sec.gov/rules/final/33-7505.htm).

[37]   The JOBS Act added § 4(a)(6) to the '33 Act. The new provision authorizes an exemption from registration for certain crowdfunding transactions, and the SEC adopted Reg. CF in 2015. It is codified at 17 C.F.R. §§ 227.100 to .503.

[38]   The following kinds of companies are not eligible to use Reg. CF:

1. non-U.S. companies;
2. reporting (publicly traded) companies;
3. certain investment companies;
4. companies that are disqualified under Reg. CF disqualification rules;
5. companies that have failed to comply with the annual reporting requirements under Reg. CF during the two years immediately preceding the filing of the offering statement; and
6. companies that have no specific business plan or have indicated their business plan is to engage in a merger or acquisition with an unidentified company or companies.

that complies with the terms of the exemption.[39] The amount that each investor may contribute is also subject to strict limits, which change based on each investor's individual annual income or net worth. Poorer investors are limited to $2,200 and even accredited investors may contribute no more than $107,000,[40] spread across all Reg. CF offerings in which the investor participates. Further complicating the process is the requirement that Reg. CF offerings must be conducted exclusively through an online platform operated by a licensed broker dealer or funding portal registered with the SEC and FINRA.[41] In addition, there are significant disclosure obligations for the issuer, both before and after the Reg. CF offering.[42] Moreover, the

---

[39]   The maximum amount is subject to adjustment by the SEC for inflation. The total that may be raised must be reduced for all other Reg. CF offerings conducted by the issuer within 12 months. Sales pursuant to other exemptions do not reduce the amount of the Reg. CF offering.

[40]   Investors whose annual income or net worth does not exceed $107,000 may contribute no more than the greater of $2,200 or 5% of the lesser of the investor's income or net worth. If both income and net worth equal or exceed $107,000 the investor's limit is 10% of the less of income or net worth. Regardless of income and net worth, the absolute maximum that an investor may contribute in a Reg. CF offering is $107,000, and that is reduced by any investment in other Reg. CF offerings in the 12-month period.

[41]   FINRA is the self-regulatory agency responsible for overseeing securities firms and broker dealers. FINRA is the successor to the National Association of Securities Dealers and offers regulatory oversight over all securities firms that do business with the public, plus those offering professional training, testing, and licensing of registered persons. It also oversees securities arbitration and mediation, market regulation by contract for the New York Stock Exchange, the NASDAQ Stock Market, Inc., the American Stock Exchange LLC, and the International Securities Exchange, LLC; and industry utilities, such as Trade Reporting Facilities and other over-the-counter operations.

[42]   In order to conduct a Reg. CF offering, the issuer must electronically file Form C with the SEC. Instructions to that form indicate that mandatory disclosures include:

1.   information about officers, directors, and owners of 20 percent or more of the issuer;
2.   a description of the issuer's business and the use of proceeds from the offering;
3.   the price to the public of the securities or the method for determining the price;
4.   the target offering amount and the deadline to reach the target offering amount;
5.   whether the issuer will accept investments in excess of the target offering amount;
6.   certain related-party transactions; and
7.   the issuer's financial condition and financial statements.

The specific financial statement requirements are based on the amount offered and sold in reliance on Reg. CF within the preceding 12-month period. For total sales of $107,000 or less, the financial statements and federal income tax returns must be certified by the issuer's principal executive officer, unless they have been reviewed or audited by an independent public accountant. For offerings up to $535,000, statements must be reviewed or audited by an independent public accountant. For offerings exceeding $535,000, the financial statements must be reviewed or audited, except that if the issuer has previously relied on Reg. CF, the statements must be audited.

In addition to the requirement that the issuer file Form C, it must also provide progress updates on Form C-U within 5 days after reaching 50% and 100% of its target offering price, unless the intermediary provides frequent updates, in which case only a final Form C-U disclosing the total amount sold must be filed.

Once a Reg. CF offering has been conducted, the issuer is required to provide an annual report on Form C-AR within 120 days after the end of each fiscal year. The report must be filed electronically with the SEC and posted on the issuer's website. The annual report must include information similar to what is required in the offering statement, although neither an audit nor a review of the financial statements is required. The annual reporting requirement continues until:

1.   the issuer becomes a reporting company;

terms of Reg. CF prohibit most public advertising.[43] Finally, securities purchased in a Reg. CF offering may not be resold for one year, except (1) to the issuer of the securities; (2) to an "accredited investor"; (3) as part of an offering registered with the Commission; or (4) to a member of the family of the purchaser or to a family trust, or the equivalent.

These restrictions make Reg. CF unwieldy and unsuitable for many planned fundraising deals. As a result, the SEC is looking at the effectiveness of this exemption.[44]

4. ANTIFRAUD RULES UNDER THE FEDERAL SECURITIES LAWS

Even assuming that a given offering is designed to comply with one or more of the preceding exemptions, or is conducted pursuant to a registration statement, the federal securities laws contain a number of antifraud provisions that can result in enforcement actions by either the SEC or private citizens who traded on the basis of fraudulent misrepresentations or omissions. Both the '33 Act and '34 Act contain broad prohibitions against fraud, and there are a number of potential enforcement mechanisms built into the statutes including private enforcement, civil action by the SEC, SEC administrative actions, and criminal prosecution.

A. PRIVATE ENFORCEMENT— EXPRESS CAUSES OF ACTION

Both the '33 Act and the '34 Act contain express private rights of actions for certain participants in the U.S. securities markets. Under the '33 Act, sections 11, 12, and 9 all contain provisions authorizing private claimants to pursue remedies for specific violations of the securities laws.

Section 11 expressly entitles a purchaser of securities to make a claim if a registration statement contains material misstatements or omissions

---

2. the issuer has filed at least one annual report and has fewer than 300 holders of record;

3. the issuer has filed at least three annual reports and has total assets that do not exceed $10 million;

4. the issuer or another party purchases or repurchases all of the securities issued pursuant to Reg. CF, including any payment in full of debt securities or any complete redemption of redeemable securities; or

5. the issuer liquidates or dissolves in accordance with state law.

43 An issuer may not advertise the terms of a Reg. CF offering except in a notice that directs investors to the intermediary's platform and includes very limited, specified information. The issuer may, however, communicate about the terms of the offering on the intermediary's platform so long as it identifies itself as the issuer in such communications. Anyone acting for the issuer must identify that affiliation.

44 SEC staff, *Report to the Commission-Regulation Crowdfunding* (June 18, 2019) (available online at https://www.sec.gov/files/regulation-crowdfunding-2019_0.pdf).

and the purchased securities can be traced to that registration statement. There are a number of potential defenses available as well, making this a very narrow cause of action.

Section 12, and in particular § 12(a)(2), covers misstatements or omissions in a prospectus or oral communication.[45] To make a § 12(a)(2) claim, plaintiff shareholders must show the existence of a material misstatement or omission in a prospectus or oral communication. They must also show that they did not know of the misstatement or omission at the time the security was purchased. Unless the defendant has a defense, a plaintiff meeting these burdens is entitled to rescission or damages if the security has already been resold.

However, in 1995, the U.S. Supreme Court markedly limited the availability of § 12(a)(2) by holding that in this context "the word 'prospectus' is a term of art referring to a document that describes a public offering of securities by an issuer. . . ."[46] The opinion did include references to the possibility that certain exempt transactions could give rise to a § 12(a)(2) claim, and as a result the availability of this cause of action depends on how an offering is conducted. In essence, § 12(a)(2) is now limited to claims based on oral misrepresentations or untruths made in connection with a public offering or exemptions under § 3 (including Rules 147 and 147A, Reg. A, and Rule 504 of Reg. D). It does not apply to offerings conducted under § 4 of the '33 Act or regulations promulgated under that section, including Reg. CF, and Rules 506(b) and 506(c).

Finally, for these private claims, section 13 of the '33 Act sets a statute of limitations that expires the earlier of one year following discovery of the untruth or three years from the date the security was offered to the public under § 11 or sold under § 12.

Under the '34 Act, § 9(e)[47] provides for a private right of action for purchasers and sellers injured by specific forms of market manipulation. The right to recover is limited by a relatively stringent two-pronged

---

[45]   Section 12(a)(2) of the '33 Act states that:

Any person who . . . offers or sells a security . . . by the use of any means or instruments of transportation or communication in interstate commerce or of the mails, by means of a prospectus or oral communication, which includes an untrue statement of a material fact or omits to state a material fact necessary in order to make the statements, in the light of the circumstances under which they were made, not misleading . . . and who shall not sustain the burden of proof that he did not know, and in the exercise of reasonable care could not have known, of such untruth or omission, shall be liable . . . to the person purchasing such security from him.

15 U.S. Code § 77l(a). The term "prospectus" is defined in § 2(a)(10) of the '33 Act as any prospectus, notice, circular, advertisement, letter, or communication, written or by radio or television, which offers any security for sale or confirms the sale of any security," with limited exceptions (including an exception for a compliant prospectus filed in connection with a registration statement). 18 U.S. Code § 77b(a)(10).

[46]   *Gustafson v. Alloyd Co.,* 513 U.S. 561, 584 (1995).

[47]   15 U.S. Code § 78i.

causation requirement that depends on proof that the manipulation caused the damage and that it affected the price at which the securities were traded. In addition, the plaintiff must prove that the defendant acted willfully in order to recover.

The '34 Act further provides in § 18(a)[48] that private plaintiffs have the right to recover if they buy or sell securities in reliance on a material misstatement in an SEC filing at a price affected by the misstatement. There is no scienter requirement under this provision, but the plaintiff must show actual reliance, proof that the reliance caused the damages, and proof that the misstatements caused changes to the security's price that harmed the plaintiff.

B. PRIVATE ENFORCEMENT— IMPLIED CAUSES OF ACTION

The most well-known antifraud regulation in the federal securities laws is Rule 10b–5, promulgated by the SEC pursuant to Section 10b of the '34 Act. Virtually all securities fraud cases involve, in one way or another, Rule 10b–5. For those reasons, both § 10b of the '34 Act and Rule 10b–5 are excerpted here. While § 10b does not expressly create a private right of action, it is well established that purchasers of a security may bring such a claim. However, private claimants may not ger sue persons who might have aided and abetted in the creation of false and misleading representations, although the SEC is not bound by this limitation.[49]

Section 10b, codified at 15 U.S. Code § 78j

Manipulative and deceptive devices

It shall be unlawful for any person, directly or indirectly, by the use of any means or instrumentality of interstate commerce or of the mails, or of any facility of any national securities exchange—. . . . [subsection a is omitted]

(b)   To use or employ, in connection with the purchase or sale of any security registered on a national securities exchange or any security not so registered, any manipulative or deceptive device or contrivance in contravention of such rules and regulations as the Commission may prescribe as necessary or appropriate in the public interest or for the protection of investors.

---

[48]   15 U.S. Code § 78r.

[49]   *See Cent. Bank of Denver v. First Interstate Bank of Denver,* 511 U.S. 164, 176–77, 179–80, 191 (1994) (holding that private plaintiffs may not maintain a cause of action for aiding and abetting under § 10b). *See also* 15 U.S. Code § 78t(e); *SEC v. U.S. Envtl., Inc.,* 155 F.3d 107, 113 (2d Cir. 1998) (dealing with the SEC's right to bring aiding and abetting claims).

Rule 10b–5, codified at 17 C.F.R. § 240.10b–5

Employment of manipulative and deceptive devices.

It shall be unlawful for any person, directly or indirectly, by the use of any means or instrumentality of interstate commerce, or of the mails or of any facility of any national securities exchange,

(a) To employ any device, scheme, or artifice to defraud,

(b) To make any untrue statement of a material fact or to omit to state a material fact necessary in order to make the statements made, in the light of the circumstances under which they were made, not misleading, or

(c) To engage in any act, practice, or course of business which operates or would operate as a fraud or deceit upon any person,

in connection with the purchase or sale of any security.

* * *

To maintain a successful claim under Rule 10b–5, a private plaintiff must show:

1. The defendant made a material misstatement or omission;

2. The misstatement or omission was made with an intent to deceive, manipulate, or defraud;[50]

3. There is a connection between the misrepresentation or omission and the plaintiff's purchase or sale of a security;

4. The plaintiff relied on the misstatement or omission;

5. The plaintiff suffered economic loss; and

6. There is a causal connection between the material misrepresentation or omission and the plaintiff's loss.[51]

On the other hand, the SEC need not show scienter and, as mentioned above, may bring enforcement actions against those who aided and abetted the fraud. If there is sufficient intent, the SEC may turn the matter over to the DoJ, which may prosecute criminal violations of the antifraud prohibitions on behalf of the government. (The DoJ is also entitled to instigate criminal actions on its own authority.)

There is a corresponding provision under the '33 Act, found in § 17(a).[52] That section essentially prohibits the same behaviors that are targeted in Rule 10b–5. However, while the U.S. Supreme Court has yet to resolve the issue, most federal courts have concluded that § 17(a) does not support a

---

[50] This element necessitates proof of scienter.

[51] *See Dura Pharms., Inc. v. Broudo,* 544 U.S. 336, 341–42 (2005).

[52] 15 U.S. Code § 77q(a).

private cause of action for damages, although injunctive relief may be possible.[53] On the other hand, the Sixth Circuit apparently disagrees.[54] To the extent that a private right of action is allowed, and the defendants sold securities to the plaintiff, claims under sections 17(a)(2) and (3) (which track Rule 10b–5(b) and (c)) do not require proof of scienter.

C. CIVIL ENFORCEMENT BY THE SEC—JUDICIAL REMEDIES

There are a number of provisions in the federal securities laws that give the SEC enforcement authority. Originally, the SEC's authority was expected to be exercised primarily through injunctive relief, and there are therefore specific statutory provisions that authorize this form of relief.

The range of the SEC's investigatory authority is substantial. Various provisions essentially authorize the SEC to investigate past, ongoing, and prospective violations of the federal securities laws, including SEC rules and regulations.[55] When securities fraud or other misconduct is discovered, the SEC has a number of options. Many of these options involve the SEC seeking redress in the federal courts.

The first of these options is injunctive relief. Sections in various statutes specifically authorize the SEC to obtain an injunction against any person "engaged or about to engage" in prohibited activities under the securities laws in question.[56] There is no requirement of "irreparable damage" or inadequacy of legal remedies, and instead relief may be based simply on "a proper showing."

Asset freezes are also a possible remedy available to the SEC. The Sarbanes-Oxley Act of 2002 added § 21C(c)(3)(A)(i) to the '34 Act.[57] This provision authorizes the SEC to obtain temporary asset freezes to prevent "extraordinary" payments to directors, officers, or other insiders. The duration of an initial order freezing assets is 45 days, subject to extension for an additional 45 days. If a violation is charged, the freeze may continue beyond those 90 days, subject to judicial review.

The SEC also has the option of seeking to impose a bar on an individuals' future service as director or officer of a publicly traded company. The '33 Act and '34 Act both give the SEC the power to seek

---

[53]   *Maldonado v. Dominguez,* 137 F.3d 1, 7–8 (1st Cir. 1998) (citing several opinions on point).

[54]   *See AFA Private Equity Fund 1 v. Miresco Inv. Serv.,* 2005 WL 2417116 at *5–7 (E.D. Mich, 2005) (discussing Sixth Circuit precedents).

[55]   *See* § 20(a) of the '33 Act (15 U.S. Code § 77t(a)), §§ 21(a)(1) & (2) of the '34 Act (15 U.S. Code §§ 78u(a)(1) & (2)), and § 42(a) of the 1940 Act (15 U.S. Code § 80a–42(a))

[56]   *See* § 20(a) of the '33 Act (15 U.S. Code § 77t(a)), § 21(d)(1) of the '34 Act (15 U.S. Code § 78u(d)(1)), and § 43(d) of the 1940 Act (15 U.S. Code § 80a–43(d)).

[57]   15 U.S. Code § 78u–3(c)(3)(A)(i).

either a temporary or permanent court order to this effect.[58] The SEC may obtain such an order on a showing that the antifraud provisions of the securities laws have been violated and that the individual in question is unfit to serve in the specified role.

Disgorgement and other equitable remedies were allowed for many years pursuant to the equitable powers of courts, and Sarbanes-Oxley removed any doubt about the legitimacy of such remedies by adding language to the '34 Act. As it now reads, § 21(d)(5) of the '34 Act[59] explicitly authorizes federal courts to grant "any equitable relieve that may be appropriate or necessary for the benefit of investors." This has included disgorgement of illegally obtained proceeds, as well as pre-judgement interest and specific undertakings as to future actions.[60]

One of the most important options for the SEC is the right to request the imposition of monetary penalties. In 1990 Congress enacted the Securities Enforcement Remedies and Penny Stock Reform Act, which amended various federal securities laws in order to give the SEC authority to seek monetary penalties for virtually any violation of the federal securities laws.[61] Finally, if an issuer is required to restate inaccurate financial statements because of misconduct, the SEC may ask for clawbacks for CEO and CFO bonuses and trading profits.[62]

D. ADMINISTRATIVE REMEDIES

The SEC is not limited to seeking relief from federal courts. Administrative remedies include cease and desist orders,[63] and administratively imposed monetary penalties after a hearing.[64] When either of these has occurred, the SEC may also order an accounting and/or

---

[58]   *See* § 20(e) of the '33 Act (15 U.S. Code § 77t(e)) and § 21(d)(2) of the '34 Act (15 U.S. Code § 78u(d)(2)).

[59]   15 U.S. Code § 78u(d)(5).

[60]   The ability of the SEC to obtain disgorgement in federal courts is, however, currently before the U.S. Supreme Court. On November 1, 2019, the Court granted certiorari in *Liu v. SEC*, No. 18-1501 to consider whether the Court's 2017 decision in *Kokesh v. SEC*, 137 S. Ct. 1635 (2017), means that disgorgement constitutes an impermissible penalty. Since 2015, the SEC has obtained more than $2.5 billion in disgorgement remedies (most of that obviously came from proceedings that did not involve cryptoassets or transactions), so the potential impact of Liu could be huge. *See generally* Greg Stohr, *Supreme Court will consider stripping SEC of power to seize illegal profits*, L.A. TIMES (Nov. 1, 2019) (available online at https://www.latimes.com/business/story/2019-11-01/supreme-court-will-consider-stripping-sec-of-disgorgement-powers). Regardless of the outcome in *Liu*, the SEC would retain authority to seek penalties and disgorgement in administrative proceedings, and Congress could also reinstate the SEC's authority to seek disgorgement in the courts even if the Supreme Court rules against the agency in the pending case.

[61]   *See* § 20(d) of the '33 Act (15 U.S. Code § 77t(e)), § 21(d)(3) of the '34 Act (15 U.S. Code § 78u(d)(3)) and § 42(e) of the 1940 Act (15 U.S. Code § 80a–42(e))

[62]   15 U.S. Code § 7243(a).

[63]   These are authorized in § 8A of the '33 Act (15 U.S. Code § 77h–1) and § 21C(a) of the '34 Act (15 U.S. Code § 78u–3).

[64]   *See* § 8A(g) of the '33 Act (15 U.S. Code § 77h–1(g)) and § 21B of the '34 Act (15 U.S. Code § 78h–2)

disgorgement.[65] Normally, such actions require a hearing, but in certain extraordinary circumstances, the SEC may issue cease and desist orders ex parte if "notice and hearing prior to entry would be impractical or contrary to the public interest."

E. CRIMINAL ENFORCEMENT

The securities laws are a hybrid of civil and criminal provisions, meaning that civil violations can also lead to criminal penalties. Criminal enforcement of the federal securities laws is in the hands of the Department of Justice, which operates through various U.S. Attorneys Offices. The DoJ often receives referrals from the SEC, although it may also investigate and prosecute cases on its own initiative.

Violations of the '33 Act can result in a maximum $10,000 fine and/or up to 5 years imprisonment. Sarbanes-Oxley substantially heightened the criminal penalties for violations under the '34 Act. Under the '34 Act, a natural person may be fined up to $5 million and/or sent to jail for up to 20 years. In addition to potential liability under the securities statutes, Sarbanes-Oxley created several new crimes. These include fraud involving securities of reporting companies,[66] false certification of reports by CEOs and CFOs,[67] and various crimes involving record tampering.[68]

There are also other federal criminal statutes that may be relied upon in the event of serious violations of the federal securities laws. For example, cases involving securities fraud often give rise to violations of the federal mail and wire fraud statutes. Similarly, RICO (the Racketeer Influenced and Corrupt Organizations Act)[69] may also be implicated. (RICO was enacted in 1970 primarily to combat organized crime, but it may also apply to securities violations, particularly where there is a pattern of violations.) The most commonly relied upon RICO offense makes it "unlawful for any person employed by or associated with any enterprise engaged in, the activities which affect, interstate or foreign commerce, to conduct or participate, directly or indirectly, in the conduct of such enterprise's affairs through a pattern of racketeering activity or collection of an unlawful debt."[70]

Finally, federal law allows criminal prosecution of anyone who "aids, abets, counsels, commands, induces, or procures" the commission of an

---

[65]   *See* '33 Act § 8A(e) (15 U.S. Code § 77h–1(e)) and '34 Act § 21B(e) (15 U.S. Code § 78n–2(e)).

[66]   18 U.S. Code § 1348.

[67]   18 U.S. Code § 1350.

[68]   18 U.S. Code §§ 1512, 1519, & 1520.

[69]   RICO was enacted by section 901(a) of the Organized Crime Control Act of 1970 (Pub.L. 91–452, 84 Stat. 922, enacted October 15, 1970) and is codified at 18 U.S.C. §§ 1961–1968.

[70]   18 U.S. Code § 1962(c).

offense against the U.S.,[71] and attempted violations of mail or wire fraud or crimes under Sarbanes-Oxley are also criminalized.[72]

5. REGULATION OF EXCHANGES

In addition to overseeing the sale of securities, the SEC also oversees the regulation of exchanges upon which securities are often traded. Section 5 of the'34 Act makes it unlawful for any broker,[73] dealer,[74] or exchange, directly or indirectly, to effect any transaction in a security, or to report any such transaction, in interstate commerce, unless the exchange is registered as a national securities exchange under Section 6 of the Exchange Act, or is exempted from such registration.

Exchanges are particularly important in the context of cryptotransactions because without the assistance of a third party intermediary, it is often difficult for purchasers and sellers of crypto to locate each other in a timely fashion. Intermediaries who act to facilitate trading in cryptoassets may well be exchanges under the federal securities laws, bringing them within the jurisdiction of the SEC.

"Exchange" is defined in section 3(a)(1) of the '34 Act as:

> any organization, association, or group of persons, whether incorporated or unincorporated, which constitutes, maintains, or provides a market place or facilities for bringing together purchasers and sellers of securities or for otherwise performing with respect to securities the functions commonly performed by a stock exchange as that term is generally understood, and includes the market place and the market facilities maintained by such exchange.[75]

Exchange Act Rule 3b–16(a) provides a functionality test to assess whether a trading system meets the definition of exchange under this provision. Under this test, an organization, association, or other group of persons shall be considered "a market place or facilities for bringing together purchasers and sellers of securities or for otherwise performing

---

[71]   18 U.S. Code § 2(a). In 1994 the Supreme Court found that private plaintiffs are not entitled to maintain aiding and abetting claims. *Cent. Bank of Denver v. First Interstate Bank of Denver*, 511 U.S. 164, 176–77, 179–80, 191 (1994). However, the SEC is not bound by this limitation. *See* 15 U.S. Code § 78t(e); *SEC v. U.S. Envtl., Inc.*, 155 F.3d 107, 113 (2d Cir. 1998).

[72]   18 U.S. Code § 1349.

[73]   Although these materials do not focus on broker-dealer regulation, it is important to understand that a broker-dealer is a natural person, company, or other organization in the business of trading securities for its own account or on behalf of customers. A "broker" is anyone in the business of trading securities who acts to execute trade orders to buy or sell a security on behalf of a customer.

[74]   A dealer is someone in the business of trading securities who is executing trades for his, her, or its own account.

[75]   15 U.S. Code § 78c(a)(1).

with respect to securities the functions commonly performed by an exchange" if it:

1. brings together the orders for securities of multiple buyers and sellers; and

2. uses established, non-discretionary methods (whether by providing a trading facility or by setting rules) under which such orders interact with each other, and the buyers and sellers entering such orders agree to the terms of the trade.[76]

Rule 3b–16(b)[77] lists certain activities that will not cause such a group to be an exchange. The list of permitted activities include routing orders to a national securities exchange, a market operated by a national securities association, or a broker-dealer for execution. The exclusion also allows persons to enter orders for execution against bids of a single dealer along with limited matching or crossing of certain orders in a manner that is incidental to such activities.

Under the terms of § 5 of the '34 Act, a system that meets the criteria of Rule 3b–16(a) and is neither excluded under Rule 3b–16(b) nor otherwise exempt, must register as a national securities exchange under § 6 of the '34 Act. The process of registering as a securities exchange is both complicated and time-consuming. It is also subject to the SEC's determination under § 19(b) of the '34 Act that the exchange will be able to comply with all requirements to which it is subject.

Although they are subject to SEC oversight, registered national securities exchanges are self-regulatory organizations (SROs) and therefore establish their own rules regarding fees and trading. Exchanges are also responsible for the supervision of their members, and each exchange must develop and maintain monitoring, surveillance, inspection, compliance and disciplinary policies and procedures to insure that members comply with all applicable regulations. A national exchange must provide fair, reasonable, and non-discriminatory access to members. Finally, all members must be registered broker-dealers or persons associated with a registered broker-dealer.

In lieu of establishing a registered national exchange, Reg. ATS allows for the creation of alternative trading systems ("ATS"). Under this regulation, an ATS will be exempt from registering as a national securities exchange if it registers as a broker-dealer and provides the SEC with specified operational information. Although it is exempt from registration as a national securities exchange, a firm relying on Reg. ATS is subject to numerous regulatory requirements stemming either from Reg. ATS or from requirements imposed on broker-dealers.

---

[76]   17 C.F.R. § 240.3b–16(a).

[77]   Exchange Act Rule 3b–16(b) (codified at 7 C.F.R. § 240.3b–16(b)).

In general terms, an ATS is subject to significant ongoing reporting requirements. As with registered national securities exchanges, an ATS that reaches certain trading thresholds must provide fair access to the trading system. An ATS must also impose adequate safeguards and procedures to protect subscribers' confidential trading information and must maintain certain books and records. In order to prevent confusion, an ATS is not allowed to refer to itself as an "exchange," or to use derivations of names associated with national exchanges such as "stock market."

In addition, SEC and Financial Industry Regulatory Authority (FINRA) rules include all of the following requirements which would apply to an ATS because it must be a broker-dealer:

1. Under SEC Rule 15c3–3, broker-dealers must maintain physical possession or control of all fully paid securities and excess margin securities carried for the account of customers.

2. Under SEC rules 17a–4 and 17a–4 and FINRA Rule 4511, broker-dealers must make and maintain current books and records for specified periods of time.

3. There are various regulatory requirements applicable to fees, commissions, and trading markups.

4. FINRA's current examination module to determine competency must also be satisfied in order to become a registered broker-dealer.

The JOBS Act exempted certain intermediaries that operate "funding portals" from the requirement to register with the SEC as a broker-dealer. A funding portal is a crowdfunding intermediary that does none of the following:

1. offer investment advice or recommendations;

2. solicit purchases, sales, or offers to buy the securities offered or displayed on its website or portal;

3. compensate employees, agents or other persons for such solicitation or based on the sale of securities displayed or referenced on its website or portal;

4. hold, manage, possess or otherwise handle investor funds or securities, or

5. engage in such other activities as the SEC, by rule, determines appropriate.

A registered funding portal need not register as a broker-dealer but it must be a member of FINRA. The portal also remains subject to both FINRA's and the SEC's examination, enforcement and rulemaking authority. Among other requirements, a funding portal must provide investors with disclosures and certain educational materials, protect the privacy of investor information, and make efforts to ensure that no investor exceeds applicable crowdfunding investment limits in any 12-month period.

The SEC maintains lists of currently approved national securities exchanges[78] and Alternative Trading Systems,[79] and FINRA maintains a list of registered funding portals.[80]

6. EXCHANGE TRADED FUNDS (ETFs)

Although often not mentioned in basic securities regulations courses, there is one other aspect of the SEC's regulatory regime that deserves comment because it is something that has a potentially significant current role in the world of cryptotransactions. This involves the regulation of Exchange Traded Funds (ETFs) under the Investment Company Act of 1940 (the 1940 Act).

An ETF is a hybrid investment product that was not originally contemplated or directly regulated by the U.S. securities laws. An ETF is somewhat like a mutual fund that trades like stock. Like a mutual fund, an ETF holds a pool of assets that reflect an index such as the S&P 500. However, an ETF is not really a mutual fund. Investors can buy and trade shares in an ETF on an exchange, and the ETF's price fluctuates throughout the day rather than having a daily net-asset value calculated at the end of each trading day. Because ETFs trade like stock, it is possible to engage in short-sales, or to purchase them on the margin. ETFs are also low cost for investors. ETFs may be either index-based or managed by a market professional.

ETFs generally deal only with authorized participants, and they issue and redeem their shares only in transactions with those persons. In most cases, ETFs only deal in transactions involving large aggregations known as creation units, primarily for in-kind baskets of portfolio assets. As a result, they do not comply with provisions of the 1940 Act governing the sale and redemption of redeemable securities. This means that under the long-standing regulatory regime, before shares of an ETF can be sold, an ETF sponsor must receive exemptive relief from several provisions of the 1940 Act.

Despite their increasing role for investors and their rapidly growing economic significance, ETFs seem to have been stuck in regulatory

---

[78]   SEC, *National Securities Exchanges* (available online at https://www.sec.gov/fast-answers/divisionsmarketregmrexchangesshtml.html).

[79]   SEC, *Alternative Trading System ("ATS") List* (available online at https://www.sec.gov/foia/docs/atslist.htm).

[80]   FINRA, *Funding Portals We Regulate* (available online at https://www.finra.org/about/funding-portals-we-regulate).

backwater. The U.S. has no specific ETF regulation nor a consistent, comprehensive approach to treatment of ETFs. Myriad statutes and regulations wind up applying differentially, resulting in similar ETFs being treated differently. This is caused by trying to place the new investment vehicle into regulatory cubbyholes designed for very different kinds of investments. In order to obtain relief from requirements that make no sense when applied to particular ETFs, the SEC winds up reviewing applications for exemptions on an ad hoc basis, assessing each ETF individually. The review process is neither transparent nor consistent. It is also both time consuming and expensive.[81]

The first ETF in the U.S. was released January 22, 1993 by the State Street Global Investors. The S&P Trust ETF (called SPDR or "Spider") proved to be very popular, and the idea has now spread to numerous other ETFs. There were more than 100 ETFs in 2002 and nearly 1,000 by 2009. The SEC reports that by 2018, there were approximately 1,900 ETFs, representing 15% of investment company assets. Sources suggest that trading in ETF typically accounts for about 25% of daily trading volume in U.S. stock markets, although that can increase to nearly 40% on days when policy changes or surprise events occur.[82] These ETFs currently represent approximately $3.4 trillion in total assets.

In mid-2018, the SEC voted to propose a new rule to update the regulatory framework applicable to ETFs. In announcing the proposed change, the SEC appeared to recognize that ad hoc exemptive orders no longer suit the nature of the ETF market. In essence, the proposed rule 6c–11 would permit ETFs that satisfy specified conditions to come to market without the need for ad hoc exemptive relief. The rule would offer relief to both index-based and actively managed ETFs.

The proposed rule was adopted September 26, 2019.

SEC PRESS RELEASE, *SEC ADOPTS NEW RULE TO MODERNIZE REGULATION OF EXCHANGE-TRADED FUNDS*
2019–190 (Sept. 26, 2019)[83]

The Securities and Exchange Commission today announced that is [sic] has voted to adopt a new rule and form amendments that are designed to modernize the regulation of exchange-traded funds (ETFs), by

---

[81] One source suggests that "[b]etween 2007 and 2018, the median processing time from filing to approval was 221 days. The SEC also estimates that the cost for a typical ETF filing for exemptive relief is $100,000." Todd P. Zerega & Thomas Ahmadifa, *Proposed ETF Rule: An Overview*, PERKINS COIE ASSET MANAGEMENT ADVOCATE (Aug. 16, 2018) (available online at https://www.assetmanagementadvocate.com/2018/08/proposed-etf-rule-an-overview/).

[82] The source for these numbers is Rachel Evans & Carolina Wilson, *How ETFs Became the Market*, BLOOMBERG (Sept. 13, 2018) (available online at https://www.bloomberg.com/graphics/2018-growing-etf-market/?srnd=etfs).

[83] This press release is archived at https://perma.cc/628L-AJSV.

establishing a clear and consistent framework for the vast majority of ETFs operating today. The adoption will facilitate greater competition and innovation in the ETF marketplace, leading to more choice for investors. It also will allow ETFs to come to market more quickly without the time or expense of applying for individual exemptive relief. In addition, the Commission voted to issue an exemptive order that further harmonizes related relief for broker-dealers.

"Since ETFs were first developed over 27 years ago, they have provided investors with a number of benefits, including access to a wide array of investment strategies, in many cases at a low cost," said SEC Chairman Jay Clayton. "As the ETF industry continues to grow in size and importance, particularly to Main Street investors, it is important to have a consistent, transparent, and efficient regulatory framework that eliminates regulatory hurdles while maintaining appropriate investor protections."

ETFs are hybrid investment products not originally allowed under the U.S. securities laws. Their shares trade on an exchange like a stock or closed-end fund, but they also allow identified large institutions to transact directly with the fund. Since 1992, the Commission has issued more than 300 exemptive orders allowing ETFs to operate under the Investment Company Act. ETFs have grown substantially in that period, and today there are approximately 2,000 ETFs with over $3.3 trillion in total net assets. Investors use ETFs for a variety of purposes, including core components of long-term investment portfolios, investment of temporary cash holdings, and for hedging portfolios.

ETFs relying on the rule and related exemptive order will have to comply with certain conditions designed to protect investors, including conditions regarding transparency and disclosure. To help create a consistent ETF regulatory framework, one year after the effective date of the rule, the Commission is rescinding exemptive relief previously granted to certain ETFs, including those that will be permitted to operate in reliance on the rule. The rule and form amendments will be effective 60 days after publication in the Federal Register, but there will be a one-year transition period for compliance with the form amendments.

* * *

FACT SHEET

Exchange-Traded Funds

Highlights

The Commission voted to adopt a new rule and form amendments designed to modernize the regulatory framework for exchange-traded funds ("ETFs"). Rule 6c–11 will permit ETFs that satisfy certain conditions to operate within the scope of the Investment Company Act of 1940 (the

"Act"), and come directly to market without the cost and delay of obtaining an exemptive order. This should facilitate greater competition and innovation in the ETF marketplace by lowering barriers to entry. The actions announced today will replace hundreds of individualized exemptive orders with a single rule. The rule's standardized conditions are designed to level the playing field among most ETFs and protect ETF investors, while disclosure amendments adopted by the Commission will provide investors who purchase and sell ETF shares on the secondary market with new information. . . .

Scope of Rule 6c–11

Rule 6c–11 will be available to ETFs organized as open-end funds, the structure for the vast majority of ETFs today. . . .

Conditions for Reliance on Rule 6c–11

Rule 6c–11 will provide certain exemptions from the Act and also impose certain conditions. The conditions include the following:

- Transparency. Under rule 6c–11, an ETF will be required to provide daily portfolio transparency on its website.

- Custom basket policies and procedures. An ETF relying on rule 6c–11 will be permitted to use baskets that do not reflect a pro-rata representation of the fund's portfolio or that differ from the initial basket used in transactions on the same business day ("custom baskets") if the ETF adopts written policies and procedures setting forth detailed parameters for the construction and acceptance of custom baskets that are in the best interests of the ETF and its shareholders. The rule also will require an ETF to comply with certain recordkeeping requirements.

- Website disclosure. The rule will require an ETF to disclose certain information on its website, including historical information regarding premiums and discounts and bid-ask spread information. These disclosures are intended to inform investors about the costs of investing in ETFs and the efficiency of an ETF's arbitrage process.

Rescission of Certain ETF Exemptive Relief

To help create a consistent ETF regulatory framework, one year after the effective date of rule 6c–11 (discussed below), the Commission is rescinding exemptive relief previously granted to ETFs that will be permitted to operate in reliance on the rule. . . .

Amendments to Form N-1A and Form N-8B-2

The Commission is adopting several amendments to Form N-1A—the form ETFs structured as open-end funds must use to register under the Act and to offer their securities under the Securities Act. These amendments will provide more useful, ETF-specific information to investors who purchase ETF shares on an exchange. . . .

Exemptive Relief and Interpretations Under the Exchange Act

In addition to the rule and form amendments under the Investment Company Act, the Commission is issuing an exemptive order that harmonizes certain related relief under the Exchange Act. In particular, the order provides exemptive relief to broker-dealers and other persons from certain requirements under the Exchange Act with respect to ETFs relying on rule 6c–11.

     . . . .[84]

Commentators in the crypto space generally agree that having an ETF for crypto is a potentially important step in the development of the industry. They do not, however, agree on how important it is. Some have suggested that it is crucial, while others suggest that it would help legitimize crypto, and is likely to have a significant impact on pricing, but should not be regarded as essential. As of mid-2019, the SEC had declined to approve any ETF for Bitcoin or any other crypto-based interest. It is, however, clear that if the SEC was to approve a Bitcoin ETF, it would lend a significant degree of legitimacy to crypto as a potential investment.

7. THE MISSION OF THE SEC

According to the official SEC website, "[t]he mission of the SEC is to protect investors; maintain fair, orderly, and efficient markets; and facilitate capital formation. The SEC strives to promote a market environment that is worthy of the public's trust." In the link that explains "What We Do," the SEC specifically notes a profound interest "in a growing economy that produces jobs, improves our standard of living, and protects the value of our savings." This feeds into the SEC's obligation to act "with an eye toward promoting the capital formation that is necessary to sustain economic growth."

The agency's mission supports the general focus of the federal securities laws upon accurate disclosure. As explained by the SEC:

> The laws and rules that govern the securities industry in the United States derive from a simple and straightforward concept: all investors, whether large institutions or private individuals, should have access to certain basic facts about an investment prior to buying it, and so long as they hold it. To achieve this, the SEC

---

[84]   The text of the final rule, conformed to the Federal Register version, is archived at https://perma.cc/7BE3-LQH7. See also 16 CFR Parts 210, 232, 239, 270, and 274.

requires public companies to disclose meaningful financial and other information to the public. This provides a common pool of knowledge for all investors to use to judge for themselves whether to buy, sell, or hold a particular security. Only through the steady flow of timely, comprehensive, and accurate information can people make sound investment decisions.[85]

Every year the SEC brings hundreds of civil enforcement actions for violation of the securities laws. In its 2018 Annual Report,[86] the SEC's Division of Enforcement set out its priorities and principles, noting that its actions were designed to punish misconduct, deter wrongdoing, remove bad actors from the markets, and (where possible) compensate harmed investors. The priorities for its actions include a focus on investors, individual accountability, keeping pace with technology, the imposition of remedies that further enforcement objectives, and monitoring of the SEC's resources.

The SEC's effectiveness is highly dependent on its enforcement authority. Each year the SEC brings hundreds of civil enforcement actions against individuals and companies for violation of the securities laws. In FY 2018 alone, the SEC brought 821 actions and obtained judgments and orders exceeding $3.9 billion in disgorgement and penalties in line with these priorities. The violations included insider trading, accounting fraud, and securities fraud.

In the above-referenced 2018 Annual Report, the SEC's Enforcement Division emphasized the range of antifraud actions brought in 2018. For example, the report notes that in FY 2018, the SEC "suspended trading in the securities of 280 issuers in order to combat potential market manipulation and microcap fraud threats. . . ." Of the 490 stand-alone enforcement actions, 25% involved improperly conducted securities offerings, an additional 16% involved issuer reporting and disclosure problems, and 7% involved market manipulation.

It is also worth noting that one of the specific priorities of the SEC involves technology, and in connection with that priority, the SEC continues to be active in considering how the federal securities laws and regulations apply in the context of cryptotransactions.

Having finished your reading of these materials, you should now be able to answer some general questions about the U.S. securities laws.

REVIEW QUESTIONS

1. Why do we have a system of both federal and state regulation of securities?

---

[85]   SEC, *What We Do* (available online at https://www.sec.gov/Article/whatwedo.html).

[86]   SEC, *2018 Annual Report* [archived at https://perma.cc/8MW9-KES2].

2.   What is the mission of the SEC and what are its goals?

3.   How can laws adopted in the 1930s apply to cryptoassets or other interests that were not in existence at that time?

4.   What is an investment contract and why does it matter?

5.   Why do entrepreneurs (including crypto entrepreneurs) need to worry about the definition of "security"?

6.   What does it mean to "register" a security with the SEC?

7.   What is special about an IPO?

8.   Why is it so important to have so many possible exemptions from the registration requirement?

9.   What are some of the most common exemptions from the registration requirement?

10.   If a securities deal is registered with the SEC, or fits within the terms of the exemptions discussed in these materials, can the issuer still be in trouble for violating the securities laws? How?

11.   Who can enforce the securities laws?

CHAPTER 8

THE DAO AND UNREGISTERED TRANSACTIONS

■ ■ ■

There are a number of reasons why the SEC has taken such an interest in cryptoassets and cryptotransactions. One is the fact that some of the deals that have been promoted look so similar to other transactions that clearly involve the issuance and sale of securities. The same kinds of sales pitches are used, and the same kind of terminology (such as referring to "investment opportunities") have often been used in connection with sales of crypto.

This chapter looks at the sale of DAO Tokens as an offering that may have peaked the interest of the SEC because the deal resembled something the SEC would traditionally have regulated. The materials then review some early statements from SEC officials about how the agency regards crypto transactions. This chapter also considers the SAFT project and the Munchee offering as examples of particular instances where the SEC has expressed interest or concern. Finally, this chapter introduces crypto exchanges in order to provide a basis for understanding how such exchanges operate (again with an eye towards evaluating the SEC's response).

1. THE DAO

PRELIMINARY NOTES AND QUESTIONS

1.   As you read through the following materials, make sure that you take the time to understand what The DAO offered to its investors. How did The DAO market its new tokens and to whom? What disclosures were made (or likely made)?

2.   After you understand what The DAO was doing, consider the risks that investors were asked to accept in exchange for paying over their Ether (another cryptoasset with a volatile but generally rising market value) in exchange for their DAO tokens. Consider how much opportunity they had to obtain additional information before they bought into the deal.

3.   What did investors expect to receive and what did they get when they bought their DAO tokens? What was their motive for purchasing the tokens?

What would have been required (and from whom) in order for their expectations to be met?

4.   Finally, consider why the SEC got involved. Why was the SEC concerned? What was the public policy justification for expending the resources necessary to determine what had happened and why? Why did the SEC conclude that a security had been sold? Assuming that everyone involved was acting in good faith, what would it have mattered if all the parties had known in advance that this was a security? Why did the SEC not decide to file an action against the persons associated with The DAO even though its conclusion was that they had sold an unregistered security in a non-compliant manner?

———————

"The DAO" project was one of the largest early ICOs on the Ethereum platform. Usually, "DAO" stands for decentralized autonomous organization, which is an entity that is organized on a blockchain and operates through smart contracts. By coding the rules by which an organization is to operate on a blockchain, the organization becomes both decentralized and autonomous. In this particular case, The DAO (also known as The Genesis DAO) was designed as a decentralized autonomous organization, through open source coding developed by Slock.it, a German corporation created by a few members of the Ethereum community. Initiated in early May of 2016 by Slock.it and its co-founders, the original objective of The DAO was to sell DAO tokens which would then be used as a kind of venture capital fund for decentralized cryptocurrency projects. In other words, The DAO "promised to create a decentralized organization that would fund other blockchain projects" with a unique governance structure in which investment and other "decisions would be made by the token holders themselves."

In the initial phase of its existence, the creators allowed anyone to send Ether to a special wallet address in exchange for 100 DAO tokens for each Ether contributed. This offering was an unprecedented success, raising approximately $150 million in Ether at its then-current market value. Once operational, The DAO was designed to allow companies to make proposals for funding. If approved by a curator, the proposal would be submitted to a vote of The DAO token-holders, and any proposals that received a 20% vote (of the total of outstanding tokens) were funded. The DAO also included an "out" in the event that the community invested in a proposal that a particular investor objected to, and this was known as the "split function." This split function allowed users to back out of The DAO by creating a "Child DAO," to which the objecting holder's contributed Ether would be returned after 28 days.

On June 17, 2016, unidentified hackers found a loophole in this "split function," which allowed them to drain 3.6 million Ether (then worth about $70 million) by requesting multiple refunds of the same tokens before The

DAO could update its records. The end result was a division in the Ethereum community over what to do.

The community at first considered a soft fork that would have blacklisted transactions from The DAO, but this was ultimately determined not to be a viable solution. Instead, the community split on the hard fork solution, which was designed to return the stolen Ether. Approximately 89% of Ether holders voted for this alternative, and the fork occurred in July of 2016, allowing the Ethereum Foundation to recover the stolen funds by unwinding certain transactions. This "hard fork" (essentially a mandatory revision to the coding of the smart contract) had "the sole function of returning all the Ether taken from The DAO to a refund smart contract."[1]

This was not the end of troubles for The DAO. The U.S. SEC's Division of Enforcement began an investigation into whether The DAO, Slock.it, Slock.it's co-founders, and intermediaries violated U.S. securities laws by selling the DAO tokens in the U.S. without registering the offering or complying with any of the potential exemptions from registration then available under the securities laws. In July of 2017, the SEC released its report on the investigation, a portion of which is excerpted here:

SEC, *REPORT OF INVESTIGATION PURSUANT TO SECTION 21(a) OF THE SECURITIES EXCHANGE ACT OF 1934: THE DAO*
'34 Act Release No. 81207 (July 25, 2017)[2]

I. Introduction and Summary

The United States Securities and Exchange Commission's ("Commission") Division of Enforcement ("Division") has investigated whether The DAO, an unincorporated organization; Slock.it UG ("Slock.it"), a German corporation; Slock.it's co-founders; and intermediaries may have violated the federal securities laws.

. . . .

This Report reiterates these fundamental principles of the U.S. federal securities laws and describes their applicability to a new paradigm—virtual organizations or capital raising entities that use distributed ledger or blockchain technology to facilitate capital raising and/or investment and the related offer and sale of securities. The automation of certain functions through this technology, "smart contracts," or computer code, does not remove conduct from the purview of the U.S. federal securities laws. This

---

[1]   Antonio Madeira, *The DAO, The Hack, The Soft Fork and The Hard Fork*, CRYPTOCOMPARE (May 20, 2018) (available online at https://www.cryptocompare.com/coins/guides/the-dao-the-hack-the-soft-fork-and-the-hard-fork/).

[2]   Available at https://www.sec.gov/litigation/investreport/34-81207.pdf [archived at https://perma.cc/F862-YS5V].

Report also serves to stress the obligation to comply with the registration provisions of the federal securities laws with respect to products and platforms involving emerging technologies and new investor interfaces.

II. Facts

A. Background

From April 30, 2016 through May 28, 2016, The DAO offered and sold approximately 1.15 billion DAO Tokens in exchange for a total of approximately 12 million Ether ("ETH"), a virtual currency used on the Ethereum Blockchain. As of the time the offering closed, the total ETH raised by The DAO was valued in U.S. Dollars ("USD") at approximately $150 million.

. . . .

B. The DAO

"The DAO" is the "first generation" implementation of the White Paper concept of a DAO Entity, and it began as an effort to create a "crowdfunding contract" to raise "funds to grow [a] company in the crypto space." In November 2015, at an Ethereum Developer Conference in London, Christoph Jentzsch described his proposal for The DAO as a "for-profit DAO [Entity]," where participants would send ETH (a virtual currency) to The DAO to purchase DAO Tokens, which would permit the participant to vote and entitle the participant to "rewards." Christoph Jentzsch likened this to "buying shares in a company and getting . . . dividends." The DAO was to be "decentralized" in that it would allow for voting by investors holding DAO Tokens. All funds raised were to be held at an Ethereum Blockchain "address" associated with The DAO and DAO Token holders were to vote on contract proposals, including proposals to The DAO to fund projects and distribute The DAO's anticipated earnings from the projects it funded. The DAO was intended to be "autonomous" in that project proposals were in the form of smart contracts that exist on the Ethereum Blockchain and the votes were administered by the code of The DAO.

. . . .

1. DAO Tokens

DAO Token holders were not restricted from re-selling DAO Tokens acquired in the offering, and DAO Token holders could sell their DAO Tokens in a variety of ways in the secondary market and thereby monetize their investment as discussed below. Prior to the Offering Period, Slock.it solicited at least one U.S. web-based platform to trade DAO Tokens on its system and, at the time of the offering, The DAO Website and other promotional materials disseminated by Slock.it included representations that DAO Tokens would be available for secondary market trading after the Offering Period via several platforms. During the Offering Period and afterwards, the Platforms posted notices on their own websites and on social media that each planned to support secondary market trading of DAO Tokens.

. . . .

2. Participants in The DAO

Before any proposal was put to a vote by DAO Token holders, it was required to be reviewed by one or more of The DAO's "Curators." At the time of the formation of The DAO, the Curators were a group of individuals chosen by Slock.it. . . . Curators of The DAO had ultimate discretion as to whether or not to submit a proposal for voting by DAO Token holders. Curators also determined the order and frequency of proposals, and could impose subjective criteria for whether the proposal should be whitelisted. One member of the group chosen by Slock.it to serve collectively as the Curator stated publicly that the Curator had "complete control over the whitelist . . . the order in which things get whitelisted, the duration for which [proposals] get whitelisted, when things get unwhitelisted . . . [and] clear ability to control the order and frequency of proposals," noting that "curators have tremendous power."

. . . .

3. Secondary Market Trading on the Platforms

During the period from May 28, 2016 through early September 2016, the Platforms became the preferred vehicle for DAO Token holders to buy and sell DAO Tokens in the secondary market using virtual or fiat currencies. Specifically, the Platforms used electronic systems that allowed their respective customers to post orders for DAO Tokens on an anonymous basis. For example, customers of each Platform could buy or sell DAO Tokens by entering a market order on the Platform's system, which would then match with orders from other customers residing on the system. Each Platform's system would automatically execute these orders based on pre-programmed order interaction protocols established by the Platform.

None of the Platforms received orders for DAO Tokens from non-Platform customers or routed its respective customers' orders to any other trading destinations. The Platforms publicly displayed all their quotes, trades, and daily trading volume in DAO Tokens on their respective websites. During the period from May 28, 2016 through September 6, 2016, one such Platform executed more than 557,378 buy and sell transactions in DAO Tokens by more than 15,000 of its U.S. and foreign customers. During the period from May 28, 2016 through August 1, 2016, another such Platform executed more than 22,207 buy and sell transactions in DAO Tokens by more than 700 of its U.S. customers.

III. Discussion

The Commission is aware that virtual organizations and associated individuals and entities increasingly are using distributed ledger technology to offer and sell instruments such as DAO Tokens to raise capital. These offers and sales have been referred to, among other things, as "Initial Coin Offerings" or "Token Sales." Accordingly, the Commission deems it appropriate and in the public interest to issue this Report in order to stress that the U.S. federal securities law may apply to various activities, including distributed ledger technology, depending on the particular facts and circumstances, without regard to the form of the organization or technology used to effectuate a particular offer or sale. In this Report, the Commission considers the particular facts and circumstances of the offer and sale of DAO Tokens to demonstrate the application of existing U.S. federal securities laws to this new paradigm.

. . . .

[After first noting that the Securities Act of 1933 requires any security to be registered or exempt from registration prior to it being offered or sold, the SEC then concluded that The DAO tokens were securities, under the following analysis.]

Under Section 2(a)(1) of the Securities Act and Section 3(a)(10) of the Exchange Act, a security includes "an investment contract." *See* 15 U.S.C. §§ 77b–77c. An investment contract is an investment of money in a common enterprise with a reasonable expectation of profits to be derived from the entrepreneurial or managerial efforts of others. *See SEC v. Edwards*, 540 U.S. 389, 393 (2004); *SEC v. W.J. Howey Co.*, 328 U.S. 293, 301 (1946); *see also United Housing Found., Inc. v. Forman*, 421 U.S. 837, 852–53 (1975) (The "touchstone" of an investment contract "is the presence of an investment in a common venture premised on a reasonable expectation of profits to be derived from the entrepreneurial or managerial efforts of others."). This definition embodies a *"flexible rather than a static principle,* one that is capable of adaptation to meet the countless and variable schemes devised by those who seek the use of the money of others on the promise of profits." *Howey*, 328 U.S. at 299 (emphasis added). The test "permits the fulfillment of the statutory purpose of compelling full and fair disclosure relative to the issuance of 'the many types of instruments that in our commercial world fall within the ordinary concept of a security.' " *Id.* In analyzing whether something is a security, "form should be disregarded for substance," *Tcherepnin v. Knight*, 389 U.S. 332, 336 (1967), "and the emphasis should be on economic realities underlying a transaction, and not on the name appended thereto." *United Housing Found.*, 421 U.S. at 849.

. . . .

[The SEC then noted that section 5 of the Securities Exchange Act of 1934 "makes it unlawful for any broker, dealer, or exchange, directly or indirectly, to effect any transaction in a security, or to report any such transaction, in interstate commerce, unless the exchange is registered as a national securities exchange under Section 6 of the Exchange Act, or is exempted from such registration," citing 15 U.S.C. § 78e.]

Section 3(a)(1) of the Exchange Act defines an "exchange" as "any organization, association, or group of persons, whether incorporated or unincorporated, which constitutes, maintains, or provides a market place or facilities for bringing together purchasers and sellers of securities or for otherwise performing with respect to securities the functions commonly performed by a stock exchange as that term is generally understood . . . ." 15 U.S.C. § 78c(a)(1).

Exchange Act Rule 3b–16(a) provides a functional test to assess whether a trading system meets the definition of exchange under Section 3(a)(1). Under Exchange Act Rule 3b–16(a), an organization, association, or group of persons shall be considered to constitute, maintain, or provide "a marketplace or facilities for bringing together purchasers and sellers of securities or for otherwise performing with respect to securities the functions commonly performed by a stock exchange," if such organization, association, or group of persons: (1) brings together the orders for securities of multiple buyers and sellers; and (2) uses established, non-discretionary methods (whether by providing a trading facility or by setting rules) under which such orders interact with each other, and the buyers and sellers entering such orders agree to the terms of the trade.

     . . . .

The Platforms that traded DAO Tokens . . . provided users with an electronic system that matched orders from multiple parties to buy and sell DAO Tokens for execution based on non-discretionary methods.

This was one of the first official pronouncements from the SEC explaining how it intended to regulate cryptoassets such as the DAO tokens. Although The DAO was found to be an issuer of securities, and the trading platforms were found to be exchanges that should have registered as national securities exchanges, the SEC decided not to pursue an enforcement action against participants at that time. Still, the action put a halt to The DAO's efforts to fund blockchain-based projects through crypto-financing. It also signaled to the crypto community that the SEC was serious about exercising its regulatory authority over ICOs and other cryptotransactions.

NOTES AND QUESTIONS

1.   Do you agree that the investors in The DAO were relying on the essential entrepreneurial efforts of others? Given that investors were to have

a vote on any projects before they were funded, wouldn't that mean that the investors also had a significant role in long term profitability of the business?

2.   Assuming that the securities laws did not apply, would the investors have had any claims against the persons who issued them The DAO tokens as a result of the hack? Did the sellers have a duty to disclose the risk of hacking? Would making the coding for the project open-source (which they did), satisfy any such duty? Did they have a duty of care to protect purchasers from vulnerabilities such as those exploited by the hacker who took advantage of a deficiency in the split function associated with the Child DAOs? Would registering the tokens as a security have protected the investors any better?

3.   What would have been the likely consequence of having to register the tokens as securities or having to find and comply with an exemption?

2. TESTIMONY BY SEC OFFICIALS

While comments by individuals within the SEC are specifically disclaimed by the agency, and acknowledged only as the opinion of the individual making the statement, it is still worth noting when the Chairman of the SEC offers testimony before a U.S. Senate Committee. On February 6, 2018, SEC Chairman Jay Clayton offered substantial testimony about how the agency was approaching cryptocurrencies. Excerpts from that testimony appear below.

SEC TESTIMONY, *CHAIRMAN JAY CLAYTON*, *CHAIRMAN'S TESTIMONY ON VIRTUAL CURRENCIES: THE ROLES OF THE SEC AND CFTC*
(Feb. 6, 2018)[3]

. . . .

Cryptocurrencies, ICOs and related products and technologies have captured the popular imagination—and billions of hard-earned dollars—of American investors from all walks of life. . . .

Unfortunately, it is clear that some have taken advantage of this lack of understanding and have sought to prey on investors' excitement about the quick rise in cryptocurrency and ICO prices.

There should be no misunderstanding about the law. When investors are offered and sold securities—which to date ICOs have largely been—they are entitled to the benefits of state and federal securities laws and sellers and other market participants must follow these laws.

Yes, we do ask our investors to use common sense, and we recognize that many investment decisions will prove to be incorrect in hindsight. However, we do not ask investors to use their common sense in a vacuum,

---

[3]   This testimony is archived at https://perma.cc/WU7R-CK4E.

but rather, with the benefit of information and other requirements where judgments can reasonably be made.

This is a core principle of our federal securities laws and is embodied in the SEC's registration requirements. Investors should understand that to date no ICOs have been registered with the SEC, and the SEC also has not approved for listing and trading any exchange-traded products (such as ETFs) holding cryptocurrencies or other assets related to cryptocurrencies. If any person today says otherwise, investors should be especially wary.

Investors who are considering investing in these products should also recognize that these markets span national borders and that significant trading may occur on systems and platforms outside the U.S. Investors' funds may quickly travel overseas without their knowledge. As a result, risks can be amplified, including the risk that U.S. market regulators, such as the SEC and state securities regulators, may not be able to effectively pursue bad actors or recover funds.

Further, there are significant security risks that can arise by transacting in these markets, including the loss of investment and personal information due to hacks of online trading platforms and individual digital asset "wallets." A recent study estimated that more than 10% of proceeds generated by ICOs—or almost $400 million—has been lost to such attacks. . . .

In order to arm investors with additional information, the SEC staff has issued investor alerts, bulletins and statements on ICOs and cryptocurrency-related investments, including with respect to the marketing of certain offerings and investments by celebrities and others. If investors choose to invest in these products, they should ask questions and demand clear answers. . . .

These warnings are not an effort to undermine the fostering of innovation through our capital markets—America was built on the ingenuity, vision and spirit of entrepreneurs who tackled old and new problems in new, innovative ways. Rather, they are meant to educate Main Street investors that many promoters of ICOs and cryptocurrencies are not complying with our securities laws and, as a result, the risks are significant.

     . . . .

Cryptocurrencies and Related Products and Trading

Speaking broadly, cryptocurrencies purport to be items of inherent value (similar, for instance, to cash or gold) that are designed to enable purchases, sales and other financial transactions. Many are promoted as providing the same functions as long-established currencies such as the U.S. dollar but without the backing of a government or other body. While cryptocurrencies currently being marketed vary in different respects, proponents of cryptocurrencies often tout their novelty and other potential beneficial features, including the ability to make transfers without an intermediary and without geographic limitation and lower transaction costs compared to other forms of payment. Critics of cryptocurrencies note that the purported benefits highlighted by proponents are unproven and other touted benefits, such as the personal anonymity of the purchasers and sellers and the absence of government regulation or oversight, could also facilitate illicit trading and financial transactions, as well as fraud.

The recent proliferation and subsequent popularity of cryptocurrency markets creates a question for market regulators as to whether our historic approach to the regulation of sovereign currency transactions is appropriate for these new markets. These markets may look like our regulated securities markets, with quoted prices and other information. Many trading platforms are even referred to as "exchanges." I am concerned that this appearance is deceiving. In reality, investors transacting on these trading platforms do not receive many of the market protections that they would when transacting through broker-dealers on registered exchanges or alternative trading systems (ATSs), such as best execution, prohibitions on front running, short sale restrictions, and custody and capital requirements. I am concerned that Main Street investors do not appreciate these differences and the resulting substantially heightened risk profile.

It appears that many of the U.S.-based cryptocurrency trading platforms have elected to be regulated as money-transmission services. Traditionally, from an oversight perspective, these predominantly state-regulated payment services have not been subject to direct oversight by the SEC or the CFTC. Traditionally, from a function perspective, these money transfer services have not quoted prices or offered other services akin to securities, commodities and currency exchanges. In short, the currently applicable regulatory framework for cryptocurrency trading was not designed with trading of the type we are witnessing in mind. As Chairman Giancarlo and I stated recently, we are open to exploring with Congress, as well as with our federal and state colleagues, whether increased federal regulation of cryptocurrency trading platforms is necessary or appropriate. We also are supportive of regulatory and policy efforts to bring clarity and fairness to this space.

The SEC regulates securities transactions and certain individuals and firms who participate in our securities markets. The SEC does not have direct oversight of transactions in currencies or commodities, including currency trading platforms.

While there are cryptocurrencies that, at least as currently designed, promoted and used, do not appear to be securities, simply calling something a "currency" or a currency-based product does not mean that it is not a security. To this point I would note that many products labeled as cryptocurrencies or related assets are increasingly being promoted as investment opportunities that rely on the efforts of others, with their utility as an efficient medium for commercial exchange being a distinct secondary characteristic. As discussed in more detail below, if a cryptocurrency, or a product with its value tied to one or more cryptocurrencies, is a security, its promoters cannot make offers or sales unless they comply with the registration and other requirements under our federal securities laws.

In this regard, the SEC is monitoring the cryptocurrency-related activities of the market participants it regulates, including brokers, dealers, investment advisers and trading platforms. Brokers, dealers and other market participants that allow for payments in cryptocurrencies, allow customers to purchase cryptocurrencies (including on margin) or otherwise use cryptocurrencies to facilitate securities transactions should exercise particular caution, including ensuring that their cryptocurrency activities are not undermining their anti-money laundering and know-your-customer obligations. As I have stated previously, these market participants should treat payments and other transactions made in cryptocurrency as if cash were being handed from one party to the other.

Finally, financial products that are linked to underlying digital assets, including cryptocurrencies, may be structured as securities products subject to the federal securities laws even if the underlying cryptocurrencies are not themselves securities. Market participants have requested Commission approval for new products and services of this type that are focused on retail investors, including cryptocurrency-linked ETFs. While we appreciate the importance of continuing innovation in our retail fund space, there are a number of issues that need to be examined and resolved before we permit ETFs and other retail investor-oriented funds to invest in cryptocurrencies in a manner consistent with their obligations under the federal securities laws. These include issues around liquidity, valuation and custody of the funds' holdings, as well as creation, redemption and arbitrage in the ETF space.

. . . .

ICOs and Related Trading

Coinciding with the substantial growth in cryptocurrencies, companies and individuals increasingly have been using so-called ICOs to raise capital for businesses and projects. Typically, these offerings involve the opportunity for individual investors to exchange currency, such as U.S. dollars or cryptocurrencies, in return for a digital asset labeled as a coin or token. The size of the ICO market has grown exponentially in the last year, and it is estimated that almost $4 billion was raised through ICOs in 2017.

Note that this number may understate the size of the ICO market (and the potential for loss) as many ICOs "trade up" after they are issued.

These offerings can take different forms, and the rights and interests a coin is purported to provide the holder can vary widely. A key question all ICO market participants—promoters, sellers, lawyers, officers and directors and accountants, as well as investors—should ask: "Is the coin or token a security?" As securities law practitioners know well, the answer depends on the facts. But by and large, the structures of ICOs that I have seen involve the offer and sale of securities and directly implicate the securities registration requirements and other investor protection provisions of our federal securities laws. As noted above, the foundation of our federal securities laws is to provide investors with the procedural protections and information they need to make informed judgments about what they are investing in and the relevant risks involved. In addition, our federal securities laws provide a wide array of remedies, including criminal and civil actions brought by the DOJ and the SEC, as well as private rights of action.

. . . .

The Commission's message to issuers and market professionals in this space [as embodied in the 2017 DAO Report] was clear: those who would use distributed ledger technology to raise capital or engage in securities transactions must take appropriate steps to ensure compliance with the federal securities laws. The Report and subsequent statements also explain that the use of such technology does not mean that an offering is necessarily problematic under those laws. The registration process itself, or exemptions from registration, are available for offerings employing these novel methods.

The statement I issued in December that was directed to Main Street investors and market professionals provided additional insight into how practitioners should view ICOs in the context of our federal securities laws. Certain market professionals have attempted to highlight the utility or voucher-like characteristics of their proposed ICOs in an effort to claim that their proposed tokens or coins are not securities. Many of these assertions that the federal securities laws do not apply to a particular ICO appear to elevate form over substance. The rise of these form-based arguments is a disturbing trend that deprives investors of mandatory protections that clearly are required as a result of the structure of the transaction. Merely calling a token a "utility" token or structuring it to provide some utility does not prevent the token from being a security. Tokens and offerings that incorporate features and marketing efforts that emphasize the potential for profits based on the entrepreneurial or managerial efforts of others continue to contain the hallmarks of a security under U.S. law. It is especially troubling when the promoters of these offerings emphasize the secondary market trading potential of these tokens, i.e., the ability to sell them on an exchange at a profit. In short, prospective purchasers are being sold on the potential for tokens to increase in value—with the ability to lock in those increases by reselling the tokens on a secondary market—or to otherwise profit from the tokens based on the efforts of others. These are key hallmarks of a security and a securities offering.

On this and other points where the application of expertise and judgment is expected, I believe that gatekeepers and others, including securities lawyers, accountants and consultants, need to focus on their responsibilities. I have urged these professionals to be guided by the principal motivation for our registration, offering process and disclosure requirements: investor protection and, in particular, the protection of our Main Street investors.

I also have cautioned market participants against promoting or touting the offer and sale of coins without first determining whether the securities laws apply to those actions. Engaging in the business of selling securities generally requires a license, and experience shows that excessive touting in thinly traded and volatile markets can be an indicator of "scalping," "pump and dump" and other manipulations and frauds. Similarly, my colleagues and I have cautioned those who operate systems and platforms that effect or facilitate transactions in these products that they may be operating unregistered exchanges or broker-dealers that are in violation of the Securities Exchange Act of 1934.

I do want to recognize that recently social media platforms have restricted the ability of users to promote ICOs and cryptocurrencies on their platforms. I appreciate the responsible step.

Enforcement

A number of concerns have been raised regarding the cryptocurrency and ICO markets, including that, as they are currently operating, there is substantially less investor protection than in our traditional securities markets, with correspondingly greater opportunities for fraud and manipulation. The ability of bad actors to commit age-old frauds with new technologies coupled with the significant amount of capital—particularly from retail investors—that has poured into cryptocurrencies and ICOs in recent months and the offshore footprint of many of these activities have only heightened these concerns.

In September 2017, the Division of Enforcement established a new Cyber Unit focused on misconduct involving distributed ledger technology and ICOs, the spread of false information through electronic and social media, brokerage account takeovers, hacking to obtain nonpublic information and threats to trading platforms. The Cyber Unit works closely with our cross-divisional Distributed Ledger Technology Working Group, which was created in November 2013. We believe this approach has enabled us to leverage our enforcement resources effectively and coordinate well within the Commission, as well as with other federal and state regulators.

To date, we have brought a number of enforcement actions concerning ICOs for alleged violations of the federal securities laws. . . . [For] example, after being contacted by the SEC last December, a company halted its ICO to raise capital for a blockchain-based food review service, and then settled proceedings in which we determined that the ICO was an unregistered offering and sale of securities in violation of the federal securities laws. Before tokens were delivered to investors, the company refunded investor proceeds after the SEC intervened.

. . . .

I also have been increasingly concerned with recent instances of public companies, with no meaningful track record in pursuing distributed ledger or blockchain technology, changing their business models and names to reflect a focus on distributed ledger technology without adequate disclosure to investors about their business model changes and the risks involved. A number of these instances raise serious investor protection concerns about the adequacy of disclosure especially where an offer and sale of securities is involved. The SEC is looking closely at the disclosures of public companies that shift their business models to capitalize on the perceived promise of distributed ledger technology and whether the disclosures comply with the federal securities laws, particularly in the context of a securities offering.

With the support of my fellow Commissioners, I have asked the SEC's Division of Enforcement to continue to police these markets vigorously and recommend enforcement actions against those who conduct ICOs or engage in other actions relating to cryptocurrencies in violation of the federal securities laws. In doing so, the SEC and CFTC are collaborating on our approaches to policing these markets . . . . We also will continue to work closely with our federal and state counterparts, including the Department of Treasury, Department of Justice and state attorneys general and securities regulators.

––––––––––––

Keep in mind that this testimony was offered at the start of 2018, and two years is a long time in the fast-moving crypto world. Therefore, this speech does not constitute the SEC's final word. However, Chairman Clayton's opinion clearly reflects a preference for a regulatory response. As you reflect on his comments, how would you answer the following questions?

NOTES AND QUESTIONS

1. Why would the SEC want crypto to be classified as a security?

2. Chairman Clayton identifies losses due to hacks as a major problem for investors. Given that issuers do not intentionally build in weaknesses for hackers to exploit, do not know of the weaknesses in advance, and are not technically responsible for hacks of third parties such as exchanges and wallet services, do these losses support the claimed need for registration and regulation?

3. Why would the SEC applaud decisions by social media sites such as Facebook to prevent advertisements for ICOs and crypto sales?

4. If the primary problem is fraud, is registration really a viable or useful response? Doesn't that simply drive up the cost for legitimate businesses while doing nothing to prevent people from lying if that is what they intend to do?

5. Based on what Chairman Clayton says, if a company specifically avoids marketing its crypto as a speculative investment, do you believe that will be enough to keep it from being a security? Should it be sufficient?

3. THE SAFT (SIMPLE AGREEMENT FOR FUTURE TOKENS)

With the preceding background in mind, consider the following documentation, prepared not by regulators in the SEC but by proponents of crypto technology. This documentation takes the form of a whitepaper drawn up by attorneys, crypto entrepreneurs, investors, and others describing documentation for an option that was specifically designed to comply with federal securities laws.

PRELIMINARY NOTES AND QUESTIONS

1. As you review the following material on the SAFT, keep in mind the following questions: Who developed the SAFT and why? What was their motivation for doing so? Were the proponents of the SAFT neutral parties or advocates for a particular position? What is the basis for your conclusion on this matter?

2. What do the drafters of the SAFT whitepaper mean by "securities token" and "utility token"? What do they mean by "direct token sale" and "prefunctional token"? How does their proposal differ from a direct sale of prefunctional tokens?

3. From a securities law standpoint, what is the relative advantage of a SAFT that is urged by its proponents as opposed to direct sales of prefunctional tokens? If an issuer has to register the SAFT itself, why is the SAFT process less burdensome than the direct sale of prefunctional tokens?

4. What elements of the *Howey* investment contract test do the SAFT proponents contend are missing from a transaction in which SAFT contract rights are converted into functional tokens? Do you agree with the analysis that the SAFT whitepaper suggests?

———————

Before getting into the details, it is important to acknowledge that as more and more people became interested in cryptoassets and token sales, deals became increasingly complex and sophisticated. Especially early on, startups sought funds from early investors in order to fund the development of new tokens. These investors would essentially buy an option or acquire a contractual right to buy tokens to be developed in the future. At first, the general assumption was that crypto was not going to be a security and that there was no need to register with the SEC.

Once regulators began to express their interest, developers and issuers wanted to keep their deals as simple and inexpensive as possible. They certainly did not want to have to register (or find available exemptions) for both the sale of the "rights" to acquire tokens in the future when they were developed, and then need to repeat the exercise when it came time to actually issue the tokens. The SAFT (or Simple Agreement for Future Tokens) was an effort to avoid the need to comply with the securities laws at multiple points during the process.

In order to understand the SAFT, it is probably necessary to examine a similar arrangement developed in connection with sales of traditional equity interests, the simple agreement for future equity (SAFE), which was developed in late 2013. This protocol and the documentation associated with it were developed by Y Combinator, which was started in 2005 as a vehicle to provide early stage funding for start-up companies. In its main program, Y Combinator interviews and selects two groups of companies each year. In exchange for a 7% equity stake, it gives its client companies $150,000 in seed money, and offers advice and connections. It then helps its clients raise funds through sales pursuant to a SAFE.

At the time the SAFE was originally developed, startups sought to raise relatively small amounts in advance of a priced funding round which was often conducted as a Series A Preferred Stock round. When the Series A round was conducted, owners of the SAFE were provided with the Preferred Stock based on predetermined pricing. The SAFE was therefore a way to provide a small amount of start-up capital from investors who were essentially regarded as early participants in the Series A round. Over time, the process has morphed into a distinct funding round, primarily because of the need to raise additional amounts.

As early stage fundraising has evolved, Y Combinator has updated its documentation. However, as explained on the Y Combinator webpage, the

SAFE continues to offer one of the major benefits that it has had since its inception. A SAFE offers a "flexible, one-document security without numerous terms to negotiate. . . ." The Y Combinator site further explains that:

> . . .[S]afes save startups and investors money in legal fees and reduce the time spent negotiating the terms of the investment. Startups and investors will usually only have to negotiate one item: the valuation cap. Because a safe has no expiration or maturity date, there should be no time or money spent dealing with extending maturity dates, revising interest rates or the like.[4]

In the world of cryptoassets, an issuer cannot rely on a future agreement to sell "equity" because cryptocoins and tokens are not equity, even if they mimic some of the same function of those traditional securities. Therefore, instead of offering simplified documentation for the sale of future equity, a SAFT is a simplified document that provides for the sale of future tokens. In essence, a SAFT is a contract in which an investor makes a payment in exchange for a contractual right to receive tokens when certain conditions (often including development of the token itself) are met.

The most carefully thought-out and documented SAFT, and the one which appears to have garnered both the most attention and the largest following, is the project jointly developed by Cooley LLP, working in conjunction with Protocol Labs, various token creators, legal experts, and investors. Their SAFT project, including a detailed whitepaper and sample documentation, was released to the public in late 2017.[5] The goal of this project, as explained in the whitepaper, was to provide a framework that would operate in compliance with existing federal regulations pursuant to which investors would fund development of "genuinely functional utility tokens" that would then be delivered to the investors.[6] The paper readily conceded that the SAFT transaction itself would involve the sale of interests that would likely be investment contracts under the U.S. securities laws, but the plan was that the resulting utility tokens would not be securities under the *Howey*[7] investment contract test.

The following excerpts from that SAFT whitepaper are included to help provide background into the project. The goal is that this material will aid in your understanding of the SEC's current and developing approach to token offerings and ICOs. As you read through these materials, keep in

---

[4]   Carolynn Levy, *Safe Financing Documents*, Y COMBINATOR (Sept. 2018) (available online at https://www.ycombinator.com/documents/).

[5]   *Announcing The SAFT Project*, PROTOCOL LABS BLOG (Oct. 2, 2017) (available online at https://protocol.ai/blog/announcing-saft-project/).

[6]   Juan Batiz-Benet, Jesse Clayburgh, & Marco Santori, *The SAFT Project: Toward a Compliant Token Sale Framework*, PROTOCOL LABS (Oct. 2, 2017) [archived at https://perma.cc/EQ8N-E3TJ].

[7]   *SEC v. W.J. Howey, Co.*, 328 U.S. 293, 298–99 (1946).

mind the preliminary questions that appear at the start of this section. They are designed to help you focus on some of the most important aspects that can be learned from reviewing this document.

THE SAFT PROJECT: TOWARD A COMPLIANT TOKEN SALE FRAMEWORK

Juan Batiz-Benet, Jesse Clayburgh, & Marco Santori (October 2, 2017)[8]

There are two categories of tokens in circulation today that are relevant to this discussion. The first kind of token is meant to serve simply as a highly-liquid substitute for a traditional security like corporate stock, a limited partnership interest, and the like. These so-called "securities tokens"[9] can offer obvious benefits over the traditional securities infrastructure. For example, they can be traded, cleared, and settled nearly instantaneously, leaving an indelible chain of title. Today, though, these benefits are overshadowed by regulatory and policy uncertainty—especially when used in the public markets. This whitepaper does not discuss securities tokens in detail.

Instead, we focus on so-called "utility tokens." This category of blockchain tokens contains assets that do not purport to replace legacy financial services products. They are designed to offer intrinsic utility that powers a decentralized, distributed network that delivers to the users of the network a consumptive good or service. For example, when their networks are functional, some tokens will act as currencies, like bitcoins do. Some will act as staking or betting mechanisms, membership rights, or loan collateral. Some will simply act as cryptographic "coupons" redeemable for mundane goods and services like bags of ground coffee or boxes of razor blades. With a particular emphasis on legal and policy effects, we describe the often-used "direct token presale" model, which involves the direct sale of a utility token to the public prior to the functionality of the token, and compare it to the SAFT framework. . . .

---

[8] The original SAFT whitepaper contains this explicit disclaimer: "This document does not constitute legal advice and should not be relied on by any person. It is designed for general informational purposes only. Developers, purchasers, investors and any other participant in a token system should consult their own counsel." The whitepaper and documentation represents the then-current thinking as influenced by Cooley LLP, Protocol Labs, various token creators, other legal experts, and investors. Most footnotes have been omitted. The document from which the excerpt is taken is archived in its entirety at https://perma.cc/XDP4-MQU5.

[9] Author's note: The dichotomy established in this document does not necessarily track the way others categorize cryptoassets. Certainly, to date, the SEC has declined to accept the notion that only "securities tokens" are subject to regulation as securities. In addition, while the whitepaper categorizes cryptocurrencies like Bitcoin as utility tokens. (It does this in the next paragraph.) That is also a characterization that may be subject to considerable dispute. However, the discussion is far from over. *SEC v. Kik Interactive Inc.*, a lawsuit filed in mid-2019 in the Southern District of New York and discussed in some detail in chapter 10, raises the issue of how to appropriately classify functional tokens, as well as the legal viability of the SAFT.

The Direct Token Presale

In a typical direct token presale, a software development team forms a legal entity. . . . Prior to the creation of any functional token, the entity accepts money from public, retail purchasers in exchange for a right to the token. The developers are, to greater or lesser extents, skilled in applied cryptography, computer programming, or both.

. . . .

Prior to the direct token presale, the entity has usually produced a technical whitepaper to postulate the feasibility and value of the unbuilt network. It has released the whitepaper for peer review, which occurs primarily via email, online or offline meetings, social media networks, or private online chat rooms. It has also generally engaged in extensive public relations campaigns to market the direct token presale. These marketing efforts include the creation and dissemination of websites, banner advertisements, press releases, and collaboration with media outlets. Thus, a great many of the purchasers in a token sale are unaccredited, retail investors.

However, entities offering token sales that raise large amounts of capital generally do not rely solely (or even mostly) on these broad solicitations. They typically spend months pitching and negotiating with professional investors to seed these sales. Very often, these professional investors meet the SEC's accredited investor definition requirements. By some informal accounts, funds from accredited investors make up between 60%–80% of the total funds raised in a direct token presale. Prior to the direct token presale, some portion of the tokens is "allocated" to the developers' entity and some to the developers individually as a type of compensation for the developers' efforts. Some networks allocate a portion of the tokens to be "mined" as a reward for users who run the network software and maintain the network's operation. The entity then sells rights to some portion of its tokens to the public, collecting in exchange anywhere from a few hundred thousand dollars to hundreds of millions of dollars.

In this way, the direct token presale is a sale of a utility token before it can function on the network or offer its intended utility. Some developers simply record each sale and promise to deliver a token when the network is built and functional. Some developers, immediately upon the execution of the sale, create and issue a pre-functional token—one that cannot yet function as intended on the network beyond the limited ability to be issued and traded on a secondary market exchange. Once the tokens exist and are tradeable, the purchasers and the entity are free to trade the tokens on any exchange that might list them.

The entity then builds the network. It uses the proceeds of the token pre-sales to fund development, including developers' salaries, office rent, utility bills, and the like. Though the entity is rarely obligated to its purchasers to build the network, almost all have embarked upon the task nonetheless.[10] As of the date of this writing, it is too early to tell whether these projects trend toward completion or abandonment. That said, the great majority of them seem, outwardly, to be working diligently toward completion.

One of the critical characteristics of the direct token presale model, for purposes of our later comparison to the SAFT Project, is that, in the typical direct token presale, tokens are sold widely to the public at a time when purchasers are still reliant on the developers to build a functional network. In a SAFT, no prefunctional tokens are ever created or sold, let alone released to the public and traded on exchanges.

. . . .

The Federal Securities Laws

It is illegal to offer or sell securities in the United States unless the offer and sale are exempt under the federal securities laws or made pursuant to an effective registration statement filed with the SEC. One kind of a security under federal law is an "investment contract."

We believe that the "investment contract" analysis is the best fit for analyzing most direct token presales under the federal securities laws.

. . . .

The *Howey* Test

Courts since the 1930s have generated significant analysis of what is meant by the term "investment contract." The Supreme Court in its 1946 decision in *SEC v. W.J. Howey Co.*, [326 U.S. 293, 298–99 (1946),] provided the seminal definition of that term. An investment contract was a "contract, transaction or scheme whereby a person invests his money in a common enterprise and is led to expect profits solely from the efforts of the promoter or a third party." Many courts in the succeeding seventy-one years have further expounded on each of the constituent parts of this test, now known as the *Howey* test.

Courts often break the *Howey* test into four prongs to determine (i) whether there exists an investment of money, (ii) whether there exists a common enterprise, (iii) whether there exists an expectation of profits, and (iv) whether the expectation of profits is solely from the efforts of others. If all prongs are satisfied, then a contract, scheme, or arrangement passes

---

[10]   Author's note: It is not clear that this statement has turned out to be accurate. "A recent study prepared by ICO advisory firm Statis Group revealed that more than 80 percent of initial coin offerings (ICOs) conducted in 2017 were identified as scams." Ana Alexandre, *New Study Says 80 Percent of ICOs Conducted in 2017 Were Scams*, COINTELEGRAPH (July 13, 2018) [archived at https://perma.cc/U7FR-6KX3]. According to these reports, of the $1.34 billion invested in ICO scams, most went to three projects: Pincoin ($660 million); Arisebank ($600 million) and Savedroid ($50 million).

the *Howey* test and constitutes a security. If any one of the prongs is not met, the arrangement fails the *Howey* test and there is no security. A comprehensive analysis of the application of the federal securities laws to any particular direct token presale is outside the scope of this whitepaper. However, we do note some of the more significant direct token presale trends in each of the following sections, organized by prong.

Investment of Money

A direct token presale typically requires participant purchasers to deliver a government currency or another digital asset such as bitcoin or ether in order to receive tokens in exchange. Although the original *Howey* test clearly references "money," more recent decisions have held that an investment of blockchain tokens such as bitcoin, or even an investment of labor, can satisfy this prong. Indeed, even donations can satisfy this prong. As a result, this prong of *Howey* is often met by direct token presales.

Common Enterprise

Direct token presales often admit of a common enterprise. Courts are split on what is the correct threshold for finding the existence of a common enterprise. The majority of courts apply the so-called horizontal commonality test. Under this approach, a common enterprise exists where multiple investors pool assets and share together in the profits and risks of the enterprise. A minority of courts instead apply the vertical commonality test. There are two variations on the vertical commonality formulation. Under the narrow vertical commonality variation, a common enterprise exists where the fortunes of the investors are bound up with the actual fortunes of the promoter or issuer of the security. Under the broad vertical commonality variation, a common enterprise exists where the fortunes of the investors are bound up with the mere efforts of the promoter or issuer.

Some direct token presales satisfy one or more of the variations on this prong, and some do not. Take horizontal commonality, for example. The developers have laid the groundwork for meeting this prong when (i) tokens are fungible, (ii) the entity pools all the money raised from selling the tokens, and (iii) the entity uses the pooled funds to build the network. Vertical commonality is rarer. To be sure, token purchasers might rely on the efforts of the developers to create the network, but that fact might support the "efforts of others" prong of the *Howey* test, not the broad variation of the vertical commonality prong, in which the fortunes of the investors must be bound up with the efforts of the issuer. Likewise, narrow vertical commonality is rare, since the purchasers' profit from the token sale is rarely dependent upon the ultimate profitability of the developers or their entity. The value of a truly decentralized network is decoupled from the financial success of the original developers. Moreover, the mission of many developers' entities is to expend all of its resources to develop an open, permission-less network that acts as a public good, slowly and expectedly entering insolvency as it does so.

Expectation of Profits

An expectation of profit generally means expected capital appreciation resulting from the development of the initial investment or expected participation in earnings resulting from the use of investor funds. There can be such an expectation where expected profits "come primarily from the discount below the current price" of a commodity. There is no expectation of profit where a purchaser is motivated primarily by the desire to use or consume the item purchased.

How much expectation of profit is permissible before the arrangement satisfies this prong? In *United Housing Foundation v. Forman*, [421 U.S. 837 (1975),] a purchaser of shares in cooperative housing almost certainly expected to sell the shares for more than the purchase price. . . .

To satisfy this prong, the purchaser's expectation of profit must predominate the expectation of using the thing purchased.

Direct token presales often satisfy this prong. In most direct token presales today, purchasers seem predominantly motivated by a desire to profit from the transaction. Most seem to hope to sell the token at a higher price than they paid. Some commentators have ignored this trend, or justified it by arguing that the developers' promise of future functionality is a substitute for a genuinely consumptive motive on the part of the purchaser. . . .

From the Efforts of Others

Assuming the purchaser's expectation of profit predominates any consumptive motive, this prong considers the source of that expectation. It asks "whether the efforts made by those other than the investor are the undeniably significant ones, those essential managerial efforts which affect the failure or success of the enterprise." An analysis of this prong in the token sale context requires a deep understanding of the rights, powers (and, sometimes, obligations) attendant to the token in question. Sadly, this prong and the prior prong are often conflated or collapsed into one another. We take up this issue in the following sections, through the lens of token functionality.

Already-functional Utility Tokens Are Unlikely to Pass the *Howey* Test

Sellers of already-functional utility tokens have very strong arguments against characterization as a security: Such tokens rarely satisfy both the "expectation of profits" and "from the efforts of others" prongs of the *Howey* test.

Generally speaking, there are two categories of purchasers of already-functional utility tokens. First, there are purchasers who buy tokens to actually use them—as network fees, membership coupons, value-staking mechanisms, currencies, etc. Their consumptive desires predominate their profit-seeking motives. Second, there are purchasers who buy a token expecting to profit merely from resale on a secondary market. These purchasers might have an "expectation of profit" under *Howey,* but it is usually not predominantly "from the efforts of others." Sales to purchasers in both of these two categories fail the *Howey* test.

The first category is self-evident. A profit motive simply does not predominate the transaction. The second category is more controversial. Critics of sales in this category might argue that the expectation of profit from resale on a secondary market is just speculative activity seeking capital appreciation. These critics might cite myriad federal court decisions holding that an expectation of mere "capital appreciation" on a secondary market, is sufficient to satisfy the *Howey* test.

This oft-repeated criticism does not stand up to scrutiny. At heart, the criticism collapses the "efforts of others" prong into the "expectation of profit" prong. It does so by relying on decisions which do not actually turn on the secondary market appreciation issue, and do not analyze it in much depth. Decisions that do so repeatedly hold that an expectation of profit from the mere increase in value on a secondary market is not from the "efforts of others." In *Noa v. Key Futures,* [638 F.2d 77 (9th Cir. 1980),] for example, a case involving a forward contract for silver bars, the Ninth Circuit found no expectation of profits from the efforts of others because once the purchase of silver bars was made, the profits to the investor depended primarily upon the fluctuations of the silver market, not the managerial efforts of Key Futures. *SEC v. Belmont Reid,* [794 F.2d 1388 (9th Cir.),] a case involving a forward contract for gold coins, held similarly because profits to the coin buyer depended primarily upon the fluctuations of the gold market, not the managerial efforts of others. In another case involving a futures contract for sugar, a federal court in New York held the presence of a speculative motive on the part of the purchaser or seller did not, on its own, evidence the existence of an investment contract. [*Sinva v. Merrill Lynch,* 253 F. Supp. 359, 367 (S.D.N.Y. 1966).]

To be sure: Gold, silver, and sugar are different from tokens in important ways. For example, in the case of a token sale, the seller may continue to improve the network and the secondary market price of the token may appreciate as a result. This characteristic is not shared by precious metals or sugar. So should utility tokens really be treated similarly?

For already-functional utility tokens, we think so. Because there is no central authority to exert "monetary policy," the secondary market price of a decentralized token system is driven exclusively by supply and demand. Supply and demand can be due to a variety of factors. One of those factors could be the efforts of the development team creating the token's functionality; but once that functionality is created, any "essential" efforts have by definition already been applied. It would be difficult to argue that any improvement on an already-functional token is an "essential" managerial effort.

Furthermore, the market effect of a mere improvement on an already functional utility token is likely dwarfed by the multitude of other factors that act on it. For example, the value of a token that powers a decentralized market for buying and selling graphics processing power in real time would likely fluctuate depending upon, among many other factors, the retail or wholesale availability of high-powered professional graphics cards. The value of a token that entitles a token holder to one box of the seller's razor blades might fluctuate with the popularity of beards in the company's target markets. The value of a token that permits users to store encrypted passwords conveniently on a blockchain might increase when a high-profile data breach is announced or decrease when a major keylogging botnet is disabled. Indeed, the value of bitcoin, another (mundane example of an) already-functional utility token, often fluctuates with changes in global geopolitical instability. The forces that could affect supply and demand for a functional utility token are countless. Supply and demand for functional tokens are affected by a variety of forces that determine the price on a secondary market—just like demand for gold in the commodity cases. It is no coincidence that blockchain tokens have been referred to as "digital gold." For functional utility tokens, mere price appreciation on a secondary market is not a substitute for the essential managerial efforts of others.

Indeed, for the purposes of the *Howey* analysis, the secondary market itself is a red herring. When a token purchaser resells a token on an exchange platform for more than the purchase price, it is not the exchange platform that created the price difference. To the contrary, the market is merely the venue where the token purchaser executes the sale. The relevant inquiry is not: "Did the purchaser expect profit from the sale on a secondary market?" It is: Of all the myriad forces affecting the secondary market price, do the "efforts of others" predominate or do the aggregated myriad forces predominate? In the case of the graphics-processing token, the predominant force one day could be the supply of rare metals required for fabricating graphics chips or the announcement of the next installment of a popular video game franchise. The next day, it could be a workers' strike at a major chip fabricator in Taiwan or the invention of a new compression algorithm. For an encrypted-password-storage token, it could very well be a data breach one day, a new law expanding (or limiting) data privacy the next day, or the announcement of a new hacking tool on the following day. For the razor blade token, it can be a trend among celebrities to don beards or the invention of an at-home laser hair removal process. These are the same kind of market forces and mechanics contemplated by the gold, silver, and sugar cases. The potential forces affecting any particular functional token are countless. It would be difficult to establish that, against this backdrop of global supply and demand dynamics, the developers' efforts still stand out as the "undeniably significant" effect on the price after the developers have expended their "essential" efforts and delivered a functional product.

Thus, an already-functional utility token is less likely to be a security for two independent grounds. First, it is more likely that purchasers have bought them to use them (since, unlike pre-functional utility tokens, they can be used immediately to satisfy imminent needs). Second, purchasers who buy them with an eye toward profit upon resale can expect those profits to be determined by a variety of market factors that predominate the efforts of the seller in updating the token's functionality.

There are, of course, limits to this position. Not all already-functional utility tokens will fail the *Howey* test simply by virtue of being functional. A later section of this whitepaper sets forth some of the limits on this position and, therefore, on the SAFT framework itself. Still, for an already-functional utility token, a great variety of forces can predominate the effects of the "efforts of others" on the purchaser's "expectation of profit." In the case of a pre-functional utility token, though, there is often just one force that clearly predominates.

. . . .

The Federal Money Services Laws

Federal law makes it a crime for anyone to knowingly conduct, control, manage, supervise, direct, or own all or part of a money transmitting business which is not licensed under state and federal law, referred to as an "unlicensed money transmitting business." We believe that some direct token presales may be characterized as unlicensed money transmitting businesses.

We focus our analysis on federal regulation promulgated by the Financial Crimes Enforcement Network ("FinCEN"). FinCEN, a bureau within the U.S. Department of the Treasury, oversees registration of money transmitting businesses. Through its regulations, FinCEN requires registration of a "money services business," a term that is defined to include "money transmitters." A "money transmitter" can be either: (i) a person that provides money transmission services, or (ii) any other person engaged in the transfer of funds. Money transmitter status is a matter of facts and circumstances, and explicitly excludes several categories of persons, including, in relevant part, anyone that only provides the medium for money transfers (such as a communications network), and anyone that accepts and transmits funds solely to facilitate the purchase of goods or services. FinCEN has explicitly stated that this exclusion applies to persons brokering the sale of commodity contracts or similar instruments.

FinCEN has published guidance to clarify whether a person dealing in cryptocurrency (which it terms "convertible virtual currency" or "CVC"), would fall under the definition of a money transmitter. In its guidance, FinCEN has stated that users of CVC are not money transmitters, but those who both issue and redeem CVC (administrators) and those who exchange CVC for either fiat or other CVC (exchangers) who accept and transmit funds as a business would be deemed money transmitters.

In further rulings, FinCEN has taken the position that a user is not a money transmitter if it is buying and selling CVC to make investments on its own account. Specifically, FinCEN has stated that non-money transmission activities in the context of CVC include "(in the case of a corporate user) making distributions to shareholders." In addition, FinCEN has explicitly stated that investments for a company's own account, even CVC investments, do not constitute money transmission activity.

Of particular importance to tokens, FinCEN originally took the position that "a person that creates units of convertible virtual currency and sells those units to another person for real currency or its equivalent is engaged in transmission to another location and is a money transmitter." In a subsequent ruling, however, presumably presented with additional data about the mining industry, it then added an important caveat to this position. It stated that "how a user obtains a virtual currency may be described using any number of other terms, such as . . .'mining,' 'creating,' . . .[or] 'manufacturing' "; that:

> it may be necessary for a user to convert Bitcoin that it has mined into a real currency or another convertible virtual currency, either because the seller of the goods or services the user wishes to purchase will not accept Bitcoin, or because the user wishes to diversify currency holdings in anticipation of future needs or for the user's own investment purposes;

and finally, that:

> in undertaking such a conversion transaction, the user is not acting as an exchanger, notwithstanding the fact that the user is accepting a real currency or another convertible virtual currency and transmitting Bitcoin.

Thus, FinCEN now arguably takes the straightforward position that a person can create a CVC and then sell it on its own account without being a money transmitter. The potential application of this reasoning to tokens is obvious. Yet, FinCEN has consistently maintained that "[a]n administrator or exchanger that (1) accepts and transmits a convertible virtual currency, or (2) buys or sells convertible virtual currency for any reason is a money transmitter." Thus, there is a risk that direct token presales violate the money transmission laws.

. . . .

The SAFT

The SAFT is a framework which seeks to navigate the federal securities and money-transmitter laws, provide greater flexibility for tax management. It further seeks to apply both investor protections and consumer protections, but timed to minimize their negative impacts and maximize their positive effects. The SAFT framework works for tokens which are not themselves independently securities. That is to say, it works for utility tokens, not securities tokens. The SAFT would have little or no beneficial effect for a DAO Token-like arrangement, for example.

The SAFT is based on the Y Combinator Simple Agreement for Future Equity, or "SAFE," which has been widely used to finance early stage companies for many years. Both the SAFE and the SAFT memorialize an exchange of investment capital in an early stage or developing company for the right to something of value in the future for the investor—preferred stock in the case of the SAFE, and functional utility tokens in the case of a SAFT.

In short, the SAFT provides investors with the right to fully-functional utility tokens, delivered once the network is created and the tokens are functional. The SAFT is very likely a security, namely an investment contract. Once the tokens have been imbued with utility and are genuinely functional, the SAFT investors' rights in the SAFT automatically convert into a right to delivery of the tokens. For the now-functional utility tokens, there is a very strong argument that the tokens themselves are not securities. The same should apply to any ultimate sale of the tokens to retail purchasers, whether by the SAFT investors or by the seller.

Still, a SAFT is not a SAFE, and a SAFT is not "safe." Indeed, no court, regulator, or taxing authority has yet interpreted the SAFT framework, nor can the SAFT claim the transactional history and ubiquity of the SAFE.

As described above, SAFTs were created with the express purpose of reducing regulatory risk for ICO issuers. This is reflected even in the subtitle of the whitepaper introducing the SAFT concept, "Toward a Compliant Token Sale Framework." Some of the largest ICOs have relied upon the SAFT structure for exactly that reason. This includes the 2017 Filecoin offering and the 2018 Telegram offering. Filecoin raised more than $250 million in its offering, and Telegram was even more successful. Its potential target was originally set at $1.2 billion to be raised in a combination private offering followed by a public sale. That target amount was subsequently raised, and Telegram actually raised approximately $1.7 billion in private sales, according to documents filed with the SEC. It was at that point when Telegram ran into regulatory difficulties that caused it to cancel its planned public sale.

In March of 2018, the SEC sent a wave of subpoenas and information requests to companies engaged in ICOs. Moreover, it appears that the SEC was specifically focusing its investigative efforts on SAFTs. This was confirmed both by stories in the Wall Street Journal and from CoinDesk, both of which quote a reportedly knowledgeable source who had unambiguously stated: "The SEC is targeting SAFTs."[11]

Given the whitepaper's explanation as to why utility tokens should not be securities, it may not be immediately obvious why the SEC has apparently taken such a potentially aggressive stance against the SAFT. The reality, however, is that investors may be more interested in speculation rather than any "utility" of either a promised or even existing token. Crowdfund Insider describes itself as "the leading news and information web site covering the emerging global industry of disruptive finance including crowdfunding, Blockchain . . . and other forms of Fintech." In its coverage of ICOs, this source specifically noted that "if you invest in an ICO, the play is to speculate on the price of the crypto once it is traded on a cryptocurrency exchange."[12] To the extent that speculation is governing decisions to purchase crypto, the case for treating the sale of tokens as involving the sale of a security is heightened.

Similarly, the whitepaper draws a number of conclusions that, with the benefit of hindsight, may not be warranted. For example, at one point, the whitepaper compares the SAFT to forward contracts in gold and silver. Both of those kinds of transaction were found by lower courts not to involve the sale of securities on the grounds that they did not involve the expectation of profits from the efforts of others. Instead, investors were relying on myriad market forces to set the future price of the underlying commodities. The comparison to crypto, especially newly developed crypto and crypto that is not yet traded on regulated exchanges, seems to be relatively weak.

In many cases, the issuer and original development team behind a new cryptoasset continues to be extremely important in its ongoing value. Gold

---

[11]   The Wall Street Journal story appeared in February. Jean Eaglesham & Paul Vigna, *Cryptocurrency Firms Targeted in SEC Probe*, WALL ST. J. (updated Feb. 28, 2018) (available online at https://www.wsj.com/articles/sec-launches-cryptocurrency-probe-1519856266?mod=searchresults&page=1&pos=1). CoinDesk report came out a few days later, in early March. Brady Dale, *What If the SEC Is Going After the SAFT?*, COINDESK (Mar. 6, 2018) (available online at https://www.coindesk.com/sec-going-saft).

[12]   JD Alois, *Most US Crowdfunding Platforms will Become Broker Dealers and Some May Become ATSs*, CROWDFUND INSIDER (Mar. 11, 2018) (available online at https://www.ycombinator.com/documents/).

and silver have tangible existence; crypto does not. Without a base promoting its usefulness, and making sure that the usefulness continues, it is not at all obvious that market forces drive pricing of even fully functional utility tokens.

Consider Ripple's XRP token. It has functionality (in that it provides access), Ripple has explicitly avoided recommending it as an investment for the public,[13] and it has a relatively broad trading market that doubtless affects price. However, the actions of Ripple in matters such as deciding how to release its store of tokens and its ongoing efforts at promoting the usefulness of the token in the financial services sector also clearly influence the value of the token.[14] Thus the fact that XRP is a "utility token" is not likely to be the determinative factor under *Howey*.

This is not to say that the whitepaper is always wrong. When a cryptoasset is released to the public and the issuer or creator has no essential role to play in the pricing of that asset, it may indeed mean that the interest is not properly characterized as a security. A case in point here would be Bitcoin itself. Obviously, the efforts of the pseudonymous Satoshi Nakamoto were absolutely essential to the creation and original launch of Bitcoin. But once Bitcoin was released, Nakamoto had little more to do with the success of the venture. Given that the true identity of the Bitcoin creator has never been released, it is fairly clear that it is the efforts of others at work in the pricing of this cryptocurrency. Moreover, those others are now so widely dispersed that there is no one person or group of influencers to whom investors can turn. This means that when a member of the public "invests" in Bitcoin, they are not doing so in reliance on the efforts of the developer or any other identifiable person or group, and instead are speculating on how market forces will play out. This is certainly not how securities have traditionally worked.

4. MUNCHEE

The distinction advanced in the SAFT whitepaper between security tokens and utility tokens was not new. Commentary among self-proclaimed crypto-pioneers widely bought into the notion that "utility" tokens should not be regarded as securities.

One source explained the distinction as follows in September of 2018, shortly before the final release of the SAFT whitepaper described above:

---

[13]   "In the homepage of Tipple guide, a sentence states 'Ripple (the company) **does not** promote XRP as a speculative investment.'" Alex Y, *What Is Ripple Coin (XRP)? Where Can I Buy Ripple?*, MANAGE YOUR FINANCE (available online at https://managingyourfinance.com/what-is-ripple-coin-xrp-where-i-can-buy-ripple) (noting that the company does promote the token to banks).

[14]   Larry Cermak, *Do Ripple executives' statements imply that XRP is a security?* THE BLOCK (Dec.6, 2018) (available online at https://www.theblockcrypto.com/2018/12/06/do-ripple-executives-statements-imply-that-xrp-is-a-security/).

Utility tokens are simply app coins or user tokens. They enable future access to the products or services offered by a company. Therefore, utility tokens are not created to be an investment.

. . . .

A security token is a digital asset that derives its value from an external asset that can be traded. Therefore, these tokens are subject to federal laws that govern securities.[15]

A similarly strict demarcation between utility and security tokens was drawn by Toju Ometoruwa in 2016.[16] While Ometoruwa acknowledged that "securities tokens" would be evaluated under the *Howey* test and would need to be sold in accordance with the federal securities laws, he also argued that utility tokens were essentially unregulated, even if the promised tokens were never developed. His understanding of "utility token" therefore was quite different from that advanced in the SAFT whitepaper.

In fact, the way in which the public appears to understand utility tokens and security tokens seems to be relatively simplistic (albeit not entirely consistent). For example, another source claimed that merely disclaiming intent to market a token as an investment should keep the interest from being a security. As explained by this commentator, a "[u]tility token or an 'app token' is a token that has a practical use in a company's ecosystem. Usually a company will launch these tokens and will explicitly add that said tokens are NOT being designed as investments; this practice makes sure to exempt the token from federal laws governing securities."[17]

The SEC was plainly not impressed with this analysis. SEC Chairman Jay Clayton had previously released a public statement warning that "certain market professionals have attempted to highlight utility characteristics of their proposed initial coin offerings in an effort to claim that their proposed tokens or coins are not securities. Many of these assertions appear to elevate form over substance. Merely calling a token a 'utility' token or structuring it to provide some utility does not prevent the token from being a security."[18]

The SEC's involvement with Munchee Inc., a California business that had created an iPhone application designed to allow users to post

---

[15]   Katalyse.io, *Security Tokens vs. Utility Tokens—How different are they?* HACKERNOON (Sept. 27, 2018) [archived at https://perma.cc/2EBX-3LWZ].

[16]   Toju Ometoruwa, *Security vs. Utility Tokens: The Complete Guide*, CRYPTOPOTATO (Sept. 16, 2016) [archived at https://perma.cc/DU64-QETN].

[17]   Torsten Hartmann, *Are security tokens the new standard? What is the difference between security vs. utility tokens*, CAPTAINALTCOIN (Nov. 11, 2018) (available online at https://captain altcoin.com/security-vs-utility-tokens/).

[18]   SEC, Public Statement, *Statement of Cryptocurrencies and Initial Coin Offerings* (Dec. 11, 2017) [archived at https://perma.cc/Y5LE-47BF].

restaurant reviews, further demonstrates the SEC's position with regard to so-called utility tokens.

In many respects, Munchee Inc. (Munchee) was a typical company with an interest in raising funds through an ICO. It had developed its iPhone App and wanted to raise approximately $15 million to improve the application through the sale of blockchain-based digital tokens or coins (MUNs). On Oct. 1, 2017, Munchee announced that its plans to launch an ICO in which 500 million MUNs would be sold to the public. At the same time, Munchee posted a "whitepaper," describing the tokens, how they would be sold, what the proceeds would be used for, and projections about how the MUNs could increase in value and be traded.

The documentation explained that the MUNs would be integrated into the company's existing iPhone application and used for a range of additional transactions, including advertisements and food sales. The distribution method was described as involving sales on various websites located in the U.S. and across the globe.

The entire plan was relatively typical of ICOs of the time. The plan of distribution included a "pre-sale" at a discount for early purchasers, retention of a sizeable proportion of the tokens (55%) for use by the company to support its business, and future development of additional functionality. The documentation released by Munchee described a two-year period in which the company planned to develop a smart contracts on the Ethereum blockchain to automatically upgrade the MUNs. Finally, Munchee promised action to develop a liquid secondary market for its tokens. The whitepaper claimed that MUNs could be traded on at least one U.S.-based crypto exchange within 30 days after the conclusion of the ICO. Munchee also indicated plans to trade in the tokens to ensure liquidity.

The whitepaper also addressed how Munchee believed that it fit into the existing regulatory environment. Munchee explicitly referenced the SEC's earlier DAO Report and stated that the company had done a *Howey* analysis." The whitepaper concluded that "as currently designed, the sale of MUN utility tokens does not pose a significant risk of implicating federal securities laws." Munchee based this conclusion on the fact that the MUNs would be used in the iPhone application and that they were therefore "utility tokens" and not "securities."

In the days following the release of the whitepaper, Munchee posted information about its tokens and the planned ICO on Munchee's primary webpage and a variety of social media platforms and message boards. On October 31, 2017, Munchee launched the ICO. One day later, on November 1, the SEC staff called, and Munchee voluntarily halted its ICO within hours. Munchee not only unilaterally terminated its ICO but also rescinded the contracts of sale it had entered into with investors and returned their funds. Notwithstanding the immediate cooperation of Munchee, the SEC decided to pursue the matter further.

Applying the *Howey* test, the SEC found that the MUNs were securities and that Munchee had violated the Securities Act by selling MUNs to the public without complying with the registration requirements. In light of the prompt remedial action taken by Munchee, the SEC elected not to impose a civil penalty. Instead, it imposed a cease and desist order on any future violations of Sections 5(a) and (c) of the Securities Act by Munchee. Excerpts from that order (including both the underlying facts and the SEC's legal analysis of those facts) are excerpted here.

IN RE MUNCHEE INC.

SEC Release No. 10445, File No. 3–18304 (Dec. 11, 2017)

ORDER INSTITUTING CEASE AND DESIST PROCEEDINGS . . .

I.

The Securities and Exchange Commission ("Commission") deems it appropriate that cease-and-desist proceedings be, and hereby are, instituted pursuant to Section 8A of the Securities Act of 1933 ("Securities Act") against Munchee Inc. ("Munchee" or "Respondent").

II.

In anticipation of the institution of these proceedings, Respondent has submitted an Offer of Settlement (the "Offer") which the Commission has determined to accept.

. . . .

III.

On the basis of this Order and Respondent's Offer, the Commission finds that:

Summary

Munchee is a California business that created an iPhone application ("app") for people to review restaurant meals. In October and November 2017, Munchee offered and then sold digital tokens ("MUN" or "MUN token") to be issued on a blockchain or a distributed ledger. Munchee conducted the offering of MUN tokens to raise about $15 million in capital so that it could improve its existing app and recruit users to eventually buy advertisements, write reviews, sell food and conduct other transactions using MUN. In connection with the offering, Munchee described the way in which MUN tokens would increase in value as a result of Munchee's efforts and stated that MUN tokens would be traded on secondary markets.

Based on the facts and circumstances set forth below, MUN tokens were securities pursuant to Section 2(a)(1) of the Securities Act. MUN tokens are "investment contracts" under *SEC v. W. J. Howey Co.*, 328 U.S. 293 (1946), and its progeny, including the cases discussed by the Commission in its Report of Investigation Pursuant To Section 21(a) Of The Securities Exchange Act of 1934: The DAO (Exchange Act Rel. No. 81207) (July 25, 2017) (the "DAO Report"). Among other characteristics of an "investment contract," a purchaser of MUN tokens would have had a reasonable expectation of obtaining a future profit based upon Munchee's efforts, including Munchee revising its app and creating the MUN "ecosystem" using the proceeds from the sale of MUN tokens. Munchee violated Sections 5(a) and 5(c) of the Securities Act by offering and selling these securities without having a registration statement filed or in effect with the Commission or qualifying for exemption from registration with the Commission. On the second day of sales of MUN tokens, the company was contacted by Commission staff. The company determined within hours to shut down its offering, did not deliver any tokens to purchasers, and returned to purchasers the proceeds that it had received.

Respondent

Munchee is a privately-owned Delaware corporation based in San Francisco.

Facts

1.   Munchee is a California business that created an app (the "Munchee App") for use with iPhones. The company began developing the app in late 2015 and launched the app in the second quarter of 2017.

2.   The Munchee App allows users to post photographs and reviews of meals that they eat in restaurants. The Munchee App is available only in the United States.

3.   Munchee and its agencies control the content on multiple web pages. . . .

Munchee Offers To Sell MUN To The General Public

4.   By Fall 2017, Munchee had developed a plan to improve the Munchee App during 2018 and 2019 that included raising capital through the creation of the MUN token and incorporating the token into the Munchee App. The MUN is a token issued on the Ethereum blockchain. Munchee created 500 million MUN tokens and stated that no additional tokens could be created.

5.   On or about October 1, 2017, Munchee announced it would be launching an "initial coin offering" or "ICO"[1] to offer MUN tokens to the

---

[1]   An "initial coin offering" or "ICO" is a recently developed form of fundraising event in which an entity offers participants a unique digital "coin" or "token" in exchange for consideration (most commonly Bitcoin, Ether, or fiat currency). The tokens are issued and distributed on a

general public. Munchee posted the MUN White Paper that described MUN tokens, the offering process, how Munchee would use the offering proceeds to develop its business, the way in which MUN tokens would increase in value, and the ability for MUN token holders to trade MUN tokens on secondary markets. . . .

6.   MUN tokens were to be available for purchase by individuals in the United States and worldwide . . . .

7.   Pursuant to the MUN White Paper, Munchee sought to raise about $15 million in Ether by selling 225 million MUN tokens out of the 500 million total MUN tokens . . . .

8.   The MUN White Paper referenced the DAO Report and stated that Munchee had done a *"Howey* analysis" and that "as currently designed, the sale of MUN utility tokens does not pose a significant risk of implicating federal securities laws." The MUN White Paper, however, did not set forth any such analysis.

Munchee's Plan To Create An "Ecosystem" And Take Other Steps To Increase The Value Of MUN

9.   Munchee offered MUN tokens in order to raise capital to build a profitable enterprise. Munchee said that it would use the offering proceeds to run its business, including hiring people to develop its product, promoting the Munchee App, and ensuring "the smooth operation of the MUN token ecosystem."

10.   While Munchee told potential purchasers that they would be able to use MUN tokens to buy goods or services in the future after Munchee created an "ecosystem," no one was able to buy any good or service with MUN throughout the relevant period.

11.   On the Munchee Website, in the MUN White Paper and elsewhere, Munchee described the "ecosystem" that it would create. . . . As a result, MUN tokens would increase in value. . . .

12.   In the MUN White Paper, on the Munchee Website and elsewhere, Munchee and its agents further emphasized that the company would run its business in ways that would cause MUN tokens to rise in value. . . .

13.   Munchee intended for MUN tokens to trade on a secondary market.

"blockchain" or cryptographically-secured ledger. Tokens often are also listed and traded on online platforms, typically called virtual currency exchanges, and they usually trade for other digital assets or fiat currencies. Often, tokens are listed and tradeable immediately after they are issued.

Issuers often release a "white paper" describing the particular project they seek to fund and the terms of the ICO. Issuers often pay others to promote the offering, including through social media channels such as message boards, online videos, blogs, Twitter, and Facebook. There are websites and social media feeds dedicated to discussions about ICOs and the offer, sale and trading of coins and tokens

. . . .

Munchee Promoted MUN Tokens And Purchasers Had A Reasonable Expectation Of Obtaining A Future Profit

14. Purchasers reasonably would have viewed the MUN token offering as an opportunity to profit. Purchasers had a reasonable expectation that they would obtain a future profit from buying MUN tokens if Munchee were successful in its entrepreneurial and managerial efforts to develop its business. Purchasers would reasonably believe they could profit by holding or trading MUN tokens, whether or not they ever used the Munchee App or otherwise participated in the MUN "ecosystem," based on Munchee's statements in its MUN White Paper and other materials. Munchee primed purchasers' reasonable expectations of profit through statements on blogs, podcasts, and Facebook that talked about profits.

[Specific allegations about how Munchee promoted potential profitability of the MUN tokens are omitted.]

MUN Token Purchasers Reasonably Expected They Would Profit From The Efforts Of Munchee And Its Agents

21. Purchasers would reasonably have had the expectation that Munchee and its agents would expend significant efforts to develop an application and "ecosystem" that would increase the value of their MUN tokens.

22. Munchee highlighted the credentials, abilities and management skills of its agents and employees. For example, in the MUN White Paper and elsewhere, Munchee highlighted that its founders had worked at prominent technology companies and highlighted their skills running businesses and creating software.

. . . .

[Additional allegations about how Munchee promoted its efforts are omitted].

Munchee Starts To Sell MUN On October 31, 2017

25. On or about October 31, 2017, Munchee started selling MUN tokens. Purchasers could pay one (1) Ether or one-twentieth (1/20) of a Bitcoin to buy 4,500 MUN. On or about November 1, 2017, Ether was trading on virtual currency exchanges for about $300 USD and Bitcoin was trading for about $6,500 USD.

Munchee Stopped Selling MUN When It Was Contacted By Commission Staff

26. On November 1, 2017, Munchee stopped selling MUN tokens hours after being contacted by Commission staff. Munchee had not

delivered any tokens to purchasers, and the company promptly returned to purchasers the proceeds that it had received.[2]

27. About 40 people purchased MUN tokens from Munchee. In aggregate, they paid about 200 Ether (or about $60,000 in USD at the time of the offering).

<u>**Legal Analysis**</u>

28. Under Section 2(a)(1) of the Securities Act, a security includes "an investment contract." See 15 U.S.C. § 77b. An investment contract is an investment of money in a common enterprise with a reasonable expectation of profits to be derived from the entrepreneurial or managerial efforts of others. *See SEC v. Edwards,* 540 U.S. 389, 393 (2004); *SEC v. W.J. Howey Co.,* 328 U.S. 293, 301 (1946); *see also United Housing Found., Inc. v. Forman,* 421 U.S. 837, 852–53 (1975) (The "touchstone" of an investment contract "is the presence of an investment in a common venture premised on a reasonable expectation of profits to be derived from the entrepreneurial or managerial efforts of others."). This definition embodies a *"flexible rather than a static principle,* one that is capable of adaptation to meet the countless and variable schemes devised by those who seek the use of the money of others on the promise of profits." *Howey,* 328 U.S. at 299 (emphasis added). The test "permits the fulfillment of the statutory purpose of compelling full and fair disclosure relative to the issuance of 'the many types of instruments that in our commercial world fall within the ordinary concept of a security.' " *Id.* In analyzing whether something is a security, "form should be disregarded for substance," *Tcherepnin v. Knight,* 389 U.S. 332, 336 (1967), "and the emphasis should be on economic realities underlying a transaction, and not on the name appended thereto." Forman, 421 U.S. at 849.

29. As the Commission discussed in the DAO Report, tokens, coins or other digital assets issued on a blockchain may be securities under the federal securities laws, and, if they are securities, issuers and others who offer or sell them in the United States must register the offering and sale with the Commission or qualify for an exemption from registration.

A.   The MUN Tokens Were Securities

30. As described above, the MUN tokens were securities as defined by Section 2(a)(1) of the Securities Act because they were investment contracts.

31. Munchee offered and sold MUN tokens in a general solicitation that included potential investors in the United States. Investors paid Ether

---

[2]   Munchee and the investors entered into a contract of sale for MUN in which investors were irrevocably bound. On November 1, 2017, Munchee unilaterally terminated the contracts of sale, returning the money to investors. Any offer by Munchee to buy the investors' securities would have required registration of the transaction or an exemption from registration.

or Bitcoin to purchase their MUN tokens. Such investment is the type of contribution of value that can create an investment contract.

32. MUN token purchasers had a reasonable expectation of profits from their investment in the Munchee enterprise. The proceeds of the MUN token offering were intended to be used by Munchee to build an "ecosystem" that would create demand for MUN tokens and make MUN tokens more valuable. Munchee was to revise the Munchee App so that people could buy and sell services using MUN tokens and was to recruit "partners" such as restaurants willing to sell meals for MUN tokens. The investors reasonably expected they would profit from any rise in the value of MUN tokens created by the revised Munchee App and by Munchee's ability to create an "ecosystem"—for example, the system described in the offering where restaurants would want to use MUN tokens to buy advertising from Munchee or to pay rewards to app users, and where app users would want to use MUN tokens to pay for restaurant meals and would want to write reviews to obtain MUN tokens. In addition, Munchee highlighted that it would ensure a secondary trading market for MUN tokens would be available shortly after the completion of the offering and prior to the creation of the ecosystem. Like many other instruments, the MUN token did not promise investors any dividend or other periodic payment. Rather, as indicated by Munchee and as would have reasonably been understood by investors, investors could expect to profit from the appreciation of value of MUN tokens resulting from Munchee's efforts.

33. Investors' profits were to be derived from the significant entrepreneurial and managerial efforts of others—specifically Munchee and its agents—who were to revise the Munchee App, create the "ecosystem" that would increase the value of MUN (through both an increased demand for MUN tokens by users and Munchee's specific efforts to cause appreciation in value, such as by burning MUN tokens), and support secondary markets. Investors had little choice but to rely on Munchee and its expertise. At the time of the offering and sale of MUN tokens, no other person could make changes to the Munchee App or was working to create an "ecosystem" to create demand for MUN tokens.

34. Investors' expectations were primed by Munchee's marketing of the MUN token offering. To market the MUN token offering, Munchee and its agents created the Munchee Website and the MUN White Paper and then posted on message boards, social media and other outlets. They described how Munchee would revise the Munchee App and how the new "ecosystem" would create demand for MUN tokens. They likened MUN to prior ICOs and digital assets that had created profits for investors, and they specifically marketed to people interested in those assets—and those profits—rather than to people who, for example, might have wanted MUN tokens to buy advertising or increase their "tier" as a reviewer on the Munchee App. Because of the conduct and marketing materials of Munchee

and its agents, investors would have had a reasonable belief that Munchee and its agents could be relied on to provide the significant entrepreneurial and managerial efforts required to make MUN tokens a success.

35. Even if MUN tokens had a practical use at the time of the offering, it would not preclude the token from being a security. Determining whether a transaction involves a security does not turn on labelling—such as characterizing an ICO as involving a "utility token"—but instead requires an assessment of "the economic realities underlying a transaction." *Forman,* 421 U.S. at 849. All of the relevant facts and circumstances are considered in making that determination. *See Forman,* 421 U.S. at 849 (purchases of "stock" solely for purpose of obtaining housing not purchase of "investment contract"); *see also SEC v. C.M. Joiner Leasing Corp.,* 320 U.S. 344, 352–53 (1943) (indicating the "test . . . is what character the instrument is given in commerce by the terms of the offer, the plan of distribution, and the economic inducements held out to the prospect").

B.   Munchee Offered And Sold MUN Tokens In Violation Of The Securities Act

36. As described above, Munchee offered and sold securities to the general public, including potential investors in the United States, and actually sold securities to about 40 investors. No registration statements were filed or in effect for the MUN token offers and sales and no exemptions from registration were available.

37. As a result of the conduct described above, Munchee violated Section 5(a) of the Securities Act, which states that unless a registration statement is in effect as to a security, it shall be unlawful for any person, directly or indirectly, to make use of any means or instruments of transportation or communication in interstate commerce or of the mails to sell such security through the use or medium of any prospectus or otherwise; or to carry or cause to be carried through the mails or in interstate commerce, by any means or instruments of transportation, any such security for the purpose of sale or for delivery after sale.

38. Also as a result of the conduct described above, Munchee violated Section 5(c) of the Securities Act, which states that it shall be unlawful for any person, directly or indirectly, to make use of any means or instruments of transportation or communication in interstate commerce or of the mails to offer to sell or offer to buy through the use or medium of any prospectus or otherwise any security, unless a registration statement has been filed as to such security.

Munchee's Remedial Actions

39. In determining to accept the Offer, and to not impose a civil penalty, the Commission considered remedial acts promptly undertaken by Respondent and cooperation afforded the Commission staff.

. . . .

NOTES AND QUESTIONS

1.   There were no allegations of fraud or intentional misconduct in connection with this particular ICO. Given that, who is the SEC protecting by preventing the Munchee ICO from proceeding as planned?

2.   The SEC order emphasizes the importance of the fact that during the relevant period (presumably during the ICO) " "no one was able to buy any good or service with" the MUN tokens. This clearly suggests that a pre-functional token is more likely to be classified as a security, but does the inverse also hold true? Is a functional token significantly less likely to be a token (as the SAFT whitepaper suggested)? In answering this question, consider the following language: "Even if the Munchee tokens had a practical use at the time of the offering, it would not preclude the token from being a security. Determining whether a transaction involves a security does not turn on labelling—such as characterizing an ICO as involving a 'utility token'—but instead requires an assessment of 'the economic realities underlying a transaction.' All of the relevant facts and circumstances are considered in making that determination." (*See* Order, ¶ 35.)

3.   The order also emphasizes the planned Munchee "ecosystem," in which Munchee would run the company so as to cause the tokens to increase in value. What is the relevance of this fact to the SEC's conclusion that the MUN tokens were securities? What would have happened if Munchee had, instead, reported that the efforts of Munchee customers and MUN tokenholders would be responsible for success of the token? Could Munchee have offered incentives to tokenholders who took actions designed to increase the value of the tokens and still argue that the "essential efforts" for creating profits would be those of the tokenholders rather than the company?

4.   The order also relies on the fact that Munchee promised to use efforts to create and support a secondary market, both by promising that the MUN tokens would be traded on at least one crypto exchange within 30 days of the conclusion of the ICO and additional promises related to Munchee's agreement to support and maintain the value of the tokens on the secondary market. Why are these activities relevant to whether the tokens are properly classified as securities?

5. CRYPTO EXCHANGES—THE EXAMPLE OF COINBASE

There is another aspect to crypto that is of considerable importance to issuers and users of cryptoassets. The value of most crypto depends on the ability of purchasers to trade it. This is certainly true for cryptocurrencies that are designed to replace fiat. Without a market for crypto, it will have limited or no utility, usefulness, or value. How do owners who wish to sell their crypto find buyers who wish to buy it?

As referenced in Chapter 7, the federal securities laws, and in particular the '34 Act (technically the Securities Exchange Act of 1934) also cover securities exchanges. Among other things, § 5 of the '34 Act essentially makes it unlawful for any exchange to effect any transaction in a security unless the exchange is registered as a national securities exchange or exempt from this requirement. Section 3(a)(1) of the '34 Act defines an "exchange" as anyone or any group "which constitutes, maintains, or provides a market place or facilities for bringing together purchasers and sellers of securities" or which performs functions commonly performed by stock exchanges.[19] Applicable regulations utilize a functional test to determine whether a trading system is an exchange under this provision. Under Exchange Act Rule 3b–16(a), a trading system constitutes an exchange if it (1) brings together the orders for securities of multiple buyers and sellers; and (2) uses established, non-discretionary methods (whether by providing a trading facility or by setting rules) pursuant to which buyers and sellers enter into agreed-upon trades.

In considering how compliant businesses seeking to provide these kinds of services may operate, it is worth considering the history of one of the largest such ventures: Coinbase.[20] Coinbase was founded in 2012 by Brian Armstrong and Fred Ehrsam. According to the company's website, Coinbase "is the easiest place to buy, sell, and manage your cryptocurrency portfolio."[21] It is based in San Francisco, California.

Coinbase claims a widespread investor base, including several Wall Street companies and Y Combinator, and was the first crypto trading platform to achieve a market value in excess of $1 billion. Today, Coinbase is one of the largest and most popular Bitcoin trading platforms, supporting more than 10 languages across 30 different countries. Coinbase is also licensed in most U.S. states.[22]

Although it was originally an online platform that sold Bitcoin and offered relatively basic wallet services, Coinbase now offers a wide range of services, including Coinbase Pro (formerly the GDAX exchange). Throughout the operating history of the company, Coinbase has worked to

---

[19]   15 U.S. Code § 78c(a)(1).

[20]   For a more examination of Coinbase, *see Coinbase—Security, Exchange, Vault, Wallet, Fees and More*, BITCOINEXCHANGEGUIDE (May 5, 2017) (available online at https://bitcoin exchangeguide.com/coinbase/).

[21]   *See* https://www.coinbase.com (slogan as of Sept. 25, 2019). Prior statements include the claim that Coinbase is "a digital currency wallet and platform where merchants and consumers can transact with new digital currencies like bitcoin, ethereum, and litecoin."

[22]   Although this book does not focus in great detail on state regulations, this topic is introduced and covered in general fashion in chapter 14. According to the Coinbase website, United States Coinbase, Inc., the company which operates Coinbase and GDAX in the U.S., is licensed to engage in money transmission in most U.S. jurisdictions. Coinbase is also registered as a Money Services Business with FinCEN, meaning that Coinbase complies with the Bank Secrecy Act requirements including Patriot Act obligations. Coinbase, *Legal FAQ* (available online at https://www.coinbase.com/legal/faq).

establish and maintain relationships with governing and regulatory bodies around the world.

In March of 2018, the SEC issued a public statement about unregistered online trading platforms.[23] In this statement, the SEC acknowledged the popularity of such platforms, which allow investors to buy and sell digital assets, including coins and tokens which may have been acquired in ICOs.

The SEC further expressed concern that many of these traded assets meet the definition of "security" under federal law, and therefore the platforms should be subject to regulation as exchanges or alternative trading systems. Instead, although many of these platforms look and operate like traditional online securities exchanges, they have neither registered nor found an exemption. Moreover, despite frequent claims that the exchanges offer only "high quality assets" or hold themselves to "the strictest of standards," these claims are neither reviewed nor verified.

As a result, the SEC cautioned the trading public that they "should not assume the trading protocols meet the standards of an SEC-registered national securities exchange."[24] Regardless of whether the exchange looks like a traditional exchange, or creates the impression that they are performing the same services as a traditional securities exchange, the SEC has concluded that "there is no reason to believe that such information has the same integrity as that provided by national securities exchanges."[25]

Shortly after the SEC's public statement, in early April 2018, the Wall Street Journal reported that Coinbase had made moves to register with the SEC as a licensed brokerage firm and compliant trading venue.[26] Other sources confirmed the significance of this development:

> The San Francisco based company is one of the largest platforms in the world for trading Bitcoin and other cryptocurrencies. It is currently valued at $1.6 billion according to the Wall Street Journal. The company declined to officially comment on its application, however the report indicates that Coinbase representatives have met with SEC officials in recent weeks to begin the process of registering with the agency. This step would allow Coinbase to add digital tokens that the SEC has ruled as

---

[23] SEC, Public Statement, *Statement on Potentially Unlawful Online Platforms for Trading Digital Assets* (Mar. 7, 2018) [archived at https://perma.cc/V6N7-YRHL].

[24] *Id.*

[25] *Id.*

[26] Dave Michaels, *Cryptocurrency Firm Coinbase in Talks to Become SEC-Regulated Brokerage*, THE WALL ST. J. (Ap. 6, 2018) (available online at https://www.wsj.com/articles/cryptocurrency-firm-coinbase-in-talks-to-become-sec-regulated-brokerage-1523043315).

securities and could up the ante for other crypto exchanges to follow suit and register as well.[27]

In June 2018, it was reported that Coinbase had acquired Keystone Capital Corporation, a financial services firm and regulated broker-dealer, and had initiated the process to become a fully regulated broker-dealer, in compliance with both SEC and FINRA requirements. The announcement was made June 6, 2018, by Asiff Hirji, President and COO of the exchange. "Today we're excited to announce that we're on track to become a US-regulated blockchain securities trading venue. We believe this is an important moment not only for Coinbase, but the entire crypto ecosystem."[28]

The SEC and FINRA approved Coinbase' acquisition, and a month later this was hailed as the first fully registered site allowed to list, sell, and facilitate trades in crypto securities. The approval also meant that Coinbase is now authorized as an alternative trading system (ATS), meaning that it does not need to become a registered national securities exchange in order to comply with the U.S. securities laws.[29]

NOTES AND QUESTIONS

1.   What services do crypto exchanges provide? Why is the availability of functioning, compliant exchanges important, and to whom? Do exchanges have any control over the functioning of crypto that is traded on their platform?

2.   From the perspectives of persons who invest in crypto, is there a difference between the services available on an exchange and an ATS? What distinguishes between the various options?

3.   What did Coinbase do that enabled it to become an ATS? Who can use the Coinbase ATS services? How does having Coinbase become an ATS serve the interests of the public, the SEC, FinCEN, or other federal regulators?

---

[27]   John McMahon, *Coinbase Seeks SEC Approval to Become Licensed Brokerage*, NEWSBTC (Ap. 10, 2018) (available online at https://www.newsbtc.com/2018/04/10/coinbase-seeks-sec-approval-become-licensed-brokerage/).

[28]   Asiff Hirji, Our path to listing SEC-regulated crypto securities, Coinbase Blog (Jun 6, 2018) (available online at https://blog.coinbase.com/our-path-to-listing-sec-regulated-crypto-securities-a1724e13bb5a).

[29]   For more information about this process, see *Coinbase Is Officially A Regulated Securities Broker-Dealer*, XBT.NET BLOG (updated Jul. 17, 2018) (available online at https://xbt.net/blog/coinbase-is-officially-a-regulated-securities-broker-dealer/).

CHAPTER 9

FRAUDULENT OFFERINGS

■ ■ ■

Another reason for the SEC's interest in crypto is the considerable potential for fraud that exists, particularly (although not exclusively) in connection with so-called initial coin offerings (ICOs). The amount of money in cryptocurrencies grew exponentially in 2017, triggering an explosion in the interest in "the hottest thing in tech." Many businesses turned to ICOs are a way to raise capital. Unfortunately, wherever there is that much money at stake, there are scams and fraud. ICOs are no exception.

This chapter introduces the kinds of fraud to which crypto offerings may be susceptible, and then considers a range of real world examples. These examples go a long way to explaining the SEC's conservative approach to cryptotransactions.

1. KINDS OF FRAUD

There are a wide range of factors that contribute to the possibility that a cryptocurrency offering will involve some kind of fraudulent activity. Many offerings involve tokens that have not yet been developed, making claims unverifiable because they involve future conduct. Some wallets and wallet services are vulnerable to hackers. Exchanges may suffer similar vulnerabilities, and may also be unregulated or act as if they are outside the reach of U.S. regulators. Cryptographic hashing practices make tracing increasingly difficult, so criminals may be able to conduct their scams in relative obscurity.

The risk for investors is substantial. The FBI has warned: "A single scam can destroy a company, devastate families by wiping out their life savings, or cost investors billions of dollars (or even all three). Today's fraud schemes are more sophisticated than ever. . . ."[1]

In the world of crypto, it is not uncommon for a promoter to falsely hold himself out as having substantial skills, connections, and/or influence in the crypto community. CEOs, investors, programmers/developers, and/or paid spokespersons make wildly optimistic projections completely divorced from reality. Websites are set up to look legitimate, and may

---

[1] FBI, *What We Investigate, White-Collar Crime* (available online at https://www.fbi.gov/investigate/white-collar-crime).

include detailed whitepapers designed to make a particular deal look enticing. Crypto scams often follow established patterns and may involve Ponzi schemes, pump and dump operations, phishing attacks, and/or bait and switch fraud.

The SEC explains Ponzi schemes as those which "involve[ ] the payment of purported returns to existing investors from funds contributed by new investors. Ponzi scheme organizers often solicit new investors by promising to invest funds in opportunities claimed to generate high returns with little or no risk."[2] Early participants may enjoy the promised high returns, but most investors in this kind of operation will make no money and stand to lose their entire contribution. In addition, many Ponzi schemes seek to encourage investors to recruit additional participants, because that is the only way in which an investor will see any return. Ponzi schemes eventually collapse when there are insufficient new investors to meet the demand for returns.

"Pump and dump" schemes are rooted in the securities markets and were traditionally associated with penny stocks. Because the markets are similar in many respects, the same kind of scheme can apply to cryptocurrency sales. In a pump and dump offering, a fraudster will distribute highly enthusiastic but false, misleading, and/or exaggerated claims about the merits of the investment. Usually, the scam artists involved will hold significant stakes in the interests being recommended, and once interest in (and the price of) the potential investment has peaked or at least risen to a sufficient level, they will sell ("dump") whatever they own on the market. The SEC describes this pattern as follows:

> Pump-and-dump schemes often occur on the Internet where it is common to see messages posted that urge readers to buy a stock quickly or to sell before the price goes down, or a telemarketer will call using the same sort of pitch. Often the promoters will claim to have 'inside' information about an impending development or to use an 'infallible' combination of economic and stock market data to pick stocks. In reality, they may be company insiders or paid promoters who stand to gain by selling their shares after the stock price is "pumped" up by the buying frenzy they create. Once these fraudsters "dump" their shares and stop hyping the stock, the price typically falls, and investors lose their money.[3]

Phishing scams work a little differently. Instead of inducing victims to purchase relatively worthless investments at inflated prices, the goal of a phishing effort is to obtain access to confidential information. The target of a phishing attempt will typically receive some type of electronic

---

[2]   SEC, *Fast Answers, Ponzi Schemes* [archived at https://perma.cc/7JEM-NF8M].

[3]   SEC, *Fast Answers, "Pump-and-Dumps" and Market Manipulations* [archived at https://perma.cc/X8U2-JH3Y].

communication which purports to be from a trustworthy source. The victim is then induced to provide confidential information which facilitates further fraud through things like identity theft or credit card fraud. One common example of a phishing scheme involves a phone or email contact from a source that appears to be very similar to one the victim utilizes, seeking to recover and/or verify customer information due to something such as a lapse in security or other technical mishap. In lieu of this, a scammer may claim to be conducting an audit as a result of unauthorized activity, with a request for verification of basic information from the recipient. Another alternative may be as basic as a fake login page, where a user is asked to divulge confidential information such as usernames, passwords, or similar data. Any of these could be used in connection with a potential investment in a cryptoasset, particularly where the target is asked to divulge information about the target's wallet or private keys.

Finally, bait and switch is also a possibility. Bait and switch involves an operation that pretends to be a legitimate service, product, and/or website. Victims are drawn to the operation by extravagant (and fraudulent) promises of high rates of return, low risk, or something else that is very attractive to prospective investors. When the victim demands payoff or otherwise becomes suspicious, the promised return disappears. This kind of scam could be particularly serious in the context of cryptocurrencies, as the victim might be induced to provide scammers with information such as private keys, which would give the fraudster access to every digital asset controlled by a compromised wallet.

2. RED FLAGS

In 2018, the SEC posted an advertisement for a mock ICO. The fake token, called the "HoweyCoin" in a not-so-subtle reference to the Supreme Court case that defined investment contract, touted "an all too good to be true investment opportunity."[4] The SEC did, of course, quickly acknowledge that the deal was "not real."

Anyone who actually clicked on the "Buy Coins Now" link in the fake ICO website was taken to a secondary page containing investor education and tips on how to avoid fraudulent offerings. The linked page included the following red flags that should tip a prospective investor off as to the questionable nature of the offering:

1. claims of high, guaranteed returns

2. celebrity endorsements

3. claims of being "SEC-compliant"

---

[4] SEC, *The SEC Has an Opportunity You Won't Want to Miss: Act Now!* SEC PRESS RELEASE 2018–88 (May 16, 2018) [archived at https://perma.cc/FZV3-RTZE].

4.   investing with a credit card

5.   pump and dump scams.[5]

Such red flags appear to be distressingly common in ICOs:

> According to new research from the Wall Street Journal, more than 15% of crypto projects raising funds through initial coin offerings (ICOs) have serious red flags that should give investors pause. The investigation, which analyzed the whitepapers of 3,300 cryptocurrency offerings and ICOs launched in 2017 and 2018, found that 513 of them likely committed plagiarism, misrepresented the identities of project founders, or promised unrealistic returns. . . . Of the 513, over 30 are already under scrutiny by regulators, and over half of the project websites are unavailable.[6]

3. *U.S. V. ZASLAVSKIY* AND RECOIN

One way to understand the SEC's approach to classification of cryptoassets is to look at the agency's own explanations. On October 27, 2017, the Department of Justice initiated a sealed complaint (later unsealed) against Maksim Zaslavskiy, alleging securities fraud in connection with general solicitations seeking investment in REcoin Group Foundation, LLC, in the form of interests in REcoin Tokens and Diamond Tokens. Zaslavskiy moved to dismiss the complaint on the grounds that the tokens were currencies not securities.

Evidencing the close cooperation between the SEC and the Department of Justice in matters involving allegations of securities fraud, the SEC sought and received permission to file a brief opposing that request. Excerpts from that brief explaining the position of the SEC insofar as it relates to the issue of when cryptoassets are securities appear below.

---

[5]   SEC, *ICO—HoweyCoins, If You Responded To An Investment Offer Like This, You Could Have Been Scammed—HoweyCoins Are Completely Fake!*, INVESTOR.GOV [archived at https://perma.cc/T62S-XPK2].

[6]   Melanie Kramer, *More Than 15% of Crypto Projects Have Serious Red Flags: Wall Street Journal*, CCN (Dec. 27, 2018) (available online at https://www.ccn.com/more-than-15-of-crypto-projects-have-serious-red-flags-wsj/).

U.S. V. ZASLAVSKIY

No. 17-CR-0647 (S.D.N.Y. 2017)

BRIEF OF SECURITIES AND EXCHANGE COMMISSION IN SUPPORT OF THE UNITED STATES IN OPPOSITION TO DEFENDANT'S MOTION TO DISMISS INDICTMENT

. . . .

INTEREST OF THE SECURITIES AND EXCHANGE COMMISSION

I.   SEC's Mission

The SEC is the primary regulator of the U.S. securities markets. Its mission is to protect investors, maintain fair, orderly and efficient markets, and facilitate capital formation. Critical to the SEC's effectiveness in promoting fair disclosures and preventing fraud in the offer and sale of securities is the ability to enforce violations of the securities laws through civil actions.

Congress enacted the federal securities laws and created the Commission after the stock market crash of 1929, when half of the new securities sold during the post-World War I period turned out to be worthless.

. . . .

Issuers and individuals increasingly have been using distributed ledger (or blockchain) technology in connection with raising capital for businesses and projects. A blockchain is a peer-to-peer database spread across a network that uses cryptography to record all transactions in the network in theoretically unchangeable, digitally-stored data packages called blocks, linked together in a chain. ICOs are blockchain-enabled offerings often targeted at retail investors—in the U.S. and globally. ICOs promise profits through the issuance of digital assets (often called coins, tokens, or cryptocurrencies) in exchange for fiat currency or other digital assets (often Bitcoins). The overall size of the ICO market has grown exponentially. It is reported that $3 billion has been raised so far in 2018; over $5 billion in 2017; and nearly $300 million in 2016. See generally www.coindesk.com/ico-tracker (last visited Mar. 19, 2018). These numbers may understate the size of the ICO market (and the potential for investor loss) as many ICOs "trade up" for some period after they are issued. Much of this form of fund-raising appears to be unlawfully conducted through unregistered and/or fraudulent offerings of securities.

II.   SEC Enforcement Actions Involving ICOs

In July 2017, the SEC issued a Report of Investigation pursuant to Section 21(a) of the Exchange Act, 15 U.S.C. § 78u(a), regarding an ICO for so-called "DAO Tokens." In the Report, the SEC considered the particular facts and circumstances presented by the offer and sale of DAO Tokens and concluded that they were securities based on long-standing legal principles, and that offers and sales of DAO Tokens were thus subject to the federal securities laws. The Report explained that issuers of distributed ledger or blockchain technology-based securities must register offers and sales of such securities unless a valid exemption from registration applies. The automation of certain functions through "smart contracts" or computer code or other technology, the Report concluded, does not remove conduct from the purview of the federal securities laws. Thus, the SEC's message to issuers and others in this space has been clear: the use of distributed ledger or blockchain technology to raise capital or engage in securities transactions does not alter the need to comply with the federal securities laws.

The SEC has been actively enforcing the federal securities laws in the ICO space. In addition to the parallel action the SEC has filed against Defendant and his entities, the SEC has brought a number of enforcement actions concerning ICOs for alleged violations of the federal securities laws. The SEC has also issued more than a dozen trading suspensions to halt trading in the stock of publicly-traded issuers who have made spurious claims relating to blockchain technology.

Several characteristics of how ICOs are conducted pose challenges for law enforcement in investigating fraud. For example, (1) tracing funds: traditional financial institutions (such as banks) often are not involved, making it harder to follow the flow of funds; (2) international scope: blockchain transactions and users span the globe and there may be restrictions on how the SEC can obtain and use information from foreign jurisdictions; (3) no central authority: as there is no central authority that collects blockchain user information, the SEC generally must rely on other sources, such as digital asset exchanges, for this type of information; (4) seizing or freezing digital assets: digital "wallets" (software that "stores" digital assets) may be encrypted and, unlike money held in a bank or brokerage account, may not be held by a third-party custodian; (5) anonymity: many digital assets are specifically designed to be pseudonymous or anonymous; thus, attribution of a specific digital asset to an individual or entity could be difficult or impossible, especially where additional anonymizing tools are employed; and (6) evolving technology: digital assets involve new and developing technologies.

Overall, the SEC's investor concerns in this area have been communicated through numerous public statements, investor alerts and bulletins, press releases, and filed enforcement actions. Those communications and actions have been highlighted on the SEC's www. investor.gov website on a page entitled, "Spotlight on Initial Coin Offerings and Digital Assets."[7]

---

[7]   Author's note: This material has been archived at https://perma.cc/H5WV-PYJG.

IV. Continuing Efforts to Protect Investors

The SEC is acutely focused on unlawful conduct in this area. In 2017, the SEC formed a Cyber Unit within its Division of Enforcement, to address cyber-related misconduct, including involving distributed ledger technology and ICOs. The SEC is continuing to police the digital asset and ICO markets vigorously and to bring enforcement actions against those who conduct ICOs or other actions relating to digital assets in violation of the federal securities laws.

The SEC's ability to fulfill its mission and protect investors and the markets is critically dependent on the appropriate application of the federal securities laws to all types of instruments—including the Tokens at issue in this case. An improper application of the definitional provisions of the Securities and Exchange Acts or an unduly narrow reading of established precedent as applied to the Tokens here could severely hinder the SEC's efforts.

. . . .

ARGUMENT

. . . .

I. Legal Background

A. The Registration and Anti-Fraud Provisions of the Securities Laws

The Securities Act, 15 U.S.C. §§ 77a, et seq., contains registration provisions that contemplate that the offer or sale of "securities" to the public must be accompanied by the "full and fair disclosure" afforded by registration with the SEC and delivery of a statutory prospectus containing information necessary to enable potential purchasers to make an informed investment decision.

. . . .

The applicability of the [federal securities laws] . . . and the outcome of the criminal and civil actions before this Court therefore turn on the meaning of the word "securities" as it is used in the Securities and Exchange Acts.

B. "Investment Contracts" Are "Securities"

Under Section 2(a)(1) of the Securities Act and Section 3(a)(10) of the Exchange Act, a security includes "an investment contract." . . .[T]he Supreme Court's decision in . . .[*SEC v. W.J. Howey Co.*, 328 U.S. 293 (1946)] holds that an "investment contract" is an investment of money in a common enterprise with a reasonable expectation of profits to be derived from the entrepreneurial or managerial efforts of others. *See* 328 U.S. at 301; *see also SEC v. Edwards*, 540 U.S. 389, 393 (2004). *Howey* "permits the fulfillment of the statutory purpose of compelling full and fair disclosure relative to the issuance of the many types of instruments" offered in "our commercial world." 328 U.S. at 299. *Howey* states the test for both the criminal and civil enforcement of the securities laws. As the Supreme Court has recognized, Congress crafted "a definition of 'security' sufficiently broad to encompass virtually any instrument that might be sold as an investment." *Reves v. Ernst & Young*, 494 U.S. 56, 60–61 (1990).

C. The SEC's Application of *Howey* in the DAO Report

In the [DAO] Report, the Commission concluded that "DAO Tokens" were investment contracts under *Howey* because, among other factors: (1) investors in DAO Tokens purchased them using the digital asset known as Ether, which constituted an "investment of 'money,'" (2) investors had a reasonable expectation of profits because DAO promoters informed investors that the DAO was a for-profit entity "whose objective was to fund projects in exchange for a return on investment," and (3) investors expected that their profits would be derived from the entrepreneurial and managerial efforts of others given that the promoters laid out their own vision and plans for the company in promotional materials, spoke about how they would select persons to work on the projects "based on their expertise and credentials," and touted their expertise in blockchain technologies, whereas the limited voting rights and wide dispersion of investors "did not provide [investors] with meaningful control over the enterprise."

II. The Tokens Here Are Investment Contracts and Therefore Securities

The charges in the Indictment make clear that the Tokens easily satisfy each prong of *Howey*: they constitute an investment of money in a common enterprise with a reasonable expectation of profits to be derived from the entrepreneurial and managerial efforts of others.

A. Token Purchasers Invested Money

Individuals invested in REcoin and Diamond "through its website using their credit cards, virtual currency or through online funds transfer services." Such investment is the type of contribution of value that can create an investment contract under *Howey*. *See SEC v. Shavers*, No. 13 Civ. 416 (ALM), 2014 WL 4652121, *1 (E.D. Tex. Sept. 18, 2014) (holding that an investment of Bitcoin meets the first prong of *Howey*).

Defendant's insistence that people who chose to buy a Token were "simply exchanging one medium of currency for another," essentially concedes that the first prong of *Howey* is satisfied. The first prong of *Howey* contemplates that the "'investment' may take the form of 'goods and services,' or some other *exchange of value*.'" *Uselton v. Com. Lovelace Motor Freight, Inc.*, 940 F.2d 564, 574 (10th Cir. 1991) (citation omitted) (emphasis added). Accordingly, an investment occurred here regardless of how Defendant now seeks to relabel it.

B.   In a Common Enterprise[2]

Defendant told investors in the REcoin Tokens that their assets would be pooled and invested into real estate selected by Defendant and his "experienced team" so that "people from all over the world'" could share in "real estate investments 'with some of the highest potential returns." After offering a "conversion of REcoin Tokens into Diamond [T]okens," Defendant made similar representations with respect to the Diamond Tokens, namely, that investor funds would be used to purchase diamonds selected by Defendant and his "experienced team," and that the company "forecast a minimum growth of 10% to 15% per year." The second prong of *Howey* is therefore met because the "fortunes of each investor depend upon the profitability of the enterprise as a whole" and there was a "tying of each individual investor's fortunes to the fortunes of the other investors by the pooling of assets, usually combined with the pro-rata distribution of profits." *Revak v. SEC Realty Corp.,* 18 F.3d 81, 87 (2d Cir. 1994). . . .[3]

Defendant's contrary argument, that there is no commonality because each individual can dispose of a Token on his or her own, is misguided. The second prong of *Howey* focuses on whether an individual's fortunes with respect to the investment are tied together to others', as they were undisputedly linked here. An individual's ability to exchange or dispose of an investment contract on his or her own—which exists with respect to many forms of investments that are straight-forward examples of investment contracts (*see, e.g., Edwards,* 540 U.S. at 391–92 (purchaser of payphone lease investment contract had option to sell back lease to promoter))—is not germane to and does not alter this analysis.

C.   With a Reasonable Expectation of Profits

The various promotional materials disseminated by Defendant informed investors that REcoin and Diamond were for-profit entities such that the value of the investments would be expected to increase based on the profitability of the business. Specifically, as the REcoin whitepaper

---

[2]   The Commission does not require commonality per se or view a "common enterprise" as a distinct element of the term "investment contract." In its opinion in *In re Barkate,* the Commission stated that a "common enterprise" is not a distinct requirement for an "investment contract" under *Howey.* Release No. 49542, 82 SEC Docket 2130, 2004 WL 762434, *3 n.13 (Apr. 8, 2004), *aff'd sub nom, Barkate v. SEC,* 125 F. App'x 892 (9th Cir. 2005). The Second Circuit has stated that a showing of "horizontal commonality" can establish a common enterprise. *See generally Revak v. SEC Realty Corp.,* 18 F.3d 81, 87–88 (2d Cir. 1994). Broadly defined, horizontal commonality is the pooling of investor assets in the common enterprise, such that the fortunes of investors are tied to each other, whereas vertical commonality focuses on the relationship between the promoter and the investor. In any event, as explained further herein, the Indictment shows the existence of commonality in this case.

[3]   The investments here also satisfy the strict vertical commonality test because investors' fortunes in the Tokens were tied to Defendant's profits. *See Revak,* 18 F.3d at 87 (in the absence of horizontal commonality, strict vertical commonality may also be sufficient). . . .

stated, the supposed REcoin Token was "an attractive investment opportunity" because it would "grow[ ] in value." Similarly, the Diamond Token was forecasted for a "minimum growth of 10% to 15% per year" and Defendant informed investors that he was looking to list the Diamond Token "on external exchanges [to] make more profit." Accordingly, investors in the Tokens had a reasonable expectation of an increase in the value of their purchase, a type of profit specifically recognized as satisfying *Howey*. *Edwards*, 540 U.S. at 394 (explaining that expected profits can include "dividends, other periodic payments, or *the increased value of the investment.*") (emphasis added).

D.   Derived from the Managerial Efforts of Others

Defendant represented that the REcoin investment would grow in value based on his managerial efforts both in selecting the assets that would back the investments and in developing the supposed environment in which the Tokens could be used. Defendant stated that "REcoin is led by an experienced team of brokers, lawyers, and developers and invests its proceeds into global real estate based on the soundest strategies." He also stated that the value of the Diamond Tokens would grow based on his development of the Diamond "ecosystem." Defendant likewise explained that his success of his efforts to list Diamond Tokens on exchanges was among the sources of the investors' returns. This suffices to meet *Howey*'s last prong, in which the essential inquiry is "whether the efforts made by those other than the investor are the undeniably significant ones, those essential managerial efforts which affect the failure or success of the enterprise." *SEC v. Glenn W. Turner Enters., Inc.*, 474 F.2d 476, 482 (9th Cir. 1973); *see also Cont'l Mktg., Corp. v. SEC*, 387 F.2d 466, 470–71 (10th Cir. 1967) (promoters' efforts to "develop" a "structure into which investors entered" was part of efforts to increase the value of the investment).

Seeking to minimize the central role Defendant held himself out as playing in these ventures, Defendant argues that "adoptors [sic] with shared professional interests would work together to create an ecosystem" that would lead to an increase in the venture's value. However, Defendant cannot minimize the importance of the supposed investment expertise of him and his team. Given Defendant's statement that "people from all over the world" were free to purchase the Tokens, the investors in these Tokens "could not reasonably be believed to be desirous or capable of undertaking" these projects "on their own," and thus had to rely on the Defendant's managerial expertise. *SEC v. Aqua-Sonic Prods. Corp.*, 687 F.2d 577, 583–84 (2d Cir. 1982); *see also Leonard*, 529 F.3d at 88 (investors need not literally rely "solely" on the efforts of others). Even if an investor's efforts help to make an enterprise profitable, those efforts do not negate a promoter's significant managerial efforts. *See, e.g., Glenn W. Turner*, 474 F.2d at 482 (finding that a multi-level marketing scheme was an investment contract and that investors relied on the promoter's managerial efforts, despite the fact that investors put forth the majority of the labor that made the enterprise profitable, because the promoter dictated the terms and controlled the scheme).

III. Defendant's Contrary Arguments Are Unavailing

Defendant does not squarely address most of the foregoing factual contentions or their interaction with *Howey*. Rather, Defendant argues that: (1) the Tokens were "to be" or were "intended to be" "currency" as that term is used in the Exchange Act, and therefore exempt from the securities laws; (2) because there was no pro-rata distribution of profits, there was no commonality; and (3) because the REcoin investors (but not the Diamond investors) were offered voting rights, whatever profit would not be derived from the managerial effort of others. Defendant's arguments mischaracterize the facts and misstate the law.

A. Defendant's Attempt to Label the Investments Here as "Cryptocurrencies" Does Not Change Their Character as Securities

Defendant dubs the investments at issue here "cryptocurrencies" or "virtual currencies" and urges the Court to issue a broad ruling that such assets—as a class—are statutorily exempt from the definition of securities under the Securities and Exchange Acts. Defendant argues that "cryptocurrencies" or "virtual currencies" are "currency" within the meaning of the Exchange Act, 15 U.S.C. § 78c(a)(10), and are therefore exempt from the definition of "security," simply because he now has decided to call them "cryptocurrencies."[4]

First, the appropriate focus is on the economics of the offering, not its label. *See, e.g., United Hous. Found., Inc v. Forman*, 421 U.S. 837, 849 (1975). What Defendant promised purchasers at the time of the offer and sale were returns on an investment. But, even if Defendant is to be believed that his intent at the time was eventually to issue tokens to be used as "cryptocurrencies" in a blockchain-based ecosystem, building such an ecosystem would have required Defendant's efforts before any cryptocurrency could be issued by it or used within it. Defendant's supposed plan that the Tokens would, one day, be useful in that ecosystem that he had not built does not alter the nature of Defendant's promise to investors. Defendant offered and sold the investment opportunity to profit from his development of that ecosystem. Defendant's fund-raising effort to obtain capital—even assuming an intention to build that ecosystem—bears all the hallmarks of a securities offering.

---

[4]   The definition of "security" under the Exchange Act expressly excludes "currency." 15 U.S.C. § 78c(a)(10) (Section 3(a)(10) of the Exchange Act). The Securities Act's definition of "security" does not exclude "currency" (see id. § 77b(a)(1)), but courts have treated the two definitions as the same. *See Landreth Timber Co. v. Landreth*, 471 U.S. 681, 686 n.1 (1985).

Second, Defendant's effort to evade the application of the securities laws by labeling the Tokens "cryptocurrencies" should be rejected as contrary to the broad and principles-based analysis that decades of law dictate. The economic realities demonstrate that the investments offered and sold are securities, as detailed above. *See, e.g., Forman*, 421 U.S. at 849 ("Congress intended the application of these [securities] statutes to turn on the economic realities underlying a transaction, and not on the name appended thereto."); *see also* SEC Chairman Jay Clayton and CFTC Chairman Christopher Giancarlo, *Regulators are Looking at Cryptocurrency*, Wall Street Journal (Jan. 24, 2018) ("[S]ome products that are labeled cryptocurrencies have characteristics that make them securities. The offer, sale and trading of such products must be carried out in compliance with securities law. The SEC will vigorously pursue those who seek to evade the registration, disclosure and antifraud requirements of our securities laws."). Indeed, one is hardpressed to imagine what would be left of the securities laws if simply labelling an investment contract a "currency" could make it so. *See, e.g., Long v. Shultz Cattle Co.*, 881 F.2d 129, 136 (5th Cir. 1989) (examining "the economic realities of [the promoter]'s program" and rejecting the promoter's attempts to "avoid the securities laws by simply attaching the label 'consulting agreement' to a package of services which [was] clearly . . . an investment contract").

Defendant advances a number of strawman arguments concerning digital assets unlike those at issue here. For example, Defendant relies on *United States v. Ulbricht*, 31 F. Supp. 3d 540, 569–70 (S.D.N.Y. 2014), where the district court determined that Bitcoin is a type of "fund" or "monetary instrument" under a money laundering statute, 18 U.S.C. § 1956(c)(4). But Bitcoin is a completely different asset than the investment at issue here. Defendant's Tokens were not even created at the time of the offer and sale, and could not be used to buy anything. Thus, the *Ulbricht* court's decision that Bitcoin is a "fund" or "monetary instrument" says nothing about whether the Tokens Defendant offered and sold are securities.

Finally, because the question whether an investment constitutes a "security" within the meaning of the Securities and Exchange Acts is highly fact-specific, the Court need not resolve broader questions about whether all (or which) digital assets are within the purview of the Acts. Nor must the Court broadly decide whether an entire category of "cryptocurrency" is a "currency" for purposes of the exclusion set forth in Section 3(a)(10) of the Exchange Act. When one looks past labels, as the Supreme Court has instructed, what was offered in this case was plainly not a currency of any nature.

B. A Pro-Rata Distribution of Profits is Not Required and, in Any Event, Is Present Here

Defendant is also incorrect to suggest that horizontal commonality requires a pro-rata distribution of profit. The Second Circuit has explained that horizontal commonality requires "pooling of assets," which is "usually" combined with such distribution—but not that such a distribution is necessary. *Revak*, 18 F.3d at 87.

Other courts that have applied horizontal commonality recognize that it is sufficient that "each investor was entitled to receive returns directly proportionate to his or her investment stake," "either for direct distribution or as an increase in the value of the investment." *SEC v. SG Ltd.*, 265 F.3d 42, 46–47, 51 (1st Cir. 2001) (finding horizontal commonality); *accord SEC v. Infinity Grp. Co.*, 212 F.3d 180, 188 (3d Cir. 2000) (finding horizontal commonality where the "return on investment was to be apportioned according to the amounts committed by the investor" and was "directly proportional to the amount of that investment").

Here, investors would have reasonably expected profits (from real estate, diamonds, and/or tokens) that were directly proportional to their investment, as well as a pro rata distribution of profits. The REcoin whitepaper states that the profits from the REcoin enterprise would be reinvested into that enterprise—an allegation that Defendant acknowledges in his papers and does not dispute. That reinvestment of profits is nothing more than a pro-rata distribution in kind to the investors in the enterprise (in other words, a proportionate return "as an increase in the value of the investment," *SG Ltd.*, 265 F.3d at 47), such that the commonality prong is satisfied.

C. The "Voting Rights" Offered to REcoin Investors Were Illusory

Defendant argues that because the REcoin Tokens gave investors voting rights, investors retained control of the enterprise such that the last *Howey* prong is not met. Here, however, these voting rights were illusory both because there is no detail in the offering materials about how the voting process would work, and because, given the large number of REcoin investors (more than 1,000), their ability to exercise any real control would be minimal. *See Williamson v. Tucker*, 645 F.2d 404, 423 (5th Cir. 1981) ("[O]ne would not expect partnership interests sold to large numbers of the general public to provide any real partnership control; at some point there would be so many [limited] partners that a partnership vote would be more like a corporate vote, each partner's role having been diluted to the level or a single shareholder in a corporation."); *see also SEC v. Merch. Capital, LLC*, 483 F.3d 747, 754–66 (11th Cir. 2007) (finding an investment contract even where voting rights were provided to purported general partners, noting that the voting process provided limited information for investors to make informed decisions, and the purported general partners lacked control over the information in the ballots). And, of course, many types of securities come with voting rights, such as common shares in a public company.

NOTES

1. Unlike the legal opinions found in traditional legal casebooks, this is an excerpt from a legal brief filed by the SEC. As such, it is a piece of advocacy. Even so, assuming the court agrees with the positions advocated (and further assuming the case does not settle before an opinion in rendered), the arguments and authorities presented here could be adopted in whole or in part in any opinion eventually rendered by the court. Generally speaking, the legal argument section of such briefs are written in such a manner that they can be used in this fashion.

2. In the case itself, in early September 2018, the federal district court upheld the indictment but deferred the final *Howey* determination to trail. District Judge Raymond Dearie cited liberal pleading standards in allowing the case to proceed. In addition, it noted that the task of analyzing various virtual currencies and ICOs under the Supreme Court's *Howey* test was highly fact-specific, and thus it was a determination better left for the finders of fact. On the other hand, the judge also concluded "Congress's purpose in enacting the securities laws was to regulate investments, in whatever form they are made and by whatever name they are called." By characterizing the indictment as charging "a straightforward scam" the court left little doubt as to how it viewed the probable outcome if the alleged facts were proven to be true.

3. On November 15, 2018 Maksim Zaslavskiy entered a guilty plea in the criminal matter, admitting that he had lied to about 1,000 investors. As part of the plea deal, a contemporaneous civil action filed by the SEC against Zaslavskiy was also settled. He was sentenced to a year and a half in prison a year later, on November 18, 2019. As part of the judgment entered into in *SEC v. RECoin Group Foundation, LLC*, 17 Civ. 5725 (E.D.N.Y. Nov. 19, 2018), Zaslavskiy agreed to a permanent injunction banning future acts of securities fraud, from serving as an officer or director of a public company, or from participating in any offering of digital securities. He also agreed to disgorge all "ill-gotten gains" together with interest and a civil penalty to be determined by the court upon motion of the SEC, with an express acknowledgment that bankruptcy would not discharge his obligation to pay such amounts.

4. ARISEBANK

According to a now defunct website (www.arisebank.com), AriseBank claimed to have been founded in March 2017 by Jared Rise and Stanley Ford.[8] AriseBank was intended to be the world's first "decentralized" bank,

---

[8] Obviously, because the site is defunct, these statements (and those in the next few paragraphs of text) no longer appear. Reports of what the site once claimed, however, abound. *See,*

where customers could get traditional banking services denominated in cryptocurrency. According to the SEC Complaint dated January 25, 2018, AriseBank claimed to be "one of the largest cryptocurrency platforms ever built." Its business model was supposedly "focused on bringing cryptocurrency to the average consumer and using it to revolutionize banking."

AriseBank claimed, as of October 2017, to have launched the AriseCoin ICO and a beta version of its banking platform. The SEC alleged that AriseBank started actual fundraising as early as November 2017 through an offering of AriseCoin, its own cryptocoin. The ICO was scheduled to last until January 2018, with a goal of raising $1 billion. AriseCoin was scheduled to be distributed on February 10, 2018.

The offering materials included many allegedly false statements designed to induce investors to purchase AriseCoins. For example, AriseBank had issued a press release announcing that it had purchased a 100-year-old commercial bank allowing to "now offer its customers FDIC-insured accounts and transactions. . . ." In reality, neither AriseBank nor the commercial bank it had allegedly acquired had ever been FDIC insured. Similarly, AriseBank made false claims of partnerships with reputable financial companies such as Visa, and reported planned acquisitions of companies that appeared to be related to well known businesses. This included both KFMC Bank Holding Company and TPMG, both of which were described by AriseBank as traditional banks, but neither of which appear to have actually existed.

From a theoretical perspective, the idea behind AriseBank was far from worthless, but according to the SEC complaint, the company repeatedly lied to potential investors. In January 2018, the SEC sued AriseBank and its two cofounders, Jared Rice and Stanley Ford, for fraud in connection with the AriseCoin ICO. The Texas Department of Banking issued a cease-and-desist order the same month, confirming that AriseBank was not a legally authorized banking platform. In November 2018, the FBI announced that it had arrested Jared Rice, the CEO or AriseBank following his indictment on an alleged multi-million dollar scam. The SEC had also successfully frozen the assets of AriseBank under emergency provisions, and the court appointed a receiver to manage the assets and ensure they could not be liquidated.

---

i.e., Ben Lane, *Supposed cryptocurrency CEO accused of stealing $4 million from investors*, HOUSINGWIRE (Nov. 29, 2018) (available online at https://www.housingwire.com/articles/47527-supposed-cryptocurrency-ceo-accused-of-stealing-4-million-from-investors); Mark Curriden, *SEC charges Dallas crypto-currency business with fraud*, BIZJOURNALS (Jan. 30, 2018) (available online at https://www.bizjournals.com/dallas/news/2018/01/30/sec-charges-dallas-crypto-currency-business-with.html). These allegations also appear in the SEC's first amended complaint in *SEC v. AriseBank*, Civ. Act. No.: 3:18–cv–186–M (filed in the Northern District of Texas on Feb. 2, 2018) (available online at https://www.sec.gov/litigation/complaints/2018/compa24088.pdf).

In December 2018, both Rice and Ford were ordered to pay nearly $2.7 million in fines.[9] The SEC announced that AriseBank founders Rice and then-COO Ford would be liable for $2,259,543 in disgorgement plus $68,423 in prejudgment interest. They were also each required to pay civil penalties of $184,767. Finally, they were each barred from acting as officers of public companies or engaging in any future offerings of digital securities.

One other aspect of AriseBank deserves comment. AriseBank also relied upon former boxing champ Evander Holyfield as a celebrity endorser, perhaps contributing to the SEC's decision to highlight the risks of relying on these kinds of endorsements in making investment decisions.[10] Holyfield's involvement with AriseBank was not a typical paid endorsement. Instead, it was characterized as a "long-lasting strategic partnership."[11] In what was touted as a "major announcement," AriseBank claimed that it was teaming up with Holyfield to raise "millions towards humanitarian relief efforts." There is no evidence that claim was true, either.

5. CENTRA TECH

AriseBank has not been the only instance where the SEC has weighed in on crypto offerings endorsed by celebrities. In April 2018, the SEC charged Centra Tech, Inc., and its two co-founders, Sohrab "Sam" Sharma and Robert Farkas, with "orchestrating a fraudulent initial coin offering (ICO) that raised more than $32 million from thousands of investors last year. Criminal authorities separately charged and arrested both defendants."[12]

Centra Tech was a financial services startup, incorporated on July 27, 2017. It was headquartered in Miami Beach, Florida, and it held itself out as a bridge between the conventional banking world and the growing crypto

---

[9]   Charlie Osborne, *AriseBank execs forced to pay $2.7 million to settle SEC charges of cryptocurrency fraud*, ZDNET (Dec.13, 2018) (available online at https://www.zdnet.com/article/arisebank-forced-to-pay-2-7-million-to-settle-sec-charges-of-cryptocurrency-service-fraud/).

[10]   SEC Public Statement, *SEC Statement Urging Caution Around Celebrity Backed ICOs* (Nov. 1, 2017) [archived at https://perma.cc/Q7HD-TVYX]. This statement includes the following warning:

> Investors should note that celebrity endorsements may appear unbiased, but instead may be part of a paid promotion. Investment decisions should not be based solely on an endorsement by a promoter or other individual. Celebrities who endorse an investment often do not have sufficient expertise to ensure that the investment is appropriate and in compliance with federal securities laws.

[11]   Michael Taggart, *Using BitShares, Holyfield and AriseBank Will Help Raise $1 Billion For Charity*, MEDIUM (Jan. 9, 2018) (available online at https://medium.com/@michaelx777/using-bitshares-holyfield-and-arisebank-will-help-raise-1-billion-for-charity-1c517819a3e0). For additional details, see *Four Time World Heavyweight Boxer, Evander Holyfield, Signs Deal with AriseBank*, PRWEB (Jan. 9, 2018) (available online at http://www.prweb.com/releases/2018/01/prweb15066177.htm).

[12]   SEC Press Release, *SEC Halts Fraudulent Scheme Involving Unregistered ICO*, Release 2018–53 (Ap. 2, 2018) [archived at https://perma.cc/K3VA-WNMF].

community. It conducted its ICO of the company's "CTR Token" from July 30, 2017, through October 5, 2017, ostensibly to fund the development of an entire suite of products related to its core business. As part of its promotion, Centra Bank represented that it was developing a debit card backed by Visa and MasterCard that would allow users to instantly convert crypto into fiat currency. (In reality, neither Visa nor MasterCard had any relationship with Centra Tech.)

To further bolster the impression of a legitimate and well developed business, Sharma and Farkas created fictional executives with impressive biographies, posted false and misleading marketing material about the company and the promised token, and paid celebrities to tout the ICO on social media.

ICOs are still somewhat unusual transactions, and they have their own steps and procedures. They also have their own documents, even though they do not follow the scripted disclosures that the SEC traditionally required in the case of sales of conventional debt and equity securities. One notable document that has become ubiquitous in the ICO ecosystem is the whitepaper.[13]

One commentator describes ICO whitepapers as follows:

> Every project that has been hosted on a blockchain, is expected to follow an implementation roadmap, which should be adequately explained to both the current investors, as well as those that may be joining in eventually.

> In view of this, the digital currency world has consciously (or not), adopted the white paper option that should explain all that needs to be known about any particular coin or token. The white paper ICO is used to convey such information as the intent for the project, the expected soft and hard cap, the development and implementation team for the project, and every other thing the investor may expect (or not expect) as benefits for the short and long run. Thus, if a person wishes to know what a cryptocurrency brand stands for, then the best place to get the leads is from the white paper.[14]

This same source suggests two related functions for a whitepaper: (1) to lure and convince potential investors that the project has merit, and (2) to generate publicity for fund-raising. Whitepapers therefore predate an offering by days or weeks, providing potential investors with information

---

[13]   The first reference to a whitepaper in this book appears back in chapter 2, which includes an excerpt from the SAFT project whitepaper. Note the lack of consistency in whether to capitalize this term, or whether to make it one word. This text tends to use "whitepaper," but other sources take a different approach.

[14]   *The Importance Of White Paper In Every Cryptocurrency ICO*, FOUNDICO (Aug. 8, 2018) (available online at https://foundico.com/blog/the-importance-of-white-paper-in-every-cryptocurrency-ico.html).

about the new token will solve particular challenges or problems, as well as any unique methodology or approach utilized by the new token.

Another source describes a whitepaper as "an instrument that helps business explain themselves to people."[15] A whitepaper therefore identifies the problem that the new project seeks to solve and the way in which the problem is to be addressed. The whitepaper can also discuss and assess business issues. This source concludes that "[e]very legit ICO should include a white paper that explains why is the company raising the needed funds."[16]

Centra Tech in fact released multiple whitepapers regarding its ICO, although all of them have now been removed from the Centra Tech website. According to a class action complaint filed by Jacob Rensel against Centra Tech and its founders, there were at least two versions with the title "Centra Tech White Paper Final Version 1.0."[17] One of those was dated August 2017, and the later was dated sometime in September of that year. According to the class action complaint, "[t]he primary difference between the two "Final Versions" is that the September Final Version 1.0 White Paper removed some explicit language touting the profit potential of investing in the Centra ICO. For example, the August Final Version 1.0 White Paper stated, '[o]ur token deal enables clients to join our prosperity and mission while generating a profit.'"

The whitepaper also contained a "roadmap and milestones" graphic outlining supposed progress and future plans for the business. Included in the roadmap was a timeline that purported to show a detailed history for the business where the company and its founders were allegedly working on the Centra Debit Card, CTR Tokens, and eBay since 2016. The roadmap also included a specific representation that as of January 2017, Centra had a "license agreement signed with VISA USA Inc."

The class action complaint subsequently alleged that these statements were all false. Centra never provided any corroborating public documentation for its claims of an established work product history. Centra Tech was not incorporated until July 2017, and internal documents suggest that the Centra idea was new at that time. In addition, VISA USA confirmed that it had no relationship with Centra Tech at any time.

Finally, the published whitepaper also included biographical information about individuals who, in fact, never really existed. As alleged in the class action complaint, Centra Tech listed a "Michael Edwards" as another Co-Founder and Chief Executive Officer ("CEO"). However, it

---

[15]   Akshay Gokalgandhi, *Importance of a white paper for an ICO*, MEDIUM (Ap. 20, 2018) (available online at http://www.prweb.com/releases/2018/01/prweb15066177.htm).

[16]   *Id.*

[17]   The complaint in *Rensel v. Centra Tech*, Case 1:17–cv–24500–JLK (filed Dec. 13, 2017), is archived at https://perma.cc/F8KP-3VP8. Various orders in this case, which as of August, 2019 is still pending, are described later in this chapter.

turned out that Edwards was not a real person, and the photo used on Centra Tech's website was that of a Canadian professor having no relationship with the company. Edwards' fake LinkedIn profile was deleted at the same time that his bio was removed from the Centra Tech website. The alleged CFO, "Jessica Robinson," was also alleged never to have existed, and her name, bio, and LinkedIn profile were also deleted following the revelation that she was not a real person.

On April 2, 2018, the SEC filed a complaint in the U.S. District Court for the Southern District of New York in Case #: 1:18–cv–02909–DLC. An amended complaint was filed on April 20, adding Raymond Trapani as a third defendant. The allegations in that complaint help illustrate why the SEC was so concerned about the transactions involved.

SEC v. SHARMA

No.1:18–cv–02909–DLC (2018)

AMENDED COMPLAINT

Plaintiff Securities and Exchange Commission (the "Commission"), for its complaint against Defendants Sohrab "Sam" Sharma ("Sharma"), Robert Farkas ("Farkas"), and Raymond Trapani ("Trapani") (together, the "Defendants"), alleges as follows:

SUMMARY

1. From approximately July 30, 2017 through October 5, 2017, Defendants raised at least $32 million from thousands of investors through the sale of unregistered securities issued by Centra Tech, Inc. ("Centra"), an entity controlled primarily by Defendants. The Centra securities were issued in a so-called "initial coin offering" ("ICO"), a term that is meant to describe the offer and sale of digital assets issued and distributed on a blockchain. Defendants sold the Centra token ("Centra Token" or "CTR Token"), an ERC20 token issued on the Ethereum blockchain, in Centra's ICO. Defendants promoted the Centra ICO by touting nonexistent relationships between Centra and well-known financial institutions, including Visa, Mastercard and The Bancorp.

2. Defendants, individually and through Centra, engaged in an illegal unregistered securities offering and, in connection with the offering, engaged in fraudulent conduct and made material misstatements and omissions designed to deceive investors in connection with the offer and sale of securities in the Centra ICO. By doing so, Defendants violated and aided and abetted Centra's violations of Sections 5(a), 5(c), and 17(a) of the Securities Act of 1933 ("Securities Act"), and Section 10(b) of the Securities Exchange Act of 1934 ("Exchange Act") and Rule 10b–5 thereunder.

3. The Centra ICO was an illegal offering of securities for which no registration statement was filed with the Commission or was then in effect,

and as to which no exemption from registration was available. The Centra ICO was a generalized solicitation made using statements posted on the internet and distributed throughout the world, including in the United States, and the securities were offered and sold to the general public, including to United States investors, in this district and elsewhere.

4. Centra raised funds from investors to create the "Centra Line" of products, a purported financial services system that would enable holders of various hard-to-spend "cryptocurrencies" to convert their assets easily into legal tender, such as U.S. dollars, and spend "cryptocurrencies" in real time with the Visa- and Mastercard-backed "Centra Card."

5. Specifically, Defendants claimed in promotional materials on Centra's website, in various social media platforms, and in other Centra offering materials, that Centra offered a physical "crypto debit card" backed by Visa and Mastercard that was connected to a virtual "smart wallet" via an Apple or Android smartphone application.

6. Defendants also claimed that—through Centra's "partnerships" with Visa, Mastercard, and The Bancorp—the Centra wallet, debit card and application would allow users to exchange, withdraw, or spend "cryptocurrencies" anywhere in the world that accepts Visa and Mastercard.

7. Defendants created, reviewed, and distributed marketing materials promoting Centra and the ICO, which claimed that the CEO and Co-Founder of Centra was an experienced businessman named "Michael Edwards," and Sharma stated in a public interview that "Edwards" invested "a lot of capital originally" to help establish Centra.

8. Defendants also claimed directly and through Centra's marketing materials that the "Centra Token Rewards Program" entitled investors to share in Centra's future earnings. Specifically, Defendants claimed that token holders would be paid "rewards" or a "dividend reward" of 0.8% of the total revenue that Centra earned through its "revenue share" agreement with Visa and Mastercard.

9. Contrary to Defendants' false representations, and as Defendants knew or recklessly disregarded: (i) Centra did not have any "partnership" or other relationship with Visa, Mastercard, or The Bancorp; (ii) "Michael Edwards" and other Centra executives pictured in its promotional materials were fictional, and the photographs used to identify the fictional executives were photos taken from the internet or pictures of other individuals; and (iii) investors who purchased Centra Tokens would not receive future payments or "revenue share" from agreements with Visa or Mastercard.

10. The foregoing false and misleading statements, as well as additional false and misleading statements described below, appeared

variously on the company's website and in versions of white papers ("White Papers") issued and updated by Defendants in connection with the offer and sale of its securities during the Centra ICO, as well as in numerous other online fora such as social media, websites, and press releases.

VIOLATIONS

11. By engaging in the conduct set forth in this Complaint, Defendants engaged in and are engaged in ongoing securities fraud in violation of Section 17(a)(1)–(3) of the Securities Act [15 U.S.C. § 77q(a)(1)–(3)], Section 10(b) of the Exchange Act [15 U.S.C. § 78j(b)], and Rule 10b–5(a)–(c) thereunder [17 C.F.R. § 240.10b–5(a)–(c)], and, without a registration statement being in effect or filed, Defendants engaged and are engaged in the unlawful sale and offer to sell securities in violation of Sections 5(a) and 5(c) of the Securities Act [15 U.S.C. §§ 77e(a), 77e(c)].

NATURE OF THE PROCEEDING AND RELIEF SOUGHT

12. The Commission brings this action pursuant to the authority conferred upon it by Section 20(b) of the Securities Act [15 U.S.C. § 77t(b)] and Section 21(d) of the Exchange Act [15 U.S.C. § 78u(d)].

13. Through this action, Commission seeks a judgment: (a) permanently enjoining Defendants from engaging in acts, practices and courses of business alleged herein; (b) ordering Defendants to disgorge their ill-gotten gains and to pay prejudgment interest thereon; (c) imposing civil money penalties on Defendants pursuant to Section 20(d) of the Securities Act [15 U.S.C § 77t(d)] and Section 21(d)(3) of the Exchange Act [15 U.S.C. § 78u(d)(3)]; (d) prohibiting Defendants, pursuant to Section 20(e) of the Securities Act [15 U.S.C. § 77t(e)] and Section 21(d)(2) of the Exchange Act [15 U.S.C. § 78u(d)(2)], from acting as an officer or director of any public company; and (e) prohibiting Defendants, pursuant to Section 21(d)(5) of the Exchange Act [15 U.S.C. § 78u(d)(5)], from participating in any offering of digital or other securities.

. . . .

[Author's note: Detailed factual allegations and the remainder of the complaint have been omitted.[18]]

NOTES AND QUESTIONS

1. This case involved both allegations of fraud and a failure of the company to register the sale or comply with an exemption from registration. Would Centra Tech have been substantially better off if it had met the conditions for an exemption?

2. The above excerpt involves the civil action brought by the SEC. At the same time as this action was initiated, an indictment filed with the U.S.

---

[18]   The entire amended complaint is archived at https://perma.cc/UC3E-APX7.

District Court in Manhattan charged Sohrab "Sam" Sharma, Robert Farkas, and Raymond Trapani (the three co-founders of Centra Tech Inc.) with securities fraud, wire fraud, and two conspiracy counts.[19] The burden of proof is higher in a criminal action, and the degree of knowledge required is higher. What, then, is the purpose of expending the resources necessary to simultaneously pursue both civil and criminal enforcement actions?

3.   Fairly obviously, anyone defrauded by Centra Tech should have had a common law fraud claim that could have been brought and maintained in state court. From the perspectives of injured parties, what are the benefits of treating the ICO as involving the securities fraud?

4.   Assuming the SEC prevails in this action, how are members of the public (especially those defrauded by the misstatements) helped?

In fact, alongside the SEC's civil action and the government's criminal prosecution, a group of investors also sued for securities violations.

On December 13, 2017, Jacob Rensel filed a class action lawsuit against Centra Tech and its founders in the U.S. District Court for the Southern District of Florida. The gravamen of the complaint was that Centra Tech and its founders violated a range of federal securities laws, by selling Centra (CTR) Tokens without registration or an exemption and by the use of fraudulent misrepresentations about the company's business. Many of the factual allegations raised by the SEC were also of concern to the private plaintiffs.

In April 2018, Rensel sought a temporary restraining order, asking that the court impose an asset freeze and a document preservation order, among other relief. For the purpose of the motion, the defendants conceded that their CTR Tokens were securities although they reserved their right to challenge that classification later in the process. Notwithstanding the fact that the defendants "conceded" the classification of the tokens as securities for purposes of the motion, Chief Magistrate Andrea Simonton issued a Report and Recommendation on June 25, 2018, widely hailed as the first judicial determination that tokens should be treated as securities under the *Howey* investment contract test.

In her report, Magistrate Judge Simonton first found that the purchasers of the CRT Tokens had made an "investment of money." By committing assets in the form of cryptocurrencies to the venture, the plaintiffs subjected themselves to the risk of economic loss, which satisfied the first part of the *Howey* test. The second element of the *Howey* test

---

[19]   Sharma and Farkas filed a motion to dismiss the indictment, which was denied by the district court on August 13, 2019. *United States v. Sharma*, No. 18 CR. 340 (LGS), 2019 WL 3802223, at *1 (S.D.N.Y. Aug. 13, 2019). As of the writing of this text, the case is apparently still ongoing.

requires proof of a common enterprise. The Magistrate found that this requirement was met because the economic fortunes of the purchasers were "interwoven with and dependent upon the efforts and success of those seeking the investment." Finally, she considered whether the plaintiffs were relying on the essential efforts of others, as required by *Howey*. She found that this element was satisfied "because the success of Centra Tech and the . . . [products] that it purported to develop was entirely dependent on the efforts and actions of the defendants."

These findings led to the Magistrate Judge's conclusion that the CRT Tokens were securities. Notably, although most courts utilizing the *Howey* test also look to whether there was an expectation of profits, Magistrate Judge did not separately discuss whether the purchasers had a reasonable expectation of profits.

The precedential value of this particular report is unclear, given that it was rendered by a Magistrate Judge in the context of a deciding a motion for a temporary restraining order without the benefit of a trial. Even so, her assessment of *Howey* could be influential as other courts also consider the extent to which the SEC's position about cryptoassets is accurate.

On September 25, 2018, the U.S. District Court Judge entered an Order Granting In Part And Denying In Part The Defendants' Renewed Motion For A Temporary Restraining Order. While the judge did not explicitly address the issue of whether Magistrate Judge Simonton had correctly applied the *Howey* test to the CTR Tokens, he did conclude "that the Report & Recommendation is well-reasoned and accurately states the law of the case. The Report and Recommendation is thorough and exhaustive in its consideration of the Parties' arguments."

The saga of Centra Tech and its founders is not over. On June 12, 2018, the SEC's civil action was stayed until conclusion of the pending criminal proceedings. In August 2019, the District Court for the Southern District of New York denied defendants' motion to dismiss the criminal indictment in U.S. v. Sharma. U.S. v. Sharma, 2019 WL 3802223 (SDNY 2019). Motions and various proceedings were still being docketed as of early November 2019.[20] On the other hand, on the civil side, on September 16, 2019, District Judge Robert Scola denied the private plaintiffs' request to certify a class in the pending action in Florida.[21]

---

[20]   The most recently docketed items for this case may be found at U.S. v. Sharma (1:18-cr-00340) (SDNY) CourtListener, available online at (https://www.courtlistener.com/docket/8010248/united-states-v-sharma/?page=2).

[21]   The Order on Plaintiffs' Motion for Class Certification in Rensel v. Centra Tech, Inc., can be found online at https://www.scribd.com/document/429813635/Centra-Tech-Order

On August 3, 2018, Centra published a "letter" purporting to reveal the truth.[22] According to this release, Centra was forced to remain silent, and it was finally able to "shed some light on the events that happened." Centra claims to have been working with the SEC since November 2017, at which time they were told "it was a non-public order and we actually tried to refund the ICO multiple times through the SEC." Centra holds to its claim that it had a processor willing to issue branded Visa cards domestically and a MasterCard worldwide. "The processor who was going to issue us MasterCards internationally sent us documentation to finalize on or around September, which we ended up executing and delivering on. The fact that he [the SEC representative?] says we lied about our technology in their press releases are flat out wrong."

Centra makes a case for over-reaching by U.S. regulators claiming that "in a US federal regulator system, people get promoted for their work and enforcement. . . . We allege and hypothesize their agenda here is for their own self benefit rather the real protection of the people. We had offered them in multiple separate occasions to refund ICO contributors, through our corporate outside counsel, they refused every time." Centra also alleges bad faith by former employees in connection with some of the concerns expressed by the SEC about the founders' actions.

In addition to the primary actions against the company and its promoters, in late 2018, a professional boxer, Floyd Mayweather Jr, and DJ Khaled, a record executive and media personality, were charged with illegally promoting the Centra Tech ICO. The SEC accused Mayweather of failing to disclose a $100,000 promotional payment and DJ Khaled with failing to report a $50,000 fee received by him. The two celebrities eventually settled those claims, with Mayweather paying more than $600,000 in fines, and DJ Khaled agreeing to pay more than $150,000.

6. THE SEC'S FOCUS ON FRAUD

As of the end of 2018, the SEC and a variety of state securities regulators were actively investigating dozens of cases in which investors lost or claimed to have lost money in crypto investments. "The investigations are aimed at stopping illegal initial coin offerings (ICOs), Ponzi schemes and pump-and-dump scams, but very few were filed during the height of the crypto craze, when many companies were launching ICOs and the price of bitcoin was skyrocketing. More recently, with the price plummeting and investors getting more skeptical, the SEC has been filing

---

[22]   *Dear Centra Community—Let the Truth be known,* MEDIUM (Aug. 3, 2018) (available online at https://medium.com/@Centra/dear-centra-community-let-the-truth-be-known-5241777b 51d1).

more cases. The WSJ noted that in November 2018 that the SEC filed five cases compared to four in 2017."[23]

According to the SEC's Division of Enforcement 2018 Annual Report,[24] the SEC has been particularly vigilant in overseeing ICOs. The SEC has explained how it has used its enforcement authority to address illegal and fraudulent operations.

> We also have recommended enforcement actions for conduct ranging from registration violations, to unregistered broker-dealer activity, to instances in which the purported use of blockchain-related technology is merely a veneer for outright fraud. A poignant example of our impactful approach is the SEC's enforcement action against the co-founders of a purported financial services start-up. This action, coupled with the Enforcement Division's joint statement with the Commission's Office of Compliance Inspections and Examinations urging caution around celebrity promotion of ICOs, brought an almost immediate end to such promotions. [This is a reference to the Centra Tech case described above.] Another example is the SEC's action against an allegedly fraudulent ICO that targeted retail investors to fund what it claimed to be the world's first "decentralized bank." [This is a reference to Arise Bank.] We moved quickly to stop the fraud by obtaining a court order, and the action showcased our ability to obtain a receiver over digital assets.[25]

While this excerpt points to only two actions, the enforcement report also indicated that "[a]s of the close of FY 2018, the SEC had brought over a dozen stand-alone enforcement actions involving digital assets and ICOs. . . . In the past year, the Division has opened dozens of investigations involving ICOs and digital assets, many of which were ongoing at the close of FY 2018."[26]

7. FRAUD BY PERSONS OTHER THAN "ISSUERS"

In the world of conventional securities regulation, the "primary" securities market involves securities such as debt and equity interests sold by an issuer. The issuer is typically the company responsible for repaying the debt or to which the equity stake relates. It is generally the issuer that is responsible for compliance under the '33 Act, whether it be in terms of

---

[23]   *Crypto Scam Victims Unlikely To Get Their Money Back*, PYMNTS.COM (Dec. 26, 2018) (available online at https://www.pymnts.com/news/security-and-risk/2018/sec-cryptocurrency-bitcoin-scam/).

[24]   SEC, *2018 Annual Report from the Division of Enforcement* [archived at https://perma.cc/8MW9-KES2].

[25]   *Id.* at 3.

[26]   *Id.* at 7–8.

providing required disclosures, choosing to register a sale, or finding and complying with an applicable exemption for the initial distribution.[27]

In its 2018 Annual Report, the SEC's Division of Enforcement reported that it had brought 490 stand-alone cases in FY 2018, most of which did not involve cryptotransactions. Of those, approximately 25% involved securities offerings and 16% involved issuer reporting/accounting and auditing issuers. In addition, the SEC brought actions relating to investment advisors, broker-dealer misconduct, insider trading, and market manipulation.

In the context of cryptotransactions, the SEC is similarly interested in more than the conduct of issuers. For example, the SEC brought a civil action (and the Department of Justice simultaneously pursued a criminal suit) against BitFunder, a crypto exchange, and its operator, Jon E. Montroll.[28]

The SEC action was filed on February 21, 2018, and it included allegations of a variety of securities violations under both the '33 and '34 Acts.[29] According to the complaint, Montroll operated the BitFunder online platform from December 2012 to November 2013 as an unregistered securities exchange. Users of the platform could create and trade Bitcoins for virtual "shares" of various virtual currency-related enterprises. Users would deposit Bitcoins into a wallet maintained and controlled by an Australian affiliate of Montroll. According to the complaint, Montroll systematically misappropriated clients' Bitcoins maintained in the wallet that he controlled.

Beginning in July, 2013, Montroll also sold shares in certain interests called "Ukyo Notes," promising purchasers a daily interest rate. Proceeds were supposed to be used for investment purposes but instead he used at least some of the proceeds to pay personal expenses and to replenish Bitcoin accounts which he had raided.

For five weeks between July 28, 2013, and August 27, 2013, BitFunder was the subject of a cyberattack that resulted in the loss of more than 6,000 Bitcoins, then valued at approximately $775,000. Montroll failed to disclose

---

[27] In part, this is because the '33 Act exempts from the registration requirement "transactions by any person other than an issuer, underwriter, or dealer." 15 U.S. Code § 77d(a)(1). Although this is a very broad exemption, it does not cover the world of secondary transactions. While the term "dealer" is limited to persons who are in the business of "offering, buying, selling, or otherwise dealing or trading in securities issued by another person," (15 U.S. Code § 77b(a)(12)), an underwriter is not necessarily a securities professional. An "underwriter" includes anyone who had bought a security from an issuer or someone under common control with the issuer, if that purchase or resale is "with a view to" or "in connection with" a distribution. It also includes anyone who "participates or has a direct or indirect participation in any such undertaking" unless the participation is limited to the usual commission paid to a dealer. (15 U.S. Code § 77b(a)(11).

[28] See USA v. Montroll, case number 1:18–cr–00520, and SEC v. Montroll, case number 1:18–cv–01582, both filed in Manhattan in the U.S. District Court for the Southern District of New York.

[29] SEC v. Montroll, Case 1:18–cv–01582 [archived at https://perma.cc/67CQ-JKAH].

this loss, continuing to solicit and accept new deposits, misleading investors about the profitability of the enterprise.

In early November 2013, users began to experience difficulty in withdrawing Bitcoins from their accounts, which Montroll falsely attributed to technical difficulties. Montroll finally closed BitFunder on November 14, 2013.

When the SEC began investigating the incident, Montroll continued his pattern of lies and omissions. The SEC complaint was eventually filed in early 2018, and Montroll was arrested and indicted on criminal charges arising out of the same events at the same time.

In July 2018, Montroll admitted to securities fraud and obstruction, eventually explaining in a December 27, 2018, sentencing memo that he had been panicked, ashamed, and desperate. Montroll requested that he be allowed to avoid prison time, stating that "[n]either greed nor a lack of concern for the people who became victims was the motive."

The government requested a much harsher penalty, filing a government memo on January 14, 2019 asking for a prison term of about 2 ½ years for lying to the SEC and defrauding customers. The government suggested that official guidelines calling for a sentence between 27 and 33 months were reasonable for a defendant who showed "disrespect" to the SEC as it investigated his businesses.

The Manhattan U.S. attorney suggested that the value of the stolen Bitcoins had appreciated to roughly $70 million, while Montroll was scheduled to make restitution of roughly $167,000 (representing the proceeds Montroll claims he derived from the wrongdoing).

A January 21, 2019, response by Montroll repeated the defense's claim that he deserved no incarceration. The supplemental memo claimed that Montroll's "extraordinary rehabilitation, good character, his unique role in providing employment and care for many people, and his acceptance of responsibility are compelling reasons for a sentence involving no incarceration." The court, however, disagreed, and on July 11, 2019, sentenced Montroll to 14 months in prison for lying to the SEC and defrauding customers.[30] Montroll was also ordered to forfeit $167,480.

Reports suggest that Montroll expects to settle with the SEC as well, although as the date these materials were written, the final recommendation from the SEC had not been announced.[31]

---

[30]   T. Gorman, *Lessons in Handling Digital Assets, Cyber Security*, SEC ACTIONS (Jul. 15, 2019) (available online at https://www.secactions.com/lessons-in-handling-digital-assets-cyber-security/).

[31]   Maria Nikolova, *SEC awaits conclusion of criminal proceeding against BitFunder operator Jon Montroll*, FINANCEFEEDS (Jun. 20, 2019) (available online at https://financefeeds.com/sec-awaits-conclusion-criminal-proceeding-bitfunder-operator-jon-montroll/).

NOTES AND QUESTIONS

1.   The government had suggested 2 ½ years of prison time, while Montroll had suggested no incarceration at all. The court split the difference with a sentence of 14 months. Do you think that is an appropriate sentence? Given the expense of incarceration, is that sentence justified? What interests are served by the 14 month prison term ordered by the court?

2.   What kinds of penalties would you expect to see in the civil enforcement action (which is not addressed in the above materials)? Is disgorgement of the entire amount of the wrongfully obtained proceeds a sufficient remedy? Why or why not? Should the Bitcoins that he stole be valued as of the date of the thefts or at today's price? Or should they be valued at the highest trading price between 2013 and today?

Despite the active involvement of the SEC in pursuing fraud claims against persons in the crypto ecosystem, such activities continue.

For example, in June of 2019, the SEC filed claims against Longfin Corp., Venkata S. Meenavalli (its CEO), and a Longfin consultant, for falsifying company revenue and fraudulently obtaining a listing on NASDAQ.[32] Longfin, which had ceased operations in 2018, had obtained qualification under a Regulation A+ exemption, but only by making numerous false representations to the SEC. Its NASDAQ listing, since surrendered, had been similarly obtained based on materially false claims. The defendants have agreed to settlements (subject to court approval) to resolve the SEC's charges, including returning a total of more than $22.7 million plus fines of more than $3 million.[33] However, the U.S. Attorney's Office for the District of New Jersey announced on June 5, 2019 that it had obtained an indictment and was bringing criminal charges in the matter.[34] The criminal case is not necessarily affected by the consent decree and settlement with the SEC, in which the defendants do not admit to any wrongdoing.

On August 13, 2019, the SEC announced that it was pursuing fraud claims against Reginald Middleton, a self-proclaimed "financial guru," and two entities under his control, Veritaseum, Inc. and Veritaseum, LLC.[35] The SEC's complaint alleged that the defendants marketed securities

---

[32]   SEC Press Release, *SEC Adds Fraud Charges Against Purported Cryptocurrency Company Longfin, CEO, and Consultant*, Release 2019–90 [archived at https://perma.cc/P6CL-37Q3].

[33]   *Id.*

[34]   *U.S. v. Meenavalli*, U.S. District Court, District of New Jersey, No. 19–cr–00402. (The docket for this matter can be found online at https://www.courtlistener.com/docket/15748102/united-states-v-meenavalli/).

[35]   SEC Press Release, *SEC Obtains Freeze of $8 Million in Assets in Alleged Fraudulent Token Offering and Manipulation Scheme*, Release 2019–150 (Aug. 13, 2019) [archived at https://perma.cc/EUK8-RKW5].

called VERI tokens, relying on numerous material misrepresentations including lying about their prior business ventures, the extent of consumer demand for the tokens, and claims of a functional product when no such token existed.[36] The district court promptly granted a temporary restraining order, freezing approximately $8,000,000 in assets out of the $14.8 million allegedly raised in 2017 and 2018.[37]

On August 20, 2019, the SEC announced a settlement with ICO Rating, a Russian ICO research and rating provider, that had been charged with failing to disclose payments that it had received to promote their crypto securities.[38] ICO Rating did not admit to violating U.S. law, but it did agree to avoid any future violations, to disgorge funds paid plus interest, and to pay a penalty in the amount of $162,000.[39]

These continuing patterns of fraudulent misrepresentations made in connection with the sale and promotion of cryptoassets help set the foundation for the SEC's insistence that it remain active in regulating such transactions. The SEC's ongoing and evolving response will be discussed in more detail in the next chapter.

---

[36]   A copy of the SEC's complaint in the *SEC v. Reginald ("Reggie") Middleton*, CV 19–4625 (E.D. N.Y., 2019), is archived at https://perma.cc/8GZV-LQLH.

[37]   A copy of the order can be found online at https://www.sec.gov/litigation/complaints/2019/order-pr2019-150.pdf.

[38]   SEC, Press Release, *SEC Charges ICO Research and Rating Provider With Failing to Disclose It Was Paid to Tout Digital Assets*, Release 2019–157 (Aug. 20, 2019) [archived at https://perma.cc/4YLZ-82UK].

[39]   *Id.*

CHAPTER 10

IS CRYPTO A SECURITY? THE SEC, THE COURTS, AND COMMENTATORS REACT

■ ■ ■

The SEC has tried to be responsive to developments involving crypto. While not all of its actions seem to be particularly supportive of the new technology, certainly the SEC has acted in ways that directly line up with its mission to protect both the investing public and the integrity of the nation's capital markets. Along with public statements to the effect that the agency has no desire to inappropriately stifle innovation, the SEC has taken or is taking the following steps:

(1) It has repeatedly warned investors about the potential risks associated with investing in cryptoassets.

(2) It has published guidance and taken legal action against individual enterprises.

(3) It has done the same with regard to individuals in order to clarify how the securities laws apply to crypto.

(4) It has instituted cease and desist proceedings against offerings of crypto that were neither registered nor exempt and which, in the opinion of the agency, involved the sale of securities.

(5) It has investigated and initiated enforcement actions in cases involving fraud in connection with crypto offerings.

(6) It has acted to see that crypto trading platforms are complying with federal registration requirements.

(7) It continues to evaluate requests for approval of ETFs for crypto.

Some of these actions, such as warnings directed to potential investors about the risks of investing in crypto, have not garnered much of a reaction from the crypto community. Others have resulted in substantial pushback, either in the form of criticism or in extended litigation. To fully frame the discussion of where the future regulation of crypto might be headed, each of these responses require some consideration.

1. THE SEC: PROTECTING POTENTIAL INVESTORS

Before the SEC formulated a cohesive approach to crypto-based transactions, and before it released anything like guidance for crypto-entrepreneurs, it began posting investor alerts, warning potential investors about the risk of speculating in Bitcoin and other cryptocurrencies. This began as early as mid-2013, with an alert about the risk that virtual currencies were being used in Ponzi schemes.[1] In May 2014, the SEC published a second investor alert, warning potential investors about extensive risks associated with investment in Bitcoin and other virtual currencies.[2]

More recently, the SEC has been even more proactive in seeking to inform and educate the public, posting a number of alerts and bulletins relating to ICOs and questionable practices in 2017 and 2018. Here is a list of some of the investor bulletins, alerts, and statements posted in 2017 and 2018 by the SEC relating to ICOs:

- SEC, Investor.gov, *Investor Bulletin: Initial Coin Offerings* (July 25, 2017) [archived at https://perma.cc/3DRB-XBDU].

- SEC, Investor.gov, *Investor Alert: Public Companies Making ICO-Related Claims* (Aug. 28, 2017) [archived at https://perma.cc/A6KR-F92P].

- SEC, Investor.gov, *Investor Alert: Celebrity Endorsements* (Nov. 1, 2017) [archived at https://perma.cc/8LYR-NED8].

- SEC, Investor.gov, *Chairman Clayton's Statement on Cryptocurrencies and Initial Coin Offerings* (Dec. 11, 2017) [archived at https://perma.cc/EAZ6-TKHN].

- SEC, Investor.gov, *The SEC Has an Opportunity You Won't Want to Miss: Act Now!* (May 16, 2018) [archived at https://perma.cc/FZV3-RTZE].

- SEC, Investor.gov, *Investor Alert: Watch Out For False Claims About SEC And CFTC Endorsements Used To Promote Digital Asset Investments* (Oct. 11, 2018) [archived at https://perma.cc/U76G-74YV].

Some of these were very specific (such as warning about celebrity endorsements and false claims of regulatory endorsements), and some quite general (including the May 16, 2018 posting about the false Howey

---

[1]   SEC, Investor Alert, *Ponzi Schemes Using Virtual Currencies* (July 23, 2013) [archived at https://perma.cc/6KE4-BK5L].

[2]   SEC, Investor Alert, *Investor Alert: Bitcoin and Other Virtual Currency-Related Investments* (May 7, 2014) [archived at https://perma.cc/T7UK-H7RA].

Coin with links to informational postings about investment risks and the potential for fraud).

Given that one of the primary missions of the SEC is to protect investors, these types of releases and announcements are almost certain to continue. It is to be expected that as the SEC further refines its approach to cryptoassets and transactions, it will continue its policy of investor alerts and guidance. It is likely that future releases will include more specific information geared not just at educating the public but also at assisting potential developers and issuers (as well as broker-dealers and exchanges) about how to comply with applicable regulations.

2. THE SEC: ESTABLISHING GUIDELINES TO EXPLAIN WHEN CRYPTO IS A SECURITY

The extent to which the federal securities laws apply to cryptoassets and transactions has obviously been something that the SEC has been considering for some time. The 2013 and 2014 investor alerts described above provide evidence of this concern.

In June 2016, Mary Jo White, then SEC Chairwoman, noted that the key regulatory issue facing the SEC at that time was whether blockchain applications fit within existing regulatory structures or whether the new technology required the adoption of a new system for registration and regulation.[3]

To some extent, this question was answered by the SEC in its 2017 report on The DAO, described in some detail in chapter eight.[4] That report takes the position that under the traditional *Howey* investment contract test, crypto should often be regarded and regulated as a security. The report does not discuss whether an entirely new system of regulation or registration is warranted, instead recognizing (at least implicitly) that investor protection of some sort is needed now. Under the terms of The DAO report, the SEC focused on the particular facts and circumstances surrounding The DAO, and concluded that based on longstanding principles, the proposed DAO tokens were indeed investment contracts and therefore securities. The report concluded that issuers of such securities must register offers and sales unless a valid exemption from registration applies.

More recently, the position that cryptoassets are often going to be securities was bolstered by remarks from SEC Chairman Jay Clayton to

---

[3]   SEC, Mary Jo White, *Opening Remarks at the Fintech Forum* (Nov. 14, 2016) [archived at https://perma.cc/5422-PM79]; *see also* Michael del Castillo, *How the SEC's Blockchain Lead is Defining Future Regulation*, COINDESK (Nov. 17, 2016), https://perma.cc/BVJ2-B6NY (analyzing Mary Jo White's remarks).

[4]   SEC, *Report of Investigation Pursuant to Section 21(a) of the Securities Exchange Act of 1934: The DAO*, '34 ACT RELEASE NO. 81207 (July 25, 2017) [archived at https://perma.cc/F862-YS5V].

the effect every ICO he has seen has involved the sale of a security.[5] Commentators have concluded that this means there is, in effect, at least a presumption that cryptoassets are securities requiring either registration or an exemption in order to be lawfully sold in this country.[6] To the extent that this paints an accurate picture of the SEC's response to developments by crypto entrepreneurs, suggestions that functional "utility tokens" will be outside the reach of the securities laws appear inaccurate.[7] In fact, in the 2018 Annual Report by the SEC's Enforcement Division, cryptocurrency scams are now listed among the SEC's top priorities. This only makes sense if the SEC has concluded that the cryptoassets in question are securities.

Not all of the statements attributed to the SEC in various sources are formal or binding legal determinations by the agencies. While the lengthy DAO Report (mentioned above as well as in chapter eight), was the result of a formal SEC investigation, a number of pronouncements simply represent the opinion of various officials within the SEC. For example, SEC Chairman Jay Clayton has offered extensive testimony to various officials about the role of the SEC in overseeing cryptocurrencies. In his February 2018 explanation to the U.S. Senate Committee on Banking, Housing, and Urban Affairs, Chairman Clayton emphasized that "determining what falls within the ambit of a securities offer and sale is a facts-and-circumstances analysis, utilizing a principles-based framework that has served American companies and American investors well through periods of innovation and change for over 80 years."[8] This testimony was couched as the Chairman's personal opinion.

---

[5]   On February 6, 2018, the Senate heard testimony from SEC Chairman Jay Clayton that "every ICO token the SEC has seen so far is considered a security and . . . if a crypto-asset issued by a company increases in value over time depending on the performance of the company, it is considered a security." Joseph Young, *SEC Hints at Tighter Regulation for ICOs, Smart Policies for "True Cryptocurrencies,"* COINTELEGRAPH (Feb. 9, 2018) [archived at https://perma.cc/Z5KF-BXG9].

[6]   *See, e.g.,* Daniel C. Zinman, et al., *SEC Issues Warning to Lawyers on ICOs,* BLOOMBERG LAW (Feb. 22, 2018), [archived at https://perma.cc/FBB5-AWF9]. Reproduced with permission. Published February 22, 2018. Copyright 2018 by The Bureau of National Affairs, Inc. (800-372-1033) http://www.bna.com. This source examines a number of recent pronouncements and actions taken by the SEC and concludes that "the SEC has essentially adopted a rebuttable presumption that ICO tokens are securities that must comply with the registration requirements of the securities laws." *Accord* Evelyn Cheng, *The SEC Just Made it Clearer That Securities Laws Apply to Most Cryptocurrencies and Exchanges Trading Them,* CNBC (Mar. 7, 2018, 5:14 PM) (available online at https://www.cnbc.com/2018/03/07/the-sec-made-it-clearer-that-securities-laws-apply-to-cryptocurrencies.html).

[7]   *But I Have a 'Utility Token' Not a 'Security Token',* CRYPTO INV. SUMMIT (Mar. 28, 2018) (available online at https://cis.la/blog/but-i-have-a-utility-token-not-a-security-token.html). This source concludes that any token sold "for the purpose of raising capital . . . [where] purchasers are buying based upon speculation that the token will increase in value, . . . [is likely to amount to] the offering of a security . . . regardless of whether you call it a utility token or a security token.").

[8]   SEC Testimony, Chairman Jay Clayton, *Chairman's Testimony on Virtual Currencies: The Roles of the SEC and CFTC* (Feb. 6, 2018) [archived at https://perma.cc/WU7R-CK4E].

While that particular statement was the opinion of one person (albeit a very important person at the SEC), there are also plenty of formal actions confirming the SEC's reliance on the *Howey* investment contract test to determine when crypto should be treated as a security. Moreover, it appears that the courts have generally acquiesced in the position that *Howey* provides the appropriate test to gauge whether or not a cryptoasset is a security.

They do this not because the test is easy to apply, but because of its flexibility. Both the SEC and the courts have acknowledged that the test is fact intensive, requiring a consideration of the facts and circumstances, in order to ascertain whether new and innovative opportunities involve the sale of "investment contracts."

PRELIMINARY NOTES AND QUESTIONS

1. Why do you think the SEC was so insistent on trying to apply the securities laws to the transaction described in the following order?

2. There were some relatively unusual facts in the following case that led the court to decline to issue the requested injunction. What were the unusual facts and how did they relate to the *Howey* test?

3. What would be the probable consequence of a judicial determination not to issue the preliminary injunction?

4. Given the unusual facts, do you believe the November 27, 2018, order would have had much precedential value or been a persuasive authority in other cases?

SEC v. BLOCKVEST, LLC [DENYING PRELIMINARY INJUNCTION]
Case No.: 18CV2287–GPB(BLM)
(US Dist. Cal. Nov. 27, 2018)[9]

Order Denying Plaintiff's Motion For Preliminary Injunction

Before the Court is Plaintiff's order to show cause why a preliminary injunction should not issue . . . .

Factual Background

Plaintiff Securities and Exchange Commission ("SEC" or "Plaintiff") filed a Complaint against Defendants Blockvest, LLC and Reginald Buddy Ringgold, III a/k/a Rasool Abdul Rahim El alleging [various violations of the federal securities laws]. . . .

---

[9]   This order is archived at https://perma.cc/RR4H-JVDM.

Defendant Reginald Buddy Ringgold, III ("Ringgold"), is the chairman and founder of Defendant Blockvest, LLC ("Blockvest") (collectively "Defendants"), a Wyoming limited liability company that was set up to exchange cryptocurrencies but has never become operational. Blockvest Investment Group, LLC owns 100% of Blockvest LLC. Ringgold owns 51% of the membership interests of Blockvest Investment Group, LLC, 9% are unissued, 20% is owned by Michael Shepperd, and the remaining 20% is owned by Ringgold's mother.

The complaint alleges that Defendants have been offering and selling alleged unregistered securities in the form of digital assets called BLV's. It involves an initial coin offering ("ICO"), which is a fundraising event where an entity offers participants a unique digital "coin" or "token" or "digital asset" in exchange for consideration, often in the form of virtual currency—most commonly Bitcoin and Ether—or fiat currency. The tokens are issued on a "blockchain" or cryptographically secured ledger. The token may entitle its holders to certain rights related to a venture underlying the ICO, such as rights to profits, shares of assets, rights to use certain services provided by the issuer, and/or voting rights. These tokens may also be listed on online trading platforms, often called virtual currency exchanges, and tradable for virtual or fiat currencies. ICOs are typically announced and promoted through online channels and issuers usually release a "whitepaper" describing the project and the terms of the ICO. To participate, investors are generally required to transfer funds (often virtual currency) to the issuer's address, online wallet, or other account. After the completion of the ICO, the issuer will distribute its unique "tokens" to the participants' unique address on the blockchain.

According to the complaint, Blockvest conducted pre-sales of BLVs in March 2018. According to the whitepaper, the BLVs are being sold in several stages: 1) a private sale (with a 50% bonus) that ran through April 30, 2018; 2) currently, a "pre-sale" (with a 20% bonus) from July 1, 2018 through October 6, 2018; and 3) the $100 million ICO launch on December 1, 2018. On May 6, 2018, Blockvest claimed it raised $2.5 million in 7 days, and by September 17, 2018, it had sold 18% of the tokens being offered or around 9 million tokens. Blockvest purports to be the "First Licensed and Regulated Tokenized Crypto Currency Exchange & Index Fund based in the US".

According to the SEC, Blockvest and Ringgold falsely claim their ICO has been "registered" and "approved" by the SEC and using the SEC's seal on the website [and similarly endorsed by the CFTC]. . . . In order to create legitimacy and an impression that their investment is safe, Defendants also created a fictitious regulatory agency, the Blockchain Exchange Commission ("BEC"), creating its own fake government seal, logo, and mission statement that are nearly identical to the SEC's seal, logo and mission statement. Moreover, BEC's "office" is the same address as the SEC's headquarters.

In response, Ringgold asserts that Blockvest has never sold any tokens to the public and has only [one] investor, Rosegold Investments LLP, ("Rosegold") which is run by him where he has invested more than $175,000 of his own money. Blockvest utilized BLV tokens during the testing and development phase and a total of 32 partner testers were involved.

During this testing, 32 testers put a total of less than $10,000 of Bitcoin and Ethereum onto the Blockvest Exchange where half of it remains today. The other half was used to pay transactional fees to unknown and unrelated third parties. No BLV tokens were ever released from the Blockvest platform to the 32 testing participants. The BLV tokens were only designed for testing the platform and the testers would not and could not keep or remove BLV tokens from the Blockvest Exchange. Their plan was to eventually issue a "new utility Token BLVX on the NEM Blockchain for exclusive use on the BlockVest Exchange." Ringgold never received any money from the sale of BLV tokens. The deposits are from digital wallet addresses and individuals that are not easily identifiable, but Ringgold believes that only affiliated persons would have deposited Bitcoin or Ethereum on the exchange and received nothing without complaining. The Blockvest Exchange platform was never open for business.

. . . .

Ringgold recognizes that mistakes were made but no representations or omissions were made in connection with the sale and purchase of securities. They were in the early stages of development as the Chief Compliance Officer had not yet reviewed all the materials. Ringgold states it was his intention to comply with "every possible regulation and regulatory agency." Currently, he has ceased all efforts to proceed with the ICO and agrees not to proceed with an ICO until he gives SEC's counsel 30 days' notice. He claims that because all his assets are frozen, he is unable to pay his counsel or third party professionals for defending this litigation and to compensate Mike Sheppard and himself for living expenses and also to support his small children as he is their primary source of funds for living expenses. Currently, the only assets Ringgold has is Rosegold's bank account which has less than $40,000.

In reply, the SEC argues that Defendants admit to receiving funds from at least 32 investors in exchange for anticipated BLV tokens. While Defendants' accounting claims that less than $10,000 were received for BLV tokens from third parties, the documents shows transactions in excess of $180,000. The SEC claims that Defendants also admit that Rosegold, which "manages Blockvest and finances Blockvest's activities" had 17 other investors during the pre-ICO solicitations and at least eight investors wrote "coins" or "Blockvest" on the checks.

Discussion

A. Preliminary Injunction

The legal standard that applies to a motion for a TRO is the same as a motion for a preliminary injunction.

. . . .

B. Prima Facie Case of Past Securities Violations

Plaintiff alleges Defendants violated [various securities laws]. . . . In their opposition, Defendants solely challenge the SEC's claims arguing that the test BLV tokens are not "securities" as defined under the federal securities law.

. . . .

1. Whether the BLV Token is a "Security" Subject to Securities Law

Section 2(a)(1) of the Securities Act and Section 3(a)(10) of the Securities Exchange Act define "security" as inter alia, a "note, stock, treasury stock, bond, [or] investment contract." 15 U.S.C. § 77b(a)(1); 15 U.S.C. § 78c(a)(10). Although the definition of a "security" in the Securities Act of 1933 is slightly different than the Securities Exchange Act of 1934, the two definitions have been held to be "virtually identical."

In its moving papers, the SEC claims that under the three-part test articulated in *SEC v. W.J. Howey Co.*, 328 U.S. 293, 298–99 (1946), the BLV tokens are "securities." Defendants argue that the BLV tokens are not "securities" as defined under *Howey*.

Congress defined "security" to be "sufficiently broad to encompass virtually any instrument that might be sold as an investment" but did not "intend to provide a broad federal remedy for all fraud." *Reves v. Ernst & Young*, 494 U.S. 45, 61 (1990) (internal quotations omitted). Courts should look not to the form but to the "economic realities of the transaction." *United Hous. Fdn. v. Forman*, 421 U.S. 837, 838 (1975).

. . . .

Howey's three-part test requires "(1) an investment of money (2) in a common enterprise (3) with an expectation of profits produced by the efforts of others." *SEC v. Rubera*, 350 F.3d 1084, 1090 (9th Cir. 2003) (internal quotation marks omitted); *SEC v. Shavers*, Case No. 13cv416, 2014 WL 12622292, at *6 (E.D. Texas Aug. 26, 2014) (district court found investment in Bitcoin Savings and Trust to be an investment contract under *Howey*).

. . . .

In opposition [to the SEC's request for an injunction], Defendants present a different rendering of facts than the SEC. They explain that they did not raise $2.5 million from the public but instead the $2.5 million was supposed to be based on a transaction with David Drake. However, the transaction eventually collapsed and they admit the social media posts were overly optimistic. They assert they have not sold any BLV tokens to the public but instead used the BLV tokens for purposes of testing during the development phase. During this phase, 32 testers put a total of less than $10,000 of Bitcoin and Ethereum onto the Blockvest Exchange. The BLV tokens were only designed for testing the platform and no tokens were released to the 32 testing participants. In the future, they intended to issue a new utility Token BLVX on the NEM Blockchain for exclusive use on the Blockvest Exchange. Moreover, Defendants argue there is no common enterprise and the tokens do not represent an interest in or obligation of a corporation or other business. Therefore, Defendants argue the BLV token is not a "security."

In reply, Plaintiff contends that Defendants marketed Blockvest ICO as a securities offering and while they argue BLVs were utility tokens, their intent of the offering was to fund Blockvest's future business. Moreover, Defendants admit that tokens were sold on Blockvest's website for money or ether and whether investors received the tokens is not relevant in determining whether the tokens are securities.

The first "investment of money" prong of *Howey* "requires that the investor 'commit his assets to the enterprise in such a manner as to subject himself to financial loss.'" *SEC v. Rubera*, 350 F.3d 1084, 1090 (9th Cir. 2003) (quoting *Hector v. Wiens*, 533 F.2d 429, 432 (9th Cir. 1976) (per curiam)). In *Rubera*, the investors "turned over substantial amounts of money . . . with the hope that [the investment managers' efforts] would yield financial gains." *Id.* "At the outset, we note that, while the subjective intent of the purchasers may have some bearing on the issue of whether they entered into investment contracts, we must focus our inquiry on what the purchasers were offered or promised." *Warfield v. Alaniz*, 569 F.3d 1015, 1021 (9th Cir. 2009). The focus on this "investment of money" prong is "what the purchasers were offered or promised." *Id.*

. . . .

The SEC argues that Blockvest's website and whitepaper presented an offer of a unregistered security in violation of Sections 5 of the Securities Act; however, its argument presumes, without evidentiary support, that the 32 test investors reviewed the Blockvest website, the whitepaper and media posts when they clicked the "buy now" button on Blockvest's website.

At his deposition, Ringgold explained that the Blockvest website was available to the public for pre-registration for the upcoming exchange.

There were also testers working on the functionality of the exchange. The "buy now" button on the website did not disclose that it was only for testors and management but once a person moved forward, he or she could not buy any coins because the platform was not "live." But the "buy now" button was accepting cryptocurrency and 32 "internal" people who were sophisticated investors helped Defendants with managing the different functions needed to test the platform. Ringgold states he knows the identity of the 32 investors. He indicated it was clear to the 32 testers that they were testing the platform so Defendants did not obtain any earnings statements from them. Ringgold explains that the 32 investor were vetted and chosen based on Defendants' prior relationship with them.

During the vetting process, Defendants collected their name, email, address and their level of sophistication. They held several conferences and a webinar where Ringgold explained his requirements for the group of test investors. Ringgold also testified that there was also a time when the credit card function with the "buy now" button on the Blockvest website was being tested but after four transactions with people Defendants knew or referred to them by somebody on the team, they shut it down because there were issues with the functionality.

Plaintiff and Defendants provide starkly different facts as to what the 32 test investors relied on, in terms of promotional materials, information, economic inducements or oral representations at the seminars, before they purchased the test BLV tokens. Therefore, because there are disputed issues of fact, the Court cannot make a determination whether the test BLV tokens were "securities" under the first prong of *Howey*.

As to the second prong of *Howey*, Plaintiff has not demonstrated that the 32 test investors had an "expectation of profits." While Defendants claim that they had an expectation in Blockvest's future business, no evidence is provided to support the test investors' expectation of profits. "By profits, the Court has meant either capital appreciation resulting from the development of the initial investment . . . or a participation in earnings resulting from the use of investors' funds." *Forman*, 421 U.S. at 852.

At this stage, without full discovery and disputed issues of material facts, the Court cannot make a determination whether the BLV token offered to the 32 test investors was a "security." Thus, Plaintiff has not demonstrated that the BLV tokens purchased by the 32 test investors were "securities" as defined under the securities laws.

The SEC also argues that Defendants have identified 17 individuals who invested money in Rosegold. Defendants present the declarations of nine individuals who assert that they did not buy BLV tokens or rely on any representations that the SEC has alleged are false. In reply, Plaintiff notes that eight individuals wrote "Blockvest" or "coins" on their checks and Defendants admitted to providing some of them the Blockvest ICO whitepaper.

Ringgold testified that he raised around $150,000 through friends and family that invested in Rosegold. Ringgold, himself, also invested $200,000 in Rosegold. His friends and family, as well as Mike Sheppard's friends and family who invested in Rosegold did not care what they were investing in because they trusted them based on their long-time familial and friend relationship. He admitted he showed the Blockvest whitepaper to his family and close friends to get an honest opinion on the design and content of it but not to solicit an investment. He testified that none of the close friends and family who he shared the whitepaper with invested because they did not have the means.

Here, there is a disputed issue of fact whether the 17 individuals who invested in Rosegold purchased "securities" as defined under the federal securities law. Merely writing "Blockvest" or "coins" on their checks is not sufficient to demonstrate what promotional materials or economic inducements these purchasers were presented with prior to their investments. See Warfield, 569 F.3d at 1021. Accordingly, Plaintiff has not demonstrated that "securities" were sold to the 17 individuals.

In sum, the Court concludes that Plaintiff has not demonstrated a prima facie showing that there has been a previous violation of the federal securities laws.

. . . .

The SEC filed a motion for partial reconsideration, and a second hearing was held February 8, 2019. On February 14, 2019, the Court issued an order granting the SEC's motion for reconsideration (at least in part), and issued the requested preliminary injunction.

SEC v. Blockvest, LLC [Order for Reconsideration]
Case No.: 18CV2287–GPB(BLM)
(S.D. Cal, Feb. 14, 2019)

ORDER GRANTING PLAINTIFF'S MOTION
FOR PARTIAL RECONSIDERATION

. . . .

C.   Prima Facie Case of Past Securities Violations

Plaintiff alleges Defendants violated Sections 17(a)(1), (2), and (3) of the Securities Act.[10] Section 2(a)(1) of the Securities Act defines "security" as inter alia, a "note, stock, treasury stock, bond, [or] investment contract." 15 U.S.C. § 77b(a)(1). Congress defined "security" to be "sufficiently broad to encompass virtually any instrument that might be sold as an investment" but did not "intend to provide a broad federal remedy for all fraud." *Reves v. Ernst & Young*, 494 U.S. 45, 61 (1990) (internal quotations omitted). Courts should look not to the form but to the "economic realities of the transaction." *United Hous. Fdn. v. Forman*, 421 U.S. 837, 838 (1975).

In *Howey*, the Court defined whether an investment contract is a security under the Securities Act and held that an investment contract is "a contract, transaction or scheme whereby a person invests his money in a common enterprise and is led to expect profits solely from the efforts of the promoter or a third party." *SEC v. W.J. Howey Co.*, 328 U.S. 293, 298–99 (1946). The Court noted that the Securities Act prohibits not only the sale but also the offer of an unregistered, non-exempt security so the fact that purchasers choose not to accept the full offer is not relevant. *Id.* at 300–01.

. . . .

The Court agrees with the SEC that the *Howey* test is unquestionably an objective one. However, the Court disputes the SEC's assertion that the Court applied a subjective test so as to require the SEC to demonstrate a security "solely on the beliefs of some individual investors, rather than on the objective nature of the investment being offered to the public . . . ." and for it to show what specific investors relied on before they purchased the test BLV tokens. Instead, the Court, relying on Ninth Circuit authority,

---

[10]   Section 17(a) provides,

It shall be unlawful for any person in the offer or sale of any securities . . . by the use of any means or instruments of transportation or communication in interstate commerce or by use of the mails, directly or indirectly

   (1)   to employ any device, scheme, or artifice to defraud, or

   (2)   to obtain money or property by means of any untrue statement of a material fact or any omission to state a material fact necessary in order to make the statements made, in light of the circumstances under which they were made, not misleading; or

   (3)   to engage in any transaction, practice, or course of business which operates or would operate as a fraud or deceit upon the purchaser.

15 U.S.C. § 77q.

recognized it was required to objectively inquire into the "terms of promotional materials, information, economic inducements or oral representations at the seminars", or in other words, an inquiry into the "character of the instrument or transaction offered" to the "purchasers." However, because there were disputed factual issues as to the nature of the investment being offered to the alleged investors, the Court denied the preliminary injunction as to these purchasers.

[The court reaffirms its decision that, as to the 32 "test" investors and 17 initial purchasers, there was no sale of "securities."]

. . . .

The SEC provided a separate theory to support its request for a preliminary injunction. The SEC alleged, in the alternative, that the promotional materials presented on Defendants' website, the Whitepaper posted online and social media accounts concerning the ICO of the BLV token constitute an "offer" of unregistered "securities," that contain materially false statements and thus, constitute violations of Section 17(a). Defendants oppose the reconsideration motion arguing that the term "offer" requires a manifestation of intent to be bound which the SEC failed to demonstrate. The Court did not directly address this alternative theory in its original order and based upon the additional submitted briefing concludes that Defendants made an "offer" of unregistered securities which violated Section 17(a).

Section 17(a) applies to the "offer" or "sale" of securities. 15 U.S.C. § 77q. A violation of Section 17(a) does not require a completed sale of securities. *See SEC v. American Commodity Exch.*, 546 F.2d 1361, 1366 (10th Cir. 1976) ("actual sales [are] not essential" for liability to attach under § 17(a) and § 10(b)); *S.E.C. v. Tambone,* 550 F.3d 106, 122 (1st Cir. 2008) (noting that "because section 17(a) applies to both sales and offers to sell securities, the SEC need not base its claim of liability on any completed transaction at all").

The Court first considers the *Howey* factors to consider whether Defendants' promotion of the BLV token on their website and the Whitepaper constitutes a "security." On the first "investment of money" prong, Defendants' website and Whitepaper invited or enticed potential investors to provide digital or other currency in exchange for BLV tokens. This includes having a "Buy Now" button. An "investment of money" can take the form of "goods and services", *Int'l Bhd. Of Teamsters v. Daniel,* 439 U.S. 551, 560 n.12 (1979) ("This is not to say that a person's 'investment,' in order to meet the definition of an investment contract, must take the form of cash only, rather than of goods and services"); or "exchange of value." [*Hocking v. Dubois*, 885 F.2d 1449, 1471 (9th Cir. 1989).] Defendants' website and their Whitepaper's invitation to potential investors to provide digital currency in return for BLV tokens satisfies the first "investment of money" prong.

Here, the website promoted a "common enterprise" because Blockvest claimed that the funds raised will be pooled and there would be a profit sharing formula. *See Hocking*, 885 F.2d at 1459 ("The participants pool their assets; they give up any claim to profits or losses attributable to their particular investments in return for a pro rata share of the profits of the enterprise; and they make their collective fortunes dependent on the success of a single common enterprise."). Specifically, the Whitepaper stated that "[a]s a Blockvest token holder, your Blockvest will generate a pro-rated share of 50% of the profit generated quarterly as well as fees for processing transactions." The second *Howey* factor has been met.

Finally, as described on the website and Whitepaper, the investors in Blockvest would be "passive" investors and the BLV tokens would generate "passive income." In conclusion, the Court determines that the SEC has demonstrated that the promotion of the ICO of the BLV token was a "security" and satisfies the *Howey* test.

Next, the Court determines whether there was an "offer" of the BLV tokens subject to Section 17(a). The Securities Act defines "offer" to "include every attempt or offer to dispose of, or solicitation of an offer to buy, a security or interest in a security for value." 15 U.S.C. § 77b(a)(3). Section 17(a) is "intended to cover any fraudulent scheme in an offer or sale of securities, whether in the course of an initial distribution or in the course of ordinary market trading." *United States v. Naftalin*, 441 U.S. 768, 778 (1979). In *Naftalin,* the Court found that the statutory phrase, "in the offer or sale of any securities," was intended to be "define[d] broadly" and is "expansive enough to encompass the entire selling process, including the seller/agent transaction." *Id.* at 773; *see Rubin v. United States*, 449 U.S. 424, 431 (1981) (noting that section 17(a) was enacted "to protect against fraud and promote the free flow of information in the public dissemination of securities" and holding that pledge of shares of stock constitutes an "offer" or "sale" of a security).

Further, the term "offer" in securities law has a "different and far broader" meaning than contract law. *Hocking*, 885 F.2d at 1457–58.

. . . .

As described by one district judge, "[i]mpossibility of performance is not dispositive to the court's determination of whether defendants' conduct constituted an 'offer to sell.' What is dispositive to the court's determination is whether defendants' conduct conditioned the public mind." *SEC v. Thomas D. Kienlen Corp.*, 755 F. Supp. 936, 940 (D. Or. 1991) (addressing "offer" under Section 54 of the Securities Act). In *Kienlen Corp.*, the district court found that a notice mailed to clients and a brochure handed out at a meeting constituted "offers to sell" where the defendants promoted the "[g]reater safety," "improved performance," and "[l]ower costs," of their offering. *Id.* at 940–41.

In *SEC v. Arvida Corp.*, 169 F. Supp. 211 (S.D.N.Y. 1958), the court found that there was an "offer to sell" under Section 2(3) of the Securities Act, 15 U.S.C. § 77b(a)(3), where the defendant conducted a press conference where a spokesperson for the issuer answered reporters' questions, including questions regarding the proposed offering price per share. *Id.* at 215. The court found "the furnishing to the press by representatives of the issuer and the underwriters of written and oral communications concerning the forthcoming public offering of the issuer's securities, thereby causing the public distribution of such information through news media, constituted an 'offer to sell.' " *Id.*

Defendants, in their briefs and at the hearing, argued that an offer requires a "manifestation of intent to be bound" but only cite to California state contract law in support. Based on caselaw defining an "offer" under the securities laws, Defendants' argument seeks to improperly narrow the definition of "offer". Under securities law and caselaw, the definition of "offer" is broad and there is no requirement that performance must be possible or that the issuer must be able to legally bind a purchaser. *See Hocking*, 885 F.2d at 1457; *Kienlen Corp.*, 755 F. Supp. at 940–41. Thus, the Court concludes that the contents of Defendants' website, the Whitepaper and social media posts concerning the ICO of the BLV tokens to the public at large constitute an "offer" of "securities" under the Securities Act.

NOTES AND QUESTIONS

1.   What was it that led the court to change its opinion about whether or not the BLV tokens were "securities" between November of 2018 and February 2019? Would it make sense for the court to conclude that the same thing is a security when it is "offered" but not when someone actually buys it or vice versa?

2.   When the federal securities laws prohibit "offers" to sell, is the statute using the word "offer" in the legal sense (as it would be used in determining whether a binding contract has been formed) or in some other way? Why would the securities statutes use the word "offer" in a different way than it is used in contract law given that, without a binding contract, potential buyers have not committed to anything?

3.   If the court genuinely concluded that all 32 test investors and the 17 initial purchasers understood that there was no real contract, and the defendants had not yet determined whether to proceed with the offering to "real" investors, are the SEC and the court correct in determining that there was an "offer" to sell securities, even under the broader definition used in the securities laws?

3. THE SEC AND ITS FIGHT AGAINST FRAUD

Federal regulators have a significant interest in protecting members of the investing public against fraud. As explained by the SEC's Director of Enforcement:

> When market participants engage in fraud under the guise of offering digital instruments—whether characterized as virtual currencies, coins, tokens, or the like—the SEC and the CFTC will look beyond form, examine the substance of the activity and prosecute violations of the federal securities and commodities laws. The Divisions of Enforcement for the SEC and CFTC will continue to address violations and bring actions to stop and prevent fraud in the offer and sale of digital instruments.[11]

The SEC has been increasingly active in seeking to address fraud in connection with sales of cryptoassets and related transactions,[12] but fraudulent activity continues. Perhaps the most colorful observation about regulators' attempts to catch-up to the rapid developments in the crypto space was the observation that "fighting fraud in virtual currencies has almost become a game of Whack-A-Mole for regulators and federal prosecutors, who find each new iteration seemingly a few steps ahead them."[13]

Because the SEC's power is limited to transactions involving securities, a consideration of the kinds of deals in which the SEC has initiated enforcement proceedings also illustrates how the agency regards cryptoassets. The SEC includes on its webpage a listing of Cyber Enforcement actions.[14] In describing the enforcement actions involving ICOs initiated in 2018, the SEC list includes a number of unregistered, non-exempt offerings but also includes the following actions involving allegations of fraud:

- On November 29, 2018, the SEC filed and settled two different cease and desist proceedings against Floyd Mayweather, Jr., and Khaled Khaled ("DJ Khaled"), for promoting the Centra Tech ICO without properly disclosing the fact and amount of compensation paid by the issuers.

---

[11]   SEC, Public Statement, *Joint Statement by SEC and CFTC Enforcement Directors Regarding Virtual Currency Enforcement Actions* (Jan. 19, 2018) [archived at https://perma.cc/VZ6E-7G89].

[12]   *See, i.e.,* Jeff John Roberts, *Cryptocurrency Scams Are Now Among the SEC's Top Enforcement Priorities,* FORTUNE (Nov. 2, 2018) (available online at https://fortune.com/2018/11/02/sec-ico-report-cryptocurrency-scams/).

[13]   Peter J. Henning, *Policing Cryptocurrencies Has Become a Game of Whack-a-Mole for Regulators,* N.Y. TIMES: DEALBOOK (May 31, 2018) (available online at https://www.nytimes.com/2018/05/31/business/dealbook/bitcoin-cryptocurrencies-regulation.html).

[14]   The official source for this listing is SEC, *Cyber Enforcement Actions* [archived at https://perma.cc/BFC3-PG4G].

- On October 22, 2018, the SEC suspended trading in American Retail Group, Inc. after the company falsely claimed it had partnered with an "SEC-qualified custodian" in connection with a cryptotransaction, and that the company was conducting a "registered" token offering.

- On October 11, 2018, the SEC obtained an emergency court order halting a planned ICO and on-going pre-ICO sales by Blockvest LLC, based on misrepresentations about regulatory approval and claims that Blockvest would be the first "licensed and regulated" crypto fund.

- On September 11, 2018, the SEC filed settled administrative proceeding against Crypto Asset Management LP (a hedge fund manager) for falsely marketing itself as the "first regulated crypto asset fund in the United States."

- On September 9, 2018, the SEC blocked trading in Bitcoin Tracker One and Ether Tracker One because of market confusion about the nature of instruments.

- On August 14, 2018, the SEC settled claims against the founder of Tomahawk Exploration LLC, a company responsible for a fraudulent ICO that was supposed to fund oil exploration and drilling.

- On May 22, 2018, the SEC obtained a court order halting an on-going fraudulent ICO by Titanium Blockchain Infrastructure Services, Inc.

- On April 20, 2018, the SEC suspended trading in IBITX Software, Inc, because of concerns about assertions about the company's development of a new cryptocurrency and crypto platform.

- On April 4, 2018, the SEC filed a complaint against Centra Tech and two co-founders (along with an amended complaint filed April 20 adding a third co-founder) for actions in connection with coordinating a fraudulent ICO. (This matter is described *infra* in part 5 of Chapter nine.)

- On March 1, 2018, the SEC halted trading in the publicly-owned HD View 360 Inc. because of concerns regarding claims about a subsidiary with blockchain technology.

- The Bitfunder/Montroll action described in some detail in chapter nine was filed February 21, 2018, on the basis of fraud in connection with an unregistered ICO, and the complaint against AriseBank (also described in chapter nine) for a fraudulent ICO was filed January 25, 2018.

As materials in the preceding chapters make clear, the SEC's interest in crypto predates 2018. One of the earliest actions by the SEC occurred in 2014, when the agency asserted jurisdiction over a Bitcoin promotion in *SEC v. Shavers*.[15] This case, which focused primarily on a Ponzi scheme investment in Bitcoins, resulted in a settlement. Also in 2014, the SEC halted traded in the securities of a publicly traded company (Mobile Technologies Corp.) because of questions about the accuracy of representations about its business, which was allegedly involved in the development and testing of a secure mobile Bitcoin platform.

In 2017, several public companies found themselves in trouble with the SEC, resulting in the agency suspending trading in securities of several publicly-traded companies. For example, in April of 2017, the SEC raised questions about Sunshine Capital, Inc.'s assertions about the liquidity and value of DIBCOINS, a cryptocurrency developed by the company's majority shareholder. Strategic Global Investments, CIAO Group, Inc., First Bitcoin Capital Corp., and American Security Resources Corp. were all investigated in August of that year for assertions made in connection with possible ICOs, involvement with cryptomarkets, and/or the companies' capital structure as it related to cryptoassets.

4. SALES OF CRYPTO WITHOUT REGISTRATION OR EXEMPTION UNDER THE FEDERAL SECURITIES LAWS

Although the SEC's motive for pursuing enforcement actions against fraudulent actors in the crypto space is clear, it is also worth emphasizing that the SEC is not limited to pursuing claims of securities fraud. Several SEC actions have, in fact, been based on failure to register transactions, even in the absence of fraud.

In 2014, the SEC brought charges against the co-owner of SatoshiDICE and FeedZeBirds, described as "two Bitcoin-related websites."[16] In that action, Erik Voorhees was charged with publicly selling shares in the crypto ventures without registering them or complying with any available exemption. Vorheese ultimately earned approximately $15,800 in profits, which he agreed to disgorge. In addition, he was hit with a fine in the amount of $35,000. Voorhees consented to the cease and desist order and agreed to refrain from issuing any unregistered security or virtual currency for a period of five years. (The SEC Press release did note that the general solicitation for FeedZeBirds referred to the sale as an "IPO," which was inaccurate, but the failure to actually register appears to have been at the heart of the SEC action.)

---

[15]   *SEC v. Shavers*, No. 4:13–CV–6, 2013 WL 4028182 (E.D. Tex. Aug. 6, 2013).

[16]   *See* SEC, Press Release, *SEC Charges Bitcoin Entrepreneur With Offering Unregistered Securities* Release 2014–111 (June 3, 2014) [archived at https://perma.cc/7AU6-V24B].

More recently, the SEC's involvement with the Munchee ICO confirmed the reality that the SEC is not limiting its enforcement actions to transactions involving false or misleading statements. As described in chapter eight, the SEC initiated cease and desist proceedings against Munchee Inc. in December of 2017.[17]

Commentators were quick to note that the Munchee case set an important precedent, providing clear notice that the SEC was not limiting its enforcement activities to situations involving fraud:

> Section 5 of the Securities Act does not require a showing of fraud to justify an SEC refusal order or a cease and desist proceeding. Despite this, many cryptocurrency promoters posited that the SEC would focus its efforts on preventing fraud and would not bring enforcement actions against issuers that sold unregistered cryptocurrencies to fund legitimate businesses. Munchee discredited this position.[18]

This is consistent with the position publicly taken by SEC Chairman Jay Clayton. On December 11, 2017 and again on February 6, 2018, the SEC Chairman publicly stated that "by and large, the structures of the initial coin offerings that I have seen . . . involve the offer and sale of securities and directly implicate the securities registration requirements and other investor protection provisions of our federal securities laws."[19] Both of these statements include the standard disclaimer that the comments represent only the views of the chairman and no other commissioner or the SEC itself. Even with this caveat, however, reaction to these statements has been relatively intense.

Reports about the testimony in particular reiterate statements to the effect that "every ICO" the SEC or its chairman have seen so far have

---

[17]   Securities Act Release No. 10445, 118 SEC Docket 5, at 1–2 (Dec. 11, 2017) (SEC cease and desist order).

[18]   Matthew J. Higgins, *Munchee Inc.: A Turning Point for the Cryptocurrency Industry*, 97 N.C. L. Rev. 220, 222–23 (2018). This article contains a discussion of the Munchee process and offering, as well as the SEC's response. Its conclusion was that "in most cases, [issuers will] be unable to structure their ICOs to circumvent securities laws." Because the Munchee platform was operational, even if incompletely developed, the case also supports the notion that issuers "cannot avoid Securities Act registration requirements simply by claiming that the ICO-funded project is complete."

[19]   SEC, *Statement on Cryptocurrencies and Initial Coin Offerings* (Dec. 11, 2017) [archived at https://perma.cc/829E-QLT4]; and SEC, Testimony, *Chairman's Testimony on Virtual Currencies: The Roles of the SEC and CFTC* (Feb. 6, 2018) [archived at https://perma.cc/CLF9-M7RB] (containing a statement that is essentially identical).

involved the offering of securities.[20] In fact, Chairman Clayton is widely quoted as having said that "every ICO I've seen is a security."[21]

Prepared remarks and testimony from the SEC and its officials generally do not take such a hard line. Both of the statements referenced above include comments to the effect that "there are cryptocurrencies that, at least as currently designed, promoted and used, do not appear to be securities. . . ."[22] On the other hand, given the consistent tenor of unscripted remarks, in the view of the SEC Chairman at least, there appears to be something akin to a presumption that an ICO will involve the sale of security. Therefore, "[b]efore launching a cryptocurrency or a product with its value tied to one or more cryptocurrencies, its promoters must either (1) be able to demonstrate that the currency or product is not a security or (2) comply with applicable registration and other requirements under our securities laws."[23]

Subsequent to these actions, additional statements have added to the uncertainty about what cryptoassets will be treated as securities and when. On June 14, 2018, William Hinman, the Director of the SEC's Division of Corporation Finance, made remarks at the Yahoo Finance All Markets Summit on crypto held in San Francisco.[24] As is the case with remarks from Chairman Clayton, Hinman's remarks were accompanied by the standard disclaimer that the SEC "disclaims responsibility for any private publication or statement of any SEC employee or Commissioner. This speech expresses the author's views and does not necessarily reflect those of the Commission, the Commissioners or other members of the staff."

In his speech, Hinman raised the provocative questions of "whether a digital asset offered as a security can, over time, become something other than a security."[25] The question is "provocative" because there are really

---

[20]   *See, i.e.,* Joseph Young, *SEC Hints at Tighter Regulation for ICOs, Smart Policies for "True Cryptocurrencies,"* COINTELEGRAPH (Feb. 9, 2018) [archived at https://perma.cc/Z5KF-BXG9] (quoting Chairman Clayton as saying that "every ICO token the SEC has seen so far is considered a security.")

[21]   Stan Higgins, *SEC Chief Clayton: 'Every ICO I've Seen Is a Security',* COINDESK (Feb. 6, 2018) (available on line at https://www.coindesk.com/sec-chief-clayton-every-ico-ive-seen-security). In an April 26, 2018 hearing before the House Appropriations Committee, Chairman Clayton was asked to clarify how regulatory authority could be split between the CFTC and SEC. In responding to this question, he acknowledged that he has "been on the record saying there are very few, there's none that I've seen, tokens that aren't securities." Neeraj Agrawal, *Hot Takes,* COINCENTER (Ap. 27, 2018) (available online at https://coincenter.org/link/sec-chairman-clayton-bitcoin-is-not-a-security).

[22]   SEC, *Testimony, supra* note 19.

[23]   SEC, *Statement, supra* note 19. The conclusion that the position of the SEC essentially created a presumption is not original with the author of this book. *See, e.g.,* Zinman, *supra* note 6. This source looked at a number of recent pronouncements and actions taken by the SEC and concluded that "the SEC has essentially adopted a rebuttable presumption that ICO tokens are securities that must comply with the registration requirements of the securities laws." *Id.*

[24]   SEC, William Hinman Speech, *Digital Asset Transactions: When Howey Met Gary (Plastic)* (June 14, 2018) [archived at https://perma.cc/X95R-KV97].

[25]   Hinman speech, *supra* note 24.

no conventional securities that the SEC has suggested can change in this manner. Once an interest has been classified as a security, it has generally retained that classification.

Nonetheless, in his public remarks, Hinman specifically called out Bitcoin and Ether as two cryptoassets that did not, insofar as he understood them, constitute securities in today's markets. As he explained, "when I look at Bitcoin today, I do not see a central third party whose efforts are a key determining factor in the enterprise. . . . And putting aside the fundraising that accompanied the creation of Ether . . . current offers and sales of Ether are not securities transactions." These conclusions are based on his understanding that "the analysis of whether something is a security is not static and does not strictly inhere to the instrument."

In his April 2018 testimony before the House Appropriations Committee, Chairman Clayton also appeared to acquiesce in the view that Bitcoin, at least, would not be a security today. He explained that "there are different types of cryptoassets. . . . A pure medium of exchange, the one that's most often cited, is Bitcoin. As a replacement for currency, that has been determined by most people to not be a security."[26]

While there is some argument that might be made (which Hinman hints about in his remarks and Chairman Clayton also seems to support) that Bitcoin was never really a security, because there was never an issuer "promoting" it, most people seem to assume or agree that Ether was a security when it was first issued. According to Hinman, a sale of securities generally occurs when an issuer sells coins or tokens instead of issuing traditional securities "in order to raise money to develop networks on which digital assets will operate. . . ."[27] This satisfies the *Howey* test because investors contribute something of value (typically other cryptoassets, such as Bitcoin), in a common enterprise, where the investors are depending on the essential efforts of the issuer to develop the system which will provide them with profits. Since this is basically what happened when Ether was first released to the public it certainly looks like those interests were securities when first issued. Nonetheless, because of the current market and disperse ownership of Ether, Hinman has suggested that he no longer believes that this cryptoasset is a security.

In support of this conclusion, Hinman cited *Howey*, where the Supreme Court stated that its investment contract test "embodies a flexible rather than a static principle."[28] Although the Court certainly used this language, flexibility was deemed necessary to enable the law to adapt "to meet the countless and variable schemes devised by those who seek the use of the

---

[26]   Neeraj Agrawal, *SEC Chairman Clayton: Bitcoin is not a security*, COINCENTER (Ap. 27, 2018) (available online at https://coincenter.org/link/sec-chairman-clayton-bitcoin-is-not-a-security).

[27]   Hinman speech, *supra* note 24.

[28]   *Howey*, 328 U.S. at 299.

money of others on the promise of profits."[29] Prior to Hinman's remarks about crypto, there was no indication that the "flexibility" was of the sort that would allow interests to be treated as securities at one point in time, and then later on become something other than a security.

To help illustrate why this particular reaction to crypto is so significant, suppose a real estate developer decides to sell interests in a condominium project "coupled with an offer or agreement to perform or arrange certain rental or other services for the purchaser."[30] According to the SEC, the presence of a collateral agreement such as a rental pooling arrangement would mean that the developer is offering "investment contracts which must be registered unless an exemption is available." On the other hand, without those collateral arrangements at the outset, there is no sale of a security.[31] Moreover, if the interests are not securities when initially sold, a subsequent arrangement to add a rental arrangement would not convert the interest into a security.[32] There is also nothing in from the SEC suggesting that once the interest in the project is deemed to be a security, it can ever become something else, even if a subsequent purchaser buys a unit without being solicited because of any income potential or with specific proof that the primary motivation is to occupy the unit. Thus, the original classification controls. Or, in other words, once a security, always a security.

The approach that Director Hinman has suggested for cryptoassets provides insight into why it sometimes looks like the SEC is attempting to fit a square peg into a round hole. Cryptoassets do not act like traditional securities, and they do not always fit well with the existing framework.

One option is for federal legislators to step in and address the situation. In December of 2018 Representatives Warren Davidson and Darren Soto introduced the "Token Taxonomy Act," which proposed to exclude "digital tokens" from the definition of "security" under both the Securities Act of 1933 and Securities Exchange Act of 1934.[33] This particular bill would have defined "digital token" as a digital unit that:

is created—

> (i)   in response to the verification or collection of proposed transactions [i.e., is mined];

---

[29]   *Id.*

[30]   SEC Release No. 5347, *Guidelines as to the Applicability of the Federal Securities Laws to Offers and Sales of Condominiums or Units in a Real Estate Development* (Jan. 4, 1974) [archived at https://perma.cc/UJB7-9WRG].

[31]   *Id.* at p. 2.

[32]   *Id.* at p. 4.

[33]   Token Taxonomy Act, 2017 Cong. U.S. HR 7356 (Dec. 20, 2018).

(ii) pursuant to rules for the digital unit's creation and supply that cannot be altered by a single person or group of persons under common control; or

(iii) as an initial allocation of digital units . . . [i.e., is pre-mined; and]

has a transaction history that—

(i) is recorded in a distributed, digital ledger or digital data structure in which consensus is achieved through a mathematically verifiable process; and

(ii) after consensus is reached, cannot be materially altered by a single person or group of persons under common control. . . .[34]

In addition, the digital token would have to be transferable without the assistance of any intermediary, and could not be an interest that represents "a financial interest in a company, including an ownership or debt interest or revenue share."[35]

This particular approach would leave oversight of digital assets, other than "securities tokens" that operate like traditional debt or equity interests but on a blockchain, to agencies such as the CFTC and FinCEN, removing them from purview of the SEC completely.

Note that this is not the only possible legislative solution. For example, instead of removing digital tokens from the definition of security, Congress might decide to add this kind of interest to the list of exempted securities.[36] Under this approach, digital interests could be exempt from the registration requirements, but depending on the wording of the exemption, might remain subject to the antifraud requirements of the securities laws. While the SEC would retain authority to investigate fraudulent transactions (as well as giving private purchasers a cause of action in at least some circumstances), this approach would address one of Director Hinman's justifications for not treating either Bitcoin or Ether as securities.

Director Hinman argued that "[t]he impetus of the Securities Act is to remove the information asymmetry between promoters and investors. . . . [T]he Securities Act prescribes the information investors need to make an informed investment decision, and the promoter is liable for material misstatements in the offering materials. These are important safeguards, . . . appropriate for most ICOs."[37] On the other hand, once a digital asset is no longer "controlled" by a singular, identifiable issuer or developer,

---

[34]   H.R. 7356 § 2(a).

[35]   *Id.*

[36]   *See* '33 Act § 3, 15 U.S. CODE § 77c.

[37]   Hinman Speech, *supra* note 24.

Hinman acknowledged that "material information asymmetries recede. As a network becomes truly decentralized, the ability to identify an issuer or promoter to make the requisite disclosures becomes difficult, and less meaningful."[38] On the other hand, if there are fraudulent misrepresentations, the speaker can be identified and enforcement action might well be appropriate. In this situation, there could be a strong reason for the SEC to retain jurisdiction.

Some players in the crypto world have opined that Congress will eventually need to act to clarify how securities laws apply to digital assets. For example, Jake Chervinsky, an associate at Kobre & Kim law firm who specializes in litigation and government enforcement actions involving digital assets, has stated that he believes:

> Congress can—and eventually will need to—do more to clarify how the federal securities laws apply to digital assets. The foundation of the securities laws dates back to the 1930s, long before anyone could have imagined the concept of a digital asset issued via the internet through the use of blockchain technology. This old legal framework simply wasn't designed for the digital age, and as a result, it doesn't provide the regulatory clarity that the crypto industry needs to move forward.[39]

Legislative action is not the only way to address potential problems and inconsistencies with the current approach being taken by the SEC. A second possibility is that the SEC might promulgate new regulations. Certain crypto entrepreneurs have called for this additional clarity from securities regulators, and this would certainly be one way to accomplish this. For example, Jeremy Allaire, CEO and co-founder of Goldman Sachs-backed crypto finance company Circle, has opined that the lack of clarity from the SEC over how crypto should be defined is "[t]he biggest and most immediate regulatory hurdle" facing crypto today.[40]

The process of promulgating these kinds of regulations, as mentioned briefly in the very first chapter of this book, is not simple. It is neither fast nor inexpensive, but a number of commentators have indicated that they expect additional clarification from the SEC in the foreseeable future. In fact, there may be a push from institutional investors for such clarity. Shane Brett, CEO of Gecko Governance, a company working on compliance tools for blockchain, has claimed that because of volatility and uncertainty in the crypto markets, institutional money is waiting for regulatory clarity. His expectation is that this will "take the form of SEC rules for reporting

---

[38]   *Id.*

[39]   Colin Harper, *"Guidance by Enforcement": How the SEC Is Slowly Shaping ICO Regulation,* BITCOIN MAGAZINE (Nov. 30, 2018) (available online at https://bitcoinmagazine.com/articles/guidance-enforcement-how-sec-slowly-shaping-ico-regulation).

[40]   Marie Huillet, *Circle CEO Says More Regulatory Clarity From US SEC Will Help Unlock Crypto Markets,* COINTELEGRAPH (Jan. 11, 2019) [archived at https://perma.cc/6L3V-WLRW].

requirements and audit trails" but until this happens, institutional investors will decline to participate in crypto markets.[41]

The lack of regulatory clarity contributes to one of the biggest problems facing crypto—the perceived lack of legitimacy. If the SEC clarifies its position, and provides increased certainty, companies that cannot or will not adhere to laws about security, operations, customer protections, informational transparency, etc. will be forced out of the marketplace, and remaining companies can be appreciated for their ability and willingness to comply with legal requirements. This is a significant incentive for the SEC to act.

This is not to suggest that significant changes to existing securities rules should be expected from the SEC any time soon. In June 2018, SEC Chairman Jay Clayton warned that the SEC had no immediate plans to amend its rules as the apply to cryptocurrencies. In an interview with CNBC, he opined that "[w]e are not going to do any violence to the traditional definition of a security that has worked for a long time."[42] Chairman Clayton's opinion is that the current definition and approach suffices, and that sales of digital assets such as tokens in order to finance a venture and provide purchasers with a return involve securities.

Despite pronouncements like this from the SEC some observers continue to predict that the SEC is likely to take steps to clarify regulatory protocols.[43] At the very least, it seems reasonable to expect official clarification about what constitutes a security.

There have been statements from individual officials at the SEC that have not been accepted as official policy. These range from "Every ICO I've seen is a security" to "If the network on which the token or coin is to function is sufficiently decentralized . . . the assets may not represent an investment contract." There is no certainty about which position (if either) is going to be officially accepted, or about when a network is "sufficiently decentralized." In addition, as of November 15, 2019, the SEC has declined to approve any crypto ETF, although new proposals are constantly being submitted for consideration.

A range of other issues are also likely to result in additional regulation, or at least entail the possibility of regulation. For example, there is the

---

[41]   Rakesh Sharma, *How SEC Regs Will Change Cryptocurrency Markets*, INVESTOPEDIA (Ap. 13, 2018) (available online at https://www.investopedia.com/news/how-sec-regs-will-change-cryptocurrency-markets/).

[42]   Nick Marinoff, *SEC Chairman: Cryptocurrencies Like Bitcoin Are Not Securities, but Most ICOs Are*, BITCOIN MAGAZINE (June 7, 2018) (available online at https://bitcoinmagazine.com/articles/sec-chairman-cryptocurrencies-bitcoin-are-not-securities-most-icos-are).

[43]   For some sources suggesting that such a regulatory reaction is likely, consider Nick Marinoff, *Crypto: 2019 Likely Set to Be the "Year of Regulation,"* BLOCKONOMI (Dec. 19, 2018) (available online at https://blockonomi.com/crypto-2019-the-year-of-regulation/); and Daria Volkova, *2019 as the Year of Crypto Regulation: Will STOs Become a New Trend?*, COINSPEAKER (Dec. 26, 2018) (available online at https://www.coinspeaker.com/2019-crypto-regulation-stos/).

question of whether to prohibit or ban trading in so-called "privacy coins" (those which are built in such a way that ownership is extremely difficult if not impossible to trace or report) or whether to limit the way in which such transactions are conducted. For example, two regulated crypto exchanges, Gemini and Coinbase, recently allowed trading of Zcash, an altcoin specifically designed for privacy of owners.[44] Both exchanges require any withdrawal of Zcash to be made to a transparent address, which might solve the privacy concerns without banning the coins themselves.

Similarly, the SEC has yet to clarify whether a developer will be liable for bugs in their software or if a third party uses their code in a malicious manner although developers often attempt to limit their personal liability by including disclaimers in their software to the effect that the software is designed for legitimate purposes only. For example, Auger's FAQ[45] states that "Augur is not a prediction market, it is a protocol for cryptocurrency users to create their own prediction markets." The success of this strategy was called into doubt in 2018 when the SEC charged Zachary Coburn (founder of EtherDelta and responsible for the EtherDelta smart contract) with operating an unregistered national securities exchange.[46] (The role of the SEC in regulating exchanges, and this particular action in particular, will be discussed in more detail in the next section of this chapter.)

The final extent and direction of legislative or regulatory clarification of these and related issues is uncertain, but these are the kinds of concerns at the forefront of the push (and need) for regulation and clarity.

5. CRYPTO EXCHANGES

The preceding discussion focused primarily on the issuance of cryptoassets and the question of whether particular coins or tokens should be treated as securities. It is important to remember, however, that the SEC is concerned with trading in crypto as well as its initial issuance. Although most of the early SEC actions in the crypto space involved companies associated with the primary issuance and sale of tokens, the

---

[44]   On the other hand, the U.K. arm of Coinbase subsequently signaled that it was dropping support for Zcash. See Daniel Palmer, *Coinbase UK Dropping Support for Cryptocurrency Zcash*, COINDESK (Aug. 12, 2019) (available online at https://www.coindesk.com/coinbase-uk-dropping-support-for-cryptocurrency-zcash) (referring to customer reports that they had been warned to convert or remove Zcash holdings by August 26, 2019).

[45]   Augur describes itself as "a decentralized oracle and peer to peer protocol for prediction markets. Augur is free, public, open source software. . . ." Augur, *FAQs*, available online at https://www.augur.net/faq/).

[46]   This was in accordance with the suggestion from CFTC Commissioner Brian Quintenz that smart contract programmers could be prosecuted if it was reasonably foreseeable that the code would be used so as to violate federal law. CFTC, Speeches & Testimony, *Remarks of Commissioner Brian Quintenz at the 38th Annual GITEX Technology Week Conference* (Oct. 16, 2018) [archived at https://perma.cc/TC7Y-DCDG].

SEC issued its first order involving a digital token exchange in November 2018.

On November 8, 2018, the SEC announced it had settled charges against the founder of the digital token exchange EtherDelta, Zachary Coburn.[47] Portions of that Order are excerpted here (with some footnotes omitted):

IN RE ZACHARY COBURN

SEC Release No. 84553, Release No. 34-84553, 2018 WL 5840155 (Nov. 8, 2018)

ORDER INSTITUTING CEASE-AND DESIST PROCEEDINGS PURSUANT TO SECTION 21C OF THE SECURITIES EXCHANGE ACT OF 1934. . . .

I.

The Securities and Exchange Commission ("Commission") deems it appropriate that cease-and-desist proceedings be, and hereby are, instituted pursuant to Section 21C of the Securities Exchange Act of 1934 ("Exchange Act") against Zachary Coburn ("Coburn" or "Respondent").

II.

In anticipation of the institution of these proceedings, Respondent has submitted an Offer of Settlement (the "Offer"), which the Commission has determined to accept. Solely for the purpose of these proceedings . . . and without admitting or denying the findings herein, . . . Respondent consents to the entry of this Order . . . .

III.

On the basis of this Order and Respondent's Offer, the Commission finds that:

Summary

1. As described more fully below, EtherDelta is an online platform that allows buyers and sellers to trade certain digital assets—Ether and "ERC20 tokens"—in secondary market trading. ERC20 tokens refer to digital assets issued and distributed on the Ethereum Blockchain using the ERC20 protocol, which is the standard coding protocol currently used by a significant majority of issuers in Initial Coin Offerings ("ICOs").

2. EtherDelta's website, launched by Coburn on July 12, 2016, provides a user-friendly interface to EtherDelta and resembles online securities trading platforms. For example, the website makes token

---

[47] The Order, instituted in an administrative proceeding before the SEC, may be found at SEC, Securities Exchange Act of 1934, Release No. 84553 (Nov. 8, 2018), available at https://www.sec.gov/litigation/admin/2018/34-84553.pdf.

"pairs"[48] available for trading, provides access to the EtherDelta order book, and displays the current, top 500 firm bids and offers by symbol, price, and size. The website also displays account information for users of the EtherDelta platform ("Users") (tracked by the User's Ethereum address and maintained in an internal ledger) and provides fields for Users to input trading interest in any token pair. Users may enter orders to buy or sell specified quantities of any ERC20 token at a specified price (in Ether) and with a specified time-in-force. The website also displays to Users market depth[49] charts and a list of confirmed trades.

3.   On July 25, 2017, the Commission issued its [DAO Report]. . . . In the DAO Report, the Commission advised that a platform that offers trading of digital assets that are securities and operates as an "exchange," as defined by the federal securities laws, must register with the Commission as a national securities exchange or be exempt from registration.

4.   From July 12, 2016 to December 15, 2017 (the "Relevant Period"), more than 3.6 million buy and sell orders in ERC20 tokens that included securities as defined by Section 3(a)(10) of the Exchange Act were traded on EtherDelta, of which approximately 92% (3.3 million) were traded during the period following the DAO Report.

5.   As discussed further below, EtherDelta meets the criteria of an "exchange". . . . During the Relevant Period, EtherDelta was not registered with the Commission as a national securities exchange and it did not operate pursuant to any exemption from registration. . . .

Respondent

6.   Coburn, age 31, is a resident of Chicago, Illinois. From September 2010 to June 2015, Coburn was a registered representative with a Chicago-based options trading firm that was a broker-dealer registered with the Commission. In approximately June 2015, Coburn left that firm to pursue his own business interests. In March 2016, he created EtherOpt, an online platform for trading options and, in July 2016, he created EtherDelta.[50] In November 2017, Coburn entered into an agreement to sell EtherDelta to foreign buyers and, as of December 16, 2017, Coburn ceased to collect any fees from Users of the platform. Coburn does not currently operate EtherDelta.

---

[48]   Token pair refers to a trade between one digital asset and either another digital asset or fiat currency. On EtherDelta, the only token pairs available for trading were those between a particular ERC20 token and Ether

[49]   The term "market depth" refers to the number of open buy and sell orders for a particular token at different prices, and provides an indication of a particular token's liquidity.

[50]   In late 2016, Coburn shut down EtherOpt's operations.

Facts

The EtherDelta Website and Hours of Operations

7. As seen below, the EtherDelta website had features similar to online securities trading platforms. For each Ether/ERC20 token pair available for trading on EtherDelta, the website provided access to the EtherDelta order book and displayed the top 500 orders to buy and orders to sell, sorted by price and color (buy orders are green and sell orders are red). The website provided User account information and provided fields for Users to input deposit, withdrawal, and trading interest. The website also provided Users' daily transaction volumes per token, market depth charts, and a list of User's confirmed trades.

8. During the Relevant Period, the EtherDelta platform was available to anyone, including U.S. persons, and had no specified hours of operation. As long as EtherDelta's website was operational, Users could interact directly with the EtherDelta smart contract or enter orders and trade tokens through the website 24 hours a day, seven days a week. [Tabular Data not reprinted here.]

The EtherDelta Smart Contract

9. EtherDelta's business operations are defined and executed by EtherDelta's "smart contract" that runs on the Ethereum Blockchain. The EtherDelta smart contract consists of coded functions that allow for, among other things, the trading of any Ether/ ERC20 token pair. On July 8, 2016, Coburn deployed the code for the first EtherDelta smart contract, written in the programming language Solidity, onto the Ethereum Blockchain. When it was deployed, the EtherDelta smart contract created an Ethereum Blockchain address, where the smart contract "resides."

10. Because the EtherDelta smart contract runs on the Ethereum Blockchain, every interaction with EtherDelta by a User requires the User to send a message to the Ethereum Blockchain mining network to be executed on the EtherDelta smart contract.

. . . .

EtherDelta User Eligibility

11. As a prerequisite for submitting an order to the platform, a User must first have an Ethereum wallet address that is capable of sending messages to the Ethereum Blockchain. Users may create a new wallet address through EtherDelta's website or by using other wallet software that is compatible with EtherDelta. Users trade on EtherDelta pseudonymously by using one or more Ethereum addresses, each a unique string of numbers and letters. Users must also demonstrate that they have available ERC20 tokens or Ether to trade on EtherDelta.

Tokens Eligible for Trading and EtherDelta's "Official Listings"

12. Users may enter orders to buy or sell any token that is ERC20 compliant. Coburn purposely wrote the EtherDelta smart contract to include the ERC20 token coding standard and there are no rules set forth in the smart contract that limit a User from trading any particular ERC20 token on EtherDelta.

13. During the Relevant Period, EtherDelta maintained a list of "official [token] listings, a select list of ERC20 Tokens that were available for trading on EtherDelta." Prior to identifying a token as an official listing, Coburn requested certain information from a token issuer (e.g., the token's name, associated website URL, and a paragraph describing the token) and performed his own due diligence on these tokens. Official listings appeared on a drop down menu on a sidebar on EtherDelta's website for easy User accessibility. During the Relevant Period, EtherDelta had approximately 500 official token listings.

The EtherDelta Order Book

14. With respect to a given order, an EtherDelta User is identified as either a "maker" or "taker" on the EtherDelta platform. A maker is someone that posts an order to buy or sell a particular ERC20 token on the EtherDelta website, which signals to other Users their intention to trade a particular token at a specific price, size, and time. A taker is someone seeking to become the counterparty to a maker's order on the platform.

. . . .

21. In posts on Reddit, Coburn explained that: "[a]t a high level, EtherDelta functions just like a normal exchange" and "[l]ike any other exchange, EtherDelta has an order book of resting orders." However, unlike a traditional exchange, "[t]here is no 'exchange owner' holding your funds. Hence, [EtherDelta is] decentralized. . . . Centralized exchanges won't be able to show you verified business logic [in a publicly verified smart contract]."

Platform Fees

22. To promote trade volume, EtherDelta did not charge a fee to a maker for placing an order. Takers, on the other hand, were charged 0.3% of a transaction's trade volume.

Legal Analysis

A.   EtherDelta Violated Section 5 of the Exchange Act

23. Section 5 of the Exchange Act makes it unlawful for any broker, dealer, or exchange, directly or indirectly, to effect any transaction in a security, or to report any such transaction, in interstate commerce, unless the exchange is registered as a national securities exchange under Section 6 of the Exchange Act, or is exempted from such registration. Section

3(a)(1) of the Exchange Act defines an "exchange" as "any organization, association, or group of persons, whether incorporated or unincorporated, which constitutes, maintains, or provides a market place or facilities for bringing together purchasers and sellers of securities or for otherwise performing with respect to securities the functions commonly performed by a stock exchange as that term is generally understood, and includes the market place and the market facilities maintained by such exchange." 15 USC § 78c(a)(1).

24. Exchange Act Rule 3b–16(a) provides a functional test to assess whether a trading system meets the definition of exchange under Section 3(a)(1) of the Exchange Act. Exchange Act Rule 3b–16(a) provides that an organization, association, or group of persons shall be considered to constitute, maintain, or provide "a market place or facilities for bringing together purchasers and sellers of securities or for otherwise performing with respect to securities the functions commonly performed by an exchange" as those terms are used in Section 3(a)(1) of the Exchange Act if such an organization, association, or group of persons: (1) brings together the orders for securities of multiple buyers and sellers; and (2) uses established, non-discretionary methods (whether by providing a trading facility or by setting rules) under which such orders interact with each other, and the buyers and sellers entering such orders agree to the terms of the trade.

25. A system that meets the criteria of Exchange Act Rule 3b–16(a), and is not excluded under Exchange Act Rule 3b–16(b), must register, pursuant to Section 5 of the Exchange Act, as a national securities exchange under Section 6 of the Exchange Act19 or operate pursuant to an appropriate exemption. One of the available exemptions is for alternative trading systems ("ATSs"). Exchange Act Rule 3a1–1(a)(2) exempts from the definition of "exchange" under section 3(a)(1) an organization, association, or group of persons that complies with Regulation ATS.21 Regulation ATS requires an ATS to, among other things, register as a broker-dealer, file a Form ATS with the Commission to notice its operations, and establish written safeguards and procedures to protect subscribers' confidential trading information. An ATS that complies with Regulation ATS and operates pursuant to the Rule 3a1–1(a)(2) exemption would not be required by Section 5 to register as a national securities exchange.

26. EtherDelta satisfied the criteria of Exchange Act Rule 3b–16(a) and is not excluded under Rule 3b–16(b). During the Relevant Period, EtherDelta operated as a market place for bringing together the orders of multiple buyers and sellers in tokens that included securities as defined by Section 3(a)(10) of the Exchange Act. The purchasers of such digital tokens invested money with a reasonable expectation of profits, including through the increased value of their investments in secondary trading, based on the managerial efforts of others.... These established non-discretionary

methods allowed Users to agree upon the terms of their trades in tokens on EtherDelta during the Relevant Period.

27. Despite operating as a Rule 3b–16(a) system, EtherDelta did not register as a national securities exchange or operate pursuant to an exemption from such registration. Accordingly, EtherDelta violated Section 5 of the Exchange Act.

B. Coburn Caused EtherDelta to Violate Section 5 of the Exchange Act

28. During the relevant period, Coburn founded EtherDelta, wrote and deployed the EtherDelta smart contract to the Ethereum Blockchain, and exercised complete and sole control over EtherDelta's operations, including over the operations constituting the violations described above. Coburn should have known that his actions would contribute to EtherDelta's violations and thus, under Exchange Act Section 21C(a), caused EtherDelta to violate Section 5 of the Exchange Act.

Respondent's Remedial Efforts

29. In determining to accept the Offer, including the decision not to impose a greater penalty, the Commission considered remedial acts promptly undertaken by Respondent and cooperation afforded the Commission staff. Coburn's efforts facilitated the staff's investigation involving an emerging technology.

IV.

In view of the foregoing, the Commission deems it appropriate and in the public interest to impose the sanctions agreed to in Respondent's Offer.

Accordingly, pursuant to Section 21C of the Exchange Act, it is hereby ordered that:

A. Respondent Coburn cease and desist from committing or causing any violations and any future violations of Section 5 of the Exchange Act.

B. Respondent Coburn shall pay disgorgement of $300,000 and prejudgment interest of $13,000, for a total of $313,000, to the Securities and Exchange Commission for transfer to the United States Treasury . . . .

C. Respondent Coburn shall, within 10 days of this Order, pay a civil money penalty of $75,000 to the Securities and Exchange Commission for transfer to the United States Treasury . . . .

According to the facts recited in the preceding Order, EtherDelta operated an online trading platform that allowed buyers and sellers to trade cryptotokens. To facilitate trades, EtherDelta employed a number of techniques traditionally associated with online trading in securities, including both an order book and a user-friendly website that displayed information such as token symbols, volumes to be traded, and prices. Any ERC-20 compliant tokens hosted on the Ethereum blockchain could be traded on the EtherDelta platform, so long as the user had an Ethereum wallet address to or from which trades could be made.

EtherDelta did all of its start-up work, including programming and development, and it was operational before the SEC issued its July 2017 DAO Report, which was the first time that the SEC officially warned that "any entity or person engaging in the activities of an exchange must register as a national securities exchange or operate pursuant to an exemption from such registration." From July 2016 (when EtherDelta was launched) to December 15, 2017 (when Coburn sold EtherDelta), more than 3.6 million trade orders were carried out on EtherDelta. Many of those (approximately 92% or 3.3 million trades) took place after the release of the DAO report.

To resolve the matter, Coburn agreed to disgorge $300,000 and pay a $75,000 fine. The SEC explicitly announced that the relatively minimal consequences were based on the Coburn's cooperation throughout the investigation and prompt remedial acts.

NOTES AND QUESTIONS

1.   The foundational work for the EtherDelta platform all took place before the SEC had formally announced a position on cryptoassets, even though the bulk of the site's trading took place after the DAO Report was issued. How would the SEC respond if a similar trading platform was launched today with neither registration nor compliance with standards imposed on exchanges?

2.   Why is the regulation of exchanges so important to the SEC? What interests are being protected?

3.   Would it surprise you to know that, as of November 15, 2019, the EtherDelta website was still functional? The official URL for EtherDelta is https://etherdelta.com, and a visit to the webpage on that date continued to show an Order Book, a price chart, and various trades along with volume. Not surprisingly, a search of registered national securities exchanges on that date did not list EtherDelta.[51]

4.   Coburn was not the owner of the exchange, although he owned the company (EtherDelta) prior to its sale. Moreover, he was apparently the

---

[51]   *See* SEC, Fast Answers, *National Securities Exchanges* (accessed Nov. 16, 2019) [archived at https://perma.cc/V5BV-RKC8]. It was also not registered as an ATS with FINRA. *See* FINRA, *Firms we Regulate* (available online at https://www.finra.org/about/firms-we-regulate) [front page archived at https://perma.cc/UE5S-KNFT].

primary developer of the smart contract utilized by the exchange. Is his liability based on a theory of piercing the veil or some other consideration? Should he have been personally liable for the allegedly improper trading that occurred on the platform?

Rather than registering as an exchange, a token trading platform might seek instead to operate as an alternative trading system ("ATS"). This would require the platform to conduct its operations in a compliant manner, including: (i) registering with the SEC as a broker-dealer with the SEC, (ii) becoming a member of FINRA (the financial industry regulatory authority), (iii) providing the SEC with at least 20 days' notice of its intention to operate as an ATS, and (iv) complying with ongoing regulatory requirements. These requirements are fairly significant, although perhaps less burdensome than becoming a registered exchange.

Now that exchanges are on notice of these requirements, how have they responded? Certainly, the response of cryptocurrency exchanges appears to have been, at best, unenthusiastic. In June, 2018, Brett Redfearn, SEC Director of division of trading and markets, confirmed to CNBC that the SEC has been "underwhelmed by the enthusiasm for coming within the regulatory structure. . . ."[52]

The SEC's perception that exchanges have been slow to respond to regulators pushed the SEC to release a formal statement about potentially unlawful online trading platforms.

PRELIMINARY NOTES

As you read the SEC's statement, consider these questions:

1.   To whom was this statement really addressed? Was it designed to influence persons running the exchanges, investors in the exchanges, users of crypto, or issuers of crypto?

2.   What was the primary goal of the following statement? Do you think it is likely to have the desired impact? What is there about the statement that, in your opinion, makes it likely or unlikely to achieve its desired goal?

---

[52]   Kate Rooney, *SEC director 'underwhelmed' by rate of cryptocurrency exchanges self-reporting,* CNBC (June 6, 2018) (available online at https://www.cnbc.com/2018/06/06/sec-under whelmed-by-rate-of-cryptocurrency-exchanges-self-reporting.html).

SEC, *STATEMENT ON POTENTIALLY UNLAWFUL ONLINE PLATFORMS FOR TRADING DIGITAL ASSETS*
Divisions of Enforcement and Trading and Markets (Mar. 7, 2018)[53]

Online trading platforms have become a popular way investors can buy and sell digital assets, including coins and tokens offered and sold in so-called Initial Coin Offerings ("ICOs"). The platforms often claim to give investors the ability to quickly buy and sell digital assets. Many of these platforms bring buyers and sellers together in one place and offer investors access to automated systems that display priced orders, execute trades, and provide transaction data.

A number of these platforms provide a mechanism for trading assets that meet the definition of a "security" under the federal securities laws. If a platform offers trading of digital assets that are securities and operates as an "exchange," as defined by the federal securities laws, then the platform must register with the SEC as a national securities exchange or be exempt from registration. The federal regulatory framework governing registered national securities exchanges and exempt markets is designed to protect investors and prevent against fraudulent and manipulative trading practices.

Considerations for Investors Using Online Trading Platforms

To get the protections offered by the federal securities laws and SEC oversight when trading digital assets that are securities, investors should use a platform or entity registered with the SEC, such as a national securities exchange, alternative trading system ("ATS"), or broker-dealer.

The SEC staff has concerns that many online trading platforms appear to investors as SEC-registered and regulated marketplaces when they are not. Many platforms refer to themselves as "exchanges," which can give the misimpression to investors that they are regulated or meet the regulatory standards of a national securities exchange. Although some of these platforms claim to use strict standards to pick only high-quality digital assets to trade, the SEC does not review these standards or the digital assets that the platforms select, and the so-called standards should not be equated to the listing standards of national securities exchanges. Likewise, the SEC does not review the trading protocols used by these platforms, which determine how orders interact and execute, and access to a platform's trading services may not be the same for all users. Again, investors should not assume the trading protocols meet the standards of an SEC-registered national securities exchange. Lastly, many of these platforms give the impression that they perform exchange-like functions by offering order books with updated bid and ask pricing and data about executions on the system, but there is no reason to believe that such

---

[53] This statement is archived in its entirety at https://perma.cc/K5J3-F3BC.

information has the same integrity as that provided by national securities exchanges.

In light of the foregoing, here are some questions investors should ask before they decide to trade digital assets on an online trading platform:

- Do you trade securities on this platform? If so, is the platform registered as a national securities exchange . . .?

- Does the platform operate as an ATS? If so, is the ATS registered as a broker-dealer and has it filed a Form ATS with the SEC . . .?

- Is there information in FINRA's BrokerCheck® about any individuals or firms operating the platform?

- How does the platform select digital assets for trading?

- Who can trade on the platform?

- What are the trading protocols?

- How are prices set on the platform?

- Are platform users treated equally?

- What are the platform's fees?

- How does the platform safeguard users' trading and personally identifying information?

- What are the platform's protections against cybersecurity threats, such as hacking or intrusions?

- What other services does the platform provide? Is the platform registered with the SEC for these services?

- Does the platform hold users' assets? If so, how are these assets safeguarded?

. . . .

Considerations for Market Participants Operating Online Trading Platforms

A platform that trades securities and operates as an "exchange," as defined by the federal securities laws, must register as a national securities exchange or operate under an exemption from registration, such as the exemption provided for ATSs under SEC Regulation ATS. An SEC-registered national securities exchange must, among other things, have rules designed to prevent fraudulent and manipulative acts and practices. Additionally, as a self-regulatory organization ("SRO"), an SEC-registered national securities exchange must have rules and procedures governing the discipline of its members and persons associated with its members, and enforce compliance by its members and persons associated with its members with the federal securities laws and the rules of the exchange. Further, a national securities exchange must itself comply with the federal securities laws and must file its rules with the Commission.

An entity seeking to operate as an ATS is also subject to regulatory requirements, including registering with the SEC as a broker-dealer and becoming a member of an SRO. Registration as a broker-dealer subjects the ATS to a host of regulatory requirements, such as the requirement to have reasonable policies and procedures to prevent the misuse of material non-public information, books and records requirements, and financial responsibility rules, including, as applicable, requirements concerning the safeguarding and custody of customer funds and securities. The overlay of SRO membership imposes further regulatory requirements and oversight. An ATS must comply with the federal securities laws and its SRO's rules, and file a Form ATS with the SEC.

Some online trading platforms may not meet the definition of an exchange under the federal securities laws, but directly or indirectly offer trading or other services related to digital assets that are securities. For example, some platforms offer digital wallet services (to hold or store digital assets) or transact in digital assets that are securities. These and other services offered by platforms may trigger other registration requirements under the federal securities laws, including broker-dealer, transfer agent, or clearing agency registration, among other things. In addition, a platform that offers digital assets that are securities may be participating in the unregistered offer and sale of securities if those securities are not registered or exempt from registration.

In advancing the SEC's mission to protect investors, the SEC staff will continue to focus on platforms that offer trading of digital assets and their compliance with the federal securities laws.

Consultation with Securities Counsel and the SEC Staff

We encourage market participants who are employing new technologies to develop trading platforms to consult with legal counsel to aid in their analysis of federal securities law issues and to contact SEC staff, as needed, for assistance in analyzing the application of the federal securities laws.

. . . .

––––––––––

Although this statement provides evidence that the SEC wants both users of crypto and persons involved with trading platforms to consider how a particular platform might be regarded, it does not clarify precisely when the SEC will treat a platform involving digital assets as an "exchange" subject to regulation. The starting point for addressing this question is obviously the statutory definition of "exchange," but the language of the '34 Act is extremely broad and quite general:

> The term "exchange" means any organization, association, or group of persons, whether incorporated or unincorporated, which constitutes, maintains, or provides a market place or facilities for bringing together purchasers and sellers of securities or for otherwise performing with respect to securities the functions commonly performed by a stock exchange as that term is generally understood, and includes the market place and the market facilities maintained by such exchange[54]

In a series of releases and related judicial opinions dating back nearly three decades, that general definition has been refined somewhat. In those cases, the Chicago Board of Trade (the BoT) asked the SEC to determine that the "Delta System," a new proprietary trading system for options on government securities, should have registered as an exchange with the SEC. The original BoT request was in response to a no action letter granted by the SEC.[55] In that no action letter the SEC opined in 1989 that the Delta System was not required to register as an exchange because it had not yet included " 'interdealer quotation or transaction mechanisms' fielding quotations on a consistent basis.[56]

The BoT sought judicial review, and the Seventh Circuit agreed with the SEC that the Delta System did not fit neatly into any specific definition of a securities exchange. *Bd. of Trade of Chi. v. SEC* (First BoT Decision), 883 F.2d 525, 535 (7th Cir. 1989). The Seventh Circuit panel noted that it "could not find a single case" detailing factors for "sorting a trading apparatus into the 'exchange' bin." *Id.* The SEC was therefore directed on remand to issue a formal ruling.

On remand, the SEC explained its position that the Delta System was not an exchange:

> In conducting [its definitional] analysis, the central focus of the Commission's inquiry should be whether the system is designed, whether through trading rules, operational procedures or business incentives, to centralize trading and provide buy and sell quotations on a regular or continuous basis so that purchasers and

---

[54]   '34 Act § 3(a)(1), 15 U.S.C. § 78c(a)(1).

[55]   A "no action" letter is a position determination by the agency that based upon specific representations from the party requesting the letter, the agency agrees with a particular conclusion and will take "no action" if the requester follows through. Typically, a no action letter is not precedential, and applies only to the party who requested the letter.

[56]   Propriety Trading Sys., Exchange Act Release No. 26,708, 54 Fed. Reg. 15429 (Apr. 11, 1989).

sellers have a reasonable expectation that they can regularly execute their orders at those price quotations . . . .[57]

This conclusion was again appealed, and the Seventh Circuit again acquiesced in the SEC determination.[58] In the course of its final determination, the court emphasized the SEC's broad discretion and expertise.[59] Specific factors emphasized by the court include the fact that the Delta System lacked members, a trading floor, and overseers (i.e., specialists or market-makers).[60]

Given this history, perhaps it is not surprising that the limited authority on trading platforms that involve digital assets is also characterized by case-by-case determinations from the SEC. In general terms, in considering whether a particular business structure should be regulated as an exchange, the SEC appears to ask the following questions:

1. Does the nontraditional platform match customer orders in securities?

2. Would it pose a threat to investors if it is not regulated as an exchange?

3. Would a decision not to require registration as an exchange result in regulatory gaps?

4. Does the platform include traditional exchange activities such as rules of membership and continuous quoting and trading?

These are not meaningless inquiries. There are a wide range of different sites that may be used to facilitate the exchange of Bitcoins and other cryptoassets. Many of these trading platforms offer different functions, charge varying fees, and occupy market niches designed to provide a competitive edge. There are even platforms that allow users to find appropriate exchanges on a case-by-case basis, for example if the user wants to maintain confidentiality. CoinSwitch, for example, is one such source of alternative exchanges. "CoinSwitch is an aggregator of cryptocurrency exchanges, it will always have exchanges available which do not ask for user information and KYC, the company says. Currently, there are Changelly, Changer, IDEX and other anonymous exchanges available on CoinSwitch."[61]

---

[57]   Proprietary Trading Sys., Exchange Act Release No. 27,611, 55 Fed. Reg. 1890 (Jan. 12, 1990).

[58]   *Bd. of Trade of Chi. v. SEC* (Second BoT Decision), 923 F.2d 1270 (7th Cir. 1991).

[59]   *Id.* at 1272–73.

[60]   *Id.* at 1272.

[61]   Eddie Mitchell, *Exchange Aggregator Compares Prices, Allows Trading on Top Platforms Without an Account*, COINTELEGRAPH (Sept. 24, 2014) [archived at https://perma.cc/8EJU-XL2R].

Some platforms operate like traditional securities exchanges except they deal in crypto rather than fiat currencies. An example of this kind of operation is Kraken.[62] There are also options like Coinbase,[63] which allow users to deal in crypto at prices set by brokers. (Generally speaking, these kinds of platforms are more expensive to use, but may be more user-friendly.) Direct trading platforms allow users to exchange, buy, and sell orders in a peer-to-peer manner by matching orders when amounts and offered prices line up. Bitstamp operates in this way.[64]

Alternatively, there are also cryptocurrency funds that are professionally managed which allow members of the public to invest in crypto without making a direct purchase. GBTC (Grayscale Bitcoin Trust) is an example of such a fund.[65] Some exchanges claim to be completely decentralized. Bisq (formerly Bitsquare) fits this characterization. According to its website, "Bisq is an open-source, peer-to-peer application that allows you to buy and sell cryptocurrencies in exchange for national currencies."[66] In addition, different exchanges may also have other distinguishing characteristics. Some are limited to users in specific geographic regions. For example, Bitbuy.ca is limited to Canadian users (as well as being limited to BTC, ETH, LTC, and BCH).

Given the range of trading options, it is not surprising that it is often difficult to know whether a particular platform will be considered to be an exchange. In the BoT cases involving the Delta System described above, there were a number of specific attributes that the Seventh Circuit mentioned in concluding that the Delta System was not an exchange, including the lack of members, a trading floor, and market-makers.[67] Crypto exchanges may well lack some of these same attributes.

The stakes are high. Most early exchanges lacked the capability of complying with the requirements to become a compliant, registered exchange or to deliver required information and comply with protocols for becoming a regulated Alternative Trading System.[68] Current exchanges might be able to comply, but generally will not wish to do so because of the extensive (and expensive) requirements associated with being an exchange. Cryptocurrency trading platforms that do desire to comply with SEC requirements (presumably because they believe they will be treated

---

[62]　The Kraken website is found at https://www.kraken.com/en-us/.

[63]　The Coinbase website is found at https://www.coinbase.com/.

[64]　For an explanation of how the Bitstamp exchange works, see Eugene Kem, *Beginners Guide to Bitstamp: Complete Review,* BLOCKONOMI (Dec. 20, 2018) (available online at https://blockonomi.com/bitstamp-review/).

[65]　*See* Grayscale Bitcoin Trust, website at https://grayscale.co/bitcoin-trust/.

[66]　*See Bisq Exchange, Decentralized,* BISQ (available online at https://bisq.network/).

[67]　Second BoT Decision, 923 F.2d at 1272.

[68]　Additional information about some of the early trading platforms can be found in J. Scott Colesanti, *Trotting Out the White Horse: How the S.E.C. Can Handle Bitcoin's Threat to American Investors,* 65 SYRACUSE L. REV. 1 (2014).

by the SEC as exchanges) are generally choosing to become an ATS (alternative trading system) rather than registering as a national securities exchange.

To comply with Regulation ATS, an exchange must register as a broker-dealer and file an initial operation report on Form ATS. If the ATS changes its operations, it must amend the form, and must file a cessation of operation report if it stops doing business. The filing requirements are set out in Rule 301(b)(2) of Regulation ATS. On July 18, 2018, the SEC announced amendments to Regulation ATS designed to enhance operational transparency and regulatory oversight, and to protect user's confidential information. New form ATS-N is designed to allow market participants to evaluate potential conflicts of interest and security concerns relating to the ATS and any of its operators or affiliates. In addition, the ATS is required to disclose how it operates, including execution and priority procedures. Form ATS-N will be publicly available on the SEC's EDGAR (Electronic Data Gathering, Analysis, and Retrieval) System.

While these changes may be helpful to users, they do not address the question of what kinds of crypto trading platforms will be subject to these requirements. Obviously, the platform has to be trading in a cryptoasset that is classified as a security, which has led many exchanges to be cautious in deciding whether to add new interests to the kinds of crypto traded on them.[69]

We do not know, however, if merely launching a smart contract that could operate as an exchange is enough for a developer to fall within the scope of exchange regulations. In the Coburn/EtherDelta case, the SEC highlighted the fact that the lack of a central database would not exempt a decentralized platform from the exchange regulations. With regard to Coburn individually, the SEC did specifically note that he had not only launched the smart contract, but that he also exercised sole administrative control. In essence, he operated a user-friendly, outward-facing interface for conducting transactions through the smart contract, which was designed to resemble more traditional online securities trading platforms. Taken together, this brought Coburn within the ambit of the regulations.

These determinations create potential problems for at least some digital token exchange platforms. Many of them have operated without registration as a national securities exchange or under any exemption, and they should be aware that the SEC seems to be watching blockchain-enabled secondary trading platforms. Companies operating those platforms should therefore carefully consider the implications of their business. Most importantly, they should consider if they should register as

---

[69]　　*See* Nick Chong, *Crypto Exchange Seized by SEC, Why Exchanges are Cautious in Adding Tokens*, NEWSBTC (Sept. 28, 2018) (available online at https://www.newsbtc.com/2018/09/28/crypto-exchange-seized-by-sec-why-exchanges-are-cautious-in-adding-tokens/).

an exchange or qualify for an exemption. The consequence of failing to register now that the SEC has provided warning guidance on multiple occasions may be increasingly harsh.[70]

6. ETFs FOR CRYPTO

The SEC has reviewed numerous requests to approve crypto ETFs, and to date has approved none of them. In fact, in November 2018, SEC Chairman Jay Clayton publicly opined that he did not see a pathway to approval until concerns over market manipulation are addressed. At a CoinDesk Consensus: Invest Conference in late 2018, Chairman Clayton stated: "How that [manipulation] issue gets addressed, I don't have a particular path. But it needs to be addressed" before the SEC approves a crypto ETF.[71]

More recently, however, there have been suggestions that one approach towards Crypto ETFS might involve more coordination with the CFTC (which will be discussed in the next chapters). SEC Hester Peirce has noted that "[a]t the SEC we've been unwilling to . . . sign off on a bitcoin ETF, an exchange-traded product based on bitcoin. My concern about our approach in that area is it looks a little bit like a merit-based approach judging the underlying bitcoin markets."[72] The most recent action by the SEC appears to confirm this reluctance, as the SEC forced "a partial bitcoin ETF proposal submitted by 'Reality shares' to withdraw it."[73]

However, the CFTC has a less formal process, allowing exchanges to self-certify if they meet the requirements of the CEA.[74] This approach conflicts with the general direction of the SEC, creating a "market scenario which is quite confusing on regulatory stance." SEC Commissioner Peirce therefore was clear in a preference for collaboration and harmonization. In her opinion, the two agencies need to resolve questions about where agency jurisdiction ends and begins because of the desire to avoid overlap and provide effective guidance to market participants.

---

[70]   Compliance with the federal securities laws does not eliminate the need to comply with Bank Secrecy Act and state money transmission laws, or the need to satisfy CEA and CFTC regulations. For a general explanation of compliance considerations, see Morrison Foerster, *First SEC Enforcement Action Against Unregistered Digital Token Exchange*, JDSUPRA (Nov. 13, 2018) (available online at https://www.jdsupra.com/legalnews/first-sec-enforcement-action-against-477 88/).

[71]   Nikhilesh De & Stan Higgins, *SEC Chair Clayton: Crypto ETF Needs Exchanges 'Free From Manipulation*," COINDESK (Nov. 27, 2018) (available online at https://www.coindesk.com/clayton-sec-ico-funding-security-offering).

[72]   Tabbassum, *SEC and CFTC Set to Collaborate To Regulate Bitcoin ETFs and Other Investment Products*, COINGAPE (Feb. 18, 2019) (available online at https://coingape.com/sec-cftc-collaborate-regulate-bitcoin-etfs/) (reporting on remarks made during a Bipartisan Policy Center event themed "The Year Ahead for Capital Markets" held February 12, 2019 in Washington D.C.).

[73]   *Id.*

[74]   *Id.*, quoting CFTC Commissioner Brian Quintenz.

Whether or not the agencies agree to allow self-certification of exchanges under the terms of the CEA, or whether a new harmonized approach is developed, so long as ownership of Bitcoin becomes increasingly diverse, and as markets are better understood, it is fairly certain that at some point, there will be crypto ETFs acceptable to the SEC. How quickly this will happen is unclear, although market participants continue to refine their proposals, seeking regulatory authorization.

7. ACADEMIC SUGGESTIONS

In addition to comments from regulators and proposed bills that suggest future direction with regard to how the federal securities laws should apply to cryptotransactions, academic commentators are also beginning to weigh in on the subject. One of the most intriguing thoughts comes from a Research Associate at Columbia Law School.

PRELIMINARY NOTES

As you read the following excerpt from a law review article proposing a particular way for the SEC to deal with crypto, consider the following questions:

1.　In the view of the author, why do conventional requirements for registration and disclosure not work well for cryptoassets? What is there about crypto that makes the burden of disclosure on developers and promoters potentially disproportionate to its benefits to person who seek to buy cryptoassets?

2.　The author of this excerpt also suggests that it is difficult to apply *Howey* to cryptotransactions. What are the special problems that crypto poses when it comes to applying the *Howey* test?

3.　The following excerpt looks at three different cryptoassets in some detail: Bitcoin, Tezos, and Filecoin. How would the *Howey* test apply to each of those? Does the author suggest that the test produces inequitable results in all of these cases? What is the difference between these cryptoassets, and why does the author draw the conclusions that she does?

4.　The ultimate suggestion that this article makes is that securities law enforcement actions involving crypto should focus only on cases involving fraud rather than failure to register or disclose (as required by many exemptions). Who would be protected by this change? Who would be less protected? Do you agree this would be a desirable change in regulatory focus? Why or why not?

CRYPTO SECURITIES: ON THE RISKS OF INVESTMENTS IN BLOCKCHAIN-BASED ASSETS AND THE DILEMMAS OF SECURITIES REGULATION

Shlomit Azgad-Tromer, 68 AM. U. L. REV. 69, 112–30 (2018)
(Excerpted with permission of the author)

. . . .

A. Are Blockchain-based Assets Securities under U.S. Law?

1. The *Howey* test

. . . .

The test of whether an offering constitutes a security was established by the Supreme Court in *Howey*.

. . . .

The Supreme Court test for a security is based on both the purchasers' motivation, and on the dependency of the contractual enterprise's success on the efforts of the respondents. In the opinion of the Supreme Court, the purchasers [in *Howey*] were "attracted solely" by the prospect of a return on their investment. . . . It is therefore the dependency on the efforts of the respondents that made the contractual agreement "[a] common enterprise managed by [the] respondents." . . . . Purchaser motivation has served as a test for the securities nature of the offering in cases since then as well.

. . . .

2. The DAO: SEC report of investigation

In July 2017, the SEC's Division of Enforcement released a report of investigation regarding the question of whether the DAO . . . and its co-founders and intermediaries may have violated U.S. federal securities laws. In this case, the SEC determined not to pursue an enforcement action, but it did publish a valuable opinion about securities regulation on the blockchain.

. . . .

In the spring of 2016, the DAO offered and sold 1.15 billion DAO tokens in exchange for a total of approximately 12 million ETH. Holders of the DAO tokens were granted certain ownership and voting rights in choosing a portfolio of investments to be held by the DAO, via funded projects, which would serve as the underlying asset of the DAO tokens and would grant its owners a return on their investment, respectively. For a project to be included under the DAO's portfolio, a "contractor" needs to submit a proposal embedded in a smart contract deployed on the blockchain and post details about the proposal on the DAO website, providing a link to the source code. The prerequisites for submitting a proposal were ownership of at least one DAO token and a secured deposit to be forfeited in case the proposal failed to achieve a quorum of DAO token holders. Additionally, before a proposal would be brought to a vote, a group of individuals appointed by Slock.it as "curators" have to review and approve it. These appointed curators had the ultimate control as to whether a project would be submitted for voting by DAO holders. The first proposal to be funded was submitted by DAO's co-founders, Slock.it. In applying the *Howey* test to the DAO case, the SEC determined the following:

(1) The term "issuer" is broadly defined to include unincorporated organizations or persons, ruling that the term issuer is to be "flexibly construed" . . . .

(2) Cryptocurrency is "money" for the purpose of the *Howey* test. . . .

(3) The motivation of DAO purchasers was to make profits, as the DAO was a for-profit entity, pooling ETH to fund projects, proposing the sharing of profits from the returns of the funded projects.

(4) The efforts of Slock.it's co-founders and the DAO's curators were essential to the success of the DAO's enterprise. . . .

The SEC stressed that Slock.it's managerial efforts played a significant role in the DAO's success both during the offering and after the enterprise launched, on an ongoing basis. . . .

B.   The Case for Antifraud-Only Markets on the Blockchain

. . . .

[S]ome evidence suggests that the SEC has initiated more fraud investigations against issues exempt from federal registration requirements than against those that were registered. . . .[A] private liquid market for sophisticated investors will allow better flow of capital to finance innovation and entrepreneurship without jeopardizing the protection of retail investors, while allowing sophisticated investors to negotiate the information they need to assess the offering and to monitor their investment's performance on an ongoing basis. Such a private market will provide blockchain issuers with a choice of regulatory regimes, i.e., a market of informational regulatory regimes. Setting multiple choices for blockchain offerings provides a mechanism superior to a single regulator for ascertaining what information disclosure is in the investors' best interests. A priori, there is no reason to assume sophisticated investors are less proficient than the SEC in setting the agenda for disclosure requirements. A private market alongside the publicly regulated one will thus provide both blockchain issuers and sophisticated investors with choices, while also revealing investor preferences and thereby providing feedback to regulators on the efficacy of the regulated market, and the nature and type of information that should be subject to mandatory disclosure.

. . . .

Crypto markets pose unique political constraints. First, a blockchain-based asset is a digital asset positioned on a virtual space and is thus inherently global. Any effort to regulate transactions occurring on the blockchain raises questions of extraterritorial jurisdiction. Among other legal difficulties, "the SEC may not be able to effectively pursue bad actors or recover funds." Second, as of early 2018, the type of business financed on the blockchain platforms is typically entrepreneurial, with little political comparability with traditional public sources of power. Third, the blockchain territory is politically positioned as a libertarian safe haven detached from national governments and their administrative agencies. At their core, blockchain-based assets are providing a financial platform based on computation power and mathematical proof, displacing traditional reliance on states, regulators, exchanges, and intermediaries. As of early 2018, the market caps of crypto markets are perhaps not high enough to pose a threat to traditional capital markets, and the intermediaries that serve them. Yet, given the astounding growth rate in crypto markets during 2016 and 2017, traditional regulatory agencies and intermediaries should be concerned, and accordingly, have political motivation to encourage regulation of the blockchain industry.

The political relationship between the regulatory apparatus of the SEC and the blockchain territory encompasses some of the most fundamental questions in international law and policy and in political theory. These questions deal with the intersection between anarchy and capitalism, globalization and the state, free markets and regulation, all of which are beyond the scope of this paper.

. . . .

C. Proposed Doctrinal Improvements

As explained above, the *Howey* test for determining whether an investment is protected under securities laws is based both on the purchasers' motivation to earn profits, rather than consume products or services, and on the dependency of the success of the contractual enterprise on the efforts of others. Blockchain-based assets call into question the rationality of this doctrine.

The first element of the *Howey* test, the motivational element, has given rise to numerous contractual designs of "utility tokens," a term describing blockchain-based assets representing consumptive goods, for the purpose of avoiding securities regulation. In the blockchain territory, discerning consumptive from speculative aspirations is an inherently impractical, vague, and redundant mission. First, all purchasers of blockchain-based assets have a profit-oriented motivation, without reservation. Even when the underlying value of the blockchain-based asset is a consumptive good, there is often a secondary market for tokens. Second, as the analysis of risk factors above shows, blockchain-based assets with consumptive value are often offered to investors in early development stages and incur significantly higher monitoring costs. Purchasers of a blockchain-based asset with a consumptive motivation are often more vulnerable than purchasers with speculative profit motivations. Third, issuers are not well-positioned to assess the purchasers' motivation in the automated trading environment of the blockchain. Issuers rarely meet their investors in person and have little knowledge of their purchase motivation. Requiring offerors of blockchain-based assets to conduct a motivational assessment of their purchasers will inevitably trigger a high degree of uncertainty over the blockchain industry.

The second element of the *Howey* test is an assessment of whether purchasers relied on the efforts of others for success of the enterprise. Blockchain-based assets again challenge the logic of this test. Investors of blockchain-based assets are never positioned to perform the contract on their own. Inevitably, they must rely on the efforts of others on the blockchain's ecosystem to bring their investment to fruition. Yet, when these "others" are dispersed on a decentralized ledger, securities regulation does not make sense, if only for the technically implausible enforcement of mandatory disclosure requirements on a decentralized ledger when no particular party is positioned as the cheaper information gatherer. When purchasers rely on the efforts of a global community of very many others on a decentralized ledger, none of these particular agents are able to carry the costs of mandatory disclosure. Reliance on the efforts of others should be narrowed to test whether a third party—be it a person, entity or coordinated group of actors—drives the expectation of a return or has the potential to exert a controlling cost on the blockchain-based investors.

Regulators should target the identified sources of risks and focus on those risks that securities regulation can potentially mitigate. Securities regulations are particularly useful in taming controlling risks and monitoring risks, and they have some potential value in hedging systemic risks. The potential benefits of applying securities regulations are thus a function of the scope of controlling costs, monitoring costs and potential systemic risks at the particular blockchain offering. The higher the controlling and monitoring costs of the blockchain-based investment contract, the higher the potential need of regulated protection. On the other hand, the costs of regulation must be taken into account and balanced against its benefits.

. . . .

D.   Examples

1.   Bitcoin

In 2008, the pseudonymous Satoshi Nakamoto released a white paper titled "Bitcoin: A Peer-to-Peer Electronic Cash System," which introduced the mechanisms underlying modern blockchains, and in particular the decentralized consensus protocol based on proof-of-work. Shortly afterwards, the same author released open source software implementing these mechanisms, and started running this software themselves on the Internet, thereby creating the Bitcoin blockchain.

In the primary market, Bitcoin has never officially been offered to investors. In the secondary market, its purchase is open to anyone, worldwide, regardless of investor status or qualification, subject to the "proof-of-work" requirement for block-rewards, which essentially allocates the right to assign property rights in the blockchain based on computational power.

. . . .

When assessing whether securities regulation should be applied to Bitcoins, controlling costs, monitoring costs, and systemic costs should be weighed against the costs of securities regulation.

First, to assess Bitcoin's possible controlling costs, one should assess whether any particular party is in a position to allocate new blocks or authorize transactions. Bitcoin's blockchain employs a purely automated mathematical process that is open to all, where the power to allocate ownership in new blocks is allocated by computational power to solve mathematical riddles. In 2018, most of this power is held by miners, but their identity and power can shift with time. Indeed, Bitcoin's founder, Satoshi Nakamoto, has not been active on its blockchain since 2010, with no deleterious effect noticed on the blockchain's growth. By contrast, consider the expected effect of the departure of a corporate founder in a traditional corporation to assess the dramatic significance of decentralization. What would happen if Mark Zuckerberg were to leave Facebook? Some efforts to institutionalize the Bitcoin community have evolved throughout the years, but no such community has been granted the power to exert controlling costs on the blockchain. . . . [I]n June 2018, William Hinman, director of the Division of Corporation Finance at the SEC announced that because Bitcoin has been decentralized and operational for some time, imposing "the disclosure regime of the federal securities laws to the offer and resale of Bitcoin would seem to add little value."[75]

---

[75]   Author's note: This reference is to SEC Speech, *Digital Asset Transactions: When Howey Met Gary (Plastic), Remarks at the Yahoo Finance All Markets Summit: Crypto* (June 14, 2018) [archived at https://perma.cc/X95R-KV97].

. . . .

2. Tezos

In July 2017, Tezos raised in an ICO 65,627 BTC and 361,122 ETH (worth together $232 million USD at the closure). The ICO was legally designed as a fundraiser, where investors were making non-refundable donations to the Tezos foundation, a corporation seeking (but not yet granted) non-profit status in Switzerland. Tezos's ICO was open to all investor types as a public offering and was promoted in YouTube videos, a Facebook page, and on its website, without discrimination.

Assessing whether securities regulation should be applied to Tezos requires . . . evaluation of the controlling costs, monitoring costs, and systemic risks of investments in Tezos, to be weighed against the costs of securities regulation of its blockchain. Consider first Tezos's controlling costs. [Many of these arise out of the transfer of all of Tezos' intellectual property to Dynamic Ledger Solutions, Inc.] . . . . In the aftermath of the ICO closure and in light of the class actions filed against the Tezos Foundation and DLS, allegations were made suggesting additional controlling costs collected by DLS shareholders, including requested coverage of legal expenses related to the lawsuits.

. . . .

Monitoring costs at Tezos are also profound. Per Tezos's "Contribution Terms" posted on its website, investments in Tezos are "non-refundable" and should be considered "contributions" rather than "investments." Remarkably, neither Tezos Foundation nor DLS are contractually obliged to provide purchasers with the tokens. The Contribution Terms explicitly state that the project "could be fully or partially abandoned," and its network and tokens not developed. No mechanisms for external audit or milestones for monitoring the development of the network were specified in the contribution documents, and indeed, according to the media, Tezos has used the proceeds of its ICO to invest in stocks, bonds, and precious metals, not to hire engineers and code developers, an unusual pattern for a startup company.

Systemic risks are hard to quantify. Investments in Tezos were likely made by investors who had limited ability to trace the sources underlying their investment and potentially producing its cash flow.

. . . .

3. Filecoin

Filecoin is a blockchain data storage network that has completed its ICO, raising more than $257 million in September 2017. As with Bitcoin, Filecoin miners compete to mine blocks. Yet in Filecoin, tokens represent actual data storage space. Miners compete not only to allocate tokens in the new block per se, but "to amass as much storage as they can, and rent it out to clients." Filecoin mining power is proportional to active storage space on a cloud, which directly provides a useful service to clients.

Despite the allusion to public offerings with the title "ICO," Filecoin's offering was legally designed as a private placement, both in the initial offering stage and on the ongoing trade in secondary markets. The initial offering of Filecoin was exclusively open to accredited investors. Investments in Filecoin had several prerequisites, including creation of a Coinlist account, verification of identity as a US accredited investor, and submission of details required for "Know Your Customer/Anti-Money Laundering" requirements. The ongoing allocation of tokens in the secondary market is decentralized. Miners get paid for fulfilling storage requests on the Filecoin market.

. . . .

Analysis of controlling costs, monitoring costs and systemic risks of the Filecoin blockchain offering yields an eclectic pattern. Controlling costs should be separately assessed in the initial offering stage and on an ongoing basis. In the initial offering, distribution of tokens was criticized for an alleged bias giving private benefits to insiders and entrepreneurs. In the secondary market, the decentralized pattern of mining and its storage capacity requirement seem to substantially limit opportunities for tunneling and self-dealing. Monitoring costs are to be tamed in Filecoin by its automated verification process of the underlying value of the blockchain offering. Recall that Filecoin is a centralized storage network in which tokens represent respective storage capacities. Although the underlying value of the token is indeed off-chain, the automated process provided by its code allows for a clear, fast, and accurate verification process of the storage space provided. Filecoin is a good example for saving the costs of monitoring by an intermediary as the storage space it secures is a technical feature that can be automatically verified by the blockchain. Finally, systemic risk should be assessed. The inaccurate pricing is indeed less of a concern when all investors are sophisticated, especially when value of tokens is entrenched in viable storage space granted to token holders.

Notably, applying the *Howey* test on Filecoin would yield a distorted outcome. To be sure, investors of Filecoin had motivation to profit and relied on the efforts of others. But the *Howey* test does not take into account the low monitoring costs afforded by the blockchain's automatic verification process, or the dispersed mining process and its role in sustaining the blockchain-based assets, applying securities laws when they offer little remedy attuned to the identified risks investors face.

8. CONTINUING DEVELOPMENTS FROM THE SEC

On April 3, 2019, the SEC issued additional guidance about the appropriate treatment of crypto offerings.[76] An excerpt from the framework (referred to in these materials as the "Framework") appears below.[77]

SEC, *FRAMEWORK FOR "INVESTMENT CONTRACT" ANALYSIS OF DIGITAL ASSETS*
(Ap. 3, 2019.)[1]

I. Introduction

If you are considering an Initial Coin Offering, sometimes referred to as an "ICO," or otherwise engaging in the offer, sale, or distribution of a digital asset,[2] you need to consider whether the U.S. federal securities laws apply. A threshold issue is whether the digital asset is a "security" under those laws. The term "security" includes an "investment contract," as well as other instruments such as stocks, bonds, and transferable shares. A digital asset should be analyzed to determine whether it has the characteristics of any product that meets the definition of "security" under the federal securities laws. In this guidance, we provide a framework for analyzing whether a digital asset has the characteristics of one particular type of security—an "investment contract." Both the Commission and the federal courts frequently use the "investment contract" analysis to determine whether unique or novel instruments or arrangements, such as digital assets, are securities subject to the federal securities laws.

The U.S. Supreme Court's *Howey* case and subsequent case law have found that an "investment contract" exists when there is the investment of money in a common enterprise with a reasonable expectation of profits to be derived from the efforts of others. The so-called *"Howey* test" applies to any contract, scheme, or transaction, regardless of whether it has any of the characteristics of typical securities. The focus of the *Howey* analysis is not only on the form and terms of the instrument itself (in this case, the

---

[76]   SEC, *Framework for "Investment Contract" Analysis of Digital Asset* (Ap. 3, 2019) [archived at https://perma.cc/J4KQ-HW52] (hereinafter referred to as *"Framework.")* SEC, Bill Hinman & Valerie Szczepanik, *Statement on "Framework for 'Investment Contract' Analysis of Digital Assets"* (Ap. 3, 2019) [archived at https://perma.cc/5CVA-RYFB] (hereinafter referred to as *"Statement.")*

[77]   Endnotes in the *Framework* have been changed to footnotes. Numbering of the footnotes reflects the numbers originally assigned to the endnotes. Some notes have been omitted.

[1]   This framework represents the views of the Strategic Hub for Innovation and Financial Technology ("FinHub," the "Staff," or "we") of the Securities and Exchange Commission (the "Commission"). It is not a rule, regulation, or statement of the Commission, and the Commission has neither approved nor disapproved its content. Further, this framework does not replace or supersede existing case law, legal requirements, or statements or guidance from the Commission or Staff.

[2]   The term "digital asset," as used in this framework, refers to an asset that is issued and transferred using distributed ledger or blockchain technology, including, but not limited to, so-called "virtual currencies," "coins," and "tokens."

digital asset) but also on the circumstances surrounding the digital asset and the manner in which it is offered, sold, or resold (which includes secondary market sales). Therefore, issuers and other persons and entities engaged in the marketing, offer, sale, resale, or distribution of any digital asset will need to analyze the relevant transactions to determine if the federal securities laws apply.

. . . .

II. Application of *Howey* to Digital Assets

In this guidance, we provide a framework for analyzing whether a digital asset is an investment contract and whether offers and sales of a digital asset are securities transactions. As noted above, under the *Howey* test, an "investment contract" exists when there is the investment of money in a common enterprise with a reasonable expectation of profits to be derived from the efforts of others. Whether a particular digital asset at the time of its offer or sale satisfies the *Howey* test depends on the specific facts and circumstances. We address each of the elements of the *Howey* test below.

A. The Investment of Money

The first prong of the *Howey* test is typically satisfied in an offer and sale of a digital asset because the digital asset is purchased or otherwise acquired in exchange for value, whether in the form of real (or fiat) currency, another digital asset, or other type of consideration.[9]

---

[9] The lack of monetary consideration for digital assets, such as those distributed via a so-called "bounty program" does not mean that the investment of money prong is not satisfied. As the Commission explained in The DAO Report, "[i]n determining whether an investment contract exists, the investment of 'money' need not take the form of cash" and "in spite of Howey's reference to an 'investment of money,' it is well established that cash is not the only form of contribution or investment that will create an investment contract." The DAO Report at 11 (citation omitted). See *In re Tomahawk Exploration LLC,* Securities Act Rel. 10530 (Aug. 14, 2018) (issuance of tokens under a so-called "bounty program" constituted an offer and sale of securities because the issuer provided tokens to investors in exchange for services designed to advance the issuer's economic interests and foster a trading market for its securities). . . .

B. Common Enterprise

Courts generally have analyzed a "common enterprise" as a distinct element of an investment contract.[10] In evaluating digital assets, we have found that a "common enterprise" typically exists.[11]

C. Reasonable Expectation of Profits Derived from Efforts of Others

Usually, the main issue in analyzing a digital asset under the *Howey* test is whether a purchaser has a reasonable expectation of profits (or other financial returns) derived from the efforts of others. A purchaser may expect to realize a return through participating in distributions or through other methods of realizing appreciation on the asset, such as selling at a gain in a secondary market. When a promoter, sponsor, or other third party (or affiliated group of third parties) (each, an "Active Participant" or "AP") provides essential managerial efforts that affect the success of the enterprise, and investors reasonably expect to derive profit from those efforts, then this prong of the test is met. Relevant to this inquiry is the "economic reality" of the transaction and "what character the instrument is given in commerce by the terms of the offer, the plan of distribution, and the economic inducements held out to the prospect." The inquiry, therefore, is an objective one, focused on the transaction itself and the manner in which the digital asset is offered and sold.

The following characteristics are especially relevant in an analysis of whether the third prong of the *Howey* test is satisfied.

1. Reliance on the Efforts of Others

The inquiry into whether a purchaser is relying on the efforts of others focuses on two key issues:

- Does the purchaser reasonably expect to rely on the efforts of an AP?

- Are those efforts "the undeniably significant ones, those essential managerial efforts which affect the failure or success of the

---

[10]   In order to satisfy the "common enterprise" aspect of the Howey test, federal courts require that there be either "horizontal commonality" or "vertical commonality." *See Revak v. SEC Realty Corp.*, 18 F.3d. 81, 87–88 (2d Cir. 1994) (discussing horizontal commonality as "the tying of each individual investor's fortunes to the fortunes of the other investors by the pooling of assets, usually combined with the pro-rata distribution of profits" and two variants of vertical commonality, which focus "on the relationship between the promoter and the body of investors"). The Commission, on the other hand, does not require vertical or horizontal commonality per se, nor does it view a "common enterprise" as a distinct element of the term "investment contract." *In re Barkate*, 57 S.E.C. 488, 496 n.13 (Apr. 8, 2004); see also the Commission's Supplemental Brief at 14 in *SEC v. Edwards*, 540 U.S. 389 (2004) (on remand to the 11th Circuit).

[11]   Based on our experiences to date, investments in digital assets have constituted investments in a common enterprise because the fortunes of digital asset purchasers have been linked to each other or to the success of the promoter's efforts. *See SEC v. Int'l Loan Network, Inc.*, 968 F.2d 1304, 1307 (D.C. Cir. 1992).

enterprise," as opposed to efforts that are more ministerial in nature?

Although no one of the following characteristics is necessarily determinative, the stronger their presence, the more likely it is that a purchaser of a digital asset is relying on the "efforts of others":

- An AP is responsible for the development, improvement (or enhancement), operation, or promotion of the network,[15] particularly if purchasers of the digital asset expect an AP to be performing or overseeing tasks that are necessary for the network or digital asset to achieve or retain its intended purpose or functionality.

  - Where the network or the digital asset is still in development and the network or digital asset is not fully functional at the time of the offer or sale, purchasers would reasonably expect an AP to further develop the functionality of the network or digital asset (directly or indirectly). This particularly would be the case where an AP promises further developmental efforts in order for the digital asset to attain or grow in value.

- There are essential tasks or responsibilities performed and expected to be performed by an AP, rather than an unaffiliated, dispersed community of network users (commonly known as a "decentralized" network).

- An AP creates or supports a market for, or the price of, the digital asset. This can include, for example, an AP that: (1) controls the creation and issuance of the digital asset; or (2) takes other actions to support a market price of the digital asset, such as by limiting supply or ensuring scarcity, through, for example, buybacks, "burning," or other activities.

- An AP has a lead or central role in the direction of the ongoing development of the network or the digital asset. In particular, an AP plays a lead or central role in deciding governance issues, code updates, or how third parties participate in the validation of transactions that occur with respect to the digital asset.

- An AP has a continuing managerial role in making decisions about or exercising judgment concerning the network or the characteristics or rights the digital asset represents including, for example:

---

[15] In this guidance, we are using the term "network" broadly to encompass the various elements that comprise a digital asset's network, enterprise, platform, or application.

- o   Determining whether and how to compensate persons providing services to the network or to the entity or entities charged with oversight of the network.

- o   Determining whether and where the digital asset will trade. For example, purchasers may reasonably rely on an AP for liquidity, such as where the AP has arranged, or promised to arrange for, the trading of the digital asset on a secondary market or platform.

- o   Determining who will receive additional digital assets and under what conditions.

- o   Making or contributing to managerial level business decisions, such as how to deploy funds raised from sales of the digital asset.

- o   Playing a leading role in the validation or confirmation of transactions on the network, or in some other way having responsibility for the ongoing security of the network.

- o   Making other managerial judgements or decisions that will directly or indirectly impact the success of the network or the value of the digital asset generally.

- •   Purchasers would reasonably expect the AP to undertake efforts to promote its own interests and enhance the value of the network or digital asset, such as where:

  - o   The AP has the ability to realize capital appreciation from the value of the digital asset. This can be demonstrated, for example, if the AP retains a stake or interest in the digital asset. In these instances, purchasers would reasonably expect the AP to undertake efforts to promote its own interests and enhance the value of the network or digital asset.

  - o   The AP distributes the digital asset as compensation to management or the AP's compensation is tied to the price of the digital asset in the secondary market. To the extent these facts are present, the compensated individuals can be expected to take steps to build the value of the digital asset.

  - o   The AP owns or controls ownership of intellectual property rights of the network or digital asset, directly or indirectly.

  - o   The AP monetizes the value of the digital asset, especially where the digital asset has limited functionality.

In evaluating whether a digital asset previously sold as a security should be reevaluated at the time of later offers or sales, there would be additional considerations as they relate to the "efforts of others," including but not limited to:

- Whether or not the efforts of an AP, including any successor AP, continue to be important to the value of an investment in the digital asset.

- Whether the network on which the digital asset is to function operates in such a manner that purchasers would no longer reasonably expect an AP to carry out essential managerial or entrepreneurial efforts.

- Whether the efforts of an AP are no longer affecting the enterprise's success.

2.   Reasonable Expectation of Profits

An evaluation of the digital asset should also consider whether there is a reasonable expectation of profits. Profits can be, among other things, capital appreciation resulting from the development of the initial investment or business enterprise or a participation in earnings resulting from the use of purchasers' funds. Price appreciation resulting solely from external market forces (such as general inflationary trends or the economy) impacting the supply and demand for an underlying asset generally is not considered "profit" under the *Howey* test.

The more the following characteristics are present, the more likely it is that there is a reasonable expectation of profit:

- The digital asset gives the holder rights to share in the enterprise's income or profits or to realize gain from capital appreciation of the digital asset.

  o   The opportunity may result from appreciation in the value of the digital asset that comes, at least in part, from the operation, promotion, improvement, or other positive developments in the network, particularly if there is a secondary trading market that enables digital asset holders to resell their digital assets and realize gains.

  o   This also can be the case where the digital asset gives the holder rights to dividends or distributions.

- The digital asset is transferable or traded on or through a secondary market or platform, or is expected to be in the future.

- Purchasers reasonably would expect that an AP's efforts will result in capital appreciation of the digital asset and therefore be able to earn a return on their purchase.

- The digital asset is offered broadly to potential purchasers as compared to being targeted to expected users of the goods or services or those who have a need for the functionality of the network.

    o   The digital asset is offered and purchased in quantities indicative of investment intent instead of quantities indicative of a user of the network. For example, it is offered and purchased in quantities significantly greater than any likely user would reasonably need, or so small as to make actual use of the asset in the network impractical.

- There is little apparent correlation between the purchase/offering price of the digital asset and the market price of the particular goods or services that can be acquired in exchange for the digital asset.

- There is little apparent correlation between quantities the digital asset typically trades in (or the amounts that purchasers typically purchase) and the amount of the underlying goods or services a typical consumer would purchase for use or consumption.

- The AP has raised an amount of funds in excess of what may be needed to establish a functional network or digital asset.

- The AP is able to benefit from its efforts as a result of holding the same class of digital assets as those being distributed to the public.

- The AP continues to expend funds from proceeds or operations to enhance the functionality or value of the network or digital asset.

- The digital asset is marketed, directly or indirectly, using any of the following . . . . [Eight possible alternatives are omitted]

Following the preceding discussion, there are six additional considerations to be used in evaluating whether a digital asset sold as a security should be reevaluated at the time of later offers or sales, and eleven additional "relevant considerations" in Part 3 of the Framework's analysis (along with five subparts).

This Framework was clearly intended to provide guidance for developers, issuers, and their counsel in determining whether a particular cryptoasset (referred to as a digital asset in the new document) should be treated as security. However, the overall usefulness of a framework that is not an official rule or pronouncement, which includes 38 different considerations, some with additional subparts, and which neither prioritizes nor indicates the degree of significance for any particular consideration, is likely to do more to confuse matters than to help.

In an additional attempt to explain its current approach, the SEC also released its first no-action letter issued in the context of a proposed offering of cryptoassets. An excerpt from that no-action letter follows.

PRELIMINARY QUESTIONS

1.   As you read the SEC's response to TurnKey Jet, can you ascertain what kind of tokens the company (referred to as TKJ in the SEC's response) proposed to offer?

2.   Were the tokens already functional? What was the anticipated function of those tokens?

3.   Was the plan to allow the tokens to be transferred or resold, and if so, to whom?

4.   Will the value of the tokens fluctuate? Could they go up in value?

SEC, *TURNKEY JET, INC. NO ACTION LETTER*[78]
(Ap. 3, 2019)

. . . .

Based on the facts presented, the Division will not recommend enforcement action to the Commission if, in reliance on your opinion as counsel that the Tokens are not securities, TKJ offers and sells the Tokens without registration under the Securities Act and the Exchange Act. Capitalized terms have the same meanings as defined in your letter.

In reaching this position, we particularly note that:

- TKJ will not use any funds from Token sales to develop the TKJ Platform, Network, or App, and each of these will be fully developed and operational at the time any Tokens are sold;

- the Tokens will be immediately usable for their intended functionality (purchasing air charter services) at the time they are sold;

- TKJ will restrict transfers of Tokens to TKJ Wallets only, and not to wallets external to the Platform;

- TKJ will sell Tokens at a price of one USD per Token throughout the life of the Program, and each Token will represent a TKJ obligation to supply air charter services at a value of one USD per Token;

- If TKJ offers to repurchase Tokens, it will only do so at a discount to the face value of the Tokens (one USD per Token) that the holder seeks to resell to TKJ, unless a court within the United States orders TKJ to liquidate the Tokens; and

---

[78]   This no-action letter is archived at https://perma.cc/MV5U-75GT.

- The Token is marketed in a manner that emphasizes the functionality of the Token, and not the potential for the increase in the market value of the Token.

This position is based on the representations made to the Division in your letter. Any different facts or conditions might require the Division to reach a different conclusion. Further, this response expresses the Division's position on enforcement action only and does not express any legal conclusion on the question presented.

. . . .

———————

Shortly after the release of the Framework and the *Turnkey Jet* no-action letter, SEC Commissioner Hester Peirce gave a speech addressing her concerns about these new developments.[79] Her assessment of the Framework and the new no-action letter was as follows:

> The SEC staff recently issued a framework to assist issuers with conducting a *Howey* analysis of potential token offerings. The document is a thorough 14 pages. It points to features of an offering and actions by an issuer that could signal that the offering is likely a securities offering. If this framework helps issuers understand what the different *Howey* factors might look like in an ICO context, it may be valuable. I am concerned, however, that it could raise more questions and concerns than it answers.
>
> While *Howey* has four factors to consider, the framework lists 38 separate considerations, many of which include several sub-points. A seasoned securities lawyer might be able to infer which of these considerations will likely be controlling and might therefore be able to provide the appropriate weight to each. Whether the framework gives anything new to the seasoned securities lawyer used to operating in the facts and circumstances world of *Howey* is an open question. I worry that non-lawyers and lawyers not steeped in securities law and its attendant lore will not know what to make of the guidance. Pages worth of factors, many of which seemingly apply to all decentralized networks, might contribute to the feeling that navigating the securities laws in this area is perilous business. Rather than sorting through the factors or hiring an expensive lawyer to do so, a wary company may reasonably decide to forgo certain opportunities or to pursue them in a more crypto-friendly jurisdiction overseas.

---

[79]   That speech can be accessed in its entirety at SEC, Speech, Hester Peirce, *How We Howey* (May 9, 2019) [archived at https://perma.cc/729A-CG6C].

On the same day the Corporation Finance staff issued the Framework, the staff also issued the first token no-action letter in response to an inquiry from TurnKey Jet, a charter jet company. The company intended to effectively tokenize gift cards. Customer members could purchase tokens that would be redeemable, dollar for dollar, for charter jet services. The tokens could be sold only to other members. This transaction is so clearly not an offer of securities that I worry the staff's issuance of a digital token no-action letter—the first and so far only such letter—may in fact have the effect of broadening the perceived reach of our securities laws. If these tokens were securities, it would be hard to distinguish them from any medium of stored value. Is a Starbucks card a security? If we are going that far, I can only imagine what name the barista will write on my coffee cup.[80]

QUESTION

Do you agree with Commissioner Peirce, or do you see the overall benefit of the SEC's continuing efforts at explaining its approach to cryptoassets?

Finally, it appears that the SEC's approach to determining when crypto is a security is heading to court in a big way. The SEC filed a complaint against the Canadian social media company Kik Interactive Inc. on June 4, 2019, alleging that their $100 million ICO was an unregistered securities distribution. The summary and conclusion included in that complaint appears below.[81]

SEC v. KIK INTERACTIVE INC. [COMPLAINT]
No. 19-cv-5244 (S.D.N.Y. 2019)

COMPLAINT

Plaintiff United States Securities and Exchange Commission (the "SEC") alleges as follows against Defendant Kik Interactive Inc. ("Kik"):

SUMMARY

1. From May to September 2017, Kik offered and sold one trillion digital tokens called "Kin." More than 10,000 investors worldwide purchased Kin for approximately $100 million in U.S. dollars and digital assets—over half of this sum coming from investors located in the United States. However, Kik's offer and sale of Kin was not registered with the

---

[80]   *Id.*, fn omitted.

[81]   The entire complaint can be found at https://www.sec.gov/litigation/complaints/2019/comp-pr2019-87.pdf, and is archived at https://perma.cc/HT2V-AVNV.

SEC, and investors did not receive he disclosures required by the federal securities laws.

2.   Congress enacted the Securities Act of 1933 to regulate the offer and sale of securities. In contrast to ordinary commerce, which often operates under the principle of caveat emptor, Congress enacted a regime of full and fair disclosure, requiring those who offer and sell securities to the investing public to provide sufficient, accurate information to allow investors to make informed decisions before they invest. Such disclosure is ordinarily provided in a "registration statement," which provides public investors with financial and managerial information about the issuer of the securities, details about the terms of the securities offering, the proposed use of investor proceeds, and an analysis of the risks and material trends that would affect the enterprise.

3.   Section 5(a) of the Securities Act [15 U.S.C. § 77e(a)] provides that, unless a registration statement is in effect as to a security or an exemption from registration applies, it is unlawful for any person, directly or indirectly, to sell securities in interstate commerce. Section 5(c) of the Securities Act [15 U.S.C. § 77e(c)] provides a similar prohibition against offers to sell or offers to buy, unless a registration statement has been filed or an exemption from registration applies. Thus, Sections 5(a) and 5(c) of the Securities Act prohibit the unregistered offer or sale of securities in interstate commerce absent an exemption.

4.   The definition of "security" includes a range of investment vehicles, including stocks, bonds, and "investment contracts." Investment contracts are transactions where an individual invests money in a common enterprise and reasonably expects profits to be derived from the entrepreneurial or managerial efforts of others. In a variety of circumstances, courts have found that investment vehicles other than stocks and bonds constitute investment contracts, including interests in orange groves, animal breeding programs, railroads, airplanes, mobile phones, and enterprises existing only on the Internet. As the Supreme Court of the United States has noted, Congress defined security broadly to embody a "flexible rather than a static principle, one that is capable of adaptation to meet the countless and variable schemes devised by those who seek the use of the money of others on the promise of profits."

5.   Kik, a private Canadian company founded in 2009, owns and operates a mobile messaging application called Kik Messenger. Despite Kik Messenger's initial success and the company's receipt of venture capital funding, Kik's costs have always far outpaced its revenues, and the company has never been profitable.

6.   In late 2016 and early 2017, Kik faced a crisis. Fewer and fewer people were using Kik Messenger. The company expected to run out of cash to fund its operations by the end of 2017, but its revenues were

insignificant, and executives had no realistic plan to increase revenues through its existing operations. In late 2016 and early 2017, Kik hired an investment bank to try to sell itself to a larger technology company, but no one was interested.

7.   Faced with a shrinking financial "runway," Kik decided to "pivot" to an entirely different business and attempt what a board member called a "hail Mary pass": Kik would offer and sell one trillion digital tokens in return for cash to fund company operations and a speculative new venture.

8.   Starting in early 2017, Kik began to devise a plan to offer and sell digital tokens. The plan became public on or about May 25, 2017, when Kik announced the Kin token offering by publishing a "white paper" and issuing press releases, and through a speech by Kik's Chief Executive Officer ("CEO") at a blockchain industry conference in Manhattan. Through these and other outlets, Kik enthusiastically described the Kin offering and Kik's plans to create, develop, and support what Kik called the "Kin Ecosystem," in which, at an unspecified future date (if the project was successful), Kin could be used to buy goods and services.

9.   From the initial May 2017 announcement through September 2017, Kik relentlessly pitched Kin and the prospect that Kik's future efforts to develop the Kin Ecosystem would drive an increase in Kin's value. Kik emphasized that only a finite number of tokens would be created and that rising demand for the tokens would cause their value to appreciate. Kik promised that it would spur such demand by dedicating company expertise and resources—including proceeds from Kin sales—to specific, Ecosystem-enhancing projects, including: the redesign of Kik Messenger to incorporate Kin; the creation of what Kik called a "rewards engine" to compensate companies that fostered Kin transactions; and the implementation of a new, Kin-specific "transaction service" to address flaws in existing blockchain technology. Kik also assured prospective buyers that, following distribution of the tokens, buyers would be able to trade Kin on secondary trading platforms, often described as "exchanges," enabling conversion of Kin to either a digital asset (e.g., Bitcoin or Ether) or fiat currency (e.g., U.S. dollars).

10.   Throughout its Kin promotional campaign, Kik also declared that the company would share with buyers a common interest in profiting from Kin's success: in addition to selling one trillion tokens through its then-ongoing offering, Kik would create and allocate to itself three trillion Kin tokens over a two-and-a-half-year period. Kik told potential buyers that, by allotting 30 percent of the outstanding supply of Kin to itself, the company would align its financial interests with those of other Kin investors, which would give the company an incentive to take entrepreneurial and managerial steps to increase the demand for the token. And, Kik described

Kin as an opportunity for both Kik and early Kin investors to "make a ton of money."

11. Starting with the May 2017 announcement, Kik offered and sold the one trillion Kin tokens in a single offering aimed at both wealthy investors and the general public.

12. From May to September 2017, Kik offered and sold tokens to professional investment funds and other select, wealthy investors using purchase agreements that Kik called "Simple Agreements for Future Tokens" or "SAFTs." Kik's SAFTs entitled purchasers to the future delivery of the Kin that they purchased when they entered into the agreements. Under the SAFTs, investors bought Kin at a discount to the price that the general public would pay, and Kik promised to deliver the tokens pursuant to a schedule, half at the time that it delivered tokens to the general public and half on the one-year anniversary of the first delivery. Kik's sale of Kin through these purchase agreements was denominated in U.S. dollars, and Kik raised approximately $49 million.

13. From May through September 2017, Kik also offered Kin to the general public and had public investors sign up for this public sale, even while the company was offering and selling discounted Kin to investment funds and other wealthy investors using its SAFTs. Kik's September 2017 sale of Kin to the general public was denominated in Ether, and Kik received approximately $50 million worth of this digital asset.

14. On September 26, 2017, Kik delivered to the public investors all of the Kin that they had purchased, and delivered to the investors who bought at a discount through SAFTs half of the tokens they had purchased, pursuant to the contracts' terms.

15. Of the nearly $100 million in cash and Ether received by Kik, over $55 million was raised from United States-based investors.

16. Throughout Kik's 2017 offering and sale of Kin, the decentralized economy that Kik had marketed did not exist. In addition, when Kik distributed Kin on September 26, 2017, no one—not even Kik—offered goods or services in return for Kin.

17. On July 25, 2017, approximately seven weeks before Kik started the public sale of Kin, the SEC issued what is often called the "DAO Report." The DAO Report "advise[d] those who would use . . . distributed ledger or blockchain-enabled means for capital raising, to take appropriate steps to ensure compliance with the U.S. federal securities laws," and found that digital assets at issue in that matter were securities. Even prior to the DAO Report, however, Kik had been informed by one of its consultants that the Kin offering was, potentially, an offering of securities that needed to be registered with the SEC and that "unregistered public securities offerings are not legal in the U.S."

18. Under the federal securities laws, Kik offered and sold securities from the initial May 2017 announcement of Kin through September 2017. But, Kik has never filed with the SEC a registration statement for its offer and sale of securities. By failing to prepare and file a registration statement, Kik did not provide important information to investors regarding the investment opportunity promoted by Kik, such as information about Kik's current financial condition (including that the company's expenses far exceeded its revenue), future plans of operation and budget, the proposed use of investor proceeds, and detailed disclosure of material trends and the most significant factors that made the offering speculative and risky. Kik thus failed to disclose information relevant for investors to evaluate Kik's promises about the investment potential of Kin and the Kin project.

19. Kin is currently trading on unregulated trading platforms at about half of the value that public buyers paid in the offering, and, during the intervening period, it has often traded much lower.

20. By engaging in the conduct set forth in this Complaint without a registration statement being in effect or filed, Kik has engaged in the unlawful offer and sale of securities in violation of Sections 5(a) and 5(c) of the Securities Act [15 U.S.C. §§ 77e(a), 77e(c)].

21. Unless Kik is permanently restrained and enjoined, it will continue to engage in the acts, practices, and courses of business set forth in this Complaint and in acts, practices, and courses of business of similar type and object.

. . . .

CONCLUSION

190. Investors' purchases of Kin were an investment of money, in a common enterprise, with an expectation of profits for both Kik and the offerees, derived primarily from the future efforts of Kik and others to build the Kin Ecosystem and drive demand for Kin. Consequently, Kik's offer and sale of Kin in 2017 was an offer and sale of securities.

191. Because Kik offered and sold securities, Kin investors were entitled to all of the protections and disclosures of the federal securities laws—protections and disclosures that were all the more important given the novel technology at issue here.

. . . .

———————

The claims for relief in the above complaint acknowledge that Kik filed a Form D in connection with the SAFT, but the SEC contends that the entire distribution constituted a single offering and thus was not in compliance with the Rule 506 exemption claimed by the company for the

SAFT portion of the sales. The SEC therefore asked the court to enjoin Kik from violating section 5 of the '33 Act; to order disgorgement of the "ill-gotten gains or unjust enrichment" from the offering, together with interest; to impose a civil penalty (fine); and for such other relief as the court determines to be just, equitable, or necessary.

After reading the above complaint, it would be easy to simply assume that Kik is a bad actor and that the securities laws should apply to prevent sales like this from taking place without registration. As is often true in the real world, however, facts are frequently in dispute. The carefully crafted reply brief in the case, filed by Kik's attorneys at Cooley LLP, makes a number of points that are worth careful consideration. Do note that it is rather unusual for there to be an introductory section in an answer filed in federal court, but Cooley clearly had a reason for taking this step.

PRELIMINARY NOTES AND QUESTIONS

1.   If the underlying issue is whether the interests involved are securities and the sales involved were all part of a single distribution, why did Kik's attorneys go to the effort of pulling out selected factual allegations in the introductory section of the answer? What strategic benefit does the introduction provide, and what legal benefit might it support? Are those the same thing?

2.   Does reading the following material change your opinion as to whether the Kik sale "needs" to be regulated by an agency such as the SEC?

3.   You were probably taught that complaints and answers deal with factual allegations. Why are there so many citations to legal authority in this answer? Are the various legal citations and explanations helpful at this stage? Why (or why not)?

SEC V. KIK INTERACTIVE INC. [ANSWER]
Case No. 19-cv-55244 (SDNY 2019)

ANSWER TO COMPLAINT

. . . .

Kik Interactive Inc. ("Kik" or the "Company") hereby answers the Complaint of the Securities and Exchange Commission ("SEC" or the "Commission") as follows, and reserves its rights to request dismissal of the Complaint on any and all grounds. To the extent not expressly admitted, all allegations of the Complaint are denied.

I.   INTRODUCTION

If the Commission had strong evidence that Kik offered or promised TDE purchasers an opportunity to profit from Kik's efforts, as part of a common enterprise, the Commission would have simply outlined all the relevant facts and let those facts speak for themselves. Instead, the Commission's Complaint reflects a consistent effort to twist the facts by removing quotes from their context and misrepresenting the documents and testimony that the Commission gathered in its investigation. The result is a Complaint that badly mischaracterizes the totality of the facts and circumstances leading up to Kik's sale of Kin in 2017. These tactics may have gotten the Commission a decent news cycle, but they will not withstand meaningful scrutiny at summary judgment or trial.

The Commission repeatedly twists the facts throughout its Complaint. Here are just three examples.

First, the Complaint alleges that a Kik consultant warned that the "Kin offering" was, potentially, an offering of securities that needed to be registered with the Commission. The Complaint alleges that:

> *"Even prior to the DAO Report, however, Kik had been informed by one of its consultants that the Kin offering was, potentially, an offering of securities that needed to be registered with the SEC and that 'unregistered public securities offerings are not legal in the U.S.'"*

But the Commission omits the full quote from the consultant, in which the consultant distinguishes digital currencies, such as Kin, from securities:

> *"[U]nregistered public securities offerings are not legal in the U.S.* ***In the case of a community currency, there is a good basis to argue that this is not a security. You're just selling units of property that you created that are used for a particular purpose in your app."***

In other words, the consultant said the opposite of what the Commission claims he said in its Complaint.

Second, the Commission incorrectly claims that Kik promised to increase Kin's price through its efforts. For example, the Commission alleges:

> *"Similarly, at the June 28, 2017 San Francisco Bitcoin Meet-up, Kik's CEO explained that setting aside Kin for the company at the beginning made sure that Kik was committed to working to increase Kin's value: 'I think what we can guarantee is we are all in on this. You know, this is—this is something we've been working to—towards for a long time, but this is something that is in our financial best interest, because of the 30 percent, but actually, like, just to be honest, like, this is something we have to do. We cannot compete with Facebook.'"*

But the Commission omits what Mr. Livingston said immediately before the quoted language, which made clear that Kik could not guarantee Kin's value because its value would depend on basic economic principles of supply and demand. The full quote reads:

> *"So we can not guarantee value with Kin. I think once you create a cryptocurrency it sits on exchanges and the price of it is set by the market based on supply and demand. So you know supply is fixed and demand goes down the price is going to go down. But I think what we can guarantee is we're all in on this. You know this is something we've been working to— towards for a long time but this is something that is in our financial best interests because of the 30 percent, but actually, like, just to be honest like this is something we have to do. We cannot compete with Facebook."*

In other words, in contrast to the Commission's misleading and selective quotation, Mr. Livingston's statement is wholly inconsistent with the Commission's claims.

Third, the Commission alleges that Kik continually emphasized its individual efforts to establish Kin's value and increase Kin's future value. The Complaint alleges:

> *"Similarly, in the May 25, 2017 video that Kik issued when announcing the Kin project, the company emphasized that 'Kik has both the experience and the resources and the user base to really make this happen.' "*

However, the Complaint fails to include the very next sentence of the video, which made clear that the success of the Kin economy depended on consumers and other developers, aside from Kik, to grow and build the economy as intended. The full statement says:

> *"I think we can make a better experience for consumers but also a better future for society in general. Kik has both the experience and the resources and the user base to really make this happen. The success of this project really comes down to how many other people can we get excited to compete with us, to join us, to work with us and to build this together."*

These are just three examples of a pattern that appears repeatedly throughout the Commission's Complaint. Indeed, apparently recognizing the weakness of its claim, the Commission has rejected its higher governmental duty to first and foremost seek justice, and has instead employed a strategy to twist the facts, creating a highly selective and misleading depiction of the record as set forth below. When viewed fairly, and in context, the evidence in this case will paint a dramatically different picture of the facts and circumstances surrounding Kik's sale of Kin in

2017, which will make clear that Kik did not violate the federal securities laws.

II. ANSWER TO SPECIFIC ALLEGATIONS

1. . . . .**ANSWER**. Kik admits that it offered and sold one trillion Kin in 2017. Kik denies the remaining allegations in this paragraph. The Commission is wrong that Kik sold Kin in a single "offer and sale." In reality, the distribution of Kin involved two entirely separate transactions: (1) a pre-sale of contractual rights, pursuant to SAFTs ("Simple Agreements for Future Tokens") and (2) the sale of Kin to the public (the "TDE"), pursuant to "Terms of Use." Because of substantial differences between the pre-sale and the TDE, Kik decided to structure the pre-sale as a sale to accredited investors exempt from registration with the Commission under SEC Regulation D.

In the pre-sale, which occurred prior to the TDE, Kik sold the conditional right to receive Kin in the future at a discount, to accredited investors (the "pre-sale"). Pre-sale participants received private placement memoranda ("PPM"), and signed SAFT agreements. Under the SAFTs, pre-sale participants would receive 50 percent of their Kin if and when a "Network Launch" (initial functionality of Kin within Kik) occurred and the remaining 50 percent of their Kin a year later. If a Network Launch did not occur, pre-sale participants would forfeit 30 percent of the amount they contributed. Kik capped the pre-sale at $50 million, all received in U.S. dollars, despite receiving millions more in interest, to ensure that the public would have an opportunity to purchase Kin in the TDE. Kik also filed a Form D with the SEC in September 2017 to formalize the exemption.

In the TDE, Kik sold around $50 million worth of Kin to around 10,000 public purchasers, more than two thirds of whom live outside of the United States. As opposed to purchasing the right to receive Kin in the future, as memorialized in the SAFTs, TDE purchasers bought Kin tokens directly under the completely different "Terms of Use," and paid in Ether—not U.S. dollars. Unlike in the pre-sale, within the first 24 hours of the TDE, purchasers could not buy more than $4,400 worth of Kin to "ensure all registered participants had a fair chance to purchase" Kin. Because Kik did not sell an "investment contract" or any other enumerated "security" in the TDE, Kik did not register the TDE with the SEC.

. . . .

4. . . . . **ANSWER**. Tellingly, the Commission misstates the test established by the Supreme Court in *Howey* when it alleges that "[i]nvestment contracts are transactions where an individual invests money in a common enterprise and reasonably expects profits to be derived . . . ." In fact, the Supreme Court has defined an investment contract as "a transaction or scheme whereby a person invests his money in a common enterprise and is *led to expect profits solely* . . . ." And although the

Supreme Court has stated that *Howey* embodies a "flexible" standard, it is far from limitless. "Investment contract" was included in the definition of "security" for the "limited purpose of identifying unconventional instruments that *have the essential properties of a debt or equity security.*" *Wals v. Fox Hills Dev. Corp.*, 24 F.3d 1016, 1018 (7th Cir. 1994) (emphasis added). Courts, including the Supreme Court, have held in many cases that there is no "investment contract," and thus no "security," where one or more parts of the test articulated in *Howey* are not met.

. . . .

7.   . . . . **ANSWER**. Kik admits that an email written by a member of Kik's Board contains the words "hail Mary pass," but Kik denies the remaining allegations in this paragraph. The Commission took several hours of testimony from the Board member quoted, but did not bother to ask any questions about the email. Now, the Commission cites the quoted language to characterize Kin as a desperate and final attempt to save a dying company, with little chance of success. But that is not the case. Kik's Board and Executive Team alike believed that Kin was a bold idea that could solve the monetization challenges faced by all developers (not just Kik) in the existing advertising-based economy, by changing the way people buy and sell digital products and services. Consistent with the Board and Executive Team's view at the time, another Board member wrote:

> *The more I think about it, I think this is a great idea. People call it a hail Mary but to me that is a longshot and I really do not think it is a long shot.*

The Commission also asked Mr. Livingston directly whether "people consider[ed] the crypto project a Hail Mary on Kik's board," and he explained:

> *I think when people first heard the idea, they, like almost everyone else I've ever introduced this idea to, thought it was crazy. But also, they—like everyone else, as they spent more time with it, they heard more about it, they understood more about it, realized that like Jim realized here, **not only was this not a long shot, but it was a great shot.***

Indeed, many of Kik's competitors (such as Line, KaKao, Telegram, and Facebook) have since announced their own cryptocurrencies, thereby validating the ambitious vision that Kik conceived at a time when others were not bold enough to pursue it.

And while it is difficult to explain the Commission's apparent contempt for the idea that a company would sell a product to generate revenue, Kin was not simply a means to fund operations, nor was it necessary for Kik to stay in business. Kik believed that it could have received traditional financing if it had wanted to, as it had many times in the past, but realized that it would not address Kik's fundamental challenge to monetize within an advertising-based model. The Commission is also well aware that Kik was not facing imminent financial ruin: as Kik's then-CFO and member of the Board informed the Staff multiple times, "*it wasn't time to hit a panic button or anything*," and he did not think that Kik was in a "precarious position." And publicly, at the TechCrunch event that the Commission repeatedly references, Mr. Livingston squarely rejected the notion that it created Kin "because [it couldn't] get money from investors." Instead, Kik decided to create a new business model centered around a cryptocurrency to fuel a new digital economy that could allow smaller players to compete with large, dominant players.

. . . .

17. . . . . **ANSWER**. Kik admits that the SEC issued the DAO Report on July 25, 2017. Kik denies the remaining allegations, including any suggestion that Kik did not "take appropriate steps to ensure compliance with the U.S. federal securities laws." Given that the token at issue in the DAO Report was completely distinguishable from Kin, and without the benefit of any other SEC guidance at the time, the DAO Report actually provided reassurance to Kik. In fact, in August 2017, Mr. Livingston publicly commented that it made "complete sense to [Kik] and [was] fully expected" that the SEC would determine that the DAO was a security because, among other things, the token at issue in the DAO Report entitled participants to vote and receive "rewards," which the DAO co-founder compared to "buying shares in a company and getting . . . dividends." Further, the DAO expressly informed investors that it would fund projects in exchange for a return on investment. In contrast, Mr. Livingston then observed that, at the time of Kik's 2017 sales of Kin, "when you look at the utility token side, *there [was] no guidance given on that*."

In the midst of this uncertainty, Kik still made significant efforts to understand and comply with all applicable laws and regulations, and did its best to "anticipate where the rules will land and provide . . . the most thoughtful, buttoned up way to not only do a token distribution event but also to build one of these decentralized networks." For example, Kik retained United States counsel; hired an experienced General Counsel; conducted robust KYC, AML, and OFAC screening; ensured that its product was functional and operational at the time of TDE; and hired a third-party auditor who confirmed that Kin was analogous to "inventory," and that Kik should therefore pay taxes on the revenue from the sale—something it would not have done if the TDE were a securities offering.

. . . .

19. . . . . **ANSWER**. Kik admits that at the time of the Complaint was filed, Kin's price, according to CoinMarketCap, was about half of what it

was at the time of the TDE. Kik denies the remaining allegations of this paragraph. Kin's price "during the intervening period" has at times exceeded its TDE price. Regardless, this allegation has no relevance to whether Kik sold an "investment contract," but is instead designed to prejudice the Company.

. . . .

In essence, Kik's answer paints a vastly different picture of the issuance of the Kin Tokens, and of Kik's activities and intentions, than that suggested in the SEC's complaint. From a legal standpoint, Kik's attorneys are arguing that there were two distinct offers involved. The first stage, conducted pursuant to a SAFT (which as you may recall from earlier materials was drafted with the help of Cooley lawyers as well as other experienced crypto and entrepreneurial professionals),[82] was conducted in a manner designed to comply with rule 506 of Reg. D.[83] All purchasers of the right to buy a token in the future, conditioned on its launch, were accredited investors, as that term is defined in Reg. D. The second part of the offering was for fully functional Kin tokens, and (as described in portions of the answer not excerpted above) it was initiated only after the pre-sale under the SAFT was complete, and only to purchasers who registered and underwent screening for KYC and AML compliance.

NOTES AND QUESTIONS

1.   Having read both the complaint and the answers to selected portions of that document, how do you perceive what Kik did? Did the sales of Kin tokens involve the kind of transaction (or transactions, if you agree that the SAFT portion and subsequent sale of functional tokens are distinct) in which purchasers (or investors, depending on your perspective) require the protection of the U.S. securities laws?

2.   Who is being protected by the SEC's action in this case? Kik has reportedly raised a several million dollar legal defense fund that the company has said will be used to "defend crypto."[84] The litigation will doubtless be expensive and time-consuming. In your opinion, is this a wise use of SEC resources? Why or why not?

3.   While we have not yet covered international regulations, those will be discussed in general form in chapter fifteen. Not surprisingly, Canada also

---

[82]   The SAFT is defined in chapter 2, and is discussed in more detail in chapters 8, part 3 and chapter 13, part 2.

[83]   Reg. D is described in chapter 7, part 3.B.2. The concept of accredited investors is covered in chapter 7 at part 3.B.3.

[84]   Stephen Palley, *SEC v. Kik—Kik files aggressive answer to SEC lawsuit*, THE BLOCK (Aug. 6, 2019) (available online at https://www.theblockcrypto.com/2019/08/06/sec-v-kik-kik-files-aggressive-answer-to-sec-lawsuit/).

regulates securities deals. To the extent that the deal requires regulatory intervention, why wouldn't the existence of regulations in Kik's home country be sufficient to protect purchasers?

CHAPTER 11

CRYPTO AND THE REGULATORS—
THE CFTC

■ ■ ■

It is probably worth providing a couple of general definitions before diving into commodities regulation and the role of the Commodities Futures Trading Commission (CFTC). A "derivative" (in the context of securities and commodities regulation) is a contract between two or more parties involving a financial security whose value is based upon, or derived from, an underlying asset or group of assets. The most common underlying assets (or groups of assets) include stocks, bonds, commodities, currencies, and market indexes. Forwards, futures, options, and swaps are some of the most common examples of derivatives.

A "forward" contract is a customized contract between two parties, with performance due on a specific date in the future, but at a price agreed upon at the time the contract is arranged. These contracts are bilateral in nature, the contract price is typically individually negotiated, and the terms are therefore not in the public domain. The contract has to be settled or performed by delivery of the specified asset to the other party on the contract's expiration date. To undo the contract, the original counter-party must agree to reverse the deal. This is an individually negotiated arrangement between two parties, and because it is individually arranged, it is not an exchange-based instrument.

A "futures" contract is an agreement to sell or buy financial instruments or physical commodities for a future delivery in a designated month at an agreed price. Futures contracts are generally traded on organized exchanges (in order to provide liquidity), and include relatively standardized terms. Because performance is typically not contemplated (or in other words, the parties often do not intend to actually deliver the underlying commodity), and because terms other than price are standardized, parties can reverse the deal with any member of the exchange. For futures traded on exchanges, almost all features or terms are imposed, meaning that the only negotiated term is the price at which the future trade would occur. Even delivery dates are generally established, with some exchanges having limited delivery options. This makes it easier to "settle" contracts without actually delivering the underlying commodity.

An "option" is a contract permitting the buyer of the option to buy or sell the underlying commodity at a designated price until a designated date. The buyer pays a "premium" for this right, which imposes no obligation on the option-holder to go through with the transaction. Once the designated date passes, the right to enforce the contract expires. "Put" options allow the buyer to force the other party to buy the underlying commodity at the designated price, while "call" options allow the buyer to force the other party to sell the underlying asset at the option price.

A "swap" is an agreement between two parties to exchange cash flows over time, either on a determined date or in many cases on multiple dates. In other words, the two parties exchange cash flows or liabilities from two different financial instruments. Most swaps involve cash flows based on a particular principal amount, although the principal does not usually trade hands. Most commonly, one party agrees to pay a fixed rate while the other party pays a floating rate. Swaps do not trade on exchanges and instead are primarily executed as individually customized, over-the-counter contracts between financial institutions or businesses.

As was mentioned near the end of the previous chapter (in the section dealing with approval of crypto exchanges), the CFTC and the SEC have regulatory authority that, at times, overlaps. Sometimes this creates opportunities, and sometimes it creates confusion and conflict. In order to understand where those lines are, it is important to understand the genesis, history, and mission of the CFTC.

1. THE HISTORY OF THE CFTC

Trading in futures-style derivatives was slow to develop in the U.S., due at least in part to a widespread historical distaste for speculation and gambling. Trading in futures can be viewed in this light because of the very real possibility (and sometimes probability or even certainty) that the parties to the contract do not actually intend to deliver the underlying asset or commodity.

Justh v. Holliday, 2 Mackey 346 (D.C. Sup. 1883), was an early Supreme Court case involving both a futures contract and a historical figure who is more famous for other reasons. This case involved General George Armstrong Custer, who, in addition to being involved in one of the most controversial and tragic battles in U.S. history, apparently had quite a fondness for gambling. In *Justh*, the U.S. Supreme Court made its distaste for gambling arrangements quite clear, holding that a contract purporting to call for the delivery of an asset at a future date when no bona fide delivery was contemplated was void against public policy both as a gaming contract and for involving gambling. The Court concluded that "[w]here a contract is made for the delivery or acceptance of securities at a future day, at a price named, and neither party, at the time of making the contract, intends to deliver or accept the shares, but merely to pay differences, according to the rise or fall of the market, the contract is void, either by virtue of statute or as contrary to public policy."[1]

Despite ongoing public criticism of both speculators and speculation, trading in futures provided a range of potential benefits for producers and processors of agricultural commodities in particular. Most notably, the liquidity provided by the presence of speculators in agricultural commodities allowed farmers to reduce their risk by entering into contracts for future delivery at preset prices, protecting some profit margin.

Congress, in attempting to balance both the legitimate need for futures trading, and the risks that it presents, first tried to require all grain futures transactions to be consummated on an exchange approved by the Secretary of Agriculture. Congress originally sought to achieve this result by imposing a prohibitive tax on noncomplying sales as part of the 1921 Futures Trading Act. The next year, this exercise of legislative power was found to be unconstitutional in *Hill v. Wallace*, 259 U.S. 44 (1922). This determination was quickly followed by Congressional enactment of the Grain Futures Act, which was promptly upheld under the commerce powers in *Chicago Board of Trade v. Union*, 262 U.S. 1 (1923).

A few years later the Grain Futures Act became the Commodities Exchange Act (the CEA), and its coverage was expanded to include a wider variety of agricultural commodities and futures contracts. The scope of the CEA was expanded again in 1968, and in 1974 further amendments created the Commodities Futures Trading Commission (CFTC), again expanding the scope of regulation and adding remedies for persons harmed by those who violate the statutory requirements.

As it currently stands, the CFTC is organized into divisions and offices. The divisions include: the Division of Clearing and Risk (which oversees derivatives clearing organizations); the Division of Enforcement (which investigates and prosecutes violations of the CEA); the Division of Market Oversight (which oversees exchanges); and the Swap Dealers and Intermediary Oversight Division (which oversees regulation and compliance by intermediaries and self-regulatory organizations, and compliance by swap dealers).[2] Under the current version of the CEA, the term "commodity" includes all agricultural products except onions,[3] "and

---

[1]   *Justh v. Holliday*, 2 Mackey at 348.

[2]   CFTC, *CFTC Organization* [archived at https://perma.cc/34EJ-L35V].

[3]   7 U.S. Code § 1a(9) defines commodity to include agricultural products, while onions are excluded by virtue of Public Law 85–839 (7 U.S. Code § 13–1), a 1958 law that banned futures trading in onions. Onions are excluded because Congress in 1958 reacted to "onion grower hysteria" and a 1955 incident involving cornering the market on onion futures on the Chicago Mercantile Exchange. Schuyler M. Moore, *The Future of Money While Private Offerings, Tax Credits, and Advertisers Have All Played A Significant Role in Film Financing, More Direct Methods May Revitalize the Market*, L.A. Law., at 20, 27 (May 2013). This same source also describes why box office receipts are excluded from the definition of commodity. *Id.*

all services, rights, and interests (except motion picture box office receipts . . .) in which contracts for future delivery are presently or in the future dealt in." 7 U.S. Code § 1a(9). An "excluded commodity" includes "an interest rate, exchange rate, currency, security, security index, credit risk or measure, debt or equity instrument, index or measure of inflation. . . ." 7 U.S. Code § 1a(19)(i).

As a result of these provisions, there are certainly times when the CFTC has been careful to differentiate between a physical resource and a "financial instrument such as a currency or interest rate."[4] However, for the last several decades the CEA has covered not only tangible resources but also a wide array of financial instruments, including foreign currencies, U.S. and foreign government securities, and U.S. and foreign stock indices.

This broad approach to defining the limits of CFTC jurisdiction is not surprising. As noted in 2014 by then-Chairman Timothy Massad, in testimony before a U.S. Senate Committee, "[t]he CEA defines the term commodity very broadly so that in addition to traditional agricultural commodities, metals, and energy, the CFTC has oversight of derivatives contracts related to Treasury securities, interest rate indices, stock market indices, [and] currencies . . . to name just a few underlying products."[5]

This definition is important because every derivative contract has an underlying asset or commodity. Transactions in the actual commodity involving immediate delivery of the item are said to occur in the "spot," "physical," or "actual" market, and are not subject to CFTC regulation except to the extent necessary to prevent fraud or manipulation. Even forward contracts, which involve a contract calling for deferred delivery (a bilateral agreement where delivery is in fact contemplated), are subject to regulation by the CFTC only to the extent that fraud or price manipulation is involved.

If, however, the transaction involves a futures contract, the CFTC has exclusive jurisdiction over the transaction. Under current rules overseen by the CFTC, a futures contract must be conducted through an exchange that is a "designated contract market" regulated by the CFTC. 7 U.S. Code § 6. Each regulated exchange imposes standardized terms on all transactions that take place on that exchange, with the only non-standard term being price of the commodity (which is negotiated).

---

[4]   See CFTC, *A Guide to the Language of the Futures Industry*, CFTC GLOSSARY (defining the word "Commodity") [archived at https://perma.cc/5FEY-XY3K].

[5]   CFTC, *Testimony of Chairman Timothy Massad before the U.S. Senate Committee on Agriculture, Nutrition & Forestry*, CFTC SPEECHES & TESTIMONY (Dec. 10, 2014) [archived at https://perma.cc/MP7T-NX86].

2. RELATIONSHIP BETWEEN THE CFTC AND THE SEC

Perhaps not surprisingly, tension between the SEC and CFTC about the scope of their authority is longstanding. When the CFTC was originally created, it might have appeared that the possibility for jurisdictional conflict between the two agencies was minor. At that time, most futures training involved agricultural products. With the pronounced and ever-increasing convergence between the derivatives and securities markets, however, conflict has seemingly become unavoidable.[6]

Professor Jerry Markham, a prolific scholar recognized for his contributions to an understanding of how U.S. financial markets are regulated, has explained that historically, "[t]he CFTC and the SEC often clash over the application of their respective jurisdiction over derivatives."[7] For example, the SEC attempted to obtain jurisdiction over futures contracts where the underlying commodity was a security in the 1978 CFTC reauthorization hearing. Despite support from the Government Accountability Office, Congress denied the SEC's request, although it did require the CFTC to "maintain communication" with the SEC.[8]

Over the years, the tension between the two agencies has often been pronounced.[9] For example, the CFTC acted to approve futures trading on stock indexes, a move that proved to be very popular. The history of this action is described in *Board of Trade of City of Chicago v. SEC*, 677 F.2d 1137, 1171 n.11 (7th Cir. 1982), *cert. granted, judgment vacated*, 459 U.S. 1026 (1982). The SEC responded by approving certain trading options on the Chicago Board of Exchange, but the commodity exchanges challenged the SEC's authority to do this, and the Seventh Circuit ruled against the SEC.

Eventually, Congress acted to allocate jurisdiction between the two agencies based on an accord that the Chairmen of the CFTC and SEC had reached. The so-called "Shad-Johnson Accords" (named for the two chairmen), were enacted into law in 1982.[10] In essence, the CFTC was given authority over index-based futures trading but not futures on single stocks, and the SEC retained jurisdiction over options trading on stock

---

[6]   For a history of some of the conflict between the two agencies, see Jerry W. Markham, *Merging the SEC and CFTC—A Clash of Cultures*, 78 U. CIN. L. REV. 537, 552–94 (2009).

[7]   RONALD FILLER & JERRY W. MARKHAM, REGULATION OF DERIVATIVE FINANCIAL INSTRUMENTS (SWAPS, OPTIONS AND FUTURES) 39 (West Academic, 2014).

[8]   JERRY W. MARKHAM, THE HISTORY OF COMMODITY FUTURES TRADING AND ITS REGULATION 99–100 (1986).

[9]   The SEC does not single out the CFTC when it comes to disputes over jurisdiction. Before the CFTC was approved, for example, the SEC had been fighting with banking regulators over securities clearing and settlement functions. Jerry W. Markham, *Regulatory battles between CFTC and SEC*, 13A COMMODITIES REG. § 28:2.

[10]   *See* Futures Trading Act of 1982, Pub. L. No. 97–444, 96 Stat. 2294 (codified in scattered sections of 7 U.S. Code).

exchanges, including options on indexes. Also as part of the legislation, the SEC was given an effective veto over approval of commodity futures contracts on indexes.[11] As proof that the "accords" did not completely smooth over the territorial disputes between the two agencies, this veto authority led to another dispute with the CFTC that in turn resulted in another temporary inter-agency agreement.[12]

Several years later, the SEC attempted an end-run around the CFTC's authority. It first approved options trading on two Dow Jones indexes, but then attempted to deny trading of commodity futures on those same indexes. The Seventh Circuit was again asked to intervene.

PRELIMINARY NOTES AND QUESTIONS

1. As you read through the following excerpt from that Seventh Circuit opinion, note the description of futures, and the explanation of how hedging can work to minimize risk for market participants. Based on the description in this case, do you understand why futures trading came to be accepted in the agricultural markets even in spite of cultural opposition to gambling?

2. Derivatives trading has long expanded beyond the original agricultural commodities that were initially contemplated. Do the modern expansions of derivatives trading reflect societal approval of (or at least acquiescence in) gambling? Are there valid societal reasons to allow systematic trading in such interests?

4. Given that no one has identified a rational basis for the distinction, why do you believe Congress chose to allow the CFTC regulated boards of trade to include options on single securities, but not futures contracts on single securities? What political justification might have been advanced for such a compromise? Whose interests are being protected?

3. With regard to the particular indexed funds at issue, why was the SEC willing to allow them to be traded on stock markets but unwilling to agree with the CFTC that they could be traded on boards of trade? From a public policy perspective, are there advantages or disadvantages to allowing both stock markets and futures exchanges to trade the same kinds of interests?

4. In the final analysis, why did the Seventh Circuit vacate the decision of the SEC declining to approve trading of the indexed funds on the boards of trade?

---

[11] *See generally* Don L. Horwitz and Jerry W. Markham, *Sunset on the Commodity Futures Trading Commission: Scene II*, 39 BUS. LAW. 67, 73–74 (1983).

[12] *See* Edward J. Kane, *Regulatory Structure in Futures Markets: Jurisdictional Competition Between the SEC, the CFTC, and Other Agencies*, 4 J. FUT. MARKETS 367, 375 (1984).

BOARD OF TRADE OF CITY OF CHICAGO V. SEC
187 F.3d 713 (7th Cir. 1999)

EASTERBROOK, CIRCUIT JUDGE.

Although the Dow Jones Industrial Average may be the world's most famous stock market index, the Dow Jones Transportation Average is its most venerable, having been established in 1884. The Dow Jones Utilities Average, which dates from 1929, is another well known indicator. An index uses a few stocks to approximate the performance of a market segment. For example, the 20 stocks in the transportation index are designed to track a portfolio of approximately 145 transportation stocks with a capitalization exceeding $200 billion. The 15 stocks in the utilities index stand in for a utilities segment of 145 firms with a capitalization near $300 billion. When Charles Dow designed these indexes, long before instantaneous worldwide networks, a "computer" was a person who calculated tables of artillery trajectories in longhand on foolscap. In that era a reference to a few stocks as an approximation of many was a valuable time-saving device. Today it is easy to follow the average value-weighted price of a whole market, which an electronic computer can produce at the touch of a button. Each investor can specify and follow the portfolio that seems most interesting or important. Still, indexes have retained their fascination with the media and the public, and they have developed a new use—as the base of futures contracts. Our case presents the question whether futures exchanges may trade contracts based on the Dow Jones Utilities Average and the Dow Jones Transportation Average. For many years Dow Jones was unwilling to license its indexes (rather, the trademarks used to denote them) for use in futures contracts. In 1997 it changed its mind and set in train these proceedings.

"A futures contract, roughly speaking, is a fungible promise to buy or sell a particular commodity at a fixed date in the future. Futures contracts are fungible because they have standard terms and each side's obligations are guaranteed by a clearing house. Contracts are entered into without prepayment, although the markets and clearing house will set margin to protect their own interests. Trading occurs in 'the contract', not in the commodity." *Chicago Mercantile Exchange v. SEC*, 883 F.2d 537, 542 (7th Cir.1989). The classic futures contract involves a commodity such as wheat, but in principle any measure of value can be used. Financial futures usually take the form of a contract that depends on the value of an index at some future date. Thus, for example, the buyer (the "long") of a futures contract based on the Standard & Poor's 500 Index future might promise to pay 100 times the value of that index on a defined future date, and the seller (the "short") will receive that price. Either side may close the position by buying or selling an offsetting obligation before the expiration date of the contract.

Financial futures contracts are useful for hedging or portfolio adjustment. They facilitate risk management—that is, assignment of the inevitable risks of markets to those best able to bear them. Someone who owns a mutual fund containing all of the Standard & Poor's 500 stocks can cut risk in half by selling a futures contract based on the S & P 500 index, or double the market return (and the risk of loss) for the same financial outlay by buying a S & P 500 futures contract. A futures contract based on a market segment (such as utilities) also may be used for portfolio adjustment. Suppose the investor wants to hold a diversified portfolio of stocks that does not include utilities. This investor might own a broadly representative mutual fund and then sell a futures contract based on a utilities index. Similarly, a person who wants to obtain the returns (and take the risks) of particular market segments that do not have their own mutual fund—for example, a combination of utilities and transportation stocks, but no industrials—could purchase an appropriate combination of futures contracts. Using these contracts for portfolio adjustment is attractive because the transactions costs of trading futures are much smaller (by an order of magnitude) than the costs of trading the underlying stocks in equivalent volumes. A pension fund that wants to move from stocks to the equivalent of a mixed stock-and-bond portfolio, without incurring the costs of trading the stocks, can do so by selling a futures contract on an index.

For many years the traditional futures markets, such as the Chicago Board of Trade, have been at odds with the traditional stock markets, such as the New York Stock Exchange, about where financial futures would be traded—and whether they would be traded at all. The stock exchanges prefer less competition; but, if competition breaks out, they prefer to trade the instruments themselves. The disagreement has spilled over to the regulatory bodies. The Securities and Exchange Commission, which regulates stock markets, has sided with its clients; the Commodities Futures Trading Commission, which regulates boards of trade, has done the same. In 1982 this court held that institutions within the CFTC's domain are authorized to trade financial futures (including options on these futures), and, because of an exclusivity clause in the Commodity Exchange Act, that the stock markets are not. Because the stock exchanges long had traded options, a financial derivative related to futures, a political donnybrook accompanied the regulatory dispute among the markets and agencies. Shortly after our opinion issued, Congress amended the Commodity Exchange Act to reflect a compromise among the CFTC, the SEC, and the Exchanges.

Congress allocated securities and options on securities to exchanges regulated by the SEC, futures and options on futures to boards of trade regulated by the CFTC. If an instrument is both a security and a futures contract, then it falls within the CFTC's domain. (This is the basis of

Chicago Mercantile Exchange, which held that a novel "index participation" is a futures contract that belongs to boards of trade.) Options on single securities are allowed, but futures contracts on single securities are not. This allocation appears to be a political compromise; no one has suggested an economic rationale for the distinction. Having drawn this line, however, Congress had to make it stick. Futures contracts thus must reflect "all publicly traded equity or debt securities or a substantial segment thereof'. 7 U.S. Code § 2a(ii)(III). Finally, both agencies participate in the process of reviewing applications to trade new financial futures contracts. Before a new contract may start trading, both the SEC and the CFTC must certify that it meets the statutory criteria. Regulation of the trading process belongs exclusively to the CFTC.

A year after this statute was enacted, the SEC and the CFTC issued a Joint Policy Statement spelling out the kinds of financial futures that the agencies believed suitable for trading. 49 Fed. Reg. 2884 (Jan. 24, 1984). The Joint Policy Statement is not a regulation and lacks legal force, but for many years the markets observed its limits when proposing new contracts. One element of the Joint Policy Statement is that any index used as the basis of a futures contract contain at least 25 domestic equity issuers. The Dow Jones Transportation Average is based on 20 stocks, the Utilities Average on 15. The second element is that, in a price-weighted index, no single security may have a weight exceeding 10% of the entire index, if its price weighting exceeds its capitalization weighting by a factor of three. In April 1997 Dow Jones replaced one firm in its Utilities Average with Columbia Gas, which accounts for 2.93% of the Utilities Average by capitalization weight, but 12.56% by price weight. The Transportation Average does not contain a stock with a similar disparity.

. . . .

When Dow Jones & Co. agreed to license its trademarks for use in financial products based on its market indexes, both stock markets and futures markets sought to trade products based on these indexes. The SEC promptly approved trading (at the stock markets) in options on the Dow Jones Industrial Average, the Dow Jones Transportation Average, and the Dow Jones Utilities Average. But when the futures exchanges sought permission to trade futures contracts based on these indexes, the SEC was less accommodating. It approved a futures contract based on the Dow Jones Industrial Average but blocked trading in the others, which have fewer than 25 stocks in the index. The SEC recognized that the Joint Policy Statement of 1984 lacks the force of law. Nonetheless, the SEC concluded, its criteria would be applied as part of the totality of the circumstances that the agency considered. But of course the circumstances an agency considers must implement the statute. One can't have a totality-of-the-circumstances approach in the abstract. Here is the critical statutory text:

[T]he [CFTC] shall have exclusive jurisdiction with respect to accounts, agreements (including any transaction which is of the character of, or is commonly known to the trade as, an "option", "privilege", "indemnity", "bid", "offer", "put", "call", "advance guaranty", or "decline guaranty") and transactions involving, and may designate a board of trade as a contract market in, contracts of sale (or options on such contracts) for future delivery of a group or index of securities (or any interest therein or based upon the value thereof): Provided, however, That no board of trade shall be designated as a contract market with respect to any such contracts of sale (or options on such contracts) for future delivery unless the board of trade making such application demonstrates and the [CFTC, with the SEC's concurrence,] expressly finds that the specific contract (or option on such contract) with respect to which the application has been made meets the following minimum requirements:

(I)   Settlement of or delivery on such contract (or option on such contract) shall be effected in cash or by means other than the transfer or receipt of any security, except an exempted security under ['33 Act § 3 or '34 Act § 3(a)(12)]. . . ;

(II) Trading in such contract (or option on such contract) shall not be readily susceptible to manipulation of the price of such contract (or option on such contract), nor to causing or being used in the manipulation of the price of any underlying security, option on such security or option on a group or index including such securities; and

(III) Such group or index of securities shall be predominately composed of the securities of unaffiliated issuers and shall be a widely published measure of, and shall reflect, the market for all publicly traded equity or debt securities or a substantial segment thereof, or shall be comparable to such measure.

7 U.S. Code § 2a(ii). The futures markets proposed contracts that would be settled in cash, so subsection (I) is satisfied. The SEC did not find that the contracts would be "readily susceptible to manipulation", so subsection (II) also is satisfied. (The SEC did express concerns related to manipulation; we discuss these below; but it did not find that the proposed contracts would be readily susceptible to manipulation.) As for subsection (III), the Dow Jones averages are "predominately composed of the securities of unaffiliated issuers" and are "widely published." They do not measure or reflect the whole market, but transportation and utilities stocks are "substantial segment[s] thereof"—or so at least the SEC assumed. It did not formally define a "substantial segment" of the market, but neither did

it deny that utilities and transportation qualify. What the SEC did conclude is that the Dow Jones Utilities and Transportation Averages do not "reflect" the utilities and transportation segments. According to the SEC, the principal shortcoming is that the indexes are not themselves "substantial segments" of the market or, as the SEC summed up, are not "broad-based."

According to the SEC's lawyers, this decision should receive the respect that *Chevron U.S.A. Inc. v. Natural Resources Defense Council, Inc.*, 467 U.S. 837 (1984), prescribes for an agency's implementation of an ambiguous statute. One potential problem with this approach is that the sense of deference to which the SEC appeals is the one associated with delegation of authority to act, and Congress has delegated to the CFTC as much as to the SEC the authority to interpret and implement § 2a(ii). Yet the CFTC disagrees with the SEC's view that the index must be "broad-based," and the CFTC contends that its view of the statute's meaning is entitled to respect from the judiciary. At least one court of appeals believes that disagreement between agencies cancels all deference and requires the court to make an independent decision. *Rapaport v. OTS*, 59 F.3d 212, 216–17 (D.C.Cir.1995). We are not so sure about this; . . . . however, it is not necessary to reach a definitive conclusion about how to proceed when these two agencies disagree over an issue under the Commodity Exchange Act. Section 2a(ii)(III) is not ambiguous—not, at least, when the question is whether an index "reflects" a substantial segment of the market.

Section 2a(ii)(III) says that the index "shall be a widely published measure of, and shall reflect, the market for all publicly traded equity or debt securities or a substantial segment thereof". The index must "reflect" a substantial segment; § 2a(ii)(III) does not require that the index be a substantial segment. The SEC's rejection of futures contracts based on the Dow Jones Utilities and Transportation Averages because the 15 or 20 stocks in the index are not themselves a substantial segment of the market cannot be reconciled with the language or structure of the statute. It is enough, according to Congress, if the index "reflects" the segment. And on this record it is undisputed that the indexes do reflect the stock-market performance of the industries they are designed to measure. The long-term correlation between the indexes and the larger portfolios of stocks in the industries exceeds 92% for both indexes.

          . . . .

Finally, a few words about manipulation. Although the SEC did not find that a futures contract based on either of the Dow Jones averages would be "readily susceptible to manipulation" of the index itself or the market segment it reflects, the SEC's order contains an undercurrent of misgiving. To the extent the SEC disagrees with the legislative judgment—that is, to the extent the SEC believes that trading in a futures contract should be forbidden when manipulation is a possibility, rather than a high probability (which we take the word "readily" to signify)—it should present that view openly to Congress, rather than engage in self-help measures that cannot be reconciled with the statute. What is more, we cannot see either in the record or in the nature of the proposed futures contracts any reason for concern.

Squeezes, corners, and other forms of manipulation in futures markets for physical commodities depend on hogging the deliverable supply. A person who owns a substantial portion of the long interest near the contract's expiration date also obtains control over the supply that the shorts need to meet their obligations. Then the long demands delivery, and the price of the commodity skyrockets. It takes time and money to bring additional supplies to the delivery point, and the long can exploit these costs to force the shorts to pay through the nose. Futures markets deal with the prospect of squeezes and corners by expanding the deliverable supply (allowing, for example, delivery in Kansas City as well as Chicago), by imposing position limits (so that no one long can hold contracts for more than the deliverable supply), and by monitoring positions so that irregularly large positions may be subject to orderly liquidation before the expiration date. But the need for these precautions, like the possibility of manipulation itself, comes from the potential imbalance between the deliverable supply and investors' contract rights near the expiration date. Financial futures contracts, which are settled in cash, have no "deliverable supply"; there can never be a mismatch between demand and supply near the expiration, or at any other time.

Although it is impossible to rule out the use of financial futures contracts to affect the price in the underlying securities, it is hard to see how the effort could be profitable to the would-be manipulator. Financial markets such as all utilities, or all transportation stocks, are so large (many hundreds of billions), liquid, and competitive that their manipulation is almost unimaginable. If someone were determined to drive the price of transportation stocks up or down, buying and selling thousands of futures contracts on the Chicago Board of Trade would be like pouring a Dixie cup of water into Lake Michigan: there would be an effect, but it would not be detectable. One test of the manipulation hypothesis is whether financial futures contracts increase aggregate price volatility, either over the long term or near the expiration date. Economists who have explored this subject agree that on balance stock-index futures contracts have reduced volatility in stock prices, and that the effect on volatility near expiration is trivial.

If the design were to manipulate the price of a single stock rather than the index or its market segment, then smaller investments of capital would suffice—but for the reasons covered in discussing surrogate trading, transactions in an index futures contract are lousy ways of approximating transactions in individual stocks. People who want to manipulate the price of Acme Widget Corp. will deal in that stock, or options in it. Data show that options reduce volatility in the security they represent. And if one-stock derivatives do not conduce to manipulation, any futures contract where the index is based on two or more stocks must be less readily manipulable. Whether even single-stock options and futures on physical commodities are subject to (reliably profitable) manipulation is an interesting question, but not one we need consider. It is enough to say that manipulation of stock prices through transactions in index futures contracts is hard to do, and a finding that these markets are "readily susceptible to manipulation of the price" would require a great deal more support than the ominous foreboding manifested in the SEC's order—an order that did not begin to discuss the vast empirical literature about the effects of options, futures contracts, and other derivatives on market efficiency.

. . . .

The order of the Securities and Exchange Commission is vacated.

NOTES

1.   The discussion of manipulation is particularly salient because, as noted in the prior chapter, fears of manipulation explain why the SEC has yet to approve a crypto ETF.

2.   Note the nature of the conflict between the SEC and CFTC, with the latter not seeking to limit the authority of the SEC or it's regulation of stock exchanges, but instead seeking to expand its reach into areas traditionally within the SEC's legal purview.

As the preceding case hints, the conflict between the CFTC and SEC can be intense. Sometimes the conflict has seemed to devolve into name-calling. For example, at one point, the SEC officials publicly accused the CFTC of using "coercion" in its regulatory efforts.[13]

On the other hand, quite aside from any jurisdictional animosity or jealousy, there are relatively clear and longstanding differences between the two agencies. Professor Markham, for example, has reported on what he sees as a "vast cultural divide between the regulatory approaches taken

---

[13]   "The Commodity Futures Trading Commission's strategy to regulate derivatives without collaborating with international securities regulators amounted to 'coercion,' according to a member of the Securities and Exchange Commission." Eric Hammesfahr, *SEC's Gallagher accuses CFTC of coercion*, CONG. Q. ROLL CALL, 2014 WL 1494110 (Apr. 17, 2014).

by the CFTC and SEC."[14] In general terms, the CFTC tends to take a more laissez-faire approach while the SEC is more often pro-regulatory.

In prior discussions about the political viability of merging the two agencies, the cultural divide between the two agencies has been repeatedly noted. Representative Barney Frank, D-Mass, and then ranking member of the House Financial Services Committee, once proclaimed that: "The existence of a separate SEC and CFTC is the single largest structural defect in our regulatory system. . . . Unfortunately, this is deeply rooted in major cultural, economic and political factors in America."[15]

Some of this difference in approach can be seen in how the two agencies deal with cryptoassets.

3. THE CFTC AND ITS MISSION

According to the CFTC website, the CFTC's mission "is to foster open, transparent, competitive, and financially sound markets. By working to avoid systemic risk, the Commission aims to protect market users and their funds, consumers, and the public from fraud, manipulation, and abusive practices related to derivatives and other products."[16]

Just as the SEC has no specific authority over the firms that issue securities or even over the merits of the securities themselves, the CFTC has not traditionally had responsibility for direct regulation of the safety and soundness of particular futures arrangements or commodities. Instead, the CFTC focuses on preventing market manipulation, abusive trading practices, and fraud, and on ensuring the financial integrity of the clearing process.

As of 2014, the CFTC's responsibilities extended to overseeing designated contract markets (DCMs) or exchanges, swap execution facilities (SEFs), derivatives clearing organizations, swap data repository, swap dealers, futures commission merchants, commodity pool operators, and other intermediaries. These include the commodity futures markets for energy and metals commodities, and for various financial products, such as interest rates, stock indexes, and foreign currency. In addition, the CFTC was given authority over swaps as part of the Dodd-Frank Wall Street Reform and Consumer Protection, and pursuant to that authorization it sets capital standards for swap dealers and major swap participants. Finally, the CFTC coordinates its work with foreign

---

[14] Jerry W. Markham, *Merging the SEC and CFTC—A Clash of Cultures*, 78 U. CINN. L. REV. 537, 591 (2009).

[15] Mark Schoeff, *Proposal to Merge SEC, CFTC will go Belly up: Washington Insiders*, INVESTMENT NEWS (Nov. 30, 2012) (available online at https://www.investmentnews.com/article/20121130/BLOG07/121139995/proposal-to-merge-sec-cftc-will-go-belly-up-washington-insiders).

[16] An explanation of the CFTC's role and missions can be found at CFTC, *Mission Visions, and Values* [archived at https://perma.cc/DL87-HK4V]. As described above, the reach of the CEA in terms of what products it covers is extremely broad.

regulators, such as its UK counterpart, the Financial Conduct Authority, which supervises the London Metal Exchange.

In March 2014 the CFTC acknowledged it was considering the regulation of Bitcoin. In 2015, the CFTC ruled that for purposes of trading, cryptocurrencies would be classified by it as commodities. In 2017, the CFTC clarified that its

> . . .jurisdiction is implicated when a virtual currency is used in a derivatives contract, or if there is fraud or manipulation involving a virtual currency traded in interstate commerce.—Beyond instances of fraud or manipulation, the CFTC generally does not oversee "spot" or cash market exchanges and transactions involving virtual currencies that do not utilize margin, leverage, or financing.[17]

In its 2017 Primer on Virtual Currencies, the CFTC noted the SEC's Report on the DAO and the SEC's conclusion that the DAO tokens were securities. Nonetheless, as stated by the CFTC, "[t]here is no inconsistency between the SEC's analysis and the CFTC's determination that virtual currencies are commodities and that virtual tokens may be commodities or derivatives contracts depending on the particular facts and circumstances."[18] The CFTC also reiterated many of the same concerns expressed by the SEC about cryptoassets, noting operational and cybersecurity concerns, along with the risk of speculation, fraud, and manipulation.[19]

In general, now that the CFTC has concluded that crypto is a commodity, all futures contracts involving it are required to be traded on a "contract" market "designated by the CFTC. The authority for this requirement is found in the following section of the CEA:

Commodity Exchange Act

7 U.S. Code § 6c—Prohibited transactions

. . . .

(b) Regulated option trading

No person shall offer to enter into, enter into or confirm the execution of, any transaction involving any commodity regulated under this chapter which is of the character of, or is commonly known to the trade as, an "option", "privilege", "indemnity", "bid", "offer", "put", "call", "advance guaranty", or "decline guaranty", contrary to any rule, regulation, or order of the Commission prohibiting any such

---

[17]   LabCFTC, *A CFTC Primer on Virtual Currencies* at p. 11 (Oct. 17, 2017) [archived at https://perma.cc/F65B-Z7LT]. An excerpt from the Primer appears later in this chapter. *See infra* note 24 and accompanying text.

[18]   *Id.* at p. 14.

[19]   *Id.* at p. 16.

transaction or allowing any such transaction under such terms and conditions as the Commission shall prescribe. Any such order, rule, or regulation may be made only after notice and opportunity for hearing, and the Commission may set different terms and conditions for different markets.

Commonly called "boards of trade" or simply "futures exchanges," these "designated contract markets" (DCMs) are defined in regulations promulgated by the CFTC and codified at 17 C.F.R. Part 38. Among other requirements, DCMs must prove that they have established rules with which all members comply that satisfy the Commission's 23 Core Principles. These core principles include establishing that:

- the contracts that the DCM trades are not readily subject to manipulation;

- the DCM has the capacity to prevent market disruptions;

- there is "appropriate and necessary" emergency authority;

- general information about the contract market is publicly available;

- trading information is published daily;

- transactions are competitive and open in a way that protects the price discovery process;

- trade information is recorded and stored securely;

- procedures protect financial integrity of transactions;

- rules protect markets and participants from abusive practices;

- disciplinary procedures are established and enforced;

- there are dispute resolution rules and procedures in place;

- the DCM has appropriate fitness standards for directors and persons with access to the facility;

- conflicts of interest are minimized and resolved where possible;

- recordkeeping requirements are complied with;

- there are adequate system safeguards against operational risk;

- the DCM has adequate financial resources.[20]

---

[20]   Appendix B to 17 C.F.R. Part 38 contains *"Guidance on, and Acceptable Practices in, Compliance With Core Principles."* For a more complete explanation of the Core Principles, see CFTC, *Designated Contract Market 23 Core Principles Chart* [archived at https://perma.cc/6R8S-NGLX].

Compliance with these requirements is assessed by Rule Enforcement Reviews, which are generally conducted every 15–18 months.

These rules all come into play whenever there is a commodity futures contract or the contract involves a derivative. Direct trades in commodities, in the so-called "spot market," are outside the scope of the CFTC's responsibility, unless the transaction involves fraud or manipulation.

4. THE CFTC AND FRAUD

On July 21, 2010, President Obama signed the Dodd-Frank Wall Street Reform and Consumer Protection Act into law. Included in that Act's provisions was an amendment to the CEA to prohibit manipulation and fraud in connection with any swap, or any contract of sale of any commodity in interstate commerce, or for future delivery.

Commodity Exchange Act

7 U.S. Code § 9—Prohibition regarding manipulation and false information

(1) **Prohibition against manipulation.** It shall be unlawful for any person, directly or indirectly, to use or employ, or attempt to use or employ, in connection with any swap, or a contract of sale of any commodity in interstate commerce, or for future delivery on or subject to the rules of any registered entity, any manipulative or deceptive device or contrivance, in contravention of such rules and regulations as the Commission shall promulgate .... provided no rule or regulation promulgated by the Commission shall require any person to disclose to another person nonpublic information that may be material to the market price, rate, or level of the commodity transaction, except as necessary to make any statement made to the other person in or in connection with the transaction not misleading in any material respect. . . .

(2) **Prohibition regarding false information.** It shall be unlawful for any person to make any false or misleading statement of a material fact to the Commission, including in any registration application or any report filed with the Commission under this chapter, or any other information relating to a swap, or a contract of sale of a commodity, in interstate commerce, or for future delivery on or subject to the rules of any registered entity, or to omit to state in any such statement any material fact that is necessary to make any statement of a material fact made not misleading in any material respect, if the person knew, or reasonably should have known, the statement to be false or misleading.

(3) **Other manipulation.** In addition to the prohibition in paragraph (1), it shall be unlawful for any person, directly or

indirectly, to manipulate or attempt to manipulate the price of any swap, or of any commodity in interstate commerce, or for future delivery on or subject to the rules of any registered entity.

* * *

This provision of the CEA is modeled closely on the language of section 10(b) of the Securities Exchange Act of 1934, although there are some important distinctions. Differences between the wording of '34 Act § 10(b) and CEA § 9 include, but are not limited to, the express prohibition of the "attempt to use" any "manipulative or deceptive device or contrivance" in the CEA and the absence of a "purchase or sale" requirement.

Because of the similarities between the CEA prohibition and '34 Act § 10(b) the CFTC intentionally modeled its rule on SEC Rule 10b–5:

CFTC Rules

17 CFR § 180.1—Prohibition on the employment, or attempted employment, of manipulative and deceptive devices.

(a) It shall be unlawful for any person, directly or indirectly, in connection with any swap, or contract of sale of any commodity in interstate commerce, or contract for future delivery on or subject to the rules of any registered entity, to intentionally or recklessly:

(1) Use or employ, or attempt to use or employ, any manipulative device, scheme, or artifice to defraud;

(2) Make, or attempt to make, any untrue or misleading statement of a material fact or to omit to state a material fact necessary in order to make the statements made not untrue or misleading;

(3) Engage, or attempt to engage, in any act, practice, or course of business, which operates or would operate as a fraud or deceit upon any person; or,

(4) Deliver or cause to be delivered, or attempt to deliver or cause to be delivered, for transmission through the mails or interstate commerce, by any means of communication whatsoever, a false or misleading or inaccurate report concerning crop or market information or conditions that affect or tend to affect the price of any commodity in interstate commerce, knowing, or acting in reckless disregard of the fact that such report is false, misleading or inaccurate. Notwithstanding the foregoing, no violation of this subsection shall exist where the person mistakenly transmits, in good faith, false or misleading or inaccurate information to a price reporting service.

In promulgating this rule, the CFTC acknowledged both the similarities in authorizing language and differences between the securities markets and the derivatives markets.[21] For those reasons, the CFTC indicated that it intended to be "guided, but not controlled, by the substantial body of judicial precedent applying the comparable language of SEC Rule 10b–5."[22] The CFTC expressed both its desire to increase certainty (because Rule 10b–5 had already withstood constitutional challenges in both civil and criminal contexts[23]) and its hope that by adopting a provision that paralleled SEC Rule 10b–5 this would be a step towards harmonization of regulations.

When the CFTC adopted interpretive regulations to explain how 7 U.S. Code § 9(1) would be applied, the agency called the section a prohibition on "manipulative and deceptive devices."[24] While the statute itself talks about the impermissibility of any "manipulative or deceptive device or contrivance" the use of the word "and" in the title to the regulation caused some to focus on the issue of whether the CFTC could pursue fraud claims that did not also involve manipulation.

In *CFTC v. Monex Credit Company,* 311 F. Supp. 3d 1173 (D.Cal. 2018), *rev'd,* 931 F.3d 966 (9th Cir. 2019), the District Court for the Central District of California considered a number of potential defenses to a CFTC enforcement action against a precious metals dealer. The defendant, among other things, claimed that § 6(c)(1) of the CEA [codified at 7 U.S. Code § 9(1)], "only confers anti-fraud jurisdiction where a particular commodity transaction manipulates or potentially manipulates the derivatives market." 311 F. Supp. at 1185. The CFTC naturally took the contrary position, claiming that provision "is not limited to futures market contracts and applies to retail commodities transactions with or without market manipulation." *Id.* The following excerpt from the district court opinion in *Monex* focuses on this particular issue. (Note that, as the citation indicates, the trial judge in this opinion was later reversed by the Ninth Circuit.)

---

[21]   *See* CFTC, *Prohibition on the Employment, or Attempted Employment, of Manipulative and Deceptive Devices and Prohibition on Price Manipulation,* 17 CFR Part 180, RIN Number 3038–AD27, 76 FED. REG. 41398 (Jul. 14, 2011) [archived at https://perma.cc/242J-E3FD].

[22]   *Id.* at 41399.

[23]   *See United States v. Persky,* 520 F.2d 283, 287 (2d Cir. 1975) (rejecting criminal defendant's claims that '34 Act § 10(b) and SEC Rule 10b–5 are unconstitutionally vague); *SEC v. Pirate Investor LLC,* 580 F.3d 233, 254 (4th Cir. 2009) (upholding civil judgment and rejecting "reliance on any ambiguity in the [section 10(b)] phrase 'in connection with' as a reason to employ the canon of constitutional avoidance . . . in light of the statute's purpose—providing a flexible regime for addressing new, perhaps unforeseen, types of fraud"), *cert. denied,* 561 U.S. 1026 (2010).

[24]   17 CFR § 180.1—*Prohibition on the employment, or attempted employment, of manipulative and deceptive devices.*

CFTC v. MONEX CREDIT COMPANY [DISTRICT COURT]
311 F. Supp. 3d 1173 (D.Cal. 2018), *rev'd*, 931 F.3d 966 (9th Cir. 2019)

THE HONORABLE JAMES V. SELNA.

. . . .

Courts must defer to an agency's construction of a statute it administers if Congress has not "spoken directly to the precise question at issue" and the agency's construction of the statute is "permissible." *Chevron U.S.A. Inc. v. Nat. Res. Def. Council, Inc.*, 467 U.S. 837, 842–43 (1984). However, if "Congress has directly spoken to the precise question at issue," courts "must give effect to the unambiguously expressed intent of Congress." *Id.* Courts apply "traditional tools of statutory construction" to ascertain whether Congress expressed such an intent. *Id.* at 843 n.9. Additionally, regulations enacted pursuant an express delegation of authority "to elucidate a specific provision of the statute by regulation . . . are given controlling weight unless they are arbitrary, capricious, or manifestly contrary to statute." *Id.* at 843–44. Therefore, the Court must first decide whether the CEA unambiguously forecloses the CFTC's interpretation and, if not, whether the interpretation is otherwise an impermissible construction of the CEA.

To determine the meaning of a statutory provision, courts "look first to its language, giving the words used their ordinary meaning." Section 6(c)(1), titled the "[p]rohibition against manipulation," makes it unlawful to use, "in connection with any swap, or a contract of sale of any commodity in interstate commerce, . . . any manipulative or deceptive device or contrivance, in contravention of such rules and regulations as the Commission shall promulgate." Terms connected by a disjunctive must ordinarily be given separate meanings. *Reiter v. Sonotone Corp.*, 442 U.S. 330, 339 (1979). Pursuant to that rule, the plain language of § 6(c)(1) suggests that Congress intended to prohibit either manipulative or deceptive conduct. However, the rule is not steadfast. *See De Sylva v. Ballentine*, 351 U.S. 570, 573 (1956) (noting that "the word 'or' is often used as a careless substitute for the word 'and'; that is, it is often used in phrases where 'and' would express the thought with greater clarity"). Another district court interpreting § 6(c)(1) has rejected the argument that its use of "or" necessarily means that the section bars two distinct types of conduct. *CFTC v. Kraft Foods Grp., Inc. ("Kraft I")*, 153 F.Supp.3d 996, 1010 (N.D. Ill. 2015) (holding that the § 6(c)(1) barred only fraudulent manipulation, not manipulation in the absence of fraud). The title of § 6(c)(1) sheds light on whether the Court should construe "or" in the disjunctive. *See Bhd. of R. R. Trainmen v. Baltimore & O. R. Co.*, 331 U.S. 519, 529 (1947) (concluding that section headings are may be used as tools for "the resolution of a doubt"). Section 6(c) is titled "Prohibition regarding manipulation and false information." While § 6(c)(1) is the "Prohibition against manipulation," § 6(c)(2) is the "Prohibition regarding false information," and § 6(c)(3) is entitled "Other manipulation." These headings imply that § 6(c)(1) and § 6(c)(3) concern forms of market manipulation, and § 6(c)(2) alone concerns false information. Section 6(c)(2) prohibits making false or misleading statements to the CFTC, but does not otherwise prohibit fraudulent conduct. While "the title of a statute and the heading of a section cannot limit the plain meaning of the text," these headings suggest that the court should construe the prohibition on the use of "manipulative or deceptive device[s] or contrivance[s]" to require both manipulative and deceptive conduct, not one or the other.

The rule against surplusage also supports interpreting "manipulative or deceptive" to require both manipulative and deceptive conduct. "It is a 'fundamental canon of statutory construction that the words of a statute must be read in their context and with a view to their place in the overall statutory scheme.'" *FDA v. Brown & Williamson Tobacco Corp.*, 529 U.S. 120, 133 (2000). Section 4b already prohibits fraud in covered retail commodity transactions. The Actual Delivery Exception exempts retail commodity transactions that result in actual delivery within 28 days from the application of § 4b. If the Court were to construe § 6(c)(1) to prohibit all fraud made in connection with any swap, or contract of sale of any commodity in interstate commerce, it would necessarily cover all retail commodity transactions, including those that result in actual delivery within 28 days. Not only would such a construction render § 4b superfluous, it would also eliminate the Actual Delivery Exception. Moreover, it would make § 6(c)(3), which already prohibits the manipulation of the price of any swap or commodity in interstate commerce, redundant. The Court may not construe § 6(c)(1) to render any other section of the CEA redundant or inoperative. Rather, the Court must "fit, if possible, all parts [of the CEA] into an harmonious whole." Construing § 6(c)(1) to prohibit fraudulent conduct alone would violate that basic principle.

However, yet another interpretive tool clashes with the rule against superfluity in this instance. "[C]ourts generally interpret similar language in different statutes in a like manner when the two statutes address a similar subject matter." *United States v. Novak*, 476 F.3d 1041, 1051 (9th Cir. 2007) (en banc). Section 10(b) of the Securities Exchange Act ("SEA") similarly prohibits "any manipulative or deceptive device or contrivance" used "in connection with the purchase or sale of any security registered on a national securities exchange or any security not so registered." Though the Supreme Court has held that the SEA "must not be construed so broadly as to convert every common-law fraud that happens to involve securities into a violation of § 10(b)," it has also explained that "the statute should be 'construed not technically and restrictively, but flexibly to effectuate its remedial purposes.'" *S.E.C. v. Zandford*, 535 U.S. 813, 819–

20 (2002). Moreover, while the Supreme Court has "recognized that the interest in 'preserving the integrity of the securities markets' was one of the purposes animating the [SEA]," it has "rejected the notion that § 10(b) is limited to serving that objective alone." *Id.* at 821–22. The Securities Exchange Commission ("SEC") routinely uses § 10(b) and Rule 10b–5 to prosecute fraud in connection with the purchase or sale of securities. *See, e.g., id.* at 825 (holding that allegations of a fraudulent scheme alone adequately stated a claim for violation of § 10(b).

The legislative history of § 6(c)(1) clarifies this ostensible conflict. Senator Cantwell introduced § 6(c)(1) as an amendment to the Senate's version of Dodd-Frank. 156 Cong. Rec. S3099–100156 Cong. Rec. S3099–100 (daily ed. May 4, 2010). Introducing the amendment, Senator Cantwell emphasized that current law made it very difficult for the CFTC to prosecute market manipulation cases because it required the CFTC to prove "specific intent" to manipulate. She noted that the CFTC had only successfully prosecuted a single case of manipulation. Senator Cantwell explained that the amendment would give the CFTC the same "anti-manipulation standard" as the Securities Exchange Commission ("SEC"), which only requires a showing of recklessness. She noted that the language of § 6(c)(1) closely tracks § 10(b) because "Federal case law is clear that when the Congress uses language identical to that used in another statute, Congress intended for the courts and the Commission to interpret the new authority in a similar manner." However, she went on to note that the SEC's manipulation authority is only intended to cause "those who attempt to affect the market or prices by artificial means unrelated to the natural forces of supply and demand." And she noted that Congress recently granted the same anti-manipulation authority to the Federal Energy Regulatory Commission ("FERC") "as a result of the Enron market manipulation," which FERC had used to bring "enforcement actions against manipulation." Consistent with Senator Cantwell's remarks, Senator Lincoln, then-Chairman of the Senate Committee on Agriculture, explained that § 753 "adds a new anti-manipulation provision to the [CEA] addressing fraud-based manipulation" and that the "new enforcement authority being provided to the CFTC supplements, and does not supplant, its existing anti-manipulation authority."

Nowhere does the legislative history contemplate extending CFTC's authority under § 6(c)(1) to allow it to combat fraud absent market manipulation. Senator Cantwell's references to § 10(b) make clear that Congress only intended to lower the scienter standard to recklessness, not adopt wholesale the full scope of enforcement available under § 10(b).

Because § 6(c)(1) unambiguously forecloses the CFTC's interpretation, the Court owes no deference to its interpretation of the statute.

   . . . .

NOTES AND QUESTIONS

1. *Chevron* deference (described at the outset of the preceding excerpt) is a fundamental principle of administrative law. In essence, after the U.S. Supreme Court decided *Chevron U.S.A., Inc. v. Natural Resources Defense Council, Inc.,* 467 U.S. 837 (1984), the rule that gives appropriate consideration and judicial deference to administrative determinations was given that title. The *Chevron* test originally held that courts should defer to administrative interpretations within their area of influence if their position was not unreasonable, so long as Congress has not spoken directly on the issue. The scope of appropriate deference has since been narrowed by the Court, which now holds that only interpretations reached through formal proceedings (including notice-and-comment rulemaking, or adjudications) qualify for deference.

2. Consider the extent to which the judge considers and relies on legislative history in his analysis. To what extent does that history bolster the *Monex* trial court's determination that fraud in the absence of manipulation should not be within the ambit of the CEA?

3. The trial court in *Monex* granted defendants' motion to dismiss, although it did give the CFTC grounds to amend its cause of action. Instead, an appeal followed. On July 25, 2019, the Ninth Circuit responded, reversing the district court. An excerpt from that opinion (focusing only on the issue of whether manipulation is required under the CEA) follows.

CFTC v. MONEX CREDIT COMPANY [ON APPEAL]
931 F.3d 966 (9th Cir. 2019)

SILER, CIRCUIT JUDGE:

A two-letter conjunction and a two-word phrase decide this case. At stake are hundreds of millions of dollars. Congress, acting shortly after the economy began to stabilize from the financial crisis that began a decade earlier, passed the Dodd-Frank Wall Street Reform and Consumer Protection Act, Pub. L. No. 111–203, 124 Stat. 1376 (2010), which amended the Commodity Exchange Act (CEA) to expand the Commodity Future Trading Commission's (CFTC) enforcement authority. This case is about the extent of those powers.

Monex Credit Company, one of the defendants and appellees, argues that the CFTC went too far when it filed this $290 million lawsuit for alleged fraud in precious metals sales. According to Monex, Dodd-Frank extended the CFTC's power only to fraud-based manipulation claims, so stand-alone fraud claims—without allegations of manipulation—fail as a matter of law.

. . . .

We REVERSE and REMAND.

. . . .

Manipulative or Deceptive

. . . .

[T]he CFTC alleges that Monex violated CEA § 6(c)(1), 7 U.S.C. § 9(1), and 17 C.F.R. § 180.1 by fraudulently deceiving its customers. There is no allegation that Monex manipulated the market, so we must decide whether § 6(c)(1) covers fraud claims in the absence of manipulation. The text:

> It shall be unlawful for any person, directly or indirectly, to use or employ, or attempt to use or employ, in connection with any swap, or a contract of sale of any commodity in interstate commerce, or for future delivery on or subject to the rules of any registered entity, any manipulative or deceptive device or contrivance, in contravention of such rules and regulations as the Commission shall promulgate.

7 U.S.C. § 9(1).

The crucial question is whether "any manipulative or deceptive device" allows stand-alone fraud claims or requires fraud-based manipulation. The district court determined that the statute unambiguously requires "both manipulative and deceptive conduct, not one or the other." Or, another way to say it, the district court held that "or" really meant "and." We disagree.

When the word "or" joins two terms, we apply a disjunctive reading. When Congress places "or" between two words, we assume that Congress intended the two terms as alternatives. While there are exceptions, this is not an instance where a disjunctive meaning would produce absurd results and statutory context compels us to treat "or" as if it were "and." We conclude that § 6(c)(1)'s language is unambiguous. Authorizing claims against "[m]anipulative or deceptive" conduct means what it says: the CFTC may sue for fraudulently deceptive activity, regardless of whether it was also manipulative.

Again, if we had any doubt, *see Conn. Nat'l Bank v. Germain*, 503 U.S. 249, 253–54 (1992), other interpretive tools support our conclusion. This CEA provision is a mirror image of § 10(b) of the Securities Exchange Act, which the Supreme Court has interpreted as a "catch-all clause to prevent fraudulent practices," *Chiarella v. United States*, 445 U.S. 222, 226 (1980), that authorizes fraud-only claims. . . . We presume that by copying § 10(b)'s language and pasting it in the CEA, Congress adopted § 10(b)'s judicial interpretations as well.

The canon against surplusage does not point to a different answer: § 6(c)(1)'s overlap with other provisions is minimal, and partial redundancy hardly justifies displacing otherwise clear text. Nor does the fact that the applicable statutory headings mention only manipulation and not fraud.

The full extent of a statutory provision rarely fits into its title, so headings are often under inclusive. Finally the CEA elsewhere references a "manipulative device or contrivance," see 7 U.S.C. § 25(a)(1)(D)(i), suggesting that Congress knew how to require market manipulation when it sought to do so. The inclusion of "deceptive" in § 6(c)(1) must have meaning.

. . . .

———————

While *Monex* was decided in the context of trading in precious metals, the case involves the kind of issue that one would expect to come up in the context of crypto. And, as we will see in the next chapter, such arguments have been advanced.

CHAPTER 12

THE CFTC, CRYPTO, THE COURTS, AND OTHER ENFORCEMENT

■ ■ ■

The preceding chapter sets out the general framework in which the CFTC operates. This chapter examines how that framework is being applied in the context of crypto, which the CFTC refers to as "virtual currency."

1. CRYPTO AS A COMMODITY

Although the CFTC has proclaimed that it does not want to "harm" innovation in the crypto ecosystem,[1] the CFTC has clearly asserted its jurisdiction over virtual currencies. Just as the SEC has expressed consistent interest in regulating cryptoassets (as described in the preceding chapters), the CFTC has also been clear in its position that crypto is a commodity. The CFTC does not, however, talk about crypto, coins, tokens, or ICOs. Instead, it uses the phrase "virtual currency" to cover the range of cryptoassets that it believes to be within its regulatory authority.

As explained by the CFTC, a virtual currency is any "digital representation of value that functions as a medium of exchange, a unit of account, and/or a store of value."[2] This is an incredibly broad definition, because any digital representation of value that can at any stage be converted into other real-world assets is almost certain to fit somewhere into that scheme. Nonetheless, under this definition, a digital interest is a commodity if it can serve as a medium of exchange, a unit of account, or a store of value. There is no requirement that these be the sole functions of the interest.

LabCFTC, a function of the CFTC, is focused on new technologies.[3] It produced a primer on virtual currencies in 2017. While the primer contains fairly standard disclosures about not being an official policy or position, and not being intended to limit current or future positions or actions, it

---

[1]   CFTC, Speeches & Testimony, *Special Address of CFTC Commissioner J. Christopher Giancarlo Before the Depository Trust & Clearing Corporation 2016 Blockchain Symposium* (Mar. 29, 2016) (available online at https://www.cftc.gov/PressRoom/SpeechesTestimony/opagiancarlo-13) (speech entitled "*Regulators and Blockchain: First, Do No Harm*").

[2]   CFTC, *An Introduction to Virtual Currency* [archived at https://perma.cc/4CS9-2MJ9].

[3]   A description of LabCFTC can be accessed on the CFTC Website at https://www.cftc.gov/LabCFTC/index.htm [archived at https://perma.cc/2ALR-QXJQ].

contains a fairly complete assessment of crypto as seen through the lens of the CFTC as of October, 2017. The following excerpts from that report illustrate how the CFTC sees crypto, its role, and the risks that it seeks to address in this emerging area.

PRELIMINARY NOTES AND QUESTIONS

1.   As you read the following document, can you think of any kinds of crypto that would not be commodities under the definitions offered in this primer?

2.   Does the CFTC's legislated mission support the agency determination that Bitcoin and other "virtual currencies" are commodities? Are there kinds of crypto that you believe should not be regulated as commodities?

3.   The CFTC identifies many of the same risks associated with "virtual currencies" that the SEC has articulated as potential risks. How does the CFTC view its authority in light of the fact that the SEC was established first and is substantially larger? (For example, the SEC's budget request for fiscal 2019 was $1.6 billion while the CFTC requested $281.5 million.) Do you believe that this duplication in enforcement authority is warranted? Should both agencies have jurisdiction over crypto, and particularly over fraud claims in the spot market?

LABCFTC, *A CFTC PRIMER ON VIRTUAL CURRENCIES*
(October 17, 2017)[4]

What is a Virtual Currency?

- Although precise definitions offered by others are varied, an IRS definition provides us with a general idea:

    - "Virtual currency is a digital representation of value that functions as a medium of exchange, a unit of account, and/or a store of value.

    - In some environments, it operates like 'real' currency . . . but it does not have legal tender status [in the U.S.].

    - Virtual currency that has an equivalent value in real currency, or that acts as a substitute for real currency, is referred to as 'convertible' virtual currency. Bitcoin is one example of a convertible virtual currency.

    - Bitcoin can be digitally traded between users and can be purchased for, or exchanged into, U.S. dollars, Euros, and other real or virtual currencies." . . .

---

4   The primer is archived at https://perma.cc/F65B-Z7LT.

Sample Potential Use Cases of Virtual Currencies

- **Store of Value**
  - Like precious metals, many virtual currencies are a "non-yielding" asset (meaning they do not pay dividends or interest), but they may be more fungible, divisible, and portable
  - Limited or finite supply of virtual currencies may contrast with 'real' (fiat) currencies

- **Trading**
  - Trading in virtual currencies may result in capital gains or losses. Note that trading in virtual currencies may involve significant speculation and volatility risk (see Virtual Currency Risks section below)

- **Payments and Transactions**
  - Some merchants and online stores are accepting virtual currencies in exchange for physical and digital goods (i.e., payments)
  - Some public Blockchain systems rely on the payment of fees in virtual currency form in order to power the network and underlying transactions

- **Transfer/Move Money**
  - Domestic and international money transfer (e.g., remittances) in order to increase efficiencies and potentially reduce related fees. . . .

The CFTC's Mission

- The mission of the CFTC is to foster open, transparent, competitive, and financially sound markets. By working to avoid systemic risk, the Commission aims to protect market users and their funds, consumers, and the public from fraud, manipulation, and abusive practices related to derivatives and other products that are subject to the Commodity Exchange Act (CEA).

- To foster the public interest and fulfill its mission, the CFTC will act:
  - To deter and prevent price manipulation or any other disruptions to market integrity;
  - To ensure the financial integrity of all transactions subject to the CEA and the avoidance of systemic risk;
  - To protect all market participants from fraudulent or other abusive sales practices and misuse of customer assets; and

–   To promote responsible innovation and fair competition among
    boards of trade, other markets, and market participants.

- Responsible innovation is market-enhancing.

Virtual Currencies are Commodities

- The definition of "commodity" in the CEA is broad.

  –   It can mean a physical commodity, such as an agricultural product
      (e.g., wheat, cotton) or natural resource (e.g., gold, oil).

  –   It can mean a currency or interest rate.

  –   The CEA definition of "commodity" also includes "all services,
      rights, and interests . . . in which contracts for future delivery are
      presently or in the future dealt in."

- The CFTC first found that Bitcoin and other virtual currencies are
  properly defined as commodities in 2015.

- The CFTC has oversight over futures, options, and derivatives
  contracts.

- The CFTC's jurisdiction is implicated when a virtual currency is used
  in a derivatives contract, or if there is fraud or manipulation involving
  a virtual currency traded in interstate commerce.

  –   Beyond instances of fraud or manipulation, the CFTC generally
      does not oversee "spot" or cash market exchanges and
      transactions involving virtual currencies that do not utilize
      margin, leverage, or financing. . . .

ICOs, Virtual Tokens, and CFT Oversight

- The Securities and Exchange Commission ("SEC") recently released a
  report about an Initial Coin Offering or "ICO" (the "DAO Report").

- The DAO Report explains that "The DAO" is an example of a
  "Decentralized Autonomous Organization," which is a "virtual"
  organization embodied in computer code and executed on a distributed
  ledger or blockchain.

- Investors exchanged Ether, a virtual currency, for virtual DAO
  "Tokens" to fund projects in which the investors would share in
  anticipated earnings. DAO Tokens could be resold on web-based
  platforms.

- Based on the facts and circumstances, the SEC determined that DAO
  Tokens are "securities" under the federal securities laws.

- There is no inconsistency between the SEC's analysis and the CFTC's
  determination that virtual currencies are commodities and that

virtual tokens may be commodities or derivatives contracts depending on the particular facts and circumstances.

— The CFTC looks beyond form and considers the actual substance and purpose of an activity when applying the federal commodities laws and CFTC regulations

Virtual Currencies Have Risks

• While virtual currencies have potential benefits, this emerging space also involves various risks, including:

— Operational Risks

— Cybersecurity Risks

— Speculative Risks

— Fraud and Manipulation Risks

• Virtual currencies are relatively unproven and may not perform as expected (for example, some have questioned whether public distributed ledgers are in fact immutable).

• Investors and users of virtual currencies should educate themselves about these and other risks before getting involved. . . .

———————

The breadth of the definition of "virtual currency" as set out in the Primer and followed by the CFTC is particularly important because the CFTC's enforcement power extends beyond futures and derivatives if fraud is involved. In the words of LabCFTC, "[v]irtual currencies have been determined to be commodities under the Commodity Exchange Act. While its regulatory oversight authority over commodity cash markets is limited, the . . . [CFTC] maintains general anti-fraud and manipulation enforcement authority over virtual currency cash markets as a commodity in interstate commerce."[5]

In fact, the CFTC has actively asserted its jurisdiction over crypto in cases not involving a futures contract, swap, or other derivative. Various commentators have suggested this is an appropriate and expected extension of CFTC authority.[6]

———————

[5] *Id.*

[6] For additional details about why the CFTC's activity in this space is predictable, see Keith Miller at. al, *CFTC Flexes Its Regulatory Muscle in a Case Involving a Virtual Currency*, PERKINS COIE, VIRTUAL CURRENCY REPORT (Jan. 29, 2018) (available online at https://www.virtualcurrencyreport.com/2018/01/cftc-flexes-its-regulatory-muscle-in-a-case-involving-a-virtual-currency/). Dennis W. Carlton, *Futures Markets: Their Purpose, Their History, Their Growth, Their Successes and Failures*, 4 J. FUTURES MARKETS 237–71 (1984) provides a historical basis for understanding the Commission's role, particularly in regulating instruments like foreign currencies, U.S. and foreign government securities, and U.S. and foreign stock indices, which is some respects are similar to various crypto offerings and exchanges.

2. THE CFTC VERSUS THE SEC
IN THE CRYPTO SPACE

None of the foregoing discussion should be taken as evidence that the authority of the CFTC, to the extent that it exists, is exclusive. Some commentators have suggested that if an interest is a commodity, it should not be a security. This is, for example, the apparent position of Houman Shadab, a professor at New York Law School, who "has authored works on the use of cryptographic technologies such as bitcoin for financial derivatives."[7] When the CFTC issued administrative enforcement action against Coinflip in 2015, Professor Shadab concluded that "[t]he action puts to rest any notion that virtual currencies qualify as securities. Otherwise, the Securities and Exchange Commission would be bringing this action, not the CFTC."[8]

Unfortunately for those who might prefer the regulation of crypto to be in the hands of a single agency, in the absence of clear guidance from Congress or controlling legal precedent from the courts, the SEC does not always agree with the CFTC. "The CFTC and SEC often clash over the application of their respective jurisdictions. . . ."[9]

As one source noted, "it is clear that both the SEC and CFTC are picking up steam in their efforts to command a presence in the fast-developing world of virtual currencies."[10] Thus, even though the CFTC has asserted jurisdiction over virtual currencies as commodities, the SEC has continued to express its opinion that cryptoassets sold through ICOs typically involve the sale of securities, subject to the requirements of the federal securities laws. The CFTC has apparently acquiesced in this view, reporting that "[t]here is no inconsistency between the SEC's analysis and the CFTC's determination . . . ."[11]

Agreement that the same interest can simultaneously be a security and a commodity does not, however, mean that the two agencies are in complete agreement about how stringently the new technology should be regulated. One commentator has suggested that there is a "turf war" "going on between the two regulators for the control of the cryptocurrency market.

---

[7]   Pete Rizzo, *CFTC Ruling Defines Bitcoin and Digital Currencies as Commodities*, COINDESK (Sept. 17, 2015) (available online at https://www.coindesk.com/cftc-ruling-defines-bitcoin-and-digital-currencies-as-commodities).

[8]   *Id.*

[9]   RONALD FILLER & JERRY W. MARKHAM, REGULATION OF DERIVATIVE FINANCIAL INSTRUMENTS (SWAPS, OPTIONS AND FUTURES) 39 (West Academic, 2014).

[10]   *Dividing Up the Sandbox: Recent Actions and Public Statements Demonstrate How the SEC and CFTC Are Dividing up the Cryptocurrency and Crypto-Token Enforcement Landscape*, JDSUPRA (Feb. 8, 2018) (available online at https://www.jdsupra.com/legalnews/dividing-up-the-sandbox-recent-actions-23253/), citing King & Spalding, *Client Alert* (Feb. 7, 2018).

[11]   Stan Higgins, *CFTC Aligns With SEC: ICO Tokens Can Be Commodities*, COINDESK (Oct. 17, 2017) (available online at https://www.coindesk.com/cftc-no-inconsistency-sec-cryptocurrency-regulation).

Although Bitcoin and Ethereum clearly fall under the CFTC's purview, the SEC is still controlling the larger initial coin offering (ICO) market."[12]

As one example of how the two agencies take different approaches to crypto, consider the issue of exchange traded funds. As noted in chapter seven, the SEC has rejected multiple requests for approval of Bitcoin ETFs. At the 2019 Bipartisan Policy Center event called "The Year Ahead for Capital Markets," SEC Commissioner Hester Peirce expressed concerned that the SEC's approach came to close to being "a merit-based approach judging the underlying bitcoin markets." In arguing that this was not necessarily the best course of action, she noted that "there are lots of markets that aren't regulated but we nevertheless build products on top of them."[13]

In rather stark contrast to this refusal to approve Bitcoin ETFs, the CFTC allows Bitcoin futures to be traded if an exchange "self-certifies" that it meets the requirements of the CEA. As CFTC Commissioner Brian Quintenz (also a participant at the February 2019 Bipartisan Policy Center event) explains, the CFTC "has a review period in which we can say no we disagree with you and here's why, but if we don't disagree, [then] they [the exchanges] have the opportunity to go ahead and self-certify that contract." Bitcoin futures contracts can thus be listed without CFTC approval but also without disapproval. The Chicago Board Options Exchange (which has been turned down by the SEC in its request to offer a Bitcoin ETF) took this approach with Bitcoin Futures, which it launched in December 2017.

Former CFTC Chairman Jim Newsome has suggested that the relatively hard-line stance being taken by Jay Clayton, the Chairman of the SEC, may be at the direction of the White House and Treasury Department.[14] This "harder line" is likely to slow the SEC's acceptance of cryptocurrency projects. For example, Dave Gedeon, head of NASDAQ Index Research and Product Development, correctly projected that the SEC would not approve any cryptocurrency exchange traded funds in 2018 because of its current stance on the need for increased investor protection.[15] The SEC has similarly refused to approve a crypto ETF as of November 15, 2019.

---

[12]   Arnab Shone, *SEC and CFTC to Consider a Joint Approach Towards Crypto*, FINANCE MAGNATES (Feb. 18, 2019) (available online at https://www.financemagnates.com/cryptocurrency/news/sec-and-cftc-to-consider-a-joint-approach-towards-crypto/).

[13]   Video of the conversation is available at Bipartisan Policy Center, *The Year Ahead for Capital Markets* (Feb. 12, 2019) at https://bipartisanpolicy.org/events/the-year-ahead-for-capital-markets/ (the comments noted here are also reported by Shone, *supra* note 12.

[14]   Ted Knutson, *Cryptocurrency Bubble Burst Unlikely, Says Ex-CFTC Chair, Now Crypto Industry Adviser*, FORBES (Mar. 8, 2018) (available online at https://www.forbes.com/sites/tedknutson/2018/03/08/cryptocurrency-bubble-burst-unlikely-says-ex-cftc-chair-now-crypto-industry-adviser/#5a897a195797).

[15]   *Id.*

3. ASSERTING AUTHORITY OVER BITCOIN TRADING PLATFORMS

In 2015, the CFTC issued its first order imposing sanctions against an unregistered Bitcoin operation trading platform.[16] The order was also the first official pronouncement from the CFTC that it was going to treat crypto as a commodity. Note that this action did not go to court, as it started as an administrative enforcement action and resulted in a settlement at that stage. Excerpts from the administrative order settling that enforcement action appear below.

PRELIMINARY NOTES AND QUESTIONS

1. As you read the parts of the order excerpted below, make sure you understand what Derivabit (doing business as Coinflip) was doing, and why the CFTC claimed jurisdiction over these activities. Be sure that you can identify the provisions of the CEA implicated by this conduct.

2. What part of the CFTC's mission is furthered by this type of enforcement action? Who is being protected?

3. If the defendants had wanted to comply with the CEA, what should they have done?

IN RE COINFLIP, INC., D/B/A/ DERIVABIT
CFTC Docket No. 15–29 (Sept 17, 2015)[17]

Order Instituting Proceedings . . . Making Findings And Imposing Remedial Sanctions

I.

The Commodity Futures Trading Commission ("Commission") has reason to believe that from in or about March 2014 to at least August 2014 (the "Relevant Period"), Coinflip, Inc., d/b/a Derivabit ("Coinflip") and Francisco Riordan ("Riordan") (the "Respondents") violated Sections 4c(b) and 5h(a)(1) of the Commodity Exchange Act, as amended (the "Act"), and Commission Regulations 32.2 and 37.3(a)(1). . . .

II.

In anticipation of the institution of an administrative proceeding, the Respondents have submitted an Offer of Settlement ("Offer"), which the Commission has determined to accept. . . .

---

[16]   CFTC, *CFTC Orders Bitcoin Options Trading Platform Operator and its CEO to Cease Illegally Offering Bitcoin Options and to Cease Operating a Facility for Trading or Processing of Swaps without Registering*, Release pr7231–15 (Sept. 17, 2015) [archived at https://perma.cc/M7CY-9XUU].

[17]   This order is archived in its entirety at https://perma.cc/YQ2N-8CHH.

A. Summary

During the Relevant Period, Respondents violated Sections 4c(b) and 5h(a)(*l*) of the Act and Commission Regulations 32.2 and 37.3(a)(*l*) by conducting activity related to commodity options contrary to Commission Regulations and by operating a facility for the trading or processing of swaps without being registered as a swap execution facility or designated contract market. Specifically, during the Relevant Period, Respondents operated an online facility named Derivabit, offering to connect buyers and sellers of Bitcoin option contracts.

B. Respondents

Coinflip, Inc. is a Delaware corporation with a principal place of business in San Francisco, California. During the Relevant period, Coinflip operated Derivabit and its website derivabit.com. Coinflip has never been registered with the Commission.

Francisco Riordan is an individual residing in San Francisco, California. Riordan is a founder, the chief executive officer, and controlling person of Coinflip. Riordan has never been registered with the Commission.

C. Facts

Coinflip Conducted Activity Related to Illegal Commodity Options

Beginning in March 2014, Coinflip advertised Derivabit as a "risk management platform . . . that connects buyers and sellers of standardized Bitcoin options and futures contracts." During this period, Coinflip designated numerous put and call options contracts as eligible for trading on the Derivabit platform. For these contracts, Coinflip listed Bitcoin as the asset underlying the option and denominated the strike and delivery prices in US Dollars. According to the derivabit.com website, a customer could place orders by registering as a user and depositing Bitcoin into an account in the user's name. Premiums and payments of settlement of the option contracts were to be paid using Bitcoin at a spot rate determined by a designated third party Bitcoin currency exchange. Users had the ability to, and in fact did, post bids or offers for the designated options contracts. Coinflip confirmed the bid or offer by communicating it to all users through its website.

During the Relevant Period, Derivabit had approximately 400 users.

Riordan Controlled Coinflip and Directed Its Operations

Riordan was the founder, engineer and Chief Executive Officer of Coinflip. He exercised control over Coinflip's daily operations and possessed the power or ability to control all aspects of the Derivabit platform. Riordan participated in key aspects of Coinflip's illegal activity, including designing and implementing the Derivabit trading platform. Riordan's control enabled him to make design and substantive changes to Coinflip's operations, including the transition from offering Bitcoin options to OTC Bitcoin Forward Contracts. Ultimately, Riordan possessed the power and ability to direct Coinflip to cease operating the Derivabit platform.

LEGAL DISCUSSION

A.   Virtual Currencies Such as Bitcoin are Commodities

Section 1a(9) of the Act defines "commodity" to include, among other things, "all services, rights, and interests in which contracts for future delivery are presently or in the future dealt in." The definition of a "commodity" is broad. *See, e.g., Board of Trade of City of Chicago v. SEC*, 677 F. 2d 1137, 1142 (7th Cir. 1982). Bitcoin and other virtual currencies are encompassed in the definition and properly defined as commodities.

B.   Coinflip Violated Sections 4c(b) Act and Commission Regulation 32.2

Section 4c(b) of the Act makes it unlawful for any person to "offer to enter into, enter into or confirm the execution of, any transaction involving any commodity . . . which is of the character of, or is commonly known to the trade as, an 'option' . . ., 'bid', 'offer', 'put', [or] 'call' . . . contrary to any rule, regulation, or order of the Commission prohibiting any such transaction. . . ." Section 32.2 of the Commission's Regulations, in turn, provides that it shall be unlawful for any person to "offer to enter into, enter into, confirm the execution of, maintain a position in, or otherwise conduct activity related to any transaction in interstate commerce that is a commodity option transaction unless: (a) [s]uch transaction is conducted in compliance with and subject to the provisions of the Act, including any Commission rule, regulation, or order thereunder, otherwise applicable to any other swap, or (b) [s]uch transaction is conducted pursuant to [Regulation] 32.3."

Between at least March 2014 and July 2014, Respondents conducted activity related to commodity option transactions, offered to enter into commodity option transactions and/or confirmed the existence of commodity option transactions. The options transactions were not conducted in compliance with Section 5h(a)(1) of the Act or Regulation 37.3(a)(*l*) . . . . Accordingly, Coinflip violated Section 4c(b) of the Act and Commission Regulation 32.2.

C.   Coinflip Violated Section 5h(a)(*l*) of the Act

Section 5h(a)(1) of the Act forbids any person from operating "a facility for the trading or processing of swaps unless the facility is registered as a swap execution facility or as a designated contract market . . . ." Section 1a(47) of the Act's definition of "swap" includes option contracts. Regulation

37.3(a)(1) similarly requires that any "person operating a facility that offers a trading system or platform in which more than one market participant has the ability to execute or trade swaps with more than one other market participant on the system or platform shall register the facility as a swap execution facility under this part or as a designated contract market under part 38 of this chapter."

During the Relevant Period, Coinflip operated a facility for the trading of swaps. However, Coinflip did not register the facility as a swap execution facility or designated contract market. Accordingly, Coinflip violated Section 5h(a)(*l*) of the Act and Regulation 37.3(a)(1).

D. Riordan Is Liable for Coinflip's Violations as Its Controlling Person . . . .

Riordan controlled Coinflip, directly or indirectly, and did not act in good faith or knowingly induced, directly or indirectly, Coinflip's acts in violation of the Act and Regulations; therefore . . . Riordan is liable for Coinflip's violations of [the CEA]. . . .

IV. FINDINGS OF VIOLATIONS

Based on the foregoing, the Commission finds that, during the Relevant Period, Respondents violated Sections 4c(b) and 5h(a)(1) of the Act, and Commission Regulations 32.2 and 37.3(a)(*l*). . . .

VI. ORDER

Accordingly, IT IS HEREBY ORDERED THAT:

A.   Respondents shall cease and desist from violating [the CEA and CFTC Regulations]. . . .

B.   Respondents and their successors and assigns shall comply with the following conditions and undertakings set forth in the Offer:

1.   Public Statements: Respondents agree that neither they nor any of their successors and assigns, agents, or employees under their authority or control shall take any action or make any public statement denying, directly or indirectly, any findings or conclusions in the Order or creating, or tending to create, the impression that the Order is without a factual basis; provided, however, that nothing in this provision shall affect Respondents' (i) testimonial obligations; or (ii) right to take legal positions in other proceedings to which the Commission is not a party. Respondents and their successors and assigns shall undertake all steps necessary to ensure that all of their agents and/or employees under their authority or control understand and comply with this agreement.

2.   Cooperation with the Commission: Respondents shall cooperate fully and expeditiously with the Commission, including

the Commission's Division of Enforcement, and any other governmental agency in this action, and in any investigation, civil litigation, or administrative matter related to the subject matter of this action or any current or future Commission investigation related thereto.

Pursuant to the requirements of the CEA and CFTC regulations, simply registering a facility (which the Coinflip operators had not done) is not sufficient to insulate a business from potential liability under federal law. The CFTC has also indicated a willingness to go after registered Bitcoin swap facilities if they fail to enforce their rules. The rules are required by CFTC regulations and impose an obligation on registered futures exchanges to observe the CFTC's 23 core principles. Some of those principles involve the platform having rules against improper trading. The following CFTC release reports on TeraExchange LLC, a registered facility that failed to enforce its own rules.

PRELIMINARY QUESTIONS

1.   Which of its rules did TeraExchange fail to enforce? Why did it fail to enforce them?

2.   Why would a business adopt rules that it was not going to follow? Did TeraExchange know it was not going to comply or was the violation accidental?

3.   Who was hurt by TeraExchange's conduct in this case?

4.   What penalty does the CFTC obtain, and why do you think the CFTC believes that it is sufficient for purposes of settlement?

CFTC, *CFTC Settles with TeraExchange LLC, a Swap Execution Facility, for Failing to Enforce Prohibitions on Wash Trading and Prearranged Trading in Bitcoin Swap*
Release Number 7240–15 (Sept. 24, 2015)[18]

Washington, DC—The U.S. Commodity Futures Trading Commission (CFTC) today issued an Order filing and simultaneously settling charges against TeraExchange LLC (Tera), a provisionally registered Swap Execution Facility (SEF), for failing to enforce its prohibition on wash trading and prearranged trading on the SEF platform. The CFTC Order requires Tera to cease and desist from future violations relating to its obligations to enforce rules on trade practices. Tera is based in Summit, New Jersey.

---

[18]   This release from the CFTC is archived at https://perma.cc/4D38-P64T.

Specifically, the CFTC Order finds that Tera offered for trading on its SEF a non-deliverable forward contract based on the relative value of the U.S. Dollar and Bitcoin, a virtual currency (the Bitcoin Swap). On October 8, 2014, the only two market participants authorized at that time to trade on Tera's SEF entered into two transactions in the Bitcoin Swap. The transactions were for the same notional amount, price, and tenor, and had the effect of completely offsetting each other. At the time, these were the only transactions on Tera's SEF.

Tera arranged for the two market participants to enter into the transactions. Tera brought together the market participants, telling one that the trade would be "to test the pipes by doing a round-trip trade with the same price in, same price out, (i.e. no P/L [profit/loss] consequences) no custodian required," according to the Order.

However, subsequent to the transactions, Tera issued a press release and made statements at a meeting of the CFTC's Global Markets Advisory Committee (GMAC) announcing the transactions, creating the impression of actual trading interest in the Bitcoin swap. Neither Tera's press release nor the statements at the GMAC meeting indicated that the October 8 transactions were pre-arranged wash sales executed for the purpose of testing Tera's systems.

As a provisionally registered SEF, Tera is required under the SEF Core Principles of the Commodity Exchange Act (CEA) and CFTC Regulations to enact and enforce rules prohibiting certain types of trade practices on the SEF, including wash trading and prearranged trading. Tera's rulebook, in fact, prohibited those practices.

The CFTC noted in the Order that "[t]hese facts should be distinguished from a situation where a SEF or other designated contract market runs pre-operational test trades to confirm that its systems are technically capable of executing transactions and, to the extent that these simulated transactions become publicly known, makes it clear to the public that the trades do not represent actual liquidity in the subject market."

. . . .

———————

These early entries into the realm of crypto regulation provided helpful guidance to companies seeking to comply with legal requirements, but have not prevented a number of enterprises from running afoul of CEA and CFTC requirements. As the price of Bitcoin rose, so did speculation involving Bitcoin derivatives. Despite relatively clear warnings from the CFTC that it intended to treat crypto as a commodity, and that it intended to enforce the requirements of the CEA and CFTC regulations against crypto based businesses, such operations repeatedly popped up.

One strategy, which proved less than successful, was for companies to attempt to locate their exchanges or businesses oversees. As the following order makes clear, the CFTC has been willing to assert jurisdiction in cases where an overseas operations serves customers in the U.S.

IN RE BFXNA INC. D/B/A BITFINEX

Dkt. No. 16–19 (CFTC June 2, 2016)[19]

Order Instituting Proceedings Pursuant to Sections 6(C) and 6(D) of the Commodity Exchange Act, as Amended, Making Findings and Imposing Remedial Sanctions

I.

The Commodity Futures Trading Commission ("Commission") has reason to believe that from in or about April 2013 to at least February 2016 (the "Relevant Period"), BFXNA Inc. d/b/a Bitfinex ("Bitfinex" or "Respondent") and, prior to January 2015, Bitfinex's predecessor in interest, iFinex Inc., violated Sections 4(a) and 4d of the Commodity Exchange Act ("Act").

. . . .

II.

In anticipation of the institution of an administrative proceeding, Bitfinex has submitted an Offer of Settlement ("Offer"), which the Commission has determined to accept. Without admitting or denying any of the findings or conclusions herein, Bitfinex consents to the entry of this Order . . . .

III.

The Commission finds the following:

A. SUMMARY

During the Relevant Period, Bitfinex operated an online platform for exchanging and trading cryptocurrencies, mainly bitcoins. Bitfinex's platform permitted users, including individuals and entities that did not meet the definition of an eligible contract participant or eligible commercial entity, to borrow funds from other users on the platform in order to trade bitcoins on a leveraged, margined, or financed basis. Bitfinex was not registered with the Commission. During the Relevant Period, Bitfinex did not actually deliver bitcoins purchased on a leveraged, margined, or financed basis to the traders who purchased them . . . . Instead, Bitfinex held the purchased bitcoins in bitcoin deposit wallets that it owned and controlled. Therefore, Bitfinex engaged in illegal, off-exchange commodity

---

[19]   This order is archived at https://perma.cc/LD3K-3DDS.

transactions and failed to register as a futures commission merchant, in violation of Sections 4(a) and 4d of the Act.

B. RESPONDENT

BFXNA Inc. d/b/a Bitfinex is a corporation formed and existing under the laws of the British Virgin Islands, and has its principal place of business . . . . [in] Hong Kong, China. Bitfinex has never been registered with the Commission in any capacity.

C. FACTS

Bitfinex operates an online platform for exchanging and trading cryptocurrencies, mainly bitcoins. Bitfinex's "Exchange Trading" feature permits users to exchange dollars for bitcoins and litecoins, and vice-versa, as well as to trade cryptocurrencies for other cryptocurrencies. Bitfinex states that it operates the "most liquid exchange in the world" for trading between bitcoins and dollars, and offers traders multiple different order types through which to place trades. Users access Bitfinex's platform and place orders through its website, www.bitfinex.com.

Another of Bitfinex's services is its "Margin Trading" feature. Through this feature, Bitfinex permits traders to borrow dollars and bitcoins from other users on the platform in order to open leveraged positions on Bitfinex's exchange. Bitfinex refers to the participants on the platform who act as lenders as "Margin Funding Providers." In order to initiate a loan, Margin Funding Providers enter offers in Bitfinex's online tool to lend funds with their own chosen terms (daily rate of return, duration, and amount), or they can lend at the "Flash Return Rate" set by the market. When an offer to borrow is accepted by a trader ("Financing Recipient"), the Financing Recipient can use the borrowed funds to buy or sell bitcoins on Bitfinex's exchange. In addition to repaying the borrowed funds, Financing Recipient are responsible for paying fees and interest to the Margin Funding Providers.

Bitfinex is not a principal, counterparty, or market-maker in any bitcoin trade. Rather, Bitfinex administers and enforces the contracts established between Margin Funding Providers and Financing Recipients.

The Bitfinex platform allows maximum leverage of 3.33-to-1 (i.e., a 30% initial margin requirement).[20] Traders may close out positions at any time without penalty for closing it. This will reimburse the Margin Funding Provider, and the position will be settled at a profit or loss. Financing Recipients can also "claim" their positions, by paying off the outstanding loan, or they can trade out of positions. If a Financing Recipient's equity in

---

[20]   Author's note: "Leverage" in this context refers to debt, so that another way of looking at this statement is that a purchaser must pay for at least 1/3 of the face value of the commodity, so that no more than 66.7% is borrowed.

a position falls below 15%, the position is forcibly liquidated in order to ensure repayment of the loan.

From April 2013 to August 2015, when a customer purchased bitcoins on Bitfinex, the purchased bitcoins were held for the benefit of the buyer in Bitfinex's omnibus settlement wallet. The individual customer interests in the omnibus settlement wallet were accounted for in real time on Bitfinex's database. However, the omnibus settlement wallet was owned and controlled by Bitfinex and Bitfinex held all "private keys" associated with its omnibus settlement wallet. Financing Recipients had no rights to access or use the bitcoins that they had purchased until Bitfinex released them, following satisfaction of the Financing Recipient's outstanding loan. Bitfinex considered bitcoins held in the omnibus wallet to belong to the Financing Recipients, but subject to a lien in the amount of any outstanding loan plus fees owed to the Margin Funding Provider.

In August 2015, Bitfinex changed its model so that bitcoins purchased using the Exchange Trading feature were held in multi-signature wallets established by a third party firm that were individually enumerated for each trader. Bitcoins purchased using the Exchange Trading feature were settled to the Blockchain on an intra-day basis. However, Bitfinex retained control over the private keys to these wallets as well.

In January 2016 and for the remainder of the Relevant Period, during the course of the Division of Enforcement's investigation, Bitfinex changed its model again so that bitcoins purchased using both the Exchange Trading and Margin Trading features were held in individually enumerated, multi-signature wallets. However, Bitfinex continued to retain control over the private keys to those wallets.

During the Relevant Period, Bitfinex's Margin Trading services were available to retail customers, and are not limited to eligible contract participants ("ECPs") or eligible commercial entities ("ECEs"). However, corporate users comprised a significant portion of Bitfinex's trading volume during the Relevant Period. In 2015, 88% of the dollars deposited to and withdrawn from Bitfinex were by corporate users.

Bitfinex's cooperation with the Commission's investigation was significant. After learning that the Commission was potentially investigating Bitfinex, on September 17, 2015—which was before the Commission had announced any enforcement action involving bitcoin— Bitfinex affirmatively contacted staff of the Division of Enforcement to offer its cooperation. During the course of the investigation conducted by the Division of Enforcement, Bitfinex consistently responded to requests for information fully and quickly, both in writing and via oral presentations.

In response to the Division of Enforcement's investigation, Bitfinex represents that it has made a number of changes to its business practices in order to attempt to come into compliance with the Act and Regulations.

IV. LEGAL DISCUSSION

A. Relevant Statutory Background

Title VII of the Dodd-Frank Wall Street Reform and Consumer Protection Act of 2010, Public Law 111–203, 124 Stat. 1376 (2010) ("the Dodd-Frank Act") amended the Commodity Exchange Act to add, among other things, new authority over certain leveraged, margined, or financed retail commodity transactions.

Section 742(a) of the Dodd-Frank Act added Section 2(c)(2)(D) to the Act. That jurisdictional provision broadly applies to any agreement, contract, or transaction in any commodity that is entered into with, or offered to (even if not entered into with), a non-eligible contract participant ("non-ECP") or non-eligible commercial entity ("non-ECE") on a leveraged or margined basis, or financed by the offeror, the counterparty, or a person acting in concert with the offeror or counterparty on a similar basis. Section 2(c)(2)(D) further provides that such an agreement, contract, or transaction shall be subject to Sections 4(a), 4(b), and 4b of the Act "as if the agreement, contract, or transaction was a contract of sale of a commodity for future delivery."

Section 2(c)(2)(D)(ii) of the Act excepts certain transactions from Commission jurisdiction. Section 2(c)(2)(D)(ii)(III)(aa) excepts a contract of sale that results in "actual delivery" within 28 days . . . . "As found by the Eleventh Circuit, the term "actual delivery" is unambiguous, and is therefore given its ordinary meaning. "Delivery" is "[t]he formal act of transferring something"; it denotes a transfer of possession and control." As such, " '[a]ctual delivery' denotes '[t]he act of giving real and immediate possession to the buyer or the buyer's agent.' "

The Commission's interpretation is consistent with the Eleventh Circuit's definition. The determination of whether "actual delivery" has occurred within the meaning of Section 2(c)(2)(D)(ii)(III)(aa) requires consideration of evidence beyond the four corners of the contract documents. In determining whether actual delivery has occurred, the Commission employs a functional approach to assess whether there has been a "real and immediate" transfer of "possession and control" to the "buyer or the buyer's agent" of the commodity. The Commission examines how the agreement, contract, or transaction is marketed, managed, and performed. Ownership, possession, title, and physical location, as well as the relationships between the buyer, seller, and possessor of the commodity, and the manner in which the sale is recorded and completed are all relevant considerations in determining whether there has been actual delivery. Thus, physical delivery of the entire quantity of the commodity, including the portion purchased using leverage, margin or financing, into the possession of the buyer, or a depository other than the seller, the seller's parent company, partners, agents and affiliates will satisfy the actual delivery exception, provided that the purported delivery is not a sham. By contrast, actual delivery will not have occurred if only a "book entry" is made by the seller purporting to show that delivery of the commodity has been made.

Congress did not express any intent to limit the reach of Section 2(c)(2)(D). Rather, in enacting the statute Congress expressed its intent that Section 2(c)(2)(D) should be applicable to a broad range of agreements, contracts, and transactions.

B.   The Commission's Jurisdiction

Section 1a(9) of the Act defines "commodity" to include, among other things, "all services, rights, and interests in which contracts for future delivery are presently or in the future dealt in." The definition of a "commodity" is broad. *See, e.g., Board of Trade of City of Chicago v. SEC,* 677 F. 2d 1137, 1142 (7th Cir. 1982). Bitcoin and other virtual currencies are encompassed in the definition and properly defined as commodities, and are therefore subject as a commodity to applicable provisions of the Act and Regulations.

Many of the customers who entered into financed transactions in bitcoin on Bitfinex were not eligible contract participants or eligible commercial entities. Indeed, many were individual investors who did not meet the $10 million discretionary investment threshold to be considered ECPs. Moreover, Bitfinex offered such transactions on a margined or leveraged basis, and/or such transactions were financed by Margin Funding Providers through Bitfinex's financing order book. Bitfinex's retail financed transactions in bitcoin therefore fell squarely within the Commission's jurisdiction under Section 2(c)(2)(D) of the Act.

Bitfinex's retail-financed commodity transactions in bitcoin did not result in actual delivery to the Financing Recipients who traded on Bitfinex's platform. Bitfinex did not transfer possession and control of any bitcoin to the Financing Recipients, unless and until all liens on the bitcoin were satisfied. Prior to satisfaction of the liens, the Financing Recipients' bitcoins were held in an omnibus settlement wallet owned and controlled by Bitfinex, and to which Bitfinex held the private keys needed to access the wallet. Bitfinex's accounting for individual customer interests in the bitcoin held in the omnibus settlement wallet in its own database was insufficient to constitute "actual delivery." Similarly, when Bitfinex changed its model in August 2015 and January 2016, it retained control over the private keys to those wallets, and the Financing Recipients had no contractual relationship with the third party firm that established the wallets.

Therefore, Bitfinex's transactions are not excepted from the Commission's jurisdiction under Section 2(c)(2)(D)(ii)(III)(aa) of the Act. Also, Bitfinex had the authority to force liquidate customers' positions without the customers' prior consent if their equity fell beneath a preset level, which further evidenced Bitfinex's possession and control over the bitcoins.

C. Bitfinex Violated Section 4(a) of the Act: Illegal, Off-Exchange Transactions

As stated above, retail commodity transactions within the scope of Section 2(c)(2)(D) of the Act are subject to enforcement under Section 4(a) of the Act, among other provisions, as if such transactions are commodity futures contracts. Section 4(a) of the Act makes it unlawful for any person to offer to enter into, enter into, execute, confirm the execution of, or conduct an office or business in the United States for the purpose of soliciting, or accepting any order for, or otherwise dealing in any transaction in, or in connection with, a commodity futures contract, unless such transaction is made on or subject to the rules of a board of trade that has been designated or registered by the CFTC as a contract market or derivatives transaction execution facility for the specific commodity.

Bitfinex offered to enter into, executed, and/or confirmed the execution of financed retail commodity transactions. None of the financed retail commodity transactions were conducted on or subject to the rules of a board of trade that has been designated or registered by the CFTC as a contract market or derivatives transaction execution facility. Bitfinex therefore violated Section 4(a) of the Act.

D. Bitfinex Violated Section 4d(a) of the Act by Failing to Register as a Futures Commission Merchant

Section 4d(a) of the Act requires all persons acting as futures commission merchants ("FCMs") to register with the Commission. Section la(28) of the Act defines a FCM, in relevant part, as an individual, partnership, corporation or trust, that is engaged in soliciting or accepting orders for retail commodity transactions, or that accepts money in connection with such transactions.

Bitfinex accepted orders for retail commodity transactions and received funds from those customers in connection with retail commodity transactions. Bitfinex was not, however, registered with the Commission in any capacity. Therefore, Bitfinex violated Section 4d(a) of the Act.

V. FINDINGS OF VIOLATION

Based on the foregoing, the Commission finds that, during the Relevant Period, Bitfinex violated Sections 4(a) and 4d of the Act.

. . . .

[Offer of Settlement and Order imposing cease and desist order, civil penalty of $75,000, and obligation to cooperate omitted.]

NOTES AND QUESTIONS

1.   As noted in the order, BFXNA Inc. d/b/a Bitfinex was organized as a corporation under the laws of the British Virgin Islands, with its principal place of business in Hong Kong, China. Neither the company nor any entity doing business as Bitfinex was registered to do business in the U.S. As a practical matter, how do you suppose the CFTC gains jurisdiction over businesses like BFXNA since it was formed and primarily located elsewhere?

2.   In this instance, the defendants voluntarily settled and agreed to cooperate. Would an administrative order do any good against international businesses that do not voluntarily settle and agree to cooperate? How would such an order be enforced?

3.   What would motivate a company like BFXNA to cooperate with the CFTC?

––––––––––

The CFTC has continued to actively monitor trading in crypto-backed derivatives. At the outset of 2018, the CFTC issued a Backgrounder on Virtual Currency Futures Markets, noting the need for additional clarity regarding federal oversight over the self-certification process for bitcoin futures products by DCMs. Excerpts from the Backgrounder explain more about the CFTC expectations for such market platforms.

CFTC, BACKGROUNDER ON OVERSIGHT OF AND APPROACH TO VIRTUAL CURRENCY FUTURES MARKETS
(January 4, 2018)[21]

. . . .

Federal and State Oversight of Virtual Currencies

US law does not provide for direct, comprehensive Federal oversight of underlying Bitcoin or virtual currency spot markets. As a result, US regulation of virtual currencies has evolved into a multifaceted, multi-regulatory approach:

- State Banking regulators oversee certain US and foreign virtual currency spot exchanges largely through state money transfer laws.

- The Internal Revenue Service (IRS) treats virtual currencies as property subject to capital gains tax.

- The Treasury's Financial Crimes Enforcement Network (FinCEN) monitors Bitcoin and other virtual currency transfers for anti-money laundering purposes.

––––––––––

[21]   This document is archived at https://perma.cc/3WBH-89ZL.

- The Securities and Exchange Commission (SEC) takes increasingly strong action against unregistered initial coin offerings.

The CFTC also has an important role to play. In 2014, the CFTC declared virtual currencies to be a "commodity" subject to oversight under its authority under the Commodity Exchange Act (CEA).

. . . .

CFTC Approach to Responsible Regulation of Virtual Currencies

The CFTC seeks to promote responsible innovation and development that is consistent with its statutory mission to foster open, transparent, competitive and financially sound derivative trading markets and to prohibit fraud, manipulation and abusive practices in connection with derivatives and other products subject to the CEA. The CFTC believes that the responsible regulatory response to virtual currencies involves the following [all but headings omitted]:

1) Consumer Education.

2) Asserting Legal Authority.

3) Market Intelligence.

4) Robust Enforcement.

5) Government-wide Coordination.

Virtual Currency Self-Certifications

On Friday, December 1, 2017, the Chicago Mercantile Exchange Inc. (CME) and the CBOE Futures Exchange (CFE) self-certified new contracts for bitcoin futures products and the Cantor Exchange self-certified a new contract for bitcoin binary options.

- The product self-certification process was deliberately designed by Congress and prior Commissions to give the initiative to DCMs to certify new products. This is consistent with a DCM's role as a self-regulatory organization (SRO) and the CFTC's principles-based approach to regulation.

- This self-certification process is one that Congress promulgated and prior Commissions have implemented. Unless it is changed, the staff of the CFTC must work responsibly within the self-certification structure.

- It is notable that the product self-certification process does NOT provide for public input, the creation of separate guaranty funds for clearing, or value judgments about the underlying spot market.

- There are limited grounds for the CFTC to "stay" self-certification such as filing a false statement in the certification.

- In the case of the CME and CFE self-certifications, no such grounds were evident.

- Had it even been possible, blocking self-certification would not have stemmed interest in Bitcoin or other virtual currencies nor their spectacular and volatile valuations. Instead, it would have ensured that the virtual currency spot markets continue to operate without federal regulatory surveillance for fraud and manipulation.

The CFTC was well prepared to handle the recent self-certifications of Bitcoin futures products. CFTC staff knew that a virtual currencies market was evolving rapidly in 2017 and that the agency would likely see proposals for the launch of Bitcoin futures.

. . . .

Background on "Heightened Review" for Virtual Currency Self-Certifications

Within the limits and parameters of the current self-certification process, CFTC staff has engaged in a "heightened review" with the DCMs and worked collaboratively through several drafts of the terms and conditions of these Bitcoin futures products to address issues. At the heart of the CFTC's heightened review is extensive visibility and monitoring of markets for virtual currency derivatives and underlying settlement reference rates. Virtual currency self-certification under heightened review means that the CFTC not only has clear legal authority, but now also will have the means to police certain underlying spot markets for fraud and manipulation.

Heightened review includes:

1) derivatives clearing organizations (DCOs) setting substantially high initial and maintenance margin for cash settled Bitcoin futures;

2) DCMs setting large trader reporting thresholds at five bitcoins or less;

3) DCMs entering direct or indirect information sharing agreements with spot market platforms to allow access to trade and trader data;

4) DCM monitoring of data from cash markets with respect to price settlements and other Bitcoin prices more broadly, and identifying anomalies and disproportionate moves in the cash markets compare to the futures markets;

5)   DCMs agreeing to engage in inquiries, including at the trade settlement level when necessary;

6)   DCMs agreeing to regular coordination with CFTC surveillance staff on trade activities, including providing the CFTC surveillance team with trade settlement data upon request; and

7)   DCMs coordinating product launches so that the CFTC's market surveillance branch can carefully monitor minute-by-minute developments.

The CFTC expects that any registered entity seeking to list a virtual currency derivative product would follow the same process, terms and conditions.

. . . .

Enforcement initiatives by the CFTC against virtual currency operations are ongoing. In the CFTC's 2018 annual enforcement report the Commission specifically noted the work of its specialized task force on virtual currency. According to that report:

> The story of virtual currency is also one about new technology. And it is a story about the need for robust enforcement to ensure technological development isn't undermined by the few who might seek to capitalize on this development for an unlawful gain. New and potentially market-enhancing technologies like virtual currencies and distributed ledger technology need breathing space to survive. And through work across the Commission, as exemplified by the work of LabCFTC, our Commission has demonstrated its continued commitment to facilitating market-enhancing innovation in the financial technology space. But part of that commitment includes acting aggressively to root out fraud and manipulation from these markets. The Virtual Currency Task Force has focused on identifying misconduct in these areas and holding bad actors accountable.[22]

Given this emphasis on anti-fraud initiatives, it is perhaps not surprising that the CFTC has sought to exert its authority over fraud in the spot markets involving virtual currencies, even where no futures contract or other derivative is involved.

---

[22]   CFTC, ANNUAL REPORT ON THE DIVISION OF ENFORCEMENT at p. 6 (Nov. 20180 [archived at https://perma.cc/W26Q-LCJG].

4. CFTC'S AUTHORITY TO REACH FRAUD NOT INVOLVING FUTURES OR DERIVATIVES

As explained in chapter eleven, the CFTC has exclusive jurisdiction over the regulation of derivatives and any fraud in connection with transactions involving those interests. It also claims jurisdiction over commodities traded in the spot market where fraud or manipulation occurs. This latter authority is somewhat more controversial.

It obviously takes a while for issues to percolate through the courts, and as a result there are very few reported decisions involving CFTC enforcement actions against crypto businesses. Of the existing opinions, one of the most important is a 2018 opinion arising out of the Eastern District of New York, focusing on Coin Drop Markets and its founder, Patrick McDonnell.

PRELIMINARY NOTES AND QUESTIONS

1.   The background on virtual currencies and Bitcoin that appears in the following opinion should be a basic review of concepts that have already been introduced in this book.

2.   Patrick McDonnell declined the services of an attorney and proceeded pro se in this matter. What arguments did he make as to why the CFTC should not prevail against him?

3.   Why does the court conclude that cryptoassets are commodities?

4.   Why does the court conclude that the CFTC has authority over fraud in the spot markets (i.e., market transactions not involving a futures or derivative contract)?

CFTC v. McDONNELL

287 F. Supp. 3d 213 (E.D.N.Y.), *adhered to on denial of reconsideration*, 321 F. Supp. 3d 366 (E.D.N.Y. 2018)

JACK B. WEINSTEIN, SENIOR UNITED STATES DISTRICT JUDGE:

I.   Introduction

The Commodity Futures Trading Commission ("CFTC") sues Patrick McDonnell and his company Coin Drop Markets. CFTC alleges defendants "operated a deceptive and fraudulent virtual currency scheme . . . for purported virtual currency trading advice" and "for virtual currency purchases and trading . . . and simply misappropriated [investor] funds." CFTC seeks injunctive relief, monetary penalties, and restitution of funds received in violation of the Commodity Exchange Act ("CEA").

Until Congress clarifies the matter, the CFTC has concurrent authority, along with other state and federal administrative agencies, and civil and criminal courts, over dealings in virtual currency. An important nationally and internationally traded commodity, virtual currency is tendered for payment for debts, although, unlike United States currency, it is not legal tender that must be accepted. 31 U.S.C. § 5103 ("United States coins and currency . . . are legal tender for all debts . . . .")

A. Commodity Futures Trading Commission ("CFTC") Standing

The primary issue raised at the outset of this litigation is whether CFTC has standing to sue defendants on the theory that they have violated the CEA. Presented are two questions that determine the plaintiff's standing: (1) whether virtual currency may be regulated by the CFTC as a commodity; and (2) whether the amendments to the CEA under the Dodd-Frank Act permit the CFTC to exercise its jurisdiction over fraud that does not directly involve the sale of futures or derivative contracts.

. . . .

B. Injunctive Relief

After hearing testimony from an investigator in the Division of Enforcement for the CFTC, the court finds the plaintiff has made a preliminary prima facie showing that the defendants committed fraud by misappropriation of investors' funds and misrepresentation through false trading advice and promised future profits. A preliminary injunction is granted in favor of the CFTC.

. . . .

II. Facts

Patrick McDonnell and his company CabbageTech, Corp., doing business as Coin Drop Markets ("defendants"), offered fraudulent trading and investment services related to virtual currency.

Customers from the United States and abroad paid defendants for "membership" in virtual currency trading groups purported to provide exit prices and profits of up to "300%" per week. Defendants advertised their services through "at least two websites, www.coindropmarkets.com and www.coindrops.club," as well as on the social media platform Twitter.

"Investors" transferred virtual currency to the defendants for "day" trading. ("McDonnell claimed that he could generate profits of 2 to 300% each day for [an] Investor . . . and that $1,000 in Litecoin [a type of virtual currency] should be earning $200 to $250 per day through trading.").

After receiving membership payment or virtual currency investments, defendants deleted their "social media accounts" and "websites and ceased communicating with . . . customers around July, 2017." Defendants provided minimal, if any, virtual currency trading advice and never achieved the promised return on investment. When customers asked for a return of their membership fee, or virtual currency investment, the defendants refused and misappropriated the funds.

III. Background of Bitcoin and Virtual Currencies

A. Description of Virtual Currencies

Virtual currencies are generally defined as "digital assets used as a medium of exchange." They are stored electronically in "digital wallets," and exchanged over the internet through a direct peer-to-peer system. They are often described as "cryptocurrencies" because they use "cryptographic protocols to secure transactions . . . recorded on publicly available decentralized ledgers," called "blockchains."

The "blockchain" serves as a digital signature to verify the exchange. "The public nature of the decentralized ledger allows people to recognize the transfer of virtual currency from one user to another without requiring any central intermediary in which both users need to trust." Some experts believe blockchain technology underlying virtual currencies will serve to "enhance [future] economic efficiency" and have a "broad and lasting impact on global financial markets in payments, banking, securities settlement, title recording, cyber security and trade reporting and analysis." Virtual currencies are not backed by any government, fiat currency, or commodity.

They have some characteristics of government paper currency, commodities, and securities.

B. Expansion and Value

The price of Bitcoin, and other virtual currencies, has risen, and then fallen, at extreme rates. Olga Kharif, *All you Need to Know About Bitcoin's Rise, From $0.01 to $15,000,* Bloomberg Businessweek, Dec. 1, 2017[23] ("The initial price of bitcoin, set in 2010, was less than 1 cent. Now it's crossed $16,000. Once seen as the province of nerds, libertarians and drug dealers, bitcoin today is drawing millions of dollars from hedge funds."). As their value has increased, online exchanges have become more accessible allowing more members of the public to trade and invest in virtual currencies.

While there are many Bitcoin exchanges around the world, Coinbase has been the dominant place that ordinary Americans go to buy and sell virtual currency. No company had made it simpler to sign up, link a bank account or debit card, and begin buying Bitcoin. The number of people with Coinbase accounts has gone from 5.5 million in January [2017] to 13.3 million at the end of November [2017], according to data from the Altana Digital Currency Fund. In late November, Coinbase was sometimes getting

---

[23]   Author's note: This article, which is quoted in the original source, is available online at https://www.bloomberg.com/news/articles/2017-12-01/understanding-bitcoin-s-rise-0-01-to-11-000-quicktake-q-a.

100,000 new customers a day—leaving the company with more customers than Charles Schwab and E-Trade.

According to coinmarketcap.com (viewed Feb. 6, 2018, at approximately 9:10 a.m. EST), there were over 1500 virtual currencies. Bitcoin had the largest market capitalization, valued at $121,264,863,386. A single Bitcoin was valued at $7,196.92. The cheapest virtual currency, Strong Hands, was valued at $0.000001. The combined market capitalization of all virtual currencies as of January 6, 2018, was roughly $795 billion; by Feb. 6, 2018, the total value had dropped to $329 billion.

C. Fraud and Crime

The rise in users and value of virtual currencies has been accompanied by increased fraud and criminal activity. Edgar G. Sánchez, *Crypto-Currencies: The 21st Century's Money Laundering and Tax Havens,* 28 U. Fla. J.L. & Pub. Pol'y 167, 169 (2017) ("[T]he newest growing concern with Bitcoin, and crypto-currencies in general, are their ability to wash money and conceal taxable income.").

Silk Road, an online drug market that allowed for purchase through Bitcoin, was one of the earliest and most audacious examples of crime enabled by virtual currencies. . . . Virtual currency exchanges have been victims of hacking and theft. . . . These and other criminal acts have led some to call for increased governmental oversight and regulation of virtual currency.

> Having delved into the prevalence of money laundering and tax evasion both globally and in the United States, and the rise of crypto-currencies and their use in disguising real money, the question remains as to what steps can be taken to legitimize crypto-currencies, or at the very least, put an end to their use for illegal purposes.

Sánchez, *supra* at 188.

D. Regulation and Oversight of Virtual Currency

Congress has yet to authorize a system to regulate virtual currency. T. Gorman, *Blockchain, Virtual Currencies and the Regulators,* Dorsey & Whitney LLP, Jan. 11, 2018 ("As the CFTC recently admitted, U.S. law does not provide for 'direct comprehensive U.S. regulation of virtual currencies. To the contrary a multi-regulatory approach is being used.'").

The CFTC, and other agencies, claim concurrent regulatory power over virtual currency in certain settings, but concede their jurisdiction is incomplete.

1. Potential Virtual Currency Regulation

Until Congress acts to regulate virtual currency the following alternatives appear to be available:

1.   **No regulation.** *See, e.g.,* Nikolei M. Kaplanov, *Nerdy Money: Bitcoin, the Private Digital Currency, and the Case Against Its Regulation,* 25 Loy. Consumer L. Rev. 111, 113 (2012) ("This Comment will show that the federal government has no legal basis to prohibit bitcoin users from engaging in traditional consumer purchases and transfers. This Comment further argues that the federal government should refrain from passing any laws or regulations limiting the use of bitcoins . . . applying any sort of regulation to bitcoin use, [ ] would be ineffective and contrary to the interest of the United States consumers.").

2.   **Partial regulation through criminal law prosecutions of Ponzi-like schemes by the Department of Justice, or state criminal agencies, or civil substantive suits based on allegations of fraud.** *See, e.g., United States v. Faiella,* 39 F.Supp.3d 544, 545 (S.D.N.Y. 2014) ("Defendants in this case are charged in connection with their operation of an underground market in the virtual currency 'Bitcoin' via the website 'Silk Road.' "); *United States v. Lord,* No. CR 15–00240–01/02, 2017 WL 1424806, at *2 (W.D. La. Apr. 20, 2017) ("Counts 2–14 charged Defendants with various other crimes associated with operating their bitcoin exchange business.").

3.   **Regulation by the Commodity Futures Trading Commission ("CFTC").** *See infra* Part III.D.2.

4.   **Regulation by the Securities and Exchange Commission ("SEC") as securities.** *See, e.g., SEC v. Plexcorps,* 17–CV–7007, 2017 WL 5988934 (E.D.N.Y. Filed Dec. 1, 2017) ("This is an emergency action to stop Lacroix, a recidivist securities law violator in Canada, and his partner Paradis-Royer, from further misappropriating investor funds illegally raised through the fraudulent and unregistered offer and sale of securities called 'PlexCoin' or 'PlexCoin Tokens' in a purported 'Initial Coin Offering.' ")

5.   **Regulation by the Treasury Department's Financial Enforcement Network ("FinCEN").** *See, e.g.,* FinCEN, *Treasury's First Action Against a Foreign-Located Money Services Business,* U.S. Department of the Treasury, Jul. 27, 2017 ("The Financial Crimes Enforcement Network (FinCEN), working in coordination with the U.S. Attorney's Office for the Northern District of California, assessed a $110,003,314 civil money penalty today against BTC-e [a virtual currency exchange] for willfully violating U.S. anti-money laundering laws.").

6.   **Regulation by the Internal Revenue Service ("IRS").** *See, e.g., United States v. Coinbase, Inc.,* No. 17–CV–01431–JSC, 2017 WL 3035164, at *1 (N.D. Cal. July 18, 2017) ("In March 2014, the IRS issued Notice 2014–21, which describes how the IRS applies U.S. tax principles to transactions involving virtual currency. (Case No. 3:16–cv–06658–JSC, Dkt. No. 2–4 at 3 ¶ 6.) In Notice 2014–21, the IRS stated its position:

virtual currencies that can be converted into traditional currency are property for tax purposes, and a taxpayer can have a gain or loss on the sale or exchange of a virtual currency, depending on the taxpayer's cost to purchase the virtual currency.").

7. Regulation by private exchanges. *See, e.g.,* Asian Review, *Japan Tries Light Touch in Bringing Cryptocurrencies out of Regulatory Limbo*, NIKKEI, Sept. 30, 2017 ("[T]here is a growing need for exchange operators to self-police to protect investors from taking on too much risk and other dangers.").

8. State regulations. *See, e.g.,* Press Release, *DFS Grants Virtual Currency License to Coinbase, Inc.,* N.Y. Department of Financial Services, Jan. 17, 2017 ("DFS has approved six firms for virtual currency charters or licenses, while denying those applications that did not meet DFS's standards. In addition to bitFlyer USA, DFS has granted licenses to Coinbase Inc., XRP II and Circle Internet Financial, and charters to Gemini Trust Company and itBit Trust Company.").

9. A combination of any of the above.

2. Oversight by CFTC

The CFTC is one of the federal administrative bodies currently exercising partial supervision of virtual currencies. Christopher Giancarlo, *Chairman Giancarlo Statement on Virtual Currencies, CFTC,* Jan. 4, 2018 ("One thing is certain: ignoring virtual currency trading will not make it go away. Nor is it a responsible regulatory strategy. The CFTC has an important role to play.").

Administrative and civil action has been utilized by the CFTC to expand its control:

> On September 17, 2015, the [CFTC] issued an [administrative] order (the Coinflip Order) filing and simultaneously settling charges against Coinflip, Inc. (Coinflip) and its chief executive officer. In the Coinflip Order, the CFTC took the view for the first time that bitcoin and other virtual currencies are commodities subject to the Commodity Exchange Act (CEA) and CFTC regulations.

Conrad Bahlke, *Recent Developments in the Regulatory Treatment of Bitcoin,* 28 No. 1 Intell. Prop. & Tech. L.J. 6 (2016) (internal citations omitted).

Legitimization and regulation of virtual currencies has followed from the CFTC's allowance of futures trading on certified exchanges. Two futures exchanges, Chicago Mercantile Exchange and the CBOE Futures Exchange, as of February 23, 2018, exceeded "$150 million in daily trading volume." The CFTC has "actively policed" futures exchanges for "violating core principles" such as "failing to enforce its prohibitions against unlawful wash trading and prearranged trades."

3. Concurrent Oversight from Other Agencies

The SEC, IRS, DOJ, Treasury Department, and state agencies have increased their regulatory action in the field of virtual currencies without displacing CFTC's concurrent authority. Most current regulatory action takes the form of pursuing criminal and fraudulent conduct after it occurs.

A new division of the Securities and Exchange Commission dedicated to so-called "initial coin offerings" (ICOs) filed its first charges on Friday, targeting a scam that reportedly raised $15 million from thousands of investors by promising a 13-fold profit in less than a month. In a criminal complaint filed in Brooklyn federal court, the new SEC division, known as the Cyber Unit, describes how Dominic Lacroix sold digital tokens known as "PlexCoins" as part of a purported plan "to increase access to cryptocurrency services" across the world.

IV. Law

A. Jurisdiction

District courts have jurisdiction over any action in which the United States is a plaintiff. U.S. Const. Art. III § 2 ("The Judicial Power shall extend to all Cases . . . [or] Controversies to which the United States shall be a Party."); 28 U.S.C. § 1345 ("Except as otherwise provided by Act of Congress, the district courts shall have original jurisdiction of all civil actions, suits or proceedings commenced by the United States, or by any agency or officer thereof expressly authorized to sue by Act of Congress."). Under 28 U.S.C. § 1331 district courts also "have original jurisdiction of all civil actions arising under the Constitution, laws, or treaties of the United States."

B. Standing

Pursuant to Title 7 U.S.C. § 13a–1(a) the CFTC may seek injunctive or other relief when it believes that a person or entity is in violation of the CEA. ("[T]he Commission may bring an action in the proper district court of the United States . . . to enjoin such act or practice, or to enforce compliance with this chapter, or any rule, regulation or order thereunder, and said courts shall have jurisdiction to entertain such actions."). Relief may be sought in the "district wherein the defendant is found or is an inhabitant or transacts business or in the district where the act or practice occurred, is occurring, or is about to occur."

1. Enforcement Power of CFTC

Exclusive jurisdiction over "accounts, agreements . . . and transactions involving swaps or contracts of sale of a commodity for future delivery" has been granted to the CFTC. Any commodity traded as a future must be traded on a commodity exchange approved by the CFTC. The CEA and its "remedial statutes" are to be "construed liberally" to allow for broad market protection. The court generally defers to an agency's interpretation of a statute "that the agency is responsible for administering."

Full deference is dependent on whether the agency's interpretation followed a formal rulemaking process. *Commodity Futures Trading Comm'n v. Sterling Trading Grp., Inc.,* 605 F.Supp.2d 1245, 1265–66 (S.D. Fla. 2009) ("*Chevron* deference is confined to those instances in which the agency renders its interpretation in the course of a rulemaking proceeding or adjudication. [E]ven if an agency's interpretation of its own statute is advanced in the course of litigation rather than through a rulemaking or agency adjudication, courts will still pay some deference to the agency's interpretation.").

a.   Virtual Currencies are Commodities

Black's Law Dictionary defines a commodity as "an article of trade or commerce." Merriam Webster defines it as "[a]n economic good . . . [or] an article of commerce . . ." Commentators have argued that based on common usage, virtual currency should be interpreted as a commodity.

> It would make sense for regulators to treat Bitcoin as a commodity. Commodities are generally defined as "goods sold in the market with a quality and value uniform throughout the world." This categorization would be appropriate because it realistically reflects the economic behavior of Bitcoin users and squares with traditional economic conceptions of exchange.

Mitchell Prentis, *Digital Metal: Regulating Bitcoin As A Commodity,* 66 Case W. Res. L. Rev. 609, 626 (2015).

Some propose that because virtual currencies provide a "store of value" they function as commodities:

> A commodity is any item that "accommodates" our physical wants and needs. And one of these physical wants is the need for a store of value. Throughout history humans have used different commodities as a store of value—even cocoa beans—but, more persistently, gold. In contrast, a security is any instrument that is "secured" against something else. As a currency is usually secured by a commodity or a government's ability to tax and defend, it is considered to be a security. By these definitions, bitcoin with a lower case "b," is a commodity, and not a currency, while Bitcoin with a capital "B" is the technology, or network, that bitcoin moves across. The analogy would be Shale technology versus shale oil.

Jeff Currie, *Bullion Bests bitcoin, Not Bitcoin,* Goldman Sachs Global Investment Research, Mar. 11, 2014.

Others argue virtual currencies are commodities because they serve as a type of monetary exchange:

> Bitcoin should primarily be considered a commodity because it serves the function of money in its community of users. Users exchange Bitcoins to obtain property that they desire. . . .

> Furthermore, while Bitcoin acts as a money commodity in its community of users, from a pricing standpoint, it is valued like other commodities. The price of traditional commodities, like gold, silver, and agricultural products, vary in accordance with their demand and scarcity. When more people want a commodity that has a fixed supply, the price rises.

> Similarly, the price of Bitcoin fluctuates according to the same fixed supply model. Bitcoins are scarce because the algorithm controlling how many Bitcoins are released into the market through mining [ ] is designed to taper the supply of bitcoins, until no more are created. Bitcoins are considered rare because there is a fixed supply of them, leading users to be willing to pay increasing prices to control them. The value of a Bitcoin is ultimately driven by supply and demand—a coin is worth whatever someone is willing to pay for it.

[Mitchell Prentis, *Digital Metal: Regulating Bitcoin As A Commodity*, 66 Case W. Res. L. Rev. 609, 628–29 (2015).]

b. Commodity Exchange Act's Definition of "Commodity"

CEA defines "commodities" as "wheat, cotton, rice, corn, oats, barley, rye, flaxseed, grain sorghums, mill feeds, butter, eggs, Solanum tuberosum (Irish potatoes), wool, wool tops, fats and oils (including lard, tallow, cottonseed oil, peanut oil, soybean oil, and all other fats and oils), cottonseed meal, cottonseed, peanuts, soybeans, soybean meal, livestock, livestock products, and frozen concentrated orange juice, and all other goods and articles . . . and all services, rights, and interests . . . in which contracts for future delivery are presently or in the future dealt in." The original grant of power to the CEA was designed to control trading in agricultural commodities. Other goods, as well as services, rights and interests, are now covered by the statute. The CEA covers intangible commodities.

c. CFTC's Interpretation of "Commodity"

After an administrative proceeding in 2015, the CFTC issued an order finding, for the first time, that virtual currencies can be classified as commodities. *In the Matter of: Coinflip, Inc.*, CFTC Docket No. 15–29 ("Bitcoin and other virtual currencies are encompassed in the definition and properly defined as commodities."). Multiple statements defining virtual currency as a commodity have been issued by the CFTC.

d. Derivative Contracts and Futures

Regulatory authority over commodities traded as futures and derivatives has been granted to CFTC.

Title 7 U.S.C. § 9(1) of the CEA makes it unlawful for any person to:

> use or employ, in connection with any swap, *or a contract of sale of any commodity in interstate commerce,* or for future delivery on or subject to the rules of any registered entity, *any manipulative or deceptive device or contrivance,* in contravention of such rules and regulations as the Commission shall promulgate by not later than 1 year after July 21, 2010 . . . (emphasis added).

17 C.F.R. § 180.1 further defines the regulatory power of the CFTC:

> (a) It shall be unlawful for any person, directly or indirectly, in connection with any swap, or contract of sale of any commodity in interstate commerce, or contract for future delivery on or subject to the rules of any registered entity, to intentionally or recklessly:
>
> > (1) Use or employ, or attempt to use or employ, any manipulative device, scheme, or artifice to defraud;
> >
> > (2) Make, or attempt to make, any untrue or misleading statement of a material fact or to omit to state a material fact necessary in order to make the statements made not untrue or misleading;
> >
> > (3) Engage, or attempt to engage, in any act, practice, or course of business, which operates or would operate as a fraud or deceit. . .

Liability, under the CEA, for commodity fraud, is shown by: "(1) the making of a misrepresentation, misleading statement, or a deceptive omission; (2) scienter; and (3) materiality."

e. Regulation of Spot Market Fraud

The CFTC has recently expanded its enforcement to fraud related to spot markets underlying the (already regulated) derivative markets. *See, e.g., CFTC v. Gelfman Blueprint, Inc.,* Case No. 17–7181, 2017 WL 4228737 (S.D.N.Y. Filed Sept. 21, 2017) (suit brought by the CFTC alleging a Bitcoin Ponzi scheme, not involving future contracts).

In *Gelfman,* as in the instant case, the CFTC relied on the broad statutory authority in Section 9(1) of the CEA, and regulatory authority under 17 C.F.R. § 180.1. Specifically, the language in § 180.1 prohibiting "any person, directly or indirectly, in connection with any . . . contract of sale of any commodity in interstate commerce" from using a "manipulative device, scheme, or artifice to defraud," or making "any untrue or misleading statement of a material fact."

The portion of the statute delegating oversight authority over "contract of sale of any commodity in interstate commerce" allows CFTC to enforce its mandate in cases not directly involving future trades. Where a futures market exists for a good, service, right, or interest, it may be regulated by CFTC, as a commodity, without regard to whether the dispute involves futures contracts.

CFTC does not have regulatory authority over simple quick cash or spot transactions that do not involve fraud or manipulation. This boundary has been recognized by the CFTC. It has not attempted to regulate spot trades, unless there is evidence of manipulation or fraud.

2. Concurrent Jurisdiction

Federal agencies may have concurrent or overlapping jurisdiction over a particular issue or area. Agencies often cooperate to enforce their overlapping powers.

C. Preliminary Injunction Standard

Under Title 7 U.S.C. § 13a–1(a) the CFTC may seek injunctive or other relief when it concludes that a person or entity is in violation of the CEA. "The CFTC is entitled to a preliminary injunction upon a prima facie showing that defendants have violated the Act and 'that there is a reasonable likelihood that the wrong will be repeated.'" When enforcing a statutorily prescribed injunction, the CFTC "need not prove irreparable injury or the inadequacy of other remedies as required in private injunctive suits."

V. Application of Law

A. CFTC Standing

The CFTC has standing pursuant to Title 7 U.S.C. § 13a–1(a) to seek injunctive and other relief related to misleading advice, and the fraudulent scheme and misappropriation of virtual currencies by defendants.

1. Virtual Currencies as Commodities

Virtual currencies can be regulated by CFTC as a commodity. Virtual currencies are "goods" exchanged in a market for a uniform quality and value. Mitchell Prentis, *Digital Metal: Regulating Bitcoin As A Commodity*, 66 Case W. Res. L. Rev. 609, 626 (2015). They fall well-within the common definition of "commodity" as well as the CEA's definition of "commodities" as "all other goods and articles . . . in which contracts for future delivery are presently or in the future dealt in."

The jurisdictional authority of CFTC to regulate virtual currencies as commodities does not preclude other agencies from exercising their regulatory power when virtual currencies function differently than derivative commodities. *See, e.g., Jay Clayton [SEC Chair] and Christopher Giancarlo [CFTC Chair], Regulators are Looking at Cryptocurrency,* Wall Street Journal, Jan. 24, 2018 ("The SEC does not have direct oversight of transactions in currencies or commodities. Yet some products that are labeled cryptocurrencies have characteristics that make them securities. The offer, sale and trading of such products must be carried out in compliance with securities law. The SEC will vigorously pursue those who seek to evade the registration, disclosure and antifraud requirements of our securities laws.").

The Chicago Mercantile Exchange Inc. ("CME") has filed an amicus brief. It claims to operate the "world's leading derivatives marketplace." It supports the view that virtual currencies are commodities subject to the CFTC's regulatory protections. It writes:

> CME offers for the Court's consideration an explanation of the possible consequences of a determination that a virtual currency such as bitcoin is not a commodity. Such a determination would put in jeopardy CME's and its market participants' expectation to rely on . . . the CFTC's regulatory protections for commodity derivatives contracts based on virtual currencies. This legal uncertainty would substantially disrupt the settled expectations of CME and numerous market participants who are trading bitcoin futures for purposes of hedging cash market exposures or making a market in bitcoin futures by offering liquidity, in addition to market professionals that clear, broker or manage virtual currency futures trading activity.

2.   CFTC Jurisdiction Over Virtual Currency Fraud

CFTC has jurisdictional authority to bring suit against defendants utilizing a scheme to defraud investors through a "contract [for] sale of [a] commodity in interstate commerce." Although the CFTC has traditionally limited its jurisdiction primarily to "future" contracts for commodities, its expansion into spot trade commodity fraud is justified by statutory and regulatory guidelines. Language in 7 U.S.C. § 9(1), and 17 C.F.R. § 180.1, establish the CFTC's regulatory authority over the manipulative schemes, fraud, and misleading statements alleged in the complaint.

B.   Prima Facie Showing of Fraud Committed by Defendants

1.   CFTC has made a prima facie showing that the defendants committed fraud by misappropriation of investors' funds and misrepresentation of trading advice and future profits promised to customers. The intentional nature of the defendants' conduct . . . is evidenced by the blatant disregard of customers' complaints and their refusal to return investors' funds.

C. Preliminary Injunction

A preliminary injunction is granted in favor of the CFTC. The court concludes that without an injunction there is a reasonable likelihood that defendants will continue to violate the CEA. A separate order outlining the terms of the relief is issued.

. . . .

SO ORDERED.

NOTE

Following a bench trial, the same Judge who entered the above preliminary injunction ruled that:

- the defendant deliberately and knowingly made misrepresentations, misleading statements, and omissions;
- the defendant misappropriated customer funds;
- the defendant's misrepresentations and omissions were material;
- the defendant acted with scienter;
- the defendant was liable under CEA as control person;
- a permanent injunction was warranted;
- restitution in amount of funds received from all customers was warranted; and
- a civil monetary penalty in an amount triple the monetary gain from the fraudulent scheme was warranted.[24]

5. THE CFTC'S AUTHORITY TO REGULATE CRYPTO THAT IS NOT LISTED ON A FUTURES EXCHANGE

McDonnell involved allegedly fraudulent claims made in connection with the solicitation of both crypto and conventional "fiat" currency from customers.[25] The opinion addressed two primary issues: whether the CFTC has authority to regulate crypto as a commodity; and whether the CEA as amended by Dodd-Frank gives the CFTC jurisdiction over fraud not directly involving the sale of futures or derivatives.[26] As explained above,

---

[24]   *CFTC v. McDonnell*, 332 F. Supp. 3d 641 (E.D.N.Y. 2018).

[25]   *CFTC v. McDonnell*, 287 F. Supp. 3d 213 (E.D.N.Y. 2018) (granting preliminary injunction and rejecting defendant's motion to dismiss); *CFTC v. McDonnell*, 321 F. Supp.3d 366 (E.D.N.Y. 2018) (denying defendant's motion for reconsideration); and *CFTC v. McDonnell*, 332 F. Supp. 3d 641 (E.D.N.Y. 2018) (finding in favor of the CFTC, imposing sanctions including granting a permanent injunction).

[26]   *McDonnell*, 287 F. Supp. 3d at 217.

the court concluded that crypto could be regulated as a commodity and that the "CFTC's broad authority extends to fraud or manipulation in derivatives markets and underlying spot markets."[27] In the views of some, the important word in this latter phrase is "underlying."[28] How can a spot market underlie a derivatives market unless there are, in fact, derivatives that someone is trading? This argument posits that, absent a market in futures contracts, the modifier "underlying" is without meaning.

This argument is based on more than the choice of wording by a district court. The definitions section in the CEA, says that the term "commodity" means thirty specifically designated agricultural products "and all services, rights and interests . . . in which *contracts for future delivery are presently or in the future dealt in.*"[29] (Emphasis added.) It is the meaning of this last phrase, which appears here in bold face font, that supports the argument that not all crypto should be regulated by the CFTC. In the case of Bitcoin, which the majority of CFTC enforcement actions to date have involved, futures markets exist and trading occurs. This is, however, not the case for the majority of cryptoassets. Most do not have any derivatives or futures that are traded, and at the current time there is little prospect for a market in those kinds of arrangements developing. Is it then possible that the CFTC's ability to pursue fraud claims in the crypto spot markets is not as broad as the CFTC might wish or expect?

PRELIMINARY NOTE AND QUESTIONS

As you read the following opinion, consider the arguments raised by the defendants as to why the CFTC should lack jurisdiction over the behavior that it sought to curb. What argument did defendants make that My Big Coin was not a commodity? What other argument did they make that the CFTC lacked jurisdiction to pursue their claims of fraud?

CFTC v. MY BIG COIN PAY, INC.
334 F. Supp. 3d 492 (D. Mass. 2018)

RYA W. ZOBEL, SR. U.S. DISTRICT JUDGE.

Defendant[s] . . . move to dismiss this case brought by plaintiff Commodity Future Trading Commission ("CFTC"). The amended complaint alleges a fraudulent "virtual currency scheme" in violation of the Commodity Exchange Act ("CEA" or "the Act") and a CFTC implementing regulation banning fraud and/or manipulation in connection with the sale of a commodity. Defendants' principal argument is that CFTC fails to state

---

[27]   *Id.*

[28]   *See, e.g.,* Michael Brooks, et. al, *The CFTC and virtual currencies: Amidst all the hype, don't forget 'commodity' is still a defined term,* PRACTITIONER INSIGHTS COMMENT., 2018 WL 2304728 (May 29, 2018).

[29]   7 U.S. Code § 1a(9).

a claim because My Big Coin ("MBC" or "My Big Coin"), the allegedly fraudulent virtual currency involved in the scheme, is not a "commodity" within the meaning of the Act. They also argue that the CEA provision and CFTC regulation are restricted to cases involving market manipulation and do not reach the fraud alleged here. Finally, they assert that plaintiff's amended complaint fails to support its allegations of misappropriation. The motion is denied.

I. Factual Background

For purposes of resolving this motion I accept as true the following well-pleaded facts, recited as alleged in the amended complaint.

[Defendants]. . . "operated a virtual currency scheme in which they fraudulently offered the sale of a fully-functioning virtual currency" called "My Big Coin". In short, defendants enticed customers to buy My Big Coin by making various untrue and/or misleading statements and omitting material facts. The falsities included that My Big Coin was "backed by gold," could be used anywhere Mastercard was accepted, and was being "actively traded" on several currency exchanges. Defendants also made up and arbitrarily changed the price of My Big Coin to mimic the fluctuations of a legitimate, actively-traded virtual currency. When victims of the fraud purchased My Big Coin, they could view their accounts on a website but "could not trade their MBC or withdraw funds . . . ." Defendants obtained more than $6 million from the scheme. . . .

Plaintiff brought suit on January 16, 2018, alleging violations of Section 6(c)(1) of the Commodities Exchange Act and CFTC Regulation 180.1(a). It also moved for a temporary restraining order and a preliminary injunction. The court granted the temporary restraining order and defendants subsequently consented to a preliminary injunction. Thereafter, plaintiff amended its complaint and defendants filed the pending motion to dismiss, which both parties extensively briefed and argued.

II. Legal Principles

"To survive a motion to dismiss, a complaint must contain sufficient factual matter, accepted as true, to 'state a claim to relief that is plausible on its face.' " . . . . For purposes of a motion to dismiss, the court accepts all well-pleaded factual allegations as true and draws all reasonable inferences in the plaintiff's favor.

III. Application

A. Jurisdiction

As an initial matter, although defendants suggest that this court does not have subject matter jurisdiction for lack of a federal question, their underlying argument that the alleged conduct did not involve a "commodity" goes to the merits of plaintiff's claim, not jurisdiction. This court has subject matter jurisdiction because the case presents a federal question and because federal law expressly authorizes CFTC to sue and the court to grant appropriate relief.

B. Whether Plaintiff Has Adequately Alleged the Sale of a "Commodity" Under the CEA

"The Commodity Exchange Act (CEA) has been aptly characterized as a 'comprehensive regulatory structure to oversee the volatile and esoteric futures trading complex.'" Accordingly, the present Act generally grants CFTC exclusive jurisdiction over futures contracts and the exchanges where they are traded. CFTC has additional powers under the statute, including the general anti-fraud and anti-manipulation authority over "any . . . contract of sale of any commodity in interstate commerce" pursuant to which it brings the claims in this case.

. . . .

"Commodity" is a defined term in the CEA. It includes a host of specifically enumerated agricultural products as well as "all other goods and articles . . . and all services rights and interests . . . in which contracts for future delivery are presently or in the future dealt in."

. . . .

Defendants contend that because "contracts for future delivery" are indisputably not "dealt in" My Big Coin, it cannot be a commodity under the CEA. They take the position that in order to satisfy the CEA's "commodity" definition, the specific item in question must itself underlie a futures contract. Plaintiff responds that "a 'commodity' for purposes of [the CEA definition] is broader than any particular type or brand of that commodity." Pointing to the existence of Bitcoin futures contracts, it argues that contracts for future delivery of virtual currencies are "dealt in" and that My Big Coin, as a virtual currency, is therefore a commodity.

The text of the statute supports plaintiff's argument. The Act defines "commodity" generally and categorically, "not by type, grade, quality, brand, producer, manufacturer, or form." For example, the Act classifies "livestock" as a commodity without enumerating which particular species are the subject of futures trading. Thus, as plaintiff urges, Congress' approach to defining "commodity" signals an intent that courts focus on categories—not specific items—when determining whether the "dealt in" requirement is met.

. . . .

Here, the amended complaint alleges that My Big Coin is a virtual currency and it is undisputed that there is futures trading in virtual currencies (specifically involving Bitcoin). That is sufficient, especially at the pleading stage, for plaintiff to allege that My Big Coin is a "commodity" under the Act. Accordingly, defendants' first ground for dismissal fails.

C. Whether Section 6(c)(1) and Regulation 180.1(a) Reach the Fraud Alleged

Defendants argue, second, that even if My Big Coin is a commodity, the complaint is still deficient because the laws under which the claims are brought "were meant to combat fraudulent market manipulation—not the kind of garden variety sales puffery that the Amended Complaint alleges." That argument fails because both Section 6(c)(1) and Regulation 180.1 explicitly prohibit fraud even in the absence of market manipulation. *See* 7 U.S.C. § 9 (banning the use of any "manipulative or deceptive device or contrivance" in connection with the sale of a commodity); 17 C.F.R. § 180.1(a) (banning the use of "any manipulative device, scheme, or artifice to defraud," the making of "any untrue or misleading statement of a material fact," or the use of "any act, practice, or course of business, which operates . . . as a fraud or deceit . . . ." in connection with the sale of a commodity). Courts have accordingly recognized CFTC's power to prosecute fraud under these provisions. *But see CFTC v. Monex Credit Co.*, 311 F.Supp.3d 1173, 1185–89 (C.D. Cal. 2018) (finding that Section 6(c)(1) prohibits only fraud-based market manipulation). Though some isolated statements in the legislative history surrounding Section 6(c)(1) suggest Congress was, perhaps, principally concerned with combating manipulation, these statements are insufficient to overcome the broad language in the statute as it was passed.

. . . .

IV. Conclusion

Defendants' motion to dismiss is denied.

NOTES AND QUESTIONS

1.   Although the token involved in the preceding case was not traded on any futures exchange, Bitcoin derivatives are traded. Why should the existence of trading in Bitcoin futures determine the jurisdictional authority of the CFTC over spot market fraud involving other cryptoassets?

2.   Defendants argued that the token it sold was not a "good or article," and instead, "like any other virtual currency, represents a set of 'services, rights or interests.'" Excerpts taken from Defendants' Motion to Dismiss, as set out in 7 BROMBERG & LOWENFELS ON SECURITIES FRAUD § 24:7 (2d ed.). Do you agree with this characterization of crypto? Is it a service, right, or interest, or is it a good or article?

3.   Although the court does not detail any of the specifics about this, the legislative history of the CEA does offer some support for the notion that the definition of commodity was not intended to be all-encompassing.

To trace the definition of commodity back to its origins, it is probably reasonable to start with the Commodity Futures Trading Commission Act of 1974 (the "1974 Act"). The 1974 Act has been characterized as "a sweeping overhaul" of the CEA. It created the CFTC and granted it extensive authority over commodity futures markets. (Prior to that time, the CFTC has been given authority to regulate a list of specifically enumerated commodities that had been expanded on numerous occasions.) By 1974, it was clear that the strategy of naming specific commodities in the definition was insufficient, as futures markets continually expanded to cover unnamed goods and services.

Commentators have explained the situation as it then existed as follows:

> Discussions were underway concerning futures markets in such things as home mortgages and ocean freight. Accordingly, Congress considered using generic categories to define the commodities subject to the jurisdiction of the CEA. These included the phrases "all other goods and articles" to cover tangible commodities in addition to the specifically enumerated agricultural commodities, and "all services, rights, and interests" to cover the intangible commodities such as home mortgages which seemed just over the horizon to Congress in 1974.
>
> . . . .
>
> The generic approach, however, generated concerns at the Treasury Department, SEC and other regulators. During the drafting process leading up to the enactment of the 1974 Act, for instance, Treasury wrote to Congress to express its concerns that the proposed legislation gave unnecessary jurisdiction to the CFTC over intangible commodities such as foreign currencies, and "a wide variety of transactions involving financial instruments," given the regulation of these markets by the Office of the Comptroller of the Currency and the Federal Reserve. The letter concluded, "[W]e strongly urge the Committee to amend the proposed legislation to make clear that its provisions would not be applicable to futures trading in foreign currencies or other financial transactions . . . other than on organized exchanges." Congress addressed the Treasury Department's concerns, in part, by including a qualifier to "all services, rights and interests." With the qualifier, the term "commodity" only included "services, rights and interests" if "contracts for future delivery are presently or in the future dealt in [such services, rights or interests]."[30]

---

[30]   7 BROMBERG & LOWENFELS ON SECURITIES FRAUD § 24:7 (2d ed.).

THOUGHT QUESTION

With this analysis in mind, do you agree with the court in *My Big Coin Pay*? Why or why not?

6. THE CFTC'S AUTHORITY TO REACH FRAUD NOT INVOLVING MANIPULATION

Recall *CFTC v. Monex Credit Company*, 311 F. Supp. 3d 1173 (D.Cal. 2018), *rev'd*, 931 F.3d 966 (9th Cir. 2019), from chapter eleven. That case involved the argument, in the context of alleged misconduct by a precious metals trader, that the CFTC did not have authority to assert fraud claims in the absence of market manipulation. This argument initially succeeded, although the trial court's ruling in *Monex* was eventually overturned by the Ninth Circuit.

McDonnell, proceeding pro se, did not raise this argument at first, but it was brought up in a subsequent motion for reconsideration. An excerpt from the court's rejection of McDonnell's request for reconsideration appears below:

CFTC v. McDONNELL

321 F. Supp. 3d 366 (E.D.N.Y. 2018)

JACK B. WEINSTEIN, SENIOR UNITED STATES DISTRICT JUDGE:

Defendant's motion to reconsider . . . challenges the court's ruling that the Commodity Futures Trading Commission ("CFTC")'s broad statutory authority, Title 7 U.S.C. § 9(1), and regulatory authority, Title 17 C.F.R. § 180.1, extends to fraud in derivatives markets and underlying spot markets.

. . . .

Defendant's motion is procedurally deficient. The decision relied upon by the defendant, *Commodity Futures Trading Comm'n v. Monex Credit Co.*, No. SACV 17–01868 JVS, 2018 WL 2306863 (C.D. Cal. May 1, 2018), is not binding authority that mandates reconsideration. Local Civil Rule 6.3 (memorandum accompanying notice of motion must set "forth concisely the matters or *controlling decisions* which counsel believes the court has overlooked.") (emphasis added); *see also Shrader v. CSX Transp., Inc.*, 70 F.3d 255, 257 (2d Cir. 1995) ("The standard for granting such a motion is strict, and reconsideration will generally be denied unless the moving party can point to controlling decisions or data that the court overlooked—matters, in other words, that might reasonably be expected to alter the conclusion reached by the court."); *Nielsen v. New York City Dep't of Educ.*, No. 04–CV–2182 (NGG), 2007 WL 2743678, at *1 (E.D.N.Y. 2007) ("The applicable standard is strict in order to dissuade repetitive arguments on issues that have already been considered fully by the court."). Defendant's motion is also untimely. *See* Local Civil Rule 6.3 ("A notice of motion for reconsideration or reargument of a court order determining a motion shall be served within fourteen (14) days after the entry of the court's determination of the original motion . . .").

Notwithstanding these procedural defects, the court has given consideration to the substance of defendant's motion for reconsideration.

. . . .

[D]efendant, relying on *Monex*, argues that the action should be dismissed because it is absent any claims specifying "fraud-based manipulation." The district court in *Monex* found that Title 7 U.S.C. § 9(1) only protects against fraud where "a particular commodity transaction manipulates or potentially manipulates the derivatives market." *Monex* took note of this court's Order and distinguished it based on non-substantive grounds.

This court has fully considered *Monex* and reaches a different conclusion. The court reaffirms its view that Title 7 U.S.C. § 9(1) gives the CFTC standing to exercise its enforcement power over the fraudulent schemes alleged in the complaint. *Commodity Futures Trading Comm'n v. McDonnell,* 287 F.Supp.3d 213, 229 (E.D.N.Y. 2018) ("Language in 7 U.S.C. § 9(1), and 17 C.F.R. § 180.1, establish the CFTC's regulatory authority over the manipulative schemes, fraud, and misleading statements alleged in the complaint.").

. . . .

On reconsideration, defendant's motion to dismiss is denied.

SO ORDERED.

NOTES AND QUESTIONS

1.   While there are very few cases involving crypto, there are other CFTC enforcement actions recognizing the authority of the CFTC to react to fraud not involving manipulation. *See, for example, CFTC v. Hunter Wise Commodities, LLC,* 21 F.Supp.3d 1317, 1348 (S.D. Fla. 2014) (finding defendants liable for violating Section 6(c)(1) and Regulation 180.1 in a fraud case not involving allegations of market manipulation).

2.   Not much has been written on the topic of whether there is a viable argument to be made that some crypto should be outside the scope of the CEA even if Bitcoin is appropriately regulated by the CFTC. For more extended discussions of the issue, consider *Virtual Currencies as Commodities,* 7 BROMBERG & LOWENFELS ON SECURITIES FRAUD § 24:6 (2d ed.), or Nicholas Fusco, *Financial Regulation—Regulating A New Sector: How Should Regulatory Agencies Classify and Regulate Virtual Currencies?—Commodity*

Futures Trading Comm'n ("CFTC") v. McDonnell et al., 287 F. Supp. 3d 213 (E.D.N.Y. 2018), 24 SUFFOLK J. TRIAL & APP. ADVOC. 136 (2019).

The preceding discussion raises four distinct issues:

(1) To what extent does the CFTC have authority to regulate crypto as a commodity?

(2) Do the Dodd-Frank Act amendments to the CEA authorize the CFTC to address fraud that does not directly involve the sale of futures or derivative contracts?

(3) In order for the CFTC to have jurisdiction, must the fraud claim involve market manipulation?

(4) Is the CFTC's jurisdiction over fraud in the spot market for crypto limited to assets that trade in the futures or derivatives markets?

To date, the CFTC has prevailed in most of the actions that it has brought. Losses in the trial courts have been over-ruled, and the CFTC's right to proceed against defendants involved in crypto transactions has generally been upheld.

CHAPTER 13

INNOVATION IN THE CRYPTO ECOSYSTEM

■ ■ ■

In the relatively short time since the advent of Bitcoin and blockchain technology, there have been a number of changes in the nascent crypto industry. The world has seen an incredible proliferation of coins and tokens, changes in the regulatory structures and rules applicable to crypto, an evolving response from industry lawyers, changes in entrepreneurial practices, and heightened international scrutiny. We have also seen the tentative involvement of very big business not just with blockchain initiatives, but into the cryptoasset sphere as well.

This material considers a handful of these changes in order to demonstrate how rapidly crypto is evolving, first from a technological standpoint. Perhaps more importantly for these materials, it also illustrates the responsiveness of various governmental agencies to this kind of innovation. Finally, it may also suggest directions for future change, particularly with regard to regulatory developments.

Because the field is changing so rapidly, it is virtually certain that by the time you are reading these materials, crypto-focused headlines will be talking about other new developments, and many of these issues discussed in this chapter will seem passé. Still, it is useful to reflect on just how quickly changes are occurring.

1. PRIVACY COINS—PROS AND CONS

Privacy is intimately connected with cryptoassets. Anonymity and privacy were central ideas behind the creation of Bitcoin, and even the identity of Satoshi Nakamoto was so successfully concealed that it is still unknown. Privacy concerns continue to be a focus of many within the crypto community. However, the earliest efforts at privacy were imperfect, at least from the perspective of users' anonymity. "While blockchain-based cryptocurrencies like Bitcoin do not directly reveal users' identities, they are often prone to deanonymization attacks. By observing the flow of transactions stored in the public blockchain, third parties can make accurate guesses about the identities of involved individuals."[1]

---

[1]   Daniel Genkin, et al., *Privacy in Decentralized Cryptocurrencies,* 61 COMMUNICATIONS OF THE ACM 78 (June 2018) (quote from Key Insights in text) (available online at https://cacm. acm.org/magazines/2018/6/228028-privacy-in-decentralized-cryptocurrencies/fulltext).

Enter the so-called "privacy coins," cryptoassets specifically designed to more completely hide a user's identity from third parties. As one pundit explained in the course of distinguishing these assets from traditional crypto like Bitcoin, Ethereum, and Litecoin, "[w]ith privacy coins, for example, users have complete anonymity, and there is no way for regulators or law enforcement officials to track the flow of these coins."[2]

Privacy coins can work in a variety of ways. Monero, often touted as one of the best privacy coins,[3] "is cryptographically private by default, utilizing several privacy features—most prominently being stealth addresses and ring confidential transactions (RingCT)."[4] Stealth addresses are random, one-time addresses that are created automatically for each transaction. RingCT is a cryptographic tool that hides the amounts involved in a transaction while still allowing for network verification. Monero also continues to work on additional privacy improvements, including a recently added router project known as Kovri,[5] which as of mid-2019 was in "heavy, active development," according to Monero's website.[6]

Dash is also often listed as a top privacy coin.[7] Dash was originally called "DarkCoin," and it specifically sought to increase anonymity of blockchain transactions. It later switched its focus, and now offers privacy as an elective feature, with "PrivateSend," which resembles Monero's RingCT.[8] Another source has explained that Dash uses mixing to

---

[2]   Nicole Lindsey, *Bans on Privacy Coins Could Have Important Implications for the Future of Privacy*, CPO MAGAZINE (Ap. 2, 2019) (available online at https://www.cpomagazine.com/data-privacy/bans-on-privacy-coins-could-have-important-implications-for-the-future-of-privacy/). This source provides an excellent background on various privacy coins and is referred to in this chapter as "*Bans on Privacy Coins.*"

[3]   "Best" in this context means among the most private, with adequate functionality evidenced by decentralization and fungibility. Monero is listed as the number one privacy coin by a number of sources. *10 Best Privacy Coins In 2019*, COINSWITCH (Mar. 18, 2019) (available online at https://coinswitch.co/news/10-best-privacy-coins-in-2019-latest-review) ("most popular"); Chris Grundy, *Compared: The Best Privacy Coins in Crypto.* THE COIN OFFERING (Mar. 2, 2019) (available online at https://thecoinoffering.com/learn/best-privacy-cryptocurrency/) ("most well-known"). It does not mean best from a moral standpoint, as "privacy coins like Monero have a distinctly unsavory reputation, even among cryptocurrency fans." *Bans on Privacy Coins, supra* note 2. Monero is often associated with malware and other illegal activities. One particularly high-profile case involved the richest man in Norway being forced to pay a $10 million Monero ransom to recover his wife after she was kidnapped. *Id.*

[4]   Aziz, *Guide on Privacy Coins: Comparison of Anonymous Cryptocurrencies*, MASTERTHECRYPTO (available online at https://masterthecrypto.com/privacy-coins-anonymous-cryptocurrencies/).

[5]   This is described by Chris Grundy, cited *supra* at note 3 and is mentioned as being in development by Aziz, *supra* note 4.

[6]   *Moneropedia, Kovri*, MONERO (as of August 15, 2019, this information was available online at https://www.getmonero.org/resources/moneropedia/kovri.html).

[7]   COINSWITCH, *supra* note 3 ("one of the best"); listed second by Chris Grundy, *supra* note 3.

[8]   Chris Grundy, *supra* note 3.

anonymize Bitcoins, in a way that requires users to trust "masternodes" to expedite the mixing process.[9]

Zcash (ZEC) has been characterized as a "strong contender for one of the best privacy coins 2019."[10] Like Dash, its privacy features are optional.

Zcash uses a new method of cryptographic privacy called "zk-SNARKs" (zero-knowledge Succinct Non-Interactive Argument of Knowledge). At the basic level, zero-knowledge proofs allow for a way to prove that the information you are sending to the other party (e.g. the amount of funds) is true, without having to broadcast said information besides the fact that it is true.[11]

A lesser known alternative privacy coin is Verge (XCG), which was originally DogeCoinDark. This privacy coin relies on the Tor Onion Router (an IP obfuscation service) to provide users with privacy.[12] It is also touted for using "an innovative Wraith Protocol technology—that allows users to switch between private and public transactions."[13]

There are of course other privacy coins, which may generally be understood as any cryptocurrency that is explicitly designed to hide data about "the identity of the user along with the amount of cryptocurrency traded and held in wallets."[14] Cryptoslate lists Privacy Coins separately from other cryptocurrencies, identifying 54 distinct alternatives.[15]

The potential benefit of privacy coins is obvious; they protect (in one way or another, and to varying extents) private financial information about users. However, they are also subject to use and abuse by criminals. The very features that make privacy coins desirable to users with legitimate privacy concerns also make the same coins attractive to criminals, who may use these coins to conduct illegal transactions, to launder funds, and to fund criminal enterprises including terrorism.

The problem of criminal utilization of privacy coins is a global issue. Even countries that have worked to be seen as pro-crypto, including Japan and France, are explicitly taking or considering actions in response to the problems posed by privacy coins. "Japan, for example, has instituted a ban on all privacy coins (such as Monero and Zcash) . . . while France is currently mulling over a proposal to enact a total ban on holding or using

---

[9]   Aziz, *supra* note 4.

[10]   COINSWITCH, *supra* note 3.

[11]   Aziz, *supra* note 4. A much more detailed explanation is available on the Zcash website. Zcash, *What are zk-SNARKs?* (available online at https://z.cash/technology/zksnarks/).

[12]   Chris Grundy, *supra* note 3.

[13]   COINSWITCH, *supra* note 3.

[14]   COINSWITCH, *supra* note 3.

[15]   Cryptoslate, *Privacy Cryptocurrencies*, available online at https://cryptoslate.com/cryptos/privacy/ (last accessed June 2019). Cryptoslate is a business that provides online blockchain news, cryptocurrencies prices, product databases, and notice of FinTech events. Cryptoslate *FAQ*, https://cryptoslate.com/faq/ (last accessed June 2019).

privacy coins."[16] Japan's rules are overseen by a self-regulatory body composed of the country's registered cryptocurrency exchanges. It has reportedly created 100 pages of rules and regulations that, among other things, include "prohibiting exchanges from accepting new coins that 'cannot be traced to previous sellers'—also known as privacy coins like Monero and Dash."[17] These rules were proposed following a substantial push from Japan's Financial Services Agency urging domestic exchanges to drop support for privacy coins, because of "their potential for abuse in money laundering."[18] France is somewhat behind Japan (whose rules went into effect in June 2019), having proposed a total ban on privacy coins in early 2019.[19] As of August 2019, there is no specific indication of what kinds of coins would be within France's ban, if it is enacted.

In the United States, of the agencies that this book focuses on, it is FinCEN that would be especially concerned with the potential impact of privacy coins. FinCEN is, however, not alone in its concern about the use of privacy coins to facilitate criminal activities. In late 2018, the Department of Homeland Security issued a pre-solicitation document through its Small Business Innovation Research Program focused on "finding a way to conduct forensic analysis on privacy-focused coins if they are used for criminal activity."[20] Having bolstered its ability to trace blockchain transactions, including those in Bitcoin, back to the source and to identify users (such as wallet holders), the U.S. government is now interested in preventing privacy coins from being used to "facilitate money laundering by rogue countries, terrorist organizations, and cybercriminals."[21]

In May 2019, FinCEN issued new guidance on Convertible Virtual Currencies (CVC), which specifically addresses privacy coins. An excerpt from that document appears below.

PRELIMINARY NOTES AND QUESTIONS

1.   Why does the U.S. not simply ban privacy coins, since other countries have taken that action? Couldn't FinCEN prohibit financial institutions that

---

[16]   *Bans on Privacy Coins, supra* note 2.

[17]   Samburaj Das, *Japan's Crypto Industry Drafts Rules to Ban Insider Trading, Privacy Coins*, CCN (June 6, 2018) (available online at https://www.ccn.com/japans-crypto-industry-drafts-rules-to-ban-insider-trading-privacy-coins/).

[18]   *Id.*

[19]   Arnab Shome, *French Finance Committee Recommends to Ban Privacy Coins*, FINANCE MAGNATES (Mar. 7, 2019) (available online at https://www.financemagnates.com/cryptocurrency/news/french-finance-committee-recommends-to-ban-privacy-coins/).

[20]   Nikhilesh De, *US Government Interested in Tracking Privacy Coins, New Document Shows*, COINDESK (Dec. 3, 2018) (available online at https://www.coindesk.com/us-homeland-security-is-interested-in-tracking-privacy-coins).

[21]   Tony Spilotro, *US Government Aims to Make Privacy Coins' Use Case Obsolete*, NEWS BTC (2018) (available online at https://www.newsbtc.com/2018/12/04/us-government-aims-to-make-privacy-coins-use-case-obsolete/).

it regulates, including crypto exchanges and trading platforms as well as wallet services that act as intermediaries, from trading in privacy coins? Could the SEC prohibit brokers and dealers from purchasing or assisting in the trading of privacy coins? Would this be a more effective approach than that suggested below?

2.   How does FinCEN regulation to minimize potential problems that could be created by privacy coins? Do you believe this is likely to be an effective approach? Is it better than banning privacy coins, or simply more politically expedient?

FINCEN GUIDANCE, *APPLICATION OF FINCEN'S REGULATIONS TO CERTAIN BUSINESS MODELS INVOLVING CONVERTIBLE VIRTUAL CURRENCIES*

FIN–20190G001 (May 9, 2019)
("2019 Guidance")[22]

The Financial Crimes Enforcement Network (FinCEN) is issuing this interpretive guidance to remind persons subject to the Bank Secrecy Act (BSA) how FinCEN regulations relating to money services businesses (MSBs) apply to certain business models involving money transmission denominated in value that substitutes for currency, specifically, convertible virtual currencies (CVCs).

This guidance does not establish any new regulatory expectations or requirements. Rather, it consolidates current FinCEN regulations, and related administrative rulings and guidance issued since 2011, and then applies these rules and interpretations to other common business models involving CVC engaging in the same underlying patterns of activity.

. . . .

4.5. Anonymity-Enhanced CVC Transactions

Anonymity-enhanced CVC transactions are transactions either (a) denominated in regular types of CVC, but structured to conceal information otherwise generally available through the CVC's native distributed public ledger; or (b) denominated in types of CVC specifically engineered to prevent their tracing through distributed public ledgers (also called privacy coins).

A money transmitter that operates in anonymity-enhanced CVCs for its own account or for the accounts of others (regardless of the frequency) is subject to the same regulatory obligations as when operating in currency, funds, or nonanonymized CVCs. In other words, a money transmitter cannot avoid its regulatory obligations because it chooses to provide money transmission services using anonymity-enhanced CVC. The regulatory framework that applies to a person participating in anonymity-enhanced

---

[22]   The entire document is archived at https://perma.cc/P4VL-NY9A.

CVC transactions depends on the specific role performed by the person, as set forth below in Section 4.5.1.

4.5.1.   Providers of anonymizing services for CVCs

Providers of anonymizing services, commonly referred to as "mixers" or "tumblers," are either persons that accept CVCs and retransmit them in a manner designed to prevent others from tracing the transmission back to its source (anonymizing services provider), or suppliers of software a transmittor would use for the same purpose (anonymizing software provider).

4.5.1(a) Anonymizing services provider

An anonymizing services provider is a money transmitter under FinCEN regulations. The added feature of concealing the source of the transaction does not change that person's status under the BSA.

FinCEN previously issued a regulatory interpretation that concluded that persons who accept and transmit value in a way ostensibly designed to protect the privacy of the transmittor are providers of secure money transmission services and are not eligible for the integral exemption.[59] In order to be exempt from status as a money transmitter under the integral exemption, the person's business must be different from money transmission itself, and the money transmission activity must be necessary for the business to operate. The subject of this previous regulatory interpretation accepted and transmitted funds in a way designed to protect a consumer's personal and financial information from a merchant, when the consumer purchased goods or services through the Internet. FinCEN determined that the added feature of protecting consumers' information did not constitute an activity separate from the funds transmission itself, because the need to protect the consumers' personal and financial information only arose in connection with the transmission of funds. FinCEN concluded that the company was engaged in the business of offering secure money transmission, rather than security for which money transmission is integrally required. Accordingly, the company qualified as a money transmitter subject to BSA obligations.

The same analysis applies to anonymizing services providers: their business consists exclusively of providing secured money transmission. Therefore, a person (acting by itself, through employees or agents, or by using mechanical or software agencies) who provides anonymizing services by accepting value from a customer and transmitting the same or another

---

[59]   *See* FIN–2008–R007, *"Whether a Certain Operation Protecting On-line Personal Financial Information is a Money Transmitter,"* Jun. 11, 2008. For a different business model, see FIN–2014–R006, "Whether a Company that Provides Online Real-Time Deposit, Settlement, and Payment Services for Banks, Businesses and Consumers is a Money Transmitter," Apr. 29, 2014. [Author's note: This source is archived at https://perma.cc/S6LR-PDQB.]

type of value to the recipient, in a way designed to mask the identity of the transmittor, is a money transmitter under FinCEN regulations.

4.5.1(b) Anonymizing software provider

An anonymizing software provider is not a money transmitter. FinCEN regulations exempt from the definition of money transmitter those persons providing "the delivery, communication, or network access services used by a money transmitter to support money transmission services." This is because suppliers of tools (communications, hardware, or software) that may be utilized in money transmission, like anonymizing software, are engaged in trade and not money transmission.

By contrast, a person that utilizes the software to anonymize the person's own transactions will be either a user or a money transmitter, depending on the purpose of each transaction. For example, a user would employ the software when paying for goods or services on its own behalf, while a money transmitter would use it to engage as a business in the acceptance and transmission of value as a transmittor's or intermediary's financial institution.

Lastly, FinCEN issued guidance stating that originating or intermediary financial institutions that replace the proper identity of a transmittor or recipient in the transmittal order with a pseudonym or reference that may not be decoded by the receiving financial institution (i.e., substituting the full name of the transmittor with a numeric code) are not complying with their obligations under the Funds Travel Rule.[61]

4.5.2.　Providers of anonymity-enhanced CVCs

A person that creates or sells anonymity-enhanced CVCs designed to prevent their tracing through publicly visible ledgers would be a money transmitter under FinCEN regulations depending on the type of payment system and the person's activity. For example:

(a) a person operating as the administrator of a centralized CVC payment system will become a money transmitter the moment that person issues anonymity enhanced CVC against the receipt of another type of value;

(b) a person that uses anonymity-enhanced CVCs to pay for goods or services on his or her own behalf would not be a money transmitter under the BSA. However, if the person uses the CVC to accept and transmit value from one person

---

61　[Author's note: Funds Travel Regulations were explained by FinCEN in guidance issued November 9, 2010. This document sets out the kinds of information that must be provided by financial institutions upon the transmittal of funds (including intermediary institutions as well as those that transmit and receive funds for another).] FinCEN Guidance, *"Funds "Travel" Regulations: Questions & Answers,"* FIN–2010–G004, at Question 16 (Nov. 09, 2010) [archived at https://perma.cc/68KS-Q7H5].

to another person or location, the person will fall under the definition of money transmitter, if not otherwise exempted.

(c) a person that develops a decentralized CVC payment system will become a money transmitter if that person also engages as a business in the acceptance and transmission of value denominated in the CVC it developed (even if the CVC value was mined at an earlier date). The person would not be a money transmitter if that person uses the CVC it mined to pay for goods and services on his or her own behalf.

4.5.3. Money Transmitters that accept or transmit anonymity-enhanced CVCs

Many money transmitters involved in CVC transactions comply with their BSA obligations, in part, by incorporating procedures into their AML Programs that allow them to track and monitor the transaction history of a CVC through publicly visible ledgers.

As mentioned above, FinCEN has issued guidance stating that transmittor's or intermediary's financial institutions that replace the proper identity of a transmittor or recipient in the transmittal order with a pseudonym or reference that may not be decoded by the receiving financial institution (i.e., substituting the full name of the transmittor with a numeric code) are not complying with their obligations under the Funds Travel Rule. A money transmitter must follow its AML risk assessment policies and procedures to determine under which circumstances the money transmitter will accept or transmit value already denominated in anonymity-enhanced CVCs. When knowingly accepting anonymity-enhanced CVCs (or regular CVC that has been anonymized), money transmitters engaged in CVC transactions subject to the Funds Travel Rule must not only track a CVC through the different transactions, but must also implement procedures to obtain the identity of the transmittor or recipient of the value.

. . . .

NOTES AND QUESTIONS

1.   How can a money transmitter accept a privacy coin and still comply with these requirements? Is there still a use for privacy coins under these rules, or is this essentially the same as banning them from use in the U.S.?

2.   Tor services are often used by developers of privacy coins. Under the 2019 Guidance, is Tor liable if issuers, developers, and exchanges create or accept coins that use Tor onion routing to evade the requirements of the BSA? Why or why not? What would Tor be treated as under this Guidance?

3.   If I buy Monero, precisely because I do not want my identity to be known, am I subject to BSA reporting obligations? Do I become subject to those

reporting obligations if I use my Monero to buy goods or services? What am I classified as under the 2019 Guidance?

Although it is the focus of the preceding excerpt, only a small part of the 2019 Guidance refers to "Anonymity-Enhanced CVC Transactions." Nonetheless, FinCEN's is obviously concerned about the role that privacy coins might play in money laundering and funding of criminal activities.[23] Although the details are substantially more complicated, as the preceding excerpt indicates, the essence of the rules for privacy coins is that "a money transmitter cannot avoid its regulatory obligations because it chooses to provide money transmission services using anonymity-enhanced CVC."[24] As noted in chapter six, once a business is a non-exempt money transmitter, it must register with FinCEN within 180 days of beginning such operations.[25] In addition, as noted in the 2019 Guidance, it must develop, implement, and maintain an effective, risk-based AML program "reasonably designed to prevent [the business] . . . from being used to facilitate money laundering and the financing of terrorist activities."[26]

In the case of persons creating or selling this kind of CVC, they are immediately subject to FinCEN regulations governing money transmitters if they operate as administrators of a centralized CVC payment system.[27] In the case of a decentralized CVC payment system, it becomes a money transmitter if it also "engages as a business in the acceptance and transmission of value denominated in the CVC it developed (even if the CVC value was mined at an earlier date)."[28]

Persons conducting ICOs are similarly likely to be subject to FinCEN requirements (absent an available exemption) if they conduct an ICO pursuant to which CVC is issued to a preferred group of early investors in exchange for another type of value, either instantaneously or on a deferred basis. The CVC may be functional or still in development. Future issuance may be through mining rather than through a direct sale to investors. According to the 2019 Guidance, "[i]n any of these scenarios, the seller of the CVC is a money transmitter, acting in the role of administrator, because at the time of issuance the seller is the only person authorized to issue and redeem (permanently retire from circulation) the new units of CVC."[29] At a minimum this requires the business to verify customer

---

[23]   2019 Guidance at § 4.5, p. 18. The classification applies since so-called privacy coins are "specifically engineered to prevent their tracing through distributed public ledgers."

[24]   *Id.* at p. 19.

[25]   31 CFR § 1022.380

[26]   2019 Guidance, § 2.1 at p. 10.

[27]   *Id.* at § 4.5.2 at p. 20.

[28]   *Id.* at § 4.5.2 at p. 21.

[29]   *Id.* at § 5.2 at p. 25.

identification, file reports, maintain records, and cooperate with law enforcement.[30]

In sum, this guidance clarifies that for the most part, persons operating in the U.S. may legally assist in the issuance, exchange, or administration of privacy coins only to the extent that privacy protocols are elective and are not being utilized. Otherwise, a transaction where the intermediary acting as the money transmitter cannot identify the actual user will not be in compliance with FinCEN requirements.

While these limitations are significant, they fall short of an outright ban. For example, they do not prohibit the ownership of privacy coins, or the use of them to buy goods and services for personal use.[31] In addition, offshore intermediaries with no assets in the territorial United States are not necessarily affected by these rules. Unless prohibited by the laws of the nation where the business is located, these third parties may be providing such services without AML, KYC, or ATF procedures in place. Additional international coordination and cooperation is therefore necessary, and likely to be forthcoming, to minimize the risks posed by privacy coins.[32] The cost of this coordination will, inevitably, be the loss of some degree of privacy and anonymity.

2. EARLY INNOVATION—THE SAFT

While privacy coins made a relatively early appearance in the crypto world, with many of such coins dating back to 2014, it took longer for the SAFT project to take off.[33] As you may recall from earlier readings, the SAFT was a project designed to provide simple documentation that could be used to assist companies in raising funds to develop functional cryptotokens with an anticipated functionality beyond serving as an alternative to fiat currency. By 2015, it was already becoming increasingly clear that U.S. regulators, and particularly the SEC, were not going to take a hands-off approach to crypto. The SAFT was therefore designed to promote the funding and development of these new assets in a manner that

---

[30]   *Id.*

[31]   2019 Guidance, § 5.3 at p. 27. Thus, for example, "[t]o the extent that a person mines CVC and uses it solely to purchase goods or services on its own behalf, the person is not an MSB under FinCEN regulations, because these activities involve neither acceptance nor transmission of the CVC within the regulatory definition of money transmission services." *Id.*

[32]   In June 2019, the Paris-based Financial Action Task Force (FATF), a coalition of countries including the United States, reacted to growing use of crypto to launder money from criminal enterprises by telling countries to tighten oversight of virtual asset service providers including cryptocurrency exchanges. *See* Anna Baydakova, Nikhilesh De, *All Global Crypto Exchanges Must Now Share Customer Data, FATF Rules*, COINDESK (June 21, 2019) (available online at https://www.coindesk.com/fatf-crypto-travel-rule). *See also* John O'Donnell, *Money-laundering Watchdog to Clamp Down on Cryptocurrencies*, REUTERS (June 21, 2019) (available online at https://www.reuters.com/article/moneylaundering-crypto-fatf/money-laundering-watchdog-to-clamp-down-on-cryptocurrencies-idUSL4N23Q3KO).

[33]   The SAFT was introduced back in chapter 8.

was intended to comply with the federal securities laws. In addition, it set out a framework that the drafters clearly hoped would convince securities regulators to treat functional utility tokens (as defined in the SAFT whitepaper) as being outside the scope of the federal securities laws.

The following excerpt from the SAFT whitepaper includes that document's abstract (which was not included in the chapter eight excerpt), and focuses on how the whitepaper authors believed the securities laws should apply to cryptoassets.

PRELIMINARY NOTES AND QUESTIONS

1.   What is the SAFT process, and how is it designed to work? When would a token developer rely on this process? What steps would the developer have to take? What kinds of tokens have to be involved?

2.   What part of the process would involve the sale of a security?

3.   If part of the deal still has to comply with the securities laws, what are the supposed advantages of this process?

THE SAFT PROJECT: TOWARD A COMPLIANT TOKEN SALE FRAMEWORK

Juan Batiz-Benet, Jesse Clayburgh, & Marco Santori (October 2, 2017)[34]

Abstract: Blockchain protocol tokens, or simply "tokens" are digital assets used in connection with decentralized services, applications, and communities (collectively, "token networks"). As of this writing, dozens of such networks are in use world-wide, with many more in development. Bitcoin and Ethereum are the most notable examples. Token networks may bring about positive paradigm shifts to computing, finance, law, government, and more. Tokens leverage computation and cryptography to represent consumptive goods (known as "utility tokens") or replacements for traditional investments (known as "securities tokens").

The public token sale, colloquially known as an "Initial Coin Offering," is a powerful new tool for creating decentralized communities, kickstarting network effects, incentivizing participants, providing faster liquidity to investors, and forming capital for creators. In these sales, network creators sell an amount of the network's tokens at a discount to users, investors, or both. Some token sales take place when or after the token network is launched, as a means to disseminate some fraction of the token supply to

---

[34]   Author's note: This document is available online at https://www.cooley.com/~/media/ cooley/pdf/reprints/saft-project-whitepaper.ashx and archived at https://perma.cc/XDP4-MQU5. It is reprinted with permission of Cooley LLP. The original SAFT whitepaper contains this explicit disclaimer: "This document does not constitute legal advice and should not be relied on by any person. It is designed for general informational purposes only. Developers, purchasers, investors and any other participant in a token system should consult their own counsel." The whitepaper and documentation represents the then-current thinking as influenced by Cooley LLP, Protocol Labs, various token creators, other legal experts, and investors.

early users. Other token sales happen long before the token network has genuine functionality; so called "direct token pre-sales" are sold at greater discounts with the goal of financing the development of the network and its launch.

Purchasers in these direct presales tend to expect profit predominantly from the seller's efforts to create functionality in the token. As such, these sellers may unintentionally be selling securities, and may have failed to comply with several U.S. laws.

We propose a path toward a new, compliant framework called the Simple Agreement for Future Tokens, or "SAFT". Together with the publication of this paper, we launch the SAFT Project—a forum for discussion and development of the SAFT framework.

The SAFT is an investment contract. A SAFT transaction contemplates an initial sale of a SAFT by developers to accredited investors. The SAFT obligates investors to immediately fund the developers. In exchange, the developers use the funds to develop genuinely functional network, with genuinely functional utility tokens, and then deliver those tokens to the investors once functional. The investors may then resell the tokens to the public, presumably for a profit, and so may the developers.

The SAFT is a security. It demands compliance with the securities laws. The resulting tokens, however, are already functional, and need not be securities under the *Howey* test. They are consumptive products and, as such, demand compliance with state and federal consumer protection laws.

To be sure, public purchasers may still be profit-motivated when they buy a post-SAFT utility token. Unlike a pre-functional token, though, whose market value is determined predominantly by the efforts of the sellers in imbuing the tokens with functionality, a genuinely functional token's value is determined by a variety of market factors, the aggregate impact of which likely predominates the "efforts of others." Sellers of already functional tokens have likely already expended the "essential" managerial efforts that might otherwise satisfy the *Howey* test.

Beyond the securities laws, the SAFT framework elegantly navigates the money services and tax laws, and addresses the significant policy concerns with the direct token presale alternative.

. . . .

Introduction to Token Sales

We believe, without overstatement, that token-based networks hold the potential to create value on an order of magnitude similar to that of the internet. The token sale plays a critical role in unlocking the value inherent in these networks. Sellers, investors, and users alike could stand to gain tremendously from this innovation if it is broadly adopted. For developers, a token sale could jump-start network effects at the earliest and most vital stages of a software project's development. For investors, tokens mean earlier liquidity and broader investment cases. Users likely stand to benefit the most inasmuch as they may participate directly in the creation and growth of the value of a network. Critically: If executed as set forth in this whitepaper, a token sale can permit users to participate financially in that creation and growth without taking on significant enterprise risk.

Because tokens transform open networks into open markets, all participants can benefit from a liquid, transparent, middleman-optional secondary market for anything that can be digitized. On-chain transactions make systemic market risks more transparent to analysts and regulators. Add to that near instant settlement times, immutable transaction records, network resiliency, and all the other benefits of underlying blockchain architecture.

. . . .

There are two categories of tokens in circulation today that are relevant to this discussion. The first kind of token is meant to serve simply as a highly-liquid substitute for a traditional security like corporate stock, a limited partnership interest, and the like. . . . This whitepaper does not discuss securities tokens in detail.

Instead, we focus on so-called "utility tokens." This category of blockchain tokens contains assets that do not purport to replace legacy financial services products. They are designed to offer intrinsic utility that powers a decentralized, distributed network that delivers to the users of the network a consumptive good or service. For example, when their networks are functional, some tokens will act as currencies, like bitcoins do. Some will act as staking or betting mechanisms, membership rights, or loan collateral. Some will simply act as cryptographic "coupons" redeemable for mundane goods and services like bags of ground coffee or boxes of razor blades.

. . . .

[The whitepaper then explains the context of the federal securities laws, and the *Howey* test in general. After concluding that most token sales will involve the investment of something of value in a common enterprise, the document then focuses on the expectation of profits from the efforts of others elements of *Howey*.]

Expectation of Profits

An expectation of profit generally means expected capital appreciation resulting from the development of the initial investment or expected participation in earnings resulting from the use of investor funds. There can be such an expectation where expected profits "come primarily from the discount below the current price" of a commodity. There is no expectation of profit where a purchaser is motivated primarily by the desire to use or consume the item purchased.

    . . . .

From the Efforts of Others

Assuming the purchaser's expectation of profit predominates any consumptive motive, this prong considers the source of that expectation. It asks "whether the efforts made by those other than the investor are the undeniably significant ones, those essential managerial efforts which affect the failure or success of the enterprise." An analysis of this prong in the token sale context requires a deep understanding of the rights, powers (and, sometimes, obligations) attendant to the token in question. Sadly, this prong and the prior prong are often conflated or collapsed into one another. We take up this issue in the following sections, through the lens of token functionality.

Already-functional Utility Tokens Are Unlikely to Pass the *Howey* Test

Sellers of already-functional utility tokens have very strong arguments against characterization as a security: Such tokens rarely satisfy both the "expectation of profits" and "from the efforts of others" prongs of the *Howey* test.

Generally speaking, there are two categories of purchasers of already-functional utility tokens. First, there are purchasers who buy tokens to actually use them—as network fees, membership coupons, valuestaking mechanisms, currencies, etc. Their consumptive desires predominate their profit-seeking motives. Second, there are purchasers who buy a token expecting to profit merely from resale on a secondary market. These purchasers might have an "expectation of profit" under *Howey*, but it is usually not predominantly "from the efforts of others." Sales to purchasers in both of these two categories fail the *Howey* test.

The first category is self-evident. A profit motive simply does not predominate the transaction. The second category is more controversial. Critics of sales in this category might argue that the expectation of profit from resale on a secondary market is just speculative activity seeking capital appreciation. These critics might cite myriad federal court decisions holding that an expectation of mere "capital appreciation" on a secondary market, is sufficient to satisfy the *Howey* test.

This oft-repeated criticism does not stand up to scrutiny. At heart, the criticism collapses the "efforts of others" prong into the "expectation of profit" prong. It does so by relying on decisions which do not actually turn on the secondary market appreciation issue, and do not analyze it in much depth. Decisions that do so repeatedly hold that an expectation of profit from the mere increase in value on a secondary market is not from the "efforts of others." [Discussion of caselaw omitted.]

Because there is no central authority to exert "monetary policy," the secondary market price of a decentralized token system is driven exclusively by supply and demand. Supply and demand can be due to a variety of factors. One of those factors could be the efforts of the development team creating the token's functionality; but once that functionality is created, any "essential" efforts have by definition already been applied. It would be difficult to argue that any improvement on an already-functional token is an "essential" managerial effort.

Furthermore, the market effect of a mere improvement on an already functional utility token is likely dwarfed by the multitude of other factors that act on it. . . . The forces that could affect supply and demand for a functional utility token are countless. Supply and demand for functional tokens are affected by a variety of forces that determine the price on a secondary market—just like demand for gold in the commodity cases. It is no coincidence that blockchain tokens have been referred to as "digital gold." For functional utility tokens, mere price appreciation on a secondary market is not a substitute for the essential managerial efforts of others.

Indeed, for the purposes of the *Howey* analysis, the secondary market itself is a red herring. When a token purchaser resells a token on an exchange platform for more than the purchase price, it is not the exchange platform that created the price difference.

. . . .

Thus, an already-functional utility token is less likely to be a security for two independent grounds. First, it is more likely that purchasers have bought them to use them (since, unlike pre-functional utility tokens, they can be used immediately to satisfy imminent needs). Second, purchasers who buy them with an eye toward profit upon resale can expect those profits to be determined by a variety of market factors that predominate the efforts of the seller in updating the token's functionality.

NOTES AND QUESTIONS

1. This document correctly predicts that the SEC would continue to use the *Howey* investment contract test to determine if a particular cryptoasset is a security. Nonetheless, the SEC appears to have taken issue with the whitepaper's suggestion that the eventual token called for in this process should not be a security. Can you figure out where the points of disagreement are between the SAFT proponents and the SEC?

2. Do you agree with the SEC that even functional utility tokens can be securities or do the SAFT proponents have the better argument on this point? When this issue makes it through the courts, who do you believe will ultimately prevail and why? Is this a desirable outcome?

It is difficult to know what the impact of the SAFT project was. Certainly, the SAFT does not dominate discussion of ICOs and token sales. However, an analysis of SEC filings undertaken in mid-2018 indicated that the number of filings relating to token sales involving the SAFT was at that time increasing, albeit not steadily.[35] According to this source, from August, 2017 to June 2018, the number of Regulation D[36] filings mentioning the SAFT in each month was as follows:

Month	Number of Reg. D filings (mentioning SAFT)
Aug. 2017	1
Sept. 2017	6
Oct. 2017	2
Nov. 2017	4
Dec. 2017	14
Jan. 2018	7
Feb. 2018	12
Mar. 2018	11
Apr. 2018	11
May. 2018	15
June 2018	10

Although most of the SAFT funds raised in this time frame were from U.S. Residents, citizens from Bermuda, Canada, the Cayman Islands, Estonia, Japan, Spain, and the U.K. also participated. Moreover, the issuers relying on the SAFT overwhelmingly chose Delaware as their state of formation, although organizations formed in a number of other nations also participated.

Professor Aaron Wright, director of the Cardozo Blockchain Project, published a report in November 2017, critiquing the SAFT approach. He suggested that the SAFT approach actually "increases the risk the Token will be treated as a Security and relies on a legal analysis that is not well

---

[35]   Muyao Shen, *Charts: SEC Data Shows Token Filing Figures Just Keep Rising*, COINDESK (Jul. 2, 2018) (available online at https://www.coindesk.com/charts-sec-data-shows-token-filing-figures-just-keep-rising).

[36]   Reg. D is one of the exemptions from registration for securities sales potentially available under the '33 Act. It is discussed *infra* in Part 3.B.5) of chapter 7. One of the prerequisites for the use of this exemption is the filing of a notice that the exemption has been claimed.

supported under US law."[37] The first concern that he articulated is the suggestion in the SAFT whitepaper that there are bright-line rules (such as the distinction between security and functional utility tokens) that apply in the context of the U.S. securities laws. Given recent SEC reactions to crypto sales, it is clear that no such dividing line exists. The second identified concern is the whitepaper's focus on investment. The report makes a compelling case that the focus on investment motives actually makes it more likely that the SEC would regard the underlying assets as securities. Third, Wright critiques what he calls a lack of "meaningful support under the law." This section accurately notes that the SEC has never stated that functionality of a token should be determinative of the token's classification as a security. Finally, the report notes that the approach advocated in the SAFT documentation could actively hurt consumers, something that the SEC is bound to consider when it looks at whether the securities laws should apply to particular transactions.

Notwithstanding such concerns, the SAFT has continued to be supported as a viable alternative by crypto-entrepreneurs.[38] Perhaps because of interest in the SAFT by issuers, the SEC has apparently been taking a close look at SAFT offerings. One commentator complained that "while many, unsurprisingly, believe the SEC is going after fraudulent issuers, recent reporting indicates the SEC may be working on a systematic investigation of projects working under the simple agreements for future tokens (SAFTs) framework."[39] The author of this comment cites an unnamed "knowledgeable source" as having reported candidly that "[t]he SEC is targeting SAFTs. The new approach of the SEC is to consider tokens as both utility and security at the same time, meaning a token can bring utility to a platform but at the same time can be considered as a security if you sold it to parties that mainly looked for profit on its increase in value."[40]

By the end of 2018, enthusiasm for the SAFT appeared to be waning. One report simply concludes that "SAFT sales have not found widespread use, despite initial optimism that such sales would represent a path for

---

[37]   Professor Wright is quoted in JD Alois, *Cardozo Blockchain Project Publishes New SAFT Approach for ICOs, Provides Regulatory Alternative for Nascent Token Market*, CROWD FUND INSIDER (Nov. 27, 2017) (available online at https://www.crowdfundinsider.com/2017/11/124918-cardozo-blockchain-project-publishes-new-saft-approach-icos-provides-regulatory-alternative-nascent-token-market/). This source also reprints Professor Wright's paper in its entirety.

[38]   *See, i.e.,* Scannavino Law, *SAFT: A New Legal Framework for Token Sales*, MEDIUM (Aug. 30, 2017) (available online at https://medium.com/law-decrypted/saft-a-new-legal-framework-for-token-sales-a50078a6dde8) (claiming that "the SAFT was developed to provide a clear and conservative path to compliance with current US securities laws and regulations when it is utilized in conjunction with an accredited investor verification process."); Brady Dale, *Here's How Filecoin's Token Sale Won't Irk the SEC (Like The DAO Did)*, OBSERVER (Mar. 8, 2017) (available online at https://observer.com/2017/08/filecoin-coinlist-securities-exchange-commission/) (explaining the SAFT utilized by Filecoin as "a way to run an initial coin offering (ICO) . . . [that should] satisfy Wall Street's rulemakers. . . .")

[39]   Brady Dale, *What If the SEC Is Going After the SAFT?* COINDESK (Mar. 6, 2018) (available online at https://www.coindesk.com/sec-going-saft).

[40]   *Id.*

token sales to avoid compliance pitfalls and security regulations. Blunt criticism of 'utility tokens', particularly from the SEC, and the risk of retroactive enforcement provided token holders reasons to cut losses, and likely contributed to the decline in sales."[41]

3. AIRDROPS (AND BOUNTIES)

While regulators struggle to keep up with ICOs, enterprising crypto-entrepreneurs are already experimenting with the next "thing." The crypto airdrop provides an interesting example of this experimentation. "Airdrop" is not a regulatory term of art and instead has entered popular usage as crypto entrepreneurs have turned to alternatives to public sales in order to disseminate their tokens. With regulatory authorities cracking down on unregistered coin and token distributions in the form of ICOs, and with social media sites restricting or prohibiting advertising of ICOs, alternative distribution methods have become increasingly important.

"Airdrops" are "the process whereby a cryptocurrency enterprise distributes cryptocurrency tokens to the wallets of some users free of charge. Airdrops are usually carried out by blockchain-based startups to bootstrap their cryptocurrency projects."[42] Established blockchain-based enterprises such as trading platforms or wallet services can conduct airdrops as well. The critical component of the process is that the distribution of coins or tokens is essentially free to the recipient.

Not all airdrops are conducted at the beginning of a coin or token's existence. Precursors to the currently popular airdrops occurred in the form of distributions following hard forks where the consensus on a blockchain fork was not unanimous.[43] Bitcoin, for example, has forked multiple times, resulting in the creation and "airdropping" of a number of new coins derived from the original asset.

The first significant Bitcoin fork was probably Bitcoin XT. This 2014 development was designed to increase the number of transactions per second.[44] While it initially appeared to be successful, with more than a thousand nodes running the new software by the summer of 2015, it has

---

[41] Feature, *2018 in Review: A Year in Numbers or a Year in Narratives?*, SMITH & CROWN (Feb. 26, 2019) (available online at https://sci.smithandcrown.com/research/2018-review-year-numbers-or-narratives).

[42] Katalyse.io, Mission.Org, *What are "Airdrops" in Crypto World?* HACKERNOON (Feb 14, 2018) [archived at https://perma.cc/WMU4-498W].

[43] Forks occur when there is a split and two versions of the blockchain exist. Hard and soft forks are described back in chapter 2.

[44] For a further discussion of the history of Bitcoin XT, see Mike Hearn, *An XT FAQ*, MEDIUM (Aug. 27, 2015) (available online at https://medium.com/@octskyward/an-xt-faq-38e78aa32ff0).

now fallen out of favor. The tokens created by that fork are, however, apparently still in circulation.[45]

In early 2016, Bitcoin Classic was launched in another effort to increase block size.[46] Early interest was strong, with about 2,000 nodes participating. Despite the early enthusiasm, Bitcoin Classic no longer exists.[47]

In 2015, a soft fork was implemented on the Bitcoin blockchain to allow more transactions to occur at once. In response, some users initiated a hard fork to avoid certain protocol updates that would have been required by the soft fork. Bitcoin Cash (BCH) was issued as a result of this change in 2017. Anyone who held Bitcoin at the time of the fork became an owner of BCH.[48]

These kinds of transactions paved the way for the modern airdrop, as it is not necessary for there to be a fork in order for a cryptoasset to be dropped into the wallets of crypto-users. Recognizing this, one might ask why a developer or company with a new coin or token would be willing to essentially give it away. There are, in fact, a number of valid strategies that could support such a decision.

Probably first among the motives for token start-ups is to generate awareness of the new asset. There is more value when a token is held on as many wallets as possible, and more token holders create more interest, wider exposure, and an increased trading volume, particularly if there is enough interest and demand to have the interest listed on an exchange. In essence, an airdrop can be a virtually free way to conduct marketing and generate interest among members of the crypto community.

In addition, an airdrop can be used to more evenly distribute the token supply, which is a particular benefit in a blockchain system. It can also help generate a lead database or network before a more public distribution goes live. Alternatively, depending on how it is conducted, an airdrop can also be used to reward early or loyal investors or participants in a venture. It certainly is one way to gain entrance into and interact with the existing crypto community.

The benefits are real, because once someone holds a token, they have the same motive as everyone else who owns the token or intends to invest

---

[45]   *BitTokens (BXT)*, COINMARKETCAP.COM [archived at https://perma.cc/L7BW-JPYP] (showing a market capitalization of $316,597 as of February 25, 2019).

[46]   For a discussion of Bitcoin Classic (and the other Bitcoin hard forks), see Nathan Reiff, *A History of Bitcoin Hard Forks*, INVESTOPEDIA (updated Apr. 25, 2018) (available online at https://www.investopedia.com/tech/history-bitcoin-hard-forks/).

[47]   Tom Zander, *Bitcoin Classic Closing its doors*, BITCOIN CLASSIC NEWS (available online at https://bitcoinclassic.com/news/closing.html).

[48]   For a description of this airdrop, see *Bitcoin cash (BCC)*, AIRDROPALERT (available online at https://airdropalert.com/bitcoin-cash-airdrop). BCH is the most successful hard fork of Bitcoin, and as of the end of February, 2019, is the sixth-largest cryptocurrency by market capitalization. COINMARKETCAP.COM [archived at https://perma.cc/9QS9-H6BZ] (accessed for this purpose on February 25, 2019, and showing Bitcoin Cash with a market cap in excess of $2.4 billion).

in it: the incentive is to see that the value of the token increases. Whether by word of mouth or by virtue of the fact that people tend to value something that they own more highly than if they have no connection with it, airdrops can be a powerful way to improve token value.

All airdrops require that a recipient already have a wallet that can accommodate different types of cryptocurrency. Most wallets will handle tokens that are likely to be dropped.[49] The requirements for wallet type and storage vary by project, and, in some cases, can be satisfied with an online soft wallet, and in some instances will need to be a wallet residing on a particular exchange. In addition, the wallet must be active (meaning that it must both hold a minimum level of some form of cryptocurrency before the date set by the project and demonstrate some level of activity), to avoid the creation of multiple wallets solely to claim airdropped coins or tokens.

However, some airdrops require more than an active wallet. Even sources geared at defining what constitutes an airdrop acknowledge that some distribution schemes that characterize themselves as airdrops are not completely free, at least of effort, for the recipient. For example, while noting that crypto airdrops generally refer to a distribution of "free tokens," one source also explains that "[t]o qualify for this free gift, one may need to perform certain tasks" such as posting on social media, writing a blog post, or otherwise.[50] Projects may require participants to sign-up; retweet; refer a friend; join the project's Telegram account; join the project's discord chat; post a comment or private message about the project; or complete other social media tasks geared at spreading the word about the project.[51]

There is even terminology to distinguish between a truly "free" airdrop and one that requires specific protocols to be followed. An "automatic airdrop" does not require the recipient to do anything other than hold a suitable, active wallet. A "manual" airdrop is one where specific requirements are imposed in the protocol devised by the project developers.[52] Alternative nomenclature sometimes refers to programs that require more substantial efforts from recipients as "bounty programs," rather than airdrops. Usually these require completion of specific tasks or jobs, such as creation of new graphics, translations, marketing and

---

[49]   Crypto Coin Junky, *Beginners Guide to Crypto Airdrops: Free Coins & Tokens*, MEDIUM (Oct. 5, 2018) (available online at https://medium.com/@johnhinkle_80891/beginners-guide-to-crypto-airdrops-free-coins-tokens-643a7327709b). Ethereum is not the only blockchain that supports airdrops. EOS, for example, also hosts tokens that have been airdropped.

[50]   CoinBundle Team, *What Are Airdrops*, MEDIUM (Sept. 14, 2018) (available online at https://medium.com/coinbundle/what-are-airdrops-ab97b276b0d1).

[51]   These potential tasks are discussed in sources such as Sudhir Khatwani, *Airdrops In Cryptocurrencies: Everything A Beginner Needs To Know*, COINSUTRA (updated Oct. 13, 2018) (available online at https://coinsutra.com/what-is-airdrop/).

[52]   *Beginners Guide, supra* note 49.

promotion for the project, or writing content.[53] Where one draws the line between airdrops and bounties is, however, unclear.

There are a number of reasons for investors to be cautious and regulators to be concerned about airdrops. As is the case with any innovation, unscrupulous players have been quick to enter the field.[54] One risk is that a scammer may create a fake twitter account that mimics an official cryptocurrency company's account. The fake account then poses as a developer for the team and requests private wallet keys[55] in order to airdrop coins. Alternatively, a twitter account that resembles a legitimate company may generate a request that a target send cryptocurrency to a wallet owned by the fraudster, again in order to receive the "free" tokens. This can be done along with a promise that the transferred tokens will be returned and assurance that this is only a test to insure that the wallet is active. There are a range of phishing, hacking, and identity theft scams that can be associated with airdrops, typically involving requests for information, account access, or payments that are not required in genuine airdrops. Private keys are never required by legitimate companies, and no rightful airdrop requires that tokens be sent to another address first. Ideally, before taking any affirmative steps in response to an offer of airdropped coins or tokens, official sources should be checked.

Note that there are some risks often mentioned in connection with crypto that are not mentioned here. For example, one of the most commonly cited concerns has to do with the risk that crypto is being used for illicit purposes (either for money laundering or to finance illegal operations such as those involving terrorist activities).[56] If an airdrop does not involve the transmission of any property of value to the developer in exchange for crypto, neither of these would seem to be an issue with airdrops per se. This does not, of course, mean that secondary trading transactions could not

---

[53]   *See generally* Winco, *What is the difference between Faucets, Airdrops, and Bounties?*, GOOD AUDIENCE BLOG (Oct. 10, 2018) (available online at https://blog.goodaudience.com/what-is-the-difference-between-faucets-airdrops-and-bounties-99c955a50956). A "faucet" is a website that offers very small increments of crypto in exchange for periodic visits or tasks over an extended period of time, usually as an incentive to help that site generate advertising income.

[54]   For a more detailed consideration of the kinds of airdrop scams that have been identified to date, see Alex Lielacher, *A Guide to Airdrops Part 3: Airdrop Scams*, BTCMANAGER (Mar. 26, 2018) (available online at https://btcmanager.com/a-guide-to-airdrops-part-3-airdrop-scams/?q=/a-guide-to-airdrops-part-3-airdrop-scams/), and Crystal Stranger, *Airdrops: the Good, the Bad, and the Scammy*, MEDIUM (Sept. 7, 2018) (available online at https://medium.com/cryptoweek/airdrops-the-good-the-bad-and-the-scammy-25a62eddb189).

[55]   A private key is the cryptographically protected access code that allows an owner to access his or her wallet; it is not designed to be shared with third parties. For a substantially more sophisticated explanation of public and private keys, see Leon Di, *Why Do I Need a Public and Private Key on the Blockchain?*, WETRUST (Jan. 29, 2017) (available online at https://blog.wetrust.io/why-do-i-need-a-public-and-private-key-on-the-blockchain-c2ea74a69e76).

[56]   This concern is addressed extensively in chapters 3 to 6. It is also clearly a global problem. For international reaction, you might consider checking out Libr. of Cong., *Regulation of Cryptocurrency Around the World* (June 2018) at p. 1 [archived at https://perma.cc/T7NJ-GN3Y]. In addition, the topic of international regulation of crypto is raised in chapter 15.

cause problems, but the airdrop itself should not contribute to this particular risk.

While it is exceedingly difficult to make blanket statements about new developments such as the airdrop process, it is generally safe to say that current regulation of airdrops is both complicated and confusing. Legitimate crypto-entrepreneurs operating in the U.S. are likely to be most concerned with whether airdrops will be treated as a distribution of securities and therefore within the purview of the U.S. Securities and Exchange Commission (SEC). As explained in more details in chapters seven through ten, under the current approach taken by the SEC, crypto is generally a security if it: (1) involves the investment of money or something of value; (2) in a common enterprise; (3) with the expectation of profits; (4) based on the essential entrepreneurial efforts of others.[57]

Although it is certainly possible that an airdrop would lack the first element, meaning that it should not be treated as involving the distribution of a security, this is not necessarily a foregone decision. One fear is that the SEC will treat crypto airdrops as securities in much the same way that it previously warned against giveaways of stock. In 1999, the SEC brought and settled four enforcement actions against companies that distributed "free" stock without registering their offerings.[58] In much the same way that airdrops can benefit crypto-businesses, in the case of those stock "giveaways," the SEC concluded that "issuers received value by spawning a fledgling public market for their shares, increasing their business, creating publicity, increasing traffic to their websites, and, in two cases, generating possible interest in projected public offerings."[59] In each instance, the SEC therefore had no trouble in determining that the transactions involved unregistered, non-exempt offerings of securities.

On August 14, 2018, the SEC issued a cease and desist order (the "*Tomahawk Order*") against Tomahawk Exploration LLC ("Tomahawk") and its founder for actions in connection with what it determined to be a public offering (ICO) of "Tomahawkcoins" or "TOM" tokens.[60] In the *Tomahawk Order*, the SEC found that the issuer's "Bounty Program" constituted an offer and sale of securities because the company received "online promotional services" in exchange for the token, which it classified as an equity security.[61] According to the order, "bounties" were offered for actions such as "as making requests to list TOM on token trading platforms, promoting TOM on blogs and other online forums like Twitter

---

[57]   This is known as the *Howey* test, and it is derived from *SEC v. W.J. Howey Co.*, 328 U.S. 293 (1946).

[58]   SEC, *SEC Brings First Actions To Halt Unregistered Online Offerings of So-Called "Free Stock,"* Release 99–83 (July 22, 1999) [archived at https://perma.cc/8TAT-7PEE].

[59]   *Id.*

[60]   A copy of the *Tomahawk Order* is archived at https://perma.cc/3ZGB-BD79.

[61]   SEC, Press Release, *SEC Bars Perpetrator of Initial Coin Offering Fraud*, 2018–152 (Aug. 14, 2018) [archived at https://perma.cc/G2G2-3N2P].

or Facebook, and creating professional picture file designs, YouTube videos or other promotional materials." According to the SEC, the lack of cash payment did not prevent the distribution from involving securities, because the company "received value in exchange for the bounty distributions, in the form of online marketing. . . ."[62]

Some sources were quick to treat this as a potential condemnation of airdrops,[63] although Tomahawk itself labeled the distribution a bounty program, and a relatively substantial degree of effort was required to become a recipient.

On April 3, 2019, the SEC issued additional guidance about the appropriate treatment of crypto offerings,[64] specifically mentioning airdrops, albeit in a single footnote in the new framework (*"Framework"*).[65] The relevant footnote reads as follows:

> The lack of monetary consideration for digital assets, such as those distributed via a so-called "bounty program" does not mean that the investment of money prong is not satisfied. As the Commission explained in The DAO Report, "[i]n determining whether an investment contract exists, the investment of 'money' need not take the form of cash" and "in spite of *Howey*'s reference to an 'investment of money,' it is well established that cash is not the only form of contribution or investment that will create an investment contract." *The DAO Report* at 11 (citation omitted). *See In re Tomahawk Exploration LLC*, Securities Act Rel. 10530 (Aug. 14, 2018) (issuance of tokens under a so-called "bounty program" constituted an offer and sale of securities because the issuer provided tokens to investors in exchange for services designed to advance the issuer's economic interests and foster a trading market for its securities). Further, the lack of monetary consideration for digital assets, such as those distributed via a so-called "airdrop," does not mean that the investment of money

---

[62] *Id.* at ¶ 34.

[63] *I.e.*, Robert Wernli, Jr., et al, *Airdrop of Crypto Tokens Hits Regulatory Flak*, SHEPPARD MULLIN (Aug. 28, 2018) (available online at https://www.lawoftheledger.com/2018/08/articles/cryptocurrency/crypto-tokens-regulatory-tomahawk/). *See* Brady Dale, *So Long ICOs, Hello Airdrops: The Free Token Giveaway Craze Is Here*, COINDESK (Updated Mar. 17, 2018) (available online at https://www.coindesk.com/long-icos-hello-airdrops-free-token-giveaway-craze), citing Todd Kornfeld, counsel at the Pepper Hamilton LLP law firm, as expressing concern based on SEC actions from 1999 that targeted giveaways of free equity interests. This source reports that Stream, a blockchain-based video streaming platform, "delayed its airdrop indefinitely because of concern that airdrops could also be in violation of securities law." However, although crypto must satisfy the *Howey* investment contract analysis, which among other things looks at whether there is an investment of money or something else of value, true corporate stock is always regarded as a security under U.S. law. *See United Housing Foundation v. Forman*, 421 U.S. 837 (1975) and *Landreth Timber Co. v. Landreth*, 471 U.S. 681 (1985).

[64] SEC, Bill Hinman & Valerie Szczepanik, *Statement on "Framework for 'Investment Contract' Analysis of Digital Assets"* (Ap. 3, 2019) [archived at https://perma.cc/5CVA-RYFB].

[65] SEC, *Framework for "Investment Contract" Analysis of Digital Assets* (Ap. 3, 2019) [archived at https://perma.cc/J4KQ-HW52].

prong is not satisfied; therefore, an airdrop may constitute a sale or distribution of securities. In a so-called "airdrop," a digital asset is distributed to holders of another digital asset, typically to promote its circulation.[66]

This explanation was appended to the new *Framework* for determining when crypto (referred to as a digital asset) should be treated as an investment contract. Rather than clarifying the law, however, the new framework introduces 38 different considerations, some with additional subparts, that may be important in determining when a digital asset is a security. Further complicating the issue is the fact that the *Framework* does not prioritize among the considerations.

To demonstrate the complexity that continues to plague companies contemplating a crypto airdrop, there is a blanket assertion in the *Framework* that "[t]he first prong of the *Howey* test is typically satisfied in an offer and sale of a digital asset because the digital asset is purchased or otherwise acquired in exchange for value, whether in the form of real (or fiat) currency, another digital asset, or other type of consideration."[67] None of the 38 articulated considerations provide insight into this element, instead revealing a focus on the later efforts of the issuer or associated persons to develop, improve, or maintain the network; to create a market for the tokens; to control or oversee future distributions; and to benefit from the tokens in the same way that recipients expect to.

Whether courts will agree with what appears to be a unique take on the *Howey* test, especially in the contexts of airdrops that require nothing more than the holding of an active wallet, is uncertain. At this point, therefore, the *Framework,* which was obviously intended to be helpful, may raise more questions than it answers in the context of airdrops.

4. INITIAL EXCHANGE OFFERINGS (IEOs)

Airdrops are not the only innovative distribution technique being utilized by crypto developers. An IEO is another new process by which crypto-based offerings are being conducted. Instead of directly dealing with potential investors, this particular distribution/financing model utilizes the services and facilities of a crypto exchange or trading platform in order to raise funds.

In a more conventional ICO, a token development company or team generally sells its newly created tokens directly to investors (or sells the right to obtain tokens once they are fully functional). In an IEO, the development group sells its tokens through a crypto exchange platform. The exchange essentially buys the tokens, although payment may be

---

[66]   *Framework, supra* note 65 at n.9.
[67]   *Id.* at Part II.A. This is supported by n.9.

deferred until a third party purchaser pays for the assets, or the exchange may have the right to force the developer to buy back any unsold tokens. An investor would create an account on the applicable exchange, generally funding their digital wallets with whatever tokens are used by that crypto platform. The new tokens (or possibly pre-functional tokens, or contractual rights to acquire the tokens when complete) are then purchased by the investors directly from the exchange through those wallets, with the understanding that when the IEO ends, the new tokens will be listed on that exchange and may be exchanged in secondary trading transactions by the investors.

IEOs are relatively new and appear to have been created following the late 2017 ban on ICOs by China[68] and a significant decline in ICOs worldwide during the latter-half of 2018.[69] There are now a number of launchpads that support IEOs,[70] and the overall popularity of IEOs appears to be increasing significantly.[71] According to CoinSchedule, from March 1, 2019 to May 31, 2019, 23 separate IEOs were conducted, raising a total of $1,220,355,280.[72] Some IEOs have already achieved considerable success. For example, it has been widely reported that "BitTorrent raised $7.2 million in 18 minutes, and Fetch.AI recently raised $6 million in 22 seconds on Binance's Launchpad as well."[73]

From an investor's perspective, one significant theoretical advantage to the IEO model is that the exchange performs the preliminary assessment of whether the underlying token project is worth supporting via audits, technical analysis, and additional review. There is also external validation in that the pricing, supply, and any hard/soft caps on the distribution are generally set not by the developer, but by the exchange, which has its own interests to consider. Perhaps as significantly, the

---

[68] This event is pointed to as the trigger for the development of IEOs by Benjamin Vitaris, *What Is an Initial Exchange Offering (IEO) and How It Differs From ICO?* CRYPTOPOTATO (updated Ap. 29, 2019) [archived at https://perma.cc/HRK3-NDEW].

[69] *See* Brian Curran, *What Is an IEO? Complete Guide to Initial Exchange Offerings,* BLOCKONOMI (Ap. 5, 2019) (available online at https://blockonomi.com/what-is-an-ieo/).

[70] A launchpad in this context is a fundraising platform used by an exchange. *See* Vitaris, *supra* note 68, listing Binance Launchpad, Bitmax Launchpad, Bittrex IEO, OK Jumpstart (OKEx), KuCoin Spotlight, and Huobi Prime.

[71] John Reed Stark, *The SEC's Looming Initial Exchange Offering Sweep: Part 1,* LAW360 (May 30, 2019) [available online at https://www.law360.com/securities/articles/1162809/the-sec-s-looming-initial-exchange-offering-sweep-part-1?nl_pk=90e22563-0a32-414c-8b90-a040fc4efeeb& utm_source=newsletter&utm_medium=email&utm_campaign=securities&read_more=1] (last accessed June, 2019).

[72] *Successful Token Sales Ordered by Completion Date* (IEO selected), COINSCHEDULE (available online at https://www.coinschedule.com/stats-list/IEO?dates=Mar%2001,%202019%20 to%20May%2031,%202019) (registration is required to access the site, but the process is free). The total amount raised is somewhat misleading, because it includes a single offering by Bitfinex ending May 13, 2019, which raised $1,000,000,000.

[73] Curran, *supra* note 69.

exchange where the IEO is conducted automatically lists the token after the distribution, so that resales are facilitated by this process.

From the token creator's perspective, the distribution process may be easier on a number of fronts. One significant advantage is that the exchange is responsible for compliance with the BSA's AML and KYC rules. The developer's marketing budget is reduced because the exchange generally markets the tokens that it supports. Finally, there is no need for the developer to scramble after the sale to find exchanges willing to list the new token; that work is done prior to launch when the exchange screens the project.

On the other hand, the process also introduces an intermediary to the process, one of the conventional "evils" that the blockchain was created to address. The crypto community, brought together (in part) by a shared belief in the adage that "trusted third parties are security holes,"[74] is not likely to view this in a uniformly positive light. Moreover, not all exchanges are equal. Exchanges are often the target of hackers,[75] and they may also be subject to problems created by incompetence.[76]

The regulatory reaction to IEOs is not settled. While the SEC's recent framework on how digital assets are to be assessed under the *Howey* investment contract test may be useful,[77] it does not, for example, explain how cryptoexchanges fit within the framework's approach to "Active Participants."[78] Valerie Szczepanik, associate director of the SEC's Division of Corporation Finance, senior advisor for digital assets and

---

[74]   Nick Szabo, *Trusted Third Parties are Security Holes*, SATOSHI NAKAMOTO INSTITUTE (originally published 2001) (available online at https://nakamotoinstitute.org/trusted-third-parties/).

[75]   For example, in the first half of 2018, Japanese cryptoexchanges suffered hacking losses of approximately $518 million. Daniel Palmer, *Japan Lost $540 Million to Crypto Hacks in First Half of 2018*, COINDESK (Sept. 20, 2018) (available online at https://www.coindesk.com/japan-lost-540-million-to-crypto-hacks-in-first-half-of-2018). Even in the wake of Japan's crackdown on cryptoexchange security following the infamous CoinCheck debacle, and the advent of its touted self-regulatory structure, hacks have continued to occur. In late 2018, hackers reported stole more than $59 million in crypto from the Japanese exchange Zaif. Dennis Sahlstrom, *Japanese Cryptocurrency Exchange Hacked, $60 Million Worth of Bitcoin Stolen*, TOSHI TIMES (2018) (available online at https://toshitimes.com/japanese-cryptocurrency-exchange-hacked-60-million-worth-of-bitcoin-stolen/).

[76]   In this regard, consider the QuadrigaCX spectacle, where the death of the CEO left the company without access to wallets holding millions of dollars worth of crypto. *A Canadian Mystery Mobilizes a Global Crypto Community, What Happened at QuadrigaCX?*, TRUSTNODES (Feb. 3, 2019)(available online at https://www.trustnodes.com/2019/02/03/a-canadian-mystery-mobilizes-a-global-crypto-community-what-happened-at-quadrigacx). There may be more to this story. Reports began to circulate in early 2019 that the company never had those crypto reserves at all or that some other kind of mis- or mal-feasance was involved. *See* Adam Button, *The QuadrigaCX saga keeps getting weirder*, FOREXLIVE (Feb. 4, 2019) [archived at https://perma.cc/N5HZ-NFXF]. The complete story may never be known.

[77]   *See Framework, supra* note 65. This *Framework* is discussed in more detail in chapter 10.

[78]   *See* Framework, *supra* note 65, at § II.C., p. 3, a phrase used in the document to include "a promoter, sponsor, or other third party . . . [that] provides essential managerial efforts that affect the success of the enterprise. . . ."

innovation, and co-author of the SEC's statement accompanying the recent Framework on digital assets,[79] has expressed concern about IEOs. At CoinDesk's Consensus 2019 conference, she warned that "[p]latforms seeking to list these tokens for a listing fee or bring buyers to the table for issuers are probably engaging in broker-dealer activity. . . ."[80]

Section 15(a)(1) of the '34 Act (the Securities Exchange Act of 1934) makes it unlawful for a person to "effect a transaction in securities" or "attempt to induce the purchase or sale of, any security" unless that person is registered with and licensed by FINRA as a broker or dealer. (FINRA is the self-regulatory organization designated by the SEC to license and regulate broker-dealers.)

Failure to register as a broker-dealer when required can result in the imposition of severe, and even criminal, penalties. It can also lead to liability for the token creator, since merely retaining and permitting an unlicensed intermediary to help facilitate or effect a securities transaction (such as an IEO) may be a violation of federal and many state laws. Finally, and as the next section of this chapter will discuss in more detail, attorneys and other advisors should be wary of this process, since section 20(e) of the '34 Act allows the SEC to impose aiding and abetting liability on persons who knowingly or recklessly provide substantial assistance in the violation of the '34 Act prohibitions.

Experts who have considered the matter have generally concluded that when a crypto exchange facilitates an IEO, its activities create at least a prima facie case that the platform is acting as a broker-dealer. The typical compensation offered to such exchanges, the platform's efforts in screening, managing, packaging, and marketing the underlying tokens all support this conclusion.[81]

Further supporting the probability that the SEC will undertake additional enforcement efforts against unregistered crypto exchanges participating in IEOs, on September 11, 2018, the SEC filed its first action involving a crypto trading platform for failure to register as a broker-dealer.[82] In that instance, an action was initiated against TokenLot and its owners for operating as an unregistered broker-dealer by accepting payment in the form of a portion of the total proceeds from each ICO, where TokenLot advertised an on-going ICO through social media, e-mail distributions, and paid on-line advertising. Investors generally transmitted funds to wallets controlled or maintained by TokenLot.

---

[79]   See Statement, supra note 64.

[80]   Anna Baydakova & Marc Hochstein, SEC's Crypto Czar Says Exchanges That List IEOs May Face Legal Risks, COINDESK (May 13, 2019) (available online at https://www.coindesk.com/secs-crypto-czar-says-exchanges-that-list-ieo-tokens-may-face-legal-risks).

[81]   See Stark, supra note 71.

[82]   SEC, Sec. Act. 1933 Rel. No. 10543, In Re TokenLot LLC (Sept. 11, 2018) [archived at https://perma.cc/3BEZ-7WK6].

Without admitting guilt, TokenLot and its owners agreed to a cease and desist order, disgorged nearly $500,000, destroyed unsold digital assets, paid penalties, and accepted three-year industry bars.

Although TokenLot did not involve an IEO, many of the activities that it undertook resemble the same kind of promotional activities that an IEO entails. Moreover, the TokenLot situation was even less like a broker-dealer in that TokenLot was not a contractual intermediary, as an exchange or platform is in the IEO situation.

In any event, these regulatory developments certainly give reason to pause before pursuing an IEO in the U.S. through any platform that is not also registered as a broker-dealer with FINRA.

5. THE EMPIRE STRIKES BACK: AIDING AND ABETTING LIABILITY

Crypto entrepreneurs are not the only ones attempting to stay ahead of the game. Just as businesses are experimenting with new approaches to marketing (with their emphasis on privacy, for example) or in avoiding regulation (first with the SAFT and now with airdrops and IEOs, again as examples), regulators are also considering additional enforcement options. One option is to pursue a wider variety of persons involved with non-compliant crypto businesses as aiders and abettors. Both the CFTC and the SEC possess the authority to impose such aiding and abetting liability.[83]

CEA Section 13(a) provides that "[a]ny person who . . . willfully aids, abets, counsels, commands, induces, or procures the commission of, a violation of [the CEA or CFTC rules] . . . may be held responsible for such violation as a principal." To prevail under this provision, the CFTC must prove: "(1) the CEA was violated, (2) the aider and abettor had knowledge of the wrongdoing underlying the violation, and (3) the aider and abettor intentionally assisted the primary wrongdoer."[84]

CFTC Commissioner Brian Quintenz discussed how these rules might apply in the context of crypto-transactions at the October 2018 GITEX Technology Week Conference.[85] He suggested that where "code developers could reasonably foresee, at the time they created the code, that it would

---

[83] These are not the only federal regulatory agencies with authority to bring claims for aiding and abetting in the context of cryptotransaction. The IRS, for example, has authority to impose penalties for aiding and understating tax liability. 26 U.S. Code § 6701. The penalties are, however quite limited in amount. In addition, taxation of crypto is generally outside the scope of most of these materials, so the text focuses on the CFTC, SEC, FinCEN, and the U.S. Department of Justice acting pursuant to provisions in the securities, commodities, and bank secrecy acts.

[84] *See In re Barclays PLC*, CFTC No. 12–25, at 27 (June 27, 2012) [archived at https://perma.cc/2HWP-HCAT] (citing In re Nikkhah, CFTC No. 95–13, [1999–2000 Transfer Binder] COMM. FUT. L. REP. (CCH) ¶ 28,129, at 49,888 n.28 (May 12, 2000)).

[85] CFTC, Speeches & Testimony, *Remarks of Commissioner Brian Quintenz at the 38th Annual GITEX Technology Week Conference* (Oct. 16, 2018) [archived at https://perma.cc/CWY3-R5XW].

likely be used by U.S. persons in a manner violative of CFTC regulations . . . a strong case could be made that . . .[they] aided and abetted violations of CFTC regulations."[86]

Nor are smart contract coders the only ones at risk. Other sources caution bankers to be cautious as well, noting the risk that if they become involved in cryptotransactions they may find themselves subject to aiding and abetting liability under regulatory regimes with which they are unfamiliar, such as the CEA.[87]

The SEC similarly has authority over those who aid and abet violations of the federal securities laws.[88] Some of the most pointed comments about the potential for aiding and abetting liability under the securities laws for professionals in the crypto ecosystem come from SEC Chairman Jay Clayton, who made the following remarks in a speech at the 2018 Securities Regulation Institute in Washington D.C.

> Market professionals, especially gatekeepers, need to act responsibly and hold themselves to high standards. To be blunt, from what I have seen recently, particularly in the ICO space, they can do better. Our securities laws—and 80 plus years of practice—assume that securities lawyers, accountants, underwriters, and dealers will act responsibly. It is expected that they will bring expertise, judgment, and a healthy dose of skepticism to their work . . . Legal advice (or in the cases I will cite, the lack thereof) surrounding ICOs helps illustrate this point . . . .
>
> First, most disturbing to me, there are ICOs where the lawyers involved appear to be, on the one hand, assisting promoters in structuring offerings of products that have many of the key features of a securities offering, but call it an "ICO," which sounds pretty close to an "IPO." On the other hand, those lawyers claim the products are not securities, and the promoters proceed without compliance with the securities laws, which deprives investors of

---

[86]   *Id.* For a further discussion of the extent to which developers may face such liability, see Jonathan Marcus et al, *Smart Contract Coders May Face Aiding And Abetting Liability*, LAW360 (Feb. 27, 2019) (available online at https://www.law360.com/securities/articles/1133133/smart-contract-coders-may-face-aiding-and-abetting-risk?nl_pk=90e22563-0a32-414c-8b90-a040fc4efeeb&utm_source=newsletter&utm_medium=email&utm_campaign=securities).

[87]   Marc Gottridge, *Bankers can't be too cautious with crypto*, AMERICAN BANKER (Ap. 23, 2018) (available online at https://www.americanbanker.com/opinion/bankers-cant-be-too-cautious-with-crypto).

[88]   Keep in mind that this includes authority over those who aid and abet certain violations of the BSA (Bank Secrecy Act), which is normally enforced by FinCEN. Under the BSA, broker-dealers must report suspicious transactions to FinCEN. Section 17(a) of the '34 Act and Rule 17a–8 require broker-dealers to comply with the recordkeeping, retention and reporting duties of the BSA. The SEC has brought individual actions against compliance officers for aiding and abetting in the failure of companies to file the required reports, albeit not in the context of crypto transactions. *See, i.e.,* SEC, Sec. Exch. Act 1934 Release No. 82958, *In re Eugene Terracciano* (Mar. 28, 2018) [archived at https://perma.cc/A7NP-UGNS].

the substantive and procedural investor protection requirements of our securities laws.

Second, are ICOs where the lawyers appear to have taken a step back from the key issues—including whether the "coin" is a security and whether the offering qualifies for an exemption from registration—even in circumstances where registration would likely be warranted. These lawyers appear to provide the "it depends" equivocal advice, rather than counseling their clients that the product they are promoting likely is a security. Their clients then proceed with the ICO without complying with the securities laws because those clients are willing to take the risk.

With respect to these two scenarios, I have instructed the SEC staff to be on high alert for approaches to ICOs that may be contrary to the spirit of our securities laws and the professional obligations of the U.S. securities bar.[89]

The import of this speech is clear. "Per Chairman Jay Clayton, lawyers now also risk being investigated or prosecuted right beside their ICO clients."[90]

6. ENTER THE TITANS

Finally, nothing spells change for the crypto ecosystem more than the active participation of commercial giants. The summer of 2019 involved news from two very large companies about their interest in cryptoassets. One announcement involved the world's largest social media site, Facebook, with more than two billion users every month,[91] and the other involved the world's largest brick-and-mortar retailer, Walmart, with total revenue in excess of $500 billion for the fiscal year ending January 31, 2019.[92]

On June 18, 2019, Facebook announced that it was actively planning to launch a cryptocurrency to be called Libra in 2020.[93] The release took the form of an official whitepaper.

---

[89]   SEC, Speech, Jay Clayton, *Opening Remarks at the Securities Regulation Institute* (Jan. 22, 2018) [archived at https://perma.cc/LNX5-RZ3E].

[90]   Kevin LaCroix, *Guest Post: Beware ICO Lawyers: As Regulatory Gatekeepers, You're the Next SEC Target*, THE D&O DIARY (Jan. 30, 2018) (available online at https://www.dandodiary.com/2018/01/articles/securities-laws/guest-post-beware-ico-lawyers-regulatory-gatekeepers-youre-next-sec-target/).

[91]   Alfred Lua, *21 Top Social Media Sites to Consider for Your Brand*, BUFFER (Jan 24, 2019) (available online at https://buffer.com/library/social-media-sites).

[92]   Walmart, *Company Facts* (available online at https://corporate.walmart.com/newsroom/company-facts). The data in the text reflects what was reported by the company on Aug. 15, 2019.

[93]   *See generally* Nick Statt, *Facebook Confirms it will Launch a Cryptocurrency Called Libra in 2020*, THE VERGE (June 18, 2019) (available online at https://www.theverge.com/2019/6/18/18682290/facebook-libra-cryptocurrency-visa-mastercard-digital-currency-calibra-wallet-announce).

According to the whitepaper, the Libra coin will not be directly controlled by Facebook, and instead will be under the governance of the Libra Association, a non-profit group based in Switzerland.[94] The Libra Association is designed to be a group of diverse organizations from around the world, including not only Facebook but also major investors such as Mastercard, Visa, eBay, and PayPal. The whitepaper indicates that the plan is to have approximately 100 members for the Association by the target launch date in the first half of 2020. The cost to join this exclusive group is set at $10 million, but the potential benefits are extensive.

First there is the right of control. The Libra Association will oversee Libra's development, its real-world reserves, and will vote on the Libra blockchain's governance rules. Members will also have the right to become a validator node, and they will be entitled to a share of dividends from interest earned on the Libra reserves, in an amount that is proportionate to their investment.

Libra itself will be designed as a "stablecoin," with value pegged to a basket of bank deposits and short-term government securities for a group of historically-stable Fiat currencies, including the dollar, pound, euro, Swiss franc, and yen. The precise mix of currencies has not been released, and the Association can change the mix to offset price fluctuations in any particular Fiat. The plan is to start the value somewhere close to the dollar, euro, or pound to make it easier for users to adopt the new coin.

Facebook intends to use a subsidiary, Calibra, to handle its dealings with Libra apart from its Facebook operations. This is intended to help preserve the privacy of Libra users. Calibra will serve as an initial wallet for the virtual currency and is anticipated to be built into Facebook Messenger and WhatsApp, as well as being a standalone product.

The reaction to the whitepaper and public announcement in the U.S. was swift and overwhelmingly negative. A draft bill to prevent large tech companies from issuing virtual currencies was quickly circulated to policymakers in the U.S. House of Representatives.[95] The draft bill was tentatively entitled the "Keep Big Tech Out Of Finance Act," and included a section prohibiting any "large platform utility" from creating any "digital asset that is intended to be widely used as medium of exchange, unit of account, store of value, or any other similar function, as defined by the Board of Governors of the Federal Reserve System."[96] The bill, in its early

---

[94] The whitepaper that officially announced Libra in June of 2019 did, however, note that "while final decision-making authority rests with the association, Facebook is expected to maintain a leadership role through 2019." *Libra White Paper* (available online at https://www.theverge.com/2019/6/18/18682290/facebook-libra-cryptocurrency-visa-mastercard-digital-currency-calibra-wallet-announce).

[95] Wolfie Zhao, *US May Bar Large Tech Firms From Issuing Cryptocurrencies*, COINDESK (June 15, 2019) (available online at https://www.coindesk.com/us-may-bar-large-tech-firms-from-issuing-cryptocurrencies).

[96] *Id.*

incarnation at least, would apply to tech firms with global annual revenue in excess of $25 billion, and it would impose fines of "not more than $1 million per each day of such violation."[97]

Two days of hearings were held initially, while a house judiciary subcommittee acted to extend its bipartisan investigation into the market-power of various tech giants, including Facebook.[98] A number of questions were asked and answered, although other issues remain open.[99] It was fairly clear that the U.S. reaction was not positive.[100]

While the reaction from around the world has been mixed, it has not been overwhelmingly positive. "Financial institutions of numerous countries, including . . . Japan, China, France and the United Kingdom, have expressed their concern regarding Facebook—the social media giant that has been surrounded by privacy-relate scandals like in 2018 with Cambridge Analytica. . . ."[101] Some sources questioned whether Facebook would really protect the privacy of users, especially with its prior history of lapses and abuses. Others worried that Libra could threaten the stability of the existing international monetary system or compromise competition among banking institutions. There is also the fear that Libra might become "too big to fail" (potentially requiring governments to back up a private enterprise in order to protect the global economy). One of the most commonly articulated concerns was that Libra might facilitate money laundering or the funding of criminal enterprises. As a result of these concerns, some commentators have doubted whether Libra will meet its target launch date, or whether it will ever get off the ground.[102]

On August 5, 2019, Walmart announced that it had applied for a Cryptocurrency patent for a new block-chain-based mobile payment system. Although the patent was filed January 29, 2019, the news broke in

---

[97]   *Id.*

[98]   *See generally* Assoc. Press, *Facebook's New Cryptocurrency Libra Faces US Government Backlash*, S. CHINA MORNING POST (Jul. 16, 2019) (available online at https://www.scmp.com/news/world/united-states-canada/article/3018847/facebooks-new-cryptocurrency-libra-faces-us).

[99]   *See* Josh Constine, *Highlights from Facebook's Libra Senate Hearing*, TECHCRUNCH (June, 2019) (available online at https://techcrunch.com/2019/07/16/libra-in-messenger-whats app/).

[100]   Matt Binder, *'Like a toddler' with matches: Facebook slammed by senators in Libra hearing*, MASHABLE (Jul. 16, 2019) (available online at https://mashable.com/article/facebook-libra-hearing-congress/).

[101]   Stephen O'Neal, *Facebook Libra Regulatory Overview: Major Countries' Stances on Crypto*, COINTELEGRAPH (Jul. 16, 2019) [archived at https://perma.cc/5CXF-5BVT].

[102]   Salvador Rodriguez, *The tech industry is starting to doubt Facebook will be able to launch its Libra currency by 2020*, CNBC (Jul. 10, 2019) (available online at https://www.cnbc.com/2019/07/10/tech-industry-expressing-doubt-facebook-will-launch-libra-by-2020.html). In early October 2019, PayPal pulled out of the Libra Association, being the first backer to do so. Thomas Simms, *PayPal Ditches Libra, Crypto Stagnant, Mark Cuban Hates BTC: Hodler's Digest, Sept. 30–Oct. 6*, COINTELEGRAPH (Oct. 6, 2019) [archived at https://perma.cc/53BH-8BDV]. Shortly thereafter Visa, Mastercard, and eBay backed out as well.

August, alongside official comment from Walmart that it was not actively pursuing such a cryptocurrency at this time.[103]

The new crypto, which as of the writing of these materials has not been officially named, is planned as a stablecoin pegged to the value of the dollar. Although some commentators have hypothesized that the Walmart coin might have an easier time with American regulators than Facebook's Libra,[104] that observation does not mean that this particular project will come to fruition.

Predicting how Walmart would fair if it does decide to proceed with its stablecoin is not an easy challenge. This is not Walmart's first attempt to break into banking services. In 1998 an Oklahoma state bank owned by the Walton family (which founded and still controls Walmart) converted into a national thrift with a bank charter.[105] Plans to place branches in Walmart stores, however, were thwarted at that time by Gramm-Leach-Bliley Act in 1999, which restricted the ability of a commercial entity to offer banking services. In 2001, Walmart attempted to reach an agreement with a subsidiary of Canada's Toronto Dominion Bank, but the U.S. Office of Thrift Supervision found this would give Walmart unauthorized control over the bank.[106] In 2002, Walmart was prevented by the California legislature from purchasing the Franklin Bank of California.[107] At that time, Walmart had explained the move as an effort to help reduce debit card fees.

Then, in July of 2005, Walmart attempted to obtain a license to become an industrial bank, by filing applications with the Utah Department of Financial Institutions and the Federal Deposit Insurance Corporation.[108] The stated goal of this action was to reduce banking fees incurred in connection with processing of credit, debit, and electronic check payments, enabling the company to pass these savings on to customers. Not surprisingly, banking groups vehemently opposed the request, warning that Walmart could utilize its vast commercial enterprise to drive smaller commercial banks out of business. Consumers also filed objections to the proposal, and Walmart abandoned its plans to seek a special banking charter in 2007.

---

[103]   *Walmart's Answer To Facebook's Libra: The Walmart Coin*, PYMNTS (Aug. 5, 2019) (available online at https://www.pymnts.com/news/retail/2019/walmarts-coin-facebooks-libra/).

[104]   *See, i.e.*, Max Boddy, *Expert: Walmart Crypto Project More Agreeable to Lawmakers Than Libra*, COINTELEGRAPH (Aug. 5, 2019) [archived at https://perma.cc/UJ7N-HYBS].

[105]   Kevin K. Nolan, *Wal-Mart's Industrial Loan Company: The Risk to Community Banks*, 10 N.C. BANKING Inst. 187, 191 (2006), citing Charles Davis, *US Community Bankers Rally Opposition to Wal-Mart Move*, RETAIL BANKER INT'L at 1 (Aug. 12, 2005).

[106]   Nolan, *supra* note 105 at 191.

[107]   *Id.* at 192.

[108]   Karen L. Werner, *Community Banks: Banking Coalition Seeks House Support for ILC Compromise After Wal-Mart Request*, 85 BANKING REP. 230 (2005).

The stablecoin described in Walmart's patent applications would offer Walmart some of the same advantages as the company's prior efforts to obtain a banking charter, but it also entails many of the same anti-competitive risks for other banks. Walmart is a huge commercial enterprise, and utilizing its own cryptocurrency to avoid banking fees payable to other institutions could offer the company tremendous savings as well as allowing the company to pass those savings on to consumers. It could also pose a huge threat to smaller commercial banks and lenders, and could serve as a stepping stone into other banking-like services.

While there are parallels with Facebook's recently announced plans to launch the Libra stablecoin, there are also significant differences. First, Walmart plans to peg its coin to the dollar rather than to a basket of international currencies. The Federal Reserve Bank is likely to be pleased by this distinction. Second, Walmart faces increasing competitions from online retailers such as Amazon and, in the international markets particularly, Alibaba. This make it less likely that Walmart would run the risk of creating a monopoly. Walmart also appears to lack the same "global" intention that Facebook has. Finally, it appears that the coin would operate much like a rechargeable gift card, as purchasers would essentially give cash to Walmart in exchange for the new coin, which could then be used to purchase items from the company.

On the other hand, a Walmart coin, however denominated, might be a threat to smaller banks and credit unions, and it is likely to receive a chilly welcome from crypto purists. Similarly, some individuals are likely to worry that Walmart may be less interested in protecting customers' privacy than it should be. If the proposed coin becomes a public relations problem, or is perceived as likely to become one, Walmart may never proceed with its plans for the coin.

Until Congress or other regulators rule on these and other proposals that have been made and new ones that will doubtless appear in the future, the final outcome of these initiatives is in doubt.

CHAPTER 14

REGULATION OF CRYPTO AT THE STATE LEVEL

■ ■ ■

On May 2, 2019, MIT Technology Review's Business of Blockchain conference included a panel presentation focused on "Regulation in the Blockchain Era."[1] Caitlan Long, co-founder of the Wyoming Blockchain Coalition, and Peter Van Valkenburgh, Director of Research at Coin Center, were on the panel. They are both widely regarded as experts on the topic, but they expressed significantly different views about the most desirable paradigm for regulation of crypto between federal and state authorities.

Caitlin Long argued that digital assets are property and therefore should be regulated at the state level. In her opinion, state regulation is most appropriate because states generally control property and commercial law. She has particularly praised the diligence of the Wyoming legislature in clarifying terms and regulations as applied to cryptoassets.[2] In contrast to this position, Peter Van Valkenburgh would rely on federal regulation. It is his opinion that state-level regulation, which has resulted in an inconsistent set of overlapping rules, is an inconvenience to companies and consumers.[3] It also results in rules that sometimes overprotect and sometimes fail to protect the public adequately.

Regardless of one's opinion on this issue, the reality is that states have retained considerable jurisdiction over matters relevant to crypto. They have concurrent jurisdiction over the sales of securities (unless federal law specifically exempts inconsistent state regulation, as it has done in the case of the federal registration process and some exemptions from registration).[4] In addition, it is generally recognized that while money transmitters are

---

[1] MIT Media Lab, *Business of Blockchain*, MIT TECH. REV. (May 2, 2019) [program archived at https://perma.cc/5SU9-RNSC].

[2] Her presentation is available online at https://events.technologyreview.com/video/watch/caitlin-long-financialization-cryptoassets/ (last visited June, 2019). A brief textual explanation of her comments may be found at Adrian Zmudzinski, *Crypto Regulation Experts Debate State vs. Federal Regulation in the Blockchain Era*, COINTELEGRAPH (May 4, 2019) [archived at https://perma.cc/9RSH-HR6N].

[3] His presentation is available online at https://events.technologyreview.com/video/watch/gary-gensler-crypto-regulation/ (last visited June, 2019). This presentation is also reviewed (briefly) by Zmudzinski, *supra* note 2.

[4] This is discussed *supra* in chapter 7.

subject to BSA requirements at the federal level,[5] "individual states have the authority to administer and license money transmitters."[6] States also have authority to tax cryptoassets and transactions.[7]

In 2015, two legal scholars opined that "[m]ost states have now taken positions on virtual currencies."[8] In support of that conclusion, they noted numerous state alerts and actions that followed reports from the Conference of State Bank Supervisors and the North American Securities Administrators Association.[9] While the extent of those actions at that time is debatable,[10] it is clear that significant and varied state approaches currently exist. This chapter therefore considers the existing state of such regulation, while noting that this is still evolving as states consider how to address crypto in a more comprehensive manner.

This chapter is not intended to serve as a comprehensive guide to state regulation, even as of the date of this writing. Rather, a selection of alternative approaches is included here to provide readers with a sense of the various options and approaches that are currently being taken in this sphere of regulatory influence.

1. SECURITIES LAWS

A. EFFORTS AT COORDINATION AMONG THE STATES

At the outset, it should be noted that states are not left to fend for themselves in the crypto ecosystem. They are, for example, free to borrow from the federal securities laws to the extent that they wish to do so. In addition, the North American Securities Administrators Association (NASAA)[11] has issued a number of advisories designed to help state (and foreign) agencies with the potential problems posed by crypto.

---

[5]   These are discussed *supra* in chapter 3.

[6]   For further discussion of this, see Susan Alkadri, *Defining and Regulating Cryptocurrency: Fake Internet Money or Legitimate Medium of Exchange?* DUKE L. & TECH. REV. 71, 82 (Dec. 9, 2018).

[7]   Although not a primary focus of this book, taxation (including state level regulation) is discussed *infra* in chapter 16.

[8]   Sarah Jane Hughes, Stephen T. Middlebrook, *Advancing A Framework for Regulating Cryptocurrency Payments Intermediaries*, 32 YALE J. ON REG. 495, 511 (2015).

[9]   *See, i.e.,* Conference of State Bank Supervisors & NASAA, *Model State Consumer and Investor Guidance on Virtual Currency*, CSBS.org (Apr. 23, 2014) [archived at https://perma.cc/ GMH6-GLRP].

[10]   For example, Alkadri, *supra* note 6, contends that as of her 2018 work, "[m]ost states have yet to consider cryptocurrency-specific legislation." *Id.* at 83, citing John L. Douglas, *New Wine into Old Bottles: Fintech Meets the Bank Regulatory World*, 20 N.C. BANKING INST. 17, 44–45 (2016). *Accord* Matthew E. Kohen & Justin S. Wales, *State Regulations on Virtual Currency and Blockchain Technologies—(Updated)*, CARLTON FIELDS (Oct. 17, 2017; updated Ap. 19, 2019) (available online at https://www.carltonfields.com/insights/publications/2018/state-regulations-on-virtual-currency-and-blockchain-technologies).

[11]   NASAA was organized in 1919 as a voluntary association. Its mission is to protect consumers who purchase securities. Its membership includes "67 state, provincial, and territorial

In 2014, NASAA issued its first Investor Advisory on Virtual Currency, warning investors of the potential risks of investing in the new assets.[12] In 2017, NASAA identified ICOs and other crypto contracts as emerging threats on which securities administrators might need to focus.[13] A few months later, an updated and expanded Informed Investor Advisory focusing on ICOs was issued by the NASAA, along with links to more than a dozen state-initiated enforcement actions.[14] A subsequent warning about cryptocurrencies added actions in two additional states.[15]

In May 2018, state and provincial securities regulators across the U.S. and Canada announced a coordinated international crackdown on crypto.[16] According to the early report, which was characterized as "the tip of the iceberg," 40 jurisdictions were involved in nearly 70 inquiries or investigations and 35 completed or pending enforcement actions. By August 2018 more than 200 active investigations of ICOs and crypto-related investments were underway by state and provincial authorities as part of the initiative that NASAA labeled "Operation Crytosweep."[17]

This should not, however, be taken as an indication that the states are uniform in their approach to how crypto is to be treated under state securities laws. In fact, states vary widely in their view of crypto. Some are clearly working to attract crypto entrepreneurs, and these jurisdictions have adopted securities requirements that coincide with this preference. On the other hand, some states are considerably more cautious, typically applying existing securities laws to crypto transactions. Other states have yet to signal clearly how they intend to treat these new assets. As explained by some seasoned legal practitioners:

---

securities administrators in the 50 states, the District of Columbia, Puerto Rico, the U.S. Virgin Islands, Canada, and Mexico. In the United States, NASAA is the voice of state securities agencies responsible for efficient capital formation and grass-roots investor protection." NASAA, *About Us*, http://www.nasaa.org/about-us/ [page archived at https://perma.cc/RF3Y-LLSX].

[12] NASAA, *NASAA Issues Investor Advisory on Virtual Currency* (Ap. 29, 2014) [archived at https://perma.cc/95AQ-59ZP]. The advisory itself is archived at https://perma.cc/XV29-DL9T.

[13] NASAA, *NASAA Announces Current and Emerging Investor Threats* (Dec. 13, 2017) [archived at https://perma.cc/FTQ7-6ZHY].

[14] NASAA, *Informed Investor Advisory: Initial Coin Offerings* (Ap. 2018) [archived at https://perma.cc/Y7QM-YMNV]. Most of the state enforcement actions were initiated by Massachusetts and Texas authorities, although New Jersey and North Carolina actions were also mentioned.

[15] NASAA, *Informed Investor Advisory: Cryptocurrencies* (Ap. 2018) [archived at https://perma.cc/ZN8R-4BDN] (adding examples of enforcement actions by California and South Carolina).

[16] NASAA, *State and Provincial Securities Regulators Conduct Coordinated International Crypto Crackdown* (May 21, 2018) [archived at https://perma.cc/X4M8-73TV].

[17] NASAA, *NASAA Updates Coordinated Crypto Crackdown* (Aug. 28, 2018) [archived at https://perma.cc/ZZT9-VENX]. *See also* Marc Gottridge & Evan Koster, *Merchants need a liability plan to conquer crypto payments*, PAYMENTS SOURCE (Nov. 6, 2018) (available online at https://www.paymentssource.com/opinion/merchants-need-a-fully-formed-liability-plan-to-take-crypto-payments) (commenting on the activity by state regulators).

Some states have issued guidance, opinion letters, or other information from their financial regulatory agencies regarding whether virtual currencies are "money" under existing state rules, while others have enacted piecemeal legislation amending existing definitions to either specifically include or exclude digital currencies from the definition. To use a pun those in the blockchain space should understand, there is a complete lack of consensus as to whether they do or not.[18]

To provide an indication of the range of possible approaches, information from and about the securities laws in selected American jurisdictions appears below.

B. STATES THAT CHOOSE NOT TO REGULATE

Wyoming is widely recognized as being the most pro-crypto American state. As noted by the co-founder of the Wyoming Blockchain Coalition, "Wyoming has now enacted a total of 13 blockchain-enabling laws, making it the only US state to provide a comprehensive, welcoming legal framework that enables blockchain technology to flourish, both for individuals and companies."[19] With regard to Wyoming's securities laws, the state has a very traditional definition of security, but then has an extraordinary set of provisions relating to digital assets which removes many of them from the scope of state securities regulation.

The following statutory provisions include the conventional definition of security found in the Wyoming statute, and then the newer definitions that were promulgated in order to exempt digital offerings from the state registration requirements.

WEST'S WYOMING STATUTES ANNOTATED

Title 17. Corporations, Partnerships and Associations
Chapter 4.   Securities (Refs & Annos)
(Effective: Feb. 28, 2019)

§ 17–4–102.   Definitions

(a) In this act, unless the context otherwise requires:

. . . .

(xxviii) "Security" means a note; stock; treasury stock; security future; bond; debenture; evidence of indebtedness; certificate of interest or participation in a profit-sharing agreement; collateral trust certificate; preorganization certificate or subscription; transferable

---

[18]   Kohen & Wales, *supra* note 10.

[19]   Caitlan Long, *What Do Wyoming's 13 New Blockchain Laws Mean?*, FORBES (Mar. 4, 2019) (available online at https://www.forbes.com/sites/caitlinlong/2019/03/04/what-do-wyomings-new-blockchain-laws-mean/#789ad4785fde).

share; investment contract; voting trust certificate; certificate of deposit for a security; put, call, straddle, option, or privilege on a security, certificate of deposit, or group or index of securities, including an interest therein or based on the value thereof; put, call, straddle, option, or privilege entered into on a national securities exchange relating to foreign currency; or, in general, an interest or instrument commonly known as a "security"; or a certificate of interest or participation in, temporary or interim certificate for, receipt for, guarantee of, or warrant or right to subscribe to or purchase, any of the foregoing.

. . . .

Title 34. Property, Conveyances and Security Transactions
Chapter 29. Digital Assets
(Effective: July 1, 2019)

§ 34–29–101. Definitions

(a) As used in this chapter:

(i) "Digital asset" means a representation of economic, proprietary or access rights that is stored in a computer readable format, and includes digital consumer assets, digital securities and virtual currency;

(ii) "Digital consumer asset" means a digital asset that is used or bought primarily for consumptive, personal or household purposes and includes:

(A) An open blockchain token constituting intangible personal property as otherwise provided by law;

(B) Any other digital asset which does not fall within paragraphs (iii) and (iv) of this subsection.

(iii) "Digital security" means a digital asset which constitutes a security, as defined in W.S. 17–4–102(a)(xxviii), but shall exclude digital consumer assets and virtual currency;

(iv) "Virtual currency" means a digital asset that is:

(A) Used as a medium of exchange, unit of account or store of value; and

(B) Not recognized as legal tender by the United States government.

(b) The terms in paragraphs (a)(ii) through (iv) of this section are mutually exclusive.

§ 34–29–102. Classification of digital assets as property; applicability to Uniform Commercial Code

(a) Digital assets are classified in the following manner:

(i) Digital consumer assets are intangible personal property and shall be considered general intangibles, as defined in W.S. 34.1–9–102(a)(xlii), only for the purposes of article 9 of the Uniform Commercial Code, title 34.1, Wyoming statutes;

(ii) Digital securities are intangible personal property and shall be considered securities, as defined in W.S. 34.1–8–102(a)(xv), and investment property, as defined in W.S. 34.1–9–102(a)(xlix), only for the purposes of articles 8 and 9 of the Uniform Commercial Code, title 34.1, Wyoming statutes;

(iii) Virtual currency is intangible personal property and shall be considered money, notwithstanding W.S. 34.1–1–201(b)(xxiv), only for the purposes of article 9 of the Uniform Commercial Code, title 34.1, Wyoming statutes.

(b) Consistent with W.S. 34.1–8–102(a)(ix), a digital asset may be treated as a financial asset under that paragraph, pursuant to a written agreement with the owner of the digital asset. If treated as a financial asset, the digital asset shall remain intangible personal property.

(c) A bank providing custodial services under W.S. 34–29–104 shall be considered to meet the requirements of W.S. 34.1–8–102(a)(xiv).

(d) Classification of digital assets under this section shall be construed in a manner to give the greatest effect to this chapter, but shall not be construed to apply to any other asset.

NOTES AND QUESTIONS

1. The Wyoming securities statute contains essentially the same definition of security as found in the federal securities laws. This definition (which includes the term "investment contract") has not been amended, and the term "investment contract" has not been defined to exclude cryptoassets. When is crypto not a security under the Wyoming securities laws? Will crypto ever be a security under the Wyoming securities laws? How do the state statutes accomplish these results?

2. For what purposes would cryptoassets be treated as securities under these new laws? What is the importance of having them treated as securities for some purposes and not for others?

Note that the above sections of Wyoming law are the most recent statutory provisions relating to the securities treatment of cryptoassets in that state. Originally, the Wyoming statutes spoke in terms of utility tokens, but the current iteration references "digital consumer asset." This phrase is defined in Wyo. Stat. § 34–29–101(a)(2) as "a digital asset that is used or bought primarily for consumptive, personal or household purposes," including without limitation blockchain tokens. These kinds of tokens are specifically exempted from the definition of security except insofar as that classification explains how to take and perfect security interests in the assets. The Wyoming approach has also been adopted by Arizona and has been proposed by a handful of additional states.[20]

Montana is also experimenting with exempting utility tokens from its securities laws. In May 2019, Montana House Bill 584 was signed into law by Governor Steve Bullock. This Act amended the Montana Code effective July 1, 2019, with a designated termination date of September 30, 2023. The amended provision of state law reads as follows:

Montana Code 30–10–105. Exempt transactions—rulemaking.

Except as expressly provided in this section, 30–10–201 through 30–10–207 and 30–10–211[21] do not apply to the following transactions:

. . . .

(23)(a) a utility token transaction that meets the following requirements:

(i) the purpose of the utility token is primarily consumptive;

(ii) the issuer of the utility token markets the utility token for a consumptive purpose and does not market the utility token to be used for a speculative or investment purpose;

(iii) the issuer of the utility token files a notice of intent to sell utility tokens with the securities commissioner in a form prescribed by the commissioner. If the information contained on the notice required in this section becomes inaccurate in any material respect for any reason, the issuer shall file an amendment to the notice in writing with the securities commissioner within 30 days.

(iv) either the utility token is available at the time of sale, or all of the following are met:

(A) the consumptive purpose of the utility token is available within 180 days after the time of sale or transfer of the utility token;

---

[20]   *See* Long, *supra* note 19.

[21]   The referenced provisions relate to registration of securities under Montana law.

(B) the initial buyer is prohibited from reselling or transferring the utility token until the consumptive purpose of the utility token is available; and

(C) the initial buyer provides a knowing and clear acknowledgment that the initial buyer is purchasing the utility token with the primary intent to use the utility token for a consumptive purpose and not for a speculative or investment purpose.

(b) Except as provided in this subsection (23), the securities commissioner may enter into agreements with federal, state, or foreign regulators to allow utility tokens issued, purchased, sold, or transferred in this state to be issued, purchased, sold, or transferred in another jurisdiction, and any utility tokens issued, purchased, sold, or transferred in another jurisdiction to be issued, purchased, sold, or transferred in this state.

(c) As used in this subsection (23), the following definitions apply:

(i) "Consumptive purpose" means to provide or receive goods, services, or content including access to goods, services, or content.

(ii) "Utility token" means a digital unit that is:

(A) created:

(I) in response to the verification or collection of a specified number of transactions relating to a digital ledger or database;

(II) by deploying computer code to a blockchain network that allows for the creation of digital tokens or other units; or

(III) using any combination of the methods specified in subsections (23)(c)(ii)(A)(I) or (23)(c)(ii)(A)(II);

(B) recorded in a digital ledger or database that is chronological, consensus-based, decentralized, and mathematically verified in nature, especially relating to the supply of units and their distribution;

(C) capable of being exchanged or transferred between persons without an intermediary or custodian; and

(D) issued to allow the holder of the digital unit access to a good or service delivered by the issuer without vesting the holder with any ownership interest or equity interest in the issuer."

QUESTIONS

1. How does the Montana approach, which also exempts some tokens from the state securities laws, differ from that taken in Wyoming?

2. Do you find one of these approaches easier to understand than the other?

Note that Montana law continues to use the phrase "utility token," but in order for such tokens to be exempt, they must have been designed for and been marketed for a consumptive rather than speculative purpose.

Colorado has also enacted "limited exemptions from the securities registration and securities broker-dealer and salesperson licensing requirements for persons dealing in digital tokens,"[22] and according to the state offers "limited exemptions from the securities registration" of digital tokens.[23] A few other states have considered or are considering similar actions.[24]

C. STATES THAT CHOOSE TO REGULATE

Absent legislative intervention, state securities regulators have generally been free to determine whether and how to proceed against crypto offerings under traditional regulations. Just as the SEC has applied the traditional *Howey* investment contract analysis to cryptotransactions, absent legislatively imposed exemptions, state authorities have been free to pursue enforcement actions as they deem necessary or appropriate.

In December 2017, Massachusetts announced a sweep of entities raising funds in that state through ICOs.[25] Sixteen months later, the Massachusetts securities regulator issued consent orders halting five initial coin offerings based on allegations that the offerings involved the sale of unregistered securities in violation of Massachusetts law.[26]

---

[22] Abhimanyu Krishnan, *Crypto Regulation Passed: Colorado Exempts Cryptocurrencies From Securities Laws*, INVEST IN BLOCKCHAIN (Mar. 11, 2019) (available online at https://www.investinblockchain.com/colorado-exempts-cryptocurrencies-from-securities-laws/). A copy of the Act is archived at https://perma.cc/4S6U-S5NH].

[23] In March 2019, Colorado enacted the Digital Token Act of 2019, providing limited exemptions from the securities registration and securities broker-dealer and salesperson licensing requirements for persons dealing in digital tokens. COLO. REV. STAT. § 11–51–308.7.

[24] For example, on January 3, 2019, the North Dakota House introduced H.B. 1043 and H.B. 3004, which would have exempted "an open blockchain token from specified securities transactions and dealings." The bill was, however, defeated on its second reading on January 11, 2019. The Rhode Island House proposed a bill that, among other things, would have exempted virtual-currency from securities requirements. 2019 RI H.B. 5776 (NS) (Feb. 28, 2019). The bill was referred to the House Finance Committee and has not been advanced since that time.

[25] *See* Mass. Sec. of the Commonwealth, *"Secretary Galvin Issues Orders In Connection with ICO Cryptocurrency Sweep,"* (Mar. 27, 2018), [list of actions archived at https://perma.cc/TM73-XHYM].

[26] JOSEPH C. LONG ET AL, 12 BLUE SKY LAW § 3:111 (Nov. 2018 Update).

The Massachusetts consent order in *In re 18moons, Inc.* is illustrative of the way in which Massachusetts has applied its securities laws to the sale of cryptoassets. As you read the following, remember that this is not the result of a judicial determination, but is rather a consent decree where the alleged facts have neither been admitted to nor denied by the company that was investigated.

IN RE: 18MOONS, INC.

Docket No., E–2018–001 (Mass. Mar. 27, 2018)[27]

Consent Order

I. PRELIMINARY STATEMENT

This Consent Order ("Order") is entered into by the Massachusetts Securities Division (the "Division") and 18moons, Inc. (hereinafter "18moons") with respect to . . . whether 18moons' activities and conduct violated . . . the Massachusetts Uniform Securities Act (the "Act"), and the corresponding regulations promulgated thereunder . . . (the "Regulations").

On March 26, 2018, 18moons submitted an Offer of Settlement ("Offer") to the Division. 18moons neither admits nor denies the Statement of Facts set forth in Section V and the Violations of Law set forth in Section VI herein, and consents to the entry of this Order . . . with prejudice.

II. JURISDICTION AND AUTHORITY

1. As provided for by the Act, the Division has jurisdiction over matters relating to securities. The Act authorizes the Division to regulate the offers and/or sales of securities, as well as those individuals offering and/or selling securities within the Commonwealth.

2. The Offer was made and this Order is entered in accordance with the Act. Specifically, the acts and practices investigated by the Enforcement Section took place in Massachusetts.

III. RELEVANT TIME PERIOD

3. Except as otherwise expressly stated, the conduct described herein occurred during the approximate time period of December 15, 2016 to January 25, 2018 (the "Relevant Time Period").

IV. RESPONDENT

4. 18moons, Inc. is a corporation organized under the laws of Delaware. 18moons registered as a foreign corporation in Massachusetts on December 2, 2016.

. . . .

---

[27] The Consent Order is available in its entirety at http://www.sec.state.ma.us/sct/current/sctcryptocurrency/MSD-18moons-Consent-Order-E-2018-0010.pdf.

V. STATEMENT OF FACTS

5.   18moons is a company that creates, produces and distributes children's programming.

6.   In January 2018, the 18moons Chief Financial Officer stated that the company had 1.5 million monthly active users.

7.   In late 2017, 18moons began to plan its initial coin offering of Planet Kids Coins (hereinafter "PKCs").

8.   8moons planned to offer a maximum $10 million (USD) of PKCs in February 2018, with a soft cap of $1 million (USD).

9.   18moons planned to authorize a maximum of 125,000,000 PKCs and to offer up to 100,000,000 PKCs to potential purchasers.

10. PKCs were to be implemented as Ethereum-based tokens on the Ethereum blockchain, as opposed to an independent blockchain.

11. 18moons planned that the initial price of a PKC would be $0.10 (USD).

12. 18moons structured a two-tier bonus structure whereby "early birds" would receive a 3% bonus if they purchased between 1–5 million PKCs, and a 10% bonus if they purchased between 50–100 million PKCs.

13. 18moons utilized certain social media platforms, including Bitcointalk, Reddit, Telegram, Twitter, and YouTube to make potential purchasers aware of the planned offering of PKCs.

14. After receiving the Division's January 25, 2018 subpoena, 18moons noted on its website and represented to the Division that it decided to postpone indefinitely the proposed offering of PKCs.

15. 18moons planned to make PKCs available for purchase using USD or other cryptocurrencies.

16. 18moons intended to pool funds raised from the sale of PKCs "to fuel the development and maintenance of the platform."

17. The value of PKCs were to be based on the price traded on cryptocurrency exchanges.

18. During the Relevant Time Period, 18moons was not registered in any capacity in the securities industry in Massachusetts.

19. PKCs are not registered in Massachusetts.

VI. VIOLATIONS OF LAW

Count I—Violations of MASS. GEN. LAWS ch. 110A, § 301

20. Section 301 of the Act provides:

It is unlawful for any person to offer or sell any security in the commonwealth unless:—

(1)   the security is registered under this chapter;

(2)   the security or transaction is exempted under section 402; or

(3)   the security is a federal covered security.

MASS. GEN. LAWS ch. 110A, § 301.

21. Section 401(k) of the Act provides:

"Security" means any note; stock; treasury stock; bond; debenture; evidence of indebtedness; certificate of interest or participation in any profit-sharing agreement; collateral-trust certificate; preorganization certificate or subscription; transferable share; investment contract; voting-trust certificate; certificate of deposit for a security; certificate of interest or participation in an oil, gas, or mining title or lease or in payments out of production under such a title or lease; or, in general, any interest or instrument commonly known as a "security," or any certificate of interest or participation in, temporary or interim certificate for, receipt for, guarantee of, or warrant or right to subscribe to or purchase, any of the foregoing.

. . . .

MASS. GEN.LAWS ch. 110A, § 401(k).

22. Section 14.401 of the Regulations provides:

Investment Contract, as used in Section 401(k) of the Act, includes:

(1)   any investment in a common enterprise with the expectation of profit to be derived through the essential managerial efforts of someone other than the investor. As used in 950 CMR 14.401, a "common enterprise" means an enterprise in which the fortunes of the investor are interwoven with and dependent upon the efforts and successes of those seeking the investment or a third party; and

(2)   any investment by which an offeree furnishes initial value to an offeror, and a portion of this initial value is subject to the risks of the enterprise, and the furnishing of the initial value is induced by the offeror's promises or representations which give rise to a reasonable understanding that a valuable benefit of some kind over and above the initial value will accrue to the offeree as a result of the operation of the enterprise, and the offeree does not receive the right to

exercise practical and actual control over the management of the enterprise.

950 MASS. CODE REGS. 14.401.

23. The Enforcement Section alleges that the conduct of 18moons, as described above, constitutes violations of MASS. GEN. LAWS ch. 110A, § 301.

VII. ORDER

IT IS HEREBY ORDERED:

A.　18moons shall not sell unregistered or non-exempt securities in Massachusetts;

B.　l 8moons is censured by the Division;

C.　18moons shall not make offers and sales of PKCs in Massachusetts until PKCs, or other such offerings, are registered as securities or are exempt from registration as securities in Massachusetts. For any future registered or exempt offers of securities in Massachusetts, 18moons shall file a Form U-2, Consent to Service of Process, with the Division to the extent required by MASS. GEN. LAWS. ch. 110A, § 414(g);

D.　Prior to making any offers or sales of PKCs, or other such offerings, 18moons shall provide the Enforcement Section with written notice of such securities offerings;

E.　If applicable, 18moons shall offer rescission of sales of PKCs to those investors who purchased PKCs prior to the date of this Order; and

F.　Upon issuance of the Order, if 18moons fails to comply with any of the terms set forth in the Division's Order, the Enforcement Section may take appropriate action. Additionally, after a fair hearing and the issuance of an appropriate order finding that 18moons has not complied with the Order, the Enforcement Section may move to have the Order declared null and void, in whole or in part, and re-institute the associated investigation.

. . . .

WILLIAM FRANCIS GALVIN
SECRETARY OF THE COMMONWEALTH

[signature block omitted]

Date: March 27, 2018.

NOTES AND QUESTIONS

1.　Note that there was no special definition of security referenced in the Order as being applicable to cryptoassets, although the Massachusetts statute (unlike federal law) does include a statutory definition of "investment contract." How does the state regulatory definition of investment contract differ from the federal *Howey* test?

2.   The factual underpinning of the preceding order relates to the failure of 18moons to register the offering (or comply with an available exemption) rather than to any concern about fraudulent misrepresentations. Given that there was no problem with fraud, who is being protected by this kind of state action? How are they being protected?

3.   Assume the proposed sale complied with an available exemption from registration under the federal securities laws (other than being exempt for being an intrastate offering). To what extent should this suffice to protect state investors as well?

Texas is another state that has been active in the context of crypto, but its early focus was on fraudulent offerings. In 2017, the Texas State Securities Board launched an investigation into cryptocurrency offerings directed at Texas residents.[28] The result was a finding of widespread fraud utilizing such practices as phony web sites, faked photographs, and false claims of famous investors. As a result of the investigation, the Texas securities authority issued 10 cease-and-desist orders against promoters of allegedly illegal or fraudulent initial coin offerings. The scope of Texas' inquiry went beyond fraud, however, as noted in an April 2018 Investor Alert that expressed concern over the fact that in the 32 investigations into crypto offerings "[n]o promoters were registered to sell securities in Texas, a violation of the Texas Securities Act."[29] A January 4, 2018, Emergency Cease and Desist Order issued against BitConnect, a U.K.-based crypto marketplace, further reinforces these concerns.[30] This order asserts that BitConnect was improperly offering to trade impermissibly unregistered securities, while simultaneously promising inflated and unrealistic rates of return.[31]

In its notice about the enforcement efforts, the Texas Securities regulator was careful to say that it "is not regulating the cryptocurrencies themselves, only the investments that claim to use virtual currencies in an investment program."[32] On the other hand, it has also warned that it is continuing to investigate other suspect offerings.

---

[28]   *See* Tx St. Sec. Bd, *Investor Alert: Cryptocurrencies-Widespread Fraud Found in Cryptocurrency Offerings*, at 1 (Apr. 10, 2018), [archived at https://perma.cc/5ZXL-S2F7].

[29]   *Id.*

[30]   *In re Bitconnect*, Tx St. Sec. Bd, Order No. ENF–18–CDO–1754 [archived at https://perma.cc/Y4TP-M6DU].

[31]   Tex. St. Sec. Bd, *$4 Billion Crypto-Promoter Ordered to Halt Fraudulent Sales* (Jan. 4, 2018) [archived at https://perma.cc/Y577-KEGY].

[32]   *Alert, supra* note 28.

As noted above, a number of other states have also initiated enforcement actions against crypto-based businesses.[33] However, as of this writing, none of these states have securities regulations that are tougher on cryptoassets than on other interests, and to date none have new definitions specifically bringing crypto within the purview of the state securities laws. On the other hand, as has been the case with federal law, state definitions of what constitutes a security have generally been broad enough to encompass crypto, at least in the opinion of some regulators.

D. STATES WHERE THERE IS SIGNIFICANT UNCERTAINTY

Probably the largest number of states have yet to speak clearly about how they intend to approach the securities treatment of crypto. They have neither adopted new laws or regulations, nor published any firm guidance for companies in the crypto industry.

Some states warn potential investors about the risks of investing, without clearly acting to subject businesses that sell crypto to the authority of the securities regulators. For example, in August 2014, the Louisiana Office of Financial Institutions issued a set of guidelines for cryptocurrency consumers and investors.[34] The state has not, however, made any move to subject crypto to oversight by the state securities regulator.[35] Similarly, Iowa has also warned investors to proceed with caution.[36] But like Louisiana, it has not announced if or when the state securities administrator will exercise authority over crypto offered or sold to its residents.[37] Other states have made no pronouncement at all.[38]

2. MONEY TRANSMISSION REQUIREMENTS

The preceding materials discuss state securities laws as they apply to crypto. States also regulate, or have the potential to regulate, crypto-based businesses as money transmitters.

---

[33]   *See supra* notes 16–17. Other states also participated in the crackdown. *See, i.e.,* Mn Commerce Dep't, *Minnesota Commerce Department joins other states in international cryptocurrency investment* crackdown (May 2018) [archived at https://perma.cc/9NAS-HQNP].

[34]   La. Off. Fin. Inst, *Consumer and Investor Advisory on Virtual Currency* (Aug. 2014) [archived at https://perma.cc/EVY7-JJ6J].

[35]   Alex Hamilton, *Digital states: Cryptocurrency rules and regulations across the US*, BOBS GUIDE (Feb. 8, 2019) [archived at https://perma.cc/XY8Y-B3GD].

[36]   Iowa Insurance Div., *Iowa Insurance Division Reminds Investors to Approach Cryptocurrency with Caution* (Jan. 4, 2018) [archived at https://perma.cc/86JQ-L7T7?type=image] (screenshot view).

[37]   Hamilton, *supra* note 35.

[38]   For example, Arkansas has no official position on the securities treatment of crypto. Kentucky is in the same position. Hamilton, *supra* note 35 ("There is currently no cryptocurrency-related legislation in place, or pending, in Kentucky.").

A. STATE REGULATION OF MONEY TRANSMISSION

In addition to the federal requirements of the BSA which are overseen by FinCEN, "[f]orty-seven states and the District of Columbia have money transmitter licensing requirements."[39] Unfortunately, states are no more consistent in deciding how they should apply their money transmitter requirements to crypto businesses than they are in determining how to apply their securities laws.

In 2015, to aid states desiring to impose regulations on businesses involved with the transmission and exchange of virtual currencies, the Counsel of State Bank Supervisors (CSBS) adopted a model framework suggesting that "states regulate cryptocurrency businesses as they regulate fiat money transmission and exchanges."[40] An excerpt from that framework follows:

CSBS, *STATE REGULATORY REQUIREMENTS FOR VIRTUAL CURRENCY ACTIVITIES CSBS MODEL REGULATORY FRAMEWORK*
(September 15, 2015)[41]

Introduction

. . . .

Licensing and supervision serve as a mechanism for protecting consumers, ensuring system stability, safeguarding market development, and assisting law enforcement. To further these objectives, meet the needs of states to address virtual currency activities, and promote consistent state regulation of virtual currency activities, CSBS developed a Draft Model Regulatory Framework ("Draft Framework") for state virtual currency regulatory regimes. The Draft Framework was released for public comment to seek feedback on the framework and on specific questions related to virtual currency.

. . . .

MODEL REGULATORY FRAMEWORK

Policy Statement

State regulators have determined that certain virtual currency activities raise concerns in the areas of consumer protection, marketplace stability, and law enforcement.

. . . .

---

[39]   Meghan E. Griffiths, *Virtual Currency Businesses: An Analysis of the Evolving Regulatory Landscape*, 16 TEX. TECH ADMIN. L.J. 303, 309 (2015).

[40]   Susan Alkadri, *supra* note 6 at 89–90.

[41]   This document is archived at https://perma.cc/2V33-W7QT.

Virtual Currency Defined

Virtual Currency is a digital representation of value used as a medium of exchange, a unit of account, or a store of value, but does not have legal tender status as recognized by the United States Government. Virtual Currency does not include the software or protocols governing the transfer of the digital representation of value. Virtual Currency does not include stored value redeemable exclusively in goods or services limited to transactions involving a defined merchant. Virtual Currency does not include units of value that are issued in affinity or rewards programs and that cannot be redeemed for either fiat or virtual currencies. Virtual currency, as used in this framework, includes "digital currency" and "cryptocurrency."

Covered Activities

This model regulatory framework applies to activities involving third party control of virtual currency. At a minimum, this covers entities engaged in the following virtual currency activities when carried out on behalf of another:

- Transmission
- Exchanging:
  - Sovereign currency for virtual currency or virtual currency for sovereign currency
  - Virtual currency for virtual currency
- Services that facilitate the third-party exchange, storage, and/or transmission of virtual currency (e.g. wallets, vaults, kiosks, merchant-acquirers, and payment processors).

Exclusions

Virtual currency activities outside of the covered activities described above are not covered by the policy statement or by the regulatory requirements discussed in this document. In particular, the Framework is not intended to cover:

- Merchants and consumers who use virtual currencies solely for the purchase or sale of goods or services;
- Activities that are not financial in nature but utilize technologies similar to those used by digital currency. For example, a cryptography-based distributed ledger system for non-financial recordkeeping would be outside the scope of this policy;
- Activities involving units of value that are issued in affinity or rewards programs and that cannot be redeemed for either fiat or virtual currencies; or

- Activities involving units of value that are used solely within online gaming platforms and have no market or application outside of those gaming platforms.

Activities performed by entities otherwise exempt from laws and regulations applicable to covered activities should remain exempt. Specifically, the model regulatory framework does not apply to depository institutions.

Regulatory Requirements .... [Details for each of the following requirements are omitted.]

1. Licensing Requirements

2. Use of Licensing Systems

3. Financial Strength and Stability

4. Consumer Protection

5. Cyber Security

6. Compliance (General)

7. Bank Secrecy Act/Anti-Money Laundering

8. Books and Records

9. Supervision

. . . .

NOTES AND QUESTIONS

1.   Federal regulation of crypto-based businesses includes various money transmitter requirements, which often impose the obligation to adopt a risk-based compliance plan to insure that the business satisfies AML and KYC obligations. To what extent does state regulation add significant levels of protection against money laundering and funding of criminal enterprises?

2.   What is the cost of having a double layer of enforcement? Overseeing compliance obligations requires considerable resources. Why, then, are so many states insistent on their right and need to regulate crypto businesses as money transmitters?

Another effort at encouraging uniformity while providing states with guidance as to how they might proceed with regulations of crypto was spearheaded by the Uniform Law Commission (ULC). In 2017, the ULC finalized the Uniform Regulation of Virtual-Currency Business Act ("Uniform Act") as a model statute for state adoption.[42] During the drafting process, the ULC solicited comments and input from a wide range of

---

[42]   National Conference of Commissioners on Uniform State Laws ("ULC"), UNIFORM REGULATION OF VIRTUAL-CURRENCY BUSINESSES ACT (2017), available online for download (with comments) at https://www.uniformlaws.org/viewdocument/final-act-with-comments-72?Community Key=e104aaa8-c10f-45a7-a34a-0423c2106778&tab=librarydocuments (hereinafter Uniform Act).

interested parties including the U.S. Department of the Treasury, the Federal Reserve Bank of New York, the Conference of State Bank Supervisors (CSBS), the Texas Department of Banking, the California Department of Business Oversight, the Electronic Freedom Frontier, Coinbase, Inc., the Bitcoin Foundation, and PayPal.[43]

In essence, with certain exemptions, the Uniform Act requires a license in order for a business to legally "engage in virtual-currency business activity" or to hold oneself out as doing so.[44] To give an idea of the complexity of the Uniform Act, hopefully without being overwhelming, consider these provisions. They are presented out of order, with the substantive prohibition in section 201 appearing first, followed by certain definitions from section 102, which are also presented out of order. For ease in readability, some formatting changes have been made.

UNIFORM REGULATION OF VIRTUAL-CURRENCY BUSINESSES ACT

drafted by the
NATIONAL CONFERENCE OF COMMISSIONERS
ON UNIFORM STATE LAWS[45]

SECTION 201. CONDITIONS PRECEDENT TO ENGAGING IN VIRTUAL-CURRENCY BUSINESS ACTIVITY. A person may not engage in virtual-currency business activity, or hold itself out as being able to engage in virtual-currency business activity, with or on behalf of a resident unless the person is:

(1) licensed in this state by the department under Section 202;

(2) licensed in another state to conduct virtual-currency business activity by a state with which this state has a reciprocity agreement and has qualified under Section 203;

(3) registered with the department and operating in compliance with Section 207; or

(4) exempt from licensure or registration under this [act] by Section 103(b) or (c).

SECTION 102. DEFINITIONS. In this [act]:

. . . .

(23) "**Virtual currency**":

(A) means a digital representation of value that:

---

[43] The extensive process is described in the prefatory note to the Uniform Act (with comments), at pp. 11–12.

[44] Uniform Act, *supra* note 41 at § 201.

[45] Copyright © 2017 by National Conference of Commissioners on Uniform State Laws.

    (i)   is used as a medium of exchange, unit of account, or store of value; and

    (ii) is not legal tender, whether or not denominated in legal tender; and

(B) does not include:

    (i)   a transaction in which a merchant grants, as part of an affinity or rewards program, value that cannot be taken from or exchanged with the merchant for legal tender, bank credit, or virtual currency; or

    (ii) a digital representation of value issued by or on behalf of a publisher and used solely within an online game, game platform, or family of games sold by the same publisher or offered on the same game platform.

. . . .

(25) "**Virtual-currency business activity**" means:

(A) exchanging, transferring, or storing virtual currency or engaging in virtual-currency administration, whether directly or through an agreement with a virtual-currency control-services vendor;

(B) holding electronic precious metals or electronic certificates representing interests in precious metals on behalf of another person or issuing shares or electronic certificates representing interests in precious metals; or

(C) exchanging one or more digital representations of value used within one or more online games, game platforms, or family of games for:

    (i)   virtual currency offered by or on behalf of the same publisher from which the original digital representation of value was received; or

    (ii) legal tender or bank credit outside the online game, game platform, or family of games offered by or on behalf of the same publisher from which the original digital representation of value was received.

. . . .

(5) "**Exchange**," used as a verb, means to assume control of virtual currency from or on behalf of a resident, at least momentarily, to sell, trade, or convert:

(A) virtual currency for legal tender, bank credit, or one or more forms of virtual currency; or

(B) legal tender or bank credit for one or more forms of virtual currency.

. . . .

(21) "**Transfer**" means to assume control of virtual currency from or on behalf of a resident and to:

(A) credit the virtual currency to the account of another person;

(B) move the virtual currency from one account of a resident to another account of the same resident; or

(C) relinquish control of virtual currency to another person.

. . . .

(20) "**Store**," except in the phrase "store of value," means to maintain control of virtual currency on behalf of a resident by a person other than the resident. "Storage" and "storing" have corresponding meanings.

. . . .

(3) "**Control**" means:

(A) when used in reference to a transaction or relationship involving virtual currency, power to execute unilaterally or prevent indefinitely a virtual-currency transaction; and

(B) when used in reference to a person, the direct or indirect power to direct the management, operations, or policies of the person through legal or beneficial ownership of voting power in the person or under a contract, arrangement, or understanding.

. . . .

(24) "**Virtual-currency administration**" means issuing virtual currency with the authority to redeem the currency for legal tender, bank credit, or other virtual currency.

. . . .

When you trace through these provisions, it is clear that businesses must be licensed under the Act if they intend to exchange, transfer, or store virtual currency, or if they will be engaging in virtual-currency administration. Virtual currency is very broadly defined, although the Act excludes non-convertible merchant affinity or rewards interests and most representations of value limited to online games. In addition, in order to be covered as a business engaged in the exchanging, transferring, or storing of virtual currency, the business must have control over the particular activity on behalf of a third party, which means the power to unilaterally execute or prevent a transaction.

Although the applicable provisions are not excerpted here, there are some exemptions built into the Act, including a three-tiered system of regulation designed to allow businesses to "ramp up" their activities before obtaining the license described in the Uniform Act. However, the first tier (which would exempt a business from licensure) is limited to businesses whose virtual currency business activity within a state "is reasonably expected to be valued, in the aggregate [within that state], on an annual basis at $5,000 or less." The second-tier allows a business to register rather than obtaining a license, but it is limited to entities whose annual virtual currency activity in the state is not expected to exceed $35,000. In addition to the relatively lower dollar limit, the registration requirements are similar to the licensure requirements in several respects, and the option is only available for two years, after which the entity must cease its virtual currency business or apply for a license even if it will not exceed annual in-state earnings of $35,000.

The Uniform Act also includes exemptions that appear to mirror most common exemptions in state money transmission statutes. Among these are exemptions for government agencies; banks (including the OCC's proposed special purpose national bank, but not industrial loan companies); entities providing processing or clearing services; and persons using virtual currency on their own behalf; for personal, family, or household purposes; or for academic purposes. Entities that are licensed under the state's money transmission statute and which have obtained permission to engage in virtual currency activities need not be licensed under the Uniform Act, although they must comply with certain of its provisions.

There are other exemptions from the licensing requirements, including exemptions for any person who only provides processing, clearing, or settlement services to exempt virtual currency businesses, or any person who "contributes only connectivity software or computing power to a decentralized virtual currency, or to a protocol governing transfer of the digital representation of value," or who "provides only data storage or security services" for a virtual currency business. Other exemptions exist for dealers in foreign exchange, attorneys, and title insurance companies providing escrow services, securities or commodities intermediaries, secured creditors, virtual currency control-services vendors, and persons that do not charge for their virtual currency business activities. The Uniform Act also exempts any virtual currency transaction that is subject to the Electronic Fund Transfer Act, the Securities Exchange Act of 1934, or the Commodities Exchange Act.

As of mid-2019, only a handful of states had introduced bills proposing the adoption of the Uniform Act, and no state had yet done so.[46]

Not surprisingly, despite the efforts of these national groups encouraging states to regulate businesses involved in crypto as money

---

[46]   The states with bills proposing adopting of the act as of June 1, 2019 were California, Oklahoma, Rhode Island, Nevada, and Hawaii. Information from ULC, *Regulation of Virtual Currency Business Act* [archived at https://perma.cc/2KFJ-ZNMY].

transmitters under state law, there is a wide range of opinion at the state level. Some states have explicitly chosen not to regulate crypto under state money transmission laws, either adopting new legislation that compels that result or interpreting pre-existing statutes narrowly so that crypto is not covered. Others have chosen to regulate, with some states adopting new provisions and some interpreting existing requirements broadly so as to encompass crypto businesses. Others have more complicated interpretations, sometimes covering crypto businesses and sometimes exempting them, or simply staying silent so that there is no clarity in determining how the state might approach crypto. Examples from states that fall into each of those categories follows.

These examples, which are not intended to be a comprehensive listing of all states in each category, is accurate as of mid-2019, but because this is such a dynamic and evolving area of law, it is possible and even probable that over time some states will change their position.[47] Still, this material should provide an illustration of the variety of state approaches, which makes compliance with these requirements onerous.

B. STATES THAT CHOOSE NOT TO REGULATE

Wyoming is an example of a state that has taken specific action to remove crypto from state money transmission requirements. That state has a specific statutory provision that exempts virtual currency from the Wyoming Money Transmitters Act.[48] That act defines "virtual currency" as "any type of digital representation of value that: (A) is used as a medium of exchange, unit of account or store of value; and (B) is not recognized as legal tender by the United States government."[49]

Similarly, in June 2017, New Hampshire amended its money transmitter licensing requirement to exempt "[p]ersons who engage in the business of selling or issuing payment instruments or stored value solely in the form of convertible virtual currency or receive convertible virtual currency for transmission to another location."[50] This provision does make such persons subject to the state deceptive practices restrictions.

Other states have acted through official channels short of legislative pronouncements. For example, Alaska is one jurisdiction with no blockchain, cryptocurrency, or virtual currency references in the state statutes or regulations. However, the state's Division of Banking and Services has issued guidance to the effect that it is not authorized to

---

[47]   A somewhat more updated list, which also does not purport to be all-inclusive, is described in Carol Goforth, *The Case for Preempting State Money Transmission Laws for Crypto-based Businesses*, 73 AR. L. REV. ___ (2020) (forthcoming as of the date this book was edited).

[48]   *See* WYO. STAT. ANN. § 40–22–104(a)(vi).

[49]   WYO. STAT. ANN. § 40–22–102(xxii).

[50]   N.H. REV. STAT. ANN. § 399–G:3.

regulate virtual currencies as only transactions involving fiat currencies are subject to the state's money transmitter law.[51]

A number of other states where finance and money transmitter laws do not mention virtual currencies or crypto have reached the same or similar conclusions. For example, the Illinois Department of Financial and Professional Regulation has issued guidance concluding that virtual currencies are not "money" under the Illinois money transmitters act, and therefore "[a] person or entity engaged in the transmission of solely digital currencies, as defined, would not be required to obtain a . . . license."[52] North Dakota's Department of Financial Institutions has issued guidance under that state's law to the effect that: "The purchase, sale, or exchange of virtual currency does not in and of itself require a money transmitter license."[53] Tennessee takes the same position, having issued guidance explaining that it does not consider virtual currency to be money under its money transmitter act and therefore, no license is required.[54]

C. STATES THAT CHOOSE TO REGULATE

At the other end of the spectrum are states that have specifically determined, either through legislative amendments or official interpretations, that crypto is subject to state money transmitter requirements. Perhaps as a result of the urging of national groups, a number of state legislatures have acted to provide regulatory clarity by legislative initiatives that explicitly expand coverage of state money transmitter requirements to crypto.

North Carolina amended its Money Transmitter Act[55] in 2016 to include persons who transmit virtual currency, requiring those already operating in the cryptocurrency space to apply for a license to do so. The law does provide some exemptions, including for virtual currency miners and software firms implementing smart contracts. The statute defines "virtual currency" as "[a] digital representation of value that can be digitally traded and functions as a medium of exchange, a unit of account, or a store of value . . . but does not have legal tender status as recognized by the United States Government."[56]

---

[51]   Kohen & Wales, *supra* note 10.

[52]   *See* Illinois Department of Financial and Professional Regulation, *Digital Currency Regulatory Guidance*, (June 13, 2017) (archived at https://perma.cc/QAA5-JC26).

[53]   N.D. Financial Institutions, *FAQs—Non-Depository* (available online at https://www.nd. gov/dfi/about-dfi/non-depository/frequently-asked-questions-non-depository) (answer in response to the question: "Do I need a money transmitter license to purchase, sell, or operate an exchange for virtual currency?")

[54]   Memo, Tenn. Dep't of Fin. Inst., Regulatory Treatment of Virtual Currencies under the Tennessee Money Transmitter Act (Dec. 16, 2015), 2015 WL 10385047.

[55]   This act is codified at N.C. GEN. STAT. ANN. §§ 53–208.41 et seq.

[56]   N.C. GEN. STAT. ANN. § 53–208.42(19).

Oregon amended its money transmitter statute in May 2015, to provide that cryptocurrency exchanges must register as money transmitters and obtain a license from the state's Department of Consumer and Business Services.[57] That statute has a very broad definition of "money," so that it includes "a medium of exchange that: (a) The United States or a foreign government authorizes or adopts; or (b) Represents value that substitutes for currency but that does not benefit from government regulation requiring acceptance of the medium of exchange as legal tender.[58]

Washington state, which has adopted the Uniform Money Services Act (UMSA)[59] (another uniform act promulgated by the ULC),[60] amended its definition of "money transmission" in 2014 to include "receiving money or its equivalent value (equivalent value includes virtual currency) to transmit, deliver, or instruct to be delivered to another. . . ."[61] "Virtual currency" is defined to mean "a digital representation of value used as a medium of exchange, a unit of account, or a store of value, but does not have legal tender status as recognized by the United States government."[62]

It is also possible for state regulatory authorities to interpret pre-existing money transmission requirements as applying to crypto without legislative intervention or clarification. For example, Illinois's Department of Financial and Professional Regulation issued guidance in June 2017 which concluded that "a person or entity engaged in the transmission of solely digital currencies" needs a transmitters of money act license.[63] Colorado has also concluded that crypto is covered by Colorado's conventional money transmitter statute notwithstanding the lack of express language applicable to virtual currency or cryptoassets in the act itself.[64] In Interim Guidance issued in 2018, the state concluded "[i]f a person is engaged in the business of transmitting money from one consumer to another within an exchange through the medium of

---

[57]   The Oregon Money Transmitters Act is codified at OR. REV. STAT. §§ 717.200–.320 & 717.905.

[58]   OR. REV. STAT. § 717.200.

[59]   This act is codified at REV. CODE WASH. CH. 19.230.

[60]   Like the Uniform Regulation of Virtual Currency Business Act, the UMSA has received a lukewarm welcome at the state level. Originally promulgated by the ULC in 2000, and last amended in 2004, the UMSA has been adopted in only a dozen states. *See* ULC, *Money Services Act,* Legislation (available online at https://www.uniformlaws.org/committees/community-home?communitykey=cf8b649a-114c-4bc9-8937-c4ee17148a1b&tab=groupdetails).

[61]   REV. CODE WASH. CH. 19.230.010(18).

[62]   *Id.* at 19.230.010(30).

[63]   Illinois Department of Financial and Professional Regulation, *Digital Currency Regulatory Guidance* (July 13, 2017) [archived at https://perma.cc/3LEU-HXUC].

[64]   COLO. REV. STAT. ANN. § 11–110–103 (defining a number of terms, but not referencing virtual currency or monetary value).

cryptocurrency, that act would constitute money transmission and would be subject to licensure under the Colorado law."[65]

Louisiana has similarly interpreted its state money transmitter act expansively. The Louisiana statute defines "money" or "monetary value" to mean "currency or a claim that can be converted into currency through a financial institution, electronic payments network, or other formal or informal payment system."[66] "Currency" is limited to "the coin and paper money of the United States or another country that is designated as legal tender . . . ."[67] Despite this limiting language, the state's Office of Financial Institutions has issued public guidance concluding that persons who would be classified as "exchangers" by FinCEN will be subject to licensure as money transmitters in Louisiana.[68]

D. STATES WHERE THE LAW IS UNCLEAR OR COMPLICATED

Although the states described above have at least taken some steps to clarify how money transmission requirements will apply to crypto, the reality is that "most states have not yet enacted regulations that provide virtual currency operators with any guidance on" whether state money transmitter rules apply to cryptotransactions.[69] Still other states have issued incomplete or inconsistent pronouncements, or have (at various times) taken actions that appear to be in conflict about how crypto should be approached.

A number of states have simply taken no official position on crypto-based businesses and whether they are subject to money transmitter requirements. Arizona, for example, does not mention virtual currency in its money transmitter laws,[70] and there have been no guidelines from the state Department of Financial Institutions.[71] Similarly, Arkansas has no blockchain or crypto-specific laws, regulations, or official publications relating to the state's money transmission laws.[72] On the other hand, the Arkansas Securities Department has issued no action letters in response

---

[65]   Colo. Dept. of Reg. Agencies, *Interim Regulatory Guidance, Cryptocurrency and the Colorado Money Transmitters Act* (Sept. 20, 2018) (archived at https://perma.cc/DL43-BQDD).

[66]   LA. STAT. ANN. § 6:1032(12).

[67]   *Id.* at § 6:1032(6).

[68]   *See* La. Office of Fin. Inst., *Consumer and Investor Advisory on Virtual Currency* (2014) (archived at https://perma.cc/DKN9-MRH7).

[69]   *See* Kohen & Wales, *supra* note 10 (source updated as of Ap. 19, 2019).

[70]   AZ. REV. STAT. ANN. § 6–1201.

[71]   A June 6, 2019 search of the Arizona Department of Financial Institutions website revealed no documents with the word or phrase cryptocurrency, digital asset, digital currency, or virtual currency. Sample search page archived at https://perma.cc/RCM2-89CQ.

[72]   AR. CODE §§ 23–55–101 *et seq.* Under the Arkansas statutes, "money" means "a medium of exchange that is authorized or adopted by the United States or a foreign government," but "money transmission" also includes "selling or issuing payment instruments, stored value, or receiving money or monetary value for transmission." AR. CODE § 23–55–101(10) & (12)(A).

to inquiries from crypto-based businesses, determining that the Securities Department will not recommend that the businesses be penalized for failing to procure money transmitter licenses.[73] Unfortunately, these opinion letters may not be relied upon by anyone other than the persons to whom they are directed.

Kentucky's Money Transmitter Act[74] does not explicitly include the concept of "virtual currencies" although it does require a license for the transmission of "monetary value," which includes "a medium of exchange whether or not redeemable in money."[75] Kentucky has not yet published any guidelines on the issue of whether virtual currency transmissions are subject to its act.

Iowa is also currently in an uncertain position. While the Iowa Money Services Act requires a license for the transmission of "monetary value," it does not specifically reference virtual currency,[76] and the State's Division of Banking has not published guidelines on whether virtual currency businesses are subject to the act. On the other hand, Iowa has introduced a bill "providing for exemptions for virtual currency from certain security and money transmission regulations."[77]

Florida's position on the applicability of money transmission requirements is also confused. The Florida money services businesses statute[78] does not specifically reference crypto or virtual currency. Its money transmitter licensing requirements apply to any business which receives "currency, monetary value, or payment instruments for the purpose of transmitting the same,"[79] and includes any "medium of exchange, whether or not redeemable in currency" in the definition of "monetary value."[80] The issue of whether this language covered crypto-based business was at the heart of *Florida v. Espinoza,* No. F14–293 (Fla. Cir. Ct. July 22, 2016), *rev'd* 264 So.3d 1055 (Fla. App. 2019). In *Espinoza,* the trial court found that the existing statutory language did not include crypto, but in 2017 the Florida legislature enacted Florida House Bill 1379 which added the term "virtual currency" to the state money laundering act. There was no such amendment to the state money transmission statute, but the third district court of appeals reversed the trial court's order in Espinoza in early 2019, concluding that the state money transmission

---

[73]   *See, i.e.,* Arkansas Securities Department, *CEX.IO Ltd No Action Letter,* No. 18-NA-006 (July 18, 2018) (archived at https://perma.cc/C3UG-YUPB) (agreeing that a virtual currency purchase and sale and exchange product should not need a license under the state's Uniform Money Services Act).

[74]   This act is codified at KY REV. STAT. ANN. §§ 286.11–001 *et seq.*

[75]   *Id.* at § 286.11–003(15).

[76]   IOWA CODE ANN. § 533C.101.

[77]   2019 IA H.F. 240, 88 Gen. Ass. (Feb. 6, 2019).

[78]   This legislation is codified at FLA. STAT. ANN. §§ 560.103 et seq.

[79]   *Id.* at § 560(23).

[80]   *Id.* at § 560(21).

requirements did apply to virtual currencies. The Florida Supreme Court has not weighed in on the controversy.

Wisconsin's position is even less helpful or clear.[81] To date, there are no laws specifically relating to blockchain or cryptoassets in Wisconsin. The state has taken the position that it lacks the authority to regulate virtual currencies, or the ability to license or supervise businesses who limit their activities to crypto. Despite its refusal to license such activities, the state has also concluded that businesses that deal in both crypto and fiat may need a license, which means that Wisconsin businesses working with cryptocurrency must agree not to transmit money.[82]

Hawaii is also a complicated jurisdiction. According to one legal commentator, "Hawaii appears to be moving in two divergent paths, one that forces cryptocurrency businesses to leave that State, and the other that supports the prosperity of cryptocurrency related businesses."[83] On one hand, a particularly friendly cryptocurrency bill was proposed in Hawaii in January of 2017. The stated purpose of this bill was to promote economic development by forming a digital currency working group.[84] The goal of the group would have been to explore the uses of blockchain technology by governments and businesses in order to bolster tourism and technology adoption in the state. Although the bill died in committee, it is one indication of support for crypto, since it passed through its second reading in the state senate before languishing in the state Ways and Means Committee. The Hawaiian legislature has unsuccessfully considered multiple bills that would variously include and exclude virtual currencies from its Money Transmitter Act, but to date the state's Money Transmitter Act has not been amended to specifically address virtual currencies. Nonetheless, in 2016, the state Division of Financial Institutions concluded in 2016 that digital currency businesses operating in Hawaii are required to be licensed.[85]

The primary problem posed in Hawaii as a result of this determination is a unique provision in its statute requiring licensees to hold "in trust permissible investments having an aggregate market value of not less than the aggregate amount of its outstanding transmission obligations."[86] This might not be an issue except that the Hawaii Division of Financial

---

[81]   Alex Hamilton, *Digital states: Cryptocurrency rules and regulations across the US*, BOBS GUIDE (Feb. 8, 2019) [archived at https://perma.cc/XY8Y-B3GD].

[82]   Wisconsin Department of Financial Institutions, *Virtual Currency* [archived at https://perma.cc/R6YQ-QUTQ].

[83]   Scott D. Hughes, *Cryptocurrency Regulations and Enforcement in the U.S.*, 45 W. ST. L. REV. 1, 26 (2017).

[84]   Hawaii House Bill 1481 (2017) [archived at https://perma.cc/RHS8-CT6D].

[85]   *Id.*

[86]   HAW. REV. STAT. ANN. § 489D–8.

Institutions concluded that only cash reserves would be acceptable as permissible investments.[87]

The practical import of this determination is that a money transmitter engaged with crypto would need to maintain not only sufficient digital currencies to meet customer needs, but also the cash equivalent of those assets. As Coinbase noted, this is untenable. In fact, as a result, Coinbase withdrew its operations from Hawaii.[88] A bill that would specifically include virtual currencies within the state money transmitter act while adding them to the list of permissible investments was introduced in the state Senate but does not appear to have much forward momentum.[89]

3. SPECIAL LICENSING

New York illustrates yet another approach to the regulation of crypto in the financial sector overseen by state authorities. Rather than fitting virtual currency businesses within the state's existing money transmitter framework, New York adopted a new regime specifically designed to govern crypto.[90] Under the new regime, anyone involved in any of the following activities in New York is required to obtain a BitLicense:

- virtual currency transmission;

- storing, holding, or maintaining custody or control of virtual currency on behalf of others;

- buying and selling virtual currency as a customer business;

- performing exchange services as a customer business; and/or

- controlling, administering, or issuing a virtual currency.

Beginning August 8, 2015,[91] businesses that deal with any form of digital currency in any of those ways are required to take each of the following steps:[92]

---

[87]   *See* Hawaii Money Transmitter License (application form) (updated as of Mar. 13, 2019) [archived at https://perma.cc/BM4R-XLX2].

[88]   Juan Suarez, *How Bad Policy Harms Coinbase Customers in Hawaii*, THE COINBASE BLOG (Feb. 22, 2017) (available online at https://blog.coinbase.com/how-bad-policy-harms-coinbase-customers-in-hawaii-ac9970d49b34) (noting that "No digital currency business—and frankly, no commercially viable business anywhere—has the capital to supplement every customer bitcoin with redundant dollar collateral.")

[89]   2019 HI S.B. 1364, HI 30th Legislature (Jan. 24, 2019). This bill appears to have languished in the Hawaii Senate Commerce Consumer Protection & Housing committee.

[90]   N.Y. COMP. CODES R. & REGS. tit. 23, Part 200.

[91]   Stan Higgins, *NY Bitcoin Businesses Now Have 45 Days to Apply for BitLicense*, COINDESK, https://www.coindesk.com/ny-bitcoin-business-45-days-bitlicense/ (last updated Oct. 23, 2015);

[92]   All of these are found in various subsections of N.Y. COMP. CODES R. & REGS. tit. 23, § 200.

- apply for a BitLicense from the New York Department of Financial Services;

- pay a nonrefundable application fee of $5,000;

- consent to state examination, post a surety bond in an amount determined on a case-by-case basis;

- provide various disclosures and financial information;

- establish AML rules;

- provide adequate cybersecurity protections; and

- adopt business continuity and disaster recovery programs.

The burdensome (and expensive) BitLicense process led to both swift criticism and a rapid exodus of crypto-businesses from New York.[93] It has taken several years for more than a handful of businesses to comply with all of these requirements.[94]

To date, no other state has adopted rules that are this restrictive. California has in fact considered and rejected the possibility of BitLicense-like regulations on two separate occasions.[95]

4.   OTHER STATE REGULATORS

In addition to state securities and banking authorities, state taxing authorities are also profoundly interested in cryptoassets and transactions. State tax issues may include not only income tax, but also state property and sales taxes. While taxation of crypto is generally beyond the scope of these materials, it is probably worth mentioning that states vary in their approaches to this issue at least as much as for anything else related to crypto.

Not surprisingly, many states have yet to clarify their stance on the taxation of crypto.[96] Since some states automatically rely on federal tax rules except as otherwise provided, federal tax laws[97] are therefore very influential. This, however, is not universally true.

---

[93]   Daniel Roberts, *Behind the "exodus" of bitcoin startups from New York*, FORTUNE (Aug. 14, 2015) (available online at https://fortune.com/2015/08/14/bitcoin-startups-leave-new-york-bitlicense/).

[94]   The relatively short list of institutions with a BitLicense can be found by searching "Type of Institution: Virtual Currency" on the NYDFS website. *See* N.Y. Dept. of Fin. Serv., *Who We Supervise*, https://myportal.dfs.ny.gov/web/guest-applications/who-we-supervise (last visited August 2019). On August 15, 2019, the list included 17 virtual company businesses.

[95]   Alkadri, *supra* note 6 at 85.

[96]   State-focused commentary tends to reinforce this concept. *See, i.e.,* Charlie Kearns & Dennis Jansen, *Can't Hardly Wait—Cryptocurrency and State Tax Legislation*, 28 J. MULTISTATE TAX'N 1 (Sept. 2018), 2018 WL 3993428; Kelly J. Winstead, *The North Carolina State Tax Treatment of Virtual Currency: An Unanswered Question*, 21 N.C. BANKING INST. 501 (2017).

[97]   This topic is considered *infra* in chapter 16.

A few states have legislation governing at least some aspects of the taxation of crypto. For example, during the 2017 legislative session, Nevada banned city and county-level taxes on the use of a blockchain by any person or entity.[98] On March 12, 2018, Wyoming exempted virtual currencies from ad valorem property taxation.[99] In so doing, the state clarified that virtual currency is exempt from property tax in the same manner that the state exempts cash, bank drafts, and checks. Because Wyoming's new virtual currency exemption is limited to property tax, other Wyoming state or local taxes could apply to certain virtual transactions— to the extent there is statutory authority to do so—including but not limited to exchanges of virtual currencies for tangible goods.[100] In addition, virtual currency is notably absent from the Wyoming Legal Tender Act,[101] which exempts money and certain gold and silver coins from taxation of any kind.[102]

Speaking generally, the states that have considered the sales tax treatment of cryptotransactions have generally taken one of two approaches illustrated in the preceding paragraph: (1) they follow the barter approach, or (2) they look at advertised price.

For example, the New York State Department of Taxation and Finance issued a technical memorandum on virtual currency transactions in 2014.[103] Pursuant to that guidance, New York treats transactions involving a purchase with crypto as a barter arrangement. However, since crypto is intangible, the recipient of crypto is not required to pay sales tax, but if the goods or services being exchanged for crypto are subject to tax, the recipient of those goods or services will have to pay sales tax. The guidance states that the tax is based on the value of the goods or services, determined by the fair market value of the crypto at the time of the exchange.

New York, Kentucky, New Jersey, and Wisconsin have all opted to treat crypto as property,[104] so that transactions involving Bitcoin or other crypto are treated like barter exchanges. This approach generally results in the imposition of sales tax when crypto is exchanged for tangible property or a service that would ordinarily be subject to sales tax. The amount of tax that must be paid is determining the fair market value of

---

[98]   NEV. REV. STAT. ANN. § 244.3535 (boards of county commissioners) & § 268.0979 (cities) (both effective June, 2017).

[99]   WYO. STAT. ANN. § 39–11–105(b)(6), as enacted by Wyo. S.F. 111, 6th Legis. Sess (2018).

[100]   WYO. STAT. ANN. § 39–11–105(b)(6).

[101]   This act is (codified at WYO. STAT. ANN. § 9–4–1301 et seq.

[102]   *Id.* at § 9–4–1301.

[103]   *Tax Department Policy on Transactions Using Convertible Virtual Currency*, NY Dept of Tax. & Fin., Tech. Mem TSB–M–14(5)C, (7)I, (17)S (Dec. 5, 2014) [archived at https://perma.cc/ LLX3-K7ZV].

[104]   Ky. Dep't of Rev., *Ky. Sales Tax Facts* (June 2014); N.J. Dep't of Taxation, *Technical Advisory Memorandum* TAM–2015–1(R) (July 28, 2015); Wis. Dep't of Rev., *News for Tax Professionals* (Mar. 28, 2014).

the crypto at the time of the exchange. Note that the crypto is treated as intangible property under this approach, and is therefore not subject to sales tax. Similarly, if crypto is exchanged for cash, neither party would owe sales tax because both the crypto and the fiat are considered intangible assets.

The Washington State Department of Revenue has also provided guidance in how sales taxes or business and occupancy taxes might apply where the form of payment is in crypto.[105] The Washington explanation says that the amount owed is generally based on the advertised sale price of the goods or services (in U.S. dollars). California has also issued guidance suggesting that crypto should be treated like currency because they are to be regarded like traditional forms of payment such as credit cards or checks.[106] Under this approach, the basis for sales tax purposes when a consumer purchases taxable goods or services with crypto will be the advertised price of those goods or services.

The reality is that we still have limited guidance on the taxation of cryptocurrencies from state authorities in most jurisdictions. That may well (and hopefully will) change with time.

---

[105]   "Basically, the same classification(s) apply with the virtual currency that apply on a cash, check, debit card, credit card, gift certificate or stored value card transaction." Dept. of Rev., Washington State, *Accepting Virtual Currency as Payment for Goods or Services* [archived on March 21, 2019 at https://perma.cc/9DDQ-JRRU].

[106]   Cal. Bd. of Equalization, *Special Notice: Accepting Virtual Currency as a Payment Method*, L–382 (June 2014) [archived at https://perma.cc/9W7D-LM7G]. This essentially mirrors the Washington statement described *supra* at note 105.

CHAPTER 15

REGULATION OF CRYPTO
AROUND THE GLOBE

∎ ∎ ∎

1. THE RANGE OF POLICY INTERESTS RAISED BY CRYPTO

In early 2018, cryptoassets had a global market capitalization exceeding $830 billion.[1] By mid-November 2019, that had fallen to a little over $260 billion,[2] which is still a significant amount of wealth tied up in interests of a kind that did not even exist ten years ago.[3] Moreover, this capitalization is truly global, as crypto generally cannot be confined to a single nation, and transactions regularly take place across national boundaries. By its nature, most crypto is inherently outside the reach of any single nation. This means that the benefits that it offers and the potential problems that it creates are also global in nature.

There are a number of global concerns that increase the importance of international cooperation and compliance with international norms when it comes to crypto. The largest international response has clearly involved the issue of how to address money laundering and the funding of terrorism and weapons of mass destruction. In the absence of truly effective global governmental structures,[4] reaction to these concerns has been led by various international groups and organizations, which have pushed for the adoption of minimum international standards. In addition, many of these same groups are interested in and have expressed concern about the possibility that crypto might pose a risk to international financial systems

---

[1]   *Historical Snapshot—Jan. 7, 2018*, COINMARKETCAP.COM [archived at https://perma.cc/4FDX-BY3S]. The total market capitalization for all cryptocurrencies tracked by CoinMarketCap on that date was $830,595,477,030.

[2]   *All Cryptocurrencies*, COINMARKETCAP.COM [archived at https://perma.cc/EXH4-7ELS] (accessed for this purpose November 19, 2019) (reporting a total market capitalization for all cryptocurrencies of $223,136,433,348).

[3]   Significance is, of course relative. Estimates by Credit Suisse Research Institute suggest that in 2018, total global wealth amounted to approximately 317 trillion. Credit Suisse Group, *Global Wealth Report 2018* [archived at https://perma.cc/4LYX-CG6W]. Compared to that, even $800 billion is not all that significant, and $132 billion seems quite modest, indeed.

[4]   While it is beyond the scope of this book, the impact of the lack of effective global government on current world issues has certainly not gone unremarked. A relatively brief but potentially eye-opening essay on this subject is Rana Dasgupta, *The Demise of the Nation State*, THE GUARDIAN (Ap. 5, 2018) (available online at https://www.theguardian.com/news/2018/apr/05/demise-of-the-nation-state-rana-dasgupta).

and stability,[5] although they generally agree that as of 2019, this concern calls for monitoring rather than action. If future developments do threaten financial stability, however, one can expect a relatively prompt push from these groups for a more cohesive global response. Finally, and to a lesser extent, international groups are concerned about fraudulent activities that transcend national boundaries. This has resulted in a number of meetings designed to encourage cooperation and a degree of consistency in the way in which anti-fraud efforts are pursued, particularly with regard to ICOs and other international crypto distributions, but there is far less agreement on this topic.

Of course many issues that cryptoassets present are predominantly domestic in nature, impacting national concerns. For example, crypto offers the potential for increased economic development in countries where it is accepted, which may be seen as an opportunity or a problem depending on the risks involved to other interests, and upon the nature of property ownership and the degree of support for free enterprise from any particular governmental regime. Unfortunately, as has been demonstrated clearly in the United States, there is also the possibility that new technologies such as blockchain and cryptoassets will be exploited by those who intend to defraud the uninformed and unsophisticated. While there has been some international pressure on this front, because the impacts are felt internally, most anti-fraud initiatives have been domestic in nature. In addition, it is clear that some governments seek to exert more control over their citizenry, particularly in countries where governmental authority is backed by force rather than popular choice. Religious regimes may seek to advance religious objectives, particularly to the extent that religious doctrine is viewed as being in conflict with crypto. A few nations may be trying to find ways around international sanctions, which can exist for a wide variety of reasons, or may have other reasons for considering a state-issued cryptocurrency. Some countries may have other reasons for reacting to crypto in particular ways, such as the need to utilize resources to deal with other, more pressing problems. All of these concerns shape how nations react when faced with new issues, such as those created by cryptoassets, and each of these considerations will be discussed in the remainder of this chapter.

It is also true that crypto offers the possibility that an underground economy outside traditional government fiat might develop, with concomitant reductions in tax revenues (which virtually all countries

---

[5]   Crypto was introduced as an intentionally disruptive technology, with the goal of replacing fiat. If this were to happen, both domestic and international monetary policies around the round would be profoundly impacted. While this may not be a current issue, proposals such as Libra, introduced in chapter 13, may make this an increasing concern for governments around the world.

impose in one form or another).[6] It is therefore to be expected that based on each national government's needs to promote and protect domestic policies relative to these issues, every jurisdiction will be concerned with deciding how to address these new cryptoassets to assess earnings and collect appropriate tax revenues. This particular issue, however, is sufficiently complex that it really cannot be explained in any meaningful detail here. Therefore, aside from mentioning this as a basis for considerable regulation around the world, this book does not go into significant detail on the taxation of cryptoassets by nations other than the U.S., although the final section of chapter sixteen includes a small selection of tax rulings from other nations.

As for the policy considerations and objectives that are discussed, there is a diverse set of regulatory reactions to consider. In resolving these sometimes-competing policy considerations, some countries have clearly decided it is in their interests to develop crypto-friendly regulatory regimes. At the start of 2019, this included countries like Australia, Spain, Belarus, the Cayman Islands, and Luxemburg, although some of these nations have gone about being pro-crypto in unusual ways. On the other hand, some jurisdictions have decided it is in their interests to restrict the use or availability of crypto, some going so far as to enact bans on crypto-based activities. As of the start of 2019, this included Algeria, Bolivia, China, Macau, Morocco, Nepal, Pakistan, and Vietnam.[7] Qatar and

---

[6]   Even Communist dictatorships generally impose income taxes, despite the fact that wages are often controlled by the state. North Korea, which publicly proclaims that it is "tax-free," nonetheless apparently imposes various sales taxes. "North Korea's people typically still don't pay direct taxes. However, there are still some taxes paid: The government just doesn't call them taxes. Those taxes, which tend to be user fees and value-added-type taxes (similar to our sales taxes) make up 11.4% of the country's gross domestic product (GDP). . . ." Kelly Phillips Erb, *A Quick Look At North Korea From History To Taxes*, FORBES (June 12, 2018) (available online at https://www.forbes.com/sites/kellyphillipserb/2018/06/12/a-quick-look-at-north-korea-from-history-to-taxes/#f5be6ba44c5f).

There are a limited number of countries that impose no income tax: Bermuda, Bahamas, United Arab Emirates, and Monaco. Despite the absence of an income tax, however, there are other taxes that could be affected if certain transactions are switched from fiat to crypto, especially if those transactions are unreported. Bermuda, for example, has a payroll tax that employers are supposed to collect, and it also imposes taxes upon foreign currencies. The Bahamas also impose an employment tax apportioned between employees and employers. The United Arab Emirates requires employers to remit a social security tax based on gross remuneration. Monaco imposes an inheritance and gift tax for property "situated" in Monaco.

Despite the fact that virtually all nations impose taxes, and will actively seek to protect sources of tax revenues, this topic will not be addressed in any detail in this chapter on international regulation.

[7]   These general claims of the state of international regulation as of the start of 2019 are based on research provided by the Libr. of Cong., *Regulation of Cryptocurrency Around the World* (last updated Jan. 22, 2019) [archived at https://perma.cc/2U44-5LVK] (hereinafter *Regulation of Crypto*). In addition to a general overview of all of these countries, more in-depth analysis was also available for a smaller, selected number of jurisdictions. Libr. of Cong., *Regulation of Cryptocurrency in Selected Jurisdictions* (June 2018) [archived at https://perma.cc/UMF4-Z5EA] (hereinafter *Selected Jurisdictions*). Where specific nations are identified below, that research has been updated to be current as of April 1, 2019. Because so many nations are working on crypto regulations, it is important to update any information provided here rather than relying on it as an-up-to-date reflection of the state of international regulation.

Bahrain have prohibited their citizens from participating in crypto-activities while they are within national borders, but do not preclude actions taken by citizens while they are in other countries. Still other countries impose such stringent restrictions that it appears to be quite difficult to develop, exchange, or use crypto in those places. At the beginning of 2019, this included Bangladesh, Iran, Thailand, Lithuania, Lesotho, and Colombia. A few jurisdictions, for very different reasons, have even taken steps to develop their own cryptoassets. Finally, some countries have adopted a wait-and-see approach, usually complying with minimum international standards but doing little else.

Given this incredibly broad range of responses, it is a challenge to organize materials on the international regulation of cryptoassets in a meaningful way. This chapter looks first at some of the most influential international groups and organizations and considers very briefly their reaction to crypto. It then examines in somewhat greater detail the standards and guidelines imposed or recommended by these organizations in the context of AML and CTF needs, financial stability concerns, and anti-fraud initiatives (in the context of securities regulations). The third part of this chapter considers how particular nations have addressed the following issues in the context of crypto: AML/CTF, financial stability, economic growth, the need to protect citizens from fraud, the desire to assert or maintain control; the potential to issue a national cryptocurrency; and individual economic and political situations. (Remember that although taxation is a concern of virtually all nations, that particular topic is outside the scope of this chapter, except to note that one of the most common reactions from world governments has been to establish rules regarding taxation of crypto.)

Before proceeding further, there is an important caveat. Considering how various nations have reacted to crypto with these various policy objectives in mind helps make some sense of an incredibly complicated and rapidly changing regulatory environment, but much of the information presented here is based on second-hand reports and translations.[8] The qualifications of the authors of some of the original reports have not been investigated, and of course this material is limited by the fact that the treatment of crypto is rapidly evolving. At any future point, a particular country may have moved past the regulations described here, so the information in this chapter should be taken only as a starting point for any research rather than a definitive statement of the law of any particular

---

[8]   Much of the material in this section comes from *Selected Jurisdictions, supra* at note 7. This source was particularly useful in understanding foreign sources including legislation and regulations that have not been translated into English. Note that this chapter also contains significantly more footnotes and citations than is customary in student materials, and even in this book. The purpose of this is to enable this to serve as a starting point for research and a reference guide, since there are so few legal publications dealing with crypto currently available.

nation. (This is one reason for the extraordinarily large number of footnotes in this chapter.)

2. INTERNATIONAL GROUPS AND ORGANIZATIONS

In understanding how governments have reacted to crypto, as mentioned above, there are a range of international pressures and considerations at work. In order to understand how international pressures have operated to encourage at least a measure of consistency in regard to these concerns, it is necessary to understand at a very general level some of the major organizations and groups that work at establishing and enforcing international standards.

A. THE U.N.

The United Nations (U.N.) is probably the international organization that is the closest thing to a global governing body in existence. Although it has a large mission and occupies an important role, it does have a number of limitations on its effectiveness.

The U.N., which came into existence following the end of World War II, has as its central mission the task of maintaining international peace and security.[9] It has as its members 193 nations, and two non-member observer states: the Holy See and the State of Palestine. This comprises the vast majority of recognized nations in the world today, although there are a handful of other countries recognized by at least one U.N. member that are not part of the group. (The list of non-included countries includes Abkhazia, the Cook Islands, Kosovo, Niue, Northern Cyprus, South Ossetia, Taiwan, and Western Sahara. Many of these are breakaway states, whose legal status is in dispute despite their recognition by at least one other U.N. member.)

While most of the U.N.'s initiatives do not directly involve cryptoassets, and the focus of the group is not to propose regulatory structures for the member nations, the group is very concerned with international crimes such as terrorism, human trafficking, and sales of illegal weaponry. Various U.N. initiatives therefore touch on the extent to which crypto may facilitate such illegal activity. For example, as part of the U.N. Global Counter-terrorism Strategy, the group specifically encourages members "to implement the comprehensive international standards embodied in the Financial Action Task Force's Forty Recommendations on Money Laundering and Nine Special Recommendations on Terrorist

---

9   U.N., *What We Do* (available online at https://www.un.org/en/sections/what-we-do/).

Financing, recognizing that States may require assistance in implementing them."[10]

Speaking generally, however, the U.N. not taken a formal position on cryptocurrencies or suggested any particular regulatory approach. There are examples of the U.N. using crypto and blockchain technology, such as sending U.N. volunteers to Africa to introduce cryptocurrencies.[11] Various U.N. initiatives have also adopted or taken advantage of the blockchain technology that underlies cryptoassets.[12] On the other hand, the chief of the U.N. Office on Drugs and Crime Global Cybercrime Program has warned that crypto makes it significantly harder to fight money laundering by criminals.[13]

B. THE E.U.

Another international organization likely to come to mind when thinking of crypto is the European Union (the E.U.). The E.U., which came into existence in 1993 pursuant to the Maastricht Treaty, is a union, both political and economic, of 28 member countries. The E.U. is represented in the U.N., the WTO, the G7, and the G20, and has diplomatic missions across the globe. The E.U. has been characterized as a superpower as a result of its international influence.[14] E.U. policies are focused on ensuring the free movement of people, goods, services, and capital within the Union. Nineteen E.U. nations currently use a common currency, the euro. In addition, all E.U. members are subject to standardized laws, although those laws impact only matters on which the member nations have agreed to act in concert.

Particularly with regard to crypto, the E.U. has four potential regulators: the European Commission, the European Banking Authority (EBA), the European Securities and Markets Authority (ESMA), and the European Insurance and Occupational Pensions Authority.[15] The European Commission is responsible for planning, preparing, and proposing legislation. It also responds to emerging risks that might impact the Union's financial stability, and it oversees the effectiveness of financial

---

[10]   U.N., Office of Counter-Terrorism, *UN Global Counter-Terrorism Strategy* [archived at https://perma.cc/FCF3-M95Q]. The standards developed by the Financial Action Task Force (FATF) are discussed later in this chapter.

[11]   *United Nations News*, COINTELEGRAPH [page archived as of Sept. 3, 2019 at https://perma.cc/GYL3-RNA9].

[12]   For some examples of the U.N. and U.N. nations utilizing blockchain technology, see Marie Huillet, *UN, Sierra Leone Launch Blockchain-Based 'Credit Bureau of the Future,'* COINTELEGRAPH (Sept. 28, 22018) [archived at https://perma.cc/7ZFD-TXM5].

[13]   *See* Adrian Zmudsinski, *UN Official: Cryptocurrency Makes Criminals Harder to Catch*, COINTELEGRAPH (Aug. 29, 2019) [archived at https://perma.cc/Q5UQ-S5VW].

[14]   JOHN MCCORMICK, THE EUROPEAN SUPERPOWER (2006).

[15]   These are the four regulatory authorities at the E.U. identified by the FSB as being crypto-asset regulators. FSB, *Crypto-assets Regulators Directory* (Ap. 5, 2019) (available online at https://www.fsb.org/wp-content/uploads/P050419.pdf).

sector reforms. The EBA is responsible for monitoring how technological innovations impact the financial system, and it is charged with ensuring effective and consistent regulation and supervision of the E.U. banking sector. ESMA also works to protect the stability of the E.U.'s financial sector, although its focus is protection of investors and promoting stable and orderly financial markets. Finally, the European Insurance and Occupational Pensions Authority has responsibility for the insurance sector, to the extent that crypto and ICOs might impact that industry.

One of the most important E.U. policies and directives relative to crypto is the fifth E.U. Anti-Money Laundering Directive (AMLD 5) adopted by the European Commission in 2018. The AMLD 5 requires member nations to apply a range of AML requirements to crypto exchanges and wallet services by 2020.[16] Regarding crypto assets, ESMA published advice to European institutions in January 2019, acknowledging that cryptoassets with certain characteristics are financial instruments and should be supervised as such, although this requires action by individual countries in order to be effective.[17] This follows a joint warning from ESMA, EBA and the insurance and pensions group on February 12, 2018, regarding virtual currencies, stating that they are "highly risky," unregulated, and unsuitable for investment, savings or retirement planning.[18] To a significant extent, however, the E.U. leaves the details of how to regulate cryptoassets and transactions to the discretion of member countries, so long as certain minimum standards are met.

C. THE G7 AND G20

The early 1970s were a difficult time from an economic perspective. Not only was the United States dealing with the fallout from the Nixon-Watergate scandal, but the exchange rate had collapsed in 1971, and the 1973 energy crisis had contributed to a recession for many major industrial nations around the world. One of the results of these economic difficulties was the development of the G7, or group of seven, consisting of seven of the largest and most advanced economies in the world.[19] In 1975, a summit hosted by France brought together representatives of six governments: France, West Germany, Italy, Japan, the United Kingdom, and the United States. Canada was invited to join the group in 1976, making the group of seven. The European Union is also represented in the group. From the

---

16   For a discussion of the new AMLD 5 see Juergen Krais, *EU: 5th EU Anti-Money Laundering Directive Published*, GLOBAL COMPLIANCE NEWS (July 16, 2018) (available online at https://globalcompliancenews.com/eu-5th-anti-money-laundering-directive-published-20180716/).

17   *See* ESMA, *Crypto-Assets Need Common EU-Wide Approach To Ensure Investor Protection* (Jan. 9, 2019) [archived at https://perma.cc/45CM-GHYE].

18   European Supervisory Authorities, *Warning—ESMA, EBA and EIOPA Warn Consumers on the Risks of Virtual Currencies* (Feb. 12, 2018) [archived at http://perma.cc/EAH5-XTZE].

19   Together, the G7 countries represent approximately 60% of global net wealth and account for more than 45% of the world's gross domestic product based on nominal values.

beginning, the purpose of this organization has been to facilitate shared macroeconomic initiatives, and as of the summer of 2019, the appropriate treatment of crypto is among its priorities.

A larger international group, the G20 (Group of 20) is an international forum for the governments and central bank governors from 19 countries plus the European Union.[20] It was founded with the explicit objective of promoting international financial stability and has also indicated substantial interest in crypto.

These two groups have been instrumental in encouraging the development of standards to protect nations from problems presented by money laundering and the channeling of funds into illegal enterprises, such as the funding of terrorism. They have also encouraged the formation of specific groups that have as their missions a number of concerns that are directly relevant to cryptotransactions.

D. FATF

The Financial Action Task Force (FATF) was established by the 1989 G7 summit in response to growing concerns about these problems. The Task Force is charged with examining money laundering techniques and trends, and reviewing responses while suggesting additional responses. It acts to "set standards and promote effective implementation of legal, regulatory and operational measures for combating money laundering, terrorist financing and other related threats to the integrity of the international financial system."[21] In furtherance of this obligation, FATF has developed a series of 40 Recommendations[22] that have been widely recognized as the international standard for combating of money laundering and the financing of illegal activity such as terrorism.

It is hard to overstate the importance of the FATF standards. The FATF itself consists of 38 members, but in addition, it relies on a global network of FATF-Regional Bodies. More than 200 jurisdictions have committed to the FATF recommendations.[23]

Among its other roles, FATF also identifies jurisdictions with weak AML and CFT measures. It reviews jurisdictions based on threats, vulnerabilities, and particular risks that are identified in association with

---

[20]   The G20 members are Argentina, Australia, Brazil, Canada, China, France, Germany, India, Indonesia, Italy, Japan, Mexico, South Korea, South Africa, Russia, Saudi Arabia, Turkey, the U.K., the U.S., and the European Union.

[21]   FATF, *Who We Are* [archived at https://perma.cc/WY5S-B4UK].

[22]   FATF, *International Standards on Combating Money Laundering and the Financing of Terrorism & Proliferation—The FATF Recommendations* (Updated June 2019) [archived at https://perma.cc/W9X6-FZBQ].

[23]   See the list of countries that are members of FATF or one or more of the regional bodies at https://www.fatf-gafi.org/countries/ (the list as of August 15, 2019 is archived at https://perma.cc/NF4E-TS4Z).

a given nation.[24] When a nation is identified as having problematic oversight or enforcement measures, the FATF publicly lists the nation. As of February 2019, 69 countries have been identified as having had problematic regulatory regimes. Of those, 55 have since reformed their systems to address the identified weaknesses.[25]

Most identified countries are asked to apply enhanced due diligence measures, although those with "serious, long-standing strategic deficiencies that have still failed to make progress" are faced with a call for members and non-members to apply counter-measures (such as heightened scrutiny and enhanced due diligence) to transactions involving or arising from that jurisdiction. As of mid-2019 only the Democratic People's Republic of Korea and Iran are being singled out under this call for action, while a dozen other nations are currently being monitored under a request that they improve their compliance.[26]

E. THE FSB

"The Financial Stability Board (FSB) is an international body that monitors and makes recommendations about the global financial system."[27] Located in Basel, Switzerland, it includes all G20 economies and Financial Stability Forum[28] members, as well as the European Commission. It brings together senior policy makers from various authorities including persons involved in finance, central banks, and agency regulators. It does not produce legally-binding policies, and acts instead to coordinate efforts by the participants. Members commit to adhere to the internationally agreed minimum standards and policies designed to strengthen global financial security.

In addition to members, the FSB has six regional consultative groups, which allow the board to reach authorities in 70 other jurisdictions, including many developing economies. Policy discussions often include representatives from these groups.

In the summer of 2019, the FSB, which reports regularly to the G20, produced a report on work underway by international organizations and at

---

[24]   FATF, *High-risk and Other Monitored Jurisdictions—Review Process* [archived at https://perma.cc/N96L-2E58].

[25]   FATF, *Topic: High-risk and Other Monitored Jurisdictions* [archived at https://perma.cc/CLZ2-4NXY].

[26]   FATF, *High-risk and Other Monitored Jurisdictions* (*list of countries*) [archived at https://perma.cc/6AWF-MJC9].

[27]   FSB, *About the FSB* (available online at https://www.fsb.org/about/).

[28]   The Financial Stability Forum was the predecessor to the FSB, and it included a number of international economic organizations, financial institutions, central bank authorities, and a range of nations, including the Australia, Canada, China, France, Germany, Hong Kong, Italy, Japan, the Netherlands, Singapore, Switzerland, the United Kingdom, and the United States. *See* FSF, *History of the FSB* (available online at https://www.fsb.org/history-of-the-fsb/).

the national level to address various risks of cryptoassets.[29] In this report, the FBS describes work in progress at the Basel Committee on Banking Supervision, the Committee for Payments and Market Infrastructures, the International Organization of Securities Commissions (IOSCO), FATF, the OECD and the FSB.[30] The report specifically notes the wide variance in regulatory approaches to crypto across nations, including differences in the stage of development of the applicable economic markets and differing legal and regulatory frameworks in place. It also warns that there may be gaps, overlaps, and conflicts in regulatory responses.[31]

F. THE OECD

Another international group involved with blockchain and crypto is the Organization for Economic Cooperation and Development (OECD).[32] This group appears to have been cautiously enthusiastic about blockchain technology. A 2014 working paper, which does purport to represent the official views of the Organization or any of its member countries, expressed reservations about Bitcoin but nonetheless expressed some optimism regarding the potential for economic development offered by blockchain technology.[33] This paper pointed to Ripple as an example of a potentially important and valuable innovation, and advised member states to consider comparable blockchain-based alternatives to conventional banking. A more recent pronouncement from the OECD asked global regulators to work together to facilitate the development of ICOs.[34] Despite these cautious calls for action and cooperation, no specific suggestions or standards for crypto-based businesses, cryptotransactions, or ICOs have been promulgated by the group.

---

[29]   FSB, *FSB reports on work underway to address crypto-asset risks* (May 31, 2019) (available online at https://www.fsb.org/2019/05/fsb-reports-on-work-underway-to-address-crypto-asset-risks/). This report was prepared for the G20 meeting of Finance Ministers and Central Bank Governors, June 8–9, 2019. A copy of the report can be found at FSB, *Crypto-assets—Work underway, regulatory approaches and potential gaps* (May 31, 2019) (available online at https://www.fsb.org/wp-content/uploads/P310519.pdf).

[30]   FSB report, *supra* note 29 at p. 1, executive summary.

[31]   *Id.* at 8.

[32]   The OECD was founded in 1961. It is an intergovernmental economic organization consisting of 36 member countries. Its objective is to stimulate economic progress and world trade, while describing itself as being committed to democracy and market economies. Most of its members are regarded as high-income, developed nations.

[33]   Adrian Blundell-Wignall, *The Bitcoin Question: Currency versus Trust-less Transfer Technology*, OECD WORKING PAPERS ON FINANCE, INSURANCE AND PRIVATE PENSIONS, No. 37 (OECD Publishing, 2014) (available online at https://www.oecd.org/daf/fin/financial-markets/The-Bitcoin-Question-2014.pdf). For additional information about the OECD's position on crypto, see Simon Chandler, *Crypto Discussions at Highest Level: The OECD's Love of Blockchain Obscures Its Fear of Bitcoin*, COINTELEGRAPH (Sept. 10, 2018) [archived at https://perma.cc/2F8S-W8KT].

[34]   OECD, *Initial Coin Offerings (ICOs) for SME Financing* (Jan. 15, 2019) [available online at https://www.oecd.org/finance/ICOs-for-SME-Financing.pdf] (this report applies to "small and medium-sized companies," which it abbreviates as SMEs). For a brief assessment of this working paper, see Adrian Zmudzinski, *OECD Calls for 'Delicate Balance' in Global ICO Regulation*, COINTELEGRAPH (Jan. 18, 2019) [archived at https://perma.cc/LLG5-D6NL].

G. THE IMF AND THE WORLD BANK

Another international organization whose principal purpose is to ensure financial stability of the international monetary system is the International Monetary Fund (IMF). The IMF and World Bank are both institutions within the U.N. system, and they function in tandem. The IMF focuses on macroeconomic issues, while the World Bank concentrates on longer-term economic development. In 2018, these two organizations adopted the Bali Fintech Agenda.[35]

This agenda sets out twelve key considerations for policymakers in the international community. Those considerations consist of the following priorities:

1. Embrace the promise of fintech.

2. Enable new technologies to enhance financial service provision.

3. Reinforce competition and commitment to open, free, and contestable markets.

4. Foster fintech to promote financial inclusion and develop financial markets.

5. Monitor developments closely to deepen understanding of evolving financial systems.

6. Adapt regulatory framework and supervisory practices for orderly development and stability of the financial system.

7. Safeguard the integrity of financial systems.

8. Modernize legal frameworks to provide an enabling legal landscape.

9. Ensure the stability of domestic monetary and financial systems.

10. Develop robust financial and data infrastructure to sustain fintech benefits.

11. Encourage international cooperation and information-sharing.

12. Enhance collective surveillance of the international monetary and financial system.

While several of these general policies are likely to have important ramifications for crypto in the long-term, they are so general in nature that other sources of information about possible regulatory approaches and

---

[35]   IMF Policy Paper, *The Bali Fintech Agenda* (Oct. 11, 2018) (can be downloaded in PDF format at https://www.imf.org/en/Publications/Policy-Papers/Issues/2018/10/11/pp101118-bali-fintech-agenda).

other groups that have focused on the development of specific standards are playing a much larger role on the international stage.

H. BRICS

BRICS is the acronym that refers to a group of five major emerging national economies: Brazil, Russia, India, China, and South Africa. In 2015, BRICS established the New Development Bank (formerly called the BRICS Development Bank), which can lend up to $34 billion each year, with an emphasis on infrastructure projects. BRICS has previously discussed cryptocurrency as an alternative to national currencies, but as of this publication, this has not progressed beyond discussions.[36] Nonetheless, BRICS is a group that has the potential to impact the adoption, use, and regulation of cryptocurrencies on at least a regional basis. Since many highly populated nations may be influenced by this group, it is worth watching for future developments in the area of cryptotransactions although as of mid-2019 it has made primarily focused on blockchain-based projects that do not involve cryptoassets.

An awareness of these groups helps set the stage for understanding the international response to crypto. Obviously, some of the groups[37] have been more pro-active in suggesting regulatory responses to crypto than others, and that fact is reflected in the following materials.

3. INTERNATIONALLY DEVELOPED STANDARDS AND GUIDELINES

A. INTERNATIONAL INITIATIVES RELATING TO AML/CTF

FATF's work has particular relevance for the international regulation of crypto. As described in chapters four and five of this book, one of the key concerns that regulators have about crypto is that it can be used for money laundering and the funding of criminal activities. These activities occur on

---

[36] *See* William Suberg, *BRICS to Discuss Cryptocurrency as Alternative to National Currencies*, COINTELEGRAPH (Sept. 4, 2017) [archived at https://perma.cc/96KF-ESYZ]. For the status of crypto regulation in the BRICS nations as of early 2019, see Marina Chudinovskikh & Victor Sevryugin, *Cryptocurrency Regulation in the BRICS Countries and the Eurasian Economic Union*, 6 BRICS L. J. (2019) (available online by downloading the PDF at https://www.researchgate.net/publication/331172100_Cryptocurrency_regulation_in_the_BriCs_Countries_and_the_eurasian_economic_union).

[37] There are a number of other international organizations that are not considered in any detail in this chapter. For example, there is a different listing of such organizations in FSB, *Crypto-assets Regulators Directory* (Ap. 5, 2019) (available online at https://www.fsb.org/wp-content/uploads/P050419.pdf). This authorities introduced in the text of this chapter, however, should provide evidence of the extent of efforts at coordination and cooperation (or sometimes simply compliance) on an international level.

a global scale. Thus, appropriate standards, policies, procedures, and enforcement at an international level are essential to address these issues. FATF noted these risks in 2014,[38] specifically identifying some of the very transactions (Silk Road and Liberty Reserve) discussed in chapter four of this book. In 2015, FATF issued initial guidance for how countries and businesses should approach virtual currencies.[39]

Given its awareness of potential problems posed by cryptoassets, it is not surprising that when FATF updated its recommendations in October 2018, it also specifically included guidance applicable to new technologies such as crypto. In particular, as amended, Recommendation 15 requires counties and financial institutions to act by 2020 to "identify and assess the money laundering or terrorist financing risks that may arise in relation to (a) the development of new products and new business practices, including new delivery mechanisms, and (b) the use of new or developing technologies for both new and pre-existing products."[40] The Recommendation mentions virtual assets specifically, requiring that "virtual asset service providers are regulated for AML/CFT purposes, and licensed or registered and subject to effective systems for monitoring and ensuring compliance."[41]

An interpretive note to Recommendation 15, added in June 2019, further explains that "[f]or the purposes of applying the FATF Recommendations, countries should consider virtual assets as 'property,' 'proceeds,' 'funds,' 'funds or other assets,' or other 'corresponding value.' Countries should apply the relevant measures under the FATF Recommendations to virtual assets and virtual asset service providers. . . ."[42]

These are fairly general statements, but on June 21, 2019, FATF finalized its new guidance for virtual assets and virtual assets providers in a 59-page report.[43] This document explains in some detail how countries should apply FATF standards to crypto. As it notes, "[a]lmost all of the FATF Recommendations are directly relevant" to virtual assets, and "[t]he Guidance details the full range of obligations" "following a Recommendation-by-Recommendation approach."[44]

---

[38]   FATF, *Virtual Currencies Key Definitions and Potential AML/CFT Risks* (June 2014) [archived at https://perma.cc/5TUW-9A8R].

[39]   FATF, *Guidance for a Risk-Based Approach—Virtual Currencies* (2015) [archived at https://perma.cc/5UFJ-MAMY].

[40]   *Recommendations, supra* note 22 at 15.

[41]   *Id.*

[42]   *Id.* at 70.

[43]   FATF, *Guidance For a Risk-Based Approach Virtual Assets and Virtual Asset Service Providers* (2019) [archived at https://perma.cc/A93S-3EGY].

[44]   *Id.* at 4–5.

Given the historical effectiveness of FATF procedures, it is to be expected that most nations and most compliant businesses will actively strive to meet the myriad requirements associated with having risk-based policies and procedures designed to address money laundering concerns and to avoid the risk that crypto will be used to fund criminal activities such as terrorism. In fact, the greatest degree of international consistency with regard to regulation of crypto is in this area, as will be described later with regard to selected nations.

B. GLOBAL FINANCIAL STABILITY

In part, the current level of international interest and scrutiny over the extent to which crypto poses a threat to financial security may be due to the launch of Libra in 2020, the cryptocurrency backed by Facebook and other members of the Libra Association.[45] On the other hand, international financial organizations have been monitoring crypto and its potential for impact on the global economy for some time.

In July of 2018, the FSB issued a report noting a number of concerns centered around cryptoassets, including consumer risks, and the need to protect investors, market integrity, and potentially financial stability.[46] The report was updated in October of that year, and the updated version listed concerns about price fluctuations, market volatility, and market manipulation alongside of issues about how to address oversight of trading platforms, anti-money laundering, and anti-terrorism initiatives.[47] In both documents, the FSB concluded that even when crypto market capitalization was at the $830 billion level near the end of 2017, crypto did "not pose a material risk to global financial stability."[48]

The FSB has clearly continued to work on the question of how nations should approach cryptoassets and transactions. Among its submissions for the 2019 G20 meeting, the FSB included a report on the financial stability, regulatory, and governance implications of decentralized financial

---

[45]   This development was introduced in chapter 13.

[46]   FSB, *Crypto-assets—Report to the G20 on Work by the FSB and Standard-Setting Bodies* (July 16, 2018) [archived at https://perma.cc/E3E5-6NFG] a p. 1. The FSB works through senior financial sector policy makers from the G20 countries, plus four other key financial center: Hong Kong, Singapore, Spain and Switzerland. In addition, it includes international and regional bodies like the European Central Bank and European Commission. The FSB also has six regional consultative groups involving various authorities from 70 other countries and jurisdictions, including a number of emerging market and developing economies. These regional groups enable the FSB to discuss and monitor policies while they are being drafted and implemented.

[47]   FSB, *Crypto-asset markets: Potential Channels for Future Financial Stability Implications* (Oct. 10, 2018) [archived at https://perma.cc/86XY-M9RH] at p. 1. With more than two dozen members from around the globe, the FSB works to identify potential systemic risk in the financial sector, to frame potential policy actions that can respond to those risks, and to oversee implementation of such policies. *See* FSB, *About the FSB* (available online at http://www.fsb.org/about/).

[48]   FSB, *Crypto-asset markets, supra* note 47.

technologies.[49] The Chairman of the FSB, Randal K. Quarles, also outlined the FSB's initiatives to the G20 leaders ahead of the summit. Included in his assessment was a warning that "[a] wider use of new types of crypto-assets for retail payment purposes would warrant close scrutiny by authorities to ensure that they are subject to high standards of regulation."[50]

In the face of this, it is probably not surprising that the reaction of most G7 and G20 nations to Libra has been relatively hostile. The Finance Ministers and Central Bank Governors of the G7 nations met in July, the last such meeting prior to the 2019 G7 Summit.[51] In the report of the outcomes of that meeting, the group specifically acknowledged the importance of continuing work on "the assessment of risks related to the development by the private sector of new payment products such as the Libra." Following that meeting, the G7 nations have generally expressed a range of concerns about the potential impact of the proposed coin.[52]

Those concerns do not appear to overcome the general belief that at the current time, crypto is not a threat to international global stability. A later section of this chapter considers particular responses of selected G7 and other nations to the question of whether crypto threatens financial stability.

C. SECURITIES REGULATION

Individual nations have attempted to protect their citizens and financial markets from fraudulent offerings by imposing a range of requirements in connection with the issuance and sale of various investment interests. (The U.S. approach to securities regulation is described in general terms in chapter seven of this book.) Not surprisingly, the way in which such rules apply to crypto also varies widely.

One of the problems that exists in a global world is that individuals and entities may seek to escape the reach of a given nation's laws by placing themselves and/or their assets outside the territorial boundaries of a country in which they may have operated illegally. The International Organization of Securities Commissions (IOSCO) is the international body that brings together the world's securities regulators to discuss

---

[49] FSB, *Decentralised Financial Technologies: Report on Financial Stability, Regulatory and Governance Implications* (June 6, 2019) [archived at https://perma.cc/28UX-CLKK].

[50] *FSB Chair's letter to G20 Leaders meeting in Osaka* (June 24, 2019) [archived at https://perma.cc/3S9C-PBGL].

[51] G7 France, *G7 Finance Ministers Meeting: What are the Outcomes?* (July 20, 2019) [archived at https://perma.cc/FA9R-LDPA].

[52] For stories reporting on the reaction, consider *G7 Nations to Act Against Facebook's 'Libra' Cryptocurrency Plan*, DW (July 17, 2019) (available online at https://www.dw.com/en/g7-nations-to-act-against-facebooks-libra-cryptocurrency-plan/a-49624988), and Victor Mallet, *G7 Warns On 'Serious Risks' Posed by Libra and Other Digital Coins*, FINANCIAL TIMES (July 18, 2019) (available at https://www.ft.com/content/a6cbf244-a926-11e9-984c-fac8325aaa04).

international standards that address this particular problem. As explained on its website, IOSCO "is recognized as the global standard setter for the securities sector. IOSCO develops, implements and promotes adherence to internationally recognized standards for securities regulation. It works intensively with the G20 and the Financial Stability Board (FSB). . . ."[53] The organization was established in 1983, and its membership regulates the overwhelming majority of the world's securities markets.[54]

In much the same way that FATF has assisted in the development of international standards in the financial sector, IOSCO provided 38 principles to assist in the development of international standards for the securities and derivatives industries. The IOSCO *Objectives and Principles of Securities Regulation* have been endorsed by both the G20 and the FSB as the relevant standards in this area.[55] The 38 Principles are designed to achieve three overarching objectives: protection of investors; ensuring fair, efficient, and transparent markets; and reducing systematic risk.[56] In general terms, IOSCO has suggested that "[w]here a regulatory authority has determined that a crypto-asset or an activity involving a crypto-asset falls within its jurisdiction, . . .[these Principles] provide useful guidance in considering the novel and unique issues and risks that arise in this new market."[57]

To more completely address the perceived need for international cooperation, in 2002, a Multilateral Memorandum of Understanding (MMOU) was signed by securities regulatory agencies from 27 countries.[58] Its purpose was to foster "mutual cooperation and consultation . . . to ensure compliance with, and enforcement of . . . securities and derivatives laws and regulations."[59] A 2016 enhanced version[60] was designed to "foster greater cross-border enforcement cooperation and assistance among securities regulators, enabling them to respond to the risks and challenges posed by globalisation and advances in technology since 2002." Both the

---

[53]   OICV-IOSCO, *About IOSCO* [archived at https://perma.cc/5MUA-9DNU].

[54]   Membership in IOSCO covers more than 95% of global security markets in more than 115 jurisdictions. As of August 2019, it had 227 members.

[55]   OICV-IOSCO, *Objectives and Principles of Securities Regulation* (May 2017) [archived at https://perma.cc/ZLV2-SV7D].

[56]   *Id.* at 3, Forward.

[57]   OICV-IOSCO, *Issues, Risks and Regulatory Considerations Relating to Crypto-Asset Trading Platforms*, Consultation Report (May 2019) [archived at https://perma.cc/N5UJ-NK4M] at 1.

[58]   OICV-IOSCO, *Multilateral Memorandum of Understanding Concerning Consultation and Cooperation and the Exchange of Information* (May 2002) [archived at https://perma.cc/NQA5-USY4].

[59]   *Id.* at 2, Purpose.

[60]   OICV-IOSCO, *Enhanced Multilateral Memorandum of Understanding Concerning Consultation and Cooperation and the Exchange of Information* (2016) [archived at https://perma. cc/VZG2-NNCV]. The enhanced version has only 12 signatories. The Enhanced MMOU is described at OICV-IOSCO, About IOSCO, *Enhanced Multilateral Memorandum of Understanding Concerning Consultation and Cooperation and the Exchange of Information (EMMoU)* [archived at https://perma.cc/D7BN-8SKY].

U.S. SEC and CFTC are signatories to these agreements, although only 11 other countries have signed the enhanced version, which exists alongside the original document.

Obviously, the 2002 MMOU was not designed with crypto in mind, but it does provide some impetus for cooperation among the signatories.

Other initiatives from the IOSCO more directly relate to crypto. In February 2017, the group published a report on financial technologies that specifically discussed the role and risks of tokenized assets and currencies.[61] More recently, in May 2019, a draft consultation report was issued by the group. As of this writing that report is not in final form, but it outlines issues, risks, and regulatory considerations relating to crypto trading platforms (exchanges).[62] The fact that this report is still in draft form obviously limits the impact of the recommendations but also reflects the complexity and continually evolving nature of crypto.

4. NATIONAL POLICY OBJECTIVES

In addition to internationally coordinated action on issues relating to AML/CTF, financial stability, and transnational securities regulation (including anti-fraud initiatives), national governments will also have a range of domestic policy objectives that they seek to further. For example, virtually all nations have a reasonable and predictable need to adopt policies and regulations that promote that country's economic development. Some will feel the need to exert control over their citizens by restricting access to alternate currencies, such as crypto. Some religious regimes may have particular objectives dictated by religious doctrine. Some states have decided, for a variety of reasons, that it is in their best interests to develop their own cryptocurrencies. A number of nations across the globe have other economic issues or problems that limit the resources available to respond to new technologies such as crypto.

Individual national responses to crypto are shaped by a large number of factors. Nations will differ in their approach to crypto based in part on the extent to which they have embraced public, private, or communal ownership of property. Governments concerned about political uncertainty, unrest, or civil war are likely to be constrained by the need to protect and control their citizens. Countries with particular ideological underpinnings

---

[61] OICV-IOSCO, *IOSCO Research Report on Financial Technologies (FinTech)* (Feb. 2017) [archived at https://perma.cc/5H58-N5WB].

[62] Consultation Report, *supra* note 57. The Report (which as of August 2019 is not in final form) was prepared with the assistance of members from Australia, Brazil, Canada (OSC, AMF Quebec, IIROC), China, Dubai, France, Germany, Hong Kong, India, Ireland, Italy, Japan, Republic of Korea, Kuwait, Malaysia, Mexico, The Netherlands, Nigeria, Romania, Russia, Saudi Arabia, Singapore, South Africa, Spain, Sweden, Switzerland, Turkey, United Kingdom, and the U.S. (the CFTC and the SEC).

will be focused on those considerations.[63] However, there are some patterns that exist.

First, at least partially in response to the pressures from and support of international organizations, most countries have or are exploring substantial AML/CTF initiatives in line with international norms. Most governments also seem to be aware of the importance of financial stability and the potential that crypto has to impact that, at some point in the future. In addition, the potential for fraud and misuse of the new technology is also commonly recognized, although the extent to which individual countries have been able to respond to this particular concern varies widely. Countries are trying to explore how crypto can further economic growth. More repressive regimes are working to control citizens through their policies. Religious considerations have appeared in a handful of nations. State-backed cryptocurrencies are appearing. All of these reactions will be considered in turn, with a final subsection articulating some of the current problems across the globe that explain why some nations appear to be lagging behind in the area of crypto regulation.[64]

A. AML/CTF INITIATIVES

Of all the regulations applied to crypto, the strongest and most consistent set of reactions has involved anti-money laundering and counter terrorism funding initiatives. Given the role of FATF as described above, this is perhaps not surprising. It does not appear to matter whether a given nation is seen as crypto-friendly, hostile, somewhere in the middle, or even still deciding; most nations have been willing to abide by or work toward establishing rules in compliance with minimum international standards in this regard.

For example, countries that are widely seen as being progressive and pro-crypto may shy away from burdensome regulation, but they will still impose substantial AML/CTF requirements. On a very consistent basis, countries require businesses acting as crypto-intermediaries on behalf of others to adopt risk-based policies and procedures to assure that they are overseen by effective regulators, and that they know and can identify their customers, make appropriate reports, and keep records.

1) Australia

Australia has clearly been working to position itself as a world leader in recognizing and supporting legitimate crypto-based enterprises. This

---

[63]   As noted earlier, governments also have an interest in collecting sufficient tax revenue, however denominated, to carry out their functions. International taxation is, however, a topic that will not be dealt with in any detail in this chapter. Chapter 16 does include a brief recitation of some of the positions of tax issues taken by a selection of other nations.

[64]   The final section of this chapter will also introduce, albeit briefly, the role of non-state actors in the crypto ecosystem.

does not mean that the country has failed to adopt AML/CTF based regulations applicable to crypto. The Australian government introduced and enacted legislation in 2017, bringing digital currency exchange providers under the nation's AML/CTF provisions.[65] The relevant provisions became effective April 3, 2018.[66] Under that legislation, digital currency exchanges are required to enroll in a register maintained by AUSTRAC (the Australian Transaction Reports and Analysis Centre), implement a risk-based AML/CTF program, report suspicious transactions, and maintain various records.[67] This kind of relatively stringent AML/CTF response in even the most pro-crypto nations is consistent with the recommendations by the FATF and international norms.

2) Canada

Canada has also had a sophisticated and generally positive reaction to crypto. Canada allows its citizens to invest in and trade cryptocurrencies.[68] According to the Canadian webpage on digital currencies, "[y]ou can use digital currencies to buy goods and services on the Internet and in stores that accept digital currencies. You may also buy and sell digital currency on open exchanges, called digital currency or cryptocurrency exchanges."[69]

A parliamentary act passed June 19, 2014 defined cryptocurrencies so as to bring them within the ambit of "money service business" regulations.[70] The purpose of the measure was to bring businesses involved with virtual currencies within the scope of Canada's Proceeds of Crime (Money Laundering) and Terrorist Financing Act.[71] The law essentially requires companies dealing in crypto to register with the Financial Transactions and Reports Analysis Centre of Canada (Fintrac), adopt compliance programs, "keep and retain prescribed records," report

---

[65] Parliament of Australia, *Anti-Money Laundering and Counter-Terrorism Financing Amendment Bill 2017*, [archived at https://perma.cc/3LS8-TZ5L]; *Anti-Money Laundering and Counter-Terrorism Financing Amendment Act 2017* (Cth) sch 1 pt 2, [archived at https://perma.cc/892P-DQ5W].

[66] Austrac, *Digital Currency Exchange Providers* (last updated Dec. 20, 2018) [archived at https://perma.cc/4659-6EK4].

[67] For more detailed explanations of the 2017 legislation, see Parliament of Australia, Cat Barker, *Anti-Money Laundering and Counter-Terrorism Financing Amendment Bill 2017*, BILLS DIGEST No. 47, 2017–18 (Oct. 25, 2017), [archived at https://perma.cc/ECT9-GT6M]. *See also* Productivity Commission, *Business Set-Up, Transfer and Closure* 240–44, recommendation 9.3 (Inquiry Report No. 75) (Sept. 30, 2015) [archived at https://perma.cc/CQF9-WVPZ].

[68] Financial Consumer Agency of Canada, *Digital Currency* [archived at https://perma.cc/7DJC-QZFJ].

[69] *Id.*

[70] Bill C-31, *An Act to Implement Certain Provisions of the Budget Tabled in Parliament on February 11, 2014, and Other Measures*, Second Session, Forty-first Parliament, 62–63 Elizabeth II, 2013–2014, Statutes of Canada 2014 Ch. 20 [archived at https://perma.cc/2N7QE68C].

[71] Library of Congress, Bill C-31, *supra* note 70, and Tariq Ahmad, *Canada: Canada Passes Law Regulating Virtual Currencies as "Money Service Businesses"* GLOBAL LEGAL MONITOR (July 9, 2014) [archived at https://perma.cc/BQA6-K7MV].

suspicious and terrorist-related interactions, and ascertain whether any of their customers are "politically exposed persons."[72] The law also applies to exchanges operating outside Canada,[73] to the extent that they "direct services at persons or entities in Canada."[74] Finally, the provisions prevent banks from dealing with unregistered companies that deal in virtual currencies.[75] The 2014 law was one of the "world's first national law[s] on digital currencies, and certainly the world's first treatment in law of digital currency financial transactions under national anti-money laundering law."[76] Although not fully implemented until some years later, these provisions insure that Canadian-based crypto intermediaries comply with international norms.

3) Japan

Generally recognized as being a progressive regulator for crypto,[77] Japan was also one of the first nations to begin a systematic consideration of how best to approach the new technology. This is not surprising given the extensive base of crypto investors and users in the country.[78]

Japan's Financial Services Agency (FSA) established a study and working group on "sophistication of payment and settlement operations" in 2014 and 2015.[79] The working group recommended a registration system for cryptocurrency exchanges, subjecting crypto transactions to AML

---

[72]   Christine Duhaime, *Canada Implements World's First National Digital Currency Law; Regulates New Financial Technology Transactions*, DUHAIME LAW (June 22, 2014) [archived at https://perma.cc/4TLH-LTN5].

[73]   Extraterritorial jurisdiction in international law refers to the ability of a government to extend and exercise its authority beyond its normal territorial borders. There are certainly widely accepted principles that help define when such jurisdiction is appropriate. For further information on this concept, see Anthony J. Colangelo, *What Is Extraterritorial Jurisdiction?*, 99 CORNELL L. REV. 1303 (2014). *See also* Dan E. Stigall, *International Law and Limitations on the Exercise of Extraterritorial Jurisdiction in U.S. Domestic Law*, 35 HASTINGS INT'L & COMP. L. REV. 323, 327 (2012);

[74]   Bill C-31, *supra* note 70 at § 255(2).

[75]   *Id*. at § 258.

[76]   Duhaime, *supra* note 72.

[77]   One source asserted that as of 2017, "Japan has the world's most progressive regulatory climate for cryptocurrencies." *Cryptocurrency Regulations in Japan*, CRYPTOCOMPLY (available online   at   https://complyadvantage.com/knowledgebase/crypto-regulations/cryptocurrency-regulations-japan/).

[78]   *Cryptocurrency in Japan: A Brief History*, DRAGLET BLOG (now SKALEX) (available online at https://www.draglet.com/crypto-japan/).

On a given day (in 2018), Japan is either the second or third largest economy in the world for Bitcoin. Japanese yen averages 11% of global trading volume for BTC, keeping it neck-and-neck with the South Korean won for global trading dominance after the U.S. dollar. For a country of only 127 million people, 11% of global trading volume is an outsized influence per capita on the crypto industry.

Id.

[79]   Most of the information in this section comes from sources that are written in Japanese. The information in this chapter relating to Japan therefore relies heavily on *Selected Jurisdictions, supra* note 7, for citations to and translations of original source materials in that language. Except where noted, the information relating to Japan in this chapter comes from *Selected Jurisdictions*.

regulations and introducing a system to protect investors and users. Following consideration of the report by the FSA, the government introduced a bill to amend the country's Payment Services Act; that bill was approved in 2016 and went into effect April 1, 2017. This act brought Japanese crypto activities within the purview of the FSA, which both legitimizes crypto and imposes standards for crypto-exchanges.[80] Crypto exchanges are required to be licensed by the FSA and to comply with AML and KYC requirements designed to prevent crypto from being utilized to further criminal activities.[81]

Japan is one of the nations that, despite its generally pro-crypto stance, goes further than technically required by FATF with regard to so-called privacy coins. Effective June 18, 2018, the FSA announced a ban on privacy coin trading, affecting coins such as Monera, Zcash, and Dash, which have apparently been used by organized crime groups to launder money.[82]

4) Jersey

Jersey is also widely regarded as being exceptionally friendly to crypto-enterprises. Jersey is a Dependency of the United Kingdom and is generally recognized as a tax haven with a robust financial sector. In 2015, Jersey issued a consultation on crypto, noting "[t]he creation of a business-friendly framework that encourages innovation, jobs and growth in both the financial services and digital sectors is a priority for the Government of Jersey."[83] The result of the consultation was a policy document concluding that any crypto regulatory framework should be limited to preventing money-laundering and financing of terrorism.[84] Although Jersey specifically rejected the idea of comprehensive regulation on the

---

[80]   DRAGLET, *supra* note 78.

[81]   Japan was, at that time "the first country to regulate cryptocurrency exchanges." Taiga Uranaka, *Japan grants cryptocurrency industry self-regulatory status*, REUTERS (Oct. 24, 2018) (available online at https://www.reuters.com/article/us-japan-cryptocurrency/japan-grants-crypto currency-industry-self-regulatory-status-idUSKCN1MY10W).

[82]   The FSA "announced that on June 18, there will be an outright ban on all cryptocurrencies that provide a sufficient degree of anonymity to its end users. For the most part, Japanese exchanges are listening, pulling four major privacy coins—monero (XMR), dash, Augur's reputation (REP), and Zcash (ZEC)—from their platforms." Robert Viglione, *Japan's Ban Is a Wake-Up Call to Defend Privacy Coins*, COINDESK (updated May 30, 2018) (available online at https://www.coindesk.com/japan-wake-call-get-ready-defend-privacy-coins). As the title and quoted material suggests, this author is a staunch defender of the "need" for privacy, and cautions against bans such as this, complaining that this action signals that Japan is no longer acting in a crypto-friendly manner.

[83]   Chief Minister's Department, *Regulation of Virtual Currency: Consultation Paper* (July 9, 2015; presented to the States July 10, 2015) [archived at https://perma.cc/K5PY-GZRP].

[84]   Chief Minister's Department, *Regulation of Virtual Currency Policy Document* ¶ 1.1 (Oct. 21, 2015) [archived at https://perma.cc/9QBL-YQNT]. Presumably other, more general laws such as those applicable to fraud and market manipulation would continue to apply, as well.

basis that regulation might stifle innovation,[85] it has taken specific steps to comply with the international recommendations promulgated by FATF.

Jersey's AML and counter-terrorist funding laws were extended to cover crypto on September 26, 2015.[86] "Virtual currencies" were defined as a currency in order to bring them within the existing regulatory framework,[87] which made crypto businesses subject to the Jersey Financial Services Commission. The Dependency's AML policies[88] require "money service businesses" to register with the Commission[89] and comply with various record-keeping and reporting requirements.[90] In furtherance of its general anti-regulatory stance, however, these laws apply only if the business has annual proceeds in excess of £150,000 (approximately U.S. $185,000).[91] These requirements apply to "virtual currency exchanges," which are defined as enterprises engaged in the business of providing third parties with the service of exchanging "virtual currency for money in any form, or vice versa."[92] A virtual currency exchange that is exempt as a result of having an annual turnover under £150,000 is still required to notify the Commission that it is conducting such a business.[93]

---

[85]   *Id.* at ¶ 1.2.

[86]   Proceeds of Crime (Miscellaneous Amendments) (Jersey) Regulations 2016, R&O 63/2016, [archived at https://perma.cc/F2H5-2KNV]; Proceeds of Crime (Supervisory Bodies) (Virtual Currency Exchange Business) (Exemption) (Jersey) Order 2016, REVISED LAWS OF JERSEY [archived at https://perma.cc/A8W9-7753].

[87]   The Proceeds of Crime Act defines virtual currency as:

(4)   . . . any currency which (whilst not itself being issued by, or legal tender in, any jurisdiction)—

   (a)   digitally represents value;

   (b)   is a unit of account;

   (c)   functions as a medium of exchange; and

   (d)   is capable of being digitally exchanged for money in any form.

(5)   For the avoidance of doubt, virtual currency does not include any instrument which represents or stores (whether digitally or otherwise) value that can be used only to acquire goods and services in or on the premises of, or under a commercial agreement with, the issuer of the instrument.

Proceeds of Crime Act 1999, Sched. 2, Part B, ¶¶ 4, 5 [archived at https://perma.cc/K2YU-7KA4] (hereinafter Proceeds of Crime Act 1999).

[88]   Money Laundering (Jersey) Order 2008, REVISED LAWS OF JERSEY [archived at https://perma.cc/2ENA-U4AQ].

[89]   Proceeds of Crime (Supervisory Bodies) (Jersey) Law 2008, REVISED LAWS OF JERSEY, [archived at https://perma.cc/U5CQ-EQGY].

[90]   "Customer due diligence measures" are defined in the Proceeds of Crime Act 1999, *supra* note 87, at Sched. 2, Part B, ¶ 3. The KYC requirements apply if a customer enters into transactions in excess of than £1,000 (approximately U.S. $1,220). Chief Minister's Department, Regulation of Virtual Currency Policy Document, *Regulation of Virtual Currency: Consultation Paper* (July 9, 2015; presented to the States July 10, 2015) [archived at https://perma.cc/K5PY-GZRP] at ¶ 1.14. *See also* Money Laundering (Jersey) Order 2008, REVISED LAWS OF JERSEY [archived at https://perma.cc/3Y8L-ZGQD].

[91]   Order 2008 *supra* note 90.

[92]   Proceeds of Crime Act 1999, *supra* note 87, at Sched. 2, Part B, ¶ 9(2)(a)–(b).

[93]   Proceeds of Crime (Supervisory Bodies) (Virtual Currency Exchange Business) (Exemption) (Jersey) Order 2016, REVISED LAWS OF JERSEY [archived at https://perma.cc/A8W9-7753]; see also *Jersey Strengthens Financial Crime Regulation with Extension to Cover Virtual*

To avoid potential problems with international groups, Jersey has adopted special rules applicable to businesses that it categorizes as "high value dealers." A business that trades in goods and receives crypto valued at £15,000 (approximately U.S. $18,500) or more per transaction, or in groupings of transactions, are considered to be "high value dealers."[94] As such, these business must register with and be supervised by the Commission, as well as comply with AML and counter-terrorist financing requirements.[95]

5) The Netherlands

The Netherlands is also regarded as being quite welcoming to crypto. It has "no regulation on digital currencies" outside of E.U. requirements,[96] but to illustrate how prevalent crypto use in the area has become, the unofficial nickname for the city of Arnham has become "Bitcoin City."[97] In early 2019, the Netherlands Minister of Finance began looking at advice that a crypto-business licensing system should be introduced.[98] The emphasis of the proposal was on prevention of money laundering and terrorist financing. This direction is generally consistent with the approach recommended by the Central Bank of the Netherlands (De Nederlandsche Bank, "DNB"), which published a position paper in January 2018,[99] supporting the decision of the E.U. to include crypto exchanges and wallet services within the E.U.'s AML directives.[100] Wopke Hoekstra, the Dutch Minister of Finance, has also stated in a letter to parliament that regulations should not be permitted to stifle innovation in the crypto space, but that AML compliance is necessary and appropriate for both crypto exchanges and wallet services.[101] Given the directive from FATF requiring

---

Currency, JERSEY FINANCE (Oct. 24, 2016) (available online at https://www.jerseyfinance.je/news/jersey-strengthens-financial-crime-regulation-with-extension-to-cover-virtual-currency/).

[94] Proceeds of Crime Act 1999, *supra* note 87 at Sched. 2, Part B, ¶ 4.

[95] *Id.;* Jersey Financial Services Commission, *AML/CFT Handbook for Estate Agents and High Value Dealers* [archived at https://perma.cc/H5CA-UEGK].

[96] *See* Nick Hubble, *Top Crypto Friendly (and Hostile) Countries*, CAPITAL AND CONFLICT (Mar. 20, 2018) [archived at https://perma.cc/7ZH8-GMZF]. Although it has no specific regulation treating cryptoassets as securities, the Dutch Authority for financial markets (the Autoriteit) does asses ICOs on a case-by-case basis to see if the tokens involved qualify as a security or unit in a collective investment scheme and would therefore be subject to regulation. *See also Wet op het financieel toezicht [Wft] [Financial Supervision Act]*, Sept. 28, 2006, STAATSBLAD VAN HET KONINKRIJK DER NEDERLANDEN [STB.] [OFFICIAL GAZETTE OF THE KINGDOM OF THE NETHERLANDS] 2006, no. 475, as in force on Feb. 9, 2018, art. 1:1 [archived at http://perma.cc/CA3G-Y5ZK].

[97] Hubble, *supra* note 96.

[98] Adrian Zmudzinski, *Proposed License Requirements End Anonymous Crypto Selling and Buying in the Netherlands*, COINTELEGRAPH (Jan. 20, 2019) [archived at https://perma.cc/D5D5-8XJT].

[99] DNB, *Position Paper by De Nederlandsche Bank. Roundtable Cryptocurrencies/ICO's* 1 (Jan. 22, 2018) [archived at http://perma.cc/6C3N-GF4B].

[100] *Id.* at 3.

[101] Brief van de Minister van Financiën Aan de Voorzitter van de Tweede Kamer der Staten-Generaal [Letter of the Minister of Finance to the Chairman of the House of Representatives]

the adoption of AML/CTF policies for cryptocurrencies, the Dutch Money Laundering and Terrorist Financing (Prevention) Act is expected to be extended to specifically include custodian wallet providers and persons providing exchange functions for crypto by 2020.

———————

At the other end of the regulatory spectrum, there are a number of nations that are overtly hostile to crypto. Obviously, nations that ban the issuance, trading, ownership, or use of crypto, are not going to adopt specific standards beyond prohibiting it. In this vein, however, there are a number of countries that have specifically prohibited financial and other investment platforms from owning or facilitating the ownership of cryptoassets, using the bans as a way to prevent crypto from being used for money laundering or the funding of criminal activities.

6)   China

The People's Bank of China (the country's central bank) has declared that that "[a]ny new financial product or phenomenon that is not authorized under the existing legal framework, we will crush them as soon as they dare to surface."[102] As early as 2013, China was warning its citizens about the risks of Bitcoin, and at the same time it banned bank and payment institutions from dealing in Bitcoin.[103] Banks and payment institutions were also precluded from using Bitcoin pricing for goods or services, buying or selling Bitcoins, or providing any Bitcoin-related services, either directly or indirectly. They were also prevented from trading Bitcoins with fiat currency.

Since the original notice, China has become more and more resistant to crypto, and on September 2, 2017, the country banned ICOs and crypto trading platforms in the country. The rules issued by the Bank of China conclude that accepting Bitcoin or Ethereum in exchange for new coins or tokens is essentially illegal public financing, and the public has been warned that other financial crimes may also be involved such as illegal issuance of tokens or securities, illegal fundraising, financial fraud, or pyramid selling. Moreover, crypto lacks legal status in China, and "cannot and should not be circulated and used in the market as currencies." Businesses that violate these rules may have their websites and mobile

---

Toekomst financiële sector [Future of the Financial Sector] (Mar. 8, 2018) [archived at http://perma. cc/2J54-H8QC]. [This page was translated with Google translate.]

[102]   Jimmy Aki, *China's Central Bank Wants to Put the Damper on Airdrops: Report,* BITCOIN MAGAZINE (Nov. 5, 2018) (available online at https://bitcoinmagazine.com/articles/chinas-central-bank-wants-put-damper-airdrops-report).

[103]   Most of the information in this section comes from sources that are written in Chinese. This chapter therefore rely heavily on *Selected Jurisdictions, supra* note 7, for citations to and translations of original source materials in that language. Except where noted, the information on China contained in this chapter comes from *Selected Jurisdictions.*

apps shut down, apps removed from stores, and may even lose their business licenses.

Given these prohibitions, in China there is no lawful financial activity left involving crypto as to which AML/CTF requirements would apply. This may be unfortunate, given the reports suggesting that trading in crypto continues in China, through unlicensed, unregulated, private peer-to-peer networks.[104]

7) Iran

Iran, which is currently listed as a non-compliant nation by the FATF,[105] is another jurisdiction that is clearly hostile to crypto. On April 22, 2018, the Central Bank of Iran official announced that it had banned the handling of crypto by all Iranian financial institutions, including banks, credit institutions and exchanges.[106] This was not a complete surprise, given that until this point, there had been little explicit regulation of crypto in the country.[107] As a result, however, Iranian financial institutions are precluded from dealing in crypto meaning that there is no legal crypto activity in Iran as to which AML and CTF initiatives would apply.

Even the most recent initiatives from the country, which involved the legalizing of crypto mining, continue to ban other use or trading of crypto.[108]

In between the clearly pro-crypto nations, and those that ban its use outright, are nations with a range of varying responses to cryptoassets. Many of these have some regulations, but are struggling to adopt a

---

[104]   *See* William Suberg, *Despite Ban, China Keeps Trading Cryptocurrency Thanks to Tether and VPNs, Says Report*, COINTELEGRAPH (Sept. 9, 2018) [archived at https://perma.cc/75YX-66K7].

[105]   *See supra* text accompanying notes 25–26. Iran is, however, reportedly attempting to bring its AML and CTF programs into compliance, in an effort to alleviate international pressures and sanctions. Library of Congress, Barry Lerner, *Iran: IMF Evaluates Iran's Legislative and Institutional Efforts to Combat Money Laundering and Terrorism Financing*, GLOBAL LEGAL MONITOR (Apr. 13, 2018) [archived at https://perma.cc/J5NX-YLWK].

[106]   *Iranian Financial Institutions Barred from Using Crypto-Currencies*, FINANCIAL TRIBUNE (Apr. 22, 2018) (available online at https://financialtribune.com/articles/business-and-markets/85114/iranian-financial-institutions-barred-from-using-crypto). Currency exchanges are also prohibited from buying or selling crypto or adopting measures to facilitate or promote it. *Id.*

[107]   In 2017 the Money and Credit Council of the Central Bank of Iran had passed a directive deeming "non-physical and virtual transactions against the law, meaning that Iranian [currency exchanges could] not deal in cryptocurrencies." *No Bitcoin Trade for Moneychangers*, FINANCIAL TRIBUNE (Dec. 23, 2017) (available online at https://financialtribune.com/articles/economy-business-and-markets/78454/no-bitcoin-trade-for-moneychangers); Central Bank of The Islamic Republic of Iran, *Central Banking in Iran*, at 12–13 [archived at https://perma.cc/92DQ-CM3B].

[108]   *See* Yessi Bello Perez, *Iran further solidifies stance on cryptocurrency mining, but says trading is 'unlawful'*, THE NEXT WEB (Aug. 5, 2019) (available online at https://thenextweb.com/hardfork/2019/08/05/iran-further-solidifies-stance-on-cryptocurrency-mining-but-says-trading-is-unlawful/).

comprehensive response. Nonetheless, if a nation is going to regulate crypto, most of them start with AML/CTF.

8) Argentina

Even though crypto appears to be gaining acceptance among the general population in Argentina, regulation has lagged behind. In 2014, the Argentinian Unidad de Información Financiera (UIF or Financial Information Unit) of the Ministry of Finance formally recognized electronic currency in Resolution 300/2014.[109] This resolution clearly differentiates between electronic currency (which is merely an electronic transaction involving legal tender) and virtual currencies such as Bitcoin, but it does not formally address the regulation of virtual currency. Instead, the resolution merely warns persons already required to report suspicious activity that might involve money laundering or the funding of terrorism to be especially vigilant if they participate in virtual currency transactions.

Although Argentina has announced plans to explicitly extend AML and anti-terrorism requirements to crypto,[110] as of August 2019 there are no specific regulations on the issuance, exchange, or use of cryptocurrencies, and general AML/CTF requirements are the only ones that may or may not apply to crypto businesses. Given that FATF Recommendation 5 goes into effect at the start of 2020, this is expected to change.

9) Belarus

As will be described later, Belarus is one of the nations that is experimenting with how to use crypto businesses to stimulate the local economy. In very general terms, its approach has been to create a High Technology Park as an innovative space in which a modern digital economy can function within a legal framework.[111] While operational rules for operators and exchangers were originally left for self-regulation, on February 15, 2018, the National Bank of Belarus amended its AML regulations to apply to crypto-platform operators and cryptocurrency

---

[109]   Unidad de Información Financiera [Financial Information Unit], *Resolución 300/14 Prevención del Lavado de Activos y de la Financiación del Terrorismo [Prevention of the Laundering of Assets and the Finance of Terrorism]*, para. 9, BO (July 10, 2014) [archived at https://perma.cc/G2L7-9S2Q].

[110]   Olivera Doll & Camila Russo, *Argentina Supervisaría Operaciones en Bitcoins a Partir de 2018 [Argentina would Superivse Operations In Bitcoins from 2018]*, BLOOMBERG LATAM NOTICIAS (Dec. 7, 2017) (available in Spanish online at https://www.bloomberg.com/latam/blog/argentina-supervisaria-operaciones-en-bitcoins-partir-de-2018/). [This page was translated with Google translate.] Information about Argentina, updated as of August 2019, can be found at Library of Congress, *Regulation of Cryptocurrency: Argentina* (Aug. 16, 2019) [archived at https://perma.cc/Q2R8-47MF].

[111]   Most of the information in this section comes from sources that are written in Russian. This chapter therefore rely heavily on *Selected Jurisdictions*, *supra* note 7, for citations to and translations of original source materials in that language. Except where noted, the information on Belarus contained in this chapter comes from *Selected Jurisdictions*.

exchange operators, treating them as high-risk clients similar to casino operators. On March 27, 2018, additional requirements were imposed in order to further combat the risk of money laundering and financing of terrorism.[112]

10) Russia

Russia has not had a consistent reaction to crypto. Russian authorities first began advising citizens about risks associated with crypto in 2014. In January of that year, the Central Bank of the Russian Federation warned against the use of virtual currencies although it stopped short of declaring crypto to be illegal.[113] For the next two years, there were no official pronouncements other than individual (cautionary or negative) statements about crypto, but in March 2016, the Ministry of Finance began work on a bill that would have imposed criminal sanctions on the mining and use of Bitcoin.[114] Herman Gref, CEO of Russia's largest bank, Sberbank, openly opposed the bill, and it eventually failed, as it became clear that an absolute ban on crypto would be ineffective.[115]

Russia created the Russian Association of Blockchain and Cryptocurrency, now known as the Russian Association of Cryptocurrency and Blockchain, in August 2017.[116] Its purpose was to promote the development of blockchain technology and to offer regulatory options, but its success was limited. In May 2018, three crypto bills passed the first reading in the State Duma (the lower house of the Federal Assembly of Russia), including Bill No. 419059–7, "On digital financial assets." That bill would have made cryptocurrencies and tokens property, but hearings on the bill were postponed until 2019.[117]

On January 14, 2019, Anatoly Aksakov, the Head of the State Duma Committee on the Financial Market, announced that the merits of crypto regulation would be debated in first quarter of the year.[118] He suggested that the law would go into effect by March, and would (among other things) govern crypto trading platforms and exchanges, and would be implemented

---

[112] Under these requirements, applicants for registration with the Park must submit a business plan containing comprehensive protocols to identify customers, guarantee financial stability, technological safety, and security.

[113] Library of Congress, Peter Roudik, *Russia: Bitcoin Exchanges can be Penalized*, GLOBAL LEGAL MONITOR (Feb. 6, 2014) [archived at https://perma.cc/7L8T-CXU4].

[114] Samburaj Das, *Cryptocurrencies Should Not be Banned: CEO of Russia's Largest Bank*, CCN (Jan. 24, 2018) (available online at https://www.ccn.com/cryptocurrencies-not-banned-ceo-russias-largest-bank/).

[115] *Id.*

[116] *Cryptocurrency Regulations in Russia*, BENEFIT DAILY (Nov. 2018) (available online at https://benefit-daily.com/post/cryptocurrency-regulations-in-russia).

[117] Ana Berman, *Russian Parliament to Discuss Crypto Bill Within Two Months, Official States*, COINTELEGRAPH (Jan. 14, 2019) [archived at https://perma.cc/8XEL-KDY4].

[118] David Kimberley, *Russian Parliament to Implement Crypto Regulations in February*, FINANCE MAGNATES (Jan. 14, 2019) (available online at https://www.financemagnates.com/cryptocurrency/regulation/russian-parliament-to-implement-crypto-regulations-in-february/).

along with new regulations on investment and crowdfunding platforms.[119] This did not happen, and on February 27, 2019, Russian President Vladimir Putin set July 1, 2019, as the new deadline for the adoption of regulations.[120] That date also passed with no final regulations being implemented.

As of September 2019, Russia still has no final regulations applicable to cryptoassets. However, officials have announced that they expect initial regulations to be adopted before the end of the year. According to reports, "Anatoly Aksakov, head of the Duma Financial Market Committee, has said that Russia must adopt a bill on cryptocurrency before the end of this year in order to comply with recommendations from international watchdog, the Financial Action Task Force (FATF)."[121] This action would be consistent with the 2020 deadline for compliance with FATF Recommendation 15 as it relates to cryptocurrency operations.

B. FINANCIAL STABILITY

If there was a widespread belief that crypto constituted a current threat to global financial stability, this would certainly be at the top of policy issues under consideration by governments around the world. However, for the most part, nations have concurred with the assessment of the FSB that, at the current time, no such threat exists. In fact, many governmental authorities have echoed this opinion,[122] presumably focusing on both global and domestic financial security.

On the other hand, as noted in the recent G7 and 620 summits, the potential advent of Libra, in connection with Facebook and its two billion-plus users, might make a change to this. In a letter to the G20 finance leaders, the chairman of the FSB warned that "financial stability requires continued vigilance concerning new and emerging vulnerabilities in the financial system."[123] He specifically warned that technological innovation "has the potential to change significantly the structure and functioning of

---

[119]   *Id.*

[120]   Helen Partz, *Russian President Putin Orders Government to Adopt Crypto Regulation by July 2019*, COINTELEGRAPH (Feb. 27, 2019) [archived at https://perma.cc/8EZ2-54U4].

[121]   Daniel Palmer, *Russia May Allow Crypto Trading in Upcoming Legislation: Official*, COINDESK (June 24, 2019) (available online at https://www.coindesk.com/russia-may-allow-crypto-trading-in-upcoming-legislation-official).

[122]   For example, the G20 finance minister and central bank governors, while warning about risks such as money laundering and financing of criminal operations such as terrorism, in mid-2019 jointly expressed their opinion that "crypto assets to not pose a threat to global financial stability at this point. . . ." Japanese Ministry of Fin., *Communiqué, G20 Finance Ministers and Central bank Governors Meeting, Fuuoka, Japan* (June 8–9, 2019) [archived at https://perma.cc/76J2-FSXL], at ¶ 13.

[123]   FSB, Randal K. Quarles, FSB Chair, *To G20 Finance Ministers and Central Bank Governors* (Ap. 4, 2019) [archived at https://perma.cc/39FS-JM3N].

the global financial systems," pointing out that this includes risks posed by cryptoassets.[124]

This section therefore provides some typical statements about impressions regarding the general impact of crypto from a number of nations. It also includes some national responses to the potential future risk posed by initiatives such as Libra. Because most countries have determined that, at the current time, there is no present risk to global financial stability (even if that might change with future developments), the countries listed here as having representative points of view are simply included in alphabetical order rather than being divided intro crypto friendly, hostile, and neutral or undecided regimes.

1) Australia

In 2014, a committee appointed by the Australian Treasurer released its final report on the Australian financial system,[125] setting the stage for changes in Australian regulation of crypto. A report dated August 2015, recommended a number of regulatory responses to the emergence of virtual currencies.[126] It also evaluated the potential economic impact of the new technology and considered how Australia could best take advantage of new developments.[127] The report specifically noted that the use of virtual currencies (which the report referred to as digital currencies) was still limited and posed no current risks for the financial system.[128]

2) Canada

In February 2019, the Bank of Canada issued a staff discussion paper stating that a private cryptocurrency could "increase the fragility of the financial system."[129] The Bank's governing council agreed in its 2019 annual review of the nation's financial system that "[c]rypto assets are diverse and fast-evolving, posing risk to the financial safety of consumers and investors."[130] On the other hand, that report concluded that, based on a consideration of available evidence, "[c]rypto assets do not currently

---

[124]   *Id.*

[125]   Australian Govt the Treasury, FINANCIAL SYSTEM INQUIRY FINAL REPORT 166 (Nov. 2014), [archived at https://perma.cc/52SC-VCKQ].

[126]   Senate Economic References Committee, *Digital Currency—Game Change or Bit Player* (Aug. 2015) [archived at https://perma.cc/9C8Z-L76P] (hereinafter "Committee Report").

[127]   Parliament of Australia, *Digital Currency* [archived at https://perma.cc/T5XB-BNY2].

[128]   Committee Report, *supra* note 126 at 8.

[129]   Bank of Canada, James Chapman & Carolyn A. Wilkins, *Crypto 'Money': Perspective of a Couple of Canadian Central Bankers*, Staff Discussion Paper 2019–1 (Feb. 2019) (PDF link available online at https://www.bankofcanada.ca/2019/02/staff-discussion-paper-2019-1/, and the actual paper can be found at https://www.bankofcanada.ca/wp-content/uploads/2019/02/sdp2019-1.pdf).

[130]   Governing Council of the Bank of Canada, Stephen S. Poloz et al., *The Financial System Review—2019* (updated as of May 9, 2019) (available online at https://www.bankofcanada.ca/2019/05/financial-system-review-2019/).

represent a significant vulnerability for the Canadian financial system. They lack the size and, most importantly, the connections with the traditional financial system necessary for large shocks to spread or intensify."[131] Canada does, however, intend to engage in ongoing monitoring of the situation alongside other countries. The anticipated entry of Facebook into the ecosystem, through the recently announced Libra coin, has strengthened Canada's resolve to watch developments closely.[132]

3) France

The official French position for some time has been that Bitcoin and crypto do "not pose a threat to financial markets."[133] The announcement of the anticipated launch of Libra in 2020, however, raised concerns about a possible threat to sovereignty of nations. French Economy Minister Bruno Le Maire has expressed the view that action on Libra is needed "urgently," because of the potential risk to national sovereignty if a private "currency" becomes widely used.[134]

4) Germany

Germany had not previously expressed concerns about the impact of crypto on worldwide financial stability, but some German officials have issued warnings about potential risks that could be posed by Facebook's Libra project. In advance of the 2019 G7 Summit, German Finance Minister Olaf Scholz warned that regulators would need to be careful to ensure that new crypto such as Libra does not "threaten financial stability." His suggestion was that currencies should not be privately issued because "this is a core element of state sovereignty."[135]

The head of the German Federal Financial Supervisory Authority, Felix Hufeld, has urged regulators to develop standards in response to Libra. "We certainly can not just watch. We will have to respond appropriately in any way. I can only hope that we will succeed in developing at least European, if not globally, basic standards."[136] His

---

[131]   *Id.*

[132]   The Canadian Press, *Bank of Canada to review Facebook's cryptocurrency white paper 'very carefully'* CITYNEWS 1130 (June 18, 2019) (available online at https://www.citynews1130.com/2019/06/18/bank-of-canada-to-review-facebooks-cryptocurrency-white-paper-very-carefully/).

[133]   Andres Guadamuz and Chris Marsden, *Blockchains and Bitcoin: Regulatory responses to cryptocurrencies*, 20 FIRST MONEY (Dec. 2015) (available online at https://firstmonday.org/article/view/6198/5163#p4).

[134]   *See, i.e.*, Pol O Gradaigh, *French minister: G7 ministers agree action needed on Facebook's Libra*, DPA.International (Jul 17, 2019) (available online at https://www.dpa-international.com/topic/french-minister-g7-ministers-agree-action-needed-facebook-urn%3Anewsml%3Adpa.com%3A20090101%3A190717-99-100266).

[135]   *See* FINANCIAL TIMES, *supra* note 52.

[136]   Stephen O'Neal, *Facebook Libra Regulatory Overview: Major Countries' Stances on Crypto*, COINTELEGRAPH (Jul 16, 2019) (online at https://cointelegraph.com/news/libra-vs-us-congress-all-there-is-to-know-ahead-of-hearings).

opinion is that once Libra comes into use, there are likely to be considerable control and other issues, meaning that regulators need to pay close attention to this development.

5) Japan

Even at the height of the Bitcoin bubble in 2017, when prices climbed dramatically from less than $1000 at the start of the year to approximately $20,000 per coin before crashing at the end of the year, Japan did not appear to have any concern that crypto was disrupting conventional banking or affecting monetary policy.[137] On the other hand, reports began to circulate quickly after Facebook's announcement and whitepaper release about Libra that Japan's central bank, the Bank of Japan (BOJ), had concerns about the proposed cryptocurrency. Alongside concerns Libra could be difficult to regulate were fears that it might harm the existing financial system. The governor of the BOJ, Haruhiko Kuroda, was widely quoting as saying that he would "keep careful watch" over the project. A former head of the BOJ, Hiromi Yamaoka, has made similar statements, expressing concern that "[i]f Libra becomes more widely used than the sovereign currency of a particular country, the effect of monetary policy may be severely undermined."[138]

6) India

On January 4, 2019, the Reserve Bank of India (RBI) issued a report concluding that "cryptocurrencies currently pose no threat to financial stability."[139] Nonetheless, the RBI has continued to emphasize its belief that "cryptocurrencies need 'constant monitoring,' given their rapid expansion in recent years."[140] India has not ameliorated its harsh view of crypto following the announcement of Libra, even though it is the largest market for Facebook. In fact, Facebook has already indicated that it won't be offering its Calibra products in India in the foreseeable future because of India's restrictions on the technology.[141] It is, however, hard to tell

---

[137]   Leika Kihara, *Uniform global curbs on cryptocurrency trading may be hard: BOJ official*, REUTERS (Jan. 25, 2018) (available online at https://www.reuters.com/article/us-japan-bitcoin-boj/uniform-global-curbs-on-cryptocurrency-trading-may-be-hard-boj-official-idUSKBN1FE0XR).

[138]   Leika Kihara and Takahiko Wada, *Former Japan central banker warns Facebook's Libra may undermine monetary policy*, REUTERS (August 2, 2019) (https://www.reuters.com/article/us-japan-facebook-libra/former-japan-central-banker-warns-facebooks-libra-may-undermine-monetary-policy-idUSKCN1US0SK).

[139]   Ana Berman, *India: Central Bank Report States Crypto Does Not Threaten Financial Stability*, COINTELEGRAPH (Jan. 4, 2019) [archived at https://perma.cc/BAW9-P2GN], citing RBI, REPORT ON TREND AND PROGRESS OF BANKING IN INDIA 2017–18 (Dec. 28, 2018) [archived at https://perma.cc/3QL2-S8YB]. The references to risk posed by cryptoassets appear at pp. 29–30 of that report.

[140]   Berman, *supra* note 139.

[141]   O'Neal, *Facebook Libra*, *supra* note 136.

whether India is concerned about the potential impact of crypto on global financial stability or it does not like the technology for other reasons.

7) Netherlands

The Netherlands has issued warnings to investors about the risks posed by investment in ICOs,[142] and the Central Bank of the Netherlands (De Nederlandsche Bank, "DNB") has acknowledged that virtual currencies involve certain risks and drawbacks.[143] However, the DNB published a position paper in January 2018 which, among other things, concluded that cryptocurrencies have no "implications in terms of monetary policy."[144]

8) United Kingdom

In 2014, a quarterly bulletin from the Bank of England concluded that "[d]igital currencies do not currently pose a material risk to monetary or financial stability in the United Kingdom. The Bank continues to monitor developments in this area."[145] Recent pronouncements from Cordelia Kafetz, head of the Bank of England's Fintech Hub, have made it clear that this opinion had not changed as of 2018, notwithstanding the market volatility in 2017 and increasing corporate investment in the sector.[146]

With regard to Libra specifically, the governor of the Bank of England, Mark Carney, has been keeping an open mind. Carney said Libra could have genuine use cases if it can conform to regulatory demands, saying, "[a]nything that works in this world will become instantly systemic and will have to be subject to the highest standards of regulations."[147]

C. PROTECTING CITIZENS FROM FRAUD

The preceding two sections involve issues where there is substantial consensus on whether and how to react to specific issues. These include the need to apply AML/CTF standards and procedures to institutions that are assisting in the transfer or exchange of cryptoassets and the appropriate way to handle potential concerns that crypto might at some future point threaten global financial security. While nations may agree that crypto

---

[142]   Autoriteit Financiële Markten, *Initial Coin Offerings (ICO's): Serious Risks* [archived at http://perma.cc/7LGR-W95Y]. The Autoriteit is the Dutch authority for financial markets.

[143]   DNB, *Virtual Currencies* [archived at http://perma.cc/N3KY-MSLJ].

[144]   DNB, *Position Paper by De Nederlandsche Bank. Roundtable Cryptocurrencies/ICO's* 1 (Jan. 22, 2018) [archived at http://perma.cc/6C3N-GF4B].

[145]   Robleh Ali et al, *The Economics of Digital Currencies*, BANK OF ENGLAND Q. BULL. 276 (2014).

[146]   David Beach, Bank of England: *"We don't think crypto assets are money, or a particularly good store of value"* BOBSGUIDE (July 12, 2018) (available online at https://www.bobs guide.com/guide/news/2018/Jul/12/bank-of-england-we-dont-think-crypto-assets-are-money-or-a-particularly-good-store-of-value/).

[147]   O'Neal, *Facebook Libra, supra* note 136.

poses the risk of fraud, there is, however, no substantial agreement on how to handle that risk, and nations have varied tremendously in deciding how to react. While most countries have taken the step of posting warnings about the speculative nature of any investment in crypto, some have gone so far as to ban their citizens from experimentation with the new asset class (either in the name of protecting them or for other reasons). Others regulate the issuance and sale of crypto very closely. Some regulate the distribution of crypto relatively lightly, and some have yet to issue any definitive guidance on whether crypto sales will be regulated at all in this context.

Because of the incredibly diverse range of responses, the nations talked about here will be divided into three groups: countries that ban the distribution or sale of crypto; countries that have affirmatively attempted to regulate crypto businesses to a greater or lesser extent; and countries that have yet to confirm how they are going to react. Note that in this first group, the bans are not necessarily as effective at the governments might wish. It is widely reported, for example, that Bitcoin in particular continues to be widely used in China, mostly on underground, peer-to-peer networks rather than on regulated exchanges.

The first group of countries includes those that have implemented, or attempted to implement, a ban on crypto. Because bans, if effective, should adequately protect citizens from fraud and similar scams, only two examples of this approach are mentioned here.

1) Bolivia

On May 6, 2014 the El Banco Central de Bolivia, the central bank of the country, banned the use of any currency not issued or regulated by the government. Bolivian citizens are also prohibited from setting prices in any currency not previously approved by the government and official institutions. This prohibition specifically mentioned Bitcoin and a handful of other cryptoassets, although the statement is generally understood as apply to all cryptocurrencies.[148] A nonofficial translation of the statement indicated that "[i]t is illegal to use any kind of currency that is not issued and controlled by a government or an authorized entity."[149]

The stated purpose of the ban was in part to protect the country's national currency, the boliviano, but also to protect users from uncontrolled speculation that could lead to a loss of money for persons adopting the new currency.

---

[148]   Pete Rizzo, *Bolivia's Central Bank Bans Bitcoin*, COINDESK (June 19, 2014) (available online at https://www.coindesk.com/bolivias-central-bank-bans-bitcoin-digital-currencies).

[149]   *Id.*

2) China

China's stance on crypto has become increasingly hostile over time. While Chinese regulators never recognized crypto as legal tender,[150] in a 2013 notice, Bitcoin was characterized as a virtual commodity, and citizens were allowed to engage in online trading although they were warned about various risks. That circular did, however, indicate that the government was resistant to the new technology, and it did include a ban on bank and payment institution dealings in Bitcoin.

On September 2, 2017, China took firm steps to crack down on all activities involving crypto, completely banning ICOs and crypto trading platforms in the country. The ICO rules conclude that accepting Bitcoin or Ethereum in exchange for new coins or tokens is essentially illegal public financing, and the announcement warns that other financial crimes may also be involved such as illegal issuance of tokens or securities, illegal fundraising, financial fraud, or pyramid selling.

Even "airdrops," which are essentially free give-aways of crypto, are prohibited in China in the name of protecting investors. On November 3, 2018, the People's Bank of China issued a stability report specifically warned against their use.[151] The report concluded that "companies running token giveaways are evading China's blanket ban on ICOs by issuing free tokens to the investor, while keeping a large chunk of the total supply for speculation on a crypto exchange, where speculation would drive the prices up so they can profit."[152]

Most nations, of course, do not attempt to ban the use of crypto assets, instead either attempting to regulate their use or adopting a wait-and-see approach. Almost all of those that do act to regulate crypto include public warnings about the risks of investing in crypto and some limitations designed to protect innocent participants and investors who might otherwise be defrauded by unscrupulous third parties. Note that some nations have adopted new regulatory requirements for crypto while others have placed crypto into existing regulatory structures. In addition, some countries impose relatively light regulatory burdens on crypto, and others appear to be regulating with a heavy hand, imposing significant obstacles for the new technology.

3) Australia

The Australian Securities and Investments Commission (ASIC) has taken the position that digital currencies "do not fall within the legal definition of 'financial product' under the Corporations Act 2001

---

[150]   Except as noted, this information about China also comes from *Selected Jurisdictions, supra* note 7.

[151]   Aki, *supra* note 102.

[152]   *Id.*

(Corporations Act) or the Australian Securities and Investments Commission Act 2001 (ASIC Act)."[153] On the other hand, "general consumer protection provisions found in the Competition and Consumer Act 2010" have been found "to apply to digital currencies."[154] However, the administrative agency responsible for that act (the Australian Competition and Consumer Commission) had no information or warnings on its website about digital currencies even after it was found to have authority over crypto.[155]

As of 2019, the Australian securities regulator, ASIC, continues to maintain the position that under its rules, cryptocurrencies are not financial products under either the securities or corporations laws. However, ASIC's website now provides information on cryptocurrencies, including an explanation of how different kinds of cryptoassets work, and it sets out various risks associated with buying, trading, and investing in crypto.[156]

4) Belarus

Belarus has a unique approach to crypto. In order to engage in a crypto-based business in Belarus, operations must be located in the country's High Technology Park, which is a special economic zone that has a currently legislated end-date.[157] Legal entities involved in creating, issuing, storing, or exchanging of tokens must do so through a Park resident. This not only requires developers who intend to sell their crypto to reside in the Park, but any "crypto-platform operator" (which covers any provider of informational services who acts with the purpose of facilitating the exchange, sale, or purchase of tokens) must be a resident as well. Presumably, Park residents will be more sophisticated about crypto and in a better position to evaluate whether particular cryptoassets and businesses are legitimate.

Another way that Belarus protects potential investors is by guaranteeing the financial stability of crypto-platform and crypto-exchange operators. There are substantial minimum capital requirements for these two kinds of businesses: 1 million Belarusian rubles (approximately U.S. $505,000) for crypto-platform operators and 200,000 rubles (approximately U.S. $101,000) for cryptocurrency exchange operators. On the other hand, these operations are specifically excluded from other requirements of Belarusian securities and banking laws. In

---

[153]   *Id.* (referencing Corporations Act 2001 (Cth), pt 7.1 div 3 [archived at https://perma.cc/NSZ4-6FZK]; Australia Securities and Investments Commission Act 2001 (Cth), pt. 2 div2, subdiv. B, § 12BAA [archived at https://perma.cc/VBL6-NNV6]).

[154]   Committee Report, *supra* note 126 at 10.

[155]   *Id.*

[156]   *See, e.g.,* ASIC, *Cryptocurrencies,* MONEYSMART (last updated Oct. 24, 2018) [archived at https://perma.cc/H2JZ-BEG6].

[157]   For materials about Belarus, see *Selected Jurisdictions, supra* note 7.

addition, regulation on foreign exchange is also generally inapplicable to crypto transactions.

As a result of these regulations, the protections against misuse of crypto in Belarus are that crypto-based enterprises all take place within in a limited area, and crypto businesses operating to host or help exchange crypto must have substantial assets behind them so that purchasers may pursue a claim in the event of fraudulent or other illegal behavior.

5) France

In 2017, the French Financial Market Authority (Autorité des marchés financiers, or AMF) and Prudential Supervisory Authority (Autorité de contrôle prudentiel et de resolution, or ACPR) issued a joint notice warning investors that crypto was unregulated and particularly volatile.[158] Earlier warnings had essentially contained similar information.[159] In March 2018, the AMF again warned investors about investing in crypto from unregistered sources.[160] This time, however, the AMF also suggested that "cash-settled cryptocurrency contracts may qualify as a derivative" and indicated that online trading platforms offering such contracts would need to comply with E.U. regulations imposing reporting obligations on "trade repositories."[161]

Jean-Pierre Landau, a former deputy governor of the Banque de France, was charged with evaluating regulatory options with the goals of improving the development of crypto while preventing their use for illegal activities.[162] Landau is generally regarded as a crypto-skeptic,[163] but he proposed that the AMF be authorized to certify companies that issue tokens in compliance with certain standards to protect investors.[164] At

---

[158] AMF & ACPR, *Achats de Bitcoin: l'AMF et l'ACPR mettent en garde les épargnants* [*Bitcoin Purchases: The AMF and ACPR Warn Savers*] (Dec. 4, 2017) [archived at https://perma. cc/CM6Q-EGUH].

[159] For example, the French Central Bank (Banque de France) published a report in December 2013 containing warnings that crypto is not a "real" currency, is a risky investment, and potentially is a vehicle for criminal activity. Banque de France, *Les dangers liés au développement des monnaies virtuelles: l'exemple du bitcoin* [*The Dangers of the Development of Virtual Currencies: The Bitcoin Example*], FOCUS No. 10 (Dec. 5, 2013) [archived at https://perma.cc/K93L-HLAC].

[160] AMF, News Release, *The Autorité des marchés financiers (AMF) Is Publishing a List on Its Website of Unauthorized Companies Proposing Atypical Investments without Being Authorised to Do So* (Mar. 15, 2018) [archived at https://perma.cc/P38R-L8MQ].

[161] AMF, New Release, *The AMF Considers that the Offer of Cryptocurrency Derivatives Requires Authorization and that It Is Prohibited to Advertise such Offer via Electronic Means* (Feb. 22, 2018) [archived at https://perma.cc/6323-NYAP].

[162] AFP, *Un ancien de la Banque de France chargé d'une mission sur le bitcoin* [*Former Banque de France Official Tasked with a Mission on Bitcoin*], LE POINT (Jan. 15, 2018) [archived at https://perma.cc/R6CD-GCV9].

[163] David Meyer, *France's Newly-Appointed 'Monsieur Bitcoin' Is a Notable Cryptocurrency Skeptic*, FORTUNE (Jan. 16, 2018) (available online at https://fortune.com/2018/01/16/bitcoin-crypto currency-france-regulation-jean-pierre-landau/).

[164] Bruno Le Maire, Minister of the Economy and Finance, *Op-ed, Cryptoactifs, Blockchain & ICO: Comment la France veut rester à la pointe* [*Cryptoassets, Blockchain & ICO: How France*

about this same time, France joined Germany in calling for crypto to be discussed by the G20 to help develop internally coordinated initiatives.[165]

The French Minister of Finance and Economy, Bruno Le Maire, announced on September 12, 2018, that France had adopted new regulations for ICOs.[166] In accordance with Landau's recommendations, under the new rules, the AMF is authorized to issue permits and approve companies seeking to raise funds with ICOs.

On January 30, 2019, the French Finance Commission published a 148-page report on blockchain and crypto.[167] The new French approach divides crypto into three distinct categories: security tokens, utility tokens, and currency tokens. Security tokens, that look like traditional securities, will be generally regulated as such, while cryptocurrencies will be subject to AML and anti-terrorist financing requirements. In addition, there is at least some possibility that utility tokens will be subject to certain regulation, perhaps to be specified in the future.[168]

The French response found its existing regulatory structures to be inadequate to deal with crypto, and therefore adopted new definitions and rules, while also specifically seeking guidance from the E.U. in order to increase international consistency, at least among European countries.

6) Indonesia

For several years, the central bank of Indonesia, Bank Indonesia, repeatedly warned against the buying, selling, or trading of crypto, noting that cryptocurrency is not "legitimate" in the country.[169] Two Indonsesian-based crypto exchanges, BitBayer and TokoBitcoin, closed shortly after the

---

Wants to Stay at the Forefront], NUMERAMA (Mar. 19, 2018) (available online at https://www.numerama.com/politique/336943-tribune-cryptoactifs-blockchain-ico-comment-la-france-veut-rester-a-la-pointe-par-bruno-le-maire.html). [This page was translated with Google translate.]

[165]   *Berlin et Paris veulent mobiliser le G20 sur les cryptomonnaies [Berlin and Paris Want to Mobilize the G20 on Cryptocurrencies]*, REUTERS (Feb. 9, 2018) (available at https://fr.reuters.com/article/technologyNews/idFRKBN1FT19L-OFRIN). The G20 members made note of crypto in connection with sustainability. *See* Helen Partz, *G20 Members Note Crypto Regulation in Recent Declaration on Sustainable Development*, COINTELEGRAPH (Dec. 8, 2018) [archived at https://perma.cc/MM9L-FRRM].

[166]   *France Announces Landmark Crypto-Friendly ICO Regulations*, DAILY HODL (Sept. 18, 2018) (available online at https://dailyhodl.com/2018/09/18/france-announces-landmark-crypto-friendly-ico-regulations/).

[167]   The report can be found at ASSEMBLÉE NATIONALE, RAPPORT D'INFORMATION (Jan. 30, 2019) [archived at https://perma.cc/K3KH-T4CD]. [Various secondary sources and Google translate were used to translate the contents of the report.]

[168]   For additional discussion of France's regulatory approach, see GLI, BLOCKCHAIN & CRYPTOCURRENCY REGULATION 2019—FRANCE (available online at https://www.globallegalinsights.com/practice-areas/blockchain-laws-and-regulations/france).

[169]   Molly Jane Zuckerman, *Central Bank of Indonesia Warns Against All Cryptocurrency Use, Cites High Risk*, COINTELEGRAPH (Jan. 14, 2018) [archived at https://perma.cc/KS6T-ESFA].

central bank reasserted that it was not going to accept Bitcoin as payment.[170]

In February 2019, however, Indonesia's Commodity Futures Trading Regulatory Agency, also known as Bappebti, approved regulation No. 5/2019, recognizing Bitcoin and other cryptoassets as trading commodities.[171] Indrasari Wisnu Wardhana, the head of Bappepti, reportedly said that the goal of the new approach was to "give protection to people who want to invest in crypto assets so that they aren't cheated by fraudulent sellers."[172]

One of the ways that Indonesia protects investors and users of crypto is to have very high paid-in capital requirements for traders and wallet services. Not only do such businesses require regulatory approval, but they must also meet minimum paid up capital[173] requirements of 1 trillion Indonesian rupiahs (approximately U.S. $71 million) and a minimum closing balance of 800 billion Indonesian rupiahs (approximately U.S. $57 million).[174] Crypto traders have complained about the high capital requirements, noting that they are greater than that required for conventional banks and far higher "much higher than the 2.5 billion rupiah [approximately U.S. $177,000] minimum paid-up capital for futures brokers of other commodities."[175]

7) Japan

Japan was one of the first nations to begin a systematic consideration of how best to approach the new technology. This is not surprising given the extensive base of crypto investors and users in the country.[176] On the other hand, Japanese regulators have also been forced to actively evaluate

---

[170]   *Id.*

[171]   The announcement from Bappebti was Peraturan Badan Pengawas Perdagangan Berjangka Komoditi, Nomor 5 Tahun 2019 [Regulation of the Supervisory Agency Commodity-Term Trade, No. 5 of 2019], *Tentang Ketentuan Teknis Penyelenggaraan Pasar Fisik Aset* Kripto *[Regarding Technical Provisions of Management of Crypto Asset Markets]* (Feb. 8, 2019) (in Indonesian) [archived at https://perma.cc/6EBK-V9DR]. [These materials were translated with Google translate.]

[172]   Ana Alexandre, *Indonesia: New Legislation Recognizes Crypto as Trading Commodity*, COINTELEGRAPH (Feb. 15, 2019) (available online at https://cointelegraph.com/news/indonesia-new-legislation-recognizes-crypto-as-trading-commodity).

[173]   This is simply the idea that before the business begins operations, the owners must have fully contributed a certain amount against which creditors' claims may be pursued. The problem here is not the concept, but rather the amounts required as a minimum contribution in order to begin business.

[174]   *Id.*

[175]   Tabita Diela, *Cryptocurrency traders protest Indonesia's new futures rules*, REUTERS (Feb. 13, 2019) (available online at https://www.reuters.com/article/us-indonesia-crypto/cryptocurrency-traders-protest-indonesias-new-futures-rules-idUSKCN1Q30IM).

[176]   *See* DRAGLET, *supra* note 78.

how to approach crypto because two of the biggest exchange hacks in history (Mt. Gox[177] and Coincheck) both occurred in that country.[178]

Japan's Financial Services Agency (FSA) established a study and working group on "sophistication of payment and settlement operations" in 2014 and 2015.[179] The working group recommended a registration system for cryptocurrency exchanges, subjecting crypto transactions to AML regulations, and introducing a system to protect investors and users.

There were also a number of regulatory developments affecting crypto in 2018, beginning in January, which is when Coincheck lost about $400 million in NEM tokens. Three days later, the local Finance Bureau ordered Coincheck to submit a report, issuing an order of business improvement on January 29, 2018. On January 30, FSA asked all Japanese crypto exchanges to review their systems and report back. On March 8, 2018, local Finance Bureaus issued business-improvement orders to seven exchange businesses, including Coincheck, with the result that two were ordered to suspend business.

At the same time as the government agency was reacting to the Coincheck hack and calls for additional safeguards, on March 2, 2018, the sixteen government-approved crypto exchanges formed a self-regulatory organization, the Japan Virtual Currency Exchange Association, with the express goal of making crypto safer and more legitimate for users. Moving forward, all registered exchanges are required to join it.

While some commentators have complained about the "crackdown" on crypto in Japan, others have applauded the country's regulations as thoughtful and fair. As one commentator has suggested, "[t]he decision to step in and put out firm business improvement orders to the exchanges may seem harsh, but really, it is an indication that the government wants this sector to work, but work properly."[180]

While these responses have focused predominantly on the proper functioning of crypto exchanges, Japan has also been evaluating how to regulate the issuance of crypto. Under the Japanese Financial Instruments and Exchange Act (FIEA), token offerings involve the sale of securities if they are issued with the expectation of sharing profits. Tokens meet this if these three requirements are all met:

---

[177]   The Mt. Gox hack and its resulting bankruptcy is discussed *supra*, in chapter 5. For a more focused explanation of the Mt. Gox hack and its legacy for participants, see David Meyer, *After Bitcoin Spike, Mt Gox Creditors Want to Yank the Failed Exchange Out of Bankruptcy*, FORTUNE (Dec. 13, 2017) (available online at https://fortune.com/2017/12/13/bitcoin-mtgox-bankruptcy-creditors/).

[178]   The Coincheck hack is described briefly in chapter 2.

[179]   Japanese authorities are referenced in *Selected Jurisdictions, supra* note 7.

[180]   Darryn Pollock, *What Is The State Of Crypto And Blockchain In Japan After Regulation?* FORBES (Jan. 24, 2019) (available online at https://www.forbes.com/sites/darrynpollock/2019/01/24/what-is-the-state-of-crypto-and-blockchain-in-japan-after-regulation/#34ed050955c8).

(1)   purchasers of the tokens pay with cash or other assets,

(2)   the proceeds from the sale are invested in the business, and

(3)   investors expect to receive dividends or a share of profits generated by the business.[181]

Somewhat oddly, issuers of these kinds of tokens are precluded from using the official term "crypto assets" in describing the interests.[182]

Finally, effective April 2020, cryptoasset derivatives in Japan will also be governed by the FIEA.[183]

8)   The Netherlands

While clearly wanting to be seen as pro-crypto to entrepreneurs and crypto businesses, The Netherlands has issued various warnings to investors about the risks posed by investment in ICOs,[184] and the Central Bank of the Netherlands (De Nederlandsche Bank, "DNB") has acknowledged that virtual currencies involve certain risks and drawbacks.[185] The country has, however, little in the way of formal regulation applicable to crypto, warning potential investors and then leaving the decision of whether to proceed to its citizens. Note that this is not the case of a nation that has not decided whether to act; instead the government relies on warnings to protect its citizens rather than imposing burdensome regulatory requirements on crypto-based companies.

Even nations that have not decided whether or how to regulate crypto have often taken the step of warning their citizens about potential risks, while they investigate the question of how to best regulate these new assets.

9)   Brazil

The first "official" announcement about crypto came from the Brazilian Central Bank (Banco Central do Brasil) on February 19, 2014, in the form of Policy Statement No. 25,306 on the risks related to crypto.[186] The document refers to crypto as "virtual currencies" or "encrypted currencies," and the purpose of that initial statement was not to regulate crypto but to

---

[181]   Hisashi Oki, *Japan Hopes to Set Global Crypto Law Benchmark With Latest Regulatory Update,* COINTELEGRAPH (Jun 5, 2019) [archived at https://perma.cc/VH88-DTJA], citing the Japanese law firm of Anderson Mori & Tomotsune.

[182]   *Id.*

[183]   *Id.*

[184]   Autoriteit Financiële Markten, *Initial Coin Offerings (ICO's): Serious Risks* [archived at http://perma.cc/7LGR-W95Y]. The Autoriteit is the Dutch authority for financial markets.

[185]   DNB, *Virtual Currencies* [archived at http://perma.cc/N3KY-MSLJ].

[186]   Banco Central do Brasil, *Policy Statement No. 25,306* (February 19, 2014) [archived at https://perma.cc/NC7T-TVSR].

clarify that it should not be confused with electronic money.[187] The Policy Statement also noted that there were few concrete conclusions about crypto; no recognized monetary authorities backed it; and no governmental mechanisms assured value or convertibility of crypto.[188] The plan was that the central bank would adopt measures in the future if necessary.

Brazil's Central Bank issued a follow-up statement on November 16, 2017, warning of risks from storing and conducting transactions in crypto.[189] This statement again specifically warned the public that the Central Bank did not regulate, license, or supervise crypto businesses and that there was no existing legal or regulatory framework over crypto; it also reiterated that virtual currencies were not to be confused with electronic currency.[190]

On January 12, 2018, the Brazilian Securities and Exchange Commission (Comissão de Valores Mobiliários) released a statement directed to investment funds that were investing in crypto.[191] In essence, the statement noted that there was no general consensus (either in Brazil or on the global stage) about how best to conceptualize crypto.[192] Based on that determination the commission decided against classifying crypto as financial assets that investment funds could purchase.[193] While recognizing that Brazilian investment funds might, in the future, be established specifically to invest in crypto or crypto-based derivatives offered in regulated environments in other jurisdictions, the Central Bank merely noted that discussions about crypto regulation were in the initial stages and that the ultimate direction of any regulation in Brazil was uncertain.[194]

As stated in the U.S. Library of Congress survey of selected regulations of cryptocurrencies, the Brazilian Central Bank:

> . . . concluded that, based on its understanding of the technical area, it is undeniable that there are still many other inherent risks associated with such investments (such as cybersecurity and privacy risks), and with the future legality of their acquisition or

---

[187] *Id.*, noting that electronic money (moeda eletrônica) is defined in article 6(VI) of Law No. 12,865 of October 9, 2013, and its regulations as an electronically stored resource that allows the user to make payments in Brazilian Real, the national currency. Lei No. 12.865, de 9 de Outubro de 2013, [archived at https://perma.cc/5ZNY-3KVD].

[188] *Policy Statement, supra* note 186.

[189] Banco Central do Brasil, *Communiqué 31,379* (November 16, 2017) [archived at https://perma.cc/N7KB-P5J9].

[190] *Id.*

[191] Comissão de Valores Mobiliários, Ofício Circular No. 1/2018/CVM/SIN [archived at https://perma.cc/486G-8TS4].

[192] *Id.*

[193] *Id.* Article 2(V) of CVM Instruction 555/2014 lists the financial assets applicable to investment funds registered with CVM. Instrução CVM No. 555 (Dec. 17, 2014) [archived at https://perma.cc/6LV3-X532].

[194] *Id.*

trade, and that considering all these variables it was not possible . . . reach a conclusion regarding the possibility of the constitution and structuring of indirect investments in cryptocurrencies.[195]

10) Russia

Russian authorities first began warning citizens about crypto in 2014. In January of that year, the Central Bank of the Russian Federation warned against the use of virtual currencies although it stopped short of declaring crypto to be illegal.[196] Since that time, the country has flirted with bans and restrictive approaches, but President Vladimir Putin has recently insisted that the country find a way to regulate crypto by the end of 2019.[197] The direction that the country will eventually take, however, has not been finalized as of the writing of these materials. Moreover, there are indications that the initial response will focus on AML and CTF requirements, leaving open the question of how Russia will act to protect citizens from fraudulent offerings.

D. FURTHERING ECONOMIC GROWTH

In addition to regulating crypto to limit criminal use of the technology and to protect users and investors, nations may actually seek to encourage the use and development of crypto in order to further economic growth. This has, in fact, been an explicit goal of a number of nations as they decide how to react to the new technology. They way in which different nations have gone about seeking to attract crypto entrepreneurs and investors does, however, vary considerably.

1) Belarus

As mentioned earlier, the President of Belarus signed a Decree on the development of the digital economy on December 21, 2017.[198] The Decree focused on Belarus' efforts to use its High Technology Park as an innovative space to help build a modern digital economy, and it creates a legal

---

[195]   *Selected Jurisdictions, supra* note 7 at 23.

[196]   Libr. of Cong., Peter Roudik, *Russia: Bitcoin Exchanges can be Penalized*, GLOBAL LEGAL MONITOR (Feb. 6, 2014) [archived at https://perma.cc/7L8T-CXU4].

[197]   Deadlines for the enactment of basic regulators have come and gone. On January 14, 2019, Anatoly Aksakov, the Head of the State Duma Committee on the Financial Market, announced that the merits of crypto regulation would be debated in first quarter of the year. He suggested that the law would go into effect by March, and would (among other things) govern crypto trading platforms and exchanges, and would be implemented along with new regulations on investment and crowdfunding platforms. Kimberley, *supra* note 118. This did not happen, and on Feb. 27, Russian President Vladimir Putin set July 1, 2019 as the new deadline for the adoption of regulations. Helen Partz, *Russian President Putin Orders Government to Adopt Crypto Regulation by July 2019*, COINTELEGRAPH (Feb. 27, 2019) [archived at https://perma.cc/8EZ2-54U4]. That date also passed, and the most recent pronouncement as of the date this chapter was written was that action would occur by the end of 2019. This date may be harder to bypass, as the suggestion is that it is required by FATF. *See supra* note 121 and accompanying text.

[198]   The materials on Belarus come from *Selected Jurisdictions, supra* note 7.

framework for buying, selling, exchanging, creating, and mining cryptocurrencies. The expressed objective was to position Belarus as "the first jurisdiction in the world with comprehensive legal regulation of businesses based on blockchain technology" and the first country to legalize smart contracts at the national level.[199]

One of the things that makes this approach unique is that most of the Decree applies only to individuals and entities operating in the High Technologies Park, a special economic zone. Another unusual feature is that the entire project is set up as an experiment, with end-dates built in. For example, one of the most attractive aspects of the Decree is an exemption from taxation on mining, creation, acquisition, and alienation of tokens, or upon investments attracted as a result of the creation or issuance of tokens, until 2023. In addition, until at least 2049, businesses operating in the Park only have to pay 1% of their turnover to the government. Also as a legal experiment, the Decree allows residents of the Park to use "smart contracts," and permits the incorporation of elements of English contract law, such as convertible loans, options, clauses of indemnity, and noncompetition agreements, to create a "venture ecosystem."

The Decree uses unusual terminology in talking about "cryptocurrency," which it defines as Bitcoin or other digital signs (tokens) used in international circulation as a universal means of exchange. Individuals are allowed to own, acquire, mine, store, donate, bequeath, or exchange tokens for Belarusian rubles, foreign currency, or electronic money. They are not allowed to purchase goods or services with the tokens that they own. An owner need not declare ownership of tokens, and mining or buying and selling of tokens by an individual with no employees or contractors is not considered entrepreneurial activity.

Entities involved in creating, issuing, storing, or exchanging tokens must do so through a Park resident. Similarly, any "crypto-platform operator," which includes providers of informational services who act with the purpose of facilitating the exchange, sale, or purchase of tokens, must be a resident of the High Technology Park. The consideration that such a business may accept for tokens is limited to Belarusian rubles, foreign currency, electronic money, or other tokens. A "cryptocurrency exchange operator," which covers any business that exchanges, sells, or purchases tokens using software and hardware systems on its own behalf, must also be a resident of the Park.

There are substantial minimum capital requirements for these two kinds of businesses: 1 million Belarusian rubles (approximately U.S. $505,000) for crypto-platform operators and 200,000 rubles (approximately

---

[199] President of the Republic of Belarus, Press Release, *Commentary to Decree No. 8 of December 21, 2017* (Dec. 27, 2017) (in Russian) [archived at https://perma.cc/A7B7-WJBS] [This page was translated with Google translate.]

U.S. $101,000) for cryptocurrency exchange operators. On the other hand, these operations are specifically excluded from other requirements of Belarusian securities and banking laws. In addition, regulation on foreign exchange is also generally inapplicable to crypto transactions.

Despite the relatively burdensome capital requirements, Belarus' approach is clearly designed to encourage experimentation with the new asset class and to attract crypto businesses to the area.

2) France

The French approach to crypto reflects a common reaction to two conflicting policy interests: the need to protect against fraud and the use of crypto by criminals, and the desire to encourage innovation and economic development. Both the French legislative and executive branches began active efforts to evaluate cryptocurrencies in 2018. The National Assembly (Assemblée Nationale, one of the two houses of the French Parliament and the French Parliament (the Senate) each conducted investigations into crypto and blockchain.[200] While most participants agreed that a new regulatory framework for crypto was necessary in order to minimize illegal uses of crypto and to protect investors, there was also general agreement that the government needed to avoid stifling innovation.[201]

As mentioned earlier, France has tried to accomplish all of this by dividing cryptoassets into securities tokens, utility tokens, and currency tokens, and by regulating each group separately.[202] The extent to which France has been able to successfully navigate between these competing goals is uncertain. While some hail the French regime as being pro-crypto, other sources contend that "France has one of the toughest regulatory environments in Europe and the world generally when it comes to finance and specifically cryptocurrency."[203]

---

[200]   The National Assembly initiated two missions: one related to cryptocurrencies and the other to blockchain and distributed ledge technology. *See* Assemblée Nationale, *Mission d'information sur les monnaies virtuelles [Information Mission on Cryptocurrencies]*, [archived at https://perma.cc/JNU5-4MRG], and Assemblée Nationale, *Mission d'information commune sur les usages des bloc-chaînes (blockchains) et autres technologies de certification de registres [Joint Information Mission on the Uses of Blockchains and Other Technologies for the Certification of Ledgers]* [archived at https://perma.cc/3TKA-Y7L7]. The French senate's hearings also focused on these aspects of the new technology. 24 Comptes Rendus de la Commission des Finances [Minutes of the Finance Commission], SENAT [SENATE] (Feb. 7, 2018) [archived at https://perma.cc/J9LVN8ZD].

[201]   24 Comptes Rendus de la Commission des Finances [Minutes of the Finance Commission] SENAT (SENATE) (Feb. 7, 2018) [archived at https://perma.cc/J9LVN8ZD].

[202]   *See supra* notes 167–168 and accompanying text.

[203]   P. H. Madore, *French Firm Becomes Europe's First Regulated Crypto Asset Manager Funded by an ICO*, CCN (Dec. 7, 2018) (available online at https://www.ccn.com/french-firm-becomes-europes-first-regulated-crypto-asset-manager-funded-by-an-ico/).

3) Jersey

Jersey has positioned itself as being pro-crypto by avoiding regulation as much as possible. In 2015, Jersey issued a consultation on crypto, noting "[t]he creation of a business-friendly framework that encourages innovation, jobs and growth in both the financial services and digital sectors is a priority for the Government of Jersey."[204] The result of the consultation was a policy document concluding that crypto should be regulated only to the extent necessary to prevent money-laundering and the financing of terrorism.[205] Jersey specifically rejected the idea of comprehensive regulation on the basis that regulation might stifle innovation.[206] The policy document was specifically designed to "further enhance Jersey's proposition as a world leading Fintech jurisdiction" while establishing the Dependency's commitment to encouraging innovation in the digital sector while protecting against the most significant money laundering and terrorist financing risks presented by virtual currencies.[207]

This approach is consistent with Jersey's general approach to attracting investment with a low tax, minimal regulation regime.

4) The Netherlands

Although the Netherlands[208] and the Central Bank of the Netherlands (De Nederlandsche Bank, "DNB") have both acknowledged that virtual currencies involve certain risks,[209] Dutch national authorities have explicitly recognized the potential value of crypto. Wopke Hoekstra, the Dutch Minister of Finance, explained in a letter to parliament that the Netherlands does not want to ban the cryptocurrency trade, and has suggested that it should be regulated on a European or international level.[210] He has emphasized that no regulation should be permitted to limit the potential of the blockchain technology.[211]

E. CONTROL OVER CITIZENS

At the other end of the spectrum, some governments have clearly determined that allowing free access to crypto would be counter to their

---

[204]   Chief Minister's Department, *Regulation of Virtual Currency: Consultation Paper* (July 9, 2015; presented to the States July 10, 2015) [archived at https://perma.cc/K5PY-GZRP].

[205]   Chief Minister's Department, *Regulation of Virtual Currency Policy Document* ¶ 1.1 (Oct. 21, 2015) [archived at https://perma.cc/9QBL-YQNT].

[206]   *Id.* at ¶ 1.2.

[207]   *Id.* at 2.

[208]   Autoriteit Financiële Markten, *Initial Coin Offerings (ICO's): Serious Risks* [archived at http://perma.cc/7LGR-W95Y]. The Autoriteit is the Dutch authority for financial markets.

[209]   DNB, *Virtual Currencies* [archived at http://perma.cc/N3KY-MSLJ].

[210]   *Brief van de Minister van Financiën Aan de Voorzitter van de Tweede Kamer der Staten-Generaal [Letter of the Minister of Finance to the Chairman of the House of Representatives]* (Mar. 8, 2018) [archived at http://perma.cc/2J54-H8QC].

[211]   *Id.*

nation's interests notwithstanding any potential economic gains. Sometimes the rationale behind bans or prohibitions are framed in terms of the need to protect citizens from the criminal element. On the other hand, the nature of the government regimes involved and the extent of regulation may give rise to at least a circumstantial inference that government policies in some of these countries are more about controlling the citizenry and protecting the national currency than anything else.

1) Bolivia

El Banco Central de Bolivia has explicitly banned the use of Bitcoin and other cryptocurrencies. The justification offered by the Central Bank was that a ban is necessary to protect the national currency, the boliviano, and to safeguard users from the risks of uncontrolled currencies. The need to control citizen's access to crypto may be heightened in Bolivia, where the government "may have good reason to fear a competing currency whose supply is limited and is widely seen as counter to inflation ridden fiat money."[212]

2) China

As described above, China is one of the most stringent regulators of crypto, banning ICOs, discouraging crypto mining, and banning internet and mobile access to crypto exchanges. China's reaction to Bitcoin and other cryptocurrencies has ostensibly been to avoid financial risks associated with the new asset class. Reports suggest that in early 2017, more than 90% of all Bitcoin-fiat trades worldwide involved Renminbi, the official Chinese currency.[213] In response, and "[u]nerved by the high volume, the government immediately outlawed fiat from being used in cryptocurrency purchases and even imposed travel bans on Huobi and OKCoin executives, two of the nation's largest exchanges."[214] The September 2017, ban came in a jointly issued Announcement on Preventing Financial Risks from Initial Coin Offerings (ICO Rules) for purposes of investor protection and financial risk prevention.[215]

---

[212]   Guy Bentley, *Bitcoin banned by Bolivian central bank as a threat to national currency*, CITY A.M. (June 30, 2014) (available online at https://www.cityam.com/bitcoin-banned-bolivian-central-bank-threat-national-currency/).

[213]   Marie Huillet, *Chinese Yuan Now Accounts for Less Than 1% of Bitcoin Trades, Says PBoC Report*, COINTELEGRAPH (Jul. 9, 2018) [archived at https://perma.cc/5DXD-5FKZ].

[214]   David Canellis, *China brags its cryptocurrency ban has practically killed local Bitcoin trading*, THE NEXT WEB (Jul. 9, 2018) (available online at https://thenextweb.com/hardfork/2018/07/09/china-crackdown-bitcoin/), citing People's Bank of China Circular, *Joint Notice on the Risks Associated with Bitcoin* (2017).

[215]   *Announcement on Preventing Financial Risks from Initial Coin Offerings* (Sept. 4, 2017), http://www.pbc.gov.cn/goutongjiaoliu/113456/113469/3374222/index.html (in Chinese), archived at https://perma.cc/N88N-5CV5. The translation comes from *Selected Jurisdictions, supra* note 7. The seven Chinese central government regulators joining in the announcement were the People's Bank of China, the Cyberspace Administration of China (CAC), the Ministry of Industry and Information Technology, the State Administration for Industry and Commerce (SAIC), the China

Notwithstanding the stated desire to protect investors and prevent risk, China is at the forefront of nations using technology to control its citizenry.[216] Given this predilection, one might readily suppose that the decision to limit access to crypto currencies, which put financial transactions outside the purview of governmental authorities, has also been motivated (at least in part) by a desire to control the population.

3) Venezuela

Venezuela regulates crypto under a framework that went into effect on January 31, 2019. The rules were approved in November 2018 by the Constituent National Assembly, a recently created alternative to the country's Parliament.[217]

The title to the document translates as the "Constituent Decree on the Integral System of Crypto Assets," and it contains 63 articles.[218] It includes definitions and establishes obligatory licenses for mining businesses and crypto exchanges, while setting out fines for unlicensed activities. The national crypto watchdog agency, Sunacrip, is given the power to inspect and oversee and control all crypto-related commercial activities.[219]

By moving such extensive rights of control to a government watchdog, the freedoms of individuals to participate in crypto activities have been substantially diminished. This is, perhaps not surprising, given that Venezuelan citizens were also prohibited from trading in foreign currencies from 2003 until September 2018, when the nation announced the so-called "free exchange" of currency, but with all trades taking place at rates fixed by Venezuela's Central Bank.[220]

F. RELIGIOUS CONSIDERATIONS

While Christianity is the largest religious group worldwide, Islam is the fastest-growing religion in the world. This is important for crypto

---

Banking Regulatory Commission, the China Securities Regulatory Commission, and the China Insurance Regulatory Commission.

[216]   For some interesting information on the extent to which the Chinese government is apparently going, see Paul Mozur, *Inside China's Dystopian Dreams: A.I., Shame and Lots of Cameras*, THE N.Y. TIMES (July 8, 2018) (available online at https://www.nytimes.com/2018/07/08/business/china-surveillance-technology.html); Xiao Qiang, *The Road to Digital Unfreedom: President Xi's Surveillance State*, 30 THE J. OF DEMOCRACY 53 (2019).

[217]   Ana Berman, *Venezuela: New Crypto Legal Framework Comes Into Force*, COINTELEGRAPH (Feb. 4, 2019) [archived at https://perma.cc/MB6R-NXFH]. The assembly was created in 2017.

[218]   Gaceta Oficial de al República Boliariana de Venezuela, No. 41.575 (Jan. 30, 2019) [archived at https://perma.cc/L8UE-8QXW] (in Spanish).

[219]   "According to Article 11, the body should monitor digital miners, exchanges and any other financial services that might serve as intermediaries in the Venezuelan crypto market. Moreover, the same article states that Sunacrip will be able to control "creation, emission, transfer, commercialization and exchange" of all crypto actives within Venezuela." Berman, *supra* note 217.

[220]   Paul Dobson, *Venezuela Introduces 'Free Exchange' of Currency*, VENEZUELA ANALYSIS (Sept. 10, 2018) (available online at https://venezuelanalysis.com/news/14042).

because there is concern among some Islamic scholars about whether crypto is Sharia-compliant. The problem is that "[t]he speculative nature of cryptocurrencies has triggered debate among Islamic scholars over whether cryptocurrencies are religiously permissible. . . . This leaves Islamic investors to choose between sometimes conflicting judgments. . . ."[221] One source notes that because crypto involves "products of financial engineering and objects of speculation, cryptocurrencies sit uneasily with Islam. Islamic law principles, in addition to banning interest payments, emphasize real economic activity based on physical assets and frown on pure monetary speculation."[222]

The response among countries that have adopted the principles of Sharia law has been mixed, and no international group has authority to impose uniform standards or interpretations. Saudi Arabian and United Arab Emirates central banks have not imposed bans, but have warned Muslims about the risks of trading in Bitcoin. On the other hand "[s]ome scholars in Turkey, India and Britain have labelled them impermissible," and other countries have been more definitive in their opposition to the technology.[223]

1)   Egypt

In early 2018, Egypt's Grand Mufti, the top imam in the country, endorsed a ban on Bitcoin by declaring it inconsistent with Sharia law. "Sheikh Shawki Allam, the Grand Mutfi, [sic] said the digital crypto-currency carried risks of 'fraudulence, lack of knowledge, and cheating'."[224] Egypt declared Bitcoin illegitimate in the same month.

Despite these concerns, Egypt has also been considering whether to legalize cryptocurrencies, proposing a bill that would give the Central Bank of Egypt power to regulate cryptocurrencies, potentially with expensive licensing requirements.[225]

2)   Iran

The head of the Iranian Majlis (Parliament) Economic Commission, while lacking authority to legislate in the country, has concluded "[d]eals and transactions made through Bitcoin are in no way in accordance with

---

[221]   *Islam and cryptocurrency, halal or not hala?* AL JAZEERA (Ap. 8, 2018) (archived at https://perma.cc/GCM9-K286).

[222]   Reuters News Agency, *Islam and cryptocurrency, halal or not hala?* ALJAZEERA (Ap. 9, 2018) (available online at https://www.aljazeera.com/news/2018/04/islam-cryptocurrency-halal-halal-180408145004684.html).

[223]   *Id.*

[224]   *Egypt's Grand Mufti endorses Bitcoin trading ban,* BBC NEWS (Jan. 2, 2018) (available online at https://www.bbc.com/news/world-middle-east-42541270).

[225]   John Biggs, *Egypt Lifts Ban, Will Allow Licensed Cryptocurrency Companies,* COINDESK (May 29, 2019) (available online at https://www.coindesk.com/egypt-lifts-ban-will-allow-licensed-cryptocurrency-companies).

Islamic and economic fundamentals, therefore related entities, especially the central bank, must exert the necessary supervision over these deals."[226] The extent to which Iran will continue its pronounced hostility to crypto is, however, uncertain.[227]

G. STATE-BACKED CRYPTOCURRENCIES

Finally, it is worth mentioning that some countries have decided to issue their own cryptocurrency, or are working on doing so. There are a number of reasons for this reaction, ranging from the desire to have an affordable national currency (Marshall Islands and the Eastern Caribbean Central Bank (ECCB)), escaping or evading international financial restrictions (Venezuela and Iran), to asserting government control over crypto (China).

1) Eastern Caribbean Central Bank (ECCB) Member States

A number of smaller eastern Caribbean islands (Anguilla, Antigua and Barbuda, the Commonwealth of Dominica, Grenada, Montserrat, Saint Kitts and Nevis, Saint Lucia, and Saint Vincent and the Grenadines) share a common monetary authority, the Eastern Caribbean Central Bank (ECCB). These island nations also use a common currency called the Eastern Caribbean dollar, and on March 9, 2018, the ECCB signed a memorandum of understanding geared at developing a cryptocurrency.[228] The ECCB's Digital EC Pilot project was launched on March 12, 2019. According to the ECCB webpage, "[t]he pilot involves a securely minted and issued digital version of the EC dollar (DXCD)."[229] The intent is to have the ECCB issue the digital EC dollar for distribution by "licensed bank and non-bank financial institutions" that are part of the Eastern Caribbean Currency Union, and it "will be used for financial transactions between consumers and merchants, people-to-people . . . transactions, all using smart devices."[230]

The stated motive behind the project is to address the relatively high costs associated with current payment services and banking inefficiencies in the conventional settlement system, and to remedy the reality that a

---

[226]   *Iranian Lawmakers to Discuss Bitcoin*, FINANCIAL TRIBUNE (Dec. 19, 2017) (available online at https://financialtribune.com/articles/economy-business-and-markets/78221/iranian-law makers-to-discuss-bitcoin).

[227]   For example, Iran ratified a bill acknowledging the legitimacy of crypto mining in mid-2019, although the ban on crypto use and trading remains in place. Perez, *supra* note 108.

[228]   ECCB, Strategic Plan 2017–2021, at 58, cited *by Regulation of Crypto, supra* note 7, and archived by that source at https://perma.cc/GL38-SSJP. *See also* Press Release, ECCB, *ECCB to Embark on Blockchain Pilot Initiative With Bitt Inc.* (Mar. 13, 2018), cited by *Regulation of Crypto, supra* note 7 and archived by that source at https://perma.cc/UD6D-AT44.

[229]   ECCB Digital EC Pilot Program, *About the Project*, available online at https://www.eccb-centralbank.org/p/about-the-project.

[230]   *Id.*

sizeable proportion of the population of the member nations lack access to conventional banking services.[231]

2) Marshall Islands

The Republic of the Marshall Islands consists of more than 1,000 islands located in the Pacific Ocean near the equator. Prior to gaining independence in 1986, it was a trust territory administered by the U.S., and upon independence it adopted the U.S. dollar as its official currency.

The idea of issuing a cryptocurrency as the new official currency of the nation, to be used alongside the U.S. dollar, was first introduced in February 2018.[232] A total of 24 million units of the new crypto, to be called the Sovereign, or SOV, were to be released through an ICO. Some of the funds that were expected to be raised was to be dedicated to offset health care costs for the country's roughly 53,000 citizens who have suffered the consequences of U.S. nuclear testing in the region.

While the Marshall Islands was the first country to move forward with issuing its own cryptocurrency, actual implementation of the SOV has proven to be more difficult than originally anticipated, because of concern expressed by groups such as the IMF that a government-backed crypto could too easily be used to launder funds and fund terrorism and other criminal activities. Moreover, the Marshallese President faced a vote of no confidence based on her administration's plans to proceed with the cryptocurrency.

The no confidence vote did not pass, and although it is proceeding slowly, the islands continue to work on the project. As of June, 2019, the Marshall Islands has set up a not-for-profit association to be called the SOV Development Fund to oversee the development of the SOV.

3) Senegal

Senegal was one of the earliest adopters of a national cryptocurrency, having issued the eCFA in December 2016. Named for the Sengalense fiat currency, the CFA franc, the eCFA is dependent on Senegal's central banking system and can only be issued by authorized financial institutions. It is intended to be used alongside conventional fiat, and was the product of a collaboration between Banque Régionale de Marchés (BRM), a local bank, and eCurrency Mint Limited, an Ireland-based fintech startup. The collaborators issued a statement about eCFA, declaring it to be "a high-security digital instrument that can be held in all mobile money and e-

---

[231]   ECCB Digital EC (DXCD Pilot Program, *Frequently Asked Questions* (available online at https://www.eccb-centralbank.org/p/what-you-should-know-1).

[232]   *See* Ana Alexandre, *How the Marshall Islands Envisions Its National Digital Currency Dubbed 'Sovereign,'* COINTELEGRAPH (Feb. 16, 2019) [archived at https://perma.cc/RAA7-MQZZ].

money wallets. It will secure universal liquidity, enable interoperability and provide transparency to the entire digital ecosystem in WAEMU."[233]

4) Tunisia

In 2015, Tunisia became the first country in the world to successfully issue a blockchain-based national currency. It did so with the assistance of the Swiss firm, Monetas. The Tunisian crypto is called eDinar, although it is also known as Digicash or BitDinar. Similar to the process by which fiat is handled, eDinar's issuance and distribution is overseen by La Poste, or La Poste Tunisian, a governmental body. Monetas CEO Johann Gevers explained the significance of eDinar's launch as follows:

> The Monetas deployment in Tunisia is the first application for a full ecosystem of digital payments. With the La Poste Tunisienne Android application powered by Monetas, Tunisians can use their smartphones to make instant mobile money transfers, pay for goods and services online and in person, send remittance, pay salaries and bills, and manage official government identification documents.[234]

5) Venezuela

Decree 3196 of December 8, 2017,[235] authorized the Venezuelan government to create its own cryptotoken, to be called the Petro, backed by Venezuelan oil reserves at a rate of one Petro per barrel of oil.[236] The Decree established certain operational details for the Petro,[237] but the path to its issuance was rocky. Decree 3196 provided for an ICO to be made under the auspices of the newly empowered Superintendence of Cryptoassets and Related Venezuelan Activities.[238] However, the Asamblea Nacional (the Venezuelan Congress) ruled on March 8, 2018, that issuance of the Petro would be illegal, because the national Constitution requires congressional approval and a special law in order to enter into a public debt and borrow on behalf of the Venezuelan

---

[233]   Stephen O'Neal, *CBDCs of the World: The Benefits and Drawbacks of National Cryptos, According to Different Jurisdictions*, COINTELEGRAPH (Jun 19, 2019) [archived at https://perma.cc/7AYX-L2HU]. Senegal hoped to prove that its cryptocurrency would be efficient, thereby justifying it being extended to all West African Economic and Monetary Union (WAEMU) member states, including Côte d'Ivoire, Burkina Faso, Benin, Togo, Mali, Niger and Guinea-Bissau. *Id.*

[234]   O'Neal, *supra* note 233.

[235]   Decreto 3196 Mediante el cual se Autoriza la Creación de la Superintendencia de los Criptoactivos y Actividades Conexas Venezolana [Decree 3196 Authorizing the Creation of the Venezuelan Superintendency of Cryptoassets and Related Activities], Gaceta Oficial [G.O.] (Dec. 8, 2017) [archived at https://perma.cc/CSC3-BKBV]. The translation of this document (and all other sources in Spanish that are cited here) comes from *Selected Jurisdictions, supra* note 7.

[236]   Decreto 3196, *supra* note 235 at art. 4.

[237]   *Id.* at art. 3.

[238]   *Id.* at art. 8.

government.[239] The Asamblea also contended that only the Central Bank of Venezuela is authorized to issue national currency, and that oil reserves are non-transferrable assets of the Republic.[240]

In spite of those declarations, the Venezuelan government sought to move ahead, initially promising that Petro would be legal tender for governmental institutions within 120 days of April 9, 2018.[241] After wrangling in the courts, the Petro was apparently finally approved by Venezuela's Supreme Court in November, 2018.[242]

Ironically, because the Petro was required to be purchased with foreign currencies, Venezuelans were initially precluded from legally investing in it, since it was illegal for them to buy foreign currency.[243] On the other hand, Venezuelans have been actively investing in other crypto, presumably in an effort to combat the hyper-inflation that has been plaguing the nation.[244]

The clear motivation behind the Petro was to both address the nation's hyperinflation and plummeting bolívar fuerte currency and to circumvent U.S. monetary sanctions by allowing the government to improve its access to international financing. When Venezuelan President Nicolás Maduro announced the Petro in a televised address on December 3, 2017, he specifically touted access to "new forms of international financing" as a

---

[239] Asamblea Nacional de la República Bolivariana de Venezuela, *Acuerdo sobre la Implementación del Petro [Accord on the Implementation of Petro]* (Mar. 6, 2018) [archived at https://perma.cc/L6GQ-QUXV] (citing Constitucion de la República Bolivariana de Venezuela [CRBV] art. 312, G.O. (Mar. 24, 2000) [archived at https://perma.cc/3BLG-R5P4].)

[240] *Id.* (citing CRBV art. 12).

[241] *Decreto Constituyente sobre Criptoactivos y la Criptomoneda Soberana Petro [Constitutional Decree on Cryptocurrency and the Sovereign Cryptocurrency Petro]*, G.O., at pp. 3–7 (Apr. 9, 2018) [archived at https://perma.cc/HB4D-RCAJ].

[242] Jose Antonio Lanz, *Venezuela's Supreme Court of Justice Recognized Petro Cryptocurrency as Legal Tender,* ETHERUEM WORLD NEWS (November 3, 2018) (available online at https://ethereumworldnews.com/venezuelas-supreme-court-of-justice-recognized-petro-crypto currency-as-legal-tender/). Earlier reports about the issuance of the Petro predated its actual approval. *See, i.e.,* Adam James, *Venezuela's Petro Now Purchasable With Foreign Fiat,* BITCOIN NEWS (Mar. 25, 2018) (available online at https://bitcoinist.com/venezuelan-cryptocurrency-petro-now-purchasable-foreign-fiat/), noting that "[l]ast month, Venezuela became the first country to issue its own cryptocurrency with the launch of the purportedly oil-backed Petro." Americans, however, cannot buy the Petro, as President Trump acted in mid-March of 2018 to ban such purchases. Aaron Wood, *US President Trump Bans US Citizens From Buying Petro,* COINTELEGRAPH (Mar.20, 2018) [archived at https://perma.cc/A7DV-9XBV].

[243] Camila Russo, *Venezuelans Can't Buy Maduro's Cryptocurrency With Bolivars,* BLOOMBERG POLITICS (Feb. 22, 2018) (available online at https://www.bloomberg.com/news/ articles/2018-02-22/venezuelans-unable-to-buy-maduro-s-cryptocurrency-with-bolivars) (noting that Venezuela forbids its citizens from buying foreign currency, which "effectively shuts out residents in the country" from investing in the Petro.)

[244] Helen Partz, *Bitcoin Trading Reaches All Time High in Venezuela Amidst Ongoing Economic Collapse,* COINTELEGRAPH (Feb. 7, 2019) [archived at https://perma.cc/4WKH-79KG]. *See also* Ana Berman, *Venezuela Imposes Fees and Limits on Local Crypto Remittances,* COINTELEGRAPH (Feb. 11, 2019) [archived at https://perma.cc/6MTF-3STZ] (noting that "Venezuela and Colombia account for 85 percent of trading volumes on the p2p exchange in Latin America, according to Cointelegraph en Español.")

benefit of the project.[245] He also claimed that his new cryptocurrency would fight the Trump administration's "financial blockade."[246]

6) Iran

Iran's general approach to crypto has been inconsistent, perhaps reflecting disagreement among various highly-ranked officials as to the potential benefits of the new technology. Nonetheless, for now Iran clearly belongs with the group of nations that can only be seen as hostile to crypto-based activities.

Notwithstanding the hostility to cryptocurrencies issued by third parties, plans for an Iranian virtual currency were floated by Iran's Minister of Information and Communications Technology in February 2018.[247] This possibility was also discussed by the Central Bank of Iran's Information Technology Chief, Nasser Hakimi, who recognized that a national virtual currency could replace any reliance on the U.S. dollar, which might be useful to Iran in combatting American sanctions over the Iranian nuclear program, which essentially bar Iran from accessing the U.S. financial system.[248]

Various Iranian officials are backing what they call an "indignized digital money."[249] The new currency will be backed by gold, and is specifically designed to address problems created by frozen resources. The crypto will be mined "by a small consortium of private Iranian tech companies," with the permission of the Central Bank of Iran.[250] While some sources claim that the new asset is ready to be launched, the actual status of this crypto as of mid-2019 is unclear.

7) China

Despite the fact that China has adopted a very restrictive approach to crypto generally, the deputy director of the Bank of China's Payments Department, Mu Changchun, has recently been quoted as saying that

---

[245] *Venezuela Plans a Cryptocurrency, Maduro Says*, THE N.Y. TIMES (Dec. 3, 2017) (available online at https://www.nytimes.com/2017/12/03/world/americas/venezuela-crypto currency-maduro.html).

[246] *Id.*

[247] *Iran's Banks Banned from Dealing in Crypto-currencies*, BBC NEWS (Apr. 23, 2018) (available online at https://www.bbc.com/news/technology-43865105).

[248] *CBI Governor Urges Caution on Bitcoin Trade*, FINANCIAL TRIBUNE (Dec. 31, 2017) (available online at https://financialtribune.com/articles/economy-business-and-markets/78986/cbi-governor-urges-caution-on-bitcoin-trade).

[249] The author probably means "indigenized." Michael McCrae, *Gold-Backed Iranian Cryptocurrency Is Designed To Evade Sanctions*, KITCO NEWS (Jul. 21, 2019) (available online at https://www.kitco.com/news/2019-07-21/Gold-Backed-Iranian-Cryptocurrency-Is-Designed-To-Evade-Sanctions.html).

[250] Wes Messamore, *Iran Punks Trump With Historic Gold-Backed Crypto Scheme*, CCN (Jul. 14, 2019) (available online at https://www.ccn.com/iran-punks-trump-crypto/).

China's own cryptocurrency is "close to being out."[251] This same official also indicated that "researchers have been at work on the Chinese state digital currency for over a year now," although he did not provide an anticipated launch date.[252] The reported goal of the Chinese cryptocurrency is to assert state control over crypto circulation within the country, given that the current bans and regulations have not managed to stop individual ownership and peer-to-peer trading in Bitcoin and other crypto.

H. THE NEED TO ALLOCATE RESOURCES ELSEWHERE

There are a wide variety of reasons why nations have yet to implement comprehensive regulations to govern cryptoassets. High on this list is the reality that governments often have a huge list of responsibilities that demand the time and attention of personnel, and that consume a nation's financial resources. This section does not begin to address all of the reasons why cryptocurrency regulation may not be high on any given country's list of priorities, but it does point out a few of the more significant obstacles to consistent global crypto regulation.

1) The U.K. and Brexit

On June 23, 2016, the U.K. narrowly voted to leave the E.U., triggering what has come to be known as Brexit. While the House of Commons voted against the agreement by a margin of 432 to 202, the popular vote was 51.9% for leaving and 48.1% for remaining. This vote triggered the process of withdrawing from a decades-long, multinational treaty impacting virtually all of the U.K.'s regulatory structures. While the long-term results of the U.K.'s departure from the E.U. are uncertain, the short-term cost has been staggering. According to experts at The Omni Calculator Project, a startup specializing in taking complex data and simplifying it for the public, as of October 1, 2019 Brexit had cost £136,539,543,265 (which translates to nearly U.S. $175 billion at a conversion rate of 1.27:1, the approximate average rate for the first half of 2019).[253]

These numbers do not even tell half the story. Regulators and experts were immediately called upon to draft provisions for the orderly withdrawal, revising and updating and creating independent regulations to replace the rules put in place while the U.K. was part of the E.U. This obviously means that they have not had the time and energy to spend on

---

[251] *Bitcoin beware? After banning all cryptocurrencies China 'close' to releasing its own digital coin*, RT.com (Aug. 13, 2019) (available online at https://www.rt.com/business/466389-china-own-crypto-currency/).

[252] *Id.*

[253] Omni Calculator, *How much has the Brexit cost* (available online at https://www.omnicalculator.com/finance/brexit). Sources for this estimate are provided by the Omni Calculator at https://www.omnicalculator.com/finance/brexit#sources-and-explanation-for-data.

proposing and debating regulations to cover new interests such as cryptoassets.[254]

2)   Turkey

In July 2015, a two-and-one-half year ceasefire between Turkey and the Kurdistan Workers' Party (PKK) fell apart, leading to resumption of sustained violence in Turkey. Since that date, more than 4,500 persons have been killed in armed clashes or terror attacks.[255] In addition, Turkey faces spillover from nearby wars in Syria and Iraq, including a New Year's Eve attack the morning of January 1, 2017 in Istanbul that killed 39 people and injured 79 others. Such attacks, combined with dangers posed by the Islamic State, led Turkey to send troops into Syria and Iraq, escalating tensions.

In addition, President Recep Tayyip Erdogan faced a coup attempt in 2016, and thereafter launched a massive crackdown on dissent, purging more than 100,000 officials. Western Allies have objected to some of the more authoritarian initiatives, and Erdogan's response has been increasingly hostile. Relations with the U.S. are also strained, particularly in light of the U.S. decision to ally with Kurdish forces in Syria.

Given this backdrop, it is impressive that the country was able to develop a possible economic roadmap for 2019 to 2023, that at least theoretically calls for a "blockchain-based digital central bank money."[256] The facts that the report was not developed until July of 2019 and the details have not yet been finalized are unsurprising given the tremendous pressures faced by the country.[257]

3)   The Lake Chad Basin and the Greater Sahel

The Lake Chad Basin includes Cameroon, Chad, Niger, Nigeria, The Republic of Central Africa, and Libya. In addition, the Sahel region of Africa encompasses Senegal on the Atlantic coast, and extends eastward through parts of Mauritania, Mali, Burkina Faso, Niger, Nigeria, Chad, and Sudan to Eritrea on the Red Sea coast. The nations in this entire region are generally impoverished, and a combination of Jihadis, armed groups, and criminal networks have contributing to the uprooting of more than 4

---

[254]   *See* Selva Ozelli, *How Will the UK Deal With Crypto After Brexit: Expert Take,* COINTELEGRAPH (Aug. 6, 2018) [archived at https://perma.cc/YS3T-S64Y].

[255]   *Turkey's PKK Conflict: A Visual Explainer,* CRISIS GROUP (available online at https://www.crisisgroup.org/content/turkeys-pkk-conflict-visual-explainer).

[256]   Daniel Kuhn, *Turkey's New Economic Roadmap Calls for Central Bank Cryptocurrency,* COINDESK (Jul. 10, 2019) (available online at https://www.coindesk.com/turkeys-new-economic-roadmap-calls-for-central-bank-cryptocurrency).

[257]   According to this report, the Eleventh Development Plan was submitted to the Turkish Parliament for consideration on July 8, 2019. *See* Türkiye Cumhuriyeticumhurbaşkanliği, *On Birinci Kalkinma Plani* (2019–2023) (Temmuz 2019) [archived at https://perma.cc/A84H-V9M7] (in Turkish).

million persons from their homes. Terrorist networks such as Al Qaeda and groups claiming affiliation with the Islamic State also operate in the area.

The Boko Haram insurgency has plagued Nigeria, Niger, Cameroon, and Chad, resulting in a cycle of violent rebellion and repression. The lack of effective regional response helps explain why these nations have no active regulatory response to crypto, despite having part of the population that the decentralized technology was supposed to assist.

Obviously, there are other areas and nations whose resources are focused on issues other than cryptoassets. Afghanistan, Myanmar, and the Ukraine are all facing regional hostilities and armed conflicts. Yemen is on the brink of collapse, with its population facing widespread famine. Most of sub-Saharan African countries face profound economic troubles, with 27 of the world's 28 poorest countries being in that region. The average poverty rate in the region is above 40%, and hundreds of million people live in extreme poverty (defined as subsisting on $1.25 per day, or less). Two-thirds of the people in sub-Saharan Africa do not have access to electricity. The decision by governments in these areas to focus resources on issues other than cryptocurrencies is completely comprehensible. Hopefully, at some future point, their economic position will improve enough that they are able to turn their attention to these kinds of legal issues.

5. NON-STATE ACTORS

All of the preceding material (including that in previous chapters) has focused on actions by nation states or recognized subdivisions of those state actors. What about actions by groups that have not been recognized as nations?

A full discussion of what it takes to be recognized as a state is far outside the scope of this book, but readers should be aware that recognition as a state by the international community triggers an entire range of international rights and obligations. Article 1 of the Montevidea Convention of the Rights and Duties of States, signed on December 26, 1933, contains four criteria for statehood: "The state as a person of international law should possess the following qualifications: (a) a permanent population; (b) a defined territory; (c) government; and (d) capacity to enter into relations with the other states."[258] These qualifications have generally been recognized by international organizations as accurately reflecting customary international law.

---

[258] A convenient copy of the English version text of the Montevideo Convention is maintained by the Avalon Project at Yale Law School, and is available online at https://avalon.law.yale.edu/20th_century/intam03.asp.

Application of the factors can be difficult as has been seen in connection with the question of whether ISIS or ISIL[259] should be classified as a nation state. Was its population ever permanent? Was its territory really defined? Scholars have differed on these and other questions about the nature of statehood.[260]

Formal diplomatic recognition is not necessary for a nation state to be recognized. Recognition can be achieved either explicitly or implicitly, and may be de facto or de jure. Most nations have been recognized de jure (at law), but there are some notable examples of de facto (in fact) recognition. De facto statehood recognizes only that a government exercises control over a territory, while de jure recognition is broader. Probably the most significant example of the difference can be seen in the Republic of China, commonly known as "Taiwan." This state is generally recognized as de facto independent and sovereign, but it is not universally accorded de jure status, as a result of the complex relationship with the People's Republic of China. In 1971, the U.N. withdrew de jure recognition of Taiwan in favor of mainland China.

Why does any of this matter when it comes to understanding crypto? Well, for one thing, what happens when a non-state actor issues its own cryptocurrency? The issuer is not a state, but does not accept that it is subject to the authority of any other jurisdiction. Is it then subject to the dictates of international organizations such as FATF, the FSB, and others, which generally only focus on nation states?

This is not a purely hypothetical question. On October 1, 2017, Southern Cameroons Ambazonia Consortium United Front, an Anglophone secessionist group, unilaterally declared the independence of certain portions of Cameroon, ostensibly creating the "Federal Republic Ambazonia." All of the territory claimed by the group is also claimed by the Republic of Cameroon. In 2018, the so-called Federal Republic of Ambazonia created and launched a crypto-currency, AmbaCoin.[261] Given the lack of clear status for Ambazonia, there is a genuine question of how to ensure that "AmbaCoin" complies with minimum international standards.

---

[259] For a discussion of the name of the jihadist militant group that actually called itself الدولة الإسلامية في العراق والشام, *see* Jonathan Hogeback, *Is it ISIS or ISIL?* ENCYCLOPAEDIA BRITANNICA (available online at https://www.britannica.com/story/is-it-isis-or-isil).

[260] *See* Anicée Van Engeland, *Statehood, Proto States and International Law: New Challenges, Looking at the Case of isis*, THE INTERNATIONAL LEGAL ORDER: CURRENT NEEDS AND POSSIBLE RESPONSES (Brill 2017) (original in French).

[261] *Ambacoin*, Ambacoin (available online at https://ambacoin.io/).

In addition, non-state actors may also be utilizing crypto in ways that contravene accepted international norms. Terrorist organizations and groups that adopt such methods, such as ISIS (or ISIL), have often been called out for utilizing cryptocurrencies to further their agendas.[262] They may not be interested in complying with international norms or standards, but the result of their participation in the crypto-ecosystem may ultimately be more stringent and more expensive regulation for businesses that are overseen by national governments.

---

[262]   *See, i.e.,* Luke Fitzpatrick, *Privacy In Crypto: The Impact of Rising Terrorism Concerns,* FORBES (Aug. 30, 2019) (available online at https://www.forbes.com/sites/lukefitzpatrick/2019/08/30/privacy-in-crypto-the-impact-of-rising-terrorism-concerns/#2cfdd0d57f1b) (noting that a "recent study by the Middle East Media Research Institute (MEMRI) reveals that terrorist groups are using bitcoin and crypto assets to finance their activities.")

CHAPTER 16

TAXATION OF CRYPTO

■ ■ ■

This chapter is going to begin with a caveat. Because these materials presume no significant prior exposure to tax law and are designed to introduce the myriad issues presented by taxation of crypto rather than focusing on the specifics, the fine details of the U.S. tax system are not going to be dealt with here. There will be few citations to the Internal Revenue Code and Treasury Regulations that have been promulgated by the I.R.S. There are even fewer references to state law, because those rules vary so widely from state to state.

Federal, state, and sometimes local governments impose a variety of taxes on their citizens. The federal government taxes income, while most states impose income, property, and sales taxes. In order to ensure that appropriate taxes are paid, these governmental authorities also impose recordkeeping and reporting requirements. In order to put this information in context, a little more detail about these obligations is probably necessary.

The federal government generally taxes what it considers to be "income," although there are different kinds of income.[1] Earned income is subject to income tax at certain rates, which increase as you earn more. Earned income is also subject to employment taxes (for example, taxes that are necessary to fund Social Security). Unearned income is also possible, which will not be subject to employment taxes but is subject to tax at the taxpayer's marginal rate based on their total income. This kind of unearned income would include, for example, interest income from bank checking and savings accounts. In addition, some unearned income will be taxed at a much lower rate, called the capital gains rate.[2] This is generally income

---

[1]   This is a very truncated explanation. For more details about taxable and nontaxable income, see I.R.S. Publication 525, *Taxable and Nontaxable Income*, available online at https://www.irs.gov/pub/irs-pdf/p525.pdf. For rules on calculating income from sales and disposition of assets, and appropriate characterization of any income therefrom, see I.R.S. Publication 544, *Sales and Other Disposition of Assets*, available online at https://www.irs.gov/forms-pubs/about-publication-544.

[2]   To give you an idea of the difference, in 2019, the highest marginal tax rate for individuals (not including employment taxes) is 37%, and for an unmarried individual that rate kicks in for income over $510,300. For capital gains, the first $39,375 of capital gains is subject to a 0% tax rate, while amounts up to $434,550 are taxed at $15%. Only capital gains in excess of that are taxed at 20%, the highest capital gains bracket. For more details about this in an easy-to-understand format, see Amir El-Sibaie, *2019 Tax Brackets*, TAX FOUNDATION (Nov. 28, 2018) [archived at https://perma.cc/7EEG-99BD].

from selling assets that have been owned for a while and have increased in value since they were acquired, or qualified dividends that have been received as a result of owning stock in a company. This kind of income is taxed at capital gains rates, which are generally lower than the rates imposed on most other forms of income. Determining the appropriate tax rate is based on how the income is classified, which is a significant issue for users of crypto.

The I.R.S. does not let taxpayers escape liability for taxes by trading things (i.e., using a barter system) rather than first selling them for cash and then using the proceeds to buy the new item. Bartering is taxed as if the taxpayer in the transaction had sold the item for fair market value first rather than simply swapping it. If the fair market value of the bartered item is more than what the taxpayer paid for it, then there is income that will be taxed when the item is transferred in the exchange.[3]

In order for the I.R.S. to determine how much taxpayers owe in taxes, all kinds of reports must be filed (not only from the individual taxpayers but sometimes also from the persons who are paying or distributing amounts to taxpayers). The taxpayer generally has the burden to keep records to document claims made on those forms, which are filed under penalty of perjury.

State governments can impose income tax as well. In addition, state and local governments may also choose to impose taxes on the sale of goods and/or services. Sales tax rates vary widely, not only on the basis of jurisdiction but also on the nature of the goods or services being sold. Sales tax is generally owed to the state from the seller, although it is often collected by sellers from the buyers at the time of a sale.

Willful failure to properly report what is owed accurately and to pay any taxes that are owed is a crime. If he was still alive, Al Capone could confirm that.[4]

---

[3]   This is so simplified that individuals with a background in taxation are probably cringing. The concept being discussed is the taxpayer's "basis" in the property, and basis is usually, but not always, determined by the price paid for an asset. There are a number of other possibilities, including taking the basis from the original owner for property received as a gift, taking the market value of property received on death of another, etc. For purposes of understanding the tax issues as they relate to crypto, however, it is enough to know that the I.R.S. generally imposes tax on any imputed gain in a barter transaction. If you want a more detailed and accurate explanation of basis, see I.R.S. Publication 551, *Basis of Assets*, available online at https://www.irs.gov/forms-pubs/about-publication-551.

[4]   For a very brief version of the story of infamous Chicago gangster Alphonse "Scarface" Capone and his run-in with tax authorities, see Josh Clark, *Why Was Tax Evasion the Only Thing Pinned on Al Capone?* HISTORY [archived at https://perma.cc/WPR4-ZQXK].

1. THE I.R.S. PROCLAIMS THAT CRYPTO IS PROPERTY

Although the I.R.S. was one of the earliest regulators in the U.S. to take a position regarding cryptoassets,[5] it did not act until Bitcoin had been around for a number of years.

In early 2014, the National Taxpayer Advocate urged the IRS to issue guidelines on how Bitcoin should be treated for purposes of taxation. At that point, Bitcoin had been in existence for five years, and the IRS had no guidance on how to treat transactions involving Bitcoin or other cryptocurrencies.[6]

The I.R.S. officially issued taxpayer guidance in April of 2014, describing "how existing general tax principles apply to transactions using virtual currency."[7] This early "2014 Guidance" from the I.R.S. defined virtual currency as "a digital representation of value that functions as a medium of exchange, a unit of account, and/or a store of value." For federal tax purposes, a virtual currency that has an equivalent value in "real" (or fiat) currency or acts as a substitute for fiat is deemed "convertible." Once a virtual currency is classified as convertible, it becomes "property" for tax purposes.

Pursuant to this definition, if crypto has a value in "real" currency (or is intended to be a substitute for traditional currency), there is realistically no way that it will not act as a medium of exchange, a unit of account, or a store of value. Even if both the developer/issuer and user understand and agree that the cryptoasset in question will have and be used for a function such as access to particular goods or services, the crypto is still a medium of exchange in that such access would formerly have been paid for with traditional currency. Thus, the broad definition of "virtual currency" by the I.R.S., applied across the board to all cryptoassets, allows for no difference in treatment based on how the interest is marketed, its intended function,

---

[5]   As noted in earlier chapters of this book, FinCEN's first formal announcement came on March 18, 2013. Dept. of the Treasury, FinCEN Guidance, *Application of FinCEN's Regulations to Persons Administering, Exchanging, or Using Virtual Currencies*, FIN–2013–G001 (Mar. 18, 2013). The first official confirmation from CFTC that it was treating cryptoassets as commodities came in December 2014, in the form of testimony from the CFTC Chairman. *Testimony of CFTC Chairman Timothy Massad before the U.S. Senate Committee on Agriculture, Nutrition and Forestry* (Dec. 10, 2014) [archived at https://perma.cc/8F8Q-GVC7]. The SEC, aside from a number of public bulletins, alerts, advisories, and other warnings, announced its formal position on crypto for the first time in 2017. SEC, *Report of Investigation Pursuant to Section 21(a) of the Securities Exchange Act of 1934: The DAO*, '34 ACT RELEASE NO. 81207 (July 25, 2017) [archived at https://perma.cc/F862-YS5V].

[6]   Deidre A. Liedel, *The Taxation of Bitcoin: How the IRS Views Cryptocurrencies*, 66 DRAKE L. REV. 107, 115–16 (2018).

[7]   IRS *Virtual Currency Guidance*, I.R.S. Notice 2014–21, 2014–16 I.R.B. 938 (released March 26, 2014; published April 14, 2104) [archived at https://perma.cc/W5DL-XBLB] (referred to in these materials as 2014 Guidance).

or how it is exchanged. On the other hand, this approach probably does maximize the potential for tax revenues.

Unfortunately, classifying crypto as property is only the starting point for determining how it is to be taxed. The appropriate approach to calculating and reporting taxable gain or tax owed will depend to some extent on the character of the coin or token involved and the nature of underlying transaction.

2. BUYING CRYPTO FOR FIAT CURRENCY (AS IN AN ICO)

The first possible transaction involves the purchase of crypto for fiat. The purchase of one or more coins or tokens for fiat (conventional currency) will not, in and of itself, result in a reportable transaction for the purchaser. At this point in time, there has been no item of gain or anything that should count as income for purposes of calculating tax liabilities for the purchaser.[8]

On the other side of the transaction, however, the result may be different. While the purchaser does not recognize gain or loss, the issuer or seller of the cryptoasset might experience a taxable event. Particularly in the case of an ICO, the developer/issuer may be thinking of the ICO as being like the issuance of stock or debt in exchange for investment in the business, while this may not reflect the reality of the situation. By characterizing the cryptoasset as property, the issuer in an ICO will have sold property, and this may trigger state or local sales tax liability.

Confusion on the part of persons conducting ICOs is understandable. For all that ICOs have been in the news and generally quite common in recent years, relatively little has been reported about the taxation of such distributions. This is troubling because the tax implications for the issuer in an ICO may be quite complicated.

> [L]ittle attention has been paid to the U.S. federal income tax treatment of initial coin offerings. Importantly, the type of token at issue is highly relevant to the tax analysis because any tax analysis is based on application of the Notice to the facts-and-circumstances of the initial coin offering. Given the newness of the industry, there is no "standard" utility token offering facts or "standard" security token offering facts. Instead, each initial coin offering varies—often significantly. With such variance, there are no tax conclusions that can be applied to all initial coin offerings.[9]

---

[8] This is "gross income," as defined in § 61 of the Internal Revenue Code. 26 U.S. Code § 61(a).

[9] Sarah-Jane Morin, *Tax Aspects of Cryptocurrency with A Focus on the Tax Aspects of Initial Coin Offerings*, PRAC. TAX LAW., 12, 16 (Summer 2018).

Part of the problem may be that issuers, even those trying to comply with federal regulations may have been preoccupied with requirements imposed by other regulators such as the SEC, and may also have assumed that what they are selling will be treated like stock, since it is treated as a security by the SEC.

If a cryptocoin or token is treated as being like stock, an issuer conducting a distribution would not generally have to report any gain or loss as a result of selling or exchanging the asset for money or other property.[10] Similarly, if the crypto is treated like debt (as could be the case for crypto that requires the issuer to pay interest and to eventually repurchase the asset for the purchase price), the issuer would not recognize income upon receipt of the "loan." However, these rules require that the coin or token in fact be recognized as stock or debt by the I.R.S.

Unfortunately, it is not always clear when the I.R.S. will classify interests as debt or equity, and it is possible that the I.R.S. might decline to treat crypto as either. The Tax Code lists five factors, and an I.R.S. notice released in 1994 has eight elements that may be used to distinguish debt from equity.[11] Various courts have also considered the issue, looking at all facts and circumstances.

In furtherance of this approach, courts have identified and listed a number of factors. These include all of the following:

1. The names given to the certificates evidencing the indebtedness;

2. The presence or absence of a fixed maturity date;

3. The source of payments;

4. The right to enforce payment of principal and interest;

5. Participation in management as a result of the advance;

6. The status of the contribution in relation to regular corporate creditors;

7. "Thin" or adequate capitalization of the borrower;

8. Identity of interest between the creditor and stockholder;

9. The source of interest payments;

10. The ability of the corporation to obtain loans from outside lending institutions;

11. The extent to which the advance was used to acquire capital assets;

---

[10]   The rule for stock can be found at 26 U.S. Code § 1032(a).

[11]   *See* 26 U.S. Code § 385(b) and I.R.S. Notice 94–47, 1994–1 C.B. 357.

12. The failure of the debtor to repay on the due date or to seek a postponement; and

13. The intent of the parties.[12]

There are a number of problems with applying these factors to cryptoassets. First, it is not at all clear how these factors will be weighed. Second, and even more importantly, it is not at all clear how most of these factors would apply to crypto, meaning that at best, analogies will have to be drawn.

In some and probably most cases, it is likely that a particular cryptoasset will not be classified as equity or debt. In some cases, this may be obvious. Regardless of the complexity in making this determination, once it is clear that a particular coin or token is neither debt or equity, how will the transaction be treated for federal tax purposes? The answer to this question is also unclear.

One possibility is that the issuer in an ICO might be required to treat the sale of the cryptoasset as involving prepayment for future services. If the transaction is characterized as this kind of prepayment, the buyer would pay for the cryptoasset (and as such would recognize no gain or loss if fiat currency is used). However, the issuer would be treated as having received income in exchange for agreeing to perform some future service, such as the development, maintenance, or improvement of the token or the underlying blockchain. This might be particularly likely in the case of the sale of prefunctional token.[13] If the transaction is treated as involving the prepayment of expenses, this may be a taxable event for the issuer because the Internal Revenue Code generally seeks to capture as much current income as possible.[14] Case law confirms that prepayment of expenses can be presently taxable.[15]

On the other hand, it is also possible that income received by the issuer from an ICO can be deferred in at least some circumstances. This would

---

[12]   These factors are collected in the article by Morin, cited *supra* note 9 at p. 17. A list of some of the cases applying these considerations appears in footnotes 42–43 of that source.

[13]   It had become common for issuers to sell a prefunctional token in order to raise funds to develop a functional token. This has been described as follows:

> What happens when a person buys the right to use digital tokens on a network that has not yet been launched? At the time of purchase, there is no operating network and there are no digital tokens. The purchaser is buying the right to use these tokens in the future, for whatever stated purpose the network has been created to fulfill. Is the purchase of a future token, even a token that once launched can only be used within its established network, a security under the *Howey* test?

Michael Mendleson, *From Initial Coin Offerings to Security Tokens: A U.S. Federal Securities Law Analysis*, 22 STAN. TECH. L. REV. 52, 75 (2019).

[14]   26 U.S. Code § 61 and treasury regulations generally require gross income to include all sources unless specifically excluded by some other provision.

[15]   *Auto. Club of Mich. v. Comm'r*, 353 U.S. 180 (1957); *Am. Auto. Ass'n v. United States*, 367 U.S. 687 (1961); *Schlude v. Comm'r*, 372 U.S. 128 (1963); *but see Perry Funeral Home Inc. v. Comm'r*, T.C. Memo 2003–340.

involve ICOs where the issuer is obligated under potential future circumstances to return the payment. There is some authority, albeit in the context of pre-payments to a corporate taxpayer for a very different kind of interest, that suggest tax liability for prepayments may be deferred if the issuer has a potential obligation to redeem the interests under specified circumstances.[16] Note that even if the issuer of a coin or token does have a binding obligation to repurchase the asset upon the occurrence of certain events, it is not certain that the I.R.S. will apply this analysis in the context of future services to be provided in connection with cryptoassets. This means that there is no clear answer as to how payments to an issuer in the context of an ICO will be treated for federal tax purposes.

3. EXCHANGING ONE KIND OF CRYPTO FOR OTHER CRYPTO: LIKE-KIND EXCHANGE

Suppose instead of buying a new cryptoasset for fiat, a purchaser (whether in an ICO or in a secondary trading transaction) elects to pay with some other crypto. For example, a taxpayer decides to buy NewToken (a hypothetical cryptoasset) by paying with Bitcoin. Since there is no immediate gain if a taxpayer purchases new crypto by paying with fiat currency, the taxpayer might assume that there is no gain when one kind of crypto is simply exchanged for another. The taxpayer would be wrong.

A taxpayer who receives crypto in exchange for goods or services (including other crypto), or who sells crypto in a transaction involving the receipt of other goods or services, has entered into a potentially taxable transaction. Any exchange of property, which is how the I.R.S. classifies crypto, is generally a taxable event.

Prior to the 2018 tax reform, many individuals engaged in buying and selling crypto may have assumed that what they were doing was tax free under a special rule in the Internal Revenue Code that essentially provides that no gain or loss is recognized when one like-kind property is exchanged for another like-kind property.[17] This rule is known as the like-kind exchange rule, and it used to apply to a wide range of property, including real estate and intangible property as well. Like-kind exchanges allowed taxpayers to conduct a series of purchases and sales of property "of like-kind" without paying tax until the final property is sold. However, this rule only applies if the properties being exchanged are considered to be "like-kind." The 2018 tax reform sharply and decisively removed the flexibility

---

[16]   This possibility is based on a private letter ruling issued by the I.R.S. on June 2, 2017. I.R.S. Priv. Ltr Rul. 201722004. The details of that ruling are beyond the scope of this chapter, but if more information is desired, the ruling is discussed in the article by Morin, cited *supra* at note 9 on p. 17.

[17]   26 U.S. Code § 1031 (2017).

that this rule had provided by amending the definition of like-kind to limit it to "real property."[18]

As a result, a taxpayer who buys and sells crypto, paying in other crypto at each stage, will have to separately report and pay taxes on each transaction. The like-kind exchange exemption does not apply.

4. BARTERING WITH CRYPTO

An even more complicated set of issues can arise when a U.S. taxpayer wants to pay for some other form of goods or services with crypto. What are the tax consequences of that kind of transaction? This section will look at only the federal income tax consequences of the transaction. Sales tax considerations, which are a matter of state and local law, are discussed in part nine of this chapter.

It is clear that under U.S. law, a transaction that does not involve money (i.e., fiat currency) may still result in taxable income that will need to be reported by at least one of the parties. This involves the concept of "bartering," which has been defined by the I.R.S. as "an exchange of property or services."[19] Crypto is specifically considered to be property by the I.R.S., which means that when it is used to acquire other property (not including cash) and/or services, the transaction amounts to a property-for-property exchange (i.e., "barter"). To understand what this means from a tax standpoint, both the buyer and seller must be evaluated.

When someone buys as product or service for fiat, there is usually no need to look further into the purchaser's side of the transaction. If the purchase is for cryptocurrency, however, an additional inquiry is required. As the I.R.S. concluded in the 2014 Guidance,[20] if the fair market value of the property or services that are purchased is higher than the purchaser's basis in the crypto (generally what the purchaser paid for the coin or token), then there is a taxable gain that must be reported. In order to avoid imposition of tax, there would need to be a specific exclusion such as the older like-kind exchange provision (which is no longer available in the case of crypto).

In a conventional sales transaction, the seller would have gross income as a result of the transaction (from which expenses and certain other items could be deducted in order to arrive at taxable income). This is just as true when the seller receives crypto in exchange for goods or services, but now

---

[18]   Act effective Dec. 31, 2017, Pub. L. No. 115–97, § 13303, 131 Stat. 2054 (amending section 26 U.S. Code § 1031(a)(1) by striking "property" and inserting "real property"). For a more in-depth discussion of the like-kind exchange rules, see Eli Cole, *Cryptocurrency and the § 1031 Like Kind Exchange*, 10 HASTINGS SCI. & TECH. L.J. 75 (2019).

[19]   I.R.S. Publication 525, Taxable and Non-Taxable Income, at p. 19.

[20]   2014 Guidance, see *supra* note 7, A-4 at p. 3.

the seller must also determine the fair market value of the crypto that is received in the transaction.

This analysis also applies if one form of crypto is exchanged for another, since (as described in the preceding section of this chapter) the like-kind exception is clearly no longer applicable. As explained in the 2014 Guidance, an exchange of one form of crypto for another will usually result in a taxable sale. Just as with exchanges of crypto for other kinds of property, the amount of gain or loss depends of the fair market value of the two interests on the date of the exchange.

> For U.S. tax purposes, transactions using virtual currency must be reported in U.S. dollars. Therefore, taxpayers will be required to determine the fair market value of virtual currency in U.S. dollars as of the date of payment or receipt. If a virtual currency is listed on an exchange and the exchange rate is established by market supply and demand, the fair market value of the virtual currency is determined by converting the virtual currency into U.S. dollars (or into another real currency which in turn can be converted into U.S. dollars) at the exchange rate, in a reasonable manner that is consistently applied.[21]

Because of the volatility in crypto markets, as well as inconsistent pricing among various exchanges, converting crypto to U.S. dollars on the day of receipt can substantially complicate the reporting of income and the job of the I.R.S. in monitoring compliance.

5. CRYPTO AIRDROPS—CRYPTO FOR NOTHING

Airdrops are defined briefly in chapter two, and then discussed in more detail in chapter thirteen. In essence, an airdrop involves a distribution of a cryptoasset in a manner that requires no or very little effort from the recipient and involves no exchange of tangible consideration in the form of fiat or other cryptocurrencies. According to various commentators, "[a]irdrops can be defined as the process whereby a cryptocurrency enterprise distributes cryptocurrency tokens to the wallets of some users free of charge. Airdrops are usually carried out by blockchain-based startups to bootstrap their cryptocurrency projects."[22] The critical component of the process is that the distribution of coins or tokens is essentially free to the recipient.

How does the recipient of an airdropped token deal with this unexpected bonanza? Generally, as described very briefly above, the

---

[21] *Id.*, A-5 at p. 3.

[22] Katalyse.io, Mission.Org, *What are "Airdrops" in Crypto World?* MEDIUM (Feb 15, 2018) [archived at https://perma.cc/DCN8-TB8E] (this same source also notes that in addition to issuer-based airdrops, established blockchain-based enterprises such as trading platforms or wallet services can conduct airdrops as well.)

exchange of property for other property is typically a taxable event, and any gain or loss must be reported to the I.R.S. This includes exchanges involving two distinct cryptoassets. But what if one party to the "transaction" is not contributing any property or anything else of value?

In the case of an airdrop of a new token from an issuer, the way in which the airdrop is conducted is likely to be of great significance. If the recipient gives nothing of value, there is a reasonable argument that the transaction should not result in a taxable gain since nothing of value has been exchanged. Similarly, the issuer has received nothing of value and so should have no reportable income. The moment the issuer starts requiring additional effort from the recipient, however, this changes, and the token may be regarded as payment for services rendered. At the very least, this means the recipient could be required to treat the payment as earned income, subject to employment as well as income taxes.[23]

Prior to October 9, 2019, commentators acknowledged a risk that the I.R.S. could treat an airdrop, whether directly from the issuer in connection with the distribution of a new token, or as a result of a fork[24] in an existing blockchain, as being taxable. For example, when Bitcoin split into Bitcoin Cash as a result of a "hard fork,"[25] each holder of Bitcoin at the time of the fork not only retained their Bitcoins, they also received an amount of Bitcoin Cash nominally equivalent to their holdings of Bitcoin immediately before the fork. The tax consequences of that event were uncertain. It was not clear when the recipient would be required to report "income" for tax purposes, how the amount of income should be calculated, or how the taxpayer should characterize the income for tax purposes.

One possibility was that the new coins should be viewed as a taxable windfall, in much the same way as lottery winnings are treated. This would make sense under the test for what constitutes income as laid out by the U.S. Supreme Court in *Commissioner v. Glenshaw Glass,* 348 U.S. 426 (1955). The airdropped coin or token is an accession to wealth; it is clearly realized; and the recipient has dominion and control over it. Under this approach, the recipient would recognize ordinary income equal to the fair market value as of the date of receipt.

---

[23]   There are a number of complicated issues associated with paying for services in crypto. For a consideration of some of the problems this could include, see Rebecca K. Webster, *Challenges in Compensating Employees in Cryptocurrencies,* 39 MITCHELL HAMLINE L.J. PUB. POL'Y & PRAC. 157 (2018).

[24]   Although "fork" is also defined in chapter 2, for a further explanation, see David Farmer, *What is a Bitcoin Fork?,* THE COINBASE BLOG (July 27, 2017) (available online at https://blog.coinbase.com/what-is-a-bitcoin-fork-cba07fe73ef1).

[25]   For a description of this airdrop, see *Bitcoin Cash* (BCC), AIRDROPALERT (available online at https://airdropalert.com/bitcoin-cash-airdrop). BCH is the most successful hard fork of Bitcoin, and as of the end of February, 2019, was the sixth-largest cryptocurrency by market capitalization. COINMARKETCAP [archived at https://perma.cc/9QS9-H6BZ] (accessed for this purpose on February 25, 2019, and showing Bitcoin Cash with a market cap in excess of $2.4 billion).

While superficially simple and consistent with usual tax principles, this would create some potentially significant problems. The first is in ascertaining the date upon which income is "realized." There may be delays in accessing airdropped tokens because of protocols in place with certain wallet services. In some cases, the wallets may not be accessible at all, if a key has been lost. Given the general volatility in crypto pricing, even a single day's delay could significantly affect valuation.[26]

A second issue is in determining the value on the date of transfer. Immediately following the fork with Bitcoin Cash, for instance, there was no ready market for the new coin. Even after a trading market developed, prices varied considerably among the different exchange platforms that accepted the new coin.

In order to avoid these practical problems, it was also seen as possible that the I.R.S. would treat a coin airdropped as a result of a fork as being akin to a stock dividend instead of analogizing to lottery winnings. Stock dividends and stock splits are not generally taxable events.[27] Any gain is deferred until the recipient sells or disposes of the new stock. Unfortunately for issuers and taxpayers hoping for this treatment, the current treatment of stock dividends is based on specific statutory rules that do not, by their terms, apply directly to cryptoassets.

Another alternative would have involved the I.R.S. determining that a cryptocurrency split is simply not a taxable event, under the assumption that the converted interests are substantially identical to the property that was already held by the taxpayer prior to the split. Under this approach, any gain would be deferred until the taxpayer sells or disposes of the coins at a later date.

On October 9, 2019, the I.R.S. issued a revenue ruling in question and answer format that purports to resolve this issue, at least in the case of an airdropped cryptoasset following a hard fork.[28] In that ruling, the I.R.S. proclaimed that "[c]ryptocurrency from an airdrop generally is received on the date and at the time it is recorded on the distributed ledger" provided that the taxpayer has dominion and control over the asset at that time. If the taxpayer lacks such control, receipt will be deemed to occur when "the

---

[26] For example, consider the pricing of Bitcoin over time. *See Bitcoin (USD) Price,* COINDESK, https://www.coindesk.com/price, showing the fluctuation of the price exchange of Bitcoin by comparing the value equivalent to the U.S. dollar; for example, valuing Bitcoin at $3865.99 at 9:15am CDT on March 13, 2019 and at $3842.79 at 10:35am on the same day. (Website visited March, 14, 2019). Even greater volatility is possible. CoinMarketCap keeps a historical record of trading values, and on December 25, 2017 the value of a single Bitcoin was pegged at $13,995.90 at the start of the day, while less than a week earlier it had been pegged at over $19,000. In addition, a single day later, on December 26, the value of a single Bitcoin was back up as high as $16,461.20. *See Bitcoin (Historical Data),* COINMARKETCAP, https://coinmarketcap.com/currencies/bitcoin/historical-data/?start=20130428&end=20190314.

[27] 26 U.S. Code § 305(d)(1).

[28] I.R.S. Rev. Rul. 2019-24. A copy of this ruling is archived for convenience at https://perma.cc/M8YP-8463.

taxpayer later acquires the ability to transfer, sell, exchange, or other dispose of the cryptocurrency." Moreover, under this ruling upon obtaining dominion and control of the airdropped asset, the taxpayer "has an accession to wealth and has ordinary income" based on the fair market value of the new asset when the airdrop is recorded on the distributed ledger.

This ruling does not appear to recognize that not all airdrops follow forks, and it fails to acknowledge the reality that the value of a new asset may be difficult if not impossible to ascertain immediately following an airdrop.

6. MINING CRYPTO

Mining is another term defined back in chapter two, but as a very brief refresher to the concept, this is the process by which crypto transactions on a blockchain ledger are verified in order to be added to the record. In this instance, the crypto is not paid for in the sense that there is no transfer of fiat or other virtual currency in exchange for receiving the new asset, but there is still an exchange. In this case, it would be akin to an exchange of services in return for the payment of the coin or token that is mined.

In its 2014 Guidance on virtual currencies, the I.R.S. concluded:

> If a taxpayer's "mining" of virtual currency constitutes a trade or business, and the 'mining' activity is not undertaken by the taxpayer as an employee, the net earnings from self-employment (generally, gross income derived from carrying on a trade or business less allowable deductions) resulting from those activities constitute self employment income and are subject to the self-employment tax.[29]

The same source also notes that a taxpayer using computer resources to mine a cryptocurrency will generally recognize ordinary income for U.S. federal income tax purposes upon receipt of the mined coin. The amount realized will be equal to the fair market value on the date of receipt. Note that there is no clear guidance as to what to do when the value of a particular coin is fluctuating on the day of receipt. Similarly, if there is no clear trading value (as is often the case for newer cryptoassets that are not listed on the largest crypto exchanges), there is no indication of how the I.R.S. expects taxpayers to calculate the value.[30]

---

[29] 2014 Guidance, see *supra* note 7.

[30] For additional discussion of these kinds of tax issues, see Kathleen R. Semanski, *Income, from Whatever Exchange, Mine, or Fork Derived: The Basics of U.S. Cryptocurrency Taxation*, BANKING & FIN. SERVICES POL'Y REP., June 2018, at 8, 14.

7. ORDINARY INCOME OR CAPITAL GAINS?

As if the foregoing were not difficult enough, there is another complication for taxpayers at the federal level. Should income be treated as ordinary income or as capital gains? This question comes up because while cryptocurrency can be used to purchase products and services, as well as being a form of compensation, others see and utilize crypto as an investment or capital asset. The calculation of gain or loss upon the disposition of crypto therefore depends on the correct classification of the cryptoasset.

As noted above, a taxpayer may realize gain upon sale or other disposition of a cryptocoin or token. According to the I.R.S.' 2014 Guidance, the character of that gain depends on the purpose of the asset for that particular taxpayer.

> The character of the gain or loss generally depends on whether the virtual currency is a capital asset in the hands of the taxpayer. A taxpayer generally realizes capital gain or loss on the sale or exchange of virtual currency that is a capital asset in the hands of the taxpayer. For example, stocks, bonds, and other investment property are generally capital assets. A taxpayer generally realizes ordinary gain or loss on the sale or exchange of virtual currency that is not a capital asset in the hands of the taxpayer. Inventory and other property held mainly for sale to customers in a trade or business are examples of property that is not a capital asset.[31]

In order to accurately report gain or loss, a taxpayer who owns crypto must track their basis (generally, but not always, the amount they paid for the asset)[32] for every cryptoasset that they own. This is because the reportable gain depends on the amount by which "the fair market value of property received in an exchange for virtual currency exceeds the taxpayer's adjusted basis of the virtual currency" and loss depends on the extent to which "the fair market value of the property received is less than the adjusted basis of the virtual currency."[33]

Given that some individuals trade routinely and in high volume, tracking problems may be virtually insurmountable.[34] For example, suppose a taxpayer has bought small amounts of Bitcoin over a period of years, without keeping particular track of those purchases. In addition, the

---

[31]   2014 Guidance, *supra* note 7, A-7 at pp. 3–4.

[32]   While "basis" has been mentioned several times in this chapter, the precise ways in which basis is calculated and adjusted over time are outside the scope of these materials. The primary point is the difficulty in record-keeping that this may impose for taxpayers. *See* I.R.S. Publication 551, *supra* note 3, for more information on computation of basis.

[33]   2014 Guidance, *supra* note 7, A-6 at 4.

[34]   For a more in-depth consideration of these concerns, see Morin, *supra* note 9 at 15.

taxpayer was able to mine a few blocks early on, and so has some Bitcoins as a result of those operations. Today, the taxpayer wants to use a portion of the amount that is held in various wallets to buy a flashy new car. Does the taxpayer have to identify which wallets held which Bitcoins and track basis that way? Does the taxpayer use a pro-rata method for calculating basis? Is basis calculated on a first-in-first-out (FIFO) basis or last-in-first-out (LIFO)?

Although it is clear that crypto is not really stock, and rarely operates like equity in most regards, it might still be helpful to look at how taxpayers calculate basis when they sell stock acquired over time on multiple dates. In this case, with some exceptions, the taxpayer does not try to identify the particular purchase in which the affected stock was acquired; the stock being transferred is treated as being the earliest that was acquired (FIFO).[35] There are also some stock-specific rules about how to calculate the cost basis of the stock when there were multiple purchases on a single day.[36]

It seems logical that a similar approach should be taken with regard to crypto, which (like stock) can be acquired in separate blocks on different occasions and varying prices. However, there is no current guidance from the I.R.S. on which approach taxpayers should take, making compliance with reporting requirements difficult, to say the least.[37]

8. UNDER-REPORTING AND ENFORCEMENT ISSUES AT THE FEDERAL LEVEL

Given the range of unanswered issues and the complexity associated with federal tax requirements, it is not surprising that "the majority of people using the virtual currency for illicit transactions have not reported Bitcoin as part of their taxes."[38] The reality is that most people using it for legitimate means are also likely not to have reported their trading activities.

The accuracy of this claim is not hard to demonstrate. From 2103 to 2015, despite the surge in value in Bitcoin from $13 to over $1,100, the I.R.S. received reports of gains or losses on Bitcoin from only 802 taxpayers.[39] As a result of the large numbers of traders who failed to report Bitcoin transactions, the I.R.S. issued a subpoena seeking private records

---

[35]   U.S. Treas. Reg. § 1.1012–1(c)(1)(i).

[36]   U.S. Treas. Reg. § 1.1012–1(c)(1)(ii).

[37]   Recall that as to airdrops at least, the I.R.S. has concluded that gain is ordinary income. Rev. Rul. 2019-24, *supra* note 28.

[38]   Allison M. Lovell, *Avoiding Liability: Changing the Regulatory Structure of Cryptocurrencies to Better Ensure Legal Use*, 104 IOWA L. REV. 927, 941 (2019).

[39]   Jeff John Roberts, *IRS Blinks in Bitcoin Probe, Exempts Coinbase Transactions Under $20,000*, FORTUNE (July 10, 2017) (available online at https://fortune.com/2017/07/10/bitcoin-irs-coinbase/).

from Coinbase, the largest crypto exchange, which claimed that by the end of 2015 it had approximately 5.9 million customers who had traded about $6 billion in Bitcoin through its trading platform.[40]

Originally, the I.R.S. sought records relating to "all U.S. Coinbase customers who transferred Bitcoin . . . from 2013 to 2015."[41] The request originally sought information on all transactions, and was originally granted. However, subsequent responses from customers and Coinbase itself eventually led the I.R.S. to narrow the scope of the summons, to obtain records for Coinbase users that have had bitcoin transactions worth at least $20,000 in a given year. Eventually, the court ordered Coinbase to provide the I.R.S. with the following customer information for any account that had at least $20,000 in any one kind of transaction in any one year from 2013 to 2015: 1) taxpayer ID number; 2) name; 3) birth date; 4) address; 5) records of account activity; and 6) all periodic statements of account or invoice.[42]

Even with the threat of I.R.S. lawsuits, it will probably take additional clarification from Congress or the I.R.S. in order to address the under-reporting of Bitcoin and other cryptocurrency transactions. Current rules are too complex and confusing, as illustrated by the approach taken by one popular online tax preparation service. In their 2018 online materials, TurboTax has a succinct explanation of how consumers need to report crypto transactions, but in an effort to simplify their explanation, they have also made it inaccurate.[43] Instead of recognizing that some cryptocurrency transactions may involve ordinary income, as of 2018 TurboTax showed crypto being held as a capital asset like stock. If TurboTax does not explain the I.R.S. rules, ordinary taxpayers are likely to have even more difficulty in complying with reporting requirements.

9. STATE AND LOCAL TAX ISSUES

All of the preceding material has focused on the federal taxation of cryptoassets and crypto transactions. State law introduces an entirely new level of complexity. The following material is designed to summarize some of the issues mentioned in the last section of chapter fourteen.

First there is state level income tax to consider. There are a range of approaches that states take with regard to calculation of taxable income.

---

[40]   Mark Aquillo, *Court Grants IRS Summons of Coinbase Records*, J. OF ACCOUNTANCY (March 1, 2018) (available online at https://www.journalofaccountancy.com/issues/2018/mar/irs-summons-of-coinbase-records.html).

[41]   Kelly Phillips, *IRS Nabs Big Win Over Coinbase In Bid For Bitcoin Customer Data*, FORBES (Nov. 29, 2017) (available online at https://www.forbes.com/sites/kellyphillipserb/2017/11/29/irs-nabs-big-win-over-coinbase-in-bid-for-bitcoin-customer-data/#398ea7af259a).

[42]   *United States v. Coinbase, Inc.* (3:17–cv–01431–JSC) (N.D. Cal, Nov. 29, 2017) (available online at https://www.courtlistener.com/docket/4618795/77/united-states-v-coinbase-inc/).

[43]   *How do I report Bitcoin or other cryptocurrency as a capital gain?*, TURBOTAX FAQ [archived at https://perma.cc/X5SH-UGQF] (providing information updated for the 2018 tax year).

Some do not tax income at all (from crypto transactions or otherwise).[44] Some follow most provisions in the federal income tax code, and some conform quite selectively, omitting large portions of the federal code and imposing their own definitions as the starting point for determining liability for state income taxes. In fact, no state "conforms to every provision of the Internal Revenue Code. Each state offers its own set of modifications, additions, and subtractions to the code. Each adopts its own set of rules and definitions, frequently layered atop those flowing through from the federal code."[45] This means that state law must be consulted to ascertain how cryptotransactions are to be taxed.

Although few states have specifically determined how to treat virtual currency for income tax purposes, both New Jersey and New York have addressed the issue.[46] In both of these jurisdictions, crypto is treated as property. This means that these two states follow the federal guideline for taxing gains and deducting losses, requiring virtual currency users to keep track of the fair market value of the virtual currency at the time of acquisition and use. In all probability, most states with income tax are likely to do the same, although this is still conjecture.[47]

In addition to income taxes, all but five states impose sales taxes, and Delaware (which does not have a sales tax) does impose a gross receipts tax on businesses. This raises a second issue for states (and some local governments): how do sales taxes apply to cryptotransactions? Although a majority of states have yet to speak clearly on the issue,[48] a few states have issued administrative guidance on the state tax treatment of cryptocurrency transactions. Speaking generally, the states that have considered the sales tax treatment of cryptotransactions have taken one of two approaches: (1) they follow the barter approach (which looks at the fair market value of the crypto at the time of the "sale"), or (2) they look at the advertised price (and calculate the sales tax owed based on that amount). Each state's laws will have to be reviewed to determine the rules that applies.

---

[44]   As of February 2019, states with no income tax included Alaska, Florida, Nevada, New Hampshire, South Dakota, Tennessee, Texas, Washington, and Wyoming. New Hampshire taxes on income from dividends and interest.

[45]   Jared Walczak, *Tax Reform Moves to the States: State Revenue Implications and Reform Opportunities Following Federal Tax Reform*, TAX FOUNDATION (Jan. 31, 2018) (available online at https://taxfoundation.org/state-conformity-federal-tax-reform/#4).

[46]   N.J. Dep't of Taxation, *Technical Advisory Memorandum* TAM–2015–1(R) (July 28, 2015); N.Y. Dep't of Taxation, *Technical Memorandum* TSB–M–14(5)C, (7)I, (17)S (Dec. 5, 2014).

[47]   To date, however, this is apparently the unanimous approach in those few states that have spoken. "[T]he property tax treatment implemented by the IRS has been the only method implemented at the state level" for ascertaining income tax liability. Kelly J. Winstead, *The North Carolina State Tax Treatment of Virtual Currency: An Unanswered Question*, 21 N.C. BANKING INST. 501, 519–22 (2017).

[48]   Charlie Kearns and Dennis Jansen, *Can't Hardly Wait—Cryptocurrency and State Tax Legislation*, 28–Sep J. MULTISTATE TAX'N 8, 8, 2018 WL 3993428, 1 (2018).

For example, the New York State Department of Taxation and Finance issued a technical memorandum on virtual currency transactions in 2014.[49] Pursuant to that guidance, New York treats transactions involving a purchase with crypto as a barter arrangement. However, since crypto is intangible, the recipient of crypto is not required to pay sales tax, but if the goods or services being exchanged for crypto are subject to tax, the recipient of those goods or services will have to pay sales tax. The guidance states that the tax is based on the value of the goods or services, determined by the fair market value of the crypto at the time of the exchange. Kentucky, New Jersey, and Wisconsin have also opted to treat crypto as property,[50] so that transactions involving Bitcoin or other crypto are treated like barter exchanges in those jurisdictions.

On the other hand, the Washington State Department of Revenue has also provided guidance in how sales taxes or business and occupancy taxes might apply where the form of payment is in crypto.[51] The Washington explanation says that the amount owed is generally based on the advertised sale price of the goods or services (in U.S. dollars). California has also issued guidance suggesting that crypto should be treated like currency because it should be regarded like traditional forms of payment such as credit cards or checks.[52] Under this approach, for sales tax purposes, when a consumer purchases taxable goods or services with crypto, the basis will be the advertised price of those goods or services.

Nevada also has legislation that limits taxes on crypto transactions, but it takes a slightly different approach. In 2017, the state banned city and county-level taxes on the use of a blockchain by any person or entity.[53] While counties are technically authorized to impose local sales taxes, they must mirror the state sales tax base, so that it is not possible to impose tax on such transactions unless the state decides to do so.[54]

---

[49] *Tax Department Policy on Transactions Using Convertible Virtual Currency*, NY Dept of Tax. & Fin., Tech. Mem TSB–M–14(5)C, (7)I, (17)S (Dec. 5, 2014) [archived at https://perma.cc/ LLX3-K7ZV].

[50] Ky. Dep't of Rev., *Ky. Sales Tax Facts* (June 2014); N.J. Dep't of Taxation, *Technical Advisory Memorandum* TAM–2015–1(R) (July 28, 2015); Wis. Dep't of Rev., News for Tax Professionals (Mar. 28, 2014).

[51] "Basically, the same classification(s) apply with the virtual currency that apply on a cash, check, debit card, credit card, gift certificate or stored value card transaction." Dept. of Rev., Washington State, *Accepting Virtual Currency as Payment for Goods or Services* [archived on March 21, 2019 at https://perma.cc/9DDQ-JRRU].

[52] Cal. Bd. Of Equalization, Special Notice: Accepting Virtual Currency as a Payment Method, L–382 (June 2014) [archived at https://perma.cc/9W7D-LM7G]. This essentially mirrors the Washington statement described *supra* at note 51.

[53] Nevada Chapter 391 (S.B. 398), Laws 2017, § 6 (city) and § 4 (county) (eff. June 5, 2017).

[54] The Nevada statutes allow counties, but not cities, to adopt ordinances imposing local sales taxes via incremental rates. Nev. Rev. Stat. §§ 376A.050, 377A.030(1)(a)–(d). However, because the local sales tax base must mirror the state sales tax base. Nev. Rev. Stat. §§ 360B.400, 360B.480, 372.065, 374.070, 374.728, and 377.040; N.R.S. §§ 372.795, 360.200. Therefore, the reality is that Nevada boards of county commissioners do not have effective authority to impose

The issue of whether crypto is subject to property tax also varies from state to state, although few states have taken or announced a position on how they intend to approach this issue. On March 12, 2018, Wyoming exempted virtual currencies from ad valorem property taxation.[55] In essence, this exempts crypto from property tax in the same way that cash, bank drafts, and checks are exempt.[56] The exemption is, however, limited to property taxes so other state or local taxes could be applied to cryptoassets.

Unfortunately, as crypto becomes more commonplace, the complexities of state and local taxation are likely to increase as different states take different approaches. This is also likely to create problems of jurisdiction, because it may be very difficult to determine where a particular transaction actually takes place.

10.   TAXATION AT THE INTERNATIONAL LEVEL

The question of what tax rules apply is complicated even further when one considers the international environment in which crypto operates. Numerous countries have taken a position on the taxation of transactions involving cryptocurrencies, and the approaches taken vary widely.

There are a number of sources that collect information about various national regimes. One of the most useful is the Library of Congress, which has a publication that collects laws applicable to the regulation of cryptocurrency around the world.[57] It is a very lengthy document, including general information about the regulatory regimes (including tax rules) applicable to crypto in more than 130 nations. The Library of Congress also has a narrower guide that picks out a more limited number of countries and offers a more detailed assessment of the laws applicable for cryptocurrencies in 14 selected jurisdictions.[58]

The following general information about all comes from the narrower guide referenced above. The guide also contains detailed citations and references for persons wishes to conduct additional research into international tax requirements applicable to cryptoassets.

---

local sales and use tax on virtual currencies, absent the state imposing tax on such transactions. Nev. Rev. Stat. § 372.060(1).

[55]   Wyo. Stat. Ann. § 39–11–105(b)(6), as enacted by Wyo. S.F. 111, 6th Legis. Sess (2018).

[56]   For purposes of the exemption from ad valorem taxes, 'virtual currency' is defined as "any type of digital representation of value that: (i) is used as a medium of exchange, unit of account or store of value; and (ii) is not recognized as legal tender by the United States government." Wyo. Stat. Ann. § 39–11–105(b)(6). This provision was amended to create potential liability for "marketplace facilitators." 2019 Wyoming Laws Ch. 41 (H.B. 69).

[57]   Libr. of Cong., *Regulation of Cryptocurrency Around the World* (last updated Jan. 22, 2019) [archived at https://perma.cc/2U44-5LVK].

[58]   Libr. of Cong., *Regulation of Cryptocurrency in Selected Jurisdictions* (June, 2018) [archived at https://perma.cc/8H8Z-GZ5D].

It is hard to speak in generalities regarding the taxation of crypto, because there is so little consistency in the way that nations have approached this new technology, but there are clearly jurisdictions that are more hostile to crypto than others. In fact, some nations have implemented (or attempted to implement) bans on crypto, either as a result of official or unofficial actions. In China, regulators do not recognize crypto as legal tender or a medium of exchange for retail transactions, and Chinese banks do not accept crypto or provide services related to crypto. In addition, the government has been especially active since September 2017, taking a series of regulatory measures to crack down on crypto, including banning ICOs, prohibiting the conversion of crypto into or from fiat, and preventing banks from providing any other services related to crypto. Since crypto cannot be legally converted into fiat, and since most business operations involving crypto are prohibited, it is not surprising that there are no specific rules applicable to taxation of crypto transactions in China.

Similarly, Iran's Central Bank announced on April 22, 2018 that all Iranian financial institutions were barred from handling crypto. Currency exchanges are also prohibited from buying or selling crypto, or taking any action to facilitate or promote such assets. Prior to this decision, the central bank had warned citizens about risks, although a directive passed by the Money and Credit Council, the most important policy decision-making organ of the central bank, "[had] deemed non-physical and virtual transactions against the law, meaning that Iranian [currency exchanges could] not deal in cryptocurrencies."[59]

Other jurisdictions may not be hostile, but simply have yet to act with regard to crypto. This obviously leaves a great deal of uncertainty as to how such nations will eventually decide to tax cryptoassets and transactions. This is particularly problematic because there is always the risk that the government will say that gain or loss or the fair market value of crypto should have been taken into consideration under existing tax requirements, even though they did not explicitly apply to crypto. This is the case, for example, with Brazil, which has yet to regulate crypto (aside from public statements distinguishing crypto from electronic money).

Equal uncertainty as to tax requirements exists in countries where there are at least some directives relating to crypto, but none articulating rules and standards governing taxation. According to the Library of Congress, tax experts have concluded that despite other regulatory action by Mexican authorities, as of March 2018, Mexico had no clear rules regarding taxation of cryptoassets. New regulations or at least new

---

[59] *No Bitcoin Trade for Moneychangers*, FINANCIAL TRIBUNE (Dec. 23, 2017) (available online at https://financialtribune.com/articles/economy-business-and-markets/78454/no-bitcoin-trade-for-moneychangers); Central Bank of The Islamic Republic of Iran, Central Banking in Iran, at 12–13 [archived at https://perma.cc/92DQ-CM3B].

guidance is needed in order to determine how specific tax rules will apply to crypto in Mexico.

Similarly, Jersey (a Crown dependency of the United Kingdom known as a tax haven with a large financial sector) has announced its desire to create a "business-friendly framework that encourages innovation, jobs and growth in both the financial services and digital sectors. . . ."[60] Instead of imposing taxes, Jersey imposes a number of fees on different crypto-focused businesses, with an exemption for crypto exchanges that have an annual turnover of less than £150,000 (approximately $210,000 in U.S. dollars).

Other than nations that have elected to attempt to ban crypto completely, most jurisdictions seem to have made at least some inroads into taxation of crypto. Some of these have begun to specify how crypto should be taxed, but have many issues left open. For example, France has begun the process of regulating crypto, although commentators note that there are many issues that have not been addressed. The tax treatment in France is subject to limited guidance that suggests profits from the sale of cryptoassets are taxable as capital gains. The tax rules vary depending on whether the taxpayer is engaged in buying and selling crypto as an occasional or as a habitual activity. In addition, in France the value of crypto must be included when calculating wealth tax. These guidelines still leave open a number of tax issues that have yet to be clarified.

Even countries that are not pro-crypto have considered how crypto transactions and the assets themselves should be taxed. For example, Israel has not banned crypto, but it has been reluctant to embrace the new technology, issuing multiple public warnings beginning in early 2014 about the risks of dealing in crypto. Under Israeli financial services laws, crypto (as "virtual currency") is considered a financial asset so that persons engaged in a business providing crypto services must be licensed. With regard to the tax regime in Israel, the Israel Tax Authority has proposed that the virtual currencies should be treated as a "means of virtual payment" and subject to both income tax and value added taxes as appropriate. Accordingly,

> [u]nlike a regular currency, the Israel Tax Authority will regard an increase in the value of a cryptocurrency as a capital gain rather than an exchange fluctuation, making it subject to capital gains tax. Individual investors will not be liable for value-added tax, but anyone engaging in cryptocurrency mining will be classified as a "dealer" and subject to VAT, according to the circular. Anyone trading as a business will be classified as a "financial institution" for tax purposes, meaning that they will be

---

[60] Jersey Chief Minister's Department, *Regulation of Virtual Currency: Consultation Paper* (July 9, 2015; presented to the States July 10, 2015) [archived at https://perma.cc/K5PY-GZRP].

unable to reclaim VAT on expenses but will be subject to an extra 17 percent "profit tax" applied to financial institutions.[61]

The Israel Tax Authority requires documentation of transactions involving crypto to facilitate verification of activity.

Income taxes are a particularly frequent target of regulatory pronouncements regarding crypto. For example, under Argentine tax law, profits earned from the sale of crypto are considered income and taxed as such. A 15% tax is imposed regardless of whether the sale is derived from Argentine or foreign crypto. This corresponds with the way in which Argentina treats profits on securities.

Japan has also addressed income tax consequences of cryptotransactions. According to a December 1, 2017 online post from the Japanese National Tax Agency, profit on the sales of crypto will generally be classified as miscellaneous income rather than capital gains.[62]

Some nations have been more comprehensive, considering more than income taxation. This may include other kinds of tax such as sales tax, value added taxes, and wealth taxes imposed on transfers as a result of death or gift. Australia is one nation that has been reasonably proactive with regard to considering how crypto should be treated for tax purposes. The Australian Taxation Office (ATO) first issued ruling applicable to Bitcoin in December 2014, but more recently published general guidance on the tax treatment of crypto. Under the recent ATO guidance, conducting a purchase or sale with crypto in Australia is to be treated as a barter arrangement, and taxed as such. Crypto may be considered assets for capital gains tax, but a consumer who uses crypto to purchase goods or services for personal use will not realize gain or loss if the cost of the crypto was $10,000 or less. If a business sells goods or services in exchange for crypto, it must record the value of the crypto in Australian dollars ordinary income (with a deduction for the arm's length value of any item purchased with crypto). If a business sells its crypto, it may be subject to capital gains tax. Anyone in the business of mining crypto or acting as an exchange service must include all income in its assessable income. In 2017, the ATO also published separate guidance on the application of sales tax with respect to cryptotransactions. Under the 2017 update, sales and purchases of crypto are not in and of themselves subject to sales tax, although persons in a business involving crypto (including businesses that accept crypto as payment for goods and services) will need to collect sales tax.

---

[61]   Matthew Kalman, *Israel Taxman's Guidelines Killing Cryptocurrency Boom?*, BNA (Feb. 21, 2018) [archived at https://perma.cc/J8DE-6AJQ].

[62]   NTA, 仮想通貨に関する所得の計算方法等について（情報）[*Regarding Calculation Method of Income Relating to Cryptocurrency (Information)], Individual Taxation Information*], No. 4 (Dec. 1, 2017) [archived at https://perma.cc/M22N-53MF].

Canada has also tackled the issue of how its tax regulations apply to crypto. The Canada Revenue

Agency (CRA) has determined that crypto is a commodity and not a government-issued currency. As a result, a Canadian taxpayer must report gains or losses from selling or buying digital currencies. The amounts will be taxable income or capital gains, depending on the nature of the assets and the taxpayer's purpose in holding them. According to an explanatory bulletin published by the CRA:

> In general terms, where a taxpayer does not engage in the business of trading in cryptocurrency (i.e., the taxpayer acquires such property for a long-term growth), any gain or loss generated from the disposition of cryptocurrency should be treated as on account of capital. However, where a taxpayer engages in the business of trading or investing in cryptocurrency, gains or losses therefrom should be treated as being on account of income. The cost to the taxpayer of property received in exchange for cryptocurrency (for example, another type of cryptocurrency) should be equal to the value of the cryptocurrency given up as consideration.[63]

In addition, characterization of crypto as a commodity means that when crypto is used to pay for goods or services, the transaction is treated as a barter exchange. Goods purchased using crypto must be included in the seller's income for tax purposes. In addition, the Canadian goods and services tax/harmonized sales tax also applies to the fair market value of any goods and services bought with crypto.

Mining of crypto in Canada may result in taxable income if it is undertaken as a business in a commercial manner. Income is to be determined with reference to the value of inventory at the end of the year as established by specified regulations.[64] Mining as a personal hobby is not taxable in Canada.[65]

Switzerland is even more comprehensive in its approach to taxation of crypto, having addressed income, capital gains, and wealth tax issues. In Switzerland, individual Swiss states (the cantons) levy income taxes at rates set by each state. An individual taxpayer who receives crypto in exchange for providing goods or services (other than as an employee) must include the value received as self-employment income, based on the value of the crypto in Swiss Francs at the time of receipt. Any income derived

---

[63]   Mariam Al-Shikarchy et al., *Canadian Taxation of Cryptocurrency . . . So Far*, LEXOLOGY (Nov. 14, 2017) (available online at https://www.lexology.com/library/detail.aspx?g=6283077e-9d 32-4531-81a5-56355fa54f47).

[64]   *Id.*

[65]   *Cryptocurrencies and Tax: Five Things Every Canadian Needs to Know*, WILDEBOER DELLELCE (Dec. 12, 2017) (available online at https://www.wildlaw.ca/resource-centre/legal-updates/2017/cryptocurrencies-and-tax-five-things-every-canadian-needs-to-know/).

from mining operations by individuals will be assessable income, depending on the specific work arrangement. Employees will report income as salary, and independent contractors report self-employment income. Profits from professional trading activities are taxable, and losses are deductible. Crypto held as a business asset is to be reported on the balance sheet at book value, with general accounting principles determining how to account for price fluctuations.

Under Swiss law, capital gains from movable private assets, which includes crypto, are generally not taxable. Similarly, capital losses do not result in any deduction for the holder.

Just as is the case with Swiss income tax, wealth taxes are also imposed by individual cantons. For wealth tax purpose, crypto is treated like a foreign currency, with holders taxed based on the value assigned to the crypto by the tax authorities on December 31 of the fiscal year. To illustrate this, the Swiss Federal Tax Administration valued Bitcoin on December 31, 2017 at approximately $14,500 U.S. dollars. The Swiss Federal Tax Administration determines value for the most commonly utilized cryptoassets, including Bitcoin, Cardano, Bitcoin Cash, Ethereum, IOATA, Litecoin, Tron Coin, NEM, Stellar Lumens, Palladium, Platinum, and Ripple. This list is continuously updated, and while it is only a recommendation to the cantons, most Swiss states follow them. The value is based on the average trading price on a number of different trading platforms.

Finally, some nations have taken idiosyncratic approaches to regulation of crypto, with correspondingly unique tax requirements. Belarus fits into this category, with a relatively unusual regulatory regime applicable to crypto. As a result of a Presidential Decree which took effect on March 28, 2018, only legal entities operating in the special economic zone designated as the High Technologies Park may provide crypto-related services such as trading platforms and exchanges. The same Presidential Decree exempts from income tax the income of residents of the Park, was well any individual's income from mining, creation, acquisition, or disposition of crypto. In addition, the sale of crypto is exempt from value-added tax. These tax benefits last until January 1, 2023.

This discussion picks and chooses among different nations and varying tax regimes. The sharply diverging approaches do, however, offer some insights into the complexity of handling crypto on the world stage.

APPENDIX

LIST OF ACRONYMS[1]

■ ■ ■

'33 Act—Securities Act of 1933; codified at 15 U.S. Code § 77, imposing the requirement that sales of securities be registered or exempt, as well as imposing various anti-fraud requirements on the sales of securities.

'34 Act—Securities Exchange Act of 1934; codified at 15 U.S. Code § 78, regulating public companies, broker-dealers, and securities exchanges (and covering various other aspects of the federal securities laws in the U.S.).

1940 Act—Investment Company Act of 1940; codified at 15 U.S. Code §§ 80a–1 to 80a–64, the primary source of regulation for mutual funds and closed-end funds, also impacting hedge funds, private equity funds, and holding companies.

ACPR—Autorité de contrôle prudentiel et de resolution; France's Prudential Supervisory Authority.

AMF—Autorité des marchés financiers; the French Financial Market Authority.

AML—Anti-Money Laundering; a widely used acronym used to refer to U.S. and global efforts to combat money laundering.

AMLD 5—the E.U.'s 5th Anti-Money Laundering Directive, adopted June 19, 2018; it is specifically applicable to virtual currency exchanges and wallet services.

APA—Administrative Procedures Act; a U.S. statute that establishes rules for the way in which U.S. federal agencies are to act.

ATO—Australian Taxation Office; the principal revenue collection agency of the Australian government.

ATS—Alternative Trading System; a U.S. securities trading platform that complies with Reg. ATS requirements and is therefore exempt from requirements that it register as an Exchange.

AUSTRAC—the Australian Transaction Reports and Analysis Centre; the agency charged with maintaining and analyzing transaction reports under Australia's AML/CTF programs.

---

[1] Because it would be no fun if everyone could understand what we were talking about.

BO—Boletín Oficial (Official Bulletin for Argentina); the dissemination body through which the laws sanctioned by the Congress of Argentina and Executive acts are published.

BoT—Chicago Board of Trade; one of the designated markets organized and operating in the U.S. under the terms of the CEA and self-regulated in compliance with the CFTC's Core Principles.

BRICS—refers to a group of five major emerging national economies: Brazil, Russia, India, China and South Africa. These nations are known for strong regional influence; all are G20 members. The group created the New Development Bank (formerly referred to as the BRICS Development Bank), operated by the BRICS states and with authorized lending of up to $34 billion annually. Its primary focus for lending is infrastructure projects.

BSA—Bank Secrecy Act; the U.S. legislation imposing AML and KYC requirements on (among other things) "money-transmitters."

BTC—Bitcoin Classic; one of the tokens into which Bitcoin split following one of the hard forks on the bitcoin blockchain.

Cboe—Chicago Board Options Exchange; the largest U.S. options exchange, offering options on over 2,200 companies, 22 stock indices, and 140 exchange-traded funds.

CEA—Commodities Exchange Act; the U.S. statute pursuant to which the CFTC operates.

CEO—Chief Executive Officer; the most senior executive or administrative officer in charge of managing an organization.

CFO—Chief Financial Officer; the officer of a company with primary responsibility for financial planning, management of financial risks, record-keeping, and financial reporting.

CFTC—Commodities Futures Trading Commission; the U.S. agency charged with implementing and overseeing compliance with the CEA.

CRA—Canada Revenue Agency; the Canadian equivalent of the I.R.S.

CSA—Canadian Securities Administrators; a group of securities regulators from the 10 Canadian provinces acting to protect Canadian investors from unfair, improper, or fraudulent practices while fostering fair and efficient capital markets.

CTF—Counter Terrorism Funding; an acronym used to refer to legal requirements aimed at suppressing the funding of terrorist groups and activities.

CVC—Convertible Virtual Currency; generally used by FinCEN in its May 2019 official guidance on cryptoassets.

DAO—Decentralized Autonomous Organization; further defined in chapter two. (The DAO was a specific kind of DAO, and is described in more detail in chapter eight.)

DApps—Decentralized Applications; further defined in chapter two.

DCM—Designated Contract Markets; commonly called "boards of trade" or simply "futures exchanges"; defined in U.S. regulations promulgated by the CFTC and codified at 17 C.F.R. Part 38.

DNB—De Nederlandsche Bank; the Central Bank of the Netherlands.

DoT—Department of Treasury; U.S. authority responsible for enforcing finance and tax laws, managing currency, government accounts, and public debt.

DXCD—The symbol for the ECCB's Digital EC Pilot Program cryptocurrency; the cryptocurrency planned by the ECCB to exist side-by-side the Eastern Caribbean dollar in the island nations of Anguilla, Antigua and Barbuda, the Commonwealth of Dominica, Grenada, Montserrat, Saint Kitts and Nevis, Saint Lucia, and Saint Vincent and the Grenadines.

EBA—European Banking Authority; the authority in the E.U. with responsibility for creating a harmonized set of prudential rules for E.U. financial institutions. It is responsible for maintaining financial stability in the E.U. while safeguarding the integrity and efficiency of the banking sector.

ECCB—Eastern Caribbean Central Bank; the consolidated monetary authority for a group of eight eastern Caribbean island nations.

ERC20—literally "Ethereum Request for Comment," project number 20; the technical standard that applies to most Smart Contracts hosted on the Ethereum Blockchain. This is no longer the most up-to-date standard although it is still prevalent in existing tokens.

ETC—Ethereum Classic; one of the two forms of Ether created after the hard fork following the 2016 hack of The DAO).

ETF—Exchange Traded Fund; a collection of securities—such as crypto—that tracks an underlying index or is managed by a professional manager.

ETH—Ether (the token); crypto that acts as the currency used to power the Ethereum platform.

E.U.—European Union; the political and economic union of 28 member nations; it is focused on ensuring the free movement of people, goods, services, and capital within the Union.

FATF—Financial Action Task Force; sometimes also known by its French name, Groupe d'action financière, it is an intergovernmental organization founded in 1989 on the initiative of the G7 to develop policies to combat money laundering. Its current mandate has been expanded to include policies to protect against the funding of terrorism.

FCM—Futures Commission Merchant; an individual or organization involved in the solicitation or acceptance of buy or sell orders for futures or options on futures in exchange for commissions or other payments from customers.

FIEA—(Japanese) Financial Instruments and Exchange Act; the Act setting out the governance provisions for transactions involving securities and other financial instruments in Japan.

FinCEN—Financial Crimes Enforcement Network; a bureau within the U.S. Department of Treasury, charged with overseeing enforcement of the BSA.

FINRA—Financial Industry Regulatory Authority; the not-for-profit organization authorized by Congress to protect investors by overseeing the broker-dealer industry.

FinTech—not really an acronym, but a combination two words "Financial" and "Technology"; generally used to refer to computer programs and any other technology used to support or enable banking and financial services.

Fintrac—Financial Transactions and Reports Analysis Centre of Canada; Canada's financial intelligence unit. Fintrac assists in the detection, prevention and deterrence of money laundering and the financing of terrorist activities.

FSA—Financial Services Agency; the Japanese agency and integrated financial regulator charged with overseeing the country's banking, securities, and insurance sectors in order to ensure the stability of Japan's financial system.

FSB—Financial Stability Board; an international body that monitors and makes recommendations about the global financial system.

FY—Fiscal Year; a 12-month period designated for tax or accounting purposes.

G7—Group of 7; an organization consisting of representatives from Canada, France, Germany, Italy, Japan, the United Kingdom, and the United States. The European Union also participates. The group was founded to facilitate shared macroeconomic initiatives in response to the collapse of the exchange rate in 1971, the 1973 energy crisis, and the resulting recession.

G20—Group of 20; the G20 (or Group of Twenty) is an international forum for the governments and central bank governors from 19 countries and the European Union. The group was founded in 1999 to discuss policies promoting international financial stability.

GDAX—Global Digital Asset Exchange; this was the first name for the Coinbase trading subsidiary that now operates under the name "Coinbase Pro."

ICO—Initial Coin Offering; a phrase used to refer to the distribution of a cryptoasset; while originally associated with public sales, the phrase continues to be used even in connection with private placements of crypto pursuant to exemptions from registration under applicable securities laws.

IEO—Initial Exchange Offering; a new crypto-financing model where tokens are offered through the services of a cryptoexchange rather than directly by the development team.

IMF—International Monetary Fund; an organization of 189 countries which has as its primary purpose to goal of insuring financial stability of the international monetary system. In addition, according to its website, the IMF works to "foster global monetary cooperation, secure financial stability, facilitate international trade, promote high employment and sustainable economic growth, and reduce poverty."

IOSCO (also OICV-IOSCO)—International Organization of Securities Commissions, and OICV variously standing for "Organisation internationale des commissions de valeurs," "Organização Internacional das Comissões de Valores," or "Organización Internacional de Comisiones de Valores"; the international body consisting of securities regulators from more than 200 nations. It works to develop, implement, and promote internationally recognized standards for securities regulation.

IP—Intellectual Property; a work or invention that is the result of creativity to which one has rights and which are subject to legal protection.

IPO—Initial Public Offering; generally refers to the process by which an American company issues its securities to the public for the first time.

I.R.S.—Internal Revenue Service; a bureau of the U.S. Department of Treasury, charged with administration of the federal tax code.

JOBS Act—Jumpstart Our Business Startups Act, federal legislation enacted in 2012 to encourage funding of small businesses in the U.S. by easing a number of securities regulations. It went into effect on September 23, 2013, as public law 112–106.

KYC—Know Your Customer; rules imposed on various financial institutions requiring them to take reasonable steps to identify customers and keep records relating to those customer's financial transactions.

LTC—Litecoin; an altcoin, P2P cryptocurrency and open-source software project.

MMOU—Multilateral Memorandum of Understanding; a document reflecting a common understanding among nation states that sign an agreement, explaining how they should consult, cooperate, and exchange information for specified purposes.

NADEX—North American Derivatives Exchange, Inc.; a regulated U.S.-based exchange for a range of binary options and spreads.

NASAA—North American Securities Administrators Associations; a voluntary international organizational consisting of Canadian and American securities administrators from all 50 states, the District of Columbia, Puerto Rico, the U.S. Virgin Islands, Canada, and Mexico. In the U.S., NASAA serves as the collective voice of state securities agencies.

NASDAQ—initially an acronym for the National Association of Securities Dealers Automated Quotations; founded in 1971 by the National Association of Securities Dealers (NASD), and now operated as a global electronic marketplace for securities transactions; NASDAQ also refers to the NASDAQ composite, an index of more than 3,000 stocks.

NYSE—New York Stock Exchange; located in N.Y., this is largest equity based exchange in the world based on market capitalization of listed securities.

OCC—Office of the Comptroller of the Currency; an independent bureau within the U.S. Department of the Treasury, with authority to charter, regulate, and supervise all national banks and thrift institutions.

OECD—Organization for Economic Cooperation and Development; an intergovernmental economic organization whose membership consists of 36 developed nations. The group acts to stimulate economic progress and world trade, while remaining committed to democracy and free markets.

OICV-IOSCO—see IOSCO, above.

P2P—Peer-to-Peer; a distributed application organizational structure in which the peer computers are equally empowered participants.

PKK—Kurdistan Workers' Party; a group recognized as a terrorist organization by Turkey, the U.S., and the E.U., and responsible for ongoing violence in Turkey.

PoS—Proof-of-Stake; a consensus protocol used on certain blockchain projects, described in more detail in chapter two.

PoV—Proof-of-Value; a consensus protocol used on certain blockchain projects, described in more detail in chapter two.

PoW—Proof-of-Work; the consensus protocol used for Bitcoin and several other blockchain projects, described in more detail in chapter two.

RICO—Racketeer Influenced and Corrupt Organizations Act (1970); a federal law in the U.S. imposing extended criminal penalties and civil actions for acts in connection with an ongoing criminal organization.

S&P 500—Standard and Poor's 500; an index published by Standard and Poor of 500 large companies having common stock listed on NYSE, NASDAQ, or the Cboe BZX Exchange.

SAFE—Simple Agreement for Future Equity; a set of simplified documents between an investor and accompany that provides rights to the investor for future equity without determining a specific price per share at the time of initial investment.

SAFT—Simple Agreement for Future Tokens; a contract offered by crypto developers calling for them to sell rights to buy future tokens when they are developed in exchange for funds for the development process.

SAR—Suspicious Activity Report; a document that financial institutions, and those associated with their business, must file with FinCEN when there is suspected money laundering.

SEC—Securities and Exchange Commission; an independent agency of the U.S. responsible for overseeing the federal securities laws.

SEF—Swap Execution Facility; a platform for financial swap trading in the U.S. providing pre-trade information and a mechanism for executing transactions among eligible participants.

SOV—the Sovereign; the name for the government-issued cryptocurrency to be issued by The Marshall Islands and used as legal tender in that nation alongside the U.S. dollar.

SRO—Self-Regulatory Organization; any group of organizations that band together and create their own regulations in compliance with applicable law. Under U.S. securities law SRO is a defined term. Recognize U.S. SROs include, for example, FINRA, the merged enforcement arms of the NYSE and the NASD. Under Japanese law it includes the Japan Virtual Currency Exchange Association, which is the SRO for Japanese cryptocurrency exchanges.

TGE—Token Generation Event; a process by which an issuer releases Tokens for distribution.

ULC—Uniform Law Commission (formerly known as the National Conference of Commissioners on Uniform State Laws); a non-profit, American unincorporated association that works to provide model uniform legislation for consideration by the various states.

U.N.—United Nations; an international organization founded in 1945 and consisting of 193 member nations. It has various powers as described in its charter, and can take action on global issues such as peace, security, climate change, human rights, terrorism, etc. The organization also provides a forum for member states to exchange views on various issues of international importance.

USA PATRIOT Act—the "Uniting and Strengthening America by Providing Appropriate Tools Required to Intercept and Obstruct Terrorism Act of 2001"; designed to provide law enforcement with new tools to detect and prevent terrorism.

XRP—a token issued by Ripple, a real-time gross settlement system, currency exchange and remittance network created by Ripple Labs Inc., a US-based technology company.

ZEC—Zcash; one of the more popular privacy coins.

Zk-SNARK—"Zero-Knowledge Succinct Non-Interactive Argument of Knowledge"; a proof construction that allows verification of certain information, e.g. a secret key, without revealing that information, and without any interaction between the prover and verifier; Zk-SNARK serves as the mechanism by which transactions in Zcash can be made private.

INDEX

References are to Pages

NOTE—page references include footnotes in the text,
but not headings or the table of contents.